D0026290

Contemporary Investments
Security and Portfolio Analysis   4th Ed.

Douglas Hearth
University of Arkansas

Janis K. Zaima
San Jose State University

THOMSON
SOUTH-WESTERN

Australia · Canada · Mexico · Singapore · Spain · United Kingdom · United States

THOMSON

SOUTH-WESTERN

Contemporary Investments: Security and Portfolio Analysis, 4th edition

Douglas Hearth   Janis K. Zaima

Vice President/Editorial Director:
Jack Calhoun

Vice President/Editor-in-Chief:
Mike Roche

Executive Editor:
Mike Reynolds

Developmental Editor:
Elizabeth Thomson

Senior Marketing Manager:
Charlie Stutesman

Production Editor:
Cliff Kallemeyn

Manufacturing Coordinator:
Sandee Milewski

Senior Design Project Manager:
Michelle Kunkler

Senior Media Technology Editor:
Vicky True

Media Developmental Editor:
John Barans

Senior Media Production Editor:
Mark Sears

Project Management/Composition:
BookMasters, Inc.

Printer:
Transcontinental Printing
Louiseville, Quebec

Cover and Internal Designer:
Ramsdell Design, Cincinnati, OH

Cover Image:
© Paul and Linda Marie Ambrose/
Getty Images, Inc.

Library of Congress Control Number:
2003105424

ISBN: 0-324-25811-9

To David L. Kurtz: colleague, mentor, friend
—DH

To Satsuki Zaima, and in memory of Kenneth H. Zaima
—JKZ

Preface

When we started writing the first edition of *Contemporary Investments* a decade ago, our overall objective was to create a comprehensive investments textbook which, while coverage much of the same material as other texts, would have a much different writing style and focus. Years of teaching experience tell us that investments is often a course many students look forward to taking, only to be disappointed. The textbook is often the usual suspect.

We believe, however, the fundamental problem with most investments texts is that they appear to students to be detached from the real world of investments. Much of the material in other texts seems to be cloaked in mysterious economic theory coupled with lots of statistics and mathematics. Too little time is devoted to discussing how real investors actually make decisions—and whether these decisions are right or wrong. That's really too bad; we believe students want to learn more about the practice of investments, not just the theory.

What do we do differently than most investments texts? That's a fair question. For one thing, we've written *Contemporary Investments* in a more informal, conversational style. Let's face it; many textbooks, while sincere and technically correct, are just plain boring. Further, we place more emphasis on investing in common stocks than do most texts. Stocks are arguably the most complicated but also the most interesting investment instruments. The text is also replete with real companies and real investment situations. Whenever possible, we use real-world examples to illustrate key points. We don't summarily dismiss successful investors as mere flukes, but rather try to understand why they're successful. Perhaps it's mainly luck, but perhaps it's also superior investment skills. At the same time, we're not afraid to skewer the self-described investment touts and gurus, when appropriate.

Investment theory is presented in a more lucid, less intimidating manner. A student wouldn't need a degree in higher mathematics to understand the material. We show how investment theory can help investors understand the world of investments and make better decisions. It's not that we don't believe that theory is important: we do. In fact, we believe that students need a solid foundation in investment theory in order to know how to properly apply it to real investment situations.

Investing can be fun. An investor can get a great deal of satisfaction from watching what he or she felt was a great investment exceed initial expectations.

We highlight the fun aspects of investing. At the same time, we never allow students to lose sight of the fact that investing is serious and important business. Many students aspire to a career in investments. We accommodate them, but even if a student doesn't want a career in investments, more likely than not, he or she is going to be an investor. In fact, many already are. Today most employer sponsored retirement plans are so-called defined contribution plans, plans that usually require employees to make important investment decisions. Consequently, we don't neglect issues that apply mainly to the individual investor.

Finally, throughout the text, we never forget the historical context of investments. While by its nature, investing is forward looking, we believe all investors have to understand the past while looking toward the future. Sure, the past is never a guarantee of the future—a point we make frequently—but students can learn a great deal by understanding past investment successes and failures.

In short, we've tried to create an investment text written in a user-friendly, proactive manner, while still be complete and current. We hope this text not only gives students an operational knowledge of the current field of investments, but provides stimulation for a lifetime of further study. It is our hope that students will find our text to be both interesting and understandable, and perhaps consider reading assignments to be more joy than drudgery. Students, our readers, will be the ultimate judges as to how well *Contemporary Investments*, 4th edition, accomplishes this goal.

INTENDED MARKET AND USE

We believe *Contemporary Investments*, 4th edition, can be used in the first investments class at either the undergraduate or MBA level. It requires little more than a basic understanding of finance, accounting, and economics—material students should have covered in earlier courses. The entire text can be covered in one semester (or quarter). At the same time, given the depth of in-text examples and end-of-chapter exercises, the text can easily fit into a two-semester (or two-quarter) sequence.

With almost 50 years of combined teaching experience, we know just how difficult it can be to cover all the material the instructor wants and needs to cover. It often seems like there is never enough time to cover everything. We've tried to help by structuring the text material in such a way that topics can be covered generally or in more depth, depending on the needs and preferences of instructors and their students. Therefore, instructors can easily emphasize some topics while de-emphasizing others.

The text is designed to be read in what we would call—for lack of a better term—a linear fashion; the chapters work best in the order presented. On the other hand, in designing and writing the text, we've tried to allow for some flexibility depending on instructor preferences. For instance, comparing notes with other instructors tells us that some prefer to cover all of modern portfolio theory in class earlier than we do in the text. This presents no problem. We know of other instructors who prefer to cover common stocks before bonds. Again, a student can read the chapters devoted to common stock analysis (Chapters 11 through 14) before the bond chapters (9 and 10) without becoming hopelessly confused.

CHANGES TO THE FOURTH EDITION

Although we made several changes to the fourth edition, our overriding goal while writing this new edition of *Contemporary Investments* was to maintain our emphasis upon applications as the main theme behind the book. In other words, we haven't changed our basic philosophy. Rather, in the fourth edition, we concentrated on updating material, adding some new material to reflect today's changed investment environment, updating the extensive real-world examples, adding many more computational problems, and providing additional materials to instructors in the supplements. Many of these changes were suggested by users of the prior editions. We've also rewritten many of the in-chapter boxes and added questions for critical thinking. Short profiles of famous investors are another new feature.

As suggested by users of the third edition, we have moved some of the basic material on portfolio risk and return from Chapter 17 to Chapter 2. This change gives students some exposure to how the risk and return of a portfolio are calculated and the importance of diversification early on. We believe that moving this material to an earlier chapter will benefit all students, regardless of whether or not the instructor plans on covering modern portfolio theory in depth.

As everyone knows, the investing environment has changed dramatically since the publication of the third edition. After 5 straight years of double-digit gains, the stock market has suffered through 3 consecutive losing years for the first time in more than 70 years. In fact, the bear market in stocks that began in 2000 is more severe than any that has occurred since the end of the Second World War. The collapse of stock prices has certainly changed investor perceptions and expectations. Nevertheless, we continue to believe that stocks are the best investment choice for long-term investors. Markets have always recovered before—and will again. The recent bear market also highlights the importance of wise security analysis and selection. The fourth edition reflects the changed investment environment.

At the same time, the wave of corporate scandals highlighted by the collapse of companies such as Enron and WorldCom, as well as questions concerning whether investment advice and analysis are truly unbiased, are discussed extensively throughout the text. If nothing else, today's investors need to think more for themselves. We've integrated all of these issues throughout the fourth edition of *Contemporary Investments*.

FEATURES AND PEDAGOGY

Contemporary Investments offers a number of unique and important features, some of which are new to the fourth edition, designed to aid in student learning and perk up student interest. Some of the most noteworthy of these features include:

- More emphasis on common stock investment and traditional security analysis—sometimes called the Graham and Dodd approach. Not only have common stock proved to be superior investments, even factoring in the latest bear market, they are also, in our view, the most interesting, albeit complicated investment instrument. The Graham and Dodd approach for valuing common stocks was first published 65 years ago at the height of the Great Depression. It has easily withstood the test of time and is even more valuable in today's investing environment.

- The qualitative, as well as the quantitative, factors that determine fundamental stock values are examined in depth, something most texts overlook. Although it may be difficult to define what is meant by the quality of management, it is too important a topic to ignore or even downplay. A company can *appear* to have great looking financial statements, but still be poorly or improperly managed.

- Compared to most texts, modern portfolio theory (MPT) is presented in a more intuitive and realistic manner, with a minimum of mathematics. We continually show how MPT can contribute to an overall understanding of how the investments world functions. At the same time, we discuss how—when combined with more traditional security analysis—MPT can help all types of investors make better decisions.

- We provide a more balanced treatment of how professional investors make decisions—technical and fundamental analysis—and the efficient markets hypothesis. Too many texts present technical and fundamental analysis, and the efficient markets hypothesis, as black-and-white issues. In the real world, they aren't.

- Investing raises a number of ethical issues—such as the improper use of inside information, presenting misleading and incomplete financial information, and providing biased investment advice. Throughout the text, there are numerous opportunities for class discussion on ethics and investing. These opportunities are in the form of everything from boxes to end-of-chapter exercises.

- The globalization of investing has been one of the most significant developments over the past couple of decades. Instead of the usual chapter on "international investing," we integrate international material into virtually every chapter.

- Each chapter begins with a set of learning objectives—phrased as questions—designed to guide the student's reading. The chapter summary then repeats each question and summarizes the material that applies to it.

- At the beginning of each chapter is a feature called *linkages*. Linkages consists of three parts: where we've been, where we are, and where we're going.

- Throughout the chapter, there is extensive use of real companies and real investment situations. Students will run into such well-known names as Kohl's Corporation, Home Depot, Johnson & Johnson, 3M, Southwest Airlines, and Microsoft.

- Many figures are annotated. The annotations explain what the figure is showing and the point, or points, it is trying to illustrate. This feature makes figures easier for the reader to understand.

- Virtually all chapters contain one or two boxes. Investment Insight boxes provide practical investment advice or a commentary on contemporary investment issues. The Investment History boxes relate stores of where we've been and what the past may mean for the future. Questions for critical thinking have been added to each box.

- In selected chapters, a brief one-paragraph summary (called Recap) follows difficult or complicated material. Practice exercises are also presented. The answers are included at the end of the text in an appendix. The recap sections give the reader the chance to catch his or her breath and review what was covered before pushing ahead.

- At the end of each chapter, there is an extensive set of exercises. Most chapters have at least one mini case. These problems are designed to test student comprehensive over large portions of material. All chapters have between 10 and 25 review exercises designed to test knowledge over more specific chapter material. Each chapter has at least one critical exercise (most have more than one). Critical thinking exercises require library or Internet research, data analysis, or both. Not only are these exercises designed to assess how well students comprehend chapter material, they will provide students with some "hands-on" experience with real investment data. Internet-related exercises complete the end-of-chapter exercises.

SUPPLEMENTS

Contemporary Investments has the best package of supplements of any investments text on the market today. Our basic philosophy when developing the ancillary package was to enhance the learning experience by providing a wealth of material that can be used as examples, projects, and presentations. The ancillary package consists of:

- Instructor's Resource Manual (IRM). Written by the authors, the IRM outlines each chapter, a list of the points to emphasize, and identifies areas where students often get confused. The IRM provides a list of possible student projects, worked out computational examples, integration of the lecture slides, and solutions to end-of-chapter exercises. The IRM also contains a section on standards of ethical behavior (from AIMR), a discussion of security price indexes, and a review of convexity.
- Testbank. A thorough, comprehensive testbank is available in both paper and computerized formats. The testbank contains almost 2,000 objective questions, short-answer essay questions, and problems.
- Lecture Presentation Slides. For each chapter we have prepared a computerized slide program using Microsoft PowerPoint. The slide show is designed to be used as a supplement in class lectures. Each chapter includes learning objectives, key points, and chapter exhibits, and presents the complete chapter as a dynamic lecture guide.
- Web site. http://hearth.swlearning.com is the Web site that supports *Contemporary Investments*, 4th edition. The site provides teaching resources, learning resources, links to relevant Web sites, and many more features. Visit the site throughout the term.
- Data and Wizard workbooks. Located on the Web site mentioned are two Microsoft Excel workbooks. The Data workbook contains a set of worksheets designed to accompany many of the Critical Thinking Exercises found at the end of the text chapters. The Wizard workbook consists of a set of easy-to-use, pre-built worksheets. Students enter data or information on the worksheet where indicated. A series of predetermined calculations—such as finding the duration of a bond or the Black-Scholes option price—are performed.

ACKNOWLEDGMENTS

As with all books, we have many, many people to thank. We start with those individuals who reviewed various drafts of the first edition and participated in focus groups over 10 years ago. Their comments and suggestions were invaluable. We would also like to thank the individuals—both students and instructors—who reviewed and commented on the first three editions of *Contemporary Investments*. These individuals include:

Jerry Boswell *Metropolitan State College of Denver*

Ben Branch *University of Massachusetts*

Larry Byerley *University of Pittsburg at Johnstown*

Indudeep Chhachhi *Western Kentucky University*

James D'Mello *Western Michigan University*

David Dubofsky *Virginia Commonwealth University*

Marcelo Eduardo *Mississippi College*

David M. Ellis *Texas A&M University*

John Emery *California State University–Fresno*

James F. Gatti *University of Vermont*

John M. Geppert *University of Nebraska–Lincoln*

Stevenson Hawkey *Golden Gate University*

Stephen P. Huffman *University of Wisconsin–Oshkosh*

Richard Johnson *Colorado State University*

Jeffry Manzi *Ohio University*

James M'Mello *Western Michigan University*

Saeed Mortazavi *Humboldt State University*

Henry Oppenheimer *University of Rhode Island*

Aaron Phillips *American University*

James Philpot *Ouachita Baptist University*

Steve Rich *Baylor University*

Linda L. Richardson *Siena College*

James N. Rimbey *University of Arkansas*

Ann Rock *Wayne State University*

Robert Ryan *Ithaca College*

Patricia Smith *University of New Hampshire*

Ernest Swift *Georgia State University*

Joseph Vu *De Paul University*

Andrew Whitaker *North Central College*

Edward L. Winn, Jr. *Belmont University*

These individuals helped to improve and strengthen the fourth edition:

Kristine L. Beck, Ph.D. *University of Wisconsin–Oshkosh*

Peter Bobko *Guilford College*

Mei-Kei Chiang *San José State University*

Keith Jakob *The University of Montana*

Kartono Liano *Mississippi State University*

Yuen-Ling Lin *San José State University*

James A. Milanese *University of North Carolina, Greensboro*

Anastasia M. Pikas *Niagara University*

Ali Reza *San José State University*

Contemporary Investments, 4th edition, is much better because of all of their efforts.

We worked with some great people at South-Western over the years. These include Mike Reynolds, Charlie Stutesman, Elizabeth Thomson, Cliff Kallemeyn, John Barans, Mark Sears, and Joe Squance. We have always appreciated their expertise, encouragement, and certainly their patience.

Finally, to our families: Karen, Alan, and Eric, and Ken, Jana, and Kelly. We note their love, encouragement, support, and understanding. Writing is as hard on families as it is on authors.

Brief Contents

Contents

PART 1

The World of Investments

This opening section presents an overview of the subject of investments. It introduces several important concepts and ideas that reappear throughout the remainder of the text. We discuss the importance of investment decisions, the general investment process, and some apparent investment truisms. From there we cover the essential concepts of risk and return—two concepts that dominate investment decisions. Finally, we describe in depth the wide range of contemporary investment alternatives from Treasury bills to common stocks to mutual funds.

1

Prelude: Investing and Investments

IN THIS CHAPTER . . .   TO COME . . .

Our study of investments begins by asking the fundamental question: *Why* are investment decisions important? The answer to this question involves a discussion of the history of investing and the steps in the investment process. We also introduce many of the basic themes that are carried throughout the book.

We continue to lay the foundation of investments by discussing the concepts of risk and return (Chapter 2). Both are essential factors in determining where and how much we invest. Next, we describe the wide array of investment instruments available today (Chapters 3 and 4).

CHAPTER OBJECTIVES

After reading Chapter 1, you should be able to answer the following questions:

1. Why are investment decisions important?

2. What is the history of investing?

3. What steps are involved in the investment process?

4. What are some of the important truisms in investments?

Over the next six hundred pages or so, we plan to lead you on a journey through the fascinating world of investments. We look carefully at investment alternatives such as common stocks, bonds, options, and mutual funds. We examine how the security markets function and how professionals make investment decisions. We review some past follies of investors and develop an understanding of how investors should make investment decisions. We believe that you will find the journey to be rewarding intellectually and, perhaps at some point in the future, economically as well.

What makes the topic of investments important and interesting? To help answer this question, consider the following story.

By all accounts, Donald and Mildred Othmer of New York lived quiet, unpretentious lives. Donald, who died in 1995, was a professor of chemical engineering at Brooklyn Polytechnic University. Mildred, a former teacher, died in 1998. When they died, they both were in their nineties. What came as a shock to friends was that the Othmers left combined estates worth about $800 million, the bulk of which was left to a variety of nonprofit organizations. How did they accumulate such an impressive amount of wealth? Simply put, the Othmers, like many other Americans, got rich by investing their money sensibly, leaving it invested for a long period of time, and living modestly.

In the early 1960s, the Othmers turned over their life savings, then $50,000, to famed investor Warren Buffet, an old family friend. In the early 1970s, the Othmers received shares of Buffet's new company, Berkshire Hathaway. Berkshire Hathaway invests in other companies, such as American Express, Coca-Cola, and Gillette. When the Othmers received their Berkshire shares, the price was $42 per share; at the time of Mildred's death the price had risen to $77,000 per share. Even though the Othmers were smart, or perhaps just lucky, to pick Buffet to manage their money, a similar investment, made at the same time, in the overall stock market would have grown to more than $100 million by the middle of 1998.

The rewards of investing are obvious, but investing is not without risk. For instance, over the past year, the S&P 500—a popular gauge for the overall stock market—fell about 23%. Shares of Home Depot, the world's second-largest retailer, dropped by more than 35% during the same period.

Over the long run, however, the rewards of investing far outweigh the risks. Even with the recent decline in stock prices, $10,000 invested in shares of Home Depot at the beginning of 1992 would be worth in excess of $28,000 today. This chapter introduces you to the subject of investing and investments. Now, let's begin our journey.

WHY INVEST?

Why do people invest? This question seems simple enough, and it can be answered by defining the word *invest*. According to the dictionary, *invest* means "to commit (money) in order to earn a financial return; to make use of for future benefits or advantages."[1] In a nutshell, this definition explains why people com-

---

[1] *Webster's Tenth New Collegiate Dictionary* (Springfield, MA: Merriam-Webster, 1993), p. 616.

mit money to investments: to increase their future wealth. By investing money to earn financial returns, people forgo current consumption but have more money to spend in future years. Investing $1,000 today and earning 10% over the next year will give you $1,100 one year from today. Had you invested $1,000 at the beginning of 1995 in a portfolio of common stocks of large companies, your investment would have been worth almost $5,500 by the end of 1999.

Some of the more specific reasons why individuals might invest include accumulating funds to buy a home, sending their children to college, retiring comfortably, or weathering an unexpected crisis in their lives (e.g., temporary unemployment). Also, even though investing is serious business and should never be taken lightly, some people invest because they find that it provides a fun challenge.

Investing also benefits society and the economy as a whole. Obviously, by increasing personal wealth, investing can contribute to higher overall economic growth and prosperity. For example, if investing increases the value of an individual's pension fund, at retirement that person will have more disposable income and a higher standard of living, which both benefit the economy as a whole. In addition, the process of investing helps to create financial markets in which companies can raise capital. This function also contributes to greater economic growth and prosperity.

Specific types of investments provide other benefits to society as well. Common stocks, for example, provide a mechanism for monitoring the performance of company management by stockholders who own a corporation. Municipal bonds benefit those who pay proportionally high income tax because interest from municipal bonds is exempt from federal tax. At the same time, municipal bonds provide capital for valuable public projects such as schools and roads.

THE IMPORTANCE OF INVESTMENT DECISIONS

Investment decisions may be more important today than ever before. Several reasons explain this growing importance, and the following sections discuss some of the more important ones.

Larger Menu of Investment Choices

Today's investors choose among a dizzying array of investment alternatives, many of which have only been around a few years. Consider mutual funds, for example, which divide large portfolios of investments into small shares to allow investors to commit limited funds. In 1970, 361 mutual funds operated in the United States. Today, that number has grown to close to 9,000. Even to buy something as simple as a money market mutual fund, an investor must choose from more than 850 different funds.

As the number of funds grows, so does the diversity of their investment goals. The Investment Company Institute classifies mutual funds by investment objective. In 1975, it defined 7 categories of mutual funds. Today, it uses 21 different categories of mutual funds.

The larger menu of investment choices today means that an investor can probably find an investment instrument that suits personal needs. At the same time, however, the larger menu also increases the potential for confusion and poor choices. Today's investors must do their homework extremely carefully.

Longer Life Expectancies

You probably already know that life expectancies in the United States and in most developed countries are rising. Since 1950, the life expectancy of an American turning age 65 increased by about one-third. A 65-year-old in good health can expect to live for at least another 20 years.

One effect of longer life expectancies is an increase in the duration of the average person's retirement. Accumulating funds for retirement is one major reason that people invest, and a longer retirement period means more funds need to be accumulated, which requires more careful investing. Further, the rising cost of health care will likely require greater reserves for tomorrow's retirees, compared with today's retirees, to provide the same standard of living.

Begin work tomorrow and the experts will tell you to plan on saving at least $1 million for retirement (and that's in today's dollars). What's more, much of this retirement savings will be up to you. Do not count on Social Security or a company's pension to provide more than a small percentage of what you are going to need after you retire. In fact, the trend today has been toward so-called defined contribution plans such as 401(k) plans and away from traditional pension plans, or defined benefit plans. With a 401(k), you and your employer contribute to your retirement plan each year. Most plans give employees a great deal of flexibility when it comes to deciding where to invest their retirement savings. In other words, the investment decisions an employee makes while working will, to a large extent, determine whether that person will enjoy a financially secure retirement. The collapse of Enron in 2001, and along with it the value of the retirement accounts of thousands of workers, further illustrates the need to invest retirement savings properly.

Flat Growth in Personal Income

How much have personal incomes grown in the United States over the past 10 or 20 years? Adjusted for inflation, median per-capita U.S. income increased at an annual rate of about 2% between 1980 and today. Real median per-capita income actually fell slightly between 1989 and 1991, and between 2001 and 2002. Experts believe that average personal income is unlikely to substantially outpace the rate of inflation in the coming decades.

These personal income data suggest that one should not rely merely on increasing personal income to improve one's future standard of living. The key to improving a future standard of living may well be careful investing.

Changing Labor Market

The average person entering the workplace today will change jobs about five times over his or her lifetime. Further, one in three workers will be unemployed at some point during their working years. The old ideal of going to work for a company right out of college and staying there until retirement will likely be the exception, not the rule, in tomorrow's labor market. Even IBM, which once had a reputation of virtually guaranteeing lifetime employment, reduced its work-force by more than 100,000 in the past few years.

These sobering trends imply that people will have to rely more on their own resources and less on corporate paternalism to meet major financial goals. If nothing else, the changing labor market means everyone should accumulate a larger cushion of resources to break an unexpected fall. You never know when your employer is going to downsize your job out of existence!

A BRIEF HISTORY OF INVESTING

Investing itself, as a legitimate organized human endeavor, does not have a long history. Investing is an outgrowth of economic development and the maturation of modern capitalism. About three centuries ago, the world economy featured no stock exchanges or bond markets to speak of and only a handful of banks. The Bank of England, for example, was not founded until 1694. It is considered to be history's first modern bank because it was the first institution empowered to accept deposits, issue notes to serve as paper money, make loans, and discount bills.

The London Stock Exchange, the first recognizable stock exchange, or *bourse,* was also chartered in 1694.[2] Stock markets were established in most other economically advanced countries over the next 100 years or so. (The ancestor of the New York Stock Exchange, or NYSE, for example, was founded in 1792.) Both the Bank of England and the London Stock Exchange were initially distrusted, and even despised, by many in English society. As recently as the middle of the past century, the London Stock Exchange was a struggling weakling, often threatened with extinction by Parliament.

The notion of individuals pooling their capital in an organized fashion to jointly finance and own a business venture is also a fairly new concept. Although some evidence indicates joint-stock associations existed in ancient Rome, the evolution of common stock as we know it did not start until the European commercial revolution, which sprang from the Renaissance. Joint-stock companies were first organized in Europe to finance sea voyages, exploration, and trade. A joint-stock company proved to be an efficient organizational form in which to provide the large capital needs and distribute the risks that these voyages entailed. The historical evidence suggests that the Dutch East India Company, founded in 1602, was the first corporation established with permanent capital stock. The idea of transferring shares from individual to individual soon followed. However, general incorporation laws and the notion of limited liability that protected stockholders from responsibility for all of a corporation's debts were not firmly established in either Europe or the United States until the mid-nineteenth century.

Less than a century ago, stock manipulation and insider trading were neither illegal nor uncommon in the United States. During 1929, for example, more than

---

[2]A number of bourses, or financial markets, operated before the establishment of the London Stock Exchange. The first was established in Antwerp in 1531. These bourses were not, strictly speaking, stock exchanges. Rather, they were continuous fairs where dealings in commodities, bills of exchange, and insurance took place.

100 issues traded on the NYSE were subject to active pool, or syndicate, operations that involved overt manipulation of stock prices by members of the exchange.[3] Wildly overpriced, even fraudulent, securities were bought and sold openly, with little fanfare or government interference. In 1901, U.S. Steel reportedly raised $1.4 billion in capital, including more than $500 million in common stock, supported by at least $700 million of intangible, even fictitious, assets.

Before the 1920s, those who thought of themselves as investors generally owned bonds to ensure income and safety of principal. Only the stocks of a few companies qualified as investment-grade securities. These securities consisted mostly of bank and insurance stocks, which were unlisted, backed by real capital, and could expect to raise dividends regardless of the economic environment. The stocks traded on the NYSE were generally considered to be speculative in nature. Railroads, for example, simply carried too much debt to be considered investments. It was not until the 1920s that common stocks matured as investment vehicles.

Few Americans owned any securities, however, much less any common stocks, in the early part of the twentieth century. Even in the speculative frenzy that preceded the 1929 stock market crash, probably no more than 3 million individuals out of a population of about 122 million actually owned any shares of common stock. This fact contradicts the popular view that millions of ordinary Americans were playing the stock market in the late 1920s. In fact, some historians doubt that the crash caused or even contributed significantly to the Great Depression.[4]

Stock ownership, and investing in general, were not common in U.S. households until after the end of World War II. In 1952, 6.5 million individuals owned stocks (about 4% of the population). By 1970, that number had risen to about 31 million (almost 15% of the population). Still, the vast majority of household financial assets, about 80% in 1970, consisted of savings accounts and certificates of deposit from financial institutions.

During the 1970s and 1980s, millions of Americans finally made the transition from savers to investors. This trend was stimulated by the explosive growth of money market mutual funds during the late 1970s. Fed up with earning 5.5% interest on savings deposits in banks, savers moved billions of dollars into money market funds that yielded 10% or more.[5] As interest rates began to fall during the 1980s, many of these individuals started buying stocks, bonds, and mutual fund shares; in short, they became investors. The number of mutual fund accounts grew from about 9 million in 1976 to more than 100 million today. By some estimates more than half of all American adults today could be classified as "investors."

THE INVESTMENT PROCESS

Before anyone begins an investment program, several preliminary tasks need to be completed. The first preparatory task is to inventory all the investor's assets and liabilities (both financial and nonfinancial). Add up all current financial

---

[3]This practice of stock price manipulation is illegal today.
[4]See, for example, John K. Galbraith, *The Great Crash of 1929* (Boston: Houghton-Mifflin, 1954).
[5]The assets of money market mutual funds grew from less than $4 billion in 1976 to more than $186 billion only five years later in 1981.

assets (checking and savings accounts, CDs, and so forth), and determine how much is already set aside for retirement (e.g., the current balance of any pension plan, individual retirement account). In addition, assign rough market values to all physical, or real, assets (automobiles, home furnishings, and a home if the investor owns one). Next, add up all liabilities, including things such as the current balances on any mortgage, auto, or credit card loans. Subtracting liabilities from assets gives the investor's current net worth and a pretty good picture of his or her current financial situation. The net worth influences appropriate investment goals and helps with investment planning and selection.

After completing an inventory of assets and liabilities, an investor proceeds with the analysis by asking some questions about investment goals. What should investing accomplish? Setting goals will help guide investment selection and management, closing the gap between an investor's current situation and where he or she would like to be in the future. These goals can be fairly specific (e.g., to accumulate sufficient funds to send two children to college starting 10 years from now) or they can be more general (e.g., to fund a comfortable retirement in 20 years). Whether general or specific, investment goals should be realistic, and they should bear some relationship to the investor's present and expected future situation. Investment goals are also influenced by external factors—such as economic conditions.

The next task is to review current insurance coverage. Most people can break all their insurance policies into three general areas: life, health and disability, and property and liability insurance. An investor needs adequate insurance in all three areas, but it should be the right kind of insurance. Many financial experts argue that few American households meet this goal; most are overinsured in some areas and underinsured in others. Many single people, for example, carry life insurance that they may not need while carrying no disability insurance, which they probably do need. Several books on personal financial planning discuss insurance in detail.[6]

Finally, the investor should establish an emergency fund before investing. This fund can consist of low-risk, short-term investments such as money market funds. The emergency fund serves two basic purposes: (1) provides a financial safety net in the event of an unexpected emergency, such as a long-term illness or temporary unemployment, and (2) stores funds to take advantage of changing financial conditions. Experts generally suggest that an adequate emergency fund should hold an amount approximately equal to three to six months of one's normal salary.

Risk and Return Assessment

After performing these preliminary tasks, the next step in the investment process is an assessment of risk and return priorities. This assessment involves answering the following three specific questions.

- *What holding period is appropriate?* Historically, security returns behave differently over short periods of time than over longer periods of time. Returns over long holding periods show far less volatility than do returns over short holding periods. Between 1926 and today, stock returns for

---

[6]See, for example, Louis Boone, David Kurtz, and Douglas Hearth, *Planning Your Financial Future*, 3rd ed. (Mason, OH: South-Western, 2003).

one-year holding periods ranged between 54% and −43%. By contrast, annualized stock returns for 25-year holding periods ranged between 15% and 6%. The decision to invest for the short or long term could significantly affect investment selection.

- *What expected return is necessary?* Investing offers few guarantees, so we refer to future returns as expected returns. Everyone wants the highest return possible, but as we will see, higher expected returns come at a price. Investment choices depend, in part, on the return necessary to achieve investment goals. For example, to accumulate $25,000 in 10 years to send a child to college, a parent who is willing to invest $1,500 per year (starting today) will need to earn a return of about 8% per year. If money market funds are yielding only 5%, what other alternatives would allow him or her to achieve this goal? Two solutions are to invest more each year or to find investment instruments that have expected returns higher than those of money market funds.

- *How much risk is tolerable?* The question of willingness to accept risk is difficult to answer, but it is critical. Risk tolerance is low for someone who practically suffers a nervous breakdown every time a stock drops by a few pennies. However, someone who merely shrugs when a stock drops five points ($5 per share) can tolerate more risk. The point is that each investor needs to be comfortable with his or her investment selections. Measuring an individual's risk tolerance in any kind of objective way may be next to impossible. However, certain things appear to influence tolerance for risk. These factors include age, marital status, family responsibilities, and income. For example, a retiree living on a fixed income may be less tolerant of risk than a young person with a rising income.

As we discuss in the next chapter, investment risk comes in many forms. Some forms can be measured, while others cannot. A specific investment may expose the investor to a high amount of one type of risk but a low amount of another type. When making investment decisions, investors must be careful not to fear the wrong risks.

Other Issues

In addition to current financial status and risk and return preferences, three other issues should guide preparation to invest. The first concerns tax status. An investor should always know his or her marginal tax rate (based on combined federal and state taxes). Also, an account that accommodates investment for retirement may earn tax-deferred income, which means that the owner pays no taxes on account income until the money is withdrawn at retirement.

Tax status can have a major impact on the selection of investments. For example, someone who is investing for retirement in a tax-deferred account has no reason to buy municipal bonds, the interest from which is exempt from federal income taxes. However, someone in a high marginal tax bracket who is not investing for retirement may find that municipal bonds provide valuable protection from taxes.

After considering tax status, the analysis should turn to preference for capital gains or income. As we will see, investment returns can come from both capital gains (price appreciation) and income (dividend and interest payments). Someone who expresses a preference for income is probably better off investing in bonds than in stocks. Because capital gains receive preferential tax treatment for some taxable investors, tax status may greatly influence the choice between capital gains and income.

Finally, ask yourself how much time you can afford to spend on your investments. Someone may be better off investing in mutual funds than individual securities if he or she cannot spend much time selecting and managing investments or if this work seems undesirable.

Investment Selection

With preparations completed and questions about risk/return preferences, tax effects, and other background issues resolved, the investment process proceeds with selection of the most appropriate investment instruments. Sometimes called asset allocation, this stage is probably the most complex and time-consuming in the investment process.

One reason why investment selection can be so time-consuming is the wealth of information available to today's investor. Computer technology, especially the Internet, makes it easier and cheaper to find information about various investments. In fact, today the problem isn't finding information, but sifting through the massive amount of information available. The Investment Insight box on page 12 lists some investment stops along the World Wide Web.

Although the menu of investments is long and diverse, most people invest in stocks, bonds, and money market instruments. Stocks represent ownership interest in corporations such as Amazon.com, Home Depot, or Pfizer. Suppose you own 100 shares of Wal-Mart Stores, you actually own a tiny piece of the giant retailer. As a stockholder, you share in the company's profits in the form of cash dividends as well as potential increases in the stock price as the company's profits increase. Although income is a consideration, price appreciation is the main reason people invest in common stocks. As a company grows and prospers, the value of its stock should rise.

By contrast, if you a own a bond, you are actually lending money to some organization. Bonds are issued by governments (federal, state, and local) and corporations. You are paid a predetermined amount of interest each year for lending the organization your money. At some future certain date, the bond "matures" and you are paid a predetermined amount of money, called the face value. The face value of a bond can be thought of as a loan's principal. Because bonds pay fixed amounts of interest each year, the price of a bond—though not its face value—changes as interest rates change. Bond prices rise when interest rates fall, and vice versa. The main motivation for buying bonds is income, though under certain conditions bonds do rise in price.

Owning a money market instrument also means you are lending money to an organization. They are like bonds in the sense that you receive a predetermined amount of interest and the face value at maturity. Unlike bonds, however, all money market instruments mature within one year. Some investors even refer to market instruments as *cash* because they mature in a short amount of time. Examples of money market instruments include Treasury bills (T-bills) and bank savings accounts. A T-bill is a short-term IOU issued by the U.S. Treasury, so if you buy a T-bill you are lending money to the U.S. government. In the case of a

asset allocation
The stage of the investment process in which the most appropriate investment instruments are selected.

stock
Ownership interest in a corporation.

bond
Interest-bearing certificate issued by governments and corporations.

face value
Predetermined worth of a bond investment instrument.

money market instrument
A short-term, liquid, interest-bearing investment instrument (e.g., Treasury bills, bank savings accounts).

INVESTMENT INSIGHT

Investment Stops Along the World Wide Web

The Internet is a bonanza for investors. They can use their personal computers to obtain business news, information, price quotes, and research. Often the most difficult task is knowing where to start. The following are some examples:

http://quote.yahoo.com

Yahoo's investment site. Provides price quotes and other investment information in real time, or slightly delayed. Search the entire Internet using Yahoo's search engine.

http://investor.msn.com

Microsoft Network's investment site. Nonsubscribers have access to most of the site.

www.cnbc.wsj.com

A joint venture of CNBC and *The Wall Street Journal.* Excellent source of business news.

www.quicken.com

Quicken's personal finance site, with an extensive investments section.

www.morningstar.com

Morningstar's Web site containing news, articles, and information. Users can screen stocks and mutual funds.

www.cnnfn.com

Web site of CNN's financial network. Source of news, advice, and information.

www.fidelity.com

Homepage of Fidelity Investments, the nation's largest mutual fund company and a major discount broker.

www.schwab.com

Homepage of Charles Schwab, a leading discount broker.

www.vanguard.com

Homepage of the Vanguard Group, a leading mutual fund company.

www.ml.com

Homepage of Merrill Lynch, the nation's largest brokerage firm.

www.nasd.com

Homepage of the National Association of Securities Dealers.

www.sec.gov

Homepage of the U.S. Securities & Exchange Commission; access to the Edgar database (financial reports).

---

bank savings account, you are lending money to a bank. The reasons for investing in money market instruments are liquidity, income, and safety of principal.

Table 1.1 shows how stocks, bonds, and money market instruments compare on the basis of several investment characteristics (total return, stability of principal, current income, stability of income, and growth of income). We discuss stocks, bonds, and money market instruments in much more detail in subsequent chapters, starting with Chapter 3.

strategic asset allocation

Plan for determining most advantageous mix of investment instruments in a portfolio.

Strategic Asset Allocation The two phases to asset allocation are strategic and tactical. In **strategic asset allocation**, an investor must decide on the general mix of investment instruments to include in the portfolio. Should it focus on stocks, bonds, money market instruments, or some combination of the three? If a combination of instruments is most appropriate, what proportion of each should the portfolio contain? For example, an investor's situation may dictate a mix of investment instruments in a portfolio of about 60% stocks, 30% bonds, and 10% money market instruments.

tactical asset allocation

Selection of specific investments within each general category included in a portfolio.

Tactical Asset Allocation The other phase to asset allocation is **tactical asset allocation**. It involves the selection of specific investments within each general category. Today's investment environment offers a wide range of choices, but in general, an investor can take one of two approaches to the selection of investment instruments: passive or active.

TABLE 1.1

Risk and Return
Characteristics of Stocks,
Bonds, and Money Market
Instruments

Characteristic	Stocks	Bonds	Money Market Instruments
Total return	A	B	C
Stability of principal	C	B	A
Current income	B	A	C
Stability of income	B	A	C
Growth in income	A	C	B

Note: A is best or highest.

A passive investor may try to buy the market, usually in the form of a mutual fund that attempts to replicate the performance of a broad market without many changes in portfolio composition. Such funds are called index funds. Vanguard, a large U.S. mutual fund company, offers several index funds constructed to replicate the performance of well-known worldwide capital markets indexes, both stock and bond. In fact, the Vanguard 500 Index Fund, which tracks the Standard & Poor's (S&P) 500, is one of the largest mutual funds in the United States with more than $70 billion in assets. If a portfolio should contain 50% stocks and 50% bonds, a passive investor might buy equal amounts of two such funds, one that replicates the broad stock market and one that replicates the broad bond market.

Active investors take a more vigorous approach to investment selection. They look for specific investment instruments that offer superior risk/return characteristics. This approach requires a decision whether to invest in individual securities, mutual funds, or both. An active investor might decide that so-called growth stocks are coming back into favor with investors, so he or she would shift more money into growth stocks. Perhaps, believing that long-term interest rates would fall in the next couple of years, someone might invest all available funds in long-term corporate bonds. Active investing is more time-consuming and difficult than passive investing, but many investors believe that the payoff is worth the extra effort.

Investment Management

The last stage in the investment process involves monitoring the performance of investments and making changes when necessary. Investment management techniques fall into two categories: (1) active management of portfolios and (2) buy-and-hold management.

Investors who actively manage their portfolios buy and sell more frequently than more passive investors. Active investors may shift funds between various types of instruments in anticipation of changing markets. To plan these moves, they tend to monitor the performance of their investments more closely, and they may be more concerned about short-term performance than passive investors. A passive investor, however, tends to buy a portfolio of securities and keep it pretty much intact for a long period of time. This investor may be less inclined to make changes to the portfolio in response to changing market conditions.

Investors who select securities passively (e.g., invest in index funds) are more likely to approach investment management passively as well. However, an investor could actively select securities and still take a passive buy-and-hold approach to investment management. This investor would buy a portfolio of specific securities that meet certain criteria and then hold the portfolio for a fairly long period of time, making few if any changes.

Financial experts agree that both active and passive investors should make changes to the contents of their investment portfolios as they go through life. What is best for a 30-year-old may be inappropriate for someone who is 65. A 30-year-old investing for retirement should probably have most of his or her money invested in common stocks. By contrast, a 60-year-old should probably invest half in stocks and about half in bonds and money market instruments.

SOME APPARENT TRUISMS IN INVESTMENTS

Although investments may sometimes seem to be a rational, precise, almost scientific field of study, much of investing actually involves ambiguity, subjective analysis, and opinion. One investor's favored security selection technique or other method may be scorned by another. Nevertheless, six major truisms, as we call them, appear to characterize investments without much dispute. We briefly introduce each of these truisms here and continue to discuss them throughout the entire book.

Lessons of History

As you read the pages that follow, you will confront the assumption that history teaches several important lessons about investments. In fact, the other five truisms that we discuss are all based, at least in part, on historical observation. Further, investment theory and analysis often involve the application of historical relationships. For example, much of modern portfolio theory, which we discuss in Chapters 17–19, was developed and tested using historical data.

Consider some of the lessons that speculative bubbles teach us. A speculative bubble is the rapid increase in the price of an investment with no apparent justification other than a belief, or hope, that the price will go still higher. One of history's most amusing bubbles, at least in retrospect, is chronicled in the Investment History box on page 15.

The history of bubbles teaches us two important lessons. First, the price of an investment, in the long run, will reflect its true, or intrinsic value. In the short run, however, a substantial difference between price and value can exist. Eventually, the market will correct its mistake. All bubbles burst. The second lesson is that investor emotions affect investment performance. The psychological and emotional influences on investment decision making and valuation can be significant.

However, remember an important caveat whenever you apply historical observations or relationships to evaluate current and future investment situations. The past is no guarantee of the future; the past may repeat itself, but variations are common. Go back to the history of speculative bubbles, for example. No two bubbles have been identical, either in duration or magnitude. Some periods of time have seen many bubbles, whereas others have seen few. It may be easy

INVESTMENT HISTORY

Tulip Mania

One of the most amazing speculative bubbles in history occurred in the early part of the seventeenth century and dealt with, of all things, tulips in Holland. Holland in the early seventeenth century was one of the most prosperous and economically advanced countries in Europe.

Tulips were introduced to European horticulture in Vienna (c. 1559) when an Austrian count brought some plants back from Turkey, where they had been grown for centuries. (The word tulip comes from a Turkish word meaning "turban.") The Dutch fascination with tulips started soon after. Wealthy individuals began to order tulip roots directly from Constantinople, often paying high prices, and tulips in one's garden became a social necessity. The rage for tulips eventually caught on in the Dutch middle class, as merchants and shopkeepers began to vie with one another for the most sought-after varieties of the plants. The resulting demand drove the prices of tulip bulbs sharply upward until people started to view tulips as more than decorative additions to gardens, but rather as ways to make money. Tulips became investments whose prices were bound to go higher and higher; the frenzy had begun.

By 1635, tulip mania was in full bloom in Holland. The normal business of the nation was neglected, and the population embarked in the tulip trade. People rushed to convert their property into cash, and invested it in flowers. Houses and lands were offered for sale at absurdly low prices. Traders in the bourses in Amsterdam, Rotterdam, and other Dutch towns abandoned mundane things such as loans and wheat and began actively trading tulip bulbs. Even call options were available, one could have the right to buy tulips at a fixed price for a fixed period of time.

The prices of tulips reached absurd levels. One person is reported to have offered 12 acres of land in exchange for one especially glorious bulb. A *Semper Augustus* root, the most prized of all, was sold for 5,500 florins in 1636 although it weighed less than half an ounce. At the same time, in Amsterdam, 4,600 florins would have bought a new carriage complete with two horses!

Eventually, the more prudent Dutch citizens began to see that this folly could not last forever, and they began to sell their tulip bulbs. As this conviction spread in the early part of 1637, prices started to fall faster and faster. Dealers went bankrupt and refused to honor their commitments to buy bulbs. As more and more people tried to sell their tulips, a general panic took hold and prices plunged even further. When the dust finally settled, tulips were selling for no more than common onions, and Holland's economy plunged into a severe recession.

Questions for Critical Thinking

1. What are some of the similarities between the tulip bubble and the recent bubble in Internet stocks?
2. In retrospect, it seems silly that so many people fall into the "bubble trap." If so, why do bubbles keep occurring?

to state that bubbles are inevitable, but predicting when and where they will occur is far more difficult.

As another example, consider the general history of security returns. Between the beginning of 1992 and the end of 2001, stocks outperformed T-bills by a substantial margin (12.4% per year for stocks versus about 5% for T-bills). Does that mean that stocks will outperform T-bills over the next 10 years? No one can answer yes for certain, although many believe stocks probably will. However, the next 10 years could be quite different from the past 10 years.

Here's another fact to consider, since 1972 stocks have passed through six bull markets and six bear markets.[7] Each bull and bear market, however, differed

---

[7] A bull market is one where prices are generally rising while a bear market is one where prices are generally falling.

in both duration and magnitude. The 1990 bear market lasted less than five months while the bear market that began in 2000 lasted for almost three years. The 1980 bull market lasted for about a year. By contrast, the bull market that began in 1990 lasted for almost ten years. Whenever some "expert" tells you he or she has a system that regularly beats the market, remember this warning: *Past performance is all well and good, but the past is no guarantee of the future.*

Positive Relationship Between Risk and Return

Although some important exceptions may occur, in general the relationship between risk and return is positive. Higher-risk investments must offer investors higher potential returns. Historically at least, the positive relationship between risk and return seems pretty clear.

Figure 1.1 graphs so-called *cumulative wealth indexes* of stocks, Treasury bonds, and Treasury bills. (We talk about how a cumulative wealth index is constructed in the next chapter.) All these indexes assume that an investor started with $1,000 in 1926 and held each investment through the end of 2001. The indexes show how much wealth the investments in stocks or bills would have produced at the end of each subsequent year. Stocks clearly outperformed T-bonds

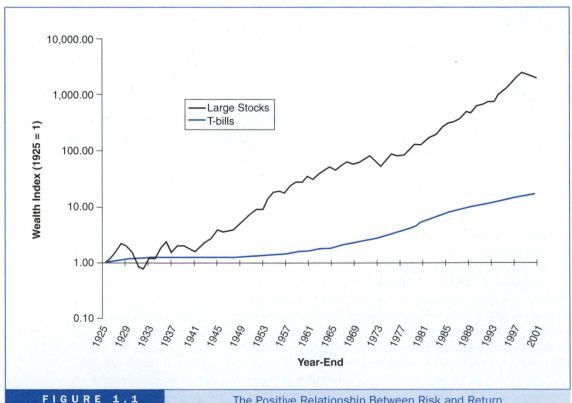

FIGURE 1.1   The Positive Relationship Between Risk and Return
Note: The wealth index shows the growth in the value of an investment over time. For instance, every $1 invested in stocks at the end of 1925 was worth approximately $2,183 by the end of 2001.

and T-bills by a wide margin. A $1,000 investment in stocks at the beginning of 1926 would have been worth almost $2.2 million by the end of 2001. Similar investments in T-bonds and T-bills would have been worth around $46,500 and $17,000, respectively, by the end of 2001. Measuring the averages, stock averaged a return of about 12.5% per year versus 5.5% for T-bonds and 3% for T-bills. At the same time, however, stocks showed far more year-to-year variation in returns than either T-bonds or T-bills. The amount returns vary from period to period is one measure of risk.

What explains the positive relationship between risk and return? The answer is risk aversion; all investors are risk averse to one degree or another (i.e., they prefer to avoid risk without some enticement). Let's say you can play a game of chance for $100. The odds are 50/50 that if you play the game, you will either lose your $100 bet or double your money. Would you play the game? If you're risk averse, you probably would not. If you play the game, you are taking a risk and the total expected payoff from the game is zero.[8] In other words, your expected wealth will be the same regardless of whether you take the risk.

Now change the odds slightly. Suppose you have a 1-in-3 chance of losing $100 and a 2-in-3 chance of making $100. (The game still costs $100 to play.) If you are risk averse, you are more likely to play the game now because the expected payoff is now positive (it is about $34), meaning that your expected wealth will increase if you play. Risk aversion leads you to demand compensation, in the form of a positive expected payoff, to voluntarily take risk.

Benefits of Diversification

The desire to avoid risk leads investors to resist putting all their investment nest eggs in one basket. Distributing available funds among several investments reduces the risk of harm from an adverse move in any one security. This diversification is beneficial to investors, as both academics and practitioners widely agree. The well-known financial advisor and writer Andrew Tobias states that the goal of investing is to:

Buy low, sell high. Having said that, the fact remains that it's rarely possible to know with any real degree of confidence what is low or high. To know that you have to know what the future will bring and no one does. As a result, the only sensible strategy for all but the most avid risk takers is to diversify.[9]

In a nutshell, diversification is beneficial because it allows investors to beat the risk/return trade-off, up to a point. Through diversification they can expose themselves to less risk, yet at the same time maintain about the same expected return. Alternatively, they can increase the expected return on their investments without significantly increasing risk.

Does diversification really work? The answer is pretty clearly yes. In Table 1.2 we show measures of risk and return for two stocks drawn from the S&P 500.

---

[8]The expected payoff from the game is found as follows: $0.5(\$100) + 0.5(-\$100) = \$0$
[9]Andrew Tobias, *The Only Other Investment Guide You'll Ever Need* (New York: Bantam Books, 1989), p. 104.

TABLE 1.2		Stock 1	Stock 2	**Portfolio (half 1 and half 2)**
Benefits of Diversification	Return	27.2%	49.9%	38.1%
	Standard deviation (a measure of risk)	25.9%	39.0%	21.3%
	Coefficient of variation (a measure of the risk/return trade-off)	0.95	0.78	0.56

Notes: A higher standard deviation indicates more risk. A lower coefficient of variation indicates a better risk/return trade-off.

(We describe how these risk and return measures are calculated in the next chapter.) The same statistics are calculated for a portfolio consisting of an equal combination of the two stocks.

The results might look, at first glance, to be the result of magic. After all, the portfolio's return is the simple average of the returns from the two individual stocks, but the standard deviation is lower. The coefficient of variation is also lower, indicating a better risk/return trade-off. This outcome is not the result of some sort of alchemy, but rather it is the result of diversification.

Not only do we know that diversification works, but perhaps more remarkably, we know why it works. Diversification works because returns on individual securities are not perfectly correlated over time. Just because one security's price rises by 10% this year, no one can say that all securities will perform exactly that way. Some securities prices will rise more, some will rise less, and some will fall. For example, between July 1984 and August 1987, the S&P 500 stock index more than doubled (up to 118%), yet stocks of drug companies were up more than 200% while oil stocks rose less than 90%. Between October 1990 and December 1992, the S&P 500 rose about 42%, but computer stocks dropped about 40%. The next chapter says even more about diversification.

Investing Knows No National Boundaries

Throughout history some investors searched outside their own countries for good investment opportunities. During the 1800s, for example, English and Scottish investment trusts provided much of the capital to build the railroads in the western United States. In the 1960s, visionaries such as John Templeton started to open up foreign stock markets to U.S. investors. Nevertheless, even 10 years ago few U.S. investors ever ventured beyond national boundaries.

Today, however, more and more U.S. investors look to international markets. For example, U.S. investors poured almost $5.5 billion into international stock mutual funds during the first six months of 1996. These investments are not limited to established foreign markets such as Canada, Germany, or Japan; intrepid investors expanded to the so-called emerging markets in countries such as Brazil, Malaysia, and Turkey.

Many forces drive contemporary investing across national boundaries. Certainly the political and economic changes that swept over the world in the late 1980s and early 1990s contributed to the globalization of investments by opening up many parts of the world to foreign investment. Another factor has been the integration of security markets worldwide. Today, U.S. T-bonds are traded in Singapore, German stocks are traded in Tokyo, and Japanese stocks are traded in New York. An investor who wants to buy or sell several thousand shares of stock in a U.S. company may be as likely to trade the shares on the London Stock Exchange as on the New York Stock Exchange. Furthermore, most governments and large corporations raise capital by selling securities worldwide.

Although investing internationally can offer U.S. investors attractive returns, it is not without its share of risk. International investing exposes you to foreign exchange risk. Changes in the value of the U.S. dollar, relative to other currencies, can result in both a positive and a negative impact on your returns. For example, during the first six months of 1996, Japanese stocks rose by 10% measured in yen. Measured in dollars, Japanese stocks rose by more than 25%. Many emerging markets are notoriously volatile.

Financial Markets Function Pretty Well

Despite the risk and novelty of international investing, our fifth truism states that the financial markets function pretty well throughout most of the world, especially in the more developed countries. Although not perfect, financial markets are generally fair, orderly, and competitive with many buyers and sellers. Furthermore, although investors should always be wary, unscrupulous traders are peddling far fewer outright fraudulent securities today compared with 75 years ago.

What makes a market function well? Three characteristics of today's financial markets illuminate this question. First, security prices adjust quickly, although not always correctly, to new information. For example, on June 9, 1993, Apple Computer's stock lost more than 10% of its value as investors reacted to negative news about the company's earnings. Had you owned Apple it is unlikely that you could have avoided the debacle because the stock dropped so rapidly after the announcement that day. Further, before the June announcement, between June 2 and June 8, Apple lost more than 14% of its value. To have avoided the June 9 sell-off, you would have had to correctly anticipate the earnings news. The issue of how security prices react to new information is discussed extensively in Chapter 7.

A second characteristic of today's financial markets is the existence of several major equilibrium pricing relationships. If specific pricing relationships among different securities get out of line, in a well-functioning market, prices will quickly adjust to correct levels specified by the pricing relationships. Consider a simple example of an equilibrium pricing relationship. An investor might purchase an option to buy 100 shares of some stock at, say, $50 per share (referred to as a call option). If the stock is currently trading for $60 per share, you know that the option must have a market price of at least $1,000 (60 minus 50, times 100). To see why, assume the option is selling for $700. Someone could buy the option, exercise it to buy the stock for $50 per share, paying $5,000 for 100 shares, and then immediately sell the stock for $60 per share. This risk-free transaction would pay $300 (ignoring transaction costs). This is an example of arbitrage. Obviously, if one person could profit from this transaction, so could everyone else, and their purchases would drive the option's price upward quickly from $700 to at least $1,000. This kind of balance between supply and demand keeps price relationships among securities near equilibrium positions.

Finally, today's smoothly functioning financial markets eliminate any easy money from the table. Each investor competes with millions of other investors for great investments; many of these competitors devote substantial resources to the search. Online trading and almost instant access to information make the financial markets even more competitive today. These advantages do not mean, however, that small individual investors cannot compete with large institutional investors, nor does it mean that investors should not look for great investments. It means simply that great investments, those that are undervalued and offer better risk/reward characteristics than the market in general, are not easy to find. Undervalued securities typically do not stay undervalued for long.

Mistakes Happen

People make investment decisions, and people are not perfect. Therefore, people make investment mistakes. One cynic noted that investments is really the study of mistakes in retrospect. Even though investing can substantially increase an investor's future wealth, it is also fraught with potential dangers. Figure 1.2 lists some of the more common pitfalls investors should try to avoid. Let's elaborate on some of them.

- *Fad investing.* Investing in something just because everyone else seems to be is rarely a good idea. Fads become bubbles, and bubbles break. An old Wall Street expression reads something like this: "When you hear that everyone is buying, ask who's selling."
- *Chasing returns.* Investors move money in and out of investments often on the basis of short-term returns. This strategy rarely works. Performance measured over a short period of time is often a poor predictor of future performance.
- *Ignoring the effects of taxes and inflation.* Taxes and inflation can turn seemingly safe investments into money losers. For example, over the last 25 years, the

---

FIGURE 1.2

Common Investment Pitfalls

Investing has the potential to substantially increase your future wealth, but is also fraught with danger. Here are some common investment pitfalls.
- Ignoring the corrosive effect of inflation and taxes on investment returns
- Fad investing
- Chasing returns
- Buying after a major price increase
- Selling after a major price decline
- Trusting self-appointed touts and investment gurus
- Not fully understanding investment risk
- Fearing the wrong risks
- Keeping a loser in the hope of eventually breaking even
- Investing with no plan or goals
- Failing to diversify sufficiently
- Underinvesting in common stocks

return from Treasury bills—what most people would consider to be a low risk investment—is actually negative once taxes and inflation are taken into account.

- *Selling after a big drop/buying after a big increase.* A great deal of evidence, both anecdotal and scientific, shows that investors often overreact to new information, both positive and negative. Many savvy investors look to buy after major price declines, and sell after major price advances.

- *Hanging on to a loser.* Say you buy a stock for $50 a share. Almost immediately it drops to $40 a share, a decline of 20%. Would you sell? Many investors would hold onto the stock hoping for a rebound. Yet in order to get back to $50, the stock will have to rise in price by 25%. Maybe it will, but then again maybe not. You have to make that determination rationally. History is full of examples of investments that never bounced back. Polaroid, for example, reached its all-time high in 1972.

- *Failing to diversify.* According to recent statistics, more than half of the typical 401(k) retirement account is invested in the employee's company's stock, meaning the account is not properly diversified. The collapse of Enron painfully illustrates what can happen when investors fail to diversify. Not only did thousands of Enron employees lose their jobs, they lost most of their retirement savings as well.

- *Trusting the self-appointed touts and gurus.* Lots of people out there are willing to give investment advice. Unfortunately, the quality of this advice can be quite variable and many advisors have a hidden agenda; they want to sell you something. As with all consumer purchases, buyer beware.

OUTLINE OF FUTURE CHAPTERS

This book is divided into seven parts. Part 1, The World of Investments, reviews risk and return, direct investment alternatives, and indirect investment alternatives. Part 2, Financial Markets and Investment Returns, discusses the organization of the financial markets, how securities and bought and sold, and how professional investors make investment decisions. Part 3, Fixed Income Securities, explores the world of bonds. Part 4, Principles of Security Analysis, outlines in detail how common stocks are analyzed and valued. Part 5 is devoted to derivative securities, and Part 6 describes modern portfolio theory. Investment management is discussed in Part 7.

SUMMARY

1. **Why are investment decisions important?**
   People invest to increase their future wealth. People also invest in order meet personal goals such as buying a home or sending children to college. Investment decisions are important today because people are living longer, and thus will need more money when they retire; because personal income is rising slowly; because the job market continues to change; and because the menu of investment choices is longer.

2. **What is the history of investing?**
   As an organized legitimate endeavor, investing does not have a long history. The first recognizable banks and stock exchanges emerged only about 350 years ago. Until the 1920s,

most stocks were considered to be wildly speculative investments. In fact, until recently, few Americans owned any stocks or other investments. It was during the late 1970s and 1980s that many Americans made the transition from savers to investors. Today, more than half of all American adults would probably be classified as "investors."

3. **What are the steps involved in the investment process?**
    The first step in the investment process is to complete some preliminary tasks, including preparing financial statements and a budget, making sure you have adequate and appropriate insurance coverage, and establishing an emergency fund. The next step is to set some realistic investment goals. Then you must assess your tolerance for risk and determine the return necessary to meet monetary goals. The fourth step is to choose the most appropriate investments. The fifth step is to manage your investments.

4. **What are some of the important truisms in investments?**
    Six important investment truisms are as follows: One, although history has much to teach us, the past is never a guarantee of the future. Two, risk and return are generally positively related in that higher risk investments must offer higher potential returns. Three, diversification is beneficial and can reduce risk without significantly reducing returns. Four, investing take place worldwide. Five, financial markets throughout much of the world function well. Six, mistakes happen. Investors should try to avoid common pitfalls.

REVIEW EXERCISES

1. What is the general reason people invest? Cite two or three additional specific reasons people invest.
2. How can investing benefit society as a whole? What are some of the societal benefits of municipal bonds?
3. List some of the reasons why investing is so important today. How have longer life expectancies affected investment decisions?
4. How long has investing been an organized, socially acceptable activity? When did millions of Americans finally make the transition from savers to investors?
5. Before you begin to invest, what preparations should you complete? What factors should influence your investment goals?
6. When you assess risk and return, what are some of the questions you need to ask yourself? What factors appear to explain differences in risk tolerance?
7. Explain the key investment differences between stocks, bonds, and money market instruments. Historically, which of the three produces the highest returns?
8. Explain the difference between strategic asset allocation and tactical asset allocation. How does a passive approach to investment management differ from an active approach?
9. Historically, do risk and return exhibit a positive or negative relationship with one another? Why should we expect to see such a relationship?
10. List some of the more common investment mistakes. What is the relationship between fad investing and speculative bubbles?

 ## CRITICAL THINKING EXERCISE

Most of the critical thinking exercises at the end of each chapter involve the analysis of actual investment data. Using Microsoft Excel or a similar spreadsheet program will make the exercises much less tedious. (You may wish to review how to use Excel and its key features.) For Chapter 1, complete the following tasks:

1. Open the Data Workbook (available on the South-Western Web site). Familiarize yourself with the various worksheets contained in the data workbook, including how the data are presented.
2. Open the Wizard Workbook (also available on the South-Western Web site). The Wizard Workbook consists of a series of preformatted worksheets designed to solve common investment program. Familiarize yourself with each worksheet.

THE INTERNET INVESTOR

http://ww

1. The Internet contains a wealth of information and assistance on many investment topics. What's more, much of it is free. To help you get the most out of the Internet Investor exercises that appear at the end of every chapter, visit www.msn.com/tutorial/default.html. List three or four things that you learned that will help you improve your "surfing" skills.
2. One excellent investment oriented Web site is www.investor.msn.com. Visit the site and write a brief summary of some of the material and tools you found on the site.
3. An initial step in the investment process is to assess your tolerance for risk. Visit the Web site, www.investoreducation.org/quiz2a.htm, and take the interactive quiz. According to the results, how much investment risk can you tolerate? Do you agree or disagree with results?

2

Fundamentals of Risk and Return

PREVIOUSLY . . .	IN THIS CHAPTER . . .	TO COME . . .
We provided an overview of investments, including a brief history of investing, the investment process, and some of the apparent truisms in investments.	We introduce the concepts of risk and return in detail, the twin pillars of investing. People invest in order to earn a rate of return. At the same time, however, all investing exposes you to risk. We review how to measure returns, how to summarize returns, the various types of risk, and how some types of risk can be measured.	The foundation of investments continues by discussing the characteristics of the major investment alternatives available today.

CHAPTER OBJECTIVES

After reading Chapter 2, you should be able to answer the following questions:

1. What are the sources of investment returns?

2. How are investment returns measured?

3. What is investment risk and how is it measured?

4. How are risk and return measured for portfolios of assets?

5. Why does diversification benefit investors?

6. What is the relationship between risk and required return?

One of the investment truisms we discussed in the prior chapter was the positive relationship between risk and return. In a nutshell, higher-risk investments must offer investors higher potential returns because investors, as a group, are risk averse. Risk aversion carries two general implications. The first is that people will pay to avoid risk—something we all do when we buy insurance. We transfer risk from ourselves to the insurance company in exchange for a fee (the insurance premium). Risk aversion also implies that people voluntarily take risk only if they are offered some sort of an inducement. Higher potential returns are one such inducement.

Historically, the positive relationship between risk and return is easy to document. For example, between 1926 and today, stocks averaged an annual return of about 12%. By contrast, Treasury bill returns averaged slightly less than 4% per year over the same period. At the same time, however, stock returns showed far more year-to-year variation than T-bills returns. As discussed later in the chapter, this higher year-to-year variation indicates higher risk. Since 1926, annual stock returns ranged from a high of greater than 54% to a low of −43%. Annual T-bill returns, by comparison, remained relatively stable, ranging between a high of 14.5% and a low of 0.1%.

The concepts of risk and return unquestionably dominate the study of investments. Investors exchange current income for future promised returns. At the same time, however, all investments expose investors to risk. Understanding risk and return is crucial when selecting and evaluating investment alternatives. In this chapter, we describe the sources of investment returns, how investment returns are measured for both individual securities as well as portfolios, the many types of investment risk, how investment risk is measured, and the relationship between risk and required returns.

SOURCES OF INVESTMENT RETURNS

The two potential sources of investment returns are income and price changes. Income is the periodic cash flow paid to the investor. Some investments pay no income, while others pay a relatively high amount. Some investments pay a fixed amount each year while the income from other investment can vary from year to year. If you own a stock, the income you receive is referred to as **dividends**. Companies that pay dividends typically pay them four times a year. The income received from bonds and money market instruments is referred to as **interest**. Most bonds pay interest twice a year.

The other source of investment returns is price changes. The prices of most investments, though not all, usually rise or fall during a period of time. We refer to an increase in the price of an investment as a **capital gain**; a decrease in the price of an investment is referred to as a **capital loss**. When added to income, capital gains obviously increase investment returns, while capital losses decrease investment returns. Price declines can create negative investment returns even if the investment pays dividends or interest.

For example, during 1994 the return from Treasury bonds was −7.8%. The following year, T-bonds returned almost 29%. What happened? Bond prices fell throughout much of 1994, and these price declines more than offset interest payments. During 1995, by contrast, bond prices rose sharply. Interest payments combined with capital gains to produce an impressive return.

dividends
Periodic income received from stock investments.

interest
Periodic income received from bonds and money market instruments.

capital gain
An increase in the price or value of an asset.

capital loss
A decrease in the price or value of an asset.

Paper vs. Real Gains and Losses

We should stop for a moment and distinguish between paper gains and losses, versus real gains and losses. A simple example will illustrate the difference. Say you buy a stock for $50 a share. A year later the stock is selling for $60 a share. In one sense you made $10 a share, but unless you sell the stock it is only a paper profit, not a real one. Similarly, if the price of the stock had fallen from $50 to $40, your $10 loss is only a paper loss unless the stock is sold.

The distinction between paper and real gains and losses creates a number of important implications for investors, one of which is taxes. Only real or, using tax jargon, *realized* capital gains or losses have tax implications. Taxable investors must pay additional federal income taxes on realized capital gains. On the other hand, realized capital losses can be deducted.

Ex-Ante vs. Ex-Post Returns

ex-post returns

Historical returns.

ex-ante returns

Expected future returns.

Between the beginning of 1992 and the end of 2001 stocks returns averaged close to 14% per year. This return is a historical return; the technical term is an **ex-post return**. It is what someone *would* have earned had they invested in stocks during this 10-year period. Let's say, some analyst forecasts stocks will return an average of 10% over the next 10 years. This return is an **ex-ante return**. It is the return we expect to earn over some future period of time.

Obviously, the only investment returns we can accurately measure are ex-post returns, but we should base investment decisions today on ex-ante returns. You can only go forward not back in time when investing. So all investors are constantly confronted with the question: How well do historical returns predict future returns? It is a difficult question to answer. As we discussed briefly in Chapter 1, the past teaches us a great deal, but the past is never a guarantee of the future.

MEASURING INVESTMENT RETURNS

Because investment returns can come from income or price changes, any proper measure of investment needs to incorporate both. Take a look at Table 2.1. It lists annual returns for Johnson & Johnson's common stock over a recent 10-year period. The returns listed are called total returns or holding period returns. Holding period returns incorporate income as well as price changes.

total returns (holding period returns)

A measure of investment returns that includes both price changes and income.

Calculating Holding Period Returns

Holding period returns are calculated over a specific period of time, say a month, quarter, or year. The formula is as follows:

$$\text{HPR}_t = (P_t - P_{t-1} + \text{CF}_t)/P_{t-1} \tag{2.1}$$

where HPR_t is the holding period return over period t, P_t is the price at the end of the period, P_{t-1} is the price at the beginning of the period, and CF_t is the income, or cash flow, received from the investment during the period.

The data necessary to calculate annual holding period returns for Johnson & Johnson are shown in Table 2.2. Let's work an example. At the beginning of

Year	Holding Period Return
1992	−10.24%
1993	−9.13
1994	24.53
1995	58.50
1996	18.10
1997	34.12
1998	28.81
1999	12.49
2000	14.00
2001	13.84

TABLE 2.1

Annual Holding Period Returns for Johnson & Johnson: 1992–2001

Year	Year-End Price	Dividend
1991	$14.31	
1992	12.63	$0.22
1993	11.22	0.25
1994	13.69	0.28
1995	21.38	0.32
1996	24.88	0.37
1997	32.94	0.43
1998	41.94	0.49
1999	46.63	0.55
2000	52.53	0.62
2001	59.10	0.70

TABLE 2.2

Price and Dividend Data for Johnson & Johnson: 1991–2001

2001, or the end of 2000, Johnson & Johnson's common stock was selling for $52.53 per share. At the end of 2001, the stock sold for $59.10. In addition, during 2001, Johnson & Johnson paid $0.70 in cash dividends. Therefore, the stock's holding period return for 2001 was

$$HPR = (\$59.10 - \$52.53 + \$0.70)/\$52.53 = 12.5\%$$

Calculating Expected Returns All of the holding period returns shown so far are ex-post returns—meaning actual historical returns. We can also use Equation 2.1 to calculate expected future returns, or ex-ante returns. For example, let's assume we expect Johnson & Johnson's stock price to increase to $62.50 by the end of 2002. Further, we expect the company to pay $0.80 in cash dividends. Therefore, the *expected* return for 2002 is calculated as follows:

$$\text{Expected return} = (\$62.50 - \$59.10 + \$0.80)/\$59.10 = 7.1\%$$

Of course this calculation provides only an expected return; the actual 2002 return may be quite different! We discuss the importance of expected returns later in the chapter.

Inflation-Adjusted Returns In your introductory finance class you perhaps discussed the difference between nominal returns and real returns. Nominal returns are dollar returns and tell us nothing about changes in the purchasing power of the dollars. Real returns that take out the effect of inflation are also referred to as inflation adjusted returns.

You calculate a real holding period return, RHPR, as follows:

$$\text{RHPR} = [(1 + \text{HPR})/(1 + \text{IR})] - 1 \tag{2.2}$$

where HPR is the nominal holding period return and IR is the rate of inflation.[1]

As we calculated earlier, Johnson & Johnson posted a nominal holding period return during 2001 of 12.5%. During 2001, the rate of inflation was 1.9%, therefore, the stock's real holding period return was

$$\text{RHPR} = (1.125/1.019) - 1 = 10.4\%$$

Inflation can have a devastating impact on investment returns. At times in the past nominal returns were positive, but real returns were negative due to high rates of inflation. The Investment History box on page 29 tells about the agony of bond investors during the 1970s.

International Returns Say you invest in a non-dollar-denominated investment. Calculating the dollar return on this investment is more complicated and will be affected by changes in exchange rates. It is best illustrated with an example.

Say you bought a British government bond for £1,000 one year ago. Today the bond's price is £1,030. During the year the bond also paid you £65 in interest. When you bought the bond the exchange rate was 1.65 ($ per £); today the exchange rate is 1.62. What was your holding period return, measured both in pounds and in dollars? Finding the HPR in pounds is simple, we just use Equation 2.1:

$$(1.030 - 1,000 + 65)/1,000 = 9.5\%$$

Now, let's find the HPR measured in U.S. dollars. First, calculate how many dollars it took to buy the bond a year ago: 1.65 × £1,000 = $1,650. Next, compute the dollar value of the bond's current price as well as the income you received: 1.62(£1,030 + £65) = $1,773.90. Now we can find the holding period return in U.S. dollars using a slightly modified version of Equation 2.1. The dollar HPR equals ($1,773.90 − $1,650)/$1,650, or 7.51%.

---

[1]A close approximation for the real holding period return can be found by simply subtracting the inflation rate from the nominal holding period return.

I N V E S T M E N T   H I S T O R Y

The Agony of Bond Investors: 1965–1981

Not *that* long ago, bonds were considered to be pretty dull investments. You simply bought bonds for income. Inflation was low and didn't vary much from year to year. Consequently, interest rates were pretty stable and bond prices rarely changed by much. In mid-1964 bonds were paying about 5.5% per year. In the face of 2.5% inflation, bond investors considered this real return to be adequate. They never anticipated what was about to happen to them.

Between 1965 and 1981, inflation averaged more than 7.5% per year, meaning bond investors earned negative real rates of return. To make matters worse, as inflation soared so did interest rates. As interest rates rise, bond prices fall. In nominal terms, the total return from bonds between 1965 and 1981 averaged 2.4% per year. The total return from bonds adjusted for inflation, however, was −4.8%. Put another way, $1,000 invested in bonds at the beginning of 1965 was worth only about $500, in real terms, by the end of 1981. The following chart shows the agony of bond investors in graphic detail. To add insult to injury, most bond investors still had to pay income taxes on the interest they received in spite of the fact that they were earning negative real rates of return.

Even though inflation generally rose during the late 1960s and 1970s, it fluctuated a great deal from year to year. As inflation started to fluctuate substantially, so did interest rates. The increased volatility in interest rates led to a sharp increase in the volatility of bond prices. In fact, bond prices were often as volatile as stock prices during this period. For example, in 1965 the annualized standard deviation of bond returns was about 1.5%. By 1980 the annualized standard deviation of bond returns was over 21%. In comparison, the annualized standard deviation of stock returns was about 24% in 1980.

Investors who bought bonds in the early 1960s suffered over the next 15 years, but those who bought bonds in the early 1980s generally prospered. As inflation fell, so did interest rates. Between 1982 and 2001, the average annual nominal rate of return on bonds was over 12%. Even adjusting for inflation, bonds have returned an average of over 9% per year since 1982.

Questions for Critical Thinking

1. Why does inflation have such a devastating impact on bond returns?
2. How can bond investors protect themselves from inflation?

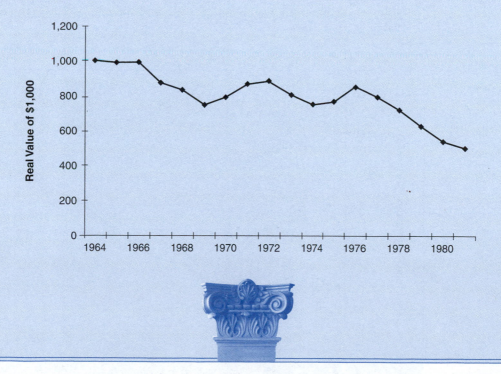

In our example, the bond had a holding period return of 9.50%, measured in pounds, but only 7.51% measured in U.S. dollars. The difference is due to the fact that the dollar got stronger relative to the pound (meaning it took more dollars to buy one pound at the beginning of the year end of the year than it did at the end of the year). At the beginning of the year, you had to pay $1.65 to buy one pound; at the end of the year, one pound bought only $1.60. Had the reverse occurred, and the pound strengthened relative to the dollar, the holding period return in dollars would have exceeded 9.5%, the holding period return in pounds. Had the exchange rate remained the same, the holding period return in dollars would have equaled 9.5%.

Total Return Indexes

A holding period return measures the change in wealth from the beginning of a period to the end of the period. Many times when evaluating an investment, we want to measure the change in the level of wealth over a period of time. A total return index allows us to measure the cumulative effect of investment returns. The value of a total return index, I_t, at the end of period t, is defined as

$$I_t = I_{t-1}(1 + \text{HPR}_t) \tag{2.3}$$

The beginning index value, I_0, is arbitrary but is usually set at 1, 100, 1,000, or some other multiple of 10.

An example of a total return index is shown in Figure 2.1. The data show the cumulative change in the level of wealth for an investor in Johnson & Johnson between the beginning of 1992 and the end of 2001 (the initial index value is set at 100).

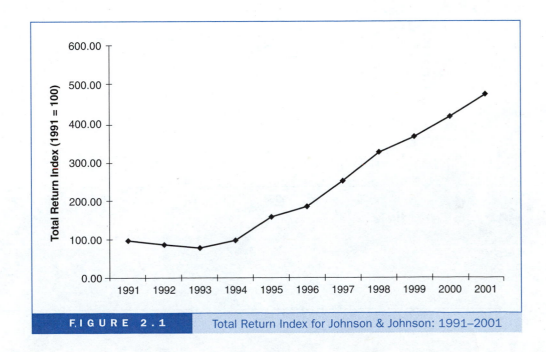

| FIGURE 2.1 | Total Return Index for Johnson & Johnson: 1991–2001 |

Total return indexes provide a variety of information. For one thing, the total return index tells us the growth of a dollar investment. In the case of Johnson & Johnson, the total return index tells us that a $100 invested in the fund at the beginning of 1992 was worth more than $479 by the end of 2001.

Total return indexes can also be used to calculate returns over holding periods of varying lengths. We can use the following equation to find a holding period return:

$$HPR = (I_t/I_{t-1}) - 1 \qquad (2.4)$$

where I_t is the index value at the end of the period and I_{t-1} is the index value at the beginning of the period.

In the case of Johnson & Johnson, the holding period return over the 10-year period shown was

$$(479.49/100.00) - 1 = 379.49\%$$

Summarizing Returns

So far, we discussed calculating holding period returns, real rates of return, returns from international investments, and total return indexes. Even though all are useful measures of return and can aid in investment analysis and selection, summary statistics of returns over a period of time are also needed. Two such statistics are the arithmetic mean and the geometric mean.

Arithmetic Mean The arithmetic mean is simply the average of all observations in a data series. If we have a set of holding period returns for an investment, we can calculate the arithmetic mean by simply summing the returns and dividing by the number of observations. More formally, the arithmetic mean, or AM, is found using the following formula:

$$AM = \frac{\sum_{t=1}^{T} HPR_t}{T} \qquad (2.5)$$

where T is the number of returns in the data series. Go back to the returns shown in Figure 2.1. We have 10 years' worth of returns, so T is equal to 10. Summing the annual holding period returns equals 185%. Dividing the sum by 10 gives us the arithmetic mean, 18.5%.[2]

Annualizing the Arithmetic Mean We can, of course, calculate holding period returns over shorter periods than years—quarters, months, or even days. Say we calculate a series of monthly holding period returns over a five-year period—we have a total of 60 monthly returns. Using Equation 2.5, we can then

[2]Any calculator with statistical functions—including all business or financial calculators—can find an arithmetic mean. Microsoft Excel also has built in statistical functions, including one that finds the arithmetic mean.

arithmetic mean

A measure of average return over a period of time.

find the **arithmetic mean**, which is the average monthly return. We can annualize this arithmetic mean using the following formula: Annualized arithmetic mean $= (1 + AM)^m - 1$, where m is the number of periods per year (12 in the case of monthly returns).

For instance, during a recent three-year period, 3M had an average monthly return of 1.2%. Annualized, its average return equals is calculated as follows:

$$(1.012)^{12} - 1 = 15.4\%$$

Geometric Mean Another measure of the "average" return over a period of time is called the geometric mean. The **geometric mean** is also referred to as the compound average annual return. The geometric mean is found using the following formula:

geometric mean

A measure of average return over a period of time (also called the compound average annual return).

$$GM = \left[\prod_{t=1}^{T} (1 + HPR_t) \right]^{1/T} - 1 \tag{2.6}$$

where Π is the product of the terms $(1 + HPR_1)$, $(1 + HPR_2)$, ... $(1 + HPR_t)$. Between the beginning of 1992 and the end of 2001, Johnson & Johnson's geometric mean is

$$[4.7949]^{1/10} - 1 = 17.0\% \text{ (rounded)}$$

So, over this 10-year period, Johnson & Johnson had a compound average annual return of 18.5%.

You may already recognize that the number inside the bracket—the product of 1 plus holding period return—is the same as the total return index we found using Equation 2.3 (setting the initial index value equal to 1). The two are the same. The total return index measures the change in wealth over a period of time, whereas the geometric mean measures the *average* annual change in wealth.

Equation 2.6 can also be used to find the compound average annual return over shorter time intervals. Let's go back to Johnson & Johnson. So far we found that the compound average annual return over the 10 years, ending in 2001, was about 17%. What was the compound average annual return over the *five*-year period ending in 2001? To answer the question, we need the total return index at the beginning of the period (the end of 1996), 1.9013, and the total return index at the end of the period, 4.7949. The compound average annual return is

$$(4.7949/1.9013)^{1/5} - 1 = 20.3\%$$

Comparing the Geometric and Arithmetic Means Let's review. Over the 10-year period ending in 2001, Johnson & Johnson had an arithmetic mean return of 18.5% and a geometric mean return of about 17%. Why are the two different? The answer is due to the fact that the two means measure different things. The geometric mean is backward looking, measuring the change in wealth over several periods of time, including compounding effects.

By contrast, the arithmetic mean represents the typical return over time. In the case of Johnson & Johnson, the typical annual return is 18.5%. The arithmetic mean also provides an indication of the expected return for an investment for use in forecasting, discounting, or estimating the cost of capital.

In fact, the arithmetic and geometric means will be equal only if an investment provides a set of equal returns for each period. If the returns vary at all from period to period, the arithmetic mean will be higher than the geometric mean. Also, more variation in returns from period to period increases the difference between the arithmetic and geometric means. Because the arithmetic and geometric means measure different things, and have somewhat different uses, it is a good idea to calculate both. You will find that most historical data for investment returns include both the arithmetic and geometric means.

RECAPRECAP

So far we discussed how to calculate holding period returns (a return measure that incorporates both price changes and income), how to adjust returns for inflation, how to compute returns for non-dollar-denominated investments, how to construct a total return index, and how to summarize returns.

To see how well you understand the material you read up to this point, answer the following questions:

1. At the beginning of 2002, a stock was selling for $50 a share; at the end of the year it was selling for $65 a share. If the stock paid $1.50 in dividends, what was its holding period return for 2002?
2. Is the return you calculated in Question 1 an ex-post or ex-ante return?
3. Assume the rate of inflation during 2002 was 3%. Find the inflation-adjusted or real return for the stock in Question 1.
4. At the beginning of 2002, you bought shares of a Japanese stock, paying ¥1,500 per share. At the end of 2002, the price per share had risen to ¥1,750. Assuming the exchange rate between the dollar and yen (yen per dollar) was 125 at the beginning of the year and 130 at the end of the year, calculate your return measured in both yen and U.S. dollars.
5. A mutual fund produced the following annual holding period returns over the preceding five years: 15.5%, 20.0%, −10.5%, 35.0%, and 27.5%. Construct a total return index. If you had invested $10,000 in this stock at the beginning of the five-year period, how much would your investment be worth at the end of the five-year period? Calculate the holding period return for the entire five-year period.
6. Using the information provided in the prior question, calculate both the arithmetic mean and the geometric mean. Why are the two different? What does each reflect?
7. Use the return data for Johnson & Johnson in Figure 2.1. Calculate the compound average annual return for the three-year period ending in 2001.

INVESTMENT RISK

We stated that the concepts of risk and return dominate investments. We also noted that all investing exposes investors to some degree of risk. Now we turn our attention to what risk is, and to what kinds of risk investors are exposed.

A Definition of Risk

Risk simply means that some uncertainty exists over what an investment's actual return will be over some period in the future. The greater the uncertainty, the greater the risk. Risk, in and of itself, is neither good nor bad; it merely

risk
Uncertainty about what an investment's return will be over some future period of time.

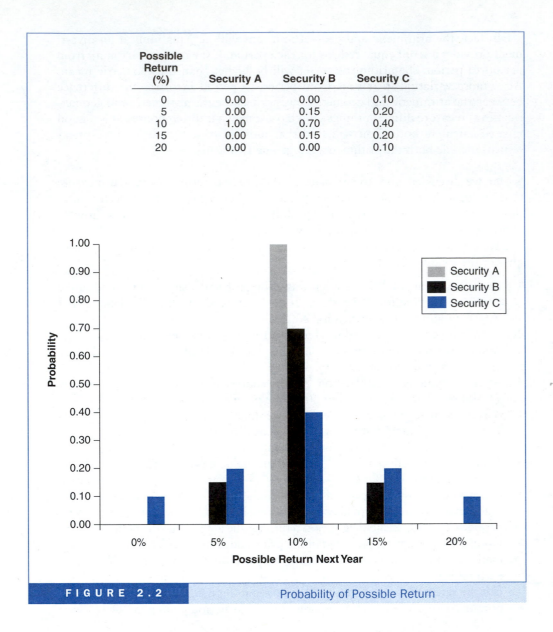

Possible Return (%)	Security A	Security B	Security C
0	0.00	0.00	0.10
5	0.00	0.15	0.20
10	1.00	0.70	0.40
15	0.00	0.15	0.20
20	0.00	0.00	0.10

FIGURE 2.2   Probability of Possible Return

exists. Risk is also often a double-edged sword, having an upside as well as a downside.

To illustrate our general definition of risk, consider three hypothetical investments: A, B, and C. Although some uncertainty is present concerning their returns, assume that all possible returns for the next year are known for all three, as are the probabilities of these returns occurring.

Figure 2.2 gives the probability distributions of next year's possible returns for all three securities. For Security A, there is a 100% chance (probability = 1.00) that its return next year will be 10%. Security B has a 15% chance (probability = 0.15) that it will return 5%, a 70% chance that it will return 10%, and a 15% chance that it will return 15%. There is a 10% chance that

Security C will return 0%, a 20% chance that it will return 5%, a 40% chance that it will return 10%, a 20% chance that it will return 15%, and a 10% chance that it will return 20%.

Recognize, initially, that all three securities have the same expected return next year, 10%. Next year's expected return for each security is simply the sum of the possible returns times the probability of each return occurring, as follows:

$$ER_A = (10\%)1.00 = 10\%$$
$$ER_B = (5\%)0.15 + (10\%)0.70 + (15\%)0.15 = 10\%$$
$$ER_C = (0\%)0.10 + (5\%)0.20 + (10\%)0.40 + (15\%)0.20 + (20\%)0.10 = 10\%$$

Given the general description of risk, which of the three securities is the riskiest? Figure 2.2 shows that Security C certainly appears to be the riskiest of the three securities. It has the greatest range of possible returns, 0% to 20%, and it has the highest probability that its actual return will differ from its expected return. There is only a 4 in 10 chance (probability = .4) that Security C's actual return will equal its expected return. By contrast, there is a 7 in 10 chance that Security B's actual return will equal its expected return. Based on our general definition of risk, Security A appears to be risk free. Apparently, its actual return cannot possibly differ from its expected return.

Types of Risk

Although our general definition of risk is a starting point, you should realize that many types of risk exist. All of these types of risk create uncertainty about future investment returns. Further different investments are more sensitive to certain types of risk. The major types of investment risk include the following:

- *Default risk:* The risk that an investment will become worthless
- *Credit risk:* The risk that the financial health of the issuer of the security (a corporation or a government) will decline causing the value of the investment to fall
- *Tax risk:* The risk that some of your investment profits will be subject to taxes
- *Purchasing power risk:* The risk that your investment returns will not keep pace with the rate of inflation
- *Interest rate risk:* The risk that interest rates will rise causing the value of the investment to fall
- *Market risk:* The risk reflected in the periodic fluctuations of security prices
- *Event risk:* The risk that something unexpected, and beyond the control of the issuer of the security, will occur causing the value of the investment to fall
- *Liquidity risk:* The risk that you may not be able to convert an investment into cash at a price close to its fair value
- *Foreign exchange risk:* The risk that the value of the dollar, relative to another currency, will change causing the dollar return on the investment to decline (applies mainly to non-dollar-denominated investments)

As mentioned, different investments expose you to different types of risk, and to varying degrees. For example, common stocks have high amounts of market risk, moderate amounts of default, credit, tax, and event risk, and, for

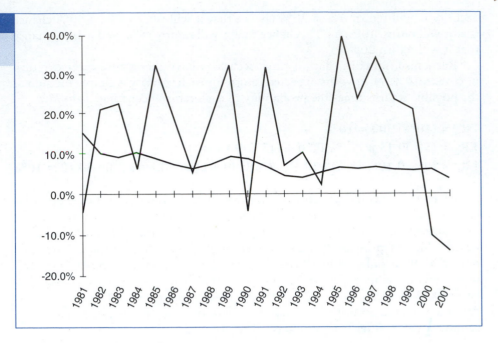

FIGURE 2.3

Stock and T-Bill Returns:
1982–2001

the most part, low amounts of liquidity risk. On the other hand, a Treasury bill exposes you to no default or credit risk, but high amounts of tax and purchasing power risk.

Many types of risk have an upside as well as a downside. For example, interest rates can fall, unexpected events can be good news, and the financial health of the issuer can improve.

Measuring Risk

The greater the uncertainty over future investment returns, the greater is the risk of an investment. How can you actually measure risk in order to compare various investments? In general, risk is associated with the variability of returns. The more variable the returns, the more risky the investment. Figure 2.3 shows the annual returns for large company stocks and T-bills between 1982 and 2001. Annual stock returns showed much more variation from year to year than T-bills ranging from a high of 37.5% to a low of −3.2%. By contrast, T-bill returns ranged from a high near 10% to a low of 3%. Based on these data, it would not be unreasonable to conclude that stocks are riskier than T-bills.

As another example, Figure 2.4 shows the monthly returns for two stocks, 3M and Starbucks, over a recent three-year period. During this period, Starbucks appears to show more month-to-month variation in returns than does 3M. Based on this observation, we could conclude that Starbucks is a riskier stock than 3M. Even though we can often make visual judgments concerning the risk of an investment, a statistical measure of risk is still needed. Standard deviation is one such measure.

Calculating the Standard Deviation You may remember from your statistics class that standard deviation measures the dispersion of a set of

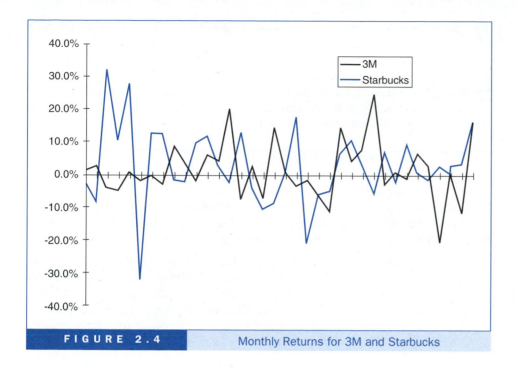

| **FIGURE 2.4** | Monthly Returns for 3M and Starbucks |

observations around its arithmetic mean.[3] The greater the standard deviation, the more dispersed the distribution. Because risk is associated with the variability of returns, the higher the standard deviation of returns, the more risky the investment.

The standard deviation is found using the following formula:

$$\text{SD} = \left[\frac{1}{T-1} \sum_{t=1}^{T} (\text{HPR}_t - \text{AM})^2 \right]^{1/2} \tag{2.7}$$

Using the data in Figure 2.1, the standard deviation of returns for Johnson & Johnson's common stock is about 20.2%.

Going back to Figure 2.3, T-bill returns exhibit less year-to-year variation than do stock returns over the period shown, suggesting that stocks have more risk than T-bills. The standard deviations confirm this assumption. Stock returns have a standard deviation near 15% while the standard deviation of T-bill returns is slightly less than 3%.

Annualizing a Standard Deviation Let's say you have a series of monthly or quarterly returns. In the prior section we saw how the arithmetic mean could be annualized. Annualizing the standard deviation is also fairly simple. You use Equation 2.7 to calculate the standard deviation (on a monthly or quarterly basis).

---

[3]The standard deviation is the square root of the variance. The variance also measures the dispersion of a distribution around its mean. Standard deviation is more widely used, however, because standard deviation is always in the same unit as the mean. Thus, if we measure a mean rate of return, the standard deviation will also be a rate of return.

You then annualize the standard deviation by multiplying the monthly or quarterly standard deviation by the square root of the periods per year, or $(\sigma \sqrt{m})$.[4]

For example, based on the monthly returns shown in Figure 2.4, we concluded that Starbucks appears to be a riskier stock than 3M. Indeed, Starbucks has the higher standard deviation. The monthly standard deviation for Starbucks is 13.5% while the monthly standard deviation for 3M is 7.1%. On an annual basis, the standard deviations of the two stocks are

$$13.5\%(\sqrt{12}) = 46.6\% \ (\text{Starbucks})$$
$$7.1\%(\sqrt{12}) = 24.6\% \ (\text{3M})$$

In the preceding section we discussed a general definition of investment risk, the various types of investment risk, and how investment risk can be measured. Answer the following questions to see how well you understand the material on investment risk.

8. Briefly explain credit risk, interest rate risk, and market risk.
9. A mutual fund produced the following annual returns over a recent 10-year period: 3.94%, 54.92%, 15.89%, 21.43%, −1.12%, 36.28%, 21.94%, 23.00%, 31.57%, 20.71%. Calculate the standard deviation of the returns.
10. Assume two stocks had standard deviations—based on quarterly returns—of 7.89% and 8.45%. Annualize the standard deviations.

Risk, Return, and Investment Selection

Investors can use the risk/return—expected, or mean return, and standard deviation—measures discussed so far to help in choosing between investments. To illustrate, consider the four hypothetical investments:

Investment	Average or Expected Return	Standard Deviation
D	15%	10%
E	15	15
F	10	10
G	20	15

Clearly, a risk-averse individual should pick D over E. Why? D and E show the same expected return, but D has a lower standard deviation. Another way of looking it is that E does not offer any incentive in the form of a higher expected return. Therefore, D dominates E. What about D and F? Again, D should be the pick of a risk-averse individual. F has the same standard deviation as D, but has a lower expected return. So, D also dominates F.

Now, would a risk-averse individual pick D or G? We really cannot say, because even though G has a higher expected return than D, it also has a higher standard deviation. Neither D nor G dominates the other. One risk-averse individual might prefer D while another risk-averse individual might just as legitimately prefer G.

[4]This formula is actually a close approximation. The more precise formula for annualizing a standard deviation is $\sqrt{[SD^2 + (1 + AM)^2]^m - (1 + AM)^{2m}}$

Another statistic—called the coefficient of variation—may help clarify investment decisions similar to the choice between D and G. The coefficient of variation, or CV, is just the standard deviation divided by the mean. It can be used as a measure of an investment's risk/return trade-off. The lower the CV, the better is the risk/return trade-off. The coefficient of variation for investment D is 10%/15% = .67, while the coefficient of variation for investment G is 15%/20% = .75. So, we could argue that D offers a slightly better risk/return trade-off than G, but we still cannot say that D dominates G.

coefficient of variation

A statistical measure of the risk/return trade-off offered by an investment.

Although statistics such as means, standard deviations, and coefficients of variations can help make investment decisions, you need to recognize that the real investment decisions are much more complicated than many of our examples. All investment decisions have to be related to the goals of the individual or organization, as well as a whole host of other considerations. In addition, the impact of such factors as compounding, taxes, and inflation need to be taken into account. What appears to be the riskier investment, might, in reality, be the best investment once you take everything into consideration. Remember, many types of risk have upsides as well as downsides. The Investment Insight box on page 40, "Fearing the Wrong Risks," discusses what can happen if you become too fixated on short-term volatility and lose sight of the bigger picture.

PORTFOLIO RISK AND RETURN

A portfolio is merely a combination of several different assets or investments. As you read this section, you will begin to understand why virtually all investment decisions need to be considered within the context of a portfolio. You will also see how the risk of individual investments can change substantially once they are evaluated within the context of a portfolio.

portfolio

Combination of several different assets or investments.

You may initially think that the risk and return for a portfolio simply reflects some sort of average of the risk and return of the individual investments that make up the portfolio. When it comes to calculating the mean, or expected return for a portfolio, you're correct. The mean return for a portfolio is merely a weighted average of the mean returns of the individual investments that make up the portfolio. For a portfolio consisting of n investments, and using historical returns, the portfolio's mean is

$$AM_p = \sum_{i=1}^{n} w_i AM_i \qquad (2.8)$$

where w_i is the percentage of the portfolio consisting of investment i and AM_i is the mean return for investment i.[5] For example, investment A has a mean return of 10%, investment B has a mean return of 12%, investment C has a mean return of 14%, and investment D has a mean return of 16%. The mean return of an equally weighted portfolio consisting of the four investments is

$$.25(10\%) + .25(12\%) + .25(14\%) + .25(16\%) = 13\%$$

_____

[5]The sum of the individual weights must equal 1.0. It also usually assumed that all the individual weights cannot be less than zero nor greater than one.

INVESTMENT INSIGHT

Fearing the Wrong Risks

If you are saving for retirement or for a newborn's college education, which is a riskier place for your savings, stocks or Treasury bills? What a silly question, you may think! Everyone *knows* that stocks are much riskier than Treasury bills. After all, you can *lose* money in the stock market—prices dropped by more than 25% on *one* day, October 19, 1987. With a Treasury bill, or something similar such as a certificate of deposit (CD), you are always guaranteed to get your money back. Look at a chart of stock prices. They resemble a yo-yo: up and down, up and down, up and down. Although all these points are true, in some important ways stocks are actually *less* risky than seemingly safe investments such as Treasury bills or CDs. Many people who, in spite of investment horizons of 10, 20, or 30 years, or even longer, avoid stocks because they think stocks are too risky. To coin a phrase, these people may be "fearing the wrong risks." They worry about losing money in the short term, not whether they will have enough money accumulated to meet future needs.

For one thing, CDs and Treasury bills offer no growth potential. They provide income, and a guarantee of getting back an initial investment, but nothing else. Inflation constantly erodes the real value of your investment. Over a short period of time, the impact of inflation isn't that significant, but over longer periods of time, it is. Take a look at the following table.

	Nominal Return (1982–2001)	Real Return (1982–2001)
Treasury bills	6.0%	2.7%
Common stocks	15.0%	11.4%

Put another way, in real terms $1,000 invested in T-bills at the beginning of 1982 would have been worth only about $1,700 by the end of 2001. By contrast, the same $1,000 would have grown to more than $8,600 over the same period had it been invested in stocks. These calculations do not factor in taxes. Interest received from T-bills and other similar investments is fully taxed as ordinary income. On the other hand, most of the return from stocks comes from capital gains, taxed at a lower rate and then only when the stocks are actually sold.

People occasionally overlook another characteristics of T-bills and CDs: interest rates go down as well as up. So even though you will never lose any money, at least in nominal terms, you could see big declines in your interest income from year to year. For example, the average interest rate paid by banks on one-year CDs fell from almost 7.5% in 1990, to less than 5% in 1991, to about 3.5% in 1992. Today, one-year bank CDs are paying less than 3%.

Next, let's look more closely at the issue of stock market volatility. Over short periods of time, the stock market does resemble a yo-yo. For example, during the past 25 years stock investors made money in 160 out of 300 months (about 60%). Stretch the time horizon to one-year intervals, however, and stocks made money in all but six years. Over rolling five-year intervals, stocks made money in all but one five-year period. In each and every rolling 10-year, or longer, interval between 1977 and 2001, stock investors made money. The key point to remember is that even though stocks bounce up and down in the short run, stock prices rise much more than they fall. Focus on the mountain, not the yo-yo of short-term ups and downs in stock prices.

The bottom line is that those investors with longer time horizons should invest some of their money in stocks or stock mutual funds. Investors in their twenties or thirties saving for retirement, should invest at least 70% of their money in stocks. Investors in their forties and fifties should keep at least half of their retirement funds in the stock market. Even investors in their sixties should still have some of their money in stocks.

Questions for Critical Thinking

1. What is the major investment objective for investors with long-term investment horizons? What is it for investors with short-term investment horizons?
2. Over the past three years, stock returns have been negative. Do recent events alter the advice that long-term investors should invest the majority of their funds in common stocks?

Finding the Standard Deviation of a Portfolio

So, finding the mean return of a portfolio is fairly simple. What about the standard deviation of a portfolio consisting of two assets or investments? The issue becomes more complicated; however, we can generally use Equation 2.7 to find a portfolio's standard deviation. Let's start with the example shown in the following table.

State of Economy	Probability	Returns		
		X	Y	Portfolio
Excellent	0.15	35%	−5%	15%
Above average	0.20	25	5	15
Average	0.30	15	15	15
Below average	0.20	5	25	15
Poor	0.15	−5	35	15
	Expected return	15.00	15.00	15
	Standard deviation	12.65	12.65	0
	Coefficient of variation	0.84	0.84	0

(*Note:* The portfolio consists of 50% X and 50% Y.)

Notice that the return for portfolio in each state of the economy reflects the fact that it consists of half X and half Y. Also, note that the expected return for the portfolio is just a weighted average of expected return for investment X and the expected return for investment Y.

On the other hand, because there is no variation in returns, the standard deviation of the portfolio is zero. The coefficient of variation is also zero. Why? Take another look at the two probability distributions; X and Y are simply mirror images of each other. When combined together in a portfolio, all the variation present in their individual probability distributions disappears.

You may be thinking that the preceding example is simply contrived. Of course it is, but the same phenomenon can be observed with real, historical investment returns. Monthly returns for a recent three-year period for Verizon Communications and Dow Chemical, along with their respective means, standard deviations, and coefficients of variation, are shown in Table 2.3. In the far right-hand column are the monthly returns for a portfolio consisting of half Verizon Communications and half Dow Chemical, along with its mean, standard deviation, and coefficient of variation. (The standard deviation was calculated using Equation 2.7.) As you can see, the portfolio's standard deviation, 12.8%, is much lower than either Verizon's or Dow's. What do these results mean?

The answer lies with the interrelationship between the returns for each of the pairs of investments. Between X and Y, for example, the better the state of the economy, the better investment X performs but the poorer Investment Y performs, and vice versa. On the other hand, the weaker the state of the economy the better Y performs and the worse X performs. You can see the same interrelationship between the historical returns for Verizon Communications and Dow Chemical—shown graphically in Figure 2.5. To some extent they moved in opposite directions from month to month. Therefore, the standard deviation of a portfolio reflects not only the standard deviation of the individual investments, but also the interrelationship between the individual investment returns.

TABLE 2.3

Monthly Returns for Dow Chemical, Verizon Communications, and an Equally Weighted Portfolio

Month	Dow Chemical	Verizon	Portfolio
1	8.68%	−3.31%	2.69%
2	5.02	−3.20	0.91
3	−6.07	0.12	−2.98
4	−12.93	−4.30	−8.62
5	6.09	−0.75	2.67
6	−7.25	10.43	1.59
7	7.41	−1.15	3.13
8	10.30	−1.40	4.45
9	−5.46	4.63	−0.42
10	5.78	1.60	3.69
11	−0.85	0.90	0.03
12	3.13	3.48	3.31
13	−0.17	3.93	1.88
14	1.69	3.15	2.42
15	−7.89	4.60	−1.65
16	3.28	−0.79	1.25
17	0.18	6.15	3.17
18	6.05	4.04	5.05
19	7.72	−3.99	1.87
20	9.35	−6.43	1.46
21	2.16	6.21	4.19
22	−5.91	−4.04	−4.98
23	−8.22	2.20	−3.01
24	−2.30	−6.13	−4.22
25	7.41	−4.86	1.28
26	1.57	6.44	4.01
27	−3.12	1.83	−0.65
28	7.72	4.36	6.04
29	−5.52	2.98	−1.27
30	−1.59	4.97	1.69
31	5.02	2.79	3.91
32	−0.46	−12.12	−6.29
33	5.95	12.74	9.35
34	−1.48	3.32	0.92
35	5.24	8.39	6.82
36	9.35	−3.39	2.98
Mean (annualized)	17.95%	15.47%	16.70%
Standard deviation (annualized)	20.86%	17.80%	12.77%
CV	1.16	1.15	0.76

Note: The portfolio consists of 50% Dow stock and 50% Verizon stock.

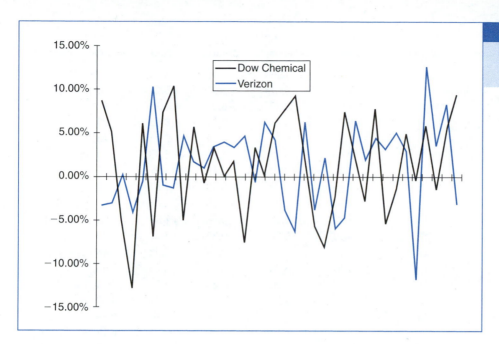

FIGURE 2.5

Monthly Returns for Dow
Chemical and Verizon
Communications

A statistical measure of the interrelationship between two variables is called
the **correlation coefficient**. As you may remember from statistics, the correlation
coefficient ranges from $+1.0$ to -1.0. A correlation coefficient of $+1.0$ indicates
that the two variables move in exactly the same directions. A correlation coefficient of -1.0 means that the two variables move in exactly the opposite directions. A correlation coefficient of zero suggests that the two variables show no
relationship. Going back to the two examples, you would expect the correlation
coefficients between each set of returns to be negative. Indeed they are; the correlation coefficient between X and Y is -1.0, while the correlation coefficient
between Verizon and Dow is -0.13.

    Calculating the standard deviation of a portfolio consisting of three or more
assets is a simple extension of the approach used to calculate the standard deviation of a two-asset portfolio. In Table 2.4, monthly returns for five stocks are
listed, along with their respective means, standard deviations, and coefficients of
variation.[6] In the far right hand column are monthly returns for an equally
weighted portfolio consisting of the five stocks, along with its mean, standard
deviation, and coefficient of variation.[7] As was the case with the prior two portfolios, notice that the portfolio's standard deviation and coefficient of variation
are lower than any of the individual stocks'. For example, of the five stocks,
Verizon has the lowest standard deviation, 17.8%, and coefficient of variation, 1.15.
By contrast, the portfolio's standard deviation is 11.1% and its coefficient of variation is 0.68. The correlation coefficients—and there is a correlation coefficient for
each pair of stocks, 10 in all—range from a high of .49 to a low of $-.13$.

correlation coefficient

A statistical measure of the interrelationship between two variables.

---

[6]The means and standard deviations have been annualized.
[7]The portfolio return for month t equals: $(R_{t,1} + R_{t,2} + R_{t,3} + R_{t,4} + R_{t,5})/5$

TABLE 2.4

Monthly Returns
for Five Stocks and a
Five-Stock Portfolio

Month	AOL Time Warner	Albertson's	Dow Chemical	Ford	Verizon	Portfolio
1	2.94%	7.35%	8.68%	−8.24%	−3.31%	1.48%
2	−7.87	0.87	5.02	−5.13	−3.20	−2.06
3	1.07	3.38	−6.07	7.24	0.12	1.15
4	−2.56	−3.75	−12.93	−8.05	−4.30	−6.32
5	1.81	0.43	6.09	2.76	−0.75	2.07
6	2.49	3.40	−7.25	−8.48	10.43	0.12
7	7.54	2.93	7.41	3.47	−1.15	4.04
8	−2.59	4.88	10.30	2.87	−1.40	2.81
9	−2.99	−1.94	−5.46	2.08	4.63	−0.74
10	8.81	−11.05	5.78	7.83	1.60	2.59
11	4.10	5.80	−0.85	1.71	0.90	2.33
12	3.94	0.00	3.13	−1.48	3.48	1.81
13	−1.54	8.03	−0.17	6.03	3.93	3.26
14	−5.64	7.06	1.69	1.22	3.15	1.50
15	−8.18	−2.20	−7.89	−6.51	4.60	−4.04
16	9.84	−7.48	3.28	−1.74	−0.79	0.62
17	−5.31	6.91	0.18	2.21	6.15	2.03
18	9.57	3.44	6.05	3.38	4.04	5.30
19	3.23	9.23	7.72	5.93	−3.99	4.42
20	−4.39	0.34	9.35	10.00	−6.43	1.77
21	0.00	3.70	2.16	5.38	6.21	3.49
22	−1.00	3.96	−5.91	1.74	−4.04	−1.05
23	−2.79	3.76	−8.22	−11.30	2.20	−3.27
24	−11.15	−0.54	−2.30	1.19	−6.13	−3.79
25	−4.04	3.35	7.41	3.47	−4.86	1.07
26	15.36	−0.59	1.57	−6.72	6.44	3.21
27	−3.25	−18.04	−3.12	1.23	1.83	−4.27
28	9.64	1.45	7.72	4.80	4.36	5.59
29	−7.98	2.15	−5.52	−1.53	2.98	−1.98
30	2.67	−1.33	−1.59	0.81	4.97	1.11
31	6.73	0.71	5.02	2.33	2.79	3.52
32	5.49	−3.55	−0.46	−4.56	−12.12	−3.04
33	4.05	−2.47	5.95	12.10	12.74	6.47
34	3.53	1.52	−1.48	7.91	3.32	2.96
35	3.76	8.96	5.24	1.33	8.39	5.54
36	13.21	1.98	9.35	8.67	−3.39	5.96
Mean (annualized)	17.42%	15.18%	17.95%	15.67%	15.47%	16.33%
Standard Deviation (annualized)	21.95%	18.96%	20.86%	19.60%	17.80%	11.13%
CV	1.26	1.25	1.16	1.25	1.15	0.68

Note: The portfolio is equally weighted among the five stocks.

Use the following data to answer the following questions:

Year	Stock A	Stock B
1993	−15.5%	55.3%
1994	39.8	8.4
1995	12.0	−12.5
1996	39.4	−8.5
1997	−15.3	23.0
1998	4.4	73.4
1999	10.0	−8.5
2000	48.0	28.7
2001	27.3	8.6
2002	36.2	19.6

11. Find the individual mean, standard deviation, and coefficient of variation for Stock A and Stock B.

12. Construct a portfolio consisting of one-half A and one-half B.

13. Find the portfolio's mean, standard deviation, and coefficient of variation. Does the portfolio represent a better risk/return trade-off than the individual stocks? Explain your answer.

DIVERSIFICATION

One of the most important concepts in finance is diversification. Diversification means spreading your money among several different investments. So when you form a portfolio, you diversify. After reading the prior section, you may have thought to yourself that the three portfolios—the hypothetical portfolio consisting of X and Y, the two-stock portfolio consisting of Verizon and Dow, and the five-stock portfolio—we constructed appear to offer better risk/return trade-offs than the individual investments. If you did, good for you! The portfolios do offer better risk/return trade-offs than the individual investments. For example, the portfolio consisting of X and Y has a higher expected return than Y and a lower standard deviation. Not only would you prefer the portfolio over Y, it dominates Y. The portfolio doesn't dominate X; however, because it has a lower expected return, many risk-averse individuals would probably prefer the portfolio over X because its coefficient of variation is much lower.

We can draw much the same conclusions with the portfolio consisting of half Verizon and half Dow Chemical. The portfolio has a higher mean return and a lower standard deviation than Verizon—meaning it actually dominates Verizon. Even though the portfolio's mean return is slightly lower than Dow's, its coefficient of variation is so much lower than Dow's that a risk-averse individual might actually prefer the portfolio to Dow.

The explanation for why the portfolios offer better risk/return trade-offs than the individual investments goes back to the correlation between the two sets of returns. (Remember, both correlation coefficients were negative.) In fact, as long as the correlation coefficient is less than 1.0, the risk/return trade-off improves if two or more individual investments are combined in a portfolio.

diversification

Spreading investment dollars among different investments; improves the risk/return trade-off.

The lower the correlation coefficient, the greater is the improvement in the risk/return trade-off.

Here's another way of thinking about diversification. Say you are invited to play a game of chance. For a bet of $500 you stand a 50% chance of winning $1,000 and a 50% chance of winning nothing, and losing your $500 bet. On the surface it is a pretty good investment. Its expected payoff is $250, or 50% [.5($1,000) + .5(−$500) = $250]. Would you play? It's hard to say. The game offers a high expected return, but it is also very risky. You stand a 50% chance of losing $500.

Let's change the game. Instead of placing one $500 bet, you place 100 sequential $5 bets. Each time, you have a 50% chance of winning $10 and a 50% chance of losing $5. The odds of you winning all 100 games, and thus winning $1,000, are pretty remote. On the other hand, the odds of you losing all 100 games, and thus losing $500, are just as remote. The odds are highest that you will win about half of the games and lose about half the games, winning about $250 in total. Each bet is just as risky as before, but *collectively* they are much less risky.

Naïve vs. Efficient Diversification

naïve diversification

Achieving diversification by adding investments randomly.

efficient diversification

Systematic process of finding the combination of investments that minimizes risk for a given level of return.

Two different approaches can be taken to diversification. The first, called **naïve diversification** achieves the benefits of diversification by adding investments pretty much at random. On the other hand, **efficient diversification** is more of a systematic process that seeks to find the combinations of investments that minimize risk for a given level of return or maximize return for a given level of risk. It is accomplished by altering both the portfolio contents and weights. We discuss both naïve and efficient diversification in Chapter 17.

Diversifiable vs. Nondiversifiable Risk

A cornerstone of modern portfolio theory, which we discuss in Chapter 17, is that the total risk of an investment, as measured by its standard deviation, can actually be broken into two parts. The first part, called **diversifiable (or individual) risk**, can be eliminated through diversification. It is also sometimes called unsystematic risk. The second part, called **nondiversifiable (or market) risk**, is risk that cannot be eliminated through diversification. This type of risk is also known as systematic. As we'll see in later chapters, it is possible for an individual stock to have a relatively high amount of total risk, yet at the same time have relatively little systematic risk.

diversifiable (individual) risk

Risk that can be eliminated through diversification (also called unsystematic risk).

nondiversifiable (market) risk

Risk that cannot be eliminated through diversification (also called systematic risk).

Because investors, like all individuals, are risk averse, they will demand higher expected returns for riskier investments. Which risk is relevant in such assessments? It is not difficult for investors to diversify, therefore the only relevant overall risk is an investment's market risk, or the amount of risk the individual investment contributes to a well-diversified portfolio. This concept is the major contribution of the capital asset pricing model (commonly referred to as CAPM). CAPM will be discussed briefly later in this chapter, and in much more detail in Chapter 18.

beta

A measure of the volatility of an individual stock relative to the overall stock market.

Beta measures the volatility of an individual stock relative to the overall stock market. A stock that has just as much volatility as the overall market has a beta of 1.0. A stock with a beta of less than 1.0 is less volatile than the market while a stock with a beta of more than 1.0 is more volatile than the market. As such, beta is a indicator of market or nondiversifiable risk and measures the amount of risk an individual stock contributes to a well-diversified portfolio. We describe how to estimate beta in Chapter 18.

RISK AND REQUIRED RETURN

As already discussed, an investor buys a security in anticipation of earning a return over some future holding period. How does the investor determine whether the expected return is adequate? Essentially, the investor compares the security's expected return to it required return. If the expected return is at least equal to the required return, then the investor will buy the security. If the security's expected return is less than the required return, then the investor will not make the investment.[8] What, then, determines the required rate of return? Three things affect required rates of return: (1) the time value of money, (2) the expected rate of inflation, and (3) the risk of the security.

One of the underlying principles of finance is that money has a time value: A dollar received today is worth more than a dollar received at some future point. The time value of money is based on two factors: inflation and risk. Even with no inflation and absolutely no risk, however, required returns on securities would still be positive. We can call this required return, assuming no inflation or risk, the real rate of return.

Now the assumption of no inflation may seem unreasonable. To adjust the real rate of return to account for inflation, while still assuming a security is risk free, the required return would become

Risk-free return =
$$(1 + \text{Real rate of return})(1 + \text{Expected rate of inflation}) - 1 \quad (2.9)$$

This risk-free return is often referred to as the nominal rate of return. Thus, a higher expected rate of inflation increases the required return, even on a risk-free security. This relationship should make sense, because investors want to be compensated for the expected erosion of the value of their returns due to inflation over a security's holding period. In other words, if they expect the rate of inflation to be 5% next year, they must earn at least 5% on their investments just to keep pace with inflation.

Figure 2.6 compares returns on T-bills between 1982 and 2001 to changes in the rate of inflation. (In many respects, a T-bill is the closest practical approximation to a risk-free security.) The figure shows both the nominal and real return on T-bills. The real return on T-bills is a reasonable approximation of the real rate of return.[9]

---

[8]In the terminology of security analysis, an investment whose expected return is greater than its required return is *undervalued*. An investment whose expected return is less than its required return is said to be *overvalued*. We cover security analysis in depth in Chapters 11–14.
[9]We used the actual rate of inflation to calculate the real return on T-bills, not the expected rate of inflation. Although this distinction may sound like semantics, it is an important distinction. Required returns are future returns, not historical ones. Whenever you invest you must form some expectation concerning future inflation, and like all forecasts, your forecast of inflation may turn out to be incorrect. This uncertainty is partly where purchasing power risk comes from.

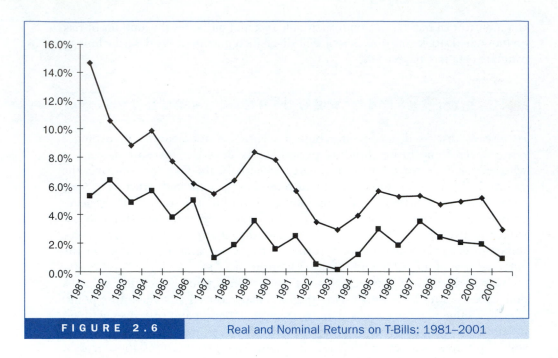

| FIGURE 2.6 | Real and Nominal Returns on T-Bills: 1981–2001 |

Nominal T-bill returns and inflation generally moved in the same direction (i.e., they rose and fell together).

However, notice that the real T-bill return fluctuated dramatically over the ten-year period, ranging from slightly more than 5% to about 0.2%.

The nominal rate of return still assumes a risk-free security. Few investors try to avoid risk entirely, however. The required return on a risky security can be written as

$$\text{Required return on a risky security} =$$
$$(1 + \text{Risk-free rate})(1 + \text{Risk premium}) - 1 \quad (2.10)$$

The risk premium reflects compensation for the amount of risk for a particular security. More risk requires a higher risk premium, which boosts the required rate of return. Securities have many potential sources of risk, and the risk premium is a function of all of them. As an example of risk premiums, look at Figure 2.7. It shows the yields on T-bills, T-bonds, and Baa-rated corporate bonds between 1988 and 2002. T-bill yields were consistently lower than T-bond yields, which, in turn, were lower than corporate bond yields. In 1992, for example, T-bills yielded 3.45%, T-bonds yielded 7.01%, and corporate bonds yielded 8.14%. Using the simple relationship in Equation 2.10, investors assigned a risk premium of about 3.56% to T-bonds and about 4.69% to corporate bonds over the risk-free T-bill rate. This suggests that investors feel that T-bonds are less risky than corporate bonds. Notice also from Figure 2.7, however, that the risk premiums were not constant during the period.

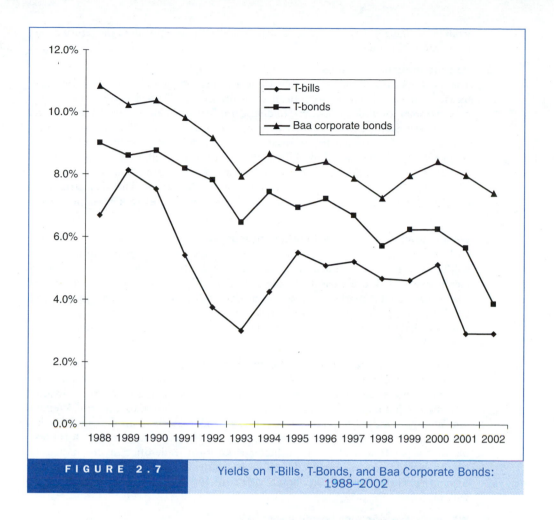

FIGURE 2.7 Yields on T-Bills, T-Bonds, and Baa Corporate Bonds: 1988–2002

Another way expressing the relationship between risk and required return is the **capital asset pricing model (CAPM)**. CAPM is calculated as follows:

$$\text{Required rate of return} = \text{Risk-free rate} + \text{beta}(\text{Market risk premium}) \qquad (2.11)$$

The market risk premium equals the required return on the overall market minus the risk-free rate. CAPM was developed from modern portfolio theory and is generally applied to common stocks. We discuss the derivation of CAPM, along with some its uses, in more detail in later chapters.

Risk and return dominate the subject of investments. Although this chapter provides only a basic overview of risk and return, it is important material that we build on throughout the rest of the text.

capital asset pricing model (CAPM)

A model developed from modern portfolio theory that calculates the required rate of return for a given stock based on the relationship between risk and return.

SUMMARY

1. What are the sources of investment returns?

Investment returns come from two sources: income (interest or dividends) and price changes. For some investments, such as common stocks, most of the return comes from price changes. For others, such as Treasury bills, virtually all of the return comes from interest income.

2.   How are investment returns measured?

The most appropriate measure of investment returns is the holding period return. It measures the total return from an investment over a specified period of time, the most common of which is a year. Holding period returns can be calculated on either an ex-post (meaning historical) basis or on an ex-ante basis. The latter is also referred to as the expected future return. Total return indexes help to measure the change in wealth over a period of time, and returns can be adjusted for inflation and exchange rates. The arithmetic mean and geometric mean are summaries of returns. The arithmetic mean measures the average, or typical return. The geometric mean measures the average compound return, or by how much an investor's wealth changed on average.

3.   What is investment risk and how is it measured?

Risk means that some uncertainty exists over what an investment's future return will be. The more uncertainty, the greater is the risk. Risk is neither good nor bad; it merely exists. Risk often has an upside as well as a downside. The different types of risk include credit, market, purchasing power, and interest rate. Some investments are more sensitive to certain types of risk than others. A statistical measure of risk is standard deviation. The greater the standard deviation of security returns, the greater is the risk.

4.   How are risk and return measured for portfolios of assets?

A combination of several assets, or investments, is called a portfolio. The mean return of a portfolio is merely a weighted average of the mean returns of the individual investments that make up the portfolio. The standard deviation of a portfolio reflects not only the standard deviations of the investments that make up the portfolio, but also the interrelationship between the returns for each pair of investments. It is possible that a portfolio will exhibit a better risk/return trade-off than the individual investments. The correlation coefficient measures the interrelationship between a pair of returns. The lower the correlation coefficient, the more the risk/return trade-off will improve.

5.   Why does diversification benefit investors?

Diversification means spreading your money among several different investments. When you form a portfolio, you diversify. Diversification improves the risk/return trade-off and the benefits of diversification increase as the number of different investments in the portfolio increases. Naïve diversification adds investments pretty much at random while efficient diversification seeks to find the combinations of investments that minimize risk for a given level of return or maximize return for a given level of risk. The total risk of an investment can be broken down into two components: individual risk (risk that can be diversified away) and market risk (risk that cannot be diversified away). Beta is a measure of market risk. The market has a beta of 1.0. Stocks with betas of less than 1.0 have less risk than the overall market while stocks with betas greater than 1.0 have more risk than the market.

6.   What is the relationship between risk and required return?

An investor buys a security in order to earn a rate of return over some future holding period. Three things affect required rates of returns on securities: (1) the time value of money, (2) the expected rate of inflation, and (3) the risk of the security. The nominal risk-free rate is a function of the real risk-free rate (representing the time value of money) and the expected rate of inflation. The required return on a risky security is a function of the nominal risk-free rate and the risk premium. The higher the risk of an investment, the higher will be the risk premium. The capital asset pricing model is one way of expressing the relationship between risk and required return.

MINI CASE 1

The following table provides month-end prices and cash dividends for Exxon Mobil for a recent two-year period. Use these data to complete the following analyses.

1. Find the holding period return for each month.
2. Calculate the arithmetic mean return and the standard deviation. Annualize the arithmetic mean and standard deviation.
3. Calculate the geometric mean. Why is the geometric mean less than the arithmetic mean?
4. Calculate a total return index. If you began the year with $10,000 invested in Exxon Mobil, how much would your investment be worth at the end of the two-year period?

Month	Price	Dividend	Month	Price	Dividend
0	71.44		13	77.46	
1	74.88		14	79.13	
2	78.44		15	81.68	.38
3	71.84	.35	16	84.79	
4	70.50		17	90.09	
5	62.60		18	90.26	.38
6	60.05	.35	19	89.55	
7	64.24		20	89.30	.69
8	63.80		21	88.99	.41
9	71.02	.38	22	88.65	
10	74.15		23	89.38	
11	72.79		24	88.70	.41
12	73.78	.38			

MINI CASE 2

Suppose three investments show the following probability distributions. Use these data to complete the following analyses.

	Returns		
Probability	Investment A	Investment B	Investment C
0.1	−22.0%	−13.0%	−10.0%
0.2	−2.0	1.0	2.0
0.4	20.0	15.0	12.0
0.2	35.0	29.0	20.0
0.1	50.0	43.0	38.0

1. Find the expected return for each investment.
2. Find the standard deviation for each investment.
3. Find the coefficient of variation for each investment.
4. Does one investment represent a better risk/return trade-off? Explain.

REVIEW EXERCISES

1. What are the two sources of investment returns? Which kinds of investment returns have potential tax implications?
2. Explain the difference between an ex-post return and an ex-ante return. Which is the only type of return that can be measured with certainty?
3. Find the holding period return of a mutual fund with a net asset value (NAV) of $12.00 at acquisition six months ago, a NAV of $12.75 today, and cash distributions during the six months of $0.50. Annualize the six-month holding period.
4. You bought a stock today for $100 per share. One year from now you expect the stock to be selling for $120 per share. In addition, you expect to receive a dividend of $5 per share. What is the expected rate of return on this stock? What is the breakdown between income and capital appreciation?
5. A mutual fund has the following net asset values and cash distributions:

Year	Net Asset Value (year-end)	Cash Distributions
1992	$13.38	–
1993	14.06	$1.15
1994	12.27	0.84
1995	14.62	0.71
1996	15.63	1.02
1997	16.65	1.26
1998	15.98	1.40
1999	20.01	1.19
2000	23.08	0.61
2001	26.93	2.80
2002	28.93	0.49

   Calculate the annual holding period return for each year listed. Starting with an initial index value of 100, compute a total return index from the end of 1992 through the end of 2002. Find the arithmetic mean and geometric mean. Why are the two different? What does each measure?
6. Using the total return index you calculated in Question 5, determine the average annual compound return from this mutual fund between the beginning of 1994 and the end of 1998. What was the average annual compound return between the end of 1998 and the end of 2002?
7. Assume during 1999 an investment had a total return of 18.5%. If the rate of inflation was 2.5%, what was this investment's real rate of return?
8. Assume an investor purchased a Canadian government bond for C$1,000 a year ago. The bond pays C$60 in interest each year. Today she sold the bond for C$1,025. Calculate the holding period return in both Canadian dollars and U.S. dollars assuming the exchange rate (US$ per one C$) was .65 when she bought the bond and .67 when she sold the bond.
9. Define risk. List three types of risk.
10. What is the difference between systematic and unsystematic risk?
11. Using the annual returns you calculated in Question 5, find the standard deviation and coefficient of variation.
12. A set of monthly returns produces a standard deviation of 12.5%. Annualize the standard deviation.
13. The following table provides ten years' worth of historical returns for three stocks. Use these data to calculate the mean return, the standard deviation, and the coefficient

of variation for each stock. Does one stock represent a better risk/return trade-off than the other two stocks? Explain.

Year	American Express	IBM	Sears
1	½ 25.0% –22.99	13.0%	34.3%
2	⅓ 34.3	–19.4	–2.3
3	–38.6	25.7	–29.1
4	3.4	–17.6	57.5
5	25.0	–38.0	25.4
6	28.1	15.3	53.0
7	11.1	31.9	–10.0
8	42.5	25.7	54.5
9	39.2	67.6	17.7
10	59.9	39.0	0.1

14. Form an equally weighted portfolio consisting of the three stocks listed in the prior exercise. Calculate the portfolio's mean, standard deviation, and coefficient of variation. Does the portfolio represent a better risk/return trade-off than the three individual stocks? Explain your answer.

15. Explain the relationship between the correlation coefficient and diversification. What is the difference between naïve diversification and efficient diversification?

16. Discuss the relationship between risk and required return.

17. What is the difference between systematic and unsystematic risk? How does this difference figure into the capital asset pricing model?

CRITICAL THINKING EXERCISES

1. This exercise requires computer work. Open the Stock Returns 1 worksheet in the Data Workbook. The worksheet contains three years' worth of monthly price and dividend data for five stocks.
   a. Calculate the holding period return for each month.
   b. Find the mean and standard deviation for each stock.
   c. Annualize the mean and standard deviations.
   d. Calculate the coefficient of variation for each stock.
   e. Form an equally weighted portfolio consisting of the five stocks. Calculate the portfolio's mean, standard deviation, and coefficient of variation. Does the portfolio appear to offer a better risk/reward trade-off than the individual stocks? Is the portfolio diversified?

2. This exercise requires computer work. Open the Stock Returns 2 worksheet in the Data Workbook. The worksheet lists annual returns from large company stocks, T-bonds, and T-bills, as well as annual inflation data between 1952 and 2001. Use the data to answer the following questions.
   a. Which were the five best years to have owned large company stocks?
   b. Which were the five worst years to have owned large company stocks?
   c. Answer Questions (a) and (b) for T-bonds and T-bills.
   d. Which five years had the highest inflation rates? Which five years had the lowest inflation rates?
   e. What do your findings in Questions (a) through (d) tell you about the historical performance of stocks and bonds relative to one another and relative to inflation?
   f. Compute annualized returns over 5-year and 10-year holding periods.
   g. Calculate the mean, standard deviation, and coefficient of variation for annualized returns over 1-, 5-, and 10-year holding periods. Discuss your findings.

1. A great deal of investment information is available on the Internet. Visit the Microsoft Investor Web site (www.investor.msn.com). On this site, find the information necessary to compute annual holding period returns for the most recent five years for the following stocks: Amgen, Best Buy, Lockheed Martin, Pfizer, and Wal-Mart.

2. One of the most important concepts in finance is diversification. Many investment firms have investor education sections on their Web sites where terms such as diversification are explained. Visit the following sites and read their explanation of diversification:

   www.personal31.fidelity.com/products/education

   www.vanguard.com/educ/inveduc.html.

   Considering the audience, what do you think of these explanations? Suggest ways they could be improved.

   (*Note:* Internet addresses change frequently. If you do not find the exact site as listed, you may need to access the company's or organization's homepage and search from there.)

3. Assume you own some German government bonds denominated in Euros and some British government bonds denominated in pounds. Using your surfing skills, obtain recent exchange rate quotations. Compare the current exchange rates with the rates one year ago. Would your return, measured in dollars, be higher than your return measured in either Euros or pounds?

3

Direct Investment Alternatives

PREVIOUSLY . . .

Following our overview of investments and investing, we introduced the concepts of risk and return in detail, the two pillars of investing. People invest in order to earn a rate of return. At the same time, however, all investing exposes the investor to risk.

IN THIS CHAPTER . . .

We explore the wide array of direct investments today. An investor cannot make intelligent decisions without some basic understanding of everything from Treasury bills to futures contracts.

TO COME...

The foundation of investments continues by discussing the characteristics of indirect investments, such as mutual funds.

CHAPTER OBJECTIVES

After reading Chapter 3, you should be able to answer the following questions:

1. What are money market instruments?

2. What are bonds and other long term fixed income securities?

3. Why invest in common stocks?

4. What are derivative securities?

5. How is investing in real assets different from investments in paper assets?

Selecting between investment alternatives used to be simple. For a typical individual, investing meant putting money into a savings account at a local bank, buying a home, monitoring a company-provided pension, holding a life insurance policy, and perhaps, for the adventuresome, owning a handful of stocks and bonds. Most Americans faced limited choices, but times have changed. Today, investors choose among literally thousands of investment alternatives, many of which did not even exist 20 years ago. Money market mutual funds, index funds, mortgage pass-through securities, stock options, financial futures, American depository receipts, and Eurobonds are a few relatively new possibilities. It is impossible to make intelligent investment decisions without some understanding of the various alternatives.

This chapter provides an overview of today's major direct investment alternatives. We will explore everything from Treasury bills to junk bonds, from blue chip stocks to call options, from pork bellies to gold.

CATEGORIZING INVESTMENT ALTERNATIVES

How many alternative investments does the worldwide market offer today? Counting all the individual security issues and investment companies, both domestic and worldwide, the number is probably 50,000, or more.[1] To make the staggering number of choices more manageable, it is useful to define some general categories in which to group investment alternatives, as illustrated in Figure 3.1.

First, we divide investment instruments into **financial assets** and **real assets**. We then divide financial assets between **direct investments** and **indirect investments**. A direct investment gives the buyer actual ownership of securities; indirect investment gives ownership of an entity that owns actual securities. Indirect investing involves investments companies, including mutual funds, closed-end funds, and unit investment trusts. (We defer our discussion of investment companies until the next chapter.) We divide direct investments in financial assets into nonmarketable assets (e.g., bank deposits and U.S. savings bonds) and **marketable securities**. By marketable, we mean an asset or security that can be sold to another investor in a secondary market. The distinction between primary and secondary markets is discussed in detail in Chapter 5. Marketable securities include money market instruments (e.g., Treasury bills and commercial paper), capital market instruments (e.g., Treasury bonds and common stocks), and derivative securities (e.g., options and futures contracts).

We can also divide real assets between direct and indirect investments. Direct investments in real assets give buyers actual ownership of such things as real estate (both owner-occupied housing and investment properties), gold, diamonds, and art work. Indirect investments in real assets provide ownership of entities such as real estate investment trusts and limited partnerships that own real assets.

Given the rather long menu of investment alternatives, it might be interesting to take a brief look at what American households actually own. Data from the Federal Reserve give us some insight into the distribution of financial assets of Americans. The data suggest a transformation in what Americans own. According

financial asset

Nonmarketable assets such as bank deposits and marketable assets such as money market instruments, bonds, and common stocks.

real asset

Real property such as real estate.

indirect investments

Investment in an entity that owns actual securities, such as a mutual fund.

marketable security

A security that can be bought and sold in a secondary financial market.

---
[1]More than 8,000 mutual funds currently operate in the United States alone.

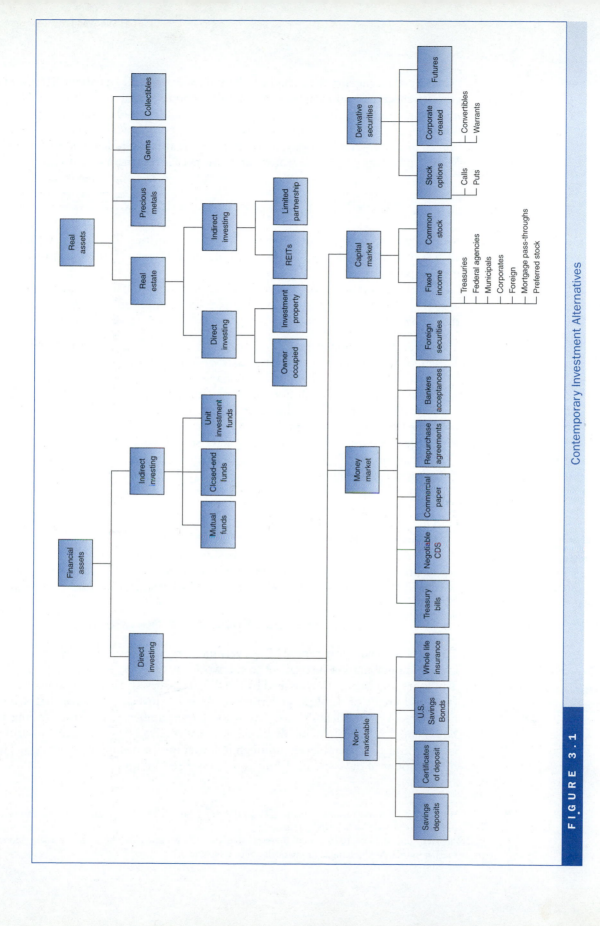

FIGURE 3.1   Contemporary Investment Alternatives

to the most recent survey by the Fed, the typical household has about $18,000 in various checking and savings accounts. By contrast, the typical household has more than $87,000 invested in stocks, bonds, and mutual funds.[2] In addition, 20 years ago fewer than one-third of American households owned any stocks, bonds, or mutual funds. Today, more than half of all households hold such assets. Many Americans progressed from simple savers to investors in recent years.

MONEY MARKET INSTRUMENTS

Money market instruments are short-term debt securities. The category includes such securities as Treasury bills, large (or marketable) certificates of deposit, commercial paper, and banker's acceptances.

Of all the major categories of investments, money market instruments are arguably the most homogeneous. All share some important features, including the following:

- *Maturity.* All money market instruments mature (i.e., pay back their face value) within one year from the date of issue. Many money market instruments have maturities of only a few days.
- *Quality.* Most, although not all, money market instruments are high-quality securities; their risk of default, or failure to repay principal, is very low. (In some cases, this risk is effectively nonexistent.)
- *Large denominations.* Another characteristic of money market instruments is their tendency to trade in large denominations. It is not unusual to see money market instruments sell in denominations of $1 million or more. This characteristic makes it difficult for small investors to own most money market instruments directly.[3]
- *Discount securities.* With the exception of bank deposits such as CDs, virtually all money market instruments are discount securities, meaning they are sold for less than their face (or par) values and do not pay periodic interest payments. When such an instrument matures, the investor receives the face value. The difference between the selling price and face value is the investor's return.

discount security

A security that is sold for less than its face value.

Short-Term U.S. Government Securities

Treasury bill (T-bill)

A short-term security issued by the U.S. Treasury.

The best-known short-term U.S. government security, and perhaps the best-known money market instrument in the world, is the U.S. Treasury bill (T-bill). T-bills are, in essence, IOUs issued by the U.S. Treasury and are backed by the full faith and credit of the U.S. government. As such, investors believe that T-bills have effectively no default risk. Given the large number of investors willing to buy them, T-bills are also highly liquid. Interest received from Treasury securities is taxable at the federal level, although it is exempt from state income taxes. The total amount of outstanding T-bills is roughly $868 billion.

---

[2]From the Survey of Consumer Finances, Federal Reserve Board. The data given are the median value of holdings for all families holding the asset.

[3]In fact, until the late 1970s, small investors had virtually no access to the money market. Money market mutual funds changed dramatically since that time.

T-bills are originally issued with three standard maturities: one month, three months, and six months. The Treasury sells bills to investors via an auction process. Three-month and six-month bills are auctioned weekly, whereas one-year bills are auctioned monthly. (We describe the Treasury's auction process in detail in Chapter 5.) T-bills are discount securities and have a minimum par value of $10,000.

T-Bill Yields and Prices Because T-bills are discount securities and do not make periodic interest payments, their yields and prices are quoted differently from many securities. T-bill prices are often quoted on a bank discount basis. The bank discount yield (BDY) is computed as follows:

$$BDY = (D/F)(360/t) \tag{3.1}$$

bank discount yield (BDY)
A method of computing the yield on T-bills.

where D is the discount [(face value)(price)], F is the face value, and t is the number of days until the bill matures.

As an example, assume that a T-bill matures in 180 days and has a discount of $2,475 and a face value of $100,000. Its BDY equals

$$(2,475/100,000)(360/180) = 4.95\%$$

The preceding formula can be rewritten to find the price of a T-bill, given its BDY:

$$Price = F[(1 - BDY)(t/360)] \tag{3.2}$$

For example, if a 180-day T-bill has a BDY of 4.95% and a face value of $100,000, its price equals

$$\$100,000[1 - .0495(180/360)] = \$97,525$$

The bill's discount would be $100,000 minus $97,525 = $2,475.

The BDY is obviously not an especially meaningful measure of the real return an investor earns from owning a T-bill. For one thing, the BDY is based on a 360-day year, not 365 or 366. Also, the BDY bases the return on the face value of the T-bill, not the amount actually invested. An alternative way of stating the yield on a T-bill is the bond equivalent yield (BEY):

$$BEY = 365(BDY)/[360 - BDY(t)] \tag{3.3}$$

bond equivalent yield (BEY)
An alternative method for computing the yield on a T-bill; closer to the actual return to the investor.

A 180-day T-bill with a BDY of 4.95% would have a BEY of

$$365(.0495)/[360 - (.0495)(180)] = 5.15\%$$

The BEY is considered to be a truer estimate than the BDY of the return an investor would actually earn from owning a T-bill. Because it is based on a 365-day year and the actual amount paid for the T-bill, the BEY is always higher than the BDY.

Short-Term Federal Agency Securities In addition to the U.S. Treasury, several federal and quasi-federal agencies are empowered to issue debt securities called federal agency securities. Approximately $300 billion in federal agency securities are outstanding; short-term obligations (i.e., those with maturities of less than one year) make up approximately 20% of outstanding federal agency securities.

Short-term federal agency securities are similar to T-bills. They are discount securities and typically have a minimum face value of $10,000. Unlike T-bills, however, federal agency securities are not backed by the full faith and credit of the U.S. government. Although some theoretical possibility of default exists with federal agency securities, investment professionals see little likelihood that Congress would allow a federal agency to default on its debt.

Commercial Paper

commercial paper

A short-term IOU issued by a corporation.

In essence, commercial paper is the corporate equivalent of a T-bill. It is a short-term IOU issued by a corporation to provide working capital. Corporations often issue commercial paper to supplement, or even as an alternative to, loans from commercial banks. Commercial paper has a maturity of less than 270 days; the most common maturity range is between 30 and 59 days.[4] Commercial paper is usually sold in large denominations ($100,000 or more) and is virtually always issued as a discount security. Today, more than $1.3 trillion in commercial paper is outstanding, up from less than $300 billion 10 years ago. Almost 90% of outstanding commercial paper was issued by financial companies. General Motors Acceptance Corporation (GMAC), General Motors' captive finance subsidiary, is the largest single issuer of commercial paper in the world.

Corporations issue commercial paper in one of two ways: as dealer-placed paper or directly placed paper. The difference is straightforward. Dealer-placed paper involves a third party, the commercial paper dealer, who purchases the paper from the issuing corporation and immediately resells it, at a slightly higher price, to investors. Directly placed paper bypasses dealers; the issuing corporation sells the paper directly to investors. Approximately 60% of outstanding commercial paper is dealer placed. Institutional investors (e.g., mutual funds, pension funds, and banks) purchase virtually all newly issued commercial paper. Because most of these investors plan to hold the paper until maturity, trading in previously issued commercial paper is not active.

Traditionally, only companies with the strongest credit ratings issued commercial paper.[5] Therefore, although defaults are not unknown, they are rare. In recent years, some companies with lower credit ratings have been able to issue commercial paper, pledging high-quality assets as collateral or backing the paper by bank letters of credit.

---

[4]Corporate securities with maturities of less than 270 days are exempt for SEC registration requirements. We describe SEC registration requirements in Chapter 5.

[5]Commercial paper has been around since colonial times. Perhaps ironically, commercial paper was first issued by companies that could not qualify for bank loans. Over the years, however, commercial paper evolved into the high-quality instrument we see today.

Banker's Acceptances

Banker's acceptances are instruments created to facilitate commercial trade transactions, many of which are international. The name comes from the fact that banks accept ultimate responsibility for paying off all the parties. Therefore, the default risk of a banker's acceptance depends more on the creditworthiness of the bank than on the financial strength of the companies that conduct the commercial transactions. Banker's acceptances are sold at discount, and their maturities range from a few days up to one year. Like commercial paper, virtually all banker's acceptances are sold to institutional investors. Today, about $25 billion in banker's acceptances are outstanding.

The easiest way to understand how banker's acceptances work is by looking at a hypothetical example. Suppose a California retail chain wants to import 5,000 "genuine" Persian rugs from the manufacturer in China for sale in the United States. The manufacturer would like immediate payment, whereas the U.S. retailer would rather pay for the rugs after it sells them, say, in 90 days. The retailer and the manufacturer come up with the following arrangement: the retailer agrees to pay $5 million for the 5,000 rugs in 90 days, and the manufacturer agrees to accept the present value of $5 million at the time the rugs are shipped. The retailer then obtains a letter of credit from its bank, Wells Fargo, which guarantees that the manufacturer will be paid 90 days after the rugs are shipped. Wells Fargo then sends the letter of credit, called a time draft, to the manufacturer's Hong Kong bank, Heng Sen Bank. Heng Sen Bank notifies the manufacturer, which then ships the rugs to the retailer. With proof of shipment, Heng Sen Bank pays the rug manufacturer the present value of $5 million, and the manufacturer leaves the picture. Heng Sen Bank presents the time draft and shipping documents to Wells Fargo, which stamps accepted on the time draft, which has created a banker's acceptance by which it agrees to pay $5 million to the holder of the banker's acceptance at maturity. Heng Sen Bank, the holder of the banker's acceptance, can either keep it, turn it over to Wells Fargo for its present value, or sell it to another money market investor. The retailer owes Wells Fargo $5 million in 90 days plus interest.

> **banker's acceptances**
>
> Instruments that facilitate commercial trade; bank accepts ultimate responsibility for paying off all the parties.

Large Certificates of Deposit

Most of you are already familiar with **certificates of deposit (CDs)**. CDs are time deposits issued by financial institutions such as banks and credit unions. CDs mature anywhere from a few weeks to a few years from the date of issue. Unlike other money market instruments, CDs are interest-bearing securities; they pay interest on their principal amounts at specified annual rates.

Although CDs can be issued in almost any denomination, an important distinction developed during the 1960s and 1970s between so-called small CDs and large CDs. Traditionally, all CDs were federally insured and could not be sold before maturity without substantial interest penalties. For a variety of historical reasons, interest rates on CDs were kept low and were subject to ceilings set by the Federal Reserve. During the 1960s and 1970s, CD rates started to fall well below rising money market rates. In an attempt to increase their direct access to the money market in the face of rising short-term rates, banks offered a new type

> **certificates of deposit (CDs)**
>
> A term savings deposit at a bank or other financial institution.

of CD. These new CDs were not federally insured, their interest rates were not subject to Federal Reserve ceilings, and they could be sold before maturity in a secondary market. These became known as large CDs because they usually had face values of at least $1 million. Today, any CD with a face value in excess of $100,000 is considered to be a large CD. Today, more than $800 billion in large CDs are outstanding, compared with about $900 billion outstanding small CDs.

The credit risk associated with large CDs depends directly on the creditworthiness of the financial institutions that issue them. Because large CDs are not federally insured, loss of principal is possible if the financial institution fails. Although the overall credit risk of large CDs is low, some recent bank failures cost large CD holders some, although rarely all, of their principal.

Repurchase Agreements

repurchase agreements

Short-term loans with government securities pledged as collateral.

Repurchase agreements, or repos, are basically short-term loans with securities as collateral. In a repurchase agreement, one party sells a package of securities (often U.S. government securities) to another party and agrees to buy back, or repurchase, the securities at a later date (ranging from overnight to months later) at a higher price. For example, suppose that a securities dealer just purchased $10 million in U.S. government bonds to sell to customers and needs to finance the purchase for a couple of days. A city government is flush with cash from tax receipts that it must soon pay out for services, but it needs a short-term investment until that time. The securities dealer sells the bonds to the city for $9,975,000, agreeing to repurchase them in 18 days for $10 million. The discount is found as follows:

$$\text{Face value} - [(\text{Repurchase rate}) \times (\text{Term}/360)(\text{Face value})]$$

The repurchase rate in this example is 5% per annum, and the term is 18 days:

$$\$10{,}000{,}000 - [(.05)(18/360)(\$10{,}000{,}000)]$$

Today, more than $350 billion in repurchase agreements are outstanding. Because repos are collateralized—backed by another asset—they are considered to be safe investments.

Short-Term Municipal Securities

In addition to the federal Treasury and other federal agencies, thousands of state and local government units in the United States (states, cities, school districts, etc.) issue securities, many of which are money market instruments. (In the terminology of investments, *government* refers to securities issued by the Treasury or federal agencies, whereas *municipal* refers to securities issued by all state and local government units.) Virtually all short-term municipals are called anticipation notes. They are issued in anticipation of revenue from another source (e.g., property tax receipts) and are almost always discount securities. They are sold in minimum denominations of at least $25,000.

The quality of short-term municipals varies, although the overall credit risk is low. Municipal securities may have some credit risk whereas government securities, specifically Treasury securities, do not. Although many issuers of municipal securities can levy taxes, unlike the federal government, they cannot legally print money. The Treasury could always print money to pay its bills (including the face value of maturing securities) if need be. State and local governments can rely only on receipt of tax payments and other revenue.

Like all municipal securities, short-term municipals possess an important feature: the interest they pay is exempt from federal income taxes. As a result, short-term municipals typically have lower yields than even T-bills.

Because of this tax feature, taxable investors should compute the **taxable equivalent yield (TEY)** when comparing municipals with other securities. The TEY is computed as follows:

$$\text{TEY} = \text{Yield on the tax-exempt security}/(1 - T) \qquad (3.4)$$

taxable equivalent yield (TEY)
Compares the yield on a tax-exempt security to the yield on a taxable security.

where T is the investor's marginal tax rate.[6] For example, if a short-term municipal security yields 3.5% and the investor has a marginal tax rate of 28%, the TEY equals 0.035/0.72, or 4.86%. Obviously as the investor's tax rate increases, the TEY increases, making municipal securities most attractive to investors in high tax brackets.

Foreign Money Market Instruments

Various money market instruments are sold in other countries. These instruments are denominated in either foreign currencies or U.S. dollars. Many foreign governments issue short-term securities similar to U.S. T-bills. Canada, for example, sells Treasury bills weekly with maturities of 90, 180, and 360 days. These discount securities have denominations as small as C$1,000. Foreign and U.S. corporations also issue commercial paper throughout the world. For example, most U.S. finance companies, such as GMAC, have Canadian operations and issue commercial paper in Canada to finance those operations.

Two of the most significant foreign money market instruments are Eurodollar deposits and Eurodollar CDs. These are simply bank deposits and CDs denominated in U.S. dollars but issued and held outside the United States or in U.S. branches of foreign banks.[7] For example, a 180-day U.S. dollar CD issued by the London branch of Citibank would be a Eurodollar CD. Today, more than $125 billion in Eurodollar deposits and Eurodollar CDs are outstanding.

One of the most widely followed money market interest rates, London interbank offered rate (LIBOR), is the rate at which five large London banks are willing to lend dollar-denominated funds to one another in the interbank market. The rates on most Eurodollar deposits and CDs are tied to the LIBOR. Many other money market and loan rates worldwide are also tied to the LIBOR.

---

[6]If the interest received is also exempt from state income taxes, T should reflect the investor's combined federal-state marginal tax rate.

[7]In addition to Eurodollars, Euroyen deposits and CDs are prominent in several major financial centers, especially in London. Euroyen deposits and CDs are simply deposits and CDs denominated in Japanese yen but issued and held outside Japan.

LONG-TERM FIXED INCOME SECURITIES (BONDS)

Money market instruments, by definition, have maturities of one year or less from the date of issue. Long-term fixed income securities (often called *bonds*) include all debt instruments that have maturities longer than one year from the date they are originally sold.[8] Aside from this obvious difference, several other important characteristics separate money market instruments from long-term fixed income securities. With the exception of CDs, money market instruments are typically discount securities. Bonds, by contrast, are usually interest bearing securities. Most bonds pay regular interest payments at fixed rates, called **coupon rates**. Interest is computed and paid at regular intervals—the most common of which is twice a year—as a percentage of the security's par, or face value.

coupon rates

Percentage of face value paid to bondholders each year as interest.

In addition, the quality of bonds varies widely. Some bonds have essentially no credit risk—Treasury bonds, for example—while other bonds have a great deal of credit risk. Further, all bonds, regardless of the amount credit risk, expose investors to more interest rate and purchasing power risk than money market instruments, and these risks generally increase as time to maturity increases. Finally, many bonds are **callable**, meaning the issuers can buy back the securities from investors, at prespecified prices, prior to maturity. Not surprisingly, issuers are far more likely to call bonds when interest rates are falling, which allows them to issue new bonds with lower coupon rates. During the last few years, for instance, many governments and corporations have called bonds.

callable (call provision)

Gives the issuer the right to buy the bond back from investors at a fixed price prior to maturity.

Government Bonds

In the language of investments, a **municipal bond** is a bond issued by a state or local government. A **government bond** is a bond issued by the U.S. Treasury or a federal agency. The U.S. Treasury issues a variety of fixed-income securities with maturities ranging between 2 and 30 years. Treasuries issued with maturities between 2 and 10 years are referred to as *notes;* those with original maturities of 30 years are referred to as *bonds.* Aside from maturity, bonds and notes differ only in that bonds are often callable starting five years before maturity; notes are generally not callable. Both notes and bonds are interest-bearing securities, trade in vigorous secondary markets, and are sold in denominations as small as $1,000. Like T-bills, T-notes and T-bonds are backed by the full faith and credit of the U.S. government and have no default risk. Currently, more than $1.5 trillion in notes and about $600 billion in bonds are outstanding. Since the mid-1990s, the Treasury tried to reduce the average maturity of its outstanding securities by emphasizing the sale of shorter-term notes. In fact, the Treasury has not sold any new bond issues since October 2001 and has called several outstanding bond issues.

municipal bond

A bond issued by a state or local government.

government bond

A bond issued by the U.S. Treasury or a federal agency.

Inflation-Indexed Securities In 1996 the Treasury sold the first so-called inflation-indexed security. These securities pay investors a fixed real rate of interest plus additional interest as compensation for inflation. Therefore, unlike most fixed

---

[8]Technically speaking, not all long-term fixed income securities are bonds. The term *bond*, however, is often used generically to refer to any debt security with a maturity in excess of one year.

income securities, inflation-indexed securities do not expose investors to purchasing power risk. They proved to be quite popular with a variety of investors; currently more than $140 billion in inflation-indexed securities are outstanding.

Federal Agency Securities Besides short-term securities, the federal agencies also issue a variety of longer-term fixed income securities to finance their operations. Federal agency securities are similar to T-notes and T-bonds. Remember, though, federal agency securities are not backed by the full faith and credit of the U.S. government, so they carry some, albeit minuscule, amount of credit risk.

Municipal Bonds

Across the United States, thousands of state and local governments issue longer-term fixed income securities in addition to the short-term securities discussed previously. The interest earned on these securities is also exempt from federal income tax. Municipal bonds are generally interest bearing, have par values of about $25,000, and are often callable.

Municipal bonds fall into two categories: general obligation bonds and revenue bonds. General obligation bonds are backed by the full faith and credit of the government that issues them. Because the issuer can spend any of its tax revenues to pay interest and principal on these bonds, general obligation bonds can be issued only by governments that have taxing authority. By contrast, revenue bonds are used to finance revenue-producing projects (from toll roads to sports facilities), and only revenues generated by the project may be used to pay bondholders. Revenue bonds can be issued by governmental units that don't have the authority to levy taxes. Thus, as a general rule, revenue bonds have more credit risk than general obligation bonds. During a typical year, about two-thirds of all municipal bonds sold are revenue bonds.

Municipal bonds are often serial issues, as opposed to term issues. In a serial bond issue, a predetermined number of bonds mature each year until the final maturity date. All term bonds mature on the same date.

As we pointed out earlier, investors must realize that municipal bonds are not free of credit risk, even if the securities are issued by a government with taxing authority. Although rare, municipal bond defaults happen. One of the largest municipal bond defaults in history occurred in December 1994 when Orange County, California, defaulted on more than $1 billion of securities. To help investors assess credit risk, many municipal bonds carry bond ratings assigned by organizations such as Moody's and Standard & Poor's. The highest rating—indicating the least amount of credit risk—is AAA (Aaa for Moody's). Bonds considered to have more credit risk are assigned lower ratings. We discuss bond ratings in more detail in Chapter 9.

Corporate Debt Issues

Corporations issue a wide variety of longer-term debt securities to raise capital for company projects. Most corporate bonds are term issues that mature after anywhere between 5 and 30 years; most have par values of $1,000.[9] In addition,

general obligation bond
Municipal bond backed by the full faith and credit of the governmental unit issuing the bond.

revenue bond
Municipal bond used to pay for revenue-producing projects; only revenues from the project can be used to pay principal and interest.

serial bond
A bond issue in which bonds mature over a period of time; commonly found in municipal bond issues.

term bond
A bond issue in which all bonds mature on the same date.

bond rating
An assessment made by an independent bond rating agency of the bond's credit risk.

_____
[9]Occasionally a company will issue a bond with a maturity in excess of 30 years. In 1995, the Walt Disney Company issued a bond with a 100-year maturity.

virtually all corporate bonds are callable. A large corporation may have several different debt issues outstanding at any one time. Shell Oil Company, for example, currently has more than 15 different long-term debt issues outstanding.

All corporate bonds expose investors to some degree of credit risk, but the amount varies widely from issue to issue. Many corporate issues are considered to be almost as safe as government bonds whereas others are seen as far more speculative. Like municipal bonds, most corporate bonds are rated. Corporate bonds with ratings above BBB (or Baa) are considered to be investment grade; those with ratings below BBB are often called junk bonds.

In general, corporate bonds can be divided into categories based on their collateral provisions. In general, corporate bonds can be divided into categories based on their collateral provisions. Some bonds, known as secured bonds, give their owners legal claims to specific assets in the event the issuers go bankrupt. A mortgage bond is secured by a lien on real assets, such as property or machinery. Unsecured bonds are known as debentures. Holders of debentures are considered to be general creditors of the issuers; if the company's assets are liquidated in bankruptcy, they have junior claims relative to mortgage bondholders. Owners of subordinated debentures have even lower claims to assets in the event of bankruptcy. Finally, income bonds are the corporate equivalent of municipal revenue bonds; they finance the purchase of income-producing assets. Unlike other corporate bonds, an income bond carries a commitment to pay interest and principal only if income from the asset is sufficient.

Mortgage Pass-Through Securities

One of the most dramatic changes to occur in the financial system over the past 20 years has been the so-called securitization of mortgages, especially home mortgages. Three federally sponsored organizations, the Federal National Mortgage Association (known as Fannie Mae), the Government National Mortgage Association (known as Ginnie Mae), and the Federal Home Loan Mortgage Corporation (known as Freddie Mac), played a major role. All three were created to purchase loans from primary mortgage lenders such as savings and loan associations to increase the supply of mortgage credit.

Traditionally all three organizations issued bonds to finance their mortgage purchases. However, in 1975, Ginnie Mae offered the first mortgage pass-through security, which pledged interest payments backed by a self-liquidating pool of mortgages, all with the same term and interest rate. As homeowners make their monthly house payments (consisting of both interest and principal), the pooled payment is passed through to the security holders. Owning a mortgage pass-through security is equivalent to owning a piece of a large pool of home mortgages. Today, Fannie Mae, Freddie Mac, and several other private financial institutions also issue mortgage pass-through securities. They have proved quite successful. Today, almost $3 trillion in mortgage pass-through securities are outstanding.

Mortgage pass-throughs are considered to be high-quality securities with minimal, if any, credit risk. All mortgages in the pool are insured, which means that the outstanding principal is paid by the insurer in the event of default. The organization that issues a mortgage pass-through security almost always guarantees timely payment of interest and principal to investors. Mortgage pass-

---

junk bond

A bond with a rating below BBB (or Baa); also called speculative-grade bond.

mortgage bond

A corporate bond in which specific assets are pledged as collateral.

debenture

A corporate bond in which no specific assets are pledged as collateral.

subordinated debenture

A bond in which investors have a junior claim to other bondholders in the event of bankruptcy.

Income bond

Corporate equivalent of a revenue bond.

mortgage pass-through security

A fixed income security backed by a self-liquidating pool of mortgages.

throughs also offer attractive yields relative to Treasury securities. Also, many investors like the monthly income from pass-throughs. The main drawback with mortgage pass-throughs is their uncertain maturities. All the loans in the pool have the same original term (usually 30 years); however, most homeowners pay off their mortgages early when they refinance or sell their homes. Because the pool is liquidated as mortgages are paid off, the pass-through could mature any time between one day and 30 years from the date of issue.

Foreign Bonds

Governments and corporations throughout the world issue debt securities outside their own countries. These bonds often have colorful names. For example, foreign bonds issued in the United States are called **Yankee bonds**, whereas foreign bonds issued in the United Kingdom are referred to as Bulldog bonds. Many U.S. corporations issue **Eurobonds** (bonds denominated in U.S. dollars but issued outside the United States). Companies also issue Euroyen bonds, bonds denominated in Japanese yen issued outside Japan. As we noted in the last chapter, however, any security denominated in a currency other than U.S. dollars exposes American investors to foreign exchange risk.

Yankee bond

Foreign bond issued in the United States.

Eurobond

Dollar-denominated bond issued outside the United States.

Preferred Stock

Preferred stock is another security issued by corporations. Preferred stock is a hybrid security; it shares characteristics of both common stock and bonds. Legally, it is a class of stock, representing an ownership or equity claim on firm assets, not a debt instrument. We include it with other fixed-income securities, such as bonds, because from an investor's standpoint, preferred stock performs much more like a bond than a stock. Preferred stock pays a set annual dividend. This fixed amount almost never changes, regardless of the issuing firm's profitability. In addition, preferred shareholders have no voting rights, and they have a senior claim, relative to common shareholders, to firm assets in the event of bankruptcy. However, failure to pay preferred stock dividends cannot force the issuer into bankruptcy, as failure to make principal and interest payments on bonds can. Although, in theory, preferred stock has no maturity, most issues are callable, and experience suggests that most preferred issues are eventually called.

Preferred stocks run the gamut from high to low quality. Like corporate and municipal bonds, preferred stocks are often rated by Standard & Poor's and Moody's. A rating reflects expert assessment of the issuer's ability to maintain the preferred stock dividend in the future. Preferred stock yields usually, although not always, exceed corporate bond yields.

For many reasons, preferred stock has long been viewed as an orphan security, not particularly popular with either issuers or investors. In fact, the total amount of preferred stock outstanding in the United States actually declined between 1970 and 1985. In recent years, however, preferred stock made a modest comeback. In 1985, approximately $6.5 billion in new preferred stock was issued, representing less than 3% of all long-term corporate securities issued that year. Today, preferred stock represents slightly more than 5% of all long-term securities issued during a typical year.

COMMON STOCK

Common stock represents an ownership claim in a corporation; bondholders are creditors, but stockholders are owners. This status leaves stockholders as residual claimants. If the company liquidates its assets, common stockholders get whatever remains after all creditors have been paid. Shares of publicly held companies (i.e., shares that can be purchased by the investing public) are traded in markets known as stock exchanges. Unlike owners of sole proprietorships or partnerships, however, common stockholders have the advantage of limited liability. In the event the company goes bankrupt, stockholders can lose no more than what they paid for their stock. Stockholders are not fully liable for corporate debts.

Although the primary benefit to investors of fixed income securities is clearly current income from interest payments, investors purchase common stocks primarily for potential capital appreciation. Many common stocks do distribute some part of corporate net income as cash dividends; however, this income should be considered a secondary reason for investing in most stocks. In theory, as the company becomes more valuable (e.g., as its earnings rise), shares of its common stock should also become more valuable, creating capital appreciation.

As an example, take a look at Figure 3.2. It shows the relationship between stock prices and earnings for Johnson & Johnson. Notice that, in general, as the firm's earnings rose, so did its stock price. Both increased by more than 11 times during the period shown.

Even though stock prices and earnings clearly show a long-term relationship, in the short term stock prices and earnings can be widely divergent. Speculative bubbles, which we discussed briefly in Chapter 1, are often extreme examples of situations where stock prices get way ahead of earnings. The Investment History box, "The Nifty Fifty," on page 70, describes a famous speculative bubble. As with all bubbles, this one eventually broke. Moreover, the bubble in technology stocks that broke in March 2000 demonstrated many eerie similarities to the Nifty Fifty.

Unlike fixed income securities, it is difficult to categorize common stocks based on factors such as quality. Wall Street professionals use loose terms such as *cyclical, defensive, growth, value,* and *blue chip* to categorize individual common stocks. The term *blue chip,* for example, was first introduced by *The Wall Street Journal* in 1904 to describe the stocks of the largest, most consistently profitable companies. In poker, the blue chips are always the most valuable. These terms are general, however, and not mutually exclusive. Two investors often put a single stock in different categories.

One of the goals of security analysis is to try to categorize individual common stocks, as well as estimate future earnings and dividends. We describe security analysis at greater length in Chapters 11 through 14.

Rights of Stockholders

Because common stockholders are legal owners of a corporation, their investments give them certain rights, including voting rights. Each share normally gives its owner one vote in elections of the company's board of directors and on other

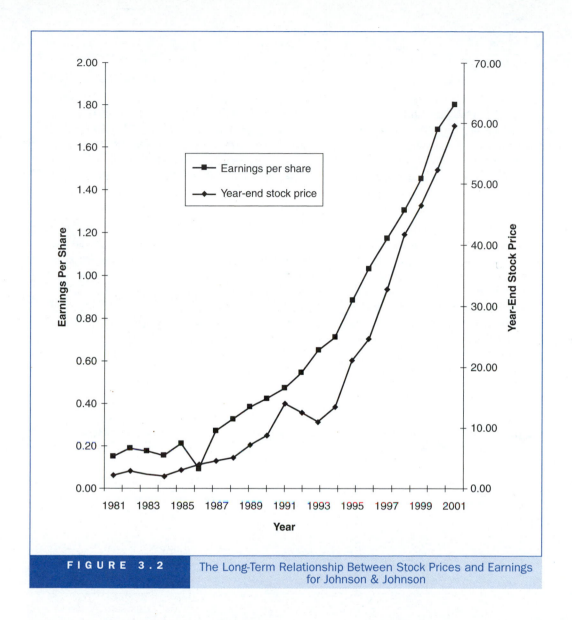

FIGURE 3.2   The Long-Term Relationship Between Stock Prices and Earnings for Johnson & Johnson

significant issues facing the company.[10] Management retains responsibility for the day-to-day operation of the company within guidelines set by stockholders and the board of directors. The role of stockholders in corporate governance relative to the roles of the board of directors and management has become quite controversial in recent years as shareholders asserted their will far more aggressively on issues such as management compensation and performance.

---

[10]The exception to this rule is a company with so-called dual classes of common stock. For example, Coors Brewing Company has two classes of common stock-Class A shares and Class B shares. Only the Class A shares carry with them voting rights, and they are all owned by members of the Coors family. Class B shares are available to the investing public.

INVESTMENT HISTORY

The Nifty Fifty

Many stock investors would have preferred to forget the 1970s. Between the beginning of 1970 and the end of 1979, the S&P 500 had an average annual total return of 5.9%, less than the average rate of inflation for the period, 7.4%. The only major stock market fad, called the Nifty Fifty, came early in the decade.

Bounced by past bubbles, many investors, especially professional money managers and mutual fund managers, decided in the early 1970s to focus exclusively on sound rational investments, avoiding any fads. This notion led them to buy shares of companies with established growth records and familiar names, such as Disney, Hewlett-Packard, and Xerox. These stocks numbered about four dozen, thus the term Nifty Fifty. They were considered to be one-decision stocks, you bought them and held them forever. Unlike many past fads, the Nifty Fifty were quality stocks. Unfortunately, a bubble caused by excessive demand carried the prices of Nifty Fifty stocks well above values justified by their prospective growth rates.

Examples from the Nifty Fifty are shown in the accompanying table. Between its low in 1970 and its high in 1972 to 1973, the S&P 500 gained about 57%. Nifty Fifty stocks did much better, as the examples in the table illustrate. Disney and Hewlett-Packard, for example, each more than quadrupled between 1970 and 1972 to 1973. At its peak in late 1972, McDonald's was selling for 82 times earnings. Yet again, sophisticated investors fell into the trap of believing that whatever price they paid for a Nifty Fifty stock, it would continue to go up. Of course, that did not happen.

The market peaked in early 1973 and then declined sharply for most of the next two years. Between early 1973 and the end of 1974, the S&P 500 lost more than 43% of its value. The prices of the Nifty Fifty held up for awhile and then collapsed. Avon Products and Disney, for example, each dropped more than 86% from their 1972 to 1973 highs. Polaroid lost more than 90% of its value between 1972 and 1974 as its price/earnings ratio fell from 115 to 16. In fact, Polaroid's stock has never recovered; it reached its all time high in the early 1970s.

Examples of the Nifty Fifty

Stock	Low 1970		High 72/73		Low 1974		Percentage Change	
	Price	P/E	Price	P/E	Price	P/E	70 to 72/73	72/73 to 74
Avon	59 1/8	34	140	65	18 5/8	10	136.8%	−86.7%
Disney	19 3/8	24	111	82	15 3/8	10	471.0	−86.1
Kodak	57 5/8	23	152	44	57 5/8	15	163.3	−62.0
HP	19 3/8	21	100	53	52	17	419.4	−48.3
McDonald's	9 1/8	19	77 1/2	82	21 1/4	13	747.9	−72.5
Polaroid	51	25	150	115	14 1/8	16	193.1	−90.6
Xerox	65 1/4	27	172	54	49	12	163.4	−71.5
S&P 500	75.6	14	118.4	19	67.1	7	56.6	−43.3

Questions for Critical Thinking

1. In what ways is the bubble in technology stocks that broke in March 2000 similar to the Nifty Fifty? Does your answer suggest that stock market bubbles are inevitable?

2. During the height of the Nifty Fifty one commentator writing in *Forbes* magazine argued that investors should never pay more than 50 times earnings for any stock, regardless of its growth prospects. Do you agree or disagree with this conclusion?

Rights to retain a proportionate ownership in a company are known as **preemptive rights**. This concern stems from dilution of the percentage of shares controlled by existing shareholders, should a company decide to sell additional shares of common stock. For example, if a company with 1 million shares outstanding were to sell another 500,000 shares to new investors, the proportion of the company owned by existing shareholders would fall to 67%. Preemptive rights prevent dilution by giving existing shareholders the right to purchase any new share offerings before other investors. Preemptive rights eventually expire after set time periods, after which any remaining shares of a new issue can be sold to outside investors.

preemptive rights

Right of shareholders to purchase newly issued shares of stock before the general public.

Foreign Stocks

American investors interested in investing in the shares of a non-U.S. company have several options. Aside from international mutual funds, investors can buy the shares directly on the foreign exchange where shares are traded. For example, an investor interested in the shares of British Petroleum could buy the shares on the London Stock Exchange. The shares would be priced in British pounds—pence actually.

However, buying shares on foreign markets can be both cumbersome and expensive. Consequently, **American depository receipts (ADRs)** are often a better alternative. ADRs are denominated in U.S. dollars and trade on U.S. stock exchanges, so they eliminate some of the risk and complication of foreign investing. More than 125 ADR issues are traded on the New York Stock Exchange alone, including such well-known companies as Royal Dutch Shell, Unilever, and Honda Motor.

An ADR is a surrogate for the underlying shares. It represents a receipt for the shares of a foreign company held in the vault of a U.S. bank. ADR shareholders are entitled to all stock and cash dividends paid by the foreign shares. ADRs can be set up either by the bank at the request of the foreign company (known as a sponsored ADR) or can be set up at the request of U.S. market makers (known as an unsponsored ADR).

American depository receipt (ADR)

Surrogate for shares of a foreign company's stock held in the vault of the U.S. bank; denominated in U.S. dollars.

DERIVATIVE SECURITIES

In recent years derivative securities gained greater prominence. A **derivative security** is one whose value depends on the value of an underlying asset, such as an agricultural commodity, an individual common stock, a stock index, or a Treasury bond. Most derivative securities are considered to be riskier investments than more traditional investments, such as stocks and bonds. As a result, derivative securities are sometimes referred to as *speculative securities*. Derivative securities can be divided into three categories: stock options, corporate-created derivative instruments, and futures contracts.

derivative security

A security whose value is tied to the value of an underlying asset; options and futures.

Stock Options

A stock option gives the holder the right, but not obligation, to buy or sell and individual stock, or stock index, at a fixed price for a fixed period of time. A **call option** is an option to buy whereas a **put option** is an option to sell. Most options expire within one year after their issue dates.

call option

The right to buy stock at a fixed price for a fixed period of time.

put option

The right to sell stock at a fixed price for a fixed period of time.

Investors use options in many ways. They can buy or sell options to speculate that the underlying stocks will rise or fall in value over a short period of time. Options can also be used to hedge various stock positions, reducing their risk by gaining the right to buy or sell at set prices, despite market movements. Options are currently available on approximately 350 individual stocks as well as several well-known stock indexes. The most actively traded options are those on the Standard & Poor's 100 stock index (OEX options). Of course, you cannot buy or sell an index. These options are settled in cash. How much cash depends on the index value on the settlement date. This process is described in Chapter 18.

To illustrate how options work, consider a December call option on Microsoft at an exercise price of $60. This call option gives the holder the right to buy 100 shares of Microsoft at a price of $60 per share at any time before late December. If Microsoft's stock price were to rise above $60 per share before late December, the holder of the option could call the stock (i.e., exercise the option). If Microsoft were to remain at or less than $60 per share before late December, the option would expire unexercised and worthless. By contrast, a December put option on Microsoft at an exercise price of $60 would give the holder the right to sell 100 shares of Microsoft at $60 per share until late December. If Microsoft's stock were to drop to $50 per share before late December, the holder of the put could buy 100 shares of Microsoft at $50 per share, then exercise the put option to sell the stock for $60 per share, making $10 per share (ignoring transaction costs as well as the cost of the option). However, if Microsoft's stock were to remain above $60 per share through late December, the put option would expire unexercised.

This simple example suggests generally how options work and how their value is tied to the value of the underlying stock (Microsoft, in the example). It leaves a number of important questions unanswered, however. For example, who sells the stock when someone exercises a call option or buys the stock when someone exercises a put? Other investors sell the same call or put option and accept the obligation to sell or buy in exchange for a fee. We answer many of the complex questions that options raise in more depth in Chapter 15.

Corporate-Created Derivative Securities

Corporations issue two kinds of securities that resemble options: convertible bonds or preferred stock issues and warrants. Like all derivative instruments, the value of these securities depends, in part, on the value of the underlying securities, which is the issuer's common stocks, for these derivatives.

convertible security

A bond or preferred stock that can be exchanged for a fixed number of shares of common stock.

Convertibles A convertible security is just like a regular corporate bond or preferred stock issue with the added feature that the investor has the option of exchanging the convertible for a fixed number of shares of the issuing company's common stock. For example, Starbucks Corporation (the parent of Starbucks Coffee) has a convertible bond outstanding that can be converted into 43 shares of Starbucks common stock. Because it allows the investor to exchange a bond with a par value of $1,000 for 43 shares of common stock, this convertible has a conversion price of $23.25. The conversion price normally remains constant, regardless of the market price of the issuer's common stock, much like the exercise price on a call option. The value of the convertible depends, in part, on the value of the issuer's common stock. If Starbucks stock is trading at $25 per share, the convertible bond will sell for at least $1,075 (43 times $25).

Convertibles are attractive to investors because they combine characteristics of bonds (the Starbucks convertible pays interest at a coupon rate of 4.5%) with the potential to share in stock price appreciation. As a result, convertibles typically have lower coupon rates (or preferred stock dividends) than do similar straight bonds or preferred stock issues (i.e., those that are not convertible).

Warrants In essence, warrants are long-term call options issued by companies. The investor redeems the warrant with the issuing corporation and receives, for a preset price, a specified number of shares of common stock. Warrants are typically issued with lives of 5 to 10 years. They are often attached to other securities (especially bonds) to make them more marketable. Because an investor can sell the warrant and still keep the security to which it was attached, warrants trade on the major stock exchanges. Like all call options, the value of a warrant rises and falls as the price of the underlying common stock rises and falls.

warrant

Long-term call option issued by corporations.

Futures Contracts

A futures contract is a real contract between parties for future delivery of a commodity at an agreed price, usually within one year. The party who agrees to deliver the commodity is said to have the short position, whereas the party who agrees to accept delivery has the long position. Let's say you go short and we go long in December corn. You agree to deliver, and we agree to accept, a specified amount of corn in December at a price on which we agree today.[11] In essence, the short position makes money if the price of the commodity falls between the contract date and the delivery date, whereas the long position makes money if the price of the commodity rises.

futures contract

A contract calling for the future delivery of an asset at a price agreed to today.

Futures contracts began in ancient Egypt and historically involved only agricultural commodities such as corn, wheat, and livestock. Today, futures contracts are available on such diverse assets as foreign currencies, T-bonds, stock indexes, precious metals, and petroleum products, in addition to traditional agricultural products. The most actively traded futures contracts involve long-term T-bonds and currencies. Futures contracts are traded throughout the world with the two largest futures exchanges located in Chicago (the Chicago Board of Trade and the Chicago Mercantile Exchange). The Singapore Futures Exchange is one of the world's largest markets for currency and other financial futures.

Basically, two groups of investors trade futures contracts: hedgers and speculators. A hedger owns or needs to buy the commodity that underlies the futures contract and uses the futures to reduce price uncertainty. A wheat farmer might use futures to guarantee the price at which a wheat crop would sell, prior to its harvest. Speculators have no need to trade commodities; they trade futures contracts to try to profit from short-term movements in commodity prices. A

---

[11]The futures contract will also specify the grade of corn to be delivered and the delivery location as well as the amount to be delivered, the delivery date, and the price.

speculator might go long in a wheat contract, believing that wheat is likely to rise in price over a short period of time. Another speculator might go short in T-bonds, believing that interest rates would soon climb higher, reducing the market prices of T-bonds.

We have a lot more to say about the investment uses of and trading in futures contracts in Chapter 16. Suffice to say at this point that although futures do not suit the needs of every investor, they can be quite useful in many investment situations.

REAL ASSETS

The discussion so far covered investing in financial assets, often called paper assets. To conclude our overview of investment alternatives, we turn our attention to real assets. Real assets are physical assets and include real estate, precious metals, gems, and collectibles (art, for example). Even though real assets occasionally produce spectacular returns, investing in real assets is problematic. The Investment Insight box on page 75 outlines some of the problems associated with investing in real assets.

Real Estate

When one thinks of real assets, real estate may come to mind first. Land, commercial property, and housing units have long been considered viable investment options, and they often provide attractive returns and even tax savings. Essentially, real investments fall into two categories: direct ownership of real estate, and indirect ownership through real estate investment trusts (REITs) or limited partnerships.

Many Americans already invest in real estate, even if they don't realize it. About 70% of all American households own their own homes. Moreover, the equity the typical owner has in his or her home, makes up a substantial portion of that household's total wealth. Owner-occupied housing has often been an excellent investment, but not always and not in every part of the country. In fact, many financial experts suggest you never buy a home *solely* on the basis on potential price appreciation. During the past 20 years, for instance, the average sales price of a home barely kept pace with the overall rate of inflation. Owning a home offers other advantages, however, including the pride of ownership and significant tax savings. Other direct real estate investments include farmland, rental property, and certain types of commercial property.

REIT (real estate investment trust)

An investment company that sells shares and uses the proceeds to purchase real estate investments.

limited partnership

A form of indirect investment in real estate in which the partners have limited liability.

Just as for financial assets, you can also invest in real estate indirectly. **Real estate investment trusts (REITs)** are corporations that invest in real estate. They pool funds from many investors and use the proceeds to purchase property, mortgage loans, or both. Shares of REITs trade on the major stock exchanges. A **limited partnership** consists of a general partner and several limited partners who invest funds in return for equity in property purchased by the partnership. The partners share in the income and/or capital appreciation produced by the property. The limited partners have limited liability; like corporate stockholders, they can lose only what they initially invested. The general partner has unlimited liability for all debts of the partnerships.

INVESTMENT INSIGHT

The Trouble with Real Assets

Given the right set of circumstances, real assets can produce impressive returns. With only a few exceptions, however, stocks and bonds produce far better returns than real assets over long periods of time. The following are some other reasons why most investors should avoid real assets:

- *No income.* With the exception of some real estate investments, all returns from real assets come in the form of price appreciation.
- *Subjective value.* It is much easier to put a fair value on a stock or bond than it is on a real asset.
- *Lack of liquidity.* Most real assets lack the liquidity of stocks and bonds. In addition, the cost of buying and selling real assets is high.
- *Safekeeping.* The investor is responsible for the safekeeping of real assets. Insurance can be quite expensive and difficult to obtain.

- *Emotional bond.* Many people who "invest" in collectibles, such as paintings, end up falling in love with them. Because they will never sell their collectibles, they will never end up making any money.

Questions for Critical Thinking

1. Historically real assets occasionally produced short periods of spectacular returns—far in excess of the returns from paper assets. What do you think are some of the characteristics of those periods?
2. Based on the reasons that explain why real asset investing is problematic, why do so many Americans invest so much of their wealth in their homes?

Precious Metals, Gems, and Collectibles

Investors have long been drawn to the glitter of gold, diamonds, and great works of art. Gold is one of the world's oldest investments and long considered a safe harbor in which money can weather any political or economic storm. Other precious metals—such as silver and platinum—have their advocates as well. Still others tout the investment potential of gems. What could be safer, they ask, than a bag full of diamonds? Some investors favor the investment potential of collectibles such as art, antiques, baseball cars, classic toys, and even Beanie Babies.

Although precious metals, gems, and collectibles can produce impressive returns at times, these investments, in our view, are even more risky than real estate. Liquidity, for example, is more of a problem with collectibles than it is with other real assets. Transaction costs can be high, and value is clearly in the eye of the beholder. How much is an original Picasso painting really worth? The auction prices of many great art works fell sharply in the early 1990s when Japanese investors stopped buying art.

Moreover, investments such as precious metals, gems, and collectibles generally returned far less value than the returns from paper assets, such as stocks and bonds. For instance, the real return from gold—that is, the return minus the rate of inflation—was actually negative between 1946 and 2001, averaging −0.3% per year. By contrast, the real return from stocks averaged 7.1% per year during the same period. Between 1982 and 2001, the real return from gold averaged −4.8% per year compared to an average real return from stocks of 10.5% per year.[12]

---

[12]Jeremy Siegel, *Stocks for the Long Run,* 3rd ed. (New York: McGraw-Hill, 2002), p. 13.

In this chapter, you were introduced to the wide array of direct investment alternatives available today. In the next chapter, we discuss how you can invest indirectly in paper assets by buying shares of investment companies.

SUMMARY

1. What are money market instruments?

Money market instruments are short-term debt securities issued by governments and corporations throughout the world. All money market instruments mature within one year, tend to be discount securities, and are generally high-quality instruments. Examples of money market instruments include Treasury bills, commercial paper, banker's acceptances, repurchase agreements, and Eurodollars.

2. What are bonds and other long-term fixed income securities?

Bonds and other fixed income securities are debt instruments issued by governments and corporations throughout the world. All have maturities in excess of one year from the date of issue. Unlike money market instruments, most bonds are interest-bearing instruments. The quality of bonds can vary substantially and most bonds are callable. Issuers of bonds include the U.S. Treasury (government bonds), state and local governments (municipal bonds), and corporations.

3. Why invest in common stocks?

Common stock represents ownership claims in corporations. The main reason for investing in common stock is expected price appreciation; over the long run stock prices tend to reflect a company's earnings. Owning common stock conveys certain rights, including voting rights and the right to buy newly issued shares of common stock. U.S. investors can buy shares of foreign companies by investing in so-called ADRs.

4. What are derivative securities?

Derivative securities are instruments that derive their value from another asset. Options give one the right to buy or sell stock at a fixed price, for a fixed period of time. Corporations issue securities with option-like features, convertibles, and warrants. A futures contract is a real contract calling for the future delivery of some asset at a price agreed upon today. Futures are available in everything from agricultural commodities to currencies to financial instruments.

5. How is investing in real assets different from investments in paper assets?

Many Americans already invest in real assets because they own their own homes. Other popular real asset investments include rental real estate, precious metals, gems, and collectibles. Real asset investing is often more risky than investing in paper assets. Historically, real assets tend to outperform paper assets only in periods of high inflation.

REVIEW EXERCISES

1. What are the general characteristics of money market instruments? Give three examples of money market instruments.
2. Assume you purchased a 90-day Treasury bill for $9,870 (it has a face value of $10,000). Find the bank discount yield and the bond equivalent yield. Which yield comes closer to measuring your true rate of return?
3. A 180-day T-bill has a face value of $10,000 and a discount yield of 4.75%. Find the price, discount, and bond equivalent yield.
4. Assume a short-term municipal is yielding 3.75%. Find the security's taxable equivalent yield for an investor in a 33% tax bracket. When should the marginal tax rate for this calculation reflect both the investor's state and federal income tax rates?

5. Define the terms *Eurodollar* and *LIBOR*. What is the relationship between Eurodollars and LIBOR?
6. What are the practical differences between federal agency securities and Treasury securities. Give an example of a federal agency security.
7. What are the differences between Treasury bills, notes, and bonds. Which of the three exposes an investor to the most risk?
8. Explain the difference between a general obligation bond and a revenue bond. Why are municipal bonds rated?
9. List several types of corporate bonds. Which type on your list is the safest?
10. What is a mortgage pass-through security? What are its investment advantages and drawbacks?
11. Why is preferred stock considered to be a hybrid security? Do investors consider preferred stock to be more like a bond or more like common stock?
12. What is the main reason for investing in common stock? What major rights does common stock give its owner?
13. What is an American depository receipt (ADR)? Why would a U.S. investor purchase ADRs rather than buy the shares directly?
14. What rights do call and put options give their owners? Why are convertible securities and warrants considered to be options?
15. List the most popular real asset investments. What are some of the general investment characteristics of real assets?

CRITICAL THINKING EXERCISE

This exercise requires library or Internet research. New stock issues—initial public offerings—can be quite risky and often disappoint. One of the most spectacular flops in recent years has been Planet Hollywood, the celebrity restaurant chain. The company went public in April 1996. Initially the stock soared and then crashed. The company's fortunes sank along with its stock price. In 1999, the company filed for bankruptcy.

Research Planet Hollywood and try to identify why the stock was hot for awhile and then cooled. What are some lessons of the Planet Hollywood debacle for investors?

THE INTERNET INVESTOR

1. Use your Web browser to research a company whose stock you may be interested in buying. Most companies provide financial results and other information on their Web sites. Other sites to visit include Quicken (www.quicken.com), Morningstar (www.morningstar.com), and Microsoft Investor (www.investor.msn.com). Prepare a brief report to your class about the company you selected.
2. As mentioned in the chapter, the U.S. Treasury began selling inflation-indexed securities a few years ago. Visit www.publicdebt.treas.gov and read about these securities. Then write a brief report explaining inflation-indexed securities in terms a layperson can understand.
3. The largest options market in the world is the Chicago Board Options Exchange. Its Web site contains an extensive investor education section. Go to www.cboe.com and prepare a brief report on some of the uses and users of stock options.

4

Mutual Funds

<table>
<tr><th>PREVIOUSLY . . .</th><th>IN THIS CHAPTER . . .</th><th>TO COME . . .</th></tr>
<tr><td>We discussed the wide array of direct investment alternatives available today—everything from Treasury bills to junk bonds, from blue chip stocks to call options, from pork bellies to gold.</td><td>We explore indirect investing through investment companies, especially mutual funds. Mutual funds are a significant part of today's investment landscape and many people will invest a majority of their investment dollars in mutual funds. We also discuss two alternatives to mutual funds: unit investment trusts and closed-end funds.</td><td>We describe the world's financial markets, how investors participate in them, and how financial markets are regulated.</td></tr>
</table>

CHAPTER OBJECTIVES

After reading Chapter 4, you should be able to answer the following questions:

1. What is a mutual fund, and how does it operate?

2. How much does mutual fund investing cost?

3. How should mutual fund performance be evaluated?

4. What are the other types of investment companies?

As we saw in the prior chapter, investors today must choose among a staggering number of investment alternatives. The stock market in the United States alone offers more than 6,000 different stock issues. Throughout the international markets, the number of stock issues worldwide is closer to 10,000. Add to that the thousands of money market, government, municipal, and corporate debt issues available, and investors face a bewildering task in choosing the right investments for their particular needs.

Many investors find that the best way to select securities intelligently in today's environment is to buy them indirectly by purchasing shares of mutual funds. Mutual funds pool funds from many investors and use these funds to purchase securities. Owning shares of a mutual fund means owning a small piece of a diversified portfolio; dividends (or interest income) and capital gains (or losses) flow through to the investor in proportion to the number of shares he or she owns.

Mutual funds are essentially creatures of the twentieth century that gained in popularity in recent years. For example, net assets of mutual funds increased at an annual rate of about 17.5% between the end of 1991 and today, to almost $7 trillion. Mutual funds are larger today than life insurance companies, savings banks, and credit unions combined. The number of shareholder accounts rose more than 200% during the last 10 years. Mutual funds played a key role in the transition during the past 30 years of so many individuals from simple savers to investors. The fact that record numbers of Americans own stock today is due, in large part, to the existence and growth of mutual funds.

In this chapter, we take a detailed look at mutual funds, how they operate, the kinds of funds available today, and how investors should choose the right fund. Even though mutual funds are by far the largest type of investment company, two other types of investment companies exist: unit investment trusts and closed-end funds.

UNDERSTANDING MUTUAL FUNDS

The ancestors of today's mutual funds can be traced back to nineteenth-century Britain. Money invested in English and Scottish investment trusts (as these companies were known) contributed substantial financing to the U.S. economy following the Civil War. British investment trusts, for example provided much of the financing to build the railroads that opened up America's western frontier.

How a Mutual Fund Operates

Today's mutual funds are fairly simple organizations. They raise money by selling shares of their own to the investing public. They use these funds to purchase various types of securities that help them achieve their stated investment objectives. For example, a money market mutual fund purchases only money market instruments such as commercial paper and Treasury bills. Mutual funds are also known as open-end investment companies because they continually sell new shares to investors. If you wish to sell shares of a mutual fund, you sell them back to the fund. The term used is *redeeming shares*. Consequently, shares of mutual funds do not trade on secondary financial markets such as the New York Stock Exchange (NYSE).

As the securities owned by the mutual fund pay interest or dividends, this income is passed along to the mutual fund's shareholders. If the securities become

open-end investment company

Another name for mutual funds; based on mutual funds' continual issue and redemption of shares.

The Fund initially sells 1 million shares priced at $10.00 per share. It buys equal dollar amounts of five stocks with the proceeds.

Stock	Purchase Price	Annual Dividend	Number of Shares Purchased	After Six Months		After One Year		Total Dividends
				Price	Total Value	Price	Total Value	
A	$ 20	$0.50	100,000	$ 30.00	$ 3,000,000	$ 34.00	$ 3,400,000	$ 50,000
B	25	0.50	80,000	24.75	1,980,000	22.50	1,800,000	40,000
C	50	1.00	40,000	67.50	2,700,000	80.00	3,200,000	40,000
D	50	1.25	40,000	48.00	1,920,000	45.00	1,800,000	50,000
E	100	2.00	20,000	100.00	2,000,000	120.00	2,400,000	40,000
Total portfolio value					$11,600,000		$12,600,000	$220,000
Per-share value					$11.60		$12.60	$0.22

TABLE 4.1   Illustration of a Hypothetical Investment Company

more or less valuable, these capital gains or losses are also passed along to the mutual fund's shareholders. Mutual funds work in a straightforward fashion, as the simple example in Table 4.1 illustrates.

The mutual fund (let's call it The Fund) sells 1 million shares at $10 per share to the investing public, raising a total of $10 million. (Assume that The Fund charges no fees or expenses to investors.) The Fund uses the $10 million to purchase equal dollar amounts of five stocks with the initial purchase prices, annual dividends, and numbers of shares purchased shown in Table 4.1.[1]

Someone who buys 1,000 shares of The Fund, a total investment of $10,000, owns 0.1% of its equally weighted portfolio of five stocks. Assume that in six months, the total value of The Fund's portfolio rises to $11.6 million, even though only two of the five stocks in the portfolio actually rise in price. The value of 1,000 shares in The Fund also rises, to $11,600. If, at the end of one year, the total value of The Fund's portfolio rises to $12.6 million, the value of 1,000 shares becomes $12,600.

Now, assume that The Fund decides to liquidate at the end of one year. The investor receives $12,600 for 1,000 shares (the $10,000 initial investment plus $2,600 in capital gains) and $220 in dividends. The owner of 0.1% of The Fund receives 0.1% of its capital gains and 0.1% of the dividends produced by its portfolio. (Remember, this example assumes no transaction costs.) The investor's return for the year equals

$$(12,600 - \$10,000 + \$220)/\$10,000 = 28.2\%$$

Not a bad return for one year! Obviously, the operations of real mutual funds are more complicated than the example, but they all work in basically the same way.

---

[1]Recognize several simplifying assumptions in the example. It assumes that investors pay no management fees or commissions, the portfolio does not change during the year, and the number of shares remains constant.

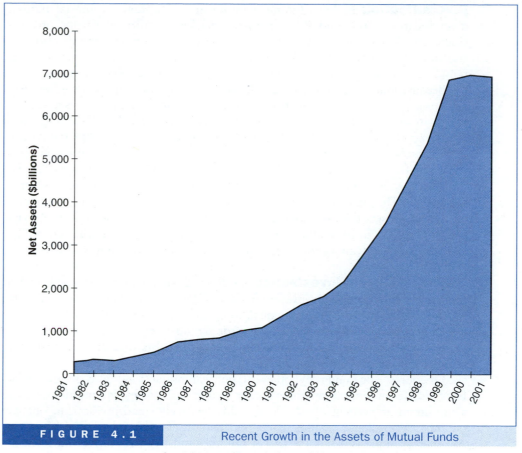

FIGURE 4.1   Recent Growth in the Assets of Mutual Funds

Source: Investment Company Institute, available at www.ici.org (accessed November 8, 2002).

The example emphasized the mutual fund's **net asset value (NAV)**. NAV is simply the market value of the mutual fund's assets minus its liabilities (if any) divided by the number of outstanding shares. The Fund's NAV equals $10.00 when it begins operations, $11.60 in six months, and $12.60 in one year. (Remember, the number of outstanding shares stays constant at 1 million.)[2]

net asset value (NAV)

Market value of the fund's assets, minus any liabilities, divided by the number of shares outstanding at any point in time.

Advantages of Mutual Funds

The popularity of mutual funds is no fluke. They offer some clear advantages to investors that more than justify their costs. (We talk more about the costs associated with mutual funds later.) We look at the three most obvious advantages of mutual funds here.

---

[2]Calculating the NAV for a real mutual fund can get quite complicated. It is a function of the number of new shares issued, the number of shares redeemed, and cash distributions, as well as the change in the value of the fund's assets.

Diversification Perhaps the most important advantage of mutual funds is diversification. Time and time again, the markets confirm the value of diversification. We demonstrated in Chapter 2 how even simple diversification can substantially improve the risk/return trade-off associated with investing (e.g., reducing an investor's risk without sacrificing too much expected return).

Because mutual funds own multiple securities, they offer investors naive diversification at a minimum. (Whether they offer efficient diversification is a question we try to answer later.) For example, Fidelity's Magellan Fund—a large stock mutual fund—owns several hundred different stocks. To see the potential benefits of this kind of diversification, take another look at the hypothetical mutual fund shown in Table 4.1. At the end of six months, two of the five stocks owned by The Fund have risen in price, two have fallen in price, and one is unchanged. Overall, the NAV of The Fund rises by $1.60 because the gain from stocks that rise in price more than offsets the loss from stocks that fall in price. At the end of one year, three stocks rise in price and two fall in price; the NAV rises another dollar. The Fund offers the advantage of diversification, as do all mutual funds.

Smaller Minimum Investments Another advantage of mutual funds is their need for smaller minimum investments. Consider The Fund again; to create this portfolio independently, buying equal dollar amounts of all five stocks in round lots (multiples of 100 shares), an investor would have to spend $50,000. The mutual fund can give the investor some of the benefits of diversification while making a much smaller investment.

Of course, The Fund is hypothetical, but real mutual funds also offer the benefit of smaller minimum investments. For example, the Magellan mutual fund has a minimum investment of $2,500; for this relatively small investment, one can obtain a piece, albeit a small one, of a portfolio of several hundred different stocks. Another example is a money market mutual fund. As you may recall from the last, many money market instruments (e.g., commercial paper and banker's acceptances) are sold in large denominations ($1 million or more). Obviously, few individual investors can directly buy any of these instruments. Small investors who put up as little as $1,000 can buy these instruments indirectly, however, by purchasing shares of a money market fund. Simply put, mutual funds allow small investors access to large diversified portfolios and securities they could not purchase on their own.

Professional Management All mutual funds provide some management services to their shareholders (e.g., basic clerical services including the preparation of some relevant tax forms). Managing even a small investment portfolio can involve a substantial amount of time-consuming clerical work. Mutual funds relieve the individual investor of much of that work.

In addition to the clerical function, most mutual funds have professional portfolio managers who decide what securities to buy, when to buy them, and when to sell them. This aspect relieves the investor of the sometimes arduous task of security analysis and selection, right? The answer is both *yes* and *no*. The investor still must select the right mutual fund (or funds) for his or her objectives, no easy job given the number of mutual funds today; also, a fund owner should always monitor its performance. Numerous other issues confront mutual fund investors. One is whether to make a single lump sum investment or make a series

INVESTMENT INSIGHT

Dollar-Cost Averaging

One popular investment strategy with mutual funds involves dollar-cost averaging. Instead of investing a lump sum all at once, you invest equal dollar amounts at regular intervals over a period of time. You may end up using this approach anyway because many retirement savings plans essentially involve dollar-cost averaging.

What is the attraction of dollar-cost averaging? Under certain conditions, it can boost your returns. Assume you are considering investing $3,000 in a mutual fund. Should you invest the entire amount today (assume the NAV is $30), or should you invest $250 a month for the next 12 months (dollar-cost average)? Look at the following table.

Beginning of Month	Investment	NAV	Shares Purchased
1	$250	$30	8.33
2	$250	$25	10.00
3	$250	$25	10.00
4	$250	$20	12.50
5	$250	$25	10.00
6	$250	$30	8.33
7	$250	$25	10.00
8	$250	$35	7.14
9	$250	$40	6.25
10	$250	$35	7.14
11	$250	$30	8.33
12	$250	$35	7.14
Total	$3,000		105.18

According to the table, you are clearly better off if you dollar-cost average. At the end of the year, you will own 105.18 shares if you dollar-cost average. On the other hand, if you invest the entire $3,000 at the beginning of the year, you will own only 100 shares at the end of the year.

Questions for Critical Thinking

1. Why do most retirement savings plans, such as 401(k) type plans, essentially involve dollar-cost averaging?
2. Under what circumstances will dollar-cost averaging produce higher returns? Under what conditions would you be better off making a single lump-sum investment?

of periodic investments. The Investment Insight box describes one popular investment strategy, known as dollar-cost averaging.

Does professional management always imply superior performance? In general, the answer to the question is no. In recent years, neither the average stock fund nor the average bond fund beat the appropriate market average. For example, during the 10-year period, ending December 31, 2001, the average large stock fund had an average annual return of about 11.3%. By contrast, the S&P 500 had an average annual return of almost 13% during the same period. There are exceptions, however. Many funds consistently beat the overall market over long periods of time.

A popular investment strategy with mutual funds—one often advocated by professionals—is dollar-cost averaging. Instead of making a single lump sum contribution, the investor makes a series of regular investments. The Investment Insight box outlines the pros and cons of dollar costing average.

Growth and Development of Mutual Funds

The Massachusetts Investment Trust, founded in 1924, is considered to be the first mutual fund organized in the United States. At the time, the idea of continuously offering and immediately redeeming shares was considered to be a radical departure in the financial community. Despite its uniqueness, the idea took hold, and other newly organized mutual funds soon followed. Most of the early mutual funds survived the 1929 stock market crash and the Great Depression.

The growth of the mutual fund industry accelerated after the end of World War II. At the end of 1940, mutual funds had net assets of $448 million; the net assets of mutual funds exceeded $2 billion by 1950, $17 billion by 1960, and $47 billion by 1970. At the end of 1970, 361 U.S. mutual funds served some 10.5 million shareholders.

Mutual funds continued to grow throughout the 1970s aided by two new types of mutual funds: money market funds and tax-exempt municipal bond funds. Money market funds became especially popular during the 1970s as small savers, who were used to earning 5.5% on their savings, were given the opportunity to earn market yields. In 1974, 16 money market funds had net assets of slightly more than $1.7 billion; by 1980, 96 money market funds had net assets in excess of $74.4 billion. By the end of 1980, 564 U.S. mutual funds had net assets of $138.4 billion.

The 1980s saw extraordinary growth in the mutual fund industry, no doubt fueled in part by the historic bull market in paper assets. Between 1980 and 1988, the number of mutual funds and shareholder accounts more than tripled; the net assets of mutual funds increased by more than 250%. During the past decade, the growth in the mutual fund industry continued. Between the end of 1988 and the end of 1998, mutual fund assets rose by almost 600%. Today, more than 8,300 mutual funds are in operation, with net assets of almost $7 trillion, and more than 280 million shareholder accounts. Figure 4.1 illustrates the recent growth in U.S. mutual funds.

International Perspective Mutual funds are also popular in other parts of the world, especially in France, Italy, Japan, Spain, and the United Kingdom. Today, the net assets of non-U.S.-based mutual funds are closing in on $5 trillion. Like their U.S. counterparts, non-U.S. mutual funds grew rapidly in recent years. For instance, the net assets of French mutual funds increased from less than $500 billion in 1997 to more than $700 billion today.

Types of Mutual Funds

In general, most mutual funds can be classified as one of four types: equity funds, hybrid funds (funds that invest in both stocks and bonds), bond and income funds, and money market funds. Figure 4.2 illustrates the distribution of mutual fund assets by type of fund for 1991 and 2001. It also shows the rapid growth of equity funds relative to other types of mutual funds. In 1991, equity funds made

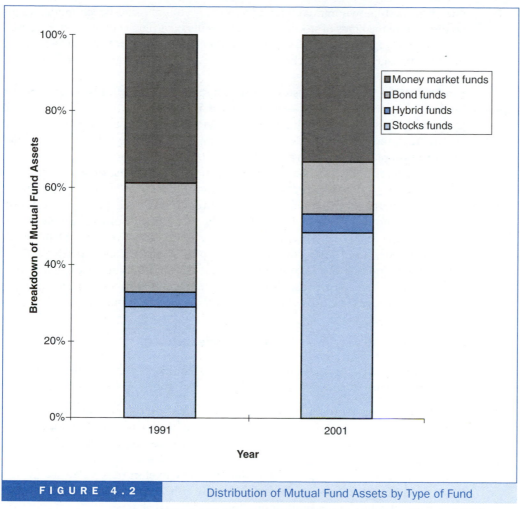

Breakdown of Mutual Fund Assets

Legend:
- ■ Money market funds
- ■ Bond funds
- ■ Hybrid funds
- □ Stocks funds

Year

FIGURE 4.2   Distribution of Mutual Fund Assets by Type of Fund

Source: Investment Company Institute, available at www.ici.org (accessed November 8, 2002).

up about 30% of mutual fund assets; by 2001, equity funds made up more than 50% of mutual fund assets.

Mutual funds can be further classified on the basis of their overall investment objectives and the types of securities that they purchase to obtain that objective. Along with the rapid growth in mutual fund assets, the number of different categories of mutual funds also expanded in recent years to meet changing investment needs. In 1975, all mutual funds fit neatly into seven categories established by the Investment Company Institute (a mutual fund trade organization). The Investment Company Institute expanded the number of different categories of mutual funds to 16 in 1985 and to the current number of 22 by 1987. Examples of mutual fund categories include aggressive growth, equity income, general bond, growth, and tax-exempt bond.

Some argue that the traditional stock mutual fund categories can lump together funds that may be, in reality, very different. To further aid investors, Morningstar—

one of the best-known mutual fund advisory services—classifies stock mutual funds on the basis of the kinds of stocks the fund typically buys (large company stocks, mid-sized company stocks, or small company stocks) and the general approach taken by the fund manager to select stocks (growth, value, or a blend of growth and value).[3]

index funds

Mutual funds designed to closely track the performance of one of several indexes.

Index Funds One of the fastest-growing types of mutual funds today is **index funds**. The largest index fund—the Vanguard 500 Index Fund—grew in size from about $1 billion in 1988 to almost $62 billion today. Index funds are designed to closely track the performance of a stock or bond market index. The most popular index funds are designed to track the S&P 500 stock index.

The case for index funds can be quite compelling. For one thing, index funds incur much lower expenses than actively managed funds. For another, index funds often outperform actively managed mutual funds. As evidence, take a look at the chart shown in Figure 4.3. It shows the performance of the Vanguard 500 Index Fund compared with the performance of the average large-blend stock fund. The index fund outperformed its group average over each period shown, sometimes by quite a bit. Before you conclude that index funds are as close to a perfect investment as you can find, however, read Investment Insight box on page 88, which lists the pros and cons of index fund investing.

Services Offered

Mutual funds offer a variety of services to shareholders, although the actual services offered vary from fund to fund. Five services are the most common:

- *Automatic reinvestment of distributions.* Instead of paying distributions (dividends and capital gains) to the shareholder in cash, the fund automatically reinvests the distributions, increasing the number of shares the shareholder owns.
- *Automatic investment plans.* The shareholder can elect to have a specific dollar amount transferred periodically (usually either monthly or quarterly) from a bank account to the fund to purchase additional shares.
- *Check writing.* All money market funds, and many bond and income funds, allow shareholders to write checks (usually for at least $500). These checks can be used just like bank checks. Sufficient shares of the fund are redeemed to cover the check. Few equity funds offer check writing services.
- *Exchange privileges.* Many funds are part of mutual fund families. The same management company may offer several different mutual funds. Fidelity Investments, for example, offers more than 100 different mutual funds. Exchange privileges allow shareholders to transfer money from one fund to another. Let's say a money market fund shareholder believes that stocks are cheap. The exchange privilege would allow this person to move all, or part of, his or her money from the money market fund to an equity fund managed by the same company. Many funds allow for exchanges by telephone.

---

[3]Generally a growth fund buys stocks the fund manager believes will grow faster than the overall market. A value fund manager looks for stocks that he or she believe are in some way "undervalued" by the market.

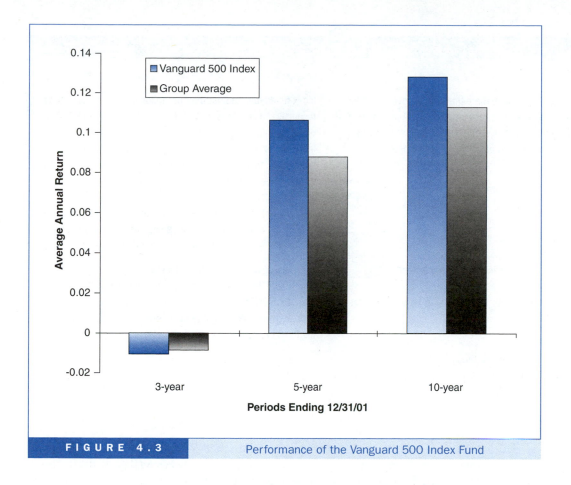

FIGURE 4.3   Performance of the Vanguard 500 Index Fund

- *Periodic statements.* All funds provide shareholders with periodic statements that show how much their shares have earned (dividends and capital gains), what their shares are currently worth, new shares purchased, shares re- deemed, and so forth. All funds also periodically distribute information on their expenses and portfolio compositions. Funds also provide important year-end tax information to shareholders.

Regulation and Taxation of Mutual Funds

As with most investments, federal agencies impose the most significant regulation on mutual funds in the United States. Many of the federal securities laws that we discuss in the next chapter apply to mutual funds. For example, federal law requires that every mutual fund provide potential investors with a current prospectus (the official offering document for the mutual fund) and limits the types of advertisements that mutual funds may use. Federal law and regulations also contain numerous provisions designed to protect the integrity of mutual fund assets and prevent funds from charging shareholders excessive fees. To buy shares, a mutual fund must be approved for sale in the investor's home state. Although most funds are approved for sale in every state, some exceptions are notable.

Virtually all mutual funds choose to be taxed as regulated investment companies under Subchapter M of the Internal Revenue Service (IRS) code. To qualify, a mutual fund must meet several requirements on asset diversification, sources of income, short-term gains, and distribution of income. The last requirement has the most significant impact on investors; to qualify under Subchapter M, a mutual fund must distribute virtually all investment income to its shareholders each year.

Regulated mutual funds pay no taxes on investment income or capital gains; rather, income and capital gains pass through to individual shareholders, who assume the tax liability. Generally, for taxable individual investors, investment income (interest and dividends) is taxed as ordinary income and increases in the value of the fund's portfolio are taxed as either short-term or long-term capital gains. Distributions of these capital gains, which are called *dividends*, are taxable for individual investors. Mutual funds are allowed to pass through the federal tax exemption on interest from municipal securities to shareholders.

To illustrate this kind of pass through, let's look at a hypothetical example. Assume during 2002, a fund distributed $3.50 per share to shareholders. Of this amount, $1.00 was dividend income and $2.50 was capital gains. An investor who owned 200 shares of this fund would be required to report an additional $200 in dividends and $500 in capital gains on his or her 2002 income tax return. Also during 2002 the fund's net asset value rose. However, as with any investment, changes in the NAV are not taxed unless you sell your shares.

MUTUAL FUND FEES AND EXPENSES

As you probably can guess, investing in a mutual fund is not free. All mutual funds charge shareholders fees and expenses, though some funds charge much more than others. Fees and expenses charged by mutual funds can be divided into two general categories: load charges and annual operating expenses.

Load Charges

A **load charge** is a fee associated with buying or redeeming shares of a mutual fund. Some mutual funds charge front-end loads, in which the investor pays the load charge when purchasing shares initially. By law, a front-end load cannot exceed 8.5% of the fund's NAV. A front-end load effectively reduces the amount of the initial investment. For example, Fidelity's Contrafund charges a 3% front-end load. If you initially invested $3,000 in the fund, you actually purchase only $2,910 worth of Contrafund shares, or 97% of $3,000.

    A back-end load refers to a fee assessed when an investor redeems shares of a mutual fund. Like a front-end load, a back-end load charge is stated as a percentage of NAV. If, for example, to redeem 1,000 shares of a fund with an NAV of $8.50 and a 3% back-end load, one would receive $8,245 for the shares $[(.97)($8.50)(1,000) = $8,245]$.

    One type of back-end load, known as a **contingent deferred sales charge (CDSC)**, is assessed, usually on a declining scale, only if shares are redeemed during the first few years of ownership. For example, the Eaton Vance National Limited Maturity Tax Free Fund has a CDSC that starts at 3% for shares redeemed less than one year after purchase; the charge declines to zero for shares held for at least four years. To determine whether a fund has a CDSC or other back-end load, look for an *r* after the name of the fund in a newspaper's listing of mutual funds. Of course, information on all fees and expenses is outlined in the fund's prospectus, which you should always read carefully before investing.

    Front-end loads are often designated, in part, as compensation for the brokers or dealers who sell mutual fund shares to investors. Back-end loads, especially CDSCs, are designed to discourage short-term trading by investors who might otherwise move money in and out of the fund frequently. Traditionally, all mutual funds charged load charges, especially front-end loads. However, no-load funds increased in popularity in recent years. Excluding money market funds, which are all no-load funds, about half of mutual fund assets today are held by no-load funds, up from about 20% 15 years ago.

Operating Expenses

All mutual funds assess management or advisory fees, along with fees to cover other operating expenses, to shareholders each year. These expenses are paid out of investment income, before it is distributed to shareholders. Instead of measuring operating expenses as a percentage of investment income, or in total dollars, a fund measures this charge as a percentage of NAV (or dollars per share). For example, the Safeco Equity Fund has annual operating expenses of 0.84% of NAV. The

load charges

Charges assessed when shares are purchased or sold.

contingent deferred sales charge (CDSC)

Back-end load that declines as the holding period increases.

majority, 0.61%, goes to pay the fund's managers. The rest goes to pay for such things as postage, brokerage costs, and the cost of printing the annual report.

Operating expenses can, of course, vary from year to year. However, most mutual funds set their advisory fees at fixed percentages of net assets. Details on operating expenses are provided in a fund's prospectus.

Some mutual funds now assess 12b-1 fees (named after the 1980 rule that allowed them). A 12b-1 fee can range up to 1.25% of NAV annually. It covers distribution costs, such as advertising, or commissions to brokers or dealers who sell the fund, in lieu of an initial load charge. Details on the 12b-1 fee, if a fund charges one, can be found in the prospectus.

12b-1 fee

Annual charge assessed by some funds; covers distribution costs and commissions to dealers and brokers.

Standardizing Fees and Expenses The Fidelity Contrafund has a 3% front-end load and annual operating expenses of 0.83%. Another stock fund, the Heartland Value Fund, has no front-end load and annual operating expenses of 1.29%. Which fund would charge a shareholder more? This question used to be difficult to answer until a few years ago when federal regulators began requiring mutual funds to publish in the prospectus a table listing fees and expenses over 1-, 3-, 5-, and 10-year periods using a standardized formula. This table allows a shareholder to compare the expenses charged by different funds.

Figure 4.4 shows the total expenses for both the Contrafund and Heartland Value fund over varying periods of time using the SEC's formula. Note that the Contrafund is more expensive over shorter holding periods due to its front-end load. However, the Heartland Value fund is more expensive over longer holding periods because it charges higher annual operating fees.

Evaluating Fees and Expenses

An investor needs to remember three things when evaluating mutual fund fees and expenses. First, fees and expenses can have a dramatic impact on the value of your investment over time, especially for funds with differences in annual operating expenses and similar investment returns. The hypothetical example in Figure 4.5 illustrates this point. We start with $10,000 in each fund and assume both funds earn 10% per year over a 10-year period. Fund A charges annual operating expenses of .75% while Fund B assesses annual operating expenses of 1.5% (we assumed that neither fund charges any loads). At the end of 10 years, you will have $24,308 in Fund A but only $21,775 in Fund B.

Second, do not make the mistake of assuming that all mutual funds with similar investment objectives charge the same. They do not. For example, the Heartland Value, Kaufmann, and Vanguard Explorer funds are all classified as small stock growth funds. All three are no-load funds, but the Explorer fund charges annual operating expenses of 0.63% compared with 1.29% for the Heartland Value fund and 2.17% for the Kaufmann fund. Today annual operating expenses for stock funds average around 1.4%, yet they range from a low of .1% to a high of more than 2.5%.

Third, no definitive evidence shows that higher fees, or load charges, are related to superior performance, or vice-versa. For example, of the top 25 stock funds, based on their five-year performance ending December 31, 2001, about half were load funds and half were no-load funds, with average annual operating expenses of about 1.4% per year.

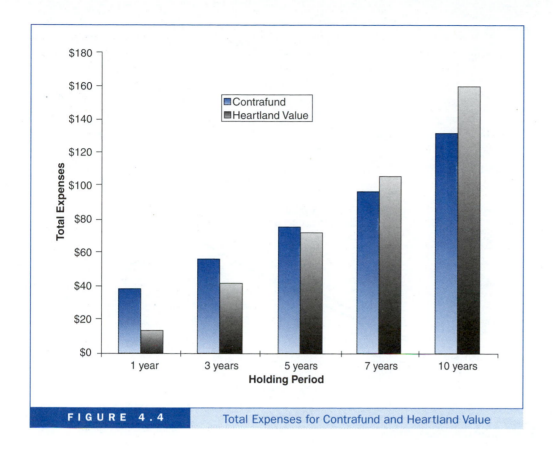

FIGURE 4.4   Total Expenses for Contrafund and Heartland Value

So how do you evaluate mutual fund fees and expenses? For one thing, do not ignore them and do not assume that you can do nothing to limit fee increases; shareholders have the right to vote on proposed changes in fees and expenses. All things being equal, of course, you should buy funds with no loads and low annual operating expenses. If your holding period may be relatively short, it is especially important to avoid load charges. The trouble is, alas, that all things are rarely equal. The fund that best suits your investment objectives may charge more.

PERFORMANCE

Performance is perhaps the single most important criterion for choosing among mutual funds. Investors need to consider several factors when assessing performance. Absolute performance is obviously important, but so is relative performance (how well the fund's performance compares with an appropriate benchmark). Also the consistency of the fund's performance and its risk level need to be considered. As with all investments, the possible relationship between historical performance and future performance must be considered as well.

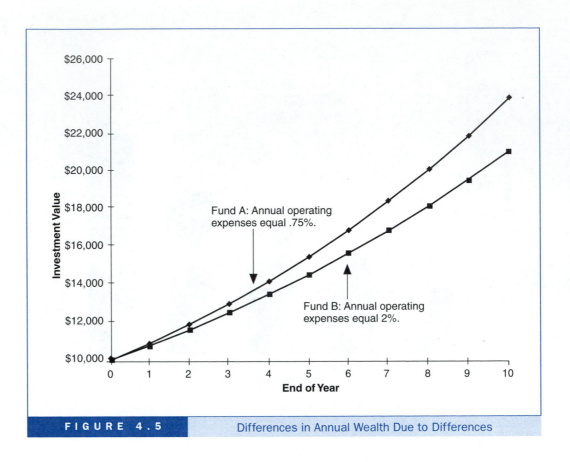

Fund A: Annual operating
expenses equal .75%.

Fund B: Annual operating
expenses equal 2%.

FIGURE 4.5	Differences in Annual Wealth Due to Differences

Evaluating Historical Performance

As an example of how to evaluate the historical performance of a mutual fund, we examine the track record of the Weitz Value fund. Even though the Weitz Value fund's past performance has been for the most part exceptional, we are not recommending it to you or anyone else. We use it merely to illustrate how investors should go about evaluating historical performance.

Measuring Returns Mutual fund returns can be measured the same way as the returns from any investment. Using the standard holding period return formula, introduced in Chapter 2, the one-period return from a mutual fund—for a single day, month, quarter, or year—is

$$(\text{NAV}_t - \text{NAV}_{t-1} + \text{DIV}_t)/\text{NAV}_{t-1}$$

where NAV_{t-1} is the net asset value at the beginning of the period, NAV_t is the net asset value at the end of the period, and DIV_t is the amount of cash (capital gains and investment income) distributed during the period to shareholders.

For instance, at the beginning of 2000 the Weitz Value fund had a NAV of $33.08; it ended the year with a NAV of $35.65. During the year, the fund distributed $3.91 per share. Therefore, its 2000 holding period return was about 19.6% [($35.65 − 33.08 + $3.91)/$33.08 = 19.6%].

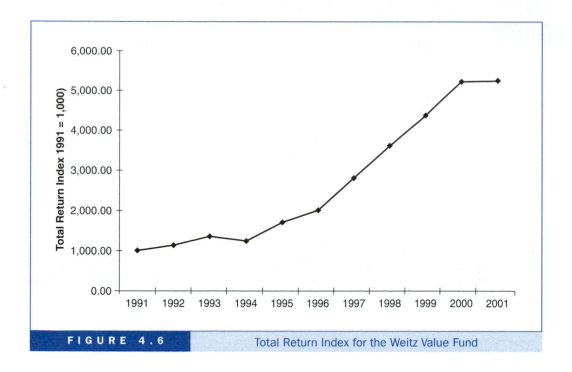

FIGURE 4.6 Total Return Index for the Weitz Value Fund

Measuring performance over longer periods of time provides more valuable information to investors than performance over just one year. After all, one year's return may be an aberration. Even the best funds have occasional bad years, and mediocre funds have their rare days in the sun.

A way of measuring performance over longer periods is to construct a total return index. (We discussed total return indexes in Chapter 2.) Figure 4.6 shows such an index for the Weitz Value fund from the end of 1991 through the end of 2001. This total return index can be interpreted as the current value of $1,000 in the Weitz Value fund from the end of 1991 through the end of 2001; this investment would have worth more than $5,200 at the end of 2001. Annualized, the Weitz Value fund returned about 18% during the 10-year period.

Performance Benchmark The Weitz Value fund returned, on average, about 18% per year between the beginning of 1989 and the end of 1998. Although this result sounds pretty impressive, without a standard for comparison, it really says little about well the fund performed relative to other alternatives. Therefore, the next step is to compare a fund's performance to appropriate benchmarks. Two benchmarks commonly used are a board market index and the average for the group to which the fund belongs. The S&P 500 is the most widely used "market" benchmark, but it is not the most appropriate for a number of stock funds. Of course, it is not an appropriate benchmark for bond and income funds. Table 4.2 lists the appropriate market benchmark for major equity and bond fund categories. Now, let's see how the Weitz Value fund compared with its two benchmarks.

Figure 4.7 compares the average annual returns for the Weitz Value fund, the S&P Midcap 400, and the average midcap value fund (the Morningstar group, to

TABLE 4.2	Type of Fund	Appropriate Benchmark for Comparison
Appropriate Performance Benchmarks	Large domestic stock	S&P 500 index
	Midcap domestic stock	S&P Midcap 400 index
	Small domestic stock	Russell 2000 index
	International stock	Morgan Stanley EAFE index
	Taxable bond	Lehman Brothers aggregate bond index
	Tax-exempt bond	Lehman Brothers municipal bond index

which the Weitz Value fund belongs) over varying periods ending December 31, 2001. In each of the periods shown, the Weitz Value fund outperformed both the group average and the S&P Midcap 400 index. For example, over the 10 years ending on December 31, 2001, the Weitz Value fund produced an average annual return of 18% compared to a group average of less than 14%. During the same period, the S&P Midcap 400 index produced an average annual return of 15.1%.

Performance and Risk The other side of the investment question, of course, is risk. Perhaps the Weitz Value fund's superior performance over the past decade was due to the fact that it is riskier than the market. The investor needs to evaluate a fund's risk as well as its return. As we noted in Chapter 2, two common risk measures are standard deviation and beta. Using quarterly returns between 1991 and 2001, the Weitz Value fund had an annualized standard deviation of 16.4% and a beta of 0.61. By contrast, the S&P Midcap 400 index had an annualized standard deviation of 19.6% and a beta of 1.0. Thus, both risk measures suggest that the Weitz Value fund was less risky than the overall market.[4]

Assessing Future Performance

Past performance is attractive, but it does not help today's investor. Future performance is much more interesting. Investors do not buy mutual funds because of what they did yesterday but how well they seem likely to do tomorrow. A key question, therefore, is how much investors should rely on the historical performance of mutual funds to assess future performance.

A school of thought, which is especially popular in parts of the academic community, argues that past performance is a poor predictor of future performance. Backed by some statistical evidence, the argument holds that individual mutual funds do not consistently, over long periods of time, post better risk-adjusted performance than the broad market averages. Some funds beat the averages some years, whereas others beat the averages in other years, but trying to predict which fund will beat the averages next year, or during the next five years, is a waste of time, random selection would do just as well. Too many investors

---

[4]We can also assess the risk of a mutual fund, relative to its return, by using three performance measures based on modern portfolio theory. These three measures, Jensen's alpha, Treynor, and Sharpe, will be developed and discussed in Chapter 20.

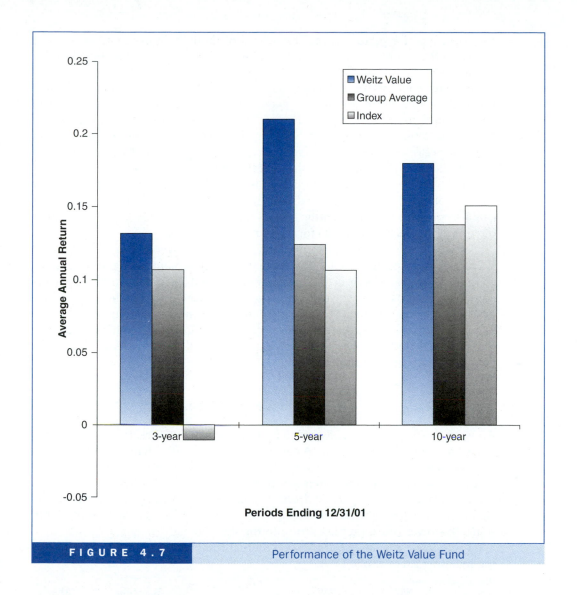

FIGURE 4.7   Performance of the Weitz Value Fund

make the mistake of buying last year's hot fund, only to see it cool off this year, so these critics claim that they are better off simply buying and holding shares of a well-diversified mutual fund that has investment objectives consistent with individual objectives and tolerance for risk, or better yet an index fund. According to this school of thought, if a fund lags behind the averages for a couple of years, shareholders are still better off holding onto the fund rather than looking for a new fund. Past performance is simply no guarantee of future performance.

Others argue that this view is nonsense. They cite evidence that past performance is a reasonable, although not perfect, predictor of future performance. For example, one can point to the performance records of several mutual funds that have consistently beaten the averages in both up and down markets. These funds may not beat the averages *every* year, but over 5-year, 10-year, or 20-year periods, they post superior performance. This school of thought argues that past records have to reflect more than just luck. A good track record, they argue, tilts the odds of success in the investor's favor.

By extension, this school of thought argues, if a fund lags behind the averages for three or four years, an investor may be wise to look elsewhere. The drop in performance may indicate that the fund manager's investment philosophy or security selection process is not working. Further, if you believe that a fund's superior performance is due, in large part, to the superior skills of its manager, you should consider selling your shares if the fund manager leaves.

The evidence that past performance is related to future performance today goes beyond the claims of mutual fund managers and other practitioners. One can also point to several scientific studies that suggest that the past performance of equity funds is a good predictor of future performance.[5]

We are in no position to resolve the controversy over how much investors should rely on past performance to gauge future performance. One of the end-of-chapter exercises asks you to identify mutual funds with outstanding performance records, as of three years ago, and then trace how well these stars have performed since. Although many funds chalk up impressive long-term performance records—such as the Weitz Value fund—and investing in these funds may improve your odds, the past is never a guarantee of the future. As you are likely to find, chasing returns rarely works.

Performance and Taxes

An issue the financial press is beginning to recognize is the relationship between taxes and mutual fund returns. As we noted earlier in the chapter, mutual funds are not taxed directly on investment income or capital gains; shareholders pay taxes on income and capital gains distributions. A mutual fund's return can be broken down into the portion from distributions and the portion due to the change in the fund's NAV. The greater the portion of the return from distributions, the lower is the after-tax return to the shareholder.

To illustrate the impact of taxes on mutual fund returns, consider the following hypothetical example:

	NAV (1998)	NAV (1999)	Distributions	Before-Tax Return	After-Tax Return*
Fund A	$10.00	$10.00	$2.00	20%	15.4%
Fund B	$10.00	$12.00	$0.00	20%	20.0%

*Assumes a 27% tax bracket.

Assume the value of particular securities owned by both funds rose during the year by the equivalent of $2.00 per share. The manager of fund A chose to sell the securities and distribute the profits to shareholders. Fund B's manager chose to keep the securities. As a result, the after-tax return to fund B's shareholders is

---

[5]See, for example, James Philpot, "Performance-Related Characteristics of Mutual Funds," Ph.D. dissertation, University of Arkansas, 1994.

higher. Of course, unrealized capital gains can turn into losses, so the fund manager must weigh the risk of losing capital gains with the tax consequences to shareholders.

Experts suggest investors examine portfolio turnover. Higher turnover means greater capital gains distributions and the amount of unrealized capital gains. Both pieces of information can be obtained from the fund's prospectus. Morningstar and other mutual fund advisory services also report tax information.

When Not to Buy Shares of Mutual Funds Most mutual funds make cash distributions at regularly scheduled intervals during the year. Some make distributions monthly, others quarterly, and still others once a year. It is a good idea never to purchase shares of a mutual fund *right* before it makes a distribution (this information can be obtained from the fund). Why? Cash distributions reduce the fund's NAV by the amount of the distribution, which means, in effect, the total value of your investment remains the same. Unfortunately, you must pay taxes on the distribution. On an after-tax basis, you come out worse off.

OTHER TYPES OF INVESTMENT COMPANIES

Mutual funds are not the only type of investment company. Two others are the unit investment trust and the closed-end investment company. Although mutual funds are much larger, these other types of investment companies are worth some consideration.

Unit Investment Trusts

A **unit investment trust** is typically an unmanaged portfolio of fixed income securities put together by a sponsor and run by an independent trustee. The sponsor sells a fixed number of shares, called *units,* and uses the proceeds, less a sales charge, to purchase a portfolio of securities. All income from the securities held by the trust is distributed to the owners of the units, along with any principal repayments. The major advantages of unit investment trusts, compared with other investment companies, are generally lower annual fees and the routine return of principal.

The securities that make up a unit investment trust's portfolio almost always remain unchanged. Unit investment trusts are usually unmanaged passive investments. A unit investment trust with a portfolio of bonds ceases to exist when the last of the bonds in the portfolio mature. An investor can usually sell units prior to maturity. The sponsor typically makes a market in the units, buying and selling them at their current NAV, although sponsors are not obligated to do so. Shares of unit investment trusts are generally the least liquid of any investment company. In addition to the initial sales charge (typically 3% to 4%), some unit investment trusts charge small annual management fees. Some sponsors also charge commissions if units are sold early.

The first unit investment trust was created in 1961; since then, more than $350 billion in units have been sold. Only municipal bond unit investment trusts were available until 1972 when the first corporate bond trust was created.

unit investment trust

Unmanaged portfolio of a specific type of security; investor purchases units or pieces of the portfolio.

Government bond trusts became available in 1978. A more recent development is the stock trust, a unit investment trust that purchases a fixed portfolio of stocks with the intention of liquidating the portfolio at some set point in time (usually after one to five years). The purpose is to offer small investors a way of purchasing a portfolio of common stocks. (Units are initially sold for as little as $1,000 each.) The units may represent diversified portfolios of stocks, specific sectors, or even stocks meeting certain investment criteria (e.g., stocks with high dividend yields or low price/earnings ratios).

Another fairly recent development is the emergence of so-called exchange-traded funds. ETF shares are created by an institutional investor depositing a specified block of securities with a trustee. In return for this deposit, the institutional investors receive a fixed amount of shares, some or all of which may be then sold to individual investors on a stock exchange. Investors buy and sell ETF shares much as they would buy or sell any listed stock. Virtually all exchange-traded funds consist of the stocks that make up several popular indexes, such as the S&P 500 and the Dow Jones 30. The ETF S&P 500 shares are called *spiders* while the ETF Dow shares are called *diamonds*. Both spiders and diamonds trade on the American Stock Exchange (AMEX).

Closed-End Investment Companies

closed-end investment company

Managed portfolios of securities with a fixed number of shares outstanding.

Like all investment companies, **closed-end investment companies** (or closed-end funds) raise money by selling shares to the investing public. They invest this money in a variety of securities consistent with their stated investment objectives. A closed-end fund usually does not sell additional shares after the initial public offering, however, and thus the number of outstanding shares is usually fixed. In addition, a closed-end fund will not redeem shares unless it liquidates. Shares of closed-end funds trade on various stock exchanges. (About 80% of closed-end fund shares are listed on the NYSE.) Investors can buy or sell shares of closed-end funds just like ordinary shares of common stock.

Some see advantages in the limits on the number of shares that closed-end investment companies have outstanding. For one thing, it limits how large a closed-end investment company can get, unlike the potentially unlimited growth of a mutual fund. Another potential advantage of a closed-end investment company, with its limited number of shares, is potential to buy shares at a discount.

Unlike unit investment trusts, virtually all closed-end funds are actively managed. Each fund has a portfolio manager, or advisor, who buys and sells securities in an attempt to maximize return for what the advisor believes is an acceptable level of risk. For example, the manager of a closed-end fund that invests in government securities might increase the average duration of the portfolio if interest rates seem likely to decline. The manager of a closed-end fund that invests primarily in common stocks might increase the percentage of the portfolio held in money market instruments if common stocks appear temporarily overvalued, making price declines likely in the near future.

More than 450 closed-end funds trade in the United States, with total net assets exceeding $180 billion. More than half of all closed-end funds invest in debt securities (either municipal or corporate bonds). However, one of the most rapidly growing type of closed-end funds is the single-country equity fund. Such a fund limits its investments to equity securities issued in a specific country.

Example of a Closed-End Fund Figure 4.8 illustrates a closed-end fund, the Germany Fund. The Germany Fund is also an example of a single-country fund. It attempts to keep a minimum of 70% of its assets invested in common and preferred stocks of Germany companies, although currently it is more than 90%. Notice that the Germany Fund shares some characteristics with mutual funds. The fund does not pay U.S. taxes on investment income and realized capital gains as long as it distributes them to shareholders. The fund is actively managed, for which the fund's investment advisor receives an annual fee. The main difference between the two, however, is the fact that the Germany Fund has a fixed number of shares outstanding.

Net Asset Value Discount Because the shares of closed-end funds trade on stock exchanges like ordinary common stocks, market prices are set by the sometimes mysterious interaction of supply and demand. In fact, the market prices of closed-end fund shares rarely equal their respective NAVs. Take another look at Figure 4.8 and compare the France Fund's year-end price with its NAV in recent years, the two were close together only at the end of 1993.

Historically, closed-end funds generally sold at discounts from their respective NAVs. In recent years, the typical discount narrowed, and some funds (e.g., the France Fund) currently sell at premiums (i.e., their share prices exceed their NAVs). In 1979, for example, equity closed-end funds sold at an average discount of 28%; today, the average discount is less than 5%. This situation raises several interesting questions. Why would a closed-end fund sell at a discount? Why does the discount vary from fund to fund? Why has the average discount narrowed in recent years?

Several reasonable explanations rather than definitive answers can be offered in response. Some suggest that the discount is due, in part, to thin secondary markets. (Remember, shares of closed-end funds are traded on stock exchanges.) As the secondary markets for the shares of these funds improved in recent years, the average discount diminished. Others suggest that the discount is due to poor average historical performance; because the funds exhibited better performance in recent years, the discount shrank. Other factors may help to explain the variation in the NAV discount, including distribution policies, taxes, management fees, and relative performance.

Dual Purpose Funds A special type of closed-end fund is a **dual purpose fund**. Unlike the typical investment company, a dual purpose fund sells two types of shares and has a predetermined life span (typically, 10 to 20 years). Investors who buy the fund's *income shares* receive all income (interest and dividends) from its assets plus a fixed redemption value when the fund liquidates. Investors who purchase the fund's *capital shares* receive everything else. Both sets of shares trade on the secondary markets. Only a handful of new dual purpose funds were formed in the past few years; currently, the market offers about six dual purpose funds.

Mutual funds and other types of investment companies are significant and attractive investment options. Many investors will invest the bulk of their funds by buying shares of investment companies.

dual purpose fund

A type of closed-end fund that sells two types of shares, income shares and capital shares.

Germany Fund

NYSE Symbol **GER**

01-MAR-03

Asset Class: Closed-end Exchange Traded Fund

Summary: This closed-end fund seeks long-term capital appreciation principally through investments in large capitalization German equity securities.

Quantitative Evaluations

Outlook (1 Lowest—5 Highest)
• **NA**

Fair Value
• **NA**

Risk
• **Average**

Earn./Div. Rank
• **NR**

Technical Eval.
• **Bearish** since 1/03

Rel. Strength Rank (1 Lowest—99 Highest)
• **24**

Insider Activity
• **NA**

Net Asset Value • 4.93
Price As Of 2/28/03 • 4.12

Prem./Disc. • -16.4%
Yield • 0.2%

Earnings vs. Previous Year
▲=Up ▼=Down ▶=No Change

10 Week Mov. Avg. – – –
30 Week Mov. Avg. ·······
Relative Strength ———

Principal Holdings - 24-DEC-02

The fund's 10 largest holdings at October 31, 2002, were: Siemens (10.6% of total assets), DaimlerChrysler (8.8%), E.ON (7.0%), Bayer (5.7%), Allianz (5.3%), Munchener Ruckvericherungs (5.2%), Deutsche Telekom (5.1%), SAP (4.7%), Volkswagen (4.2%), and BASF (4.1%). By country, the portfolio at that date was invested in Germany (85.2%), Netherlands (4.7%), Spain (3.2%), the U.K. (3.2%), France (2.7%), and Finland (1.0%). In August 2002, GER said that with the DAX Index trading at 1997 levels, equity valuations in Germany were very attractive, as it believed corporate earnings were at a turning point. In addition, interest rates and inflation were very low, both positive factors for economic growth.

Operational Review - 24-DEC-02

In the first nine months of 2002, the fund's total return based on net asset value was a negative 41.65%. In comparison, the fund's benchmark, the DAX Index, declined 40.49% during the period. Net asset value fell to $4.68 a share at September 30, 2002, from $8.02 at the end of 2001. Total investment income for the first half of 2002 amounted to $1.65 million. Total expenses aggregated $1.01 million and absorbed 61% of total investment income. Net investment income totaled $639,665 ($0.04 a share). There was a net realized and unrealized loss on investments and foreign currency transactions of $0.56 a share.

Fund Performance - 28-FEB-03

In the past 30 trading days, GER's shares have declined 13%, compared to a 7% fall in the S&P 500. Average trading volume for the past five days was 23,420 shares, compared with the 40-day moving average of 35,068 shares.

Key Fund Statistics

Dividend Rate/Share	0.01	Shareholders	3,124
Shs. outstg. (M)	16.8	Market cap. (M)	$ 69.0
Avg. daily vol. (,000)	19.9	Inst. holdings	10%
Beta	1.26		

Value of $10,000 invested 5 years ago: $ 5,081

Fiscal Year Ending Dec. 31

	2002	2001	2000	1999	1998	1997
Net Asset Value Per Share ($)						
1Q	8.19	—	—	14.19	18.49	17.02
2Q	7.51	9.16	15.61	15.26	21.59	17.99
3Q	4.68	7.12	—	14.72	15.36	18.98
4Q	—	8.02	10.89	16.93	16.07	16.23
Net Investment Income Per Share ($)						
1Q	—	—	—	—	—	-0.01
2Q	0.04	0.10	0.04	0.09	0.31	0.15
3Q	—	—	—	—	—	-0.03
4Q	—	—	—	-0.03	-0.08	-0.02
Yr.	—	0.05	-0.02	0.06	0.23	0.09

Dividend Data (Dividends have been paid since 1987.)

Amount ($)	Date Decl.	Ex-Div. Date	Stock of Record	Payment Date
0.010	Nov. 01	Nov. 15	Nov. 19	Nov. 29 '02

FIGURE 4.8A   Germany Fund

The Germany Fund, Inc.

Business Summary - 24-DEC-02

·The Germany Fund (GER) is a diversified, closed-end investment company that seeks long-term capital appreciation through investment in equity or equity-linked securities of German companies.

Investments totaled $132.1 million (at market; 98.8% of net assets) at December 31, 2001. Net assets were divided as follows: total common stock 97.1%, preferred stock 1.7%, and cash and other assets in excess of liabilities 1.2%. Insurance represented 20.3% of the portfolio, diversified telecommunications services 11.5%, chemicals 10.0%, automobiles 7.9%, industrial conglomerates 7.4%, software 6.4%, banks 5.4%, and other 31.1%.

In February 2002, the fund said it believed the underperformance of the telecommunication sector should be coming to an end, and it planned to reduce its underweight in that sector. The fund also planned to overweight the insurance sector, maintain its underweight in the banking sector, and maintain a neutral stance on the technology sector.

The fund's 10 largest holdings at December 31, 2001, were: Allianz (9.9% of the portfolio), Deutsche Telekom (9.1%), E.ON (7.5%), Munchener Ruckversicherungs (6.6%), Siemens (6.5%), SAP (6.4%), DaimlerChrysler (4.2%), BASF (3.9%), Bayer (3.6%), and Metro (3.0%).

Broken down by geographic region, the fund's portfolio at December 31, 2001, was invested in Germany (81.5%), France (7.4%), the Netherlands (4.1%), Belgium (2.3%), the U.K. (2.3%), and Finland (1.2%); cash in excess of liabilities was 1.2%.

GER invests primarily in a broad cross-section of German equity and equity-linked securities. Under normal market conditions, at least 65% of the fund's total assets will be invested in these securities. Current interest and dividend income may be considered in selecting securities. The fund may also invest up to 35% in blue chip equities of other Western European countries that have adopted the euro currency, although no more than 15% of total assets may be invested in a single country outside of Germany.

Deutsche Bank Securities and Deutsche Asset Management International GmbH, both affiliates of Deutsche Bank, Germany's largest banking institution, serve as investment manager and adviser, respectively. Under the management agreement, the manager receives an annual fee of 0.65% of the fund's average weekly net assets up to $50 million, and 0.55% of assets over $50 million. The adviser receives an annual fee of 0.35% of average weekly net assets up to $100 million and 0.25% of assets over $100 million. In 2001, the manager and investment adviser received fees of $877,499 and $476,262, respectively.

In 2000, the fund purchased 480,900 of its shares on the open market, as part of an ongoing share repurchase program. It bought back another 258,100 shares in 2001, and 210,500 in the first nine months of 2002.

Per Share Data ($)

(Year Ended Dec. 31)	2001	2000	1999	1998	1997	1996	1995	1994	1993	1992
Net Asset Value	8.02	10.89	16.93	16.07	16.23	15.76	13.52	12.89	12.87	9.78
Yr. End Price	7.05	9.50	15.13	13.88	14.25	12.63	11.38	10.75	12.50	10.12
% Difference (Prem./Disc.)	-12.10	-12.80	-10.60	-13.70	-12.20	-19.90	-15.70	-16.60	-2.90	3.50
Dividends:										
Invest. Inc.	0.06	Nil	0.04	0.23	Nil	Nil	0.12	0.12	0.06	0.12
Capital Gains	0.02	2.49	1.71	3.61	3.16	1.19	0.94	0.67	0.22	0.26
Portfolio Turnover	121%	138%	72%	81%	81%	55%	41%	31%	39%	49%

Income Statement Analysis (Million $)

	2001	2000	1999	1998	1997	1996	1995	1994	1993	1992
Total Investment Income	3.29	2.72	3.60	6.42	4.59	3.87	4.07	3.66	3.64	3.89
Net Investment Income:										
Total	0.79	-0.38	0.87	2.98	1.23	1.19	1.70	1.40	1.62	1.54
Per Share	0.05	-0.02	0.06	0.23	0.09	0.08	0.12	0.11	0.12	0.12
Realized Cap. Gains:										
Total	-15.8	18.8	19.8	46.1	47.5	18.4	13.2	9.67	4.04	3.97
Per Share	-0.95	1.12	1.34	3.18	3.38	1.30	0.94	0.72	0.30	0.30
% Net Inv. Inc./Net Assets	0.53	NM	0.40	1.20	0.50	0.60	0.90	0.80	1.10	1.10
% Expenses to:										
Net Assets	1.47	1.29	1.30	1.15	1.20	1.30	1.20	1.30	1.40	1.60
Invest. Inc.	76.8	115.0	76.2	53.5	70.9	69.2	58.4	61.9	55.6	60.3

Balance Sheet & Other Fin. Data (Million $)

	2001	2000	1999	1998	1997	1996	1995	1994	1993	1992
Net Assets	134	184	250	233	228	224	190	174	172	129
1 Year Total Return on NAV	-25.6%	-20.6%	18.1%	22.7%	23.2%	25.5%	13.1%	6.40%	36.8%	-8.80%
% Change S&P 500	-11.9	-9.10	21.0	28.6	33.4	23.0	37.6	1.30	10.1	7.60
% Change Bonds AAA	NA	NA	NA	NA	NA	NA	17.9	-13.7	13.2	0.10
Cost of Investments	129	144	143	186	275	269	220	222	192	154
Mkt. Value of Investments	132	178	245	270	354	345	266	259	229	151
% Net Asset Distribution:										
Net Cash	1.20	2.90	1.90	-16.0	-55.3	-53.9	-40.1	-48.6	-33.3	17.8
ST Oblig.	Nil	Nil	Nil	16.4	49.5	55.9	42.1	52.9	38.1	19.6
Bonds & Pfd.	1.7	8.5	7.9	9.4	11.6	1.5	6.2	2.5	2.2	6.1
Common Stk.	97.1	88.6	90.2	90.2	94.2	90.1	84.3	86.4	86.8	85.4
Other Invest.	Nil	Nil	Nil	Nil	Nil	6.4	7.5	6.8	6.2	6.6

Data as orig reptd.; bef. results of disc opers/spec. items. Per share data adj. for stk. divs. Bold denotes diluted EPS (FASB 128)-prior periods restated. E-Estimated. NA-Not Available. NM-Not Meaningful. NR-Not Ranked.

Office—31 West 52nd St., New York, NY 10019. Tel—1-800-GERMANY in the U.S.; 617 443-6918 outside of the U.S. Website—http://www.gerfund.com Pres & CEO—R. T. Hale. Chrmn—C. Strenger. CFO & Treas—J. M. Cheung. COO & Secy—R. R. Gambee. Dirs—D. Bierbaum, J. A. Bult, R. A. Burt, E. C. Schmults, H. G. Storr, C. Strenger, J. F. Strube, R. H. Wadsworth, W. Walbroel, O. Wolff Von Amerongen. Transfer Agent—Investors Bank & Trust Co., Boston. Incorporated—in Maryland in 1990. Empl—0. S&P Analyst: J. J. Schemitsch/PMW

FIGURE 4.8B

The Germany Fund, Inc.

SUMMARY

1. What is a mutual fund, and how does it operate?

Mutual funds, also known as open-end investment companies, pool funds from investors and invest in securities consistent with the fund's investment objective. Mutual fund shareholders share in the portfolio's value appreciation and income. Mutual funds continually issue new shares and redeem existing shares. The first mutual fund was created in the 1920s, but they have become a significant force in the investment field during the last 20 years. Mutual funds have also become significant in many other countries. Various mutual funds invest in money market instruments, bonds, small stocks, large value stocks, foreign stocks, and so on. Domestic mutual funds are regulated by the Securities and Exchange Commission. Investment income and realized capital gains must be passed through to shareholders in the form of dividends. Shareholders then pay taxes on those dividends.

2. How much does mutual fund investing cost?

Mutual fund fees and expenses can be divided into two categories: sales charges (also called loads) and annual operating expenses. About half of all mutual funds charge an initial sales charge; a few charge a fee when shares are sold. All funds charge annual operating expenses. Fees and expenses must be reported using a standardized formula making it much easier to compare funds. Higher fees can significantly reduce the value of an investment. Further, fees and expenses vary widely from fund to fund, with no evidence that higher fees are associated with better performance, or vice versa.

3. How should mutual fund performance be evaluated?

Performance is perhaps the most important criterion when selecting a mutual fund. Historical performance should be measured using holding period returns, over long periods of time, and compared with relevant benchmarks. Risk and the impact of taxes should also be factored in when assessing performance. Even though good past performance may improve the odds of success, investors should always remember that past performance is never a guarantee of future performance.

4. What are the other types of investment companies?

Other types of investment companies, in addition to mutual funds, include unit investment trusts, which are unmanaged portfolios consisting of specific types of securities. The investor buys units, or small pieces of the overall portfolio. The most popular type of unit investment trust consists of municipal bonds. A relatively recent development is the creation of index depository shares—unit investment trusts holding shares of all the companies making up several popular indexes. Another type of investment company is closed-end funds, which are similar to mutual funds in that most are actively managed. Both closed-end funds and unit investment trusts have a fixed number of shares outstanding. Shares of closed-end funds trade on major stock exchanges. About half of closed-end funds invest in bonds. Single-country equity funds are also prominent today.

REVIEW EXERCISES

1. List the advantages of investing in mutual funds. Elaborate on one.
2. How are mutual funds regulated and taxed? How are individual cash distributions to shareholders taxed?
3. During the 1970s, two new types of mutual funds appeared. What were they? Why were they so popular with investors almost immediately?
4. List some of the common services offered by mutual funds. What is a family of mutual funds?

5. Define *net asset value*. How is NAV affected by cash distributions?
6. List the criteria investors should use when selecting between mutual funds. What two should be examined in detail?
7. Define *sales load*. What is a contingent deferred sales charge (CDSC), or back-end load?
8. Why are mutual fund expenses standardized? Assume that you are trying to choose between a fund with a 3% initial load and annual operating expenses of 0.75% and a fund with no initial load and annual operating expenses of 1.5%. Which fund is likely to be more expensive over a one-year holding period? Over a 10-year holding period?
9. How should total returns for a mutual fund be measured? Assume that a fund began the year with a NAV of $20.00 and finished the year with a NAV of $25.00. During the year, it distributed $1.00 per share. Calculate the return to shareholders.
10. Assume that the total index on a stock fund rose from 1.6469 to 6.1403 between the end of 1992 and the end of 2002. Calculate the annual compound total rate of return. How much would an initial investment of $1,000 made at the end of 1992 be worth at the end of 2002?
11. Assume two funds began the year with NAVs of $30.00. Fund A distributed $2.00 to shareholders ($1.50 in realized in capital gains and $0.50 in investment income) and ended the year with a NAV of $32.00. Fund B distributed $0.50 to shareholders and ended the year with a NAV of $33.50. Calculate the before-tax and after-tax holding period returns (assume a marginal tax rate of 28%). If an investor owned 200 shares of Fund A, how much additional income would she be required to report on her federal tax return?
12. Explain the purpose of performance benchmarks. What are the appropriate benchmarks for a growth and income stock fund and a small stock fund?
13. Is past performance a good predictor of future performance for a mutual fund? Should you examine other factors to predict future performance?
14. Compare and contrast a unit investment trust and closed-end fund. What types of securities do most unit investment trusts purchase?
15. Define *net asset value discount*. Why do many closed-end funds trade at prices other than their respective NAVs?

CRITICAL THINKING EXERCISES

1. This exercise requires library or Internet research. Make a list of the 10 largest mutual funds, measured by net assets. How rapidly did these funds grown over the past five years? How well did they performed? Does your research lead you to any conclusions concerning the issue of size and performance? In other words, do you think a mutual fund can get too large?
2. This exercise requires library or Internet research. Using a well-known source of mutual fund information (e.g., February issues of *Money* magazine), review data for the five-year period, 1997 through 2001. Measured in terms of total one-year performance, find the five best-performing stock mutual funds each year (ignore sector funds and international funds). Record the fund and its one-year return. How well did each fund do the following year? For example, how did the top-performing funds of 1997 do in 1998? Do these one-year returns show any consistent patterns? Discuss your findings.
3. This exercise requires computer work. Open the Mutual Fund worksheet in the Data Workbook. The worksheet contains quarterly returns for 10 mutual funds, along with quarterly returns from the S&P 500. Compute the arithmetic and geometric average returns for the funds and the S&P 500. Annualize the arithmetic mean. Calculate, and annualize, the standard deviation of returns for each fund and the S&P 500. Use these data to evaluate the performance of each of the funds.

1. Go to the Morningstar Web site (www.morningstar.com). Click on the research tab and then the fund selector option. Screen the Morningstar database and find the 10 top-performing stock funds. Research each fund. Which would be the most appropriate for new mutual fund investors?

2. Virtually all mutual funds have Web sites. Two of the most comprehensive are the Janus Funds (www.janus.com) and Vanguard (www.vanguard.com). Visit each site and write a brief report answering the following questions: Do Janus and Vanguard appear to take different approaches to investing? What are some of the differences between the types of funds offered by Janus and Vanguard? Which site do you think would be more helpful to a new investor?

3. The SEC's Web site (www.sec.gov) has a great deal of information to help people make better investment decisions. Visit the SEC's Web site and read the information provided on mutual fund investing. Did it improve your understanding of mutual funds? Do you feel as though, after reading the information, you are prepared to make better decisions?

Financial Markets and Investment Returns

"Part 2 is devoted to a discussion of the financial markets and how investors make investment decisions. We believe that it is important to understand not only how investors actually make decisions but how they *should* make them as well. We begin by describing the major financial markets, both primary and secondary. Next, we discuss how investors participate in the financial markets and the devices in place to protect their interests. Then we review the concept of market efficiency. We try both to determine whether, and to what extent the financial markets are efficient, and what market efficiency implies for investment selection and analysis. Finally, we outline technical and fundamental analysis—two techniques professional investors often rely on to make investment decisions."

5

Organization of the Financial Markets

| PREVIOUSLY . . . | IN THIS CHAPTER . . . | TO COME . . . |

PREVIOUSLY . . .

We described the wide array of investment alternatives available today, both direct investments and indirect investments, such as mutual funds.

IN THIS CHAPTER . . .

We provide an overview of the world's financial markets, both primary and secondary. We describe how financial markets are classified, why financial markets are important, and how they function. We also speculate on the future evolution of financial markets.

TO COME . . .

We continue our discussion of the financial markets by describing how financial markets are regulated and how investors participate in them.

CHAPTER OBJECTIVES

After reading Chapter 5, you should be able to answer the following questions:

1. What are the different types of financial markets?

2. How do the primary financial markets function?

3. Why are secondary financial markets important?

4. How are the secondary financial markets organized?

5. How are financial markets evolving?

In a building that once housed offices of the central committee of the Polish communist party, something remarkable happened in early 1990s. The Warsaw Stock Exchange commenced operations again after a recess of 50 years. The exchange, which was originally founded in the early 1800s, was closed by Poland's new communist government in the late 1940s. The collapse of communism in the late 1980s changed both the political and economic landscapes in Poland and throughout Eastern Europe.

The Warsaw Stock Exchange began operations again on a modest scale and showed steady growth. In 1996, the general public was allowed to purchase shares in newly privatized companies. The importance of the Warsaw Stock Exchange continues to increase as state-owned companies are privatized. Poland's leaders view the Warsaw Stock Exchange as a important part of the country's transformation to a Western market-oriented democracy. They recognize that well-developed financial markets, including a stock market, foster increased economic growth and opportunity for Polish citizens.

Compared to other world financial markets, however, the Warsaw Stock Exchange is still tiny. Currently, the shares of about 200 companies are listed. Daily trading volume is less than 1 million shares. By contrast, nearly 3,000 companies are listed on the giant New York Stock Exchange, where more than 1 billion shares change hands during a typical trading day.

In our view, no one can make informed, intelligent investment decisions without a good understanding of the financial markets in which those decisions are implemented. As the opening vignette illustrates, the economic prosperity of any society is enhanced by smoothly functioning financial markets. Consequently, some knowledge of the financial markets is important for everyone, not just active investors.

WHAT IS A FINANCIAL MARKET?

A common definition of *market* is a meeting of people, or a place, for selling and buying of a good or service. This rather broad definition suggests that a financial market exists almost anytime and anywhere that anyone trades a security. The general definition does not imply that trading must take place in a physical location. It is only necessary that buyers and sellers possess the ability and opportunity to communicate with one another. No definition implies that all buyers and sellers must receive the best price possible.

Rather than asking what a market is, perhaps a more fundamental question would ask what is a **good market**? We argue that in a good financial market, trading is conducted in a fair, open, and orderly manner. To meet this standard, what characteristics should a good market have?

good market

A market where trading is conducted in a fair, orderly, and open manner.

Characteristics of a Good Market

Perhaps the single most important characteristic of a good market, for both buyers and sellers, is **liquidity**. Liquidity is the ability to quickly buy or sell an asset at a price justified by its underlying supply-and-demand conditions. In a liquid market, a seller should be able to quickly sell an asset for a cash price close to the

liquidity

The ability to quickly buy or sell an asset at a price justified by underlying supply-and-demand conditions.

market price. For example, someone wants to sell a house and receives an offer of $100,000. Suppose, however, that the underlying supply-and-demand conditions suggest that the house should be worth about $150,000. This real estate market is not liquid. Although it allows a seller to turn a house into cash, it does not set a price that is justified by the underlying supply-and-demand conditions. Of course, liquidity does not prevent an asset from falling in price, nor does it mean that an investor never has to sell an asset for a price well below the purchase price. One can lose money even in the most liquid of markets.

A good financial market should exhibit the following characteristics to be considered fair, open, and orderly:

- Sufficient information is available to determine the underlying supply-and-demand conditions, and this information is available to all market participants at about the same time. This characteristic implies that all trading should take place in full view of all market participants.
- Price continuity exists, which means that, assuming no new information has entered the market, one can buy or sell at a price close to the most recent similar trade.
- Transaction costs are low. All participants should have the opportunity to buy or sell at reasonable cost.
- All participants have equal access to the market. The market should not allow some participants to execute orders to buy or sell faster than others.
- Prices adjust quickly to new public information, and this information is disclosed at the same time to all participants.

These conditions are not absolute standards, and any assessment of how well any specific financial market meets these conditions is somewhat subjective. In the next chapter, we see that regulation of the financial markets, in the United States and most other countries, is designed primarily to ensure that these conditions exist.

The conditions of a good market do not demand a **perfect market**. For one thing, a perfect market would have to eliminate frictions, with no transaction costs, taxes, or constraining regulations. Obviously in the real world, market participants must pay transaction costs and taxes and contend with other conditions that impede their trading somewhat. Furthermore, a good market need not even be an **efficient market** all the time. Market efficiency is the extent to which security prices reflect all relevant information. Chapter 7 explores several versions of market efficiency theory, along with evidence supporting and contradicting the theory.

perfect market

A market where trading is frictionless.

efficient market

A market where security prices reflect all relevant information.

Classification of Financial Markets

Thousands of financial markets exist throughout the world. These markets, however, differ widely in terms of organization, trading practices, customers served, and types of securities traded. Let's discuss some of the ways financial markets can be classified.

primary financial market

A market where securities are sold to investors for the first time; the issuer receives the proceeds from the security sale.

Primary Markets vs. Secondary Markets One of the most obvious differences between financial markets is whether the market is a primary market or a secondary market. In **primary financial market**, securities are sold to investors for the first time. The issuer of the security—a corporation or government—receives funds from the sale. For example, the U.S. Treasury auctions securities called Treasury bills, or T-bills, on almost every Monday of the year. This market is a primary financial market because the Treasury receives funds from the security sale.

By contrast, in a **secondary financial market**, securities are bought and sold after their initial sale. In other words, the issuer of the security receives no proceeds from the sale; all the trades take place between investors. The New York Stock Exchange (NYSE) is a secondary market. All of the shares of stock traded are being sold by one set of investors and bought by another set of investors. Most financial market transactions—more than 80% by some estimates—occur in secondary markets.

secondary financial market

A market where securities are bought and sold after their initial sale; trades take place between investors.

Money vs. Capital Markets

In Chapter 3 we described money market instruments such as Treasury bills and capital market instruments such as stocks and bonds. Thus, money markets are financial markets where money market instruments are traded, while capital markets are financial markets where stocks and bonds are traded.

Debt vs. Equity

Financial markets in which debt securities are traded are known as debt markets. Financial markets in which equity securities are traded are called equity markets. The NYSE, for example, is primarily an equity market.

Organized vs. Over-the-Counter

The terms *organized* and *over-the-counter* are somewhat out of date. Traditionally, organized markets were subject to established, fixed trading rules. Over-the-counter markets followed looser trading rules. Today, most financial markets operate under established trading rules. However, **organized markets** today are considered those in which trading takes place in a physical location. The NYSE is an example of an organized market where all trading takes place on a trading floor.

organized market

A market where trading takes place in a specific location such as a trading floor.

An **over-the-counter financial market** is characterized by trading that takes place in many locations with participants linked by a computerized communications system. The Nasdaq Stock Market, the second largest stock market in the world, is considered an over-the-counter market. Traders throughout the world are linked by one of the most sophisticated computer intranets.

over-the-counter market

A market where trading takes place at many locations; traders are linked by a communications network.

Global vs. Regional Markets

Many financial markets are global in scope. The securities traded in these markets come from many countries throughout the world. Other markets are more national or regional in scope. For example, stocks from companies located throughout the world, not just those located in the United Kingdom, trade on the London Stock Exchange. By contrast, stocks traded on the Frankfurt Stock Exchange tend to be those of German companies.

In Chapter 3, we discussed derivative securities that derive their value from other instruments. Examples of derivative securities include options and futures. Option and futures markets function somewhat differently from other financial markets. These markets are discussed in greater detail in Chapters 15 and 16. For the rest of this chapter, we focus on stock and bond markets.

PRIMARY FINANCIAL MARKETS

As we noted, a primary financial market is one in which investors buy newly issued securities, and security issuers (e.g., corporations) receive the proceeds from those sales. A popular misconception is that selling stock on the New York Stock Exchange takes money away from a corporation. However, all NYSE trades involve one investor buying shares from another investor. The company received its money when it sold the stock initially in the primary market. Subsequent trades simply change the owners of the corporation and leave its financial condition unaffected.

Primary financial markets function as intermediaries between savers (investors) and borrowers (corporations and governments). Well-functioning primary markets allow borrowers to raise funds as cheaply as possible, and at the same time give savers the opportunity to earn the highest possible expected rates of return. No modern economy can exist without well-functioning primary financial markets in which firms can raise capital to fund their operations.

Primary financial markets vary widely in size and organizational complexity. Generally, they process sales of new security issues in one of three ways: (1) through open auctions, (2) through underwriting by investment bankers, or (3) through private placement with large institutional investors.

Open Auctions

Several types of securities are sold primarily through **open auctions**, where investors bid on the basis of price or yield. The most significant new security auctions sell U.S. Treasury securities, federal agency securities, and mortgage-backed securities.

open auction
A market where investors bid on the basis of price or yield.

U.S. Treasury Security Auctions As discussed in Chapter 2, the U.S. Treasury issues a variety of debt instruments. Virtually all Treasury securities are initially sold to the investing public via an auction process. These auctions are held regularly, usually on a Monday. Auctions for three-month and six-month bills are usually held every Monday (excluding holidays), auctions for one-month bills are held every Tuesday, auctions for two-year notes are held monthly, and auctions for other securities (e.g., 10-year notes) are held quarterly. The Treasury usually announces on the Wednesday before each auction how much of what types of securities it will sell the following Monday. The Treasury sells billions of dollars in securities each month.

As the fiscal agent for the federal government, the Federal Reserve actually conducts the auctions, with the Federal Reserve Bank of New York taking the leading role. Buyers can submit two types of bids: competitive bids and noncompetitive bids. A competitive bid must specify a face amount and a bid price, whereas a noncompetitive bid specifies only the face amount the buyer wants to purchase, with maximums of $5 million for notes and bonds and $1 million for bills. The Treasury accepts all noncompetitive bids, and then it reviews the competitive bids to determine the *stop-out bid,* the one with the lowest price (or highest investor yield) that it will accept. Those who submit noncompetitive bids agree to pay the average price on accepted competitive bids.

government bond dealer

Institutions that make markets in U.S. government securities.

In theory, anyone can submit a competitive bid, but in reality only the primary **government bond dealers** do so. (There are currently about 40 primary government bond dealers.) Despite the lack of formal restrictions, the Federal Reserve will deal directly only with primary dealers, which the Federal Reserve itself designates. The Federal Reserve verifies that any firm requesting primary dealer status has adequate capital and handles a reasonable volume of trading in Treasuries (at least 1% of Treasury market activity).

Primary dealers are expected to participate in every Treasury auction and are not allowed to bid for more than 35% of a total issue. Primary dealers may then resell the securities to other investors, such as pension funds. To fulfill this function, primary dealers are expected to maintain inventories of Treasury securities at all times and to participate in secondary market trading.

Federal Agency Securities As discussed in Chapter 3, several federal and quasi-federal agencies are empowered to issue debt. These federal agency securities are sold in essentially the same manner as Treasury securities. Auctions generate competitive and noncompetitive bids, which are accepted based on a minimum price and funding needs. Again, the primary government bond dealers submit virtually all the competitive bids and bid on almost every new issue. Dealers also are expected to maintain inventories of federal agency securities and to participate in secondary market trading. Because the amount of federal agency debt outstanding is much smaller than the amount of outstanding Treasury debt, sales of new federal agency issues are smaller than new Treasury issues, and the auctions are held less frequently.

Mortgage-Backed Securities Virtually all mortgage-backed securities issued by the federally sponsored mortgage agencies—GNMA, FNMA, and FHLMC (often referred to as Ginnie Mae, Fannie Mae, and Freddie Mac)—are sold via auctions similar to those for Treasury and federal agency securities. The primary government bond dealers do most of the bidding and maintain inventories of mortgage-backed securities. Some mortgage-backed securities are issued by nongovernment entities such as large financial institutions; these securities are usually underwritten and sold through investment bankers.

Underwriting and Investment Banking

Virtually all nongovernment security issues are sold to the investing public through investment bankers. Nongovernment securities include most municipal debt issues and public offerings of corporate debt and equity instruments. Bonds issued in other countries (e.g., Eurobonds) are also sold through investment bankers. Some foreign governments also tap the international credit markets by issuing bonds, which are typically underwritten as well.

Role of the Investment Banker

investment banker

Institutions that help corporations and municipalities sell securities to investors.

The **investment banker** plays several important roles in the sale of new securities. These roles can be described as origination, risk bearing, and distribution. In the origination role, the investment banker helps the issuer design the terms and set the price of the new security issue. In the risk-bearing role, the investment banker purchases the issue (called **underwriting**) and accepts responsibility for reselling it to other investors. The risks associated with mispricing the issue are borne by the investment banker, not the issuer. Finally, in the distribution role, the investment banker distributes the issue to the public. The issuer could, of course, perform these functions itself; however, most issuers (e.g., municipalities and corporations) find it much more efficient and less costly to sell new security issues through investment bankers.

Investment bankers do not provide their services for free. They charge **underwriting discounts,** purchasing securities from issuers below the prices at which they hope to resell them. Figure 5.1 shows the front page of a prospectus (the legally required document that accompanies a new issue) for a new issue of 5.9 million shares of common stock of JetBlue. Notice that the underwriting discount is stated as $1.89 per share (or about 7% of the value of the issue). The investment bankers stood to receive more than $11 million for their role in the deal.

Competitive vs. Negotiated Arrangements Issuers of securities employ investment bankers based on either competitive or negotiated arrangements. In a competitive arrangement, the issuer solicits bids from several investment bankers and then chooses the firm that offers the smallest underwriting discount, imposing the lowest cost on the issuer. In a negotiated arrangement, the issuer selects the investment banking firm and then negotiates all aspects of the issue, including the underwriting discount, with the firm. Some argue that, although competitive bidding might reduce the cost of a new security issue slightly, the extra services provided by the investment banking firm in a negotiated arrangement more than offset the extra expense to the issuer.

Most corporations issue securities by negotiated arrangements. In fact, most large corporations maintain an ongoing business relationship with one or more investment banking firms. Public utility companies, however, are still required in many states to complete competitive bidding processes.

Many states require that municipal general obligation bonds be sold through competitive bidding as well, even though this requirement seldom affects revenue bond issues. However, during the past 15 years or so a trend shows an increased use of negotiated arrangements for sales of new municipal securities. The close relationship between some issuers of municipal bonds and their investment banking firms faces strong criticism of not serving the best interests of either taxpayers or investors. Critics accuse some local officials of trading underwriting business for political contributions.

Syndication For virtually any security issue, the investment banking firm selected by the issuer, whether by negotiation or competitive bidding, forms a **syndicate** to actually sell the issue to the public. The syndicate is a group of investment banking firms, each of which purchases a portion of the issue, accepting responsibility for reselling only that portion. For example, the syndicate for the JetBlue stock issue consisted of more than 70 firms, each of which purchased at least 20,000 shares for resale to the public. Syndicates allow investment bankers to spread the risk, limit their commitment of capital, and improve the marketing of the issue.

A few corporate securities, mostly speculative equity issues, are sold by investment bankers on a best-efforts basis. In this arrangement, the investment

underwriting
The purchase of a security issue by the investment banker who accepts responsibility for selling the issue to others.

underwriting discount
Difference between the price paid to the security issuer and the price charged to investors; fee paid to investment bankers.

syndicate
A group of investment bankers who each buy, and try to resell, a portion of a new security issue.

Filed Pursuant to Rule 424(b)(1)
Registration No. 333-82576

PROSPECTUS

5,866,667 Shares

jetBlue
AIRWAYS®

COMMON STOCK

———————

We are offering 5,866,667 shares of our common stock. This is our initial public offering and no public market currently exists for our shares.

———————

Our common stock has been approved for quotation on the Nasdaq National Market under the symbol "JBLU."

———————

Investing in our common stock involves risks. See "Risk Factors" beginning on page 7.

———————

PRICE $27.00 A SHARE

———————

	Price to Public		Underwriting Discounts and Commissions		Proceeds to JetBlue
Per Share		$27.00		$1.89		$25.11
Total	$	158,400,009	$	11,088,000	$	147,312,009

We have granted the underwriters the right to purchase up to an additional 880,000 shares to cover over-allotments.

The Securities and Exchange Commission and state securities regulators have not approved or disapproved these securities, or determined if this prospectus is truthful or complete. Any representation to the contrary is a criminal offense.

Morgan Stanley & Co. Incorporated expects to deliver the shares to purchasers on April 17, 2002.

———————

FIGURE 5.1   Example of an IPO

banker does not underwrite the issue. The issuing corporation retains ownership of the stock, and the investment banking firm or syndicate merely acts as a broker to find buyers for the stock at the best possible price. The fees charged for a best-efforts issue are less than the underwriting discount, because the investment banker takes less risk.

Private Placements

Some new security issues may not be sold publicly but rather only to a select group of large institutional investors (e.g., pension funds and life insurance companies). These sales are referred to as private placements. Virtually all private placements involve corporate debt issues, although a small amount of municipal debt (less than 10%) is privately placed. In a typical year, about one-third of all new corporate debt issues are privately placed.

private placement
Private sale of securities directly to institutional investors.

A private placement typically provides a company some cost savings. The issuer avoids both the underwriting discount and the various costs associated with registering the issue with the Securities and Exchange Commission (SEC). (We describe SEC registration in the next chapter.) Institutions buy private placements because they typically carry slightly higher yields than publicly issued securities. In addition, the terms of the issue can be tailored to meet the specific needs of both the issuer and the institutional investor. Of course, the institutional investor gives up liquidity, because privately placed securities do not trade in secondary markets.

THE IMPORTANCE OF SECONDARY MARKETS

Secondary financial markets handle trading of previously issued securities between investors. Like primary markets, secondary financial markets can be classified in several different ways: auction and negotiated markets, organized and over-the-counter markets, markets with face-to-face trading, and markets where trading takes place via computer.

The importance of secondary financial markets to investors is rather obvious. Many investors want, or need, to sell securities that they acquire in the primary markets. For example, an investor might purchase a five-year T-note with the full expectation of holding it until maturity. However, the investor's situation might change, and he or she might want to sell the note after, say, three years. The secondary market for U.S. Treasury securities provides liquidity for this investor by allowing him or her to sell the note for approximately its market value.

Although it is obvious why secondary markets are important to investors, their importance to issuers may not seem as obvious. Secondary markets benefit issuers of securities in the primary markets because if investors doubted that they could sell a newly issued security in a secondary market, they might refuse to purchase it or demand a substantially higher rate of return. By giving investors the option of selling their securities, a well-functioning secondary market lowers the cost of capital for issuers.

price discovery
Secondary market information informing investors what securities are currently worth.

Aside from liquidity, secondary markets serve an important economic need for price discovery. Even if an investor plans to continue to hold a security, the secondary market still tells the investor what the security is currently worth. Furthermore, new issues of securities to be sold in the primary market are actually priced by the secondary market. For example, if five-year T-notes are yielding 5% in the secondary market, newly issued T-notes will need a 5% return to attract buyers.

Any security issue that is not privately placed trades in some kind of secondary market. However, some secondary markets function better than others (i.e., they provide more liquidity to investors). One way to assess the level of functioning is to look at the spread between the bid and ask prices of the market makers. Every secondary market has market makers, dealers willing to buy and sell the securities traded on that market. The **bid price** is the price at which the market maker is willing to buy the security, and the **ask price** is the price at which it is willing to sell the security. Market makers make their profits by selling securities at higher prices than they pay for them. A larger bid/ask spread, however, makes a secondary market less liquid.

Why, then, do some securities develop better secondary markets than others? Among the several factors involved, the most important appears to be the size of the issue (i.e., the number of individual bonds or shares of stock originally issued). Larger issues, in general, lead to more active and liquid secondary markets. Another important factor is the number of investors who originally purchased the issue. If, for example, 10 large institutions buy up an entire new security issue, it is less likely that an active secondary market will develop than if the issue had been sold to thousands of investors, any of whom may decide to sell at any time.

bid price

Price at which a market maker is willing to buy a security.

ask price

Price at which a market maker is willing to sell a security.

SECONDARY BOND MARKETS

Domestic secondary bond markets trade U.S. government securities, municipal securities, corporate debt securities, and foreign debt securities. Most U.S. secondary bond markets are over-the-counter (OTC) markets. In such a market, trading does not take place in a physical location, such as a trading floor, but rather through computer-based communications systems that link dealers. These systems allow dealers, who are often widely dispersed geographically (sometimes in other countries), to exchange offers and make deals without meeting at a single location.

U.S. Government Securities

U.S. government securities (Treasuries, federal agencies, and most mortgage-backed securities) are traded by government bond dealers, including the 40 or so primary dealers discussed earlier. Given the existence of more than $4 trillion in outstanding Treasury, federal agency, and mortgage-backed securities, this secondary market is predictably quite large and extremely active; it is considered to be the largest, most liquid financial market in the world.[1] Government bond dealers buy and sell billions of dollars' worth of government securities each day in a busy OTC financial market.

---

[1]Some Treasury bonds are also listed and traded on the New York Stock Exchange. Trading volume, however, is minuscule. Less than 1% of secondary market trades in U.S. Treasury securities occurs on the NYSE.

As you might expect, trading activity is heaviest in Treasuries and lightest in federal agencies, simply due to differences in amounts outstanding. This volume is reflected in the bid/ask spreads of each kind of security.[2] For example, the typical bid/ask spread for a Treasury security is about 12 cents per $100 in par value, whereas the typical bid/ask spread for a federal agency security is 18 cents per $100 in par value.

Municipal Bonds

Like government securities, municipal securities are traded over the counter by municipal bond dealers. Commercial banks are large investors in municipal securities, and they often function as municipal bond dealers in some secondary market activity. As a rule, municipal bonds are not actively traded, and many issues lack good secondary markets. In fact, only a handful of municipal issues are traded in any particular day. Much of this trading occurs in large trades between institutions (e.g., mutual funds and commercial banks). This sparse trading activity is reflected in the bid/ask spread, which can be as high as 250 basis points, or 2.5%. The reason for this lack of trading activity is simply that most municipal issues are relatively small.

Corporate Debt Securities

Some corporate debt instruments are traded over the counter. Others are listed and traded on some of the major stock exchanges. Today, nearly 1,500 corporate debt issues are listed on the NYSE. As the sizes of corporate debt issues vary, so does the trading activity in the secondary market. Like most municipal issues, small corporate issues do not trade frequently. The bonds listed on the NYSE tend to be the larger issues (the average par value of these issues is more than $250 million). However, in a typical trading day only about $11 million in bonds change hands on the NYSE, compared with more than $44 *billion* in common stock.

International Bond Markets

Bonds trade throughout the world. After those in the United States, the largest bond markets are located in Japan and Germany. Bond trading in Japan resembles bond trading in the United States. Trading takes place on both organized exchanges such as the Tokyo Stock Exchange (TSE) and over the counter. One difference between the U.S. and Japanese markets, however, is that a greater percentage of Japanese government bonds trade on organized exchanges in Japan than in the United States.

In Germany, banks make up the largest group of bond investors. In addition, unlike the United States and Japan, German law mandates no separation between

---

[2]The bid/ask spread is the difference between the price at which a government bond dealer is willing to buy a particular government issue (bid) and the price at which the dealer is willing to sell the security (ask). As we noted, the bid/ask spread is often considered to be a barometer for the liquidity of a financial market: the narrower the spread, the more liquid the market.

banking and securities businesses. Banks dominate underwriting, trading, and investing in securities. As a result, secondary bond trading in Germany takes place in essentially an interbank market.

As you might expect, bonds issued in a particular country tend to trade in that country. The largest market for trading Canadian government bonds, for example, is in Toronto. However, the globalization of the financial markets extends to the bond market as well. U.S. government bonds trade in London, as well as New York, and Eurobonds trade in Tokyo, as well as Zurich. The TSE, for example, is an active secondary market for U.S. government bonds.

DOMESTIC STOCK MARKETS

The United States has several secondary stock markets, some with national, indeed international, operations, and others that serve more regional needs. Trading on some U.S. stock markets is over the counter, whereas others place trading on a trading floor.

The majority of stock trading in the United States occurs on either the New York Stock Exchange or the Nasdaq. Measured in terms of the number of shares traded, Nasdaq is the largest stock market in the United States. During 2001, more than 471 billion shares were traded on Nasdaq, compared with about 307 billion on the NYSE. However, when measured in dollar terms, the NYSE is larger than Nasdaq. For instance, in 2001, about $10.5 trillion in stock was traded on the NYSE compared with about $9 trillion on Nasdaq.

Stock market indexes, the best known of which is the Dow Jones Industrials (or Dow 30), are gauges of overall stock market activity and performance. In addition to the Dow 30, other well-known indexes include the Standard & Poor's 500 (S&P 500) and the Nasdaq Composite. The various stock market indexes, however, are constructed differently and measure different segments of the stock market. Consequently, investors should use indexes with caution. The Investment Insight box on page 119 describes some of the key differences between the Dow 30 and the S&P 500.

New York Stock Exchange

The NYSE, founded in 1792, is arguably the most famous financial market in the world. It is also one of the largest. Today, the shares of more than 2,800 companies are traded on the NYSE, called the *big board* by some market participants. Most are U.S. companies; however, more than 300 stock issues of foreign companies are also listed on the exchange. Companies listed on the NYSE have a combined market value in excess of $11.7 trillion. Today, during an average day more than 1.2 billion shares, representing more than $44 billion worth of stock, trade each day.

Companies that wish to have their securities traded on the NYSE must apply directly to the exchange and meet certain listing requirements. Companies must also meet certain requirements each year and pay annual listing fees. Why do companies choose to submit to the requirements and pay the cost to list their stocks on the NYSE? Four common reasons are given: liquidity for shareholders, access to capital, prestige, and exposure.

INVESTMENT INSIGHT

Stock Market Indexes

Stock market indexes are widely reported in the financial and popular press, and are a common tool for measuring the performance of the overall stock market. Probably the best-known stock market index is the so-called Dow Jones Industrial Average (or Dow 30). It consists of the stocks of 30 large, well-known companies, all of which trade on the New York Stock Exchange. (A list of the stocks making up the Dow 30 is shown in the following table.)

The 30 Stocks in the Dow Jones Industrial Average

Alcoa	Honeywell
American Express	Intel
AT&T	IBM
Boeing	International Paper
Caterpillar	Johnson & Johnson
Citigroup	McDonald's
Coca-Cola	Merck
Disney	Microsoft
DuPont	3M
Eastman Kodak	J.P. Morgan Chase
Exxon Mobil	Philip Morris
General Electric	Procter & Gamble
General Motors	SBC Communications
Hewlett-Packard	United Technologies
Home Depot	Wal-Mart Stores

The Dow 30, a price-weighted index, is calculated as follows. The numerator is the sum of the prices of the 30 stocks making up the index. This sum is divided by a number, called the divisor. Each time a change occurs in the makeup of the Dow, or any time a stock splits, the divisor changes so the index retains continuity.

The main criticism of the Dow is that it does not represent a random sample of stocks. Certain sectors of the economy are overweighted while others are underweighted. This criticism is somewhat valid. During many periods, the performance of the Dow stocks has been higher or lower than the performance of the "typical" stock. Nevertheless, the Dow remains a popular gauge of the health of the stock market.

Another widely followed stock market index is the Standard & Poor's 500 (or S&P 500). It is made up of 500 stocks that represent approximately 95% of the total market value of all stocks traded in the United States. Stocks trading on both Nasdaq and the NYSE are included in the S&P 500.

The S&P 500 is calculated differently from the Dow. The numerator is the sum of the market values (price times number of outstanding shares) of each of the 500 stocks. The sum is divided by the so-called base period value. It is adjusted each time the composition of the index changes in order to ensure continuity.

Although most agree that the S&P 500 is a much broader measure of the overall stock market than the Dow, some argue that the S&P 500 is still an imperfect measure of the performance of stocks. Because the index is based on market values, stocks with higher market values have much more influence over the index than do stocks with low market values. The following table lists the 10 largest stocks in the S&P 500. Notice that these 10 make up almost 25% of the index. A 1% change in the price of any of these 10 stocks will have a much greater impact on the index compared to a 1% change in the price of stocks with smaller market values.

The 10 Largest Stocks in the S&P 500 (as of December 31, 2001)

Stock	Market Value ($ millions)	Percent of the Index (rounded)
GE	398,105	3.8
Microsoft	356,806	3.4
Exxon Mobil	268,833	2.6
Citigroup	259,710	2.5
Wal-Mart Stores	256,505	2.5
Pfizer	250,526	2.4
Intel	211,092	2.0
IBM	208,371	2.0
American International Group	207,431	1.9
Johnson & Johnson	181,277	1.7
Total	2,598,656	24.8

Questions for Critical Thinking

1. Explain the relative impact on both the Dow Jones Index and S&P 500 of a 10% increase in the price of General Electric's stock.
2. If you were designing an index fund to track the Dow Jones Index or the S&P 500 would you buy equal dollar amounts of each of the 30 or 500 stocks that make up the respective indexes? Why or why not?

seat

What gives a person or institution
the right to trade stock on the
floor of the New York Stock
Exchange.

specialist

A NYSE market maker.

The NYSE is an auction market. Unlike the secondary market for Treasury securities, all trading on the NYSE takes place on the exchange floor. Only members of the exchange (firms that own at least one of the 1,366 **seats**) are entitled to trade on the floor of the NYSE. Customer orders are delivered to the exchange by telephone, teletype, or computer. Buyers and sellers of an issue meet, face-to-face, at one of the 42 posts where that issue is traded, and bid against each other in an auction.

Each security listed on the NYSE is assigned to one of the 42 **specialists.** A specialist acts as a market maker and assumes the responsibility of maintaining an orderly and liquid market in each security assigned to it. Specifically, specialists have four roles: (1) they act as auctioneers, calling out quotes throughout the trading session; (2) they act as catalysts, bringing buyers and sellers together; (3) specialists act as agents for limit orders (discussed in the next chapter); and (4) they provide liquidity by buying or selling out of their own inventories when no other buyers or sellers are present. Specialists directly participate in only about 25% of all trades. A specialist must have sufficient capital to maintain an inventory of about 15,000 shares of each security assigned to it.

Like other market participants, specialists participate to make money. They earn money primarily in two ways: first, by acting as agents in limit orders, for which they receive part of the commissions, and second, by buying and selling the stocks assigned to them. As mentioned earlier, a specialist offers to buy its assigned stock at a price (the bid price) slightly below the last trade price; at the same time, it offers to sell the stock at a price (the ask price) slightly above the last trade price. Over time, specialists should end up selling their stocks at higher prices than what they pay for the shares. However, specialists are required to buy when no one else is willing to buy and to sell when no one else is willing to sell to maintain liquidity in the market. In a period when prices are rising or falling sharply, specialists put their own capital at risk. For example, during the market break on October 19, 1987, NYSE specialists lost more than $100 million. Several specialist firms were forced to merge as a result.

Nasdaq Stock Market

Nasdaq stands for the National Association of Securities Dealers Automated Quotation System. The Nasdaq Stock Market, which is owned by the National Association of Securities Dealers (NASD), is a computer-based communications network that links the member firms to serve the vast OTC market for stocks. Trading volume on the Nasdaq increased sharply in recent years, growing at an annual rate of about 20%.

Small-firm stocks, those that could not meet NYSE listing requirements, have traded over the counter for years. Various dealers make markets in these sometimes thinly traded stocks, earning the name market makers, by buying and selling from their own inventories. Before the establishment of the Nasdaq market, to buy or sell a stock traded over the counter, a broker would call around to the various market makers to receive current bid and ask prices. The broker would then buy from, or sell to, the market maker, offering the best apparent price. However, a customer could never tell whether a broker obtained the best price, because public trading information was incomplete.

As the OTC market grew in size and activity, this system became more and more cumbersome. In 1971, the National Association of Securities Dealers

(NASD) created the Nasdaq to gather all market maker quotes together for immediate reference by all member firms. The association also wanted to spruce up the somewhat unsavory reputation of the OTC market.

The current Nasdaq market offers three levels of information to members. Level 1 provides a median representative quote based on bid and ask prices, which changes constantly as individual market makers adjust their prices. Level 1 is designed for firms that want current OTC quotes but do not engage in heavy OTC trading for customers and are not OTC market makers. Level 2, designed for firms that participate in heavy OTC trading but are not market makers, provides a list of real-time quotes from all market makers in a particular stock. Level 3, designed for OTC market makers, resembles Level 2 except that it allows dealers to change their bid and ask prices continually throughout the day.

Today, nearly 5,000 stock issues trade on the Nasdaq. The most actively traded issues, a little less than 4,000, are listed on the Nasdaq National Market System (NMS). Stocks listed on the NMS must meet somewhat stricter listing requirements.

Nasdaq has been at the forefront among U.S. markets in participation in international activity. Today, more than 100 American depository receipt issues are listed on the Nasdaq system. Further, more than 250 issues are listed on both Nasdaq and foreign stock exchanges. In addition, Nasdaq operates links with the Hong Kong Stock Exchange, the Singapore Stock Exchange, and the London Stock Exchange (LSE) that accommodate around-the-clock trading.

Unlike the NYSE, all Nasdaq-listed stocks have at least two market makers, and most have many more. Recently, an average of almost 11 market makers handled each Nasdaq stock. In addition, approximately 200 stocks have more than 25 market makers. Any Nasdaq member can become a market maker for any Nasdaq-listed stock, subject to minimum capital requirements. Today, Nasdaq has more than 500 qualified market makers, including all the well-known brokerage firms.

Traditionally, companies migrated from the Nasdaq to the NYSE once they met the NYSE's listing requirements. Today, however, many companies, including such well-known ones as Amgen, Cisco Systems, Costco, Dell Computer, Intel, Microsoft, and Starbucks choose to remain on the Nasdaq even though they clearly would qualify for listing on the NYSE. The reasons for such a decision are numerous. Each company probably has its own motivations, though some believe the prestige once associated with a NYSE listing is no longer significant.

Other Domestic Stock Markets

The American Stock Exchange (AMEX), sometimes referred to as the *curb*, was founded in New York City in 1910 to provide a market for unlisted securities. In fact, the AMEX did not establish formal listing requirements until the 1930s, and it continued to trade unlisted securities until about 1946. Like the NYSE, the AMEX is considered to be a national market, and it conducts trading in much the same way as the NYSE. The AMEX began listing foreign securities and warrants before the NYSE, and since 1975, the AMEX serves as a major options market. It does still trade stock issues. Today, the AMEX lists the shares of about 900 companies. Since 1985, trading volume on the AMEX has increased at an annual rate of about 10%.

Traditionally, the AMEX traded the stocks of smaller, less well-known companies. That generalization is still true, as its listing requirements reflect. The

NYSE requires that the total market value of a listed firm's publicly held shares exceed $18 million, whereas the AMEX requires that it exceed only $3 million.

Even though AMEX trading volume rose throughout the 1990s, the AMEX's share of total stock trading volume declined. Trading on the AMEX represents less than 1% of total stock trading in the United States today. However, the AMEX has been a leader in the introduction of new products, including exchange-traded funds (described in the prior chapter). Moreover, the AMEX is also the nation's largest options market.

Regional Exchanges In addition to the two national exchanges, several smaller regional markets trade stocks in the United States. Virtually all trading on the regional exchanges (in excess of 95%) is in *dual-listed shares,* stocks listed on both a regional exchange and one of the national exchanges. For example, Disney's common stock is listed on the NYSE, along with the Boston, Cincinnati, Midwest (Chicago), Pacific (San Francisco), and Philadelphia stock exchanges. Buyers and sellers may get slightly better prices on a regional exchange, pay slightly lower transaction costs, or make trades when the NYSE is closed. The Chicago Stock Exchange, for example, remains open for 30 minutes after the NYSE closes. Some of the smaller regional brokerage firms, which are not NYSE members, often use the regional exchanges.

Third and Fourth Markets

third market

Over-the-counter trading of listed shares off the floor of the NYSE.

During the 1970s, many large institutional investors became dissatisfied with the cost of trading stocks on the NYSE. Their objection gave birth to the third market, which involves trading of NYSE-listed stocks off the exchange floor. It is considered an OTC market in which firms that are not NYSE members act as market makers for the institutional investors. More than 5 billion shares of stocks listed on the NYSE are traded in the third market each year. By most accounts, the third market is the third largest market for NYSE-listed stocks, after the Midwest Stock Exchange and, of course, the NYSE itself.

fourth market

Private trades of NYSE-listed stocks off the floor of the exchange.

The fourth market trades stocks listed on the NYSE or Nasdaq, over the counter, between institutions without the intervention of market makers. The fourth market is essentially a series of communications networks that directly match investors who want to trade large blocks of stock. Because the fourth market's trades are essentially private deals between buyers and sellers, it is difficult to obtain detailed data on its trading activity. However, by most estimates, trading volume in the fourth market exceeds several billion shares per year.

electronic communication network (ECN)

Communications networks that directly link investors, usually over the Internet, allowing them to buy or sell stocks directly with one another.

Electronic Communications Networks Electronic communications networks (ECNs) link investors, usually over the Internet, allowing them to buy or sell stocks directly with one another. ECNs offer investors a number of advantages, including faster execution and often better prices, because no market maker is involved. ECNs also offer anonymous trading, so other market participants cannot tell who is buying or selling.[3]

---

[3]Large investors complained for years that traditional brokers often leaked who was transacting. Such leaks, investors contended, often affected prices.

ECNs experienced rapid growth in recent years. By some estimates, anywhere from one-third to almost one-half of the total trading volume in Nasdaq-listed stocks takes place on the three largest ECNs—Island, Instinet, and Archipelago.

In-House Networks An emerging trend today is the **in-house network**. In-house networks are internal trading networks set up by mutual funds, pension funds, and other large institutional investors to bypass brokers and stock markets. These networks allow an institution to cross-trade between its many funds or accounts. For example, an in-house network would allow the manager of a mutual fund to sell shares of stock to another fund owned by the same fund family.

in-house network
Internal trading networks set up by various institutional investors to bypass brokers and stock markets.

INTERNATIONAL STOCK MARKETS

As noted previously, stock markets exist throughout the world. Virtually all developed and many developing countries have stock markets. Some markets are large with long histories and sophisticated trading practices. Others are much newer and smaller. Let's take a closer look at some of the major international stock markets.

London Stock Exchange

The LSE is the world's third largest stock market and the largest in Europe. It is arguably the oldest stock exchange in the world, founded in the early part of the seventeenth century. The LSE lists approximately 3,000 issues, more than 600 of which are shares of companies based outside the United Kingdom and Ireland. In addition to stocks, the LSE trades bonds (especially Eurobonds), options, and futures contracts. The London market is very much an international market; more than 66% of the world's cross-border trading (e.g., trading of U.S. stocks outside the United States) takes place in London. The figure rises to more than 95% for cross-border trading in European issues alone. Institutional investors in the United States have been known to deliberately bypass the NYSE or Nasdaq in favor of trading large blocks of stock on the LSE claiming they get better prices and faster order execution.

Figure 5.2 illustrates the recent growth in trading volume in U.K. and non-U.K. stock issues on the London Stock Exchange. The figure clearly shows the international nature of the LSE. Since the late 1990s, annual trading volume in non-U.K. stocks exceeded annual trading volume in U.K. stocks. In fact, today, two out of every three trades on the LSE involve a non-U.K. stock. In 2001, the value of non-U.K. stock trades approached £4 trillion compared with about £1.9 trillion in U.K. stock trades.

For many years the LSE's trading practices virtually mirrored those of the New York Stock Exchange. That is no longer the case. On October 27, 1986 (known in London as the "Big Bang"), member firms gained the capability to trade off the exchange floor using an automated quotation system. Trading on the exchange floor dropped so sharply that it was closed on February 28, 1991. Today, all trading on the LSE is conducted "upstairs," using a Nasdaq-type computer system.

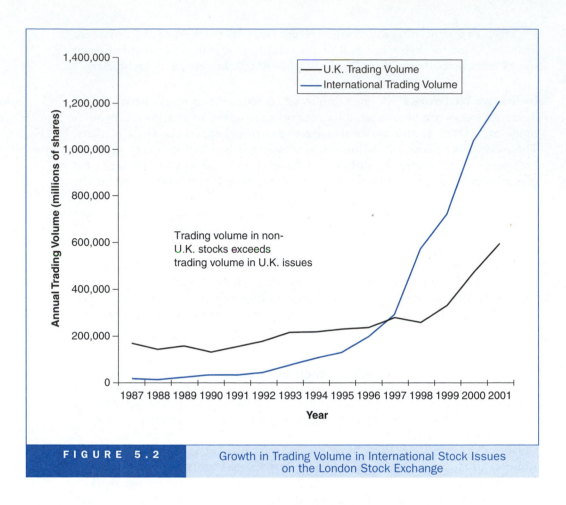

Trading volume in non-
U.K. stocks exceeds
trading volume in U.K. issues

| FIGURE 5.2 | Growth in Trading Volume in International Stock Issues on the London Stock Exchange |

Tokyo Stock Exchange

In terms of the number of shares traded, which market was larger in 1994, the NYSE or the TSE? If you answered the NYSE, you are wrong! In fact, trading volume on the TSE exceeded Nasdaq and NYSE trading volume between 1985 and 1996, sometimes by large margins. In 1988, for example, the number of shares traded on the TSE was more than twice the number of shares traded on the Nasdaq and NYSE combined.

Although the TSE is still one of the world's largest stock markets—and is by far the largest stock market in Asia—trading volume declined sharply during the early 1990s. For example, in 1992 trading volume was less than half what it was in 1989. In fact, even now, trading volume has yet to fully recover. The Tokyo Stock Exchange was also the site of a spectacular speculative bubble. The Investment History box on page 125 recounts the story of the Japanese bubble of the 1980s and early 1990s. Many aspects of this story show eerie similarities with the bubble in U.S. technology stocks that broke in 2000.

Currently, approximately 2,000 Japanese and 50 non-Japanese stock issues are listed on the TSE. It also trades bonds issued by the Japanese government and corporations, foreign bonds, options, and futures contracts. A few large American companies list their stock on the TSE, though the number declined somewhat in recent years as TSE trading volume slowed.

INVESTMENT HISTORY

The Tokyo Stock Market Bubble

During the late 1980s, the Japanese stock market was infected by the madness of crowds. Like the economy as a whole, the Japanese stock market experienced an incredible bubble. Market historians liken the Japanese stock market bubble of the late 1980s to the U.S. market in the years leading up to the Great Crash of 1929.

For many years, the Tokyo stock market was considered to be something of an investment backwater, even though Japanese stocks had risen steadily throughout the 1970s and early 1980s. The Japanese economy was growing rapidly, corporate profits were high, and inflation and interest rates were low. Like the U.S. market in the 1920s, the Japanese bull market eventually became a speculative bubble, probably sometime in the mid-1980s.

Japanese stock prices soared between 1985 and 1989. From its low in 1985 (which occurred on January 4) to its high in 1989 (which occurred on December 18), the The Tokyo Stock Price Index (TOPIX) more than tripled, increasing from a little more than 900 to almost 2,900. By contrast, the S&P 500 rose slightly more than 111% during the period. At the same time, the average price/earnings ratio of stocks listed on the Tokyo Stock Exchange rose from 35 to 71. Trading volume also exploded. In 1986, average daily trading volume was about 428 million shares; by 1988 it was more than 1 billion shares. The 1987 market break had only a temporary effect on the

frenzy. Although the Tokyo market lost about 14% on October 20, 1987, it gained back almost 9.5% the next day. For all of 1987, the TOPIX increased by almost 11%. During the next two years, 1988 and 1989, the Japanese market rose another 50%.

Finally, Japanese stocks reached a point at which more and more investors began to realize that stock prices were far out of line with their intrinsic values and started selling. Fears of slower growth in the Japanese economy and falling real estate prices, coupled with higher interest rates, also helped to break the bubble in Japanese stocks in 1990. The TOPIX dropped by more than 60%, from 2,885 to 1,103, between late 1990 and October 1992. Trading volume also declined sharply, from 283 billion shares in 1988 to about 65 billion shares in 1992.

The Tokyo stock market has yet to recover from the bubble. Since 1992, the TOPIX ranged between a high near 1,700 to a low of 980. Annual trading volume gradually increased to more than 150 billion shares, still a far cry from the heady days of the late 1980s.

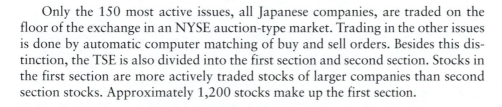

Questions for Critical Thinking

1. In what ways was the Tokyo stock market bubble similar to the bubble in U.S. technology stocks that broke in 2000?
2. Some believe that the U.S. market could experience a prolonged slump similar to Japan's. Do you agree or disagree? Explain your answer.

Only the 150 most active issues, all Japanese companies, are traded on the floor of the exchange in an NYSE auction-type market. Trading in the other issues is done by automatic computer matching of buy and sell orders. Besides this distinction, the TSE is also divided into the first section and second section. Stocks in the first section are more actively traded stocks of larger companies than second section stocks. Approximately 1,200 stocks make up the first section.

Emerging Markets

One of the most interesting developments in recent years is the emergence of new equity markets in many developing nations. New markets have sprung up in places as diverse as Chile, China, the Czech Republic, Malaysia, and Turkey. Returns from emerging markets can be quite impressive. During the first half of 1999, for example, U.S. stocks were up about 10%. Venezuela and China's markets were each up more than 40% during the same period.

Investing in these markets exposes U.S. investors to additional risk, however. For one thing, a rapid change in the value of the local currency, relative to the U.S.

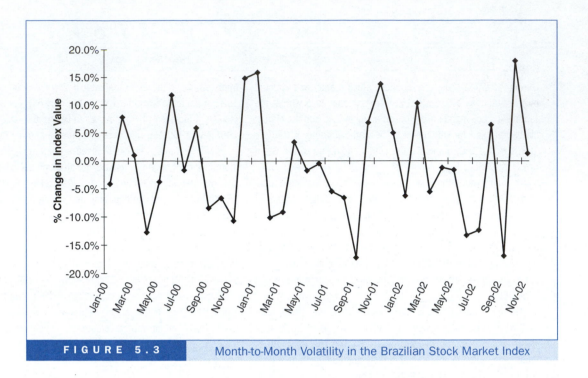

FIGURE   5.3   Month-to-Month Volatility in the Brazilian Stock Market Index

dollar, can dramatically alter returns. For example, during the first half of 1999 the Brazilian stock market was up 40%, measured in Brazilian currency, but actually down 20% when measured in U.S. dollars. For another, these markets can be quite volatile. Take a look at Figure 5.3. It shows the recent history of the Brazilian stock market. Note the wide swings in the index from month to month.

At times liquidity also poses a problem in emerging markets, which can partially explain the huge swings in prices. Further, neither trading practices nor regulation are as sophisticated in emerging markets as they are in more established stock markets.

THE FUTURE OF THE FINANCIAL MARKETS

As we move through the early years of the twenty-first century, it is difficult to know exactly what the financial markets will look like in the next 25 or 50 years; so many uncertainties cloud the crystal ball. However, given the rapid and dramatic changes the financial markets experienced during the past 20 years, we can safely say that the financial markets will continue to evolve. Three factors appear to be driving the evolution of the financial markets: institutional investors, globalization, and technology.

Today the majority of stock in most companies is owned by institutional investors (life insurance companies, pension funds, mutual funds, and so forth). Compared with individual investors, institutions trade larger blocks of stocks, and often trade more frequently. Each year institutions account for a larger and larger share of trading activity in the financial markets.[4] The speed at which orders can be executed, the trading price, and the cost of trading are critically important to institutional investors. Their dominance in the financial markets continues to prompt major changes in market structure and operations. One example is the increasing trading volume on Instinet and other fourth market networks. These networks will likely grow and expand in the coming years.

The second trend driving the evolution of the financial markets is globalization. The globalization of the financial markets is already virtually complete. Shares of more and more U.S. companies will likely be listed and traded in markets throughout the world, and shares of foreign companies will trade more widely in the United States. A future trading system may automatically route an order to buy an NYSE-listed stock to London or Hong Kong if one of those markets offers the best price. As trading moves worldwide, it moves toward around-the-clock activity. Already, as we noted, Nasdaq takes advantage of trading links with markets in London and Singapore. The London Stock Exchange is in the forefront in the development of a Pan-European stock market, one large European market linking all the continent's stock exchanges.

Driving many of these changes is technology. The pace of technological development in just the last few years is astonishing. As noted earlier, ECNs, using the Internet, capture a large share of trading volume already. Continued technological change will make 24-hour global trading much easier and cheaper.

So is continuous 24-hour trading a good thing? Perhaps. For one thing, continuous trading may make the markets function even more smoothly than they do today. Say, for example, that a company makes a significant announcement after the NYSE closes. Without continuous trading, a supply/demand imbalance might make trading hectic when the NYSE opens the next day. Continuous trading would adjust prices to the new information as soon as announcements were made.

Some believe that these changes will destroy the exchange floor as we know it. Will all trading take place within computer networks, not on the floor of stock exchanges? It is difficult to say. Trading in many world markets has moved away from exchange floors in recent years, most notably in London, Paris, and Toronto, and trades are matched by computer, not face-to-face agreements. After the Big Bang, the LSE tried to keep the floor open, but its trading volume vanished virtually overnight. In Tokyo, more issues are traded solely by computer each year. Could the floor trading system even cope with global 24-hour trading? Some doubt that it could. Like all floor markets, the NYSE depends on people who have limited stamina and cannot function beyond the current number of trading hours. To extend the trading day too long, some argue, would be too burdensome and too expensive.

In response, the NYSE argues that no conclusive evidence demonstrates that computerized trading systems such as Nasdaq are any more efficient than its floor trading system, which is already quite automated. Bid/ask spreads, for example, are no larger on the NYSE than they are on Nasdaq, and are often smaller. Further, in defending its 200-year-old specialist system, the NYSE argues

---

[4]For example, in 1998 a record 3.5 million blocks were traded on the floor of the NYSE—a block trade is defined as a trade involving at least 10,000 shares—or more than double the number of blocks traded in 1994 on the NYSE.

that the human element is still a critical part of trading. Computers cannot "feel" a stock, "work" a sensitive order, or take necessary risk. In short, computers cannot make all the decisions needed during the frenzy of trading. The exchange also likes to point out that during the 1987 market break, most specialists stayed at their posts and continued to fill orders, despite losing millions of dollars. (Specialists that failed to perform their market-making functions were disciplined by the NYSE.) Over on Nasdaq, critics allege that many market makers simply stopped answering their phones and ceased trading as stock prices plunged on October 19, 1987. Only time will tell who is right.

In this chapter we described how the world's financial markets are organized and how they operate. How investors participate in the financial markets and how they are protected will be discussed in the next chapter.

SUMMARY

1. What are the different types of financial markets?

Financial markets exist throughout the world and can be classified a number of different ways. Financial markets can be classified as primary and secondary, money and capital, debt and equity, organized and over-the-counter, and global and regional. Many of the world's financial markets meet the criteria of "good" markets. A good, well-functioning market exhibits the following characteristics: sufficient information is available to all participants; price continuity exists; transactions costs are low; all investors have equal access to the market; and prices adjust quickly to new information.

2. How do the primary financial markets function?

Securities are sold in the primary markets by open auction, through investment bankers, or through private placements. Treasury and other U.S. government securities are sold via open auction, while most corporate and municipal securities are sold through investment bankers—the term is *underwritten*. Some corporate debt issues are privately placed.

3. Why are secondary financial markets important?

Secondary markets are important because they provide investors with liquidity, which is the ability to sell a security to another investor at a price close to the security's true value. Not all secondary markets, however, are equally liquid. Often the spread between the bid and ask prices is an indication of a market's liquidity. Liquidity is beneficial for issuers as well, because liquidity lowers the cost of capital. Aside from liquidity, secondary markets provide a measure of a security's current worth. This function is referred to as price discovery.

4. How are the secondary financial markets organized?

Secondary bond and stock markets exist throughout the world; some are organized exchanges where trading takes place face-to-face while others are over-the-counter markets where trading takes place via a computerized communications network. One of the largest secondary markets is the over-the-counter market for U.S. Treasury securities. Major stock markets include the New York Stock Exchange, the Nasdaq Stock Market, the London Stock Exchange, and the Tokyo Stock Exchange.

5. How are financial markets evolving?

Financial markets changed dramatically in recent years and will continue to evolve. This evolution is being driven by three factors: the emerging dominance of institutional investors, the globalization of the financial markets, and technology.

REVIEW EXERCISES

1. What are the major characteristics of a "good" market? Pick a major financial market; does it have most of these characteristics?
2. Explain how financial markets can be classified. Are most financial market transactions conducted in the primary or secondary markets?
3. Explain the auction process for U.S. Treasury securities. Can small investors participate in a Treasury auction?
4. How is a new security issue sold via an investment banker? Why do issuers use the services of an investment bank?
5. Define *liquidity*. Why are some markets more liquid than others?
6. Explain the differences between organized and over-the-counter financial markets. Where are the various types of bonds traded?
7. Compare and contrast the NYSE specialist with the Nasdaq market maker. How does a specialist make money?
8. Define the third and fourth markets. Explain how an ECN operates.
9. List several major foreign stock exchanges. Are these markets more similar to the NYSE or the Nasdaq Stock Market in their trading practices?
10. List and discuss the three factors that appear to be driving the evolution of the financial markets. What are some of the arguments for and against round-the-clock trading?

CRITICAL THINKING EXERCISE

This exercise requires Internet or library research. Three of the best-known stock market indexes are the Dow Jones Industrials (Dow 30), the Standard & Poor's 500, and the Wilshire 5000. Research all three indexes and answer the following questions.

1. How did each of the indexes performed over the last five years? Can you explain any differences in performance?
2. How is each index constructed? How is the index adjusted whenever the contents of the index portfolio changes?
3. What is the Dow's current divisor? If one of the stocks in the index splits 2 for 1, will the divisor rise or fall?
4. When was the last time the Dow's portfolio changed? Which stocks were added, which were deleted? Why were the changes made?
5. In your opinion, which of the three indexes best represents the overall stock market? Explain your answer.

THE INTERNET INVESTOR

http://ww

1. The two largest stock markets in the world are the New York Stock Exchange (www.nyse.com) and the Nasdaq Stock Market (www.nasdaq.com). Visit both Web sites and prepare a report summarizing the similarities and differences between the two stock markets.
2. Most international stock markets have Web sites. Pick an international market and visit its Web site. Using only the information available on the Web, list some details about the market including the type of market, number of issues traded, trading procedure, and listing requirements (for both domestic and international firms).
3. The U.S. Treasury allows "small" investors to buy newly issued Treasury securities directly from the Treasury. Visit www.publicdebt.treas.gov/sec/sectrdir.htm and write a brief report explaining the program, and its advantages (or disadvantages) to small investors.

6

Investor Participation in the Financial Markets

| PREVIOUSLY . . . | IN THIS CHAPTER . . . | TO COME . . . |

We described how securities are issued and how they are bought and sold in the world's financial markets. We also speculated on the future of the financial markets.

We examine how investors participate in the financial markets, including how to choose a broker, the various types of orders investors place, and cybertrading. We also discuss the regulation of the financial markets and other ways in which investors are protected.

We discuss the concept of market efficiency. Even if the markets are not totally efficient, market efficiency has several important implications for investors.

CHAPTER OBJECTIVES

After reading Chapter 6, you should be able to answer the following questions:

1. How should investors choose a broker?

2. What are the various types of orders placed by investors?

3. What is cybertrading?

4. What are block trades and program trading?

5. Who regulates the financial markets and protects investors?

How Americans buy and sell securities has certainly changed over the past couple of decades. Gone are the days when the only way to buy or sell stocks, bonds, and most other investments was to use a traditional full-service brokerage firm, such as Merrill Lynch or Dean Witter. Investors were forced to pay commissions equal to 2%, or more, of the value of their investments each time they bought or sold securities. These hefty commissions ate away at investment profits.

Starting in the mid-1970s, instead of high, uniform commissions, a three-tiered industry developed in the brokerage business. Full-service firms continue to offer their full array of services, along with their high commissions. Next come the discount firms—such as Charles Schwab and Quick & Reilly. Discount firms offer fewer services, but charge lower commissions. At the bottom are the so-called deep-discount firms (Jack White and Brown & Company, for example). Deep-discount firms charge even lower commissions, but provide almost no service.

Starting just a couple of years ago, a major new player entered the brokerage business, electronic brokerage firms. Firms such as E*TRADE (www.etrade.com) and Ameritrade (www.ameritrade.com) allow investors to buy and sell securities through the Internet using their personal computers. Once an investor sets up an account with an electronic broker, he or she can access real or delayed price quotations, information, and even place buy and sell orders. Not only is trading online faster than using the phone, it is cheaper. For example, buying a 100 shares of stock costs about $15 using E*TRADE, one-half what a typical deep-discount firm charges, one-fourth the cost per trade using a discount broker, and one-sixth the cost of a full-service broker. As E*TRADE CEO Christos Cotsakos puts it, "For years, consumers have been paying exorbitantly high prices to get information that is selectively controlled by their brokers."

E*TRADE and other electronic brokers have proven popular with investors. In just two years, a half million investors opened accounts with E*TRADE and 500 more open new accounts each day. By one estimate, about 25% of all investment trades today are conducted using electronic brokers. Not to be left out, most discount and even a few full-service brokerage firms have started online services.

In this chapter, we describe how investors participate in the financial markets, including how investors should choose the right brokerage firm, the various types of orders investors can place, and investor protection. Knowledge of each of these topics is important if investors are to make informed decisions.

CHOOSING A BROKER

In order to buy or sell securities, investors need to first open a brokerage account. This fairly simple and straightforward process does entail a few important decisions. The first decision, of course, is to choose a brokerage firm and, in many cases, a specific broker. Investors select firms and brokers on the basis of reputation, personal contact, referral, and similar criteria. All brokerage firms require each investor to fill out an application to provide basic information regarding such characteristics as income and net worth. Many firms require that new customers have cash or cash-equivalent assets of at least $5,000.

Types of Brokerage Firms

full-service brokerage firms

Brokerage firms that offer investment advice, order execution, and record keeping to their customers.

discount brokerage firms

Brokerage firms that provide mainly order execution and record-keeping services to their customers.

deep-discount brokerage firms

Brokerage firm provides basic order execution and record keeping, but no other services, for customers.

electronic brokerage firms

Brokerage firms that allow investors to buy and sell securities over the Internet.

As we noted in the chapter's opening vignette, several types of brokerage firms are available. The investor must decide whether to set up an account with a full-service brokerage or a discount brokerage. **Full-service brokerage firms**, such as Merrill Lynch and Smith Barney, offer investment advice to their customers in addition to order execution and record keeping. A full-service firm usually assigns a specific broker to each individual customer.[1] **Discount brokerage firms**, such as Charles Schwab and Quick & Reilly, provide mainly order execution and record-keeping services, although most provide information on investment opinions from independent sources. A customer of a discount firm must likely deal with many individual brokers. **Deep-discount brokerage firms** provide order execution and record keeping, but almost no research or other services. Many deep discounters also require larger initial deposits to open accounts and a minimum number of trades per year. **Electronic brokers**—such as E*TRADE and Ameritrade—allow investors to buy and sell securities over the Internet. We discuss electronic brokers a little later in the chapter along with the rest of cybertrading.

Which type of brokerage should an investor choose? It depends on what type of investing the account will handle and the investor's need for services. Someone who makes personal investment decisions and trades frequently would probably be better off with a discount firm. However, someone who needs help making investment selections for infrequent trades may prefer a full-service firm. Also, because the customer of a full-service firm usually deals with one specific broker, it is just as important to select an appropriate broker as it is to select the right brokerage firm. The Investment Insight box on page 133 discusses some considerations when choosing a brokerage firm and a broker. The bottom line is: *You* should look for a broker who understands and accepts your personal investment objectives and risk preferences.

On the other hand, full-service firms cost more, sometimes a great deal more, compared with discount and deep-discount firms. Table 6.1 lists some sample commissions.[2] Notice that full-service firms charge five to ten times what a deep-discount firm charges. For an investor who trades infrequently and values investment advice, the difference in commissions may be a small price to pay. However, frequent traders, who make their own decisions, can save thousands of dollars by using discount, or deep-discount firms.

Most brokerage customers set up cash accounts that require them to pay the full cost, in cash, for all securities purchased, within three days. Some customers also set up margin accounts, which allow them to finance portions of their securities purchases by borrowing from the brokerage firm. The customer repays the borrowed funds with interest. We talk more about buying securities on margin a little later in the chapter.

The typical brokerage firm allows investors to buy or sell stocks, bonds, and options. Many firms today also allow investors to buy and sell shares of mutual funds. Investors interested in trading futures contracts, however, may have to set

---

[1]Brokers at most full-service firms are called *account executives*.
[2]As recently as the mid-1970s, the New York Stock Exchange required all of its members to charge fixed commissions. This NYSE rule effectively meant that all investment firms charged the same. Congress, as part of the Securities Acts Amendments of 1975, eliminated fixed commissions.

INVESTMENT INSIGHT

Picking a Stockbroker

Choosing a stockbroker is one of the most important decisions any investor makes. Here are some points to consider:

- Before selecting a broker, determine your investment goals, time horizon, and tolerance for risk. You should also prepare a financial profile (age, assets, liabilities, and so forth).
- Interview several brokers, at several different firms. Ask about their experience, educational background, and what their typical client looks like.
- Ask whether the broker has all necessary federal and state licenses. Call your state securities regulatory agency if you are not sure. The Securities and Exchange Commission (www.sec.gov) lists the state securities regulatory agencies.
- Check to see whether the broker ever faced any disciplinary action by state or federal regulators. The National Association of Securities Dealers (800-289-9999; www.nasd.com) can provide this information.
- The broker should carefully explain the commissions and fees you will be charged for various investment products. Ask if the broker receives higher commissions for certain products than

for others. If you feel the broker is recommending something just to earn a higher commission, change brokers.
- Do not submit to any pressure to open an account immediately and begin investing. Take your time and do your homework.
- Be wary of unsolicited sales calls from brokers (known in the industry as *cold calling*). Although some may be legitimate, do not buy any investment based upon a telephone solicitation, no matter how much pressure the broker puts on you. Ask the broker to send you written information about the investment and his or her background. Get another opinion about the investment from another source (Value Line, Standard & Poor's, etc.). Check on the broker with state regulators or the National Association of Securities Dealers.

Questions for Critical Thinking

1. Does it really matter to an investor how a broker is compensated?
2. Some brokerage firms are trying to recast brokers as "financial advisors." Can a broker ever be a totally objective source of investment information and recommendations?

Firm (type)	200 Shares at $25 per Share	300 Shares at $20 per Share	500 Shares at $15 per Share
E*TRADE (cyberbroker)	$ 15.00	$ 15.00	$ 15.00
Fidelity Brokerage (discount)	88.50	95.10	101.00
Merrill Lynch (full service)	129.50	164.85	205.54
Salomon Smith Barney (full service)	139.61	166.39	212.15

TABLE 6.1

Sample Commissions

Note: All of the table figures are based on published commission rates for market orders of listed and over-the-counter stocks. Actual commissions charged specific investors may vary substantially.

up another account with a firm specializing in futures trading; many traditional brokerage firms do not offer futures trading to their customers.

Most investors allow their brokers to hold securities in a **street name**, which means that the brokerage firm, not the investor, is technically listed as the owner of the security. The brokerage firm then sends the investor a monthly statement detailing monthly transactions, how much cash is in the account, and the current market value of securities owned by the investor.

street name

System by which brokerage firms hold securities for investors in the firms' names.

Virtually all brokerage firms belong to the Securities Investor Protection Corporation (SIPC), which insures brokerage accounts up to $500,000 to reimburse investors in the event the brokerage firm fails. Over the past 20 years, the SIPC paid out more than $200 million to customers of failed brokerage firms. Of course, it does not repay customers for losses due to adverse market moves. In addition to SIPC insurance, most large brokerage firms carry private insurance to further protect customers from financial loss in the event the firm fails. We strongly recommend using only brokerage firms that are SIPC members and carry insurance.

Buying Securities Without a Broker

You can buy some securities without using a broker, and thus avoid paying the brokerage commission. In the prior chapter, we briefly described how individuals can buy U.S. government securities directly from the Treasury. Investors can also buy shares of many mutual funds directly from the fund, paying no sales charges in the process.[3]

You can buy shares of common stock of many companies without paying brokerage commissions. Hundreds of companies offer dividend reinvestment plans (known as **DRIPs**). Once an investor enrolls in a DRIP, the company uses the dividends paid on shares owned by an investor to buy more shares of the company's stock. So the investor ends up buying more shares without being charged any commissions.

Another form of direct investment that is gaining popularity is no-load stock purchase programs. More than 100 companies allow first-time investors to buy shares directly from the company, often paying little if any transactions fees.

TYPES OF ORDERS

Once an investor establishes an account, various types of orders can be used to buy or sell securities. They are market orders, limit orders, and stop-loss orders. Some investors also buy stocks on margin while others sell stocks short.

Market Orders

A market order instructs the broker to buy or sell a security at the best currently prevailing price—the lowest price for a purchase or the highest price for a sale. Market orders are executed somewhat differently on the organized exchanges than on the over-the-counter market, so let's look at an example of each.

Organized Exchange Market Order Let's assume that an investor would like to buy 100 shares of Home Depot, which trades on the NYSE.[4] In response to

---

[3]As discussed in Chapter 3, funds can be classified as load funds or no-load funds. When you buy shares of a load fund you pay a sales charge; no sales charge applies when buying shares of a no-load fund. Many discount and deep-discount firms allow customers to purchase shares of hundreds of mutual funds, from dozens of fund families, without paying any brokerage fees or sales charges.

[4]Any order in a multiple of 100 shares (100, 200, 300, 500, 1,000, 10,000, and so on) is called a "round lot." Any order not in a multiple of 100 shares is called an "odd lot." Less than 1% of stock trading is in odd lots.

this request, the broker looks up the stock's symbol, HD, on a quote machine, which returns the following information: 25.25 bid, 25.27 ask, 25.26 last trade.[5] Home Depot last traded at $25.26 per share, and the stock's specialist is currently offering to buy it at $25.25 or sell it at $25.27. The investor enters a market order, which the broker transmits to the floor of the NYSE to be delivered (either physically or, more likely, electronically) to the post where HD is traded. If no sellers are present when the order arrives, the HD specialist sells 100 shares from inventory at the current ask price. If sellers are present, an auction takes place and the specialist may not be involved. Typically, specialists participated in fewer than 25% of all NYSE trades. The broker relays confirmation of the trade back to the investor, and the trade appears on the NYSE consolidated tape.[6] How long does this process take? More than 99% of all market orders are filled within two minutes!

This speed is possible because of the highly automated system at the NYSE. An electronic system matches buy and sell orders entered before the market opens and sets an opening price for each stock. The exchange's electronic order-routing system is called **SuperDOT**. It carries members' orders directly to the appropriate trading posts and then returns trade confirmations.

SuperDOT

NYSE's automated order routing and matching system.

Over-the-Counter Markets Now assume that another investor wants to buy 100 shares of Cisco Systems, which trades on the Nasdaq under the symbol CSCO. After the broker receives instructions to enter a market order, he or she consults the Nasdaq electronic quotation machine to find out the current bid and ask prices for CSCO. A broker with access to Level 2 of the Nasdaq system sees the bid and ask prices for each CSCO market maker (which probably number more than 25). Assume that the broker finds the following quotes:

Market Maker	Bid Price	Ask Price
A	14.25	14.30
B	14.23	14.28
C	14.26	14.31
D	14.27	14.31

The broker contacts Market Maker B, probably electronically, because it is offering the best (i.e., lowest) ask price for Cisco. To sell CSCO, the broker would contact Market Maker D, which currently has the highest bid price (i.e., it is willing to pay the most for Cisco).

Today, the process of entering small orders into the Nasdaq system is even simpler. In 1985, Nasdaq introduced its Small Order Execution System (SOES) to automatically execute small market orders (usually defined as orders for fewer than 1,000 shares) at the best possible price available in the Nasdaq system. SOES returns confirmation to the broker in a matter of seconds.

---

[5]All stocks have so-called ticker systems. NYSE-listed stocks have ticker symbols consisting of one, two, or three letters. Nasdaq listed stocks have four- or five-letter ticker symbols. Most ticker symbols are abbreviations of the company names (GE is General Electric, HD is Home Depot, and WMT is Wal-Mart Stores, for example). Some ticker symbols are a little more creative. For example, Anheuser-Busch trades under the ticker symbol, BUD; Harley-Davidson under the symbol, HOG.
[6]The NYSE consolidated tape lists all transactions in NYSE-listed stocks that take place on the NYSE, the regional exchanges, or over-the-counter in the third market.

Spreads and Decimal Pricing In the two prior examples you probably noticed that the NYSE specialist and Nasdaq market makers establish spreads between their respective bid and ask prices. This spread represents one way specialists and market makers make money. But what is a reasonable spread between a stock's bid and ask prices?

Critics long complained that bid/ask spreads were too wide, effectively costing investors millions of dollars each year.[7] Many pointed to the traditional practice of quoting stock prices in eighths (one-eighth equals 12.5 center per share). Most international markets, such as the London, Paris, and Toronto stock exchanges, began quoting stock prices in decimals in the 1990s. The U.S. markets were among the last to adopt decimal pricing, but, under pressure from regulators and investors, did so starting in 2000. Evidence indicates that bid/ask spreads have narrowed since the advent of decimal pricing.

An often-asked question is: Why *were* stock prices traditionally quoted in eighths? The exact origins of the system of eights is murky, but one well-known story goes as follows. When the New York Stock Exchange was established in 1792 the Spanish *peso duro* (meaning hard dollar in English) was the most widely used currency in the New World. (The new U.S. dollar was in fact based on the peso duro.) Although the U.S. Treasury quickly adopted a decimal-based currency, the NYSE stuck with the Spanish system, which divided the peso duro into eights of a dollar—pieces of eight in pirate lore. It took more than 300 years for the U.S. markets to move from eighths to decimals.

settlement date

The date (usual three days after the trade date) when securities and funds are transferred between buyer and seller.

Clearing Procedures Most market orders are settled three business days after the trade date. On the settlement date, the securities and funds are transferred between the buyer and the seller. The investor's brokerage firm is responsible for settling the transaction with the other party, either another brokerage firm or a market maker. To facilitate the clearing process, most brokerage firms use the services of a clearinghouse. The clearinghouse collects records of all transactions made by member firms, verifies each transaction, and nets out securities and cash due, or owed, by the member firms.

Limit Orders

limit order

An order that puts a limit on the price at which an investor is willing to buy or sell.

A limit order instructs a broker to buy a security for no more than a specific price or to sell for no less than a specific price. Return to the buyer of Home Depot stock, but suppose that some analysis leads to the conclusion that the current ask price, 25.27 is a little too high. The investor tells the broker to enter an order to buy Home Depot *limit* 25.20; the investor would willingly pay less than 25.20, but not more, for HD. The broker transmits the order to the post where HD is traded. If no one is willing to sell the stock for 25.20 (or less), the order remains with the specialist for entry into the *limit order book* (which today is an electronic data file). If HD eventually declines to 25.20, the specialist executes the order and informs the broker, who informs the customer. In return for this service, the specialist receives part of the commission.

---

[7]As noted in Chapter 5, the size of bid/ask spreads is one explanation for growth in the fourth market.

In 1989, Nasdaq introduced a new limit order service within its SOES. The service automatically accepts and stores limit orders for less than 1,000 shares, and it executes them when Nasdaq market maker ask quotations reach or improve on the limit prices set by the customers.

Limit orders can be valid for varying periods of time from one trading day to several trading days, one week, or longer. A limit order can also be placed *on a good till canceled* (GTC) basis, which leaves the order open ended. Brokerage firm policies regarding limit orders vary, and many charge slightly higher commissions for limit orders than for market orders.

Stop (or Stop-Loss) Orders

A stop order enters a market order that takes effect at a specified price. Stop orders are often referred to as *stop-loss orders* because they are typically used to sell stock if its value drops below some threshold. For example, an investor may have bought Home Depot at $5 per share and watched it rise to more than $25 per share. The investor still likes the outlook for the stock but worries about a temporary setback due to other stockholders selling to realize their gains (sometimes called *profit taking*). Instead of selling the stock outright for about $25.25 per share (the current bid price), the investor instructs a broker to enter a sell order at 22.50 stop. Should HD decline below $22.50, this stop order would automatically become a market order, and the stock would be sold at the prevailing price, protecting most of the investor's profit. The stop order does not guarantee a sale at $22.50 per share, only that the stock will be sold quickly at the best price currently available should its price fall below $22.50.

Stop orders can be valid for varying periods of time, or they can be open ended. As with limit orders, various brokerage firms have different policies on stop orders, and most charge higher commissions to execute them than to execute simple market orders. Stop-loss orders are often recommended during periods of extreme market volatility.

stop order

An order that automatically becomes a market order if the price of a stock drops below a specified price.

Margin Transactions

As noted earlier, margin trading involves borrowing money to buy securities. Banks lend funds to brokerage firms, which lend them, in turn, to customers to buy securities on margin. Customers typically pay between 1% and 1.5% over the rate the brokerage firm pays the bank. The brokerage firm specifies how and when the customer repays a margin loan. About $150 billion in margin debt is currently outstanding.

Technically, margin is the part of the total value of the securities that the investor pays with cash, or the investor's equity. The Federal Reserve sets minimum initial margin requirements; in other words, it specifies how much the investor must put up initially to purchase a security on margin. The current requirement of 50% has not changed since 1974. To purchase 200 shares of Coca-Cola at $50 on margin, an investor would have to put up at least $5,000 in cash (plus the commission), borrowing the other $5,000. In addition, the NYSE requires that a margin customer maintain at least a 25% margin—called the *maintenance margin requirement*—as a security's price changes. Most brokerage firms have higher maintenance requirements (30% to 40%).

The "Average" Investor

You often hear the term *average investor*, but what does the expression mean? What does the average American investor really look like? To help us answer these questions, we will rely on data compiled by the Federal Reserve. Every three years the Fed conducts a survey of consumer finances. Results from the most recent survey—conducted during December of 2001—are now available. The data provide some interesting insight into the characteristics of individual American investors.

According to the Fed, more than half of all American households now own stock, either directly or indirectly, through retirement accounts or mutual fund investments. The percentage of households owning stock increased steadily since the early 1990s, up from 36.7% in 1992 to 51.9% in 2001. At the same time, the median holdings of common stock investments increased from $13,000 to more than $34,000. For stock-owning households, the value of their stock investments represent, on average, about 56% of the total value of their financial assets.

Although the typical U.S. household can now be classified as an investor, individual households show substantial variation in stock holdings. Not surprisingly, for instance, higher-income households are much more likely to own stock than lower-income households. Almost 90% of households whose incomes put them in the top 10% own stock. By contrast, only about 12% of households that rank in the bottom 20% of income are stock owners. Older households are more likely to own stock than younger households. Homeowners are more than twice as likely to own stock compared with renters.

FIGURE 6.1	Coke Rises to $60	Coke Falls to $40	Coke Falls to $35
Illustration of a Margin Transaction			
Value	$12,000	$8,000	$7,000
Margin	7,000	3,000	2,000
Required margin	6,000	2,800	2,450
The investor . . .	Can withdraw $1,000 in cash from the account	Is not required to deposit any additional cash but cannot make additional margin purchases	Must deposit another $450 in cash into the account or the shares will be sold

Figure 6.1 illustrates how margin works. Assume you buy 200 shares of Coca-Cola at $50 on margin. Your initial margin is 50%, or $5,000. Your brokerage firm requires you maintain a margin of 35%. Assume Coke rises to $60 per share. The value of your shares rises to $12,000. You now have $7,000 in your margin account ($12,000 − $5,000). Because you are only required to have $6,000 in your margin account (50% of $12,000), some brokerage firms might allow you to withdraw $1,000 in cash from your account.

Now, instead of rising, assume Coke falls to $40. The value of your shares is $8,000 and you have only $3,000 in your margin account ($8,000 − $3,000). This percentage is 37.5 ($3,000/$8,000), and although it is below the initial margin requirement, it is still above the maintenance requirement. You would not be required to deposit any additional cash but will probably not be able to make any further margin purchases (called a *restricted account*).

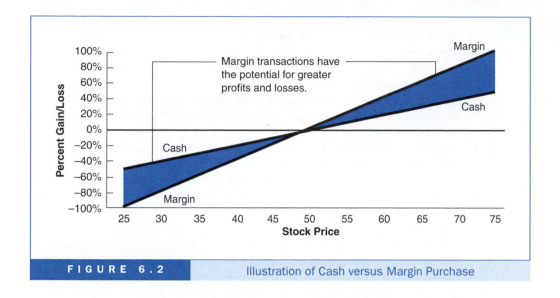

| FIGURE 6.2 | Illustration of Cash versus Margin Purchase |

Assume that Coke continues to slide, falling to $35 per share. Now your margin is down to $2,000, which is only about 28.6% of the value of the stock. You now face the dreaded **margin call**. Your broker will require that you deposit another $450 in cash into your account to bring your margin back up to 35%. Failure to do so will result in the shares being sold and the proceeds being used to repay the margin loan.

margin call

Having to deposit additional cash into a margin account.

Why should anyone buy stock on margin and pay interest on a margin loan? The answer is simply because margin trading gives investors the potential benefit of leverage, as illustrated in Figure 6.2. Buying stock on margin might increase the return to the investor, but at the same time, it increases the potential risk. Margin purchases do not suit every investor.

Figure 6.2 ignores the interest expense on the margin loan. Interest expense, of course, reduces returns to the margin investor only slightly. Banks consider margin loans to be low risk. Consequently, interest rates on margin loans are below the rates charged on credit cards, auto loans, and even home mortgages.

Short Sales

Someone who buys a security is said to be taking the *long position*. This investor purchases the stock with the expectation that it will provide a satisfactory return in the form of dividend payments plus price appreciation. What about taking the opposite position if a stock seems likely to fall in value? This move is possible by executing what is known as a **short sale**, selling borrowed stock with the expectation of buying back shares at a lower price to return to the owner at some point in the future. This transaction is perfectly legal, although certain conditions must be met. The NYSE reports that in recent years one share of stock is sold short for every ten shares purchased.

short sale

Selling shares today with the intention of buying them back at a later date.

Figure 6.3 outlines the anatomy of a short sale. The shares sold short are borrowed from another account, and the short seller must keep at least 50% of the proceeds in a margin account as collateral. The short seller is free to use the

FIGURE 6.3

Anatomy of a Short Sale

- Decide on the stock you want to sell short. It could be a poorly run company or simply one that you think is overpriced. You notice that AT&T has zoomed from 45 to 70 in just a few weeks. You believe that even though AT&T is a good company, its stock has risen too far, too fast. You decide to sell the 500 shares of AT&T short.
- Borrow the stock from another account. It must be selling for at least $5 per share and be marginable. Because AT&T is among the most widely held stocks, finding shares to borrow is no problem.
- Sell the stock. You receive $35,000, less commissions. You have to keep half of the proceeds in your account as margin. You deposit the other half in a money market account fund.
- Pay dividends to the owner of the stock—if dividends are paid while your short position is open. Assume AT&T pays a quarterly dividend of $0.33 while your short position is open. You pay the owner $165 ($0.33 × 500).
- Three months after you went short, AT&T announces that its earnings will be well below analysts' expectations. The stock price tumbles to 50. You decide to close out your short position buying 500 shares at 50 to replace the shares you borrowed. You make a profit of $20 per share—or $10,000. Your total profit is $10,000 minus commissions, plus the interest you earned over the three months, minus $165 in dividends.

balance for anything, although the brokerage firm sometimes pays the short seller interest (called a *rebate*) on the collateral. If the stock rises in price, the short seller must add to the collateral balance (much like maintaining a margin). The short seller is also responsible to the stock's owner for any cash dividends paid on the borrowed stock.

In addition to the requirements listed in Figure 6.3, the NYSE will allow a short sale only on an **uptick**. A short sale can take place at the last trade price only if that price exceeds the last different price before it. The example in Figure 6.3 worked out quite nicely, and the short seller earned a profit of about $10,000, but short selling can involve substantial risk and is recommended only for experienced, knowledgeable investors.

uptick

Most recent trade was either an increase, or no change, from the prior trade.

CYBERTRADING

With a click of a mouse and a few keystrokes, today's investors can trade securities, using their personal computer and an online account, as easily as they surf the Net. As mentioned in the opening vignette to the chapter, cybertrading exploded in recent years. Today, more than 100 brokerage firms, including many of the most established names on Wall Street, offer online trading services. By some estimates approximately 25% of all trades are cybertrades today.

Establishing an online account requires an investor to complete an application and deposit a minimum amount of cash into the account. Once the account is established, the investor receives an account name and password. The investor can simply go to the online broker's Web site and enter the personal account information, and then is ready to trade. We should note that no money changes hands over the Internet, however. All monetary transactions take place the old-fashioned way.

History of Cybertrading

Using a personal computer to trade stocks is not new. In the mid-1980s discount brokerages such as Schwab and Quick & Reilly began offering online trading using their own specialized software and networks. A few years later, brokerage firm Donaldson, Lufkin & Jenrette began offering an online trading service called PC Financial Network. It made the service available to clients of the commercial online services: America Online, CompuServe, and Prodigy.

It was the Internet that really launched online trading. The Internet is both cheaper and faster than other online trading systems, because less specialized software is needed. The Web also has potentially much wider access to investors. E*TRADE and Lombard Institutional Brokerage were among the first to use the Internet for online trading. Internet trading received a big boost in early 1996 when Schwab decided to permit stock trading over the World Wide Web. Other large discount brokerage firms followed suit later in the year.

Advantages and Disadvantages of Cybertrading

Cybertrading offers several main advantages to investors. One is cost. Commissions on cybertrades average between $5 and $30, much less than the commissions charged by full-service and even discount brokerage firms. Another advantage of cybertrading is convenience. Investors can check account balances, do research, or enter orders at any time, day or night, wherever they have access to a PC and the Internet. Online trading gives individual investors ready access to market data and information that just a few years ago was only available to securities professionals. Another issue is speed. Some claim that orders placed online may be executed faster than orders placed through more traditional means, such as over the telephone or in person.

Although cybertrading offers advantages for investors, it has drawbacks as well. The mechanics of online trading may be fairly fast and easy, but investing is still a time-consuming process. Investors still need to do their homework. Many worry that investors will confuse the speed at which they can now trade with the speed at which they should make investment decisions.

Another potential problem with online trading services is access during volatile and busy markets. All online trading service warn investors that delays in order execution are possible. In fact, no government regulations require that orders be executed within a certain amount of time. Online systems have limited capacity and can handle only so many orders at once. Consequently, the execution price can be quite different from the price when the investor placed his or her order. Experts suggest online traders use limit orders, rather than market orders during face-paced trading. Before opening an online account, ask about delays and what options are available if you cannot access you account online.

Online traders who buy on margin should be aware of the face that margin calls are not required. In other words, your broker can sell your securities without giving you a margin call. Online brokerage firms often do not provide margin calls. Read the margin agreement carefully and pay attention if your account is close to the maintenance margin requirement.

Day Trading

One of the by-products of the growth of online trading and other technical innovations, coupled with a historical bull market, was the emergence of day traders. Day traders sit in front of computer screens and, using computer software and fast Internet connections, look for short-term trends in security prices. What stocks a day trader buys or sells is of no consequence. If the day trader thinks a stock is about to rise, they buy. If they think it is about to fall, they sell. Day traders rarely hold positions for more than a few minutes, and never overnight. It is not uncommon for a day trader to buy or sell the same stocks several times during one trading day.

Day trading has been around for a long time. NYSE specialists used day trading for years as a way of making some extra money.[8] Advances in computer software and hardware, however, along with online brokerage firms and their rock-bottom commissions, allowed individuals to become day traders. Although it is impossible to come up with an exact figure on the number of full-time day traders, some estimates put the number at more than 100,000 at the height of the bull market during the late 1990s. After the bubble broke in 2000, the number of day traders declined along with the stock market.

Even when the market recovers, however, becoming a day trader probably is not the best idea. Day trading is extremely risky and by most accounts, a majority of day traders during the late 1990s lost money. Even more problematic was the fact that many day traders relied heavily on borrowed money. As a full-time job, day trading is highly stressful. It requires a great deal of concentration to pay attention to thousands of ticker symbols and prices trying to spot trends. Day traders also have high fixed costs; many seriously underestimate how much money they need to make trading just to break even.

BLOCK TRADES AND PROGRAM TRADING

As we mentioned, institutional investors account for a larger and larger share of trading volume each year. The increased presence of institutional investors increases amounts of both block trades and program trading.

Block Trading

block trade

Purchase of sale of 10,000 or more shares of stock.

The increase in institutional investing in stocks brought an increase in the number of giant **block trades**, which NYSE rules define as any trade of at least 10,000 shares with a minimum market value of $200,000. In 1970, block trades represented about 15% of NYSE trading volume; today, more than 50% of trades are block trades.[9] On the Nasdaq Stock Market, more than 40% of trading volume is made up of block trades.

---

[8]NYSE rules allow specialists to trade stocks not assigned to them, for their own accounts.

[9]This figure only includes block trades executed on the floor of the exchange or in the third market. Most trading activity in the fourth market consists of large blocks. Data on fourth market activity are only fragmentary but it is safe to assume that block trades in the fourth market consist of a few billion shares each year.

As block trading increased during the 1970s, it began to strain the specialist system. Many specialists lacked the capital necessary to buy large blocks and accommodate the huge trades. Even when they had sufficient capital, most specialists were reluctant to take the large risks involved. Consequently, institutions started trading blocks off the floor in other markets or even off the floor of the NYSE. The NYSE recognized this problem and began allowing member firms, with permission from the NYSE, to trade large blocks off the floor of the exchange.[10]

Program Trading

Institutional investors buy and sell large numbers of stocks in another technique called **program trading**. Program trading involves the use of sophisticated computer programs that can make automatic decisions to buy or sell. To take advantage of an expected marketwide increase, a pension fund might execute a program trade to buy all 500 stocks that make up the Standard & Poor's 500. Program trades are usually executed directly, using the NYSE's electronic SuperDOT system. Program trades make up about 15% of NYSE volume.

Program trades serve several purposes. A pension fund manager might execute a program trade each time the fund's sponsor makes a monthly or quarterly contribution. The program trade would deploy new cash into the stock market without substantially altering the contents of the fund's portfolio. Another use of program trading, **index arbitrage**, attempts to gain risk-free returns by exploiting differences between the prices of stock index futures and prices of the underlying stocks. We take a closer look at index arbitrage in Chapter 16.

Program trading is controversial. Some small investors complain that program trades often get priority in execution, despite NYSE rules and policies that give priority to small orders. Critics also allege that program trading tends to exaggerate market moves (both upward and downward), making stock prices more volatile. Some even blamed program trading for contributing to the 1987 market break. However, no conclusive evidence links program trading to market volatility. Nevertheless during periods of high market volatility the NYSE and other markets implement a series of so-called circuit breakers, many of which restrict program trades. Table 6.2 lists some of the circuit breakers employed by the NYSE in an attempt to control highly volatile trading days.

program trading

Trading via sophisticated computer programs that can make automatic buy or sell decisions.

index arbitrage

Using stocks and stock index futures to make a guaranteed profit over a short period of time.

INVESTOR PROTECTION

In order to function properly, investors need to have confidence in the financial markets. To a large extent, investor confidence stems from a belief that the securities markets are being sufficiently regulated. U.S. securities markets are regulated by both federal and state authorities, as well as industry self-regulation. In other countries, financial markets are also regulated, to a greater or lesser extent, by national government agencies. Recent corporate scandals involving companies such as Enron and WorldCom direct increased scrutiny toward financial market regulation.

---

[10]This rule change essentially created the third market. We described the third market in Chapter 5.

TABLE 6.2	In the aftermath following the 1987 market break, the New York Stock Exchange instituted a series of so-called circuit breakers. These breakers are tripped during periods of extreme market volatility in an attempt to maintain an orderly market. The circuit breakers include the following:
NYSE Circuit Breakers	

- *Rule 80A.* If the Dow Jones Industrial Average moves 50 points or more from the previous day's close, index arbitrage (a form of program trading) is subject to a tick test. In down markets sell orders cannot be executed on a downtick; in up markets buy orders cannot be executed on an uptick.
- *Sidecar.* If the S&P 500 futures contract declines by 12 points (equivalent to about 100 points on the Dow), all program trading market orders for S&P 500 stocks listed on the NYSE are diverted for five minutes. After the five-minute period, buy and sell orders are paired off and executed. If orderly trading cannot resume, trading in the stock is halted. New stop-loss orders in all stocks are banned for the rest of the trading day if they involve more than 2,100 shares.
- *Rule 80B.* If the Dow Jones Industrial Average declines by 10%, trading will be halted for one hour (one-half hour if the decline occurs after 2 P.M.); if the Dow drops by 20%, trading will be halted for two hours (if the decline occurs after 1 P.M., trading will be halted for one hour); and if the Dow drops by 30%, trading will be halted for the rest of the day.

Government Regulation in the United States

Regulation of U.S. securities markets is primarily a function of the federal government. Federal regulation grew out of various trading abuses during the 1920s. During the Great Depression, in an attempt to restore confidence and stability in the financial markets after the 1929 stock market crash, Congress passed a series of landmark legislative acts that formed the basis of federal securities regulation ever since.

The U.S. Securities and Exchange Commission (SEC), created in 1934, is the principal federal regulatory overseer of the securities markets. The SEC's mission is to administer securities laws and protect investors in public securities transactions. The SEC is a quasi-judicial agency with broad enforcement power. It has the power to take civil action against individuals and corporations. Actions requiring criminal proceedings are referred to the U.S. Justice Department.

insider trading

Using material nonpublic information to make investment profits.

Some of the best-known cases of regulatory intervention involved **insider trading**, broadly defined as the use of material nonpublic information to make investment profits. Many celebrated cases of insider trading occurred over the past 15 years. Some of those convicted of insider trading in recent times actually spent time in prison.

Recently, the SEC instituted a new regulation, called Regulation FD, that requires that firms share information with all investors at the same time. Regulation FD is designed to prohibit selective disclosure of information by companies to favored investment firms. Clients of these firms often received information on a company's sales or earnings before the general public. According to the SEC, one glaring example occurred when clothier Abercrombie & Fitch tipped off an analyst at one brokerage firm about the company's sluggish sales about a week before the news was revealed to the public. The analyst allegedly put out a quiet sell recommendation to a handful of his clients. When the news was made public, the price of the popular clothier's stock dropped by more than 20%. Regulation FD is designed to prohibit such selective disclosure of material information.

In the primary security markets, the SEC requires that virtually all new public issues of corporate securities be *registered*.[11] Before offering securities for sale, an issuer must file a registration statement with the SEC. As part of the registration process for a new security issue, the issuer must prepare a **prospectus**. In the prior chapter we reprinted the first page from the prospectus of JetBlue's IPO (Figure 5.1 on page 113). Figure 6.4 presents several more pages of the prospectus to show the typical contents. A prospectus gives a fairly detailed description of the company issuing the securities, including financial data, recent developments, products, research and development projects, and pending litigation. It also describes the security issue and underwriting agreement in detail.

The registration process seeks to guarantee **full and fair disclosure**. The SEC does not rule on the investment merits of a registered security issue. It is concerned only that an issuer gives investors enough information to make their own informed decisions.

In 1982, SEC Rule 415 introduced shelf registration to allow a large issuer to register a bundle of security issues once and then sell them piecemeal over a period as long as two years. The purpose is to reduce the time delays and expenses associated with registering individual security issues. Companies can now sell new securities on short notice to take advantage of favorable market conditions. Companies use shelf registrations primarily to sell new corporate bond issues.

Besides primary market registration requirements, SEC regulation extends to the secondary markets as well, keeping tabs on trading activity to make sure it is fair to all participants. Every securities exchange, including Nasdaq, must, by law, follow a set of trading rules approved by the SEC. In response to the 1987 market break, Congress passed the Market Reform Act of 1990, giving the SEC emergency authority to halt trading and restrict practices such as program trading during periods of extreme volatility.

Securities laws also require every public corporation to file several reports each year with the SEC; the contents of these reports become public information. The best known, of course, is the annual report. Public corporations prepare annual reports for their shareholders, and they file another report containing essentially the same information, Form 10-K, with the SEC. The SEC requires additional reports each time certain officers and directors buy or sell a company's stock for their own accounts (Form 4) or anytime an investor accumulates more than 5% of a company's outstanding stock (Form 13-d).

State Regulation. All states have laws regulating securities markets. In 1911, Kansas became the first state to enact a set of comprehensive securities laws. State securities laws, often referred to as **blue sky laws**, vary widely. Some states have fairly lax laws, deferring virtually all regulatory power to the SEC, whereas other states impose much stricter regulations. Unlike federal regulation, which is concerned primarily with full and fair disclosure, these states empower regulators to pass judgment on the worthiness of new security issues as investments. Some states prohibit sales of security issues approved by registration with the SEC. In

prospectus

Official offering document for a new security sale.

full and fair disclosure

SEC requirement that investors be given enough information to make informed decisions.

blue sky laws

State securities laws.

---

[11]The major exceptions are issues under $500,000 and those that mature in less than 270 days.

FIGURE 6.4 Prospectus Summary

This summary highlights selected information about our company and the common stock that we are offering. It does not contain all of the information that may be important to you. You should read this entire prospectus carefully, including the "Risk Factors" section and the financial statements and notes to those statements, which are included elsewhere in this prospectus.

JETBLUE AIRWAYS

Overview

JetBlue is a low-fare, low-cost passenger airline that provides high-quality customer service primarily on point-to-point routes. We focus on serving underserved markets and large metropolitan areas that have high average fares, and we have a geographically diversified flight schedule that includes both short-haul and long-haul routes.

We commenced service in February 2000 and established our primary base of operations at New York's John F. Kennedy International Airport, or JFK. As of February 28, 2002, we operated 108 flights per day, including 52 daily flights between JFK and Florida, 26 daily flights between JFK and upstate New York and 18 daily flights between JFK and the western United States. On August 28, 2001, we began service at our West Coast base of operations, Long Beach Municipal Airport, which serves the Los Angeles area.

To date, we have raised $175 million of equity capital, which has enabled us, among other things, to acquire a fleet of new, single-class Airbus A320 aircraft. We are scheduled to add to our operating fleet of 24 aircraft 59 new A320 aircraft by the end of 2007.

We are focused on profitability and have low operating costs because we operate a single aircraft type with high utilization and have a highly productive and incentivized workforce. Our low fares are designed to stimulate demand, and we have demonstrated our ability to increase passenger traffic in the markets we serve. In addition, we offer our customers a differentiated product, with new aircraft, low fares, leather seats, free LiveTV (a direct 24-channel satellite TV service) at every seat, pre-assigned seating and reliable performance.

The terrorist attacks on September 11, 2001 have dramatically affected the airline industry. U.S. airlines have experienced numerous difficulties in the wake of these tragic events, including but not limited to, a significant drop in demand for air travel, reduced traffic and yields, increased insurance and security costs and liquidity concerns. We, along with the rest of the industry, suffered an initial drop in demand, leading to reduced traffic and yields. Unlike many of our competitors, however, our level of operations and passenger traffic have recovered substantially to the levels we had originally anticipated before September 11, 2001, although our yields have not fully recovered. Many of our competitors have reduced their capacity, including flights in our current and potential markets. Amid these changes in industry dynamics, we intend to maintain a disciplined growth strategy by increasing frequency on our existing routes and entering attractive new markets. Our future growth plans remain intact and we have ordered additional aircraft above and beyond our pre-September 11, 2001 plans.

While the airline industry suffered unprecedented losses in 2001, we had net income of $38.5 million and operating income of $26.8 million on revenues of $320.4 million. Operating income excluded $18.7 million of compensation under the Air Transportation Safety and System Stabilization Act, or the Stabilization Act. Due to our low fares, our yields during this period were lower than all but one of the major U.S. airlines. However, our low fares together with our high quality service offering enabled us to generate a load factor (the percentage of aircraft seating capacity actually utilized) of 78.0%, higher than any of the major U.S. airlines, which had load factors ranging from 57.6% to 76.0%, with an average of 69.7% in 2001. We also generated an operating margin of 8.4%, higher than all but one of the major U.S. airlines in 2001, according to reports by those airlines.

The airline industry is highly competitive and we expect competition to continue in the future. Many of our competitors have higher maintenance costs due to the age of their fleets and significantly higher labor costs because, among other things, they have a unionized workforce with unproductive work rules and more complex operations which decrease employee productivity and increase costs. We expect our maintenance costs to significantly increase as our fleet ages, and we may experience greater labor costs in the future. We also have a limited operating history. Our accumulated deficit at December 31, 2001 was $33.1 million. Upon closing of this offering, all the outstanding shares of our convertible redeemable preferred stock will convert into common stock and $35.8 million of accrued dividends will be cancelled, resulting in an increase to stockholders' equity. As a result of these factors and other risks described in this prospectus, we may encounter difficulties in implementing our strategy and we cannot assure you that we will succeed in achieving our goals.

In recent years, airline passengers have become increasingly dissatisfied with airline travel due to flight delays and cancellations, overbooking of flights, complicated fare structures, mishandled

FIGURE 6.4 (continued)

baggage and lack of customer care. The potential to stimulate demand through low fares coupled with the high level of dissatisfaction among airline customers provides an opportunity for JetBlue. We seek to provide a high-quality flying experience, emphasizing safety, security, reliability, customer service and low fares.

Our Competitive Strengths

Our principal competitive strengths are:

Low Operating Costs. Our cost per available seat mile of 6.98 cents for 2001 was lower than any of the major U.S. airlines, which reported an average cost per available seat mile of 10.08 cents, excluding compensation under the Stabilization Act. As adjusted for the average number of miles flown per flight, we believe our cost per available seat mile was lower than all but one of the major U.S. airlines, excluding compensation under the Stabilization Act.

New All Airbus A320 Fleet. By using our strong capital base, we have been able to acquire a fleet of new aircraft. This sets us apart from most other low-fare airlines. The A320 is a reliable, fuel-efficient and versatile aircraft that can be utilized for both short-haul and long-haul flights.

Strong Brand. We believe that we have made significant progress in establishing a strong brand that helps to distinguish us from our competitors by seeking to be identified as a safe, reliable, low-fare airline that is highly focused on customer service and that provides an enjoyable flying experience.

Strong Company Culture. We have created a strong and vibrant service-oriented company culture, which is built around our five key values: safety, caring, integrity, fun and passion. We reinforce our culture by explaining to our employees the importance of customer service and safety and the need to remain productive and keep our costs low.

Well-Positioned in New York, the Nation's Largest Travel Market. Our primary base of operations at New York's JFK airport provides us access to a market of approximately 21 million potential customers in the New York metropolitan area and about 6 million potential customers within 15 miles of the airport.

Proven Management Team. Our Chief Executive Officer, David Neeleman, was the president and one of the founders of Morris Air, a successful low-fare airline that was acquired by Southwest Airlines, and a founder of WesJet. David Barger, our President and Chief Operating Officer, was vice president in charge of Continental Airlines' Newark hub from 1994 to 1998. Our Chief Financial Officer, John Owen, spent 14 years as treasurer of Southwest Airlines.

Advanced Technology. We make use of advanced technology in many ways. For instance, all of our pilots use laptop computers in the cockpit to calculate the weight and balance of the aircraft and to access their manuals in electronic format during the flight. We recently commenced installation of cabin security cameras on each of our aircraft with a live feed to the cockpit crew and, when on the ground, to our central operations center at JFK.

Our Strategy

Our goal is to establish JetBlue as a leading low-fare passenger airline by offering customers a differentiated product and high-quality customer service. The key elements of our strategy are:

Stimulate Demand. Our widely available low fares and superior product offering are designed to stimulate demand, particularly from fare-conscious leisure and business travelers who might otherwise have used alternative forms of transportation or would not have traveled at all.

Emphasize Low Operating Costs. We are focused on using technology to improve efficiency, and we believe that our fleet of identical new aircraft, ticketless reservation system, high percentage of website bookings and other initiatives, will help us reduce our costs.

Offer Point-to-Point Flights to Overpriced or Underserved Large Markets. We focus on point-to-point service to large metropolitan areas with high average fares or highly-traveled markets that are underserved. In selecting future markets, we plan to continue to follow this strategy. We further intend to penetrate our key markets by increasing the number of flights per day to existing destinations, which we believe present us with additional growth opportunities.

Differentiate Our Product and Service. We offer our passengers a unique flying experience by providing new aircraft, simple and low fares, leather seats, free LiveTV at every seat, pre-assigned seating, reliable performance and high-quality customer service.

Corporate Information

JetBlue Airways Corporation was incorporated in Delaware in August 1998. Our principal executive offices are located at 80-02 Kew Gardens Road, Kew Gardens, New York 11415 and our telephone number is (718) 286-7900. Our website address is www.jetblue.com. Information contained on our website is not a prospectus and does not constitute part of this prospectus.

FIGURE 6.4	(continued)

THE OFFERING

Common stock offered	5,866,667 shares
Common stock estimated to be outstanding immediately after this offering	40,945,496 shares
Over-allotment option	880,000 shares
Use of proceeds	We intend to use the net proceeds, together with existing cash, for working capital and capital expenditures, including capital expenditures related to the purchase of aircraft. See "Use of Proceeds."
Dividends	We have not declared or paid any dividends on our common stock. We currently intend to retain our future earnings, if any, to finance the further expansion and continued growth of our business.
Nasdaq National Market symbol	"JBLU"

Except as otherwise noted, all information in this prospectus assumes:

- the automatic conversion of all outstanding shares of our convertible redeemable preferred stock into 30,692,262 shares of common stock upon completion of this offering; and
- no exercise of the underwriters' over-allotment option.

The figures above are based on 35,078,829 shares of common stock outstanding as of February 28, 2002 and assume no exercise of outstanding options since that date. The number of shares of common stock to be outstanding after this offering excludes:

- 6,510,001 shares of common stock authorized for issuance under our stock option plans, of which 4,328,380 shares were subject to outstanding options at a weighted average exercise price of $4.38 per share as of February 28, 2002; and
- 1,500,000 shares of common stock authorized for issuance under our employee stock purchase plan following this offering.

---

one celebrated case in 1980, Massachusetts initially refused to allow the first publicly issued shares of Apple Computer to be sold in the state.[12]

Securities Regulation in Other Countries

Securities are regulated in most countries. Generally, securities regulation throughout the world is modeled more or less closely after U.S. regulation. The main goal is to ensure fair, orderly, and open securities markets. Let's briefly look at securities regulation in three other countries.

In Canada, securities regulation is more a provincial than a national responsibility. Because Toronto is Canada's largest business center and the home of the country's largest stock exchange, the Ontario Securities Commission is probably the most important regulatory body in the country. The Ontario Securities Commission is closely patterned after the U.S. SEC, often following the SEC's lead to adopt rule changes. For example, in 1993 the commission passed a series of rules concerning the disclosure of CEO pay similar to rules passed by the SEC a few years earlier.

The Ministry of Finance is the principal regulatory body for securities trading in Japan. All public security issues require the approval of the Ministry of

---

[12]Massachusetts regulators relented a few days after Apple went public in December 1980 and allowed the stock to be sold to state residents.

Finance, and its reporting and public disclosure requirements are similar to the SEC's. Further, it licenses all securities firms and brokers. The ministry used to impose severe restrictions on foreign access to the Japanese capital markets, especially the bond markets. In recent years, however, the Ministry of Finance liberalized some of these restrictions.

Germany differs from Japan and the United States in that no regulatory walls separate the banking and securities businesses. As we noted in the prior chapter, the secondary markets for both stocks and bonds in Germany are essentially interbank markets. Consequently, the German central bank, the Bundesbank, assumes the major responsibility for securities regulation in Germany. It must approve all public security issues, and it is responsible for maintaining orderly secondary markets. The German capital markets are among the most open in the world to foreign (i.e., non-German) participants.

Industry Self-Regulation

In the United States and most other countries, the securities industry is heavily self-regulated by professional associations and the major financial markets. Industry participants recognize that rules and regulations designed to ensure fair and orderly markets will promote investor confidence to the benefit of all participants. Two examples of self-regulation are the rules of conduct established by the various professionals organizations and the market surveillance techniques used by the major securities markets.

Professional Rules of Conduct Prodded initially by federal legislation, the National Association of Securities Dealers (NASD) established, and periodically updates, rules of conduct for members (both individuals and firms). These rules try to ensure that brokers perform their basic functions honestly and fairly, under constant supervision. Failure to adhere to rules of conduct can result in a variety of disciplinary actions. The NASD also established a formal arbitration procedure through which investors can attempt to resolve disputes with brokers without litigation.[13]

Many investment professionals such as security analysts and mutual fund managers are chartered financial analysts (or CFAs). CFAs are required to adhere to the Association for Investment Management & Research (AIMR) Standards of Professional Conduct. CFAs who fail to adhere to the professional conduct standards can be disciplined and even lose their CFA certification.

Market Surveillance Like all major financial markets, the NYSE uses a series of market surveillance techniques. Trading activity is monitored continuously throughout the trading day. A key technical tool is Stock Watch, an electronic monitoring system that flags unusual price and volume activity. NYSE personnel then investigate to seek explanations for unusual activity from the member firms and companies involved. In addition, all market participants must keep detailed records of every aspect of every trade (called an *audit trail*). The

---

[13]When an investor first opens an account, he or she may be required to sign a form agreeing to submit any future disputes to NASD-sponsored arbitration before filing a lawsuit.

INVESTMENT INSIGHT

Improving the Quality of Company Boards

Many critics contend that corporate boards often fail in their fundamental role of protecting the rights and interests of ordinary shareholders. Too many are dominated by insiders, or others, who owe primary allegiance to the CEO. So-called outside directors, are independent in name only.

As a result of the wave of corporate scandals involving public companies, the NYSE recently instituted a set of rules regarding the composition of corporate boards. These rules apply to all firms whose shares are listed on the exchange, and include the following main points:

- Listed companies must have a majority of independent directors.
- The definition of *independent director* is tightened. For instance, no one qualifies as "independent" unless the board affirmatively determines that the director has no material relationship with the listed company.
- To empower independent directors to serve as a more effective check on management, they must meet at regularly scheduled executive sessions without management present.
- All listed companies must be subject to a nominating/corporate governance committee composed entirely of independent directors.
  - Listed companies must have a compensation committee (the committee that determines compensation for the CEO) composed entirely of independent directors.
  - Independent directors must constitute the majority of members of the audit committee. Only the audit committee has the authority to hire or fire auditors and to approve any significant nonaudit relationship with the auditors.

Questions for Critical Thinking

1. Why is industry self-regulation so important?
2. Some contend that the NYSE's regulations make it more difficult for firms to find qualified individuals to serve on boards. Do you agree or disagree?

NYSE's enforcement division acts as its prosecutorial arm and may impose a variety of penalties on members. Further, the exchange turns over evidence to the SEC for further action if it believes that violations of federal securities laws may have occurred.

In addition to market surveillance, the NYSE also imposes a set of regulations on firms whose shares are listed on the exchange. These regulations often exceed those imposed on the firms by government regulators. For instance, the NYSE adopted a strict set of regulations concerning requirements for board members. Critics complain that complacent and ineffective boards are one of the major problems in corporate governance and contributed to the recent corporate scandals. The Investment Insight box on this page outlines these rules.

Although the NYSE probably has as effective a market surveillance system as any financial market in the world and carefully polices the activities of its members, some contend that the Nasdaq Stock Market is sometimes lax in enforcement of trading rules. After a two-year investigation, the SEC formally censured the Nasdaq in 1996. The SEC found that some market makers were engaged in price fixing by not allowing some investors news of the best prices available for particular issues. The investigation also uncovered evidence of market makers refusing to honor public quotes to buy and sell stocks, even suspicious delays in reporting trades. In response, the NASD agreed to a sweeping set of reforms, including new oversight of market makers and greater penalties for violators.

Many contend these changes lowered, though did not eliminate, the chances of small investors being ripped off, but they did boost investor confidence in the fairness of the Nasdaq Stock Market.

This chapter outlined how investor's participate in the financial markets, from choosing a broker to the types of orders investors can place. We also described the various ways investors are protected from abusive practices. In the next two chapters we take a look at how well the financial markets function and how investors make investment decisions.

SUMMARY

1. How should investors choose a broker?
In order to trade, investors usually establish an account with a brokerage firm. An investor's individual characteristics and needs should be considered when choosing a brokerage firm. Full-service firms offer detailed investment advice, along with order execution and record keeping. They also charge higher commissions. Discount brokerage firms offer less advice but charge lower commissions. Deep-discount brokerage firms offer virtually no advice, but charge rock-bottom commissions. It is possible to buy some securities without a broker by investing directly with the company.

2. What are the various types of orders placed by investors?
Most investors place market orders that instructs their broker to obtain the best possible price. Market orders are executed slightly differently on the NYSE and the Nasdaq Stock Market. Other types of orders include limit orders and stop-loss orders. Investors may be able to buy securities on margin, which means they borrow some of the funds used to purchase the securities. Margin buying increases the investor's potential return as well as the risk. A short sale is the process of selling a stock now with the hope of buying it back later at a lower price. Short selling is a way of speculating on price declines and can be quite risky.

3. What is cybertrading?
Today thousands of investors use their personal computers and the Internet to trade. Online trading and brokerage firms are growing rapidly, mainly because of price and convenience. However, online trading has drawbacks and is not for all investors. Day trading is the process of trading stocks over short periods of time to take advantage of expected short-term price movements. Day trading is extremely risky and most day traders lose money.

4. What are block trades and program trading?
Block trades involve trades of at least 10,000 shares, or $200,000 worth of securities. About half of all trades in the stock market are block trades. Many block trades are handled off the floor of the exchanges in the third market. Program trading involves the computerized execution of trades at prespecified prices. One of the best-known forms of program trading involves the simultaneous trading of stocks and stock index futures. Some argue that program trading aggravates market volatility, and the NYSE has rules to limit program trading during highly volatile trading days.

5. Who regulates the financial markets and protects investors?
Financial markets are heavily regulated. In the United States, the federal Securities and Exchange Commission is the main regulatory body. Its regulations are designed to ensure fair and orderly markets where information is fully and fairly disclosed. Securities regulations in other countries follow the U.S. model. In addition, the financial markets are self-regulated. Most professional associations require members to adhere to a code of conduct.

MINI CASE

This mini case illustrates the various types or orders and trades.

Today is Monday, January 6. You placed an order this morning to buy 500 shares of The Gap. Answer the following questions about the order, assuming that The Gap is currently trading for $30 a share and your broker charges a commission of .75% of the total trade value.

1. If you placed a market order, how much would you owe your broker, and when would the payment be due?
2. If you placed a limit order to buy (limit 28), and made it good till canceled, what would happen to your order?
3. If you bought the stock on margin, with an initial margin requirement of 50% and a maintenance requirement of 30%, how much cash would you be required to deposit initially?
4. Using the information from Question 3, at what price would you face a margin call?
5. Compute your return on both a cash transaction and a margin transaction, assuming you bought The Gap at $30 and sold it one year later for $50. Assume your margin loan carries an annual rate of interest of 4.5%.

REVIEW EXERCISES

1. Explain the various types of brokerage firms. In general, what type of investor is better off using a full-service firm? A discount, or deep-discount firm?
2. Is it possible to buy stock without using a broker? Explain how dividend reinvestment plans work.
3. Explain how a market order would be executed on the NYSE and on the Nasdaq. What role does the NYSE specialist and Nasdaq market maker play in market orders?
4. What is a limit order? How does a stop-loss order differ from a limit order?
5. Assume you buy 200 shares of stock at $100 on margin. Your broker requires a 50% initial margin and a 35% maintenance margin. If the stock rises to $110, what will be the total in your margin account? Assume the stock price falls to $90, what will be the total in your margin account.
6. Using the information from Question 5, find the price at which you will face a margin call. What will happen if you fail to meet the margin call?
7. Explain why online trading grew so rapidly in recent years. What is day trading?
8. Explain block trades and program trading. Discuss why both increased in recent years.
9. What federal agency has most of the regulatory responsibility over the financial markets? When, and why was this agency created?
10. Define the term *full and fair disclosure*. Give an example of a trading practice that violates federal securities law.

CRITICAL THINKING EXERCISES

1. This exercise requires library or Internet research. Major financial markets regularly publish information on "short interest." Markets list the stocks with the largest short positions, along with the issues that experienced the greatest change in short activity. Find a recent report on short interest and answer the following questions:
   a. List the three stocks with the largest short positions. Why do you believe so much short activity occurred with these five stocks?
   b. Identify the three stocks that show the greatest change in short activity (both increases as well as decreases in the number of short positions). List some reasons why so much change occurred in the short activity of these stocks.

2. This exercise requires library or Internet research. Regulation FD is designed to prohibit selective disclosure of material nonpublic information. The regulation, however,
   is controversial. Some contend that, far from increasing the amount of information
   companies disclose, Regulation FD will cause companies to clam up. Using your
   research skills, research the current state of Regulation FD. Do you feel it increased or
   decreased the amount of information companies disclose? Choose several large public
   companies and see how they instituted Regulation FD. (A good starting point is the
   investor section of each company's Web site.)

THE INTERNET INVESTOR

1. The National Association of Securities Dealers (NASD) is directly involved in industry
   self-regulation of the financial markets. Go to its Web site (www.nasd.com) and read
   about NASD programs regarding dispute resolution between investors and brokerage
   firms. Prepare a short report on how the arbitration process works.
2. Visit the Web site of a brokerage firm that offers online trading (such as E*TRADE,
   www.etrade.com, or Charles Schwab, www.schwab.com) to learn more about online
   trading. Most electronic brokerage firms also offer a trading demonstration. Use the
   demonstration to see how you obtain price information, company news, place buy or
   sell orders, and check account balances.
3. Use your Web browser to research a company whose stock you may be interested in
   buying. Most companies provide financial results and other information on their
   Web sites. Other sites to visit include Quicken (www.quicken.com), Morningstar
   (www.morningstar.net), Microsoft Investor (investor.msn.com), and the SEC's Edgar
   database (www.sec.gov/edgar). Prepare a brief report to your class about the company
   you selected.

7

Market Efficiency:
Concept and Reality

PREVIOUSLY . . .	IN THIS CHAPTER . . .	TO COME . . .
We discussed how the financial markets are organized and regulated, and how investors participate in the financial markets.	We examine the efficient markets hypothesis, the notion that security prices reflect all available information. This hypothesis presents many important implications for investors. Although more and more evidence suggests that the markets are less efficient than often believed, one can still conclude that it is difficult to beat the market consistently on a risk-adjusted basis.	We discuss the two techniques by which many professional investors make their decisions and recommendations: technical and fundamental analysis. We describe both techniques, as well as examine their successes and failures.

CHAPTER OBJECTIVES

After reading Chapter 7, you should be able to answer the following questions:

1. What is the efficient markets hypothesis?

2. What are the three traditional forms of market efficiency?

3. How is the efficient markets hypothesis tested?

4. What evidence supports the efficient markets hypothesis?

5. Can investors profit from anomalies?

One of the most controversial and far-reaching concepts to emerge from invest-ments theory over the past 40 years is the **efficient markets hypothesis (EMH)**, sometimes referred to as the random walk theory. In a nutshell, EMH states that securities prices fluctuate randomly around their respective intrinsic values. Intrinsic values, in turn, rationally reflect all relevant publicly available informa-tion and perhaps even privately available information as well. Prices adjust quickly to new information, which also enters the market in a random fashion. A logical conclusion from the efficient markets hypothesis is that no person or system can accurately and consistently predict short-term movements in securities prices.

> **efficient markets hypothesis (EMH)**
>
> The notion that security prices reflect all available information.

The efficient markets hypothesis has many strong proponents; most financial economists and many Wall Street practitioners believe in the EMH, at least up to a point. The proponents cite large amounts of evidence, both scientific and anec-dotal, to support the concept of market efficiency. A fair amount of evidence sug-gests, for example, that past price patterns provide virtually no information about future price patterns.

Not surprisingly, many others dismiss ideas such as efficient markets and security prices following random walks as nonsense. The detractors point to evi-dence, some anecdotal and some more scientific, and many common situations that seem to contradict the concept of market efficiency. In his book, *What Works on Wall Street*, respected money manager James O'Shaughnessy writes:

The long-term evidence in this book contradicts the random walk theory. Far from stocks following a random walk, the evidence reveals a purposeful stride. The 43 years of data found in this book prove strong return predictability. The market clearly and consistently rewards certain attributes.[1]

In this chapter, we examine both the concept and reality of market efficiency. In doing so, we try to answer two main questions: Just how efficient are the mar-kets? and What does it all mean for investors?

RANDOM WALKS AND EFFICIENT MARKETS

In the early 1950s, a statistician named Maurice Kendall was analyzing several eco-nomic time series using a new tool, the computer, when he discovered, to his surprise, that changes in stock prices appeared to be almost random in nature. On any given day, a positive price change was as likely as a negative price change. Furthermore, Kendall concluded, past price patterns could not reliably predict future price patterns.

At first glance, Kendall's findings, which several other researchers replicated, seemed to suggest that stock markets behaved almost irrationally. Perhaps prices were determined, not by rational valuation, but by the erratic behavior of investors. Some financial economists soon realized, however, that Kendall's find-ings might mean something quite different. Perhaps, random price changes were not the results of irrational markets but rather the results of well-functioning markets in which prices rationally reflect all available information and adjust quickly to new information. The concept of market efficiency was born.

---

[1]James O'Shaughnessy, *What Works on Wall Street* (New York: McGraw-Hill, 1996), p. 5.

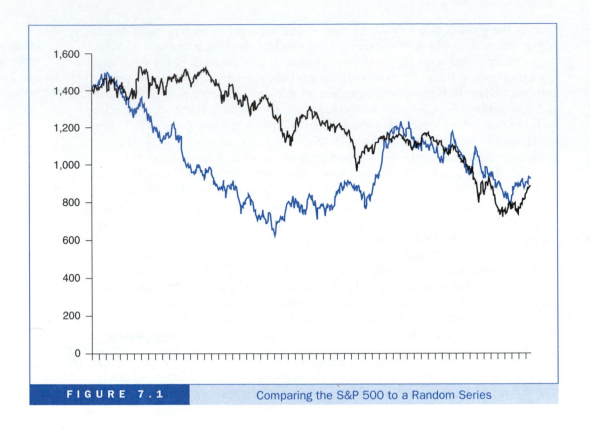

What Is a Random Walk?

random walk

A stochastic time series in which each successive change in a variable is drawn independently from a distribution with a constant mean and variance.

Kendall's discovery about the time series behavior of stock prices is commonly referred to as a random walk. Mathematically, a **random walk** is a stochastic time series in which each successive change in a variable is drawn independently from a probability distribution with a constant mean and variance. What does it mean to say that stock prices follow a random walk?

To answer this question, assume the following time series best describes the behavior of stock prices:

$$P_t = P_{t-1} + a_t \tag{7.1}$$

where $a \simeq N(\mu, \sigma^2)$. Equation 7.1 identifies a random walk as one of many possibilities. It says that today's price is equal to yesterday's price, plus a random variable, a. Each random variable is drawn from a normally distributed population with a mean of μ and a variance of σ^2. The change in price, $P_t - P_{t-1}$ equals the random variable, a_t.

Take a look at the charts shown in Figure 7.1 and Figure 7.2. In the first chart, one of the two series is the daily close for the S&P 500 over a recent three-year period. The other series consists of a random walk, much like the one defined by Equation 7.1. The random series also begins at the same point, but each subsequent value equals the prior value plus a random variable. Each random variable is drawn from a normal distribution with a mean of −0.65 and a

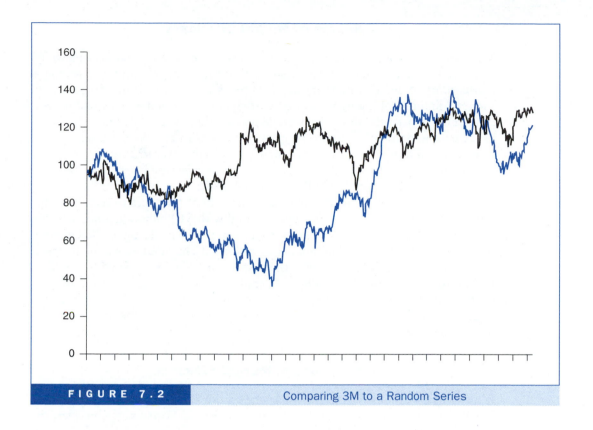

FIGURE 7.2   Comparing 3M to a Random Series

standard deviation of 17.05 (the same mean and standard deviation of the daily changes for the S&P 500). In the second chart, shown in Figure 7.2, one of the two series is the daily closing price for 3M, while the second is a random series constructed in a similar fashion to the random series shown in Figure 7.1.

By examining both charts, can you tell which series is which? If you guessed that the index and stock price are the blue series, you are correct. The black series are the random walks. This example demonstrates an important point: It is easy to see patterns in stock prices, even if none exist. The series produced by the random walks appear to look a lot like the stock index and stock price series.

Random Walks and Forecasting

Suppose that a time series of stock prices is best described by the random walk model in Equation 7.1 and someone wants to forecast its behavior. What will the forecast look like? Assume that, based on a history of price observations, P_0, P_1, P_2, . . . P_T, an analyst wants to forecast tomorrow's price, P_{T+1}. Based on all the information contained in the historical price series, if the series follows a random walk, then it turns out that the best forecast of tomorrow's price is actually today's price, P_T plus the mean of the random variable, a. We talk about this forecast a bit more later, but as you can probably already see, if stock prices do follow a random walk, the value of investment techniques that rely solely on historical price patterns can be seriously questioned.

Source of Market Efficiency

Why should anyone expect financial markets to be efficient markets in which prices reflect all available information? In a word, the answer to this question is *competition*. Financial markets in most parts of the world are competitive. Literally millions of highly motivated participants (both individuals and institutions) hunt constantly for above-average profits (the "best" investments).

After one participant discovers an investment with an above-average return, how long will it take before other participants also discover it? Probably not long in a highly competitive market. As participants discover the investment, they bid up its price quickly, eliminating the abnormal profit.

Further, many participants can devote substantial resources to search for the best investments. Say that a stock mutual fund with $10 billion in assets believes that buying the right stocks will boost its annual performance by 0.5%. One-half of 1% of $10 billion is $50 million. How much will this fund be willing to spend on research and analysis to uncover the best stocks? The fund probably would be willing to spend up to $50 million. Beating so many investors who have such deep pockets to the best investments is not easy. Perhaps this elusive search for abnormal profits by so many investors is the single most important source of market efficiency.

Implications of Market Efficiency

If the markets are really efficient, what implications would the market efficiency theory have for some popular investment techniques? For some techniques, the EMH has quite a bit to say.

technical analysis

Investment technique based on the notion that security prices follow recurrent and predictable patterns.

Technical Analysis As discussed in the next chapter, many professional investors and investment advisors rely on one of two techniques when making investment decisions: technical and fundamental analysis. Technical analysis is based on the notion that security prices follow recurrent and fairly predictable patterns. Thus, by looking at historical prices an investor can reasonably predict future prices. As pointed out already, if stock prices follow a random walk, the best forecast of tomorrow's price is today's price plus the mean of some random variable. This formula is rarely a reliable forecast. Furthermore, the EMH argues that current security prices already reflect all available information. Therefore, even if information were contained in historical prices, the EMH concludes that current prices already reflect this information. Consequently, the EMH hypothesis argues that technical analysis will not produce above average investment profits over the long run.

fundamental analysis

Investment technique based on the notion that every security eventually sells for its intrinsic value.

Fundamental Analysis Fundamental analysis is based on the belief that every security eventually sells for its intrinsic value, and therefore fundamental analysts constantly hung for under- or overvalued securities. The EMH argues that if analysts rely solely on historical data, and current, publicly available information, their recommendations cannot consistently produce abnormal profits because security prices already fully reflect this information. Rather, an analyst must have superior forecasting ability to beat the market, gaining insight into the fundamental factors that drive stock prices before other market participants recognize them. As explored in the next chapter, forecasting these fundamental factors is quite difficult.

Active vs. Passive Portfolio Management In Chapter 1, we briefly discussed the differences between passive and active portfolio management; a buy-and-hold philosophy versus more frequent trading in anticipation of price movements. The EMH casts doubts on the possibility that an actively managed portfolio can produce consistently superior returns over a passively management one (assuming both have similar risk characteristics). Because the EMH argues that security prices already reflect all available information, regularly finding under- or overvalued securities is difficult, especially because active investors pay higher transactions costs (brokerage commissions, for example) and perhaps taxes.[2]

Market efficiency, however, does not imply that a specific investor should never make changes to his or her portfolio. Changes should be made as a person's income, family situation, and other factors change. Even in an efficient market, the appropriate portfolio for a 25-year-old is significantly different from that of a 65-year-old.

TRADITIONAL FORMS OF MARKET EFFICIENCY

Earlier, we noted that market efficiency implies that security prices rationally reflect all available information. Using different assumptions about the meaning of the phrase *all available information,* we traditionally distinguished between three levels, or forms, of market efficiency: the weak form, the semi-strong form, and the strong form. Let's briefly define each.

Weak Form Market Efficiency

Weak form market efficiency states that current security prices fully reflect all historical information. Further, weak form efficiency states that investors cannot earn abnormal returns by using historical information. Historical information includes not just price information, but information on trading volume, short interest, odd lots, and other variables. Weak form efficiency also implies that security prices do not follow patterns that are either recurrent or predictable. Instead, it suggests that security prices follow a random walk.

A technical analyst may develop a trading model based on past prices over the prior 60 months, buying stock when his or her model gives one signal and selling when the model gives another. Weak form market efficiency does not imply that the trading model would not generate a profit, just that the profit would match that of someone who simply bought and held the same stock over the same period (adjusting for differences in risk and transactions costs).

> **weak form market efficiency**
> Current prices fully reflect all historical information.

Semi-Strong Form Market Efficiency

Semi-strong form market efficiency states that security prices reflect all public information and react almost instantaneously to new public information. Public information includes all historical information and adds all public information

> **semi-strong form market efficiency**
> Prices fully reflect all public information.

---

[2]For taxable investors, capital gains are taxed only when realized—when a security is actually sold at a profit. Capital gains that are not realized are not taxed. Because active investors trade more frequently than passive investors, they realize more capital gains and, therefore, lose some of their profits to taxes.

on a company's product lines, its financial policies, the quality of its management, and so forth. Therefore, semi-strong form efficient markets are also weak form efficient, although weak form efficiency does not necessarily imply semi-strong form efficiency.

As an example of semi-strong form efficiency, consider a company that announces quarterly earnings 10% higher than analysts were forecasting. This news is good, and the price of the company's stock should increase after the announcement. Semi-strong form efficiency says, however, that buying the stock after the public earnings announcement would fail to consistently produce abnormal returns. Why? The reason is simply because prices would adjust quickly to the new information, so the price at the time of the purchase would fully reflect the new information.

Strong Form Market Efficiency

strong form market efficiency

Prices fully reflect all public and private information

Strong form market efficiency makes the extreme statement that security prices reflect not only all public information, but all private information as well. Again, price reactions to new information, whether public or private, occur rapidly. Thus, even insiders with access to confidential information (e.g., corporate officers) cannot make abnormal returns consistently.

Few would dispute that corporate insiders may be able to access valuable information before the general investing public. Indeed, as we discussed in the prior chapter, a principal focus of securities regulation is to prevent insiders from exploiting their potential information advantage. Laws that prohibit such practices as insider trading are examples of attempts to limit the information advantage of insiders. Government regulators, as well as the NYSE and other major financial markets, closely monitor records of trading activity, looking for abuses of inside information.

TESTING MARKET EFFICIENCY

As you review the evidence on market efficiency in the next two sections, keep in mind the type of tests and the benchmarks used, as well as several other related topics. These issues make interpreting the evidence somewhat subjective. In our opinion, the debate on market efficiency is likely to continue indefinitely and may never be settled one way or the other.

Types of Tests

Several methods can be used test the EMH. Analysts have devised direct and indirect tests of market efficiency. Direct tests assess the success of specific investment strategies or trading rules. An example of a direct test would be a test of the accuracy of predictions by some specific technical indicator, such as moving averages or filters. Indirect tests include statistical tests of prices or returns. For example, if prices follow a random walk, the serial correlation of returns should be close to zero.

One can also test the efficient markets hypothesis by some scientific methodology or simply by looking for anecdotal evidence. A scientific experiment develops a research design based on a proven methodology. For example, we could scientifically examine market reactions to unexpected earnings announcements using a large sample over time. Results from the study would determine how rapidly the market responds to new public information. Anecdotal evidence involves looking for examples consistent, or inconsistent, with the EMH.

The conundrum, of course, is that all types of tests can be criticized. Critics can argue that the test was applied improperly, was inadequate to measure its target, or both. For example, direct tests of technical trading rules can always be criticized because testing these trading rules requires applying them mechanically. These tests cannot hope to capture the subjective portion of technical analysis that, technicians argue, helps investors exploit historical price patterns. Even if a test provides evidence consistent with the EMH, critics can always argue that the results were due to the test used, not necessarily the truth of the EMH.

Establishing a Benchmark

Tests of the EMH must usually establish some sort of a benchmark. For example, to say that some trading rule works, giving evidence inconsistent with the EMH, a test must find that a portfolio using the trading rule outperformed a similar portfolio that did not use the trading rule, generating abnormal profits. Like the type of test used, critics can always question whether the benchmark chosen was appropriate.

The most common benchmark is the so-called buy-and-hold portfolio. As an example, a test may want to evaluate a trading rule that indicates when to switch between a stock index fund and a money market fund. How well does the trading rule perform? It would have to earn higher profits (or returns) than the profits from simply buying and holding the stock index fund over the same period of time. Of course, the test must also account for differences in risk and transaction costs between the two investment strategies. Active trading strategies usually involve higher transaction costs, and they often expose a portfolio to more risk as well. Furthermore, because most investors pay taxes on realized capital gains, active strategies are usually less tax-efficient.

The Time Factor

On October 11, 1987, eight days before the market event popularly known as Meltdown Monday, Elaine Garzarelli, then a well-known technical analyst, predicted the upcoming market break. Was this prediction the result of her special insight into the market, application of her trading rules, or market inefficiency, or was this prediction merely luck? Of course, we will never know. In retrospect, it is easy to find investment strategies that produced abnormal profits. Believers will call it skill, and skeptics will call it luck. The proper test evaluates how well the strategy works over different time periods.

The time period(s) selected can, of course, always be criticized. One analyst, when confronted with a less-than-stellar recent record, commented to a television audience, that the current market was unusual and his system would begin to work once the market returned to "normal." Such an assertion cannot be proved or disproved without testing it over every single possible time period, a rather daunting task.

Kiss and Tell

Suppose that someone discovered an investment strategy that really worked and made a lot of money. Why would this person want to tell anyone? He or she could try to make money writing a book or an investment newsletter describing the strategy, but it would probably generate more money if kept secret. Suppose an analyst discovers that stocks beginning with the letter *K* rise on Wednesdays and fall on Fridays. Buying K stocks on Tuesdays and selling them on Thursdays makes the analyst lots of money. The dilemma, of course, is that once others know about the strategy, it will likely stop working. K stocks will probably start rising on Mondays and falling on Wednesdays as other investors try to anticipate the market. To avoid reducing its effectiveness, the analyst would probably keep the strategy a secret for as long as possible.

Seriously, some argue that the inclination to keep successful strategies secret introduces a bias into tests of market efficiency and trading rules. (It is called *sample selection bias*.) Only those strategies that do not work are widely reported and, consequently, tested. Strategies that do work are not reported, so the results are biased in favor of the EMH, showing that trading rules do not produce abnormal profits by testing inferior trading rules. If the successful trading rules are kept secret, perhaps we can never fairly test the true ability of investors or the validity of the EMH.

Qualitative vs. Quantitative Efficiency

We know that some investors pay more to trade than others. We also know that some investors can obtain information more cheaply than others. Perhaps we should replace the quantitative question "Are the markets efficient?" with the more qualitative question "How efficient are the markets?" In other words, market efficiency may mean different things to different investors.

We use an actual example to illustrate this point. One familiar NYSE specialist firm has a small trading operation in addition to its normal specialist duties. The trading operation attempts to make money for the firm by buying and selling NYSE-listed stocks other than those for which the firm is the specialist. The firm's traders use a variety of technical indicators and trading rules, and the trading operation appears to make abnormal profits pretty consistently.

Does that mean that the NYSE is not efficient? Not necessarily. For one thing, the specialist, being a member of the NYSE, pays virtually no transaction costs when it trades. For another, the firm rarely holds a position for more than a few minutes and never overnight. Through electronic links with the NYSE's SuperDOT system, the specialist firm's traders might buy 3,000 shares of Disney at 18 and then sell the shares a minute later for 18.15, making $450 (before transaction costs). The specialist tries to take advantage of what its traders believe are small temporary mispricing of NYSE-listed stocks. The vast majority of investors, even many so-called day traders, could never profitably duplicate this firm's trading strategy. (Perhaps this example suggests that the markets are efficient for the vast majority of investors, although not necessarily for a few investors with special advantages. In fact, one could argue that these investors help to contribute to market efficiency by correcting mispricing.)

TRADITIONAL TESTS OF THE EFFICIENT MARKETS HYPOTHESIS

In this section, we review some of the traditional tests of the three forms of the EMH, most of which appear to support the concept of market efficiency, at least in its weak and semi-strong forms. We examine tests based on historical prices, how rapidly the market reacts to new public information, and the value of private, or inside, information.

The vast majority of tests of the efficient markets hypothesis examined the efficiency of U.S. stock markets. A few studies attempted to test the efficiency of non-U.S. markets for stocks and other securities. The studies suggest that foreign markets may be at least as efficient as U.S. markets.

Usefulness of Historical Prices

Tests of trading based on historical prices essentially evaluate the weak form theory of market efficiency: that security prices fully reflect all historical information. These tests fall into two general categories: tests of the random nature of security prices and returns, and tests of specific trading rules.

Tests of the Random Nature of Security Prices and Returns Tests of the randomness of securities prices over time relied primarily on two statistical techniques: serial correlation and a so-called runs test. Both of these techniques have many other applications, as discussed in detail in most standard business statistics textbooks. Briefly, serial correlation measures the strength of the relationship between the current value of a time series (e.g., stock returns) and past share values. If stock prices follow something like the random walk described in Equation 7.1, serial correlation coefficients should be close to zero.

A runs test counts the number of times that price changes, each one designated positive or negative, change signs over a specific time period. For example, say 10 days of price changes produce this series: $+, +, -, -, -, +, -, +, +$. This sequence has five runs (the first three positive changes, the next three negative changes, a positive change, a negative change, and the final two positive changes). Now consider the following sequence of 10 price changes: $+, +, +, +, +, +, -, -, -, -$. This sequence has just two runs (the first six positive changes and the final four negative changes). Too many, or too few, runs suggests that a series is not random.

The results of these statistical tests from many studies strongly suggested that stock prices and returns are essentially random, thus providing evidence in support of weak form market efficiency. For example, a test of price changes for each of the Dow Jones Industrial Average's 30 stocks over several years found that the average serial correlation coefficient was virtually equal to zero. This study also conducted runs tests on price changes for each of the 30 Dow stocks (also over a period of several years) and found evidence supporting the contention that the price series were essentially random.

Let's conduct our own test of the randomness of security prices, using the two series shown in Figure 7.1, one the S&P 500 index, the other a random series. We

TABLE 7.1		Series	
Test of Randomness: S&P 500 vs. a Random Series	Autocorrelation (lag)	S&P 500	Random Walk
	−1	.0033	−.0527
	−2	−.0847	−.0317
	−3	−.0304	.0550
	−4	.0255	.0435
	−5	−.0098	−.0117
	Runs Test		
	Actual	118	112
	Expected*	114	114

[a]Based on an assumption that the series is random.

compute several serial correlation coefficients and conduct a runs test on the daily changes for each series. We expect changes in the random walk should probably be random, but what about price changes for the index? The results are shown in Table 7.1.

The serial correlation coefficients are essentially equal to zero. These results confirm that today's price change provides virtually no information about tomorrow's price change. The results of the runs tests reinforce the random nature of price changes for both series. The actual numbers of runs in both series are not significantly different from the number of runs expected for a random series.

Tests of Trading Rules In addition to tests of the randomness of security prices and returns, several studies examined trading rules based on historical prices to see whether they produce abnormal profits. Weak form efficiency, of course, states that such trading rules cannot produce abnormal profits. Again, the extensive evidence generally supports weak form efficiency. Let's look at one example of a trading rule, filter rules.

Essentially, a filter rule states that if a stock rises $X\%$ from its most recent low (called a support level), buy it because it defines an up trend. Similarly, if a stock declines by $Y\%$ from its most recent high (called a resistance level), then sell the stock and hold cash (or sell the stock short if you do not own it) because the stock defines a down trend.

How well do filter rules perform? Not very well, suggests some of the scientific evidence. One study compared buy-sell filters between 0.5% and 5% on each of the Dow Jones Industrial Average's 30 stocks against a simple buy-and-hold portfolio of those stocks. Only the smallest filter, 0.5%, outperformed the buy-and-hold portfolio, on average. The difference in performance, however, disappeared once the authors considered the higher transaction costs associated with the actively managed portfolio. Portfolios based on the larger filters all underperformed the buy-and-hold portfolio, even before accounting for higher transaction costs.

In a more recent study, Jeremy Siegel found that using a modified filter rule to make buy and sell decisions produced an average annual return of about 7.4% between 1990 and 2001. Figuring in transactions costs reduced this average annual return to 5.2%. By contrast, the average annual return from a buy-and-hold strategy was slightly more than 14% over the same period.[3]

We repeat a caveat about tests of trading rules: to allow testing, mechanical buy-and-sell criteria must be established. As we discussed earlier in this chapter, forecasts based on trading rules are often more subjective than objective by nature and difficult to replicate. No test can really evaluate the subjective portion of trading decisions.

Market Reaction to New Public Information

A huge amount of widely varying new public information enters the financial markets each day. Semi-strong form market efficiency states that security prices reflect all this information and react quickly to it. The reaction is so fast, in fact, that no one can consistently earn abnormal profits simply by buying or selling in response to the new public information. Studies examined market reactions to almost every conceivable type of new public information. Results of these studies generally support the semi-strong form of market efficiency. Let's look at some anecdotal evidence first.

On October 20, 1999, IBM announced that its third quarter earnings were substantially less than analysts had been expecting. Investors bolted for the doors and the stock lost about 20% of its value falling from 112.75 to near 90. Would you have avoided this debacle by selling IBM shares on October 20? Probably not unless you had access to the information early. You see, IBM made the announcement *after* the New York Stock Exchange closed for the day.[4] By the time the stock opened for trading the next day, October 21, the flood of sell orders overnight had already driven the opening price down to 90 1/8. IBM closed that day at 89.

This type of anecdotal evidence of semi-strong form market efficiency can be seen almost every day. Companies regularly make significant announcements with both negative and positive implications. In the majority of cases, much of the reaction either takes place before the announcement, or so quickly that most investors cannot profit from trading on the information. Scan today's business news on the Internet and you will probably find several examples similar to IBM's rapid price changes in response to new public information.

Scientific Evidence Of course, anecdotal evidence in and of itself does not prove that investors cannot earn abnormal returns by acting on new public information. To find stronger evidence in support of semi-strong form market efficiency, we need to turn to the various scientific studies. These studies, often called event studies, typically examine market reactions to specific kinds of announcements. They analyze a large group of similar announcements using a statistical methodology that measures returns different from what would be expected, given no new information (called abnormal returns or residuals). Semi-strong form market efficiency implies that no abnormal returns should consistently occur after the announcement date.

---

[3]Jeremy Siegel, *Stocks for the Long Run,* 3rd ed. (New York: McGraw-Hill, 2002), p. 293.
[4]Significant information is often released after the close of trading. The fact that new potentially market-moving information is released throughout the day is one reason cited by proponents of expanded after-hours trading.

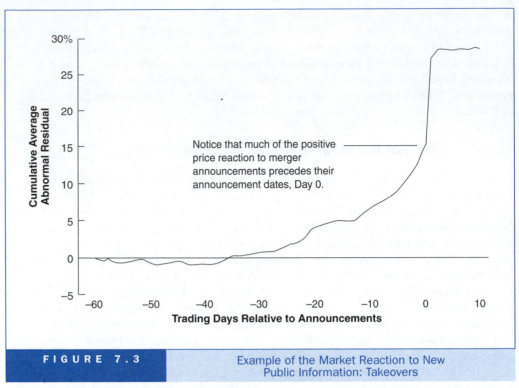

Notice that much of the positive price reaction to merger announcements precedes their announcement dates, Day 0.

| FIGURE 7.3 | Example of the Market Reaction to New Public Information: Takeovers |

Source: Arthur Keown and John Pinkerton, "Merger Announcements and Insider Trading Activity," *The Journal of Finance,* September 1981, pp. 855–70. Reprinted by permission of Blackwell.

To illustrate this approach, and the evidence presented by the vast majority of these studies, let's look at a classic study that examined market reactions to merger/takeover announcements.[5] As you know, shareholders of public companies that are taken over (often referred to as target shareholders) receive premium prices for their shares (prices higher than the existing market price). As a result, we would logically expect stock prices to jump in response to a takeover announcement. If the market is semi-strong form efficient, then this jump should occur before or on the announcement date, not afterward.

Figure 7.3 summarizes the researchers results. It plots the cumulative average abnormal return (CAAR) against time relative to day of the announcement (day 0). The CAAR starts to rise, slowly at first, starting about 30 days before the announcement (day −30) and the trend continues right up to the announcement date (day 0).[6] The two largest increases occur on the day before the announcement date (day −1) and the announcement date itself. The CAAR then exhibits random

---

[5]Arthur Keown and John Pikerton, "Merger Announcements and Insider Trading," *Journal of Finance,* September 1981, pp. 855–870.

[6]The CAAR is the sum of the average abnormal return up to day t, or $CAAR_t = AAR_t + CAAR_{t-1}$. In the absence of new information, the expected value of AAR is zero. Therefore, in the absence of new information, the CAAR should exhibit random drift near zero. If investors react the new information, then the CAAR should rise (positive information) or fall (negative information).

drift after the announcement date (day 11 through day 110). These findings suggest that any significant price reaction of a target company stock due to a takeover announcement occurs before the announcement date. No one can earn an abnormal profit by acting on this new public information after it enters the market. This study's results are, therefore, consistent with semi-strong form market efficiency.

One must guard against overinterpreting the results of this and other event studies. Assume that company A offers to buy company B for $50 cash per share. The price of company B's stock will jump on the announcement. If it does not jump to $50 per share, does it mean that the market is not semi-strong form efficient? Not necessarily; think of all the things that can happen once a takeover offer becomes public. For one, company A's bid may fail. Even if A does buy B, who knows, when the announcement is first made, just how long it will take to complete the deal. Alternatively, company A may be forced to raise its offer price. The point is that takeovers, and many other transactions, are complex and uncertain. As this uncertainty is resolved after the announcement, significant price reactions are likely to occur. The resolution of uncertainty can be thought of as new public information.

Value of Private Information

Tests of the value of inside, or private, information seek to evaluate strong-form market efficiency. These tests are perhaps the most difficult to conduct because it is impossible to pinpoint exactly when new private information, or inside information, enters the market. Further, the definition of inside information is ambiguous. Not surprisingly, the results from these studies are quite mixed.

One group of studies began with the assumption that mutual fund managers and securities analysts may have access to information before the general investing public. Securities analysts, for example, constantly talk to the companies they follow and may be able to learn some new information before it is made public. These studies then examined the performance of mutual funds or security analyst recommendations, compared with some benchmark.

Results from these studies generally show that neither mutual fund managers nor securities analysts appear, on average, to be capable of consistently outperforming the overall market, after adjusting for risk. In fact, the average stock mutual fund underperformed the S&P 500 over the past 10 years.

Does this evidence support strong form market efficiency, or does it cast doubt on the assumption that mutual fund managers have access to private information? Obviously, this question cannot be answered.

Event Studies Event studies provided more evidence about strong form efficiency. Notice that Figure 7.3 showed evidence of positive price movements in takeover stocks well before the public announcements. Does this evidence suggest that insiders were using private information about upcoming takeovers to make abnormal profits? The authors of the study thought so. They wrote, "Impending merger announcements are poorly held secrets, and trading on this nonpublic information abounds."[7]

---

[7]Keown and Pinkerton, "Merger Announcements," p. 855. Results of this and other studies prompted the SEC to crack down on insider trading starting in the mid-1980s.

Many more-recent event studies show the same pattern as Figure 7.3. Prices rise, or fall, before the public announcement date. Further, the rise or fall in prices is often gradual, not immediate, suggesting that one can earn abnormal returns by possessing material nonpublic information. Perhaps the markets are not strong form efficient. However, because no one knows when private information becomes available, or even what really constitutes private information, perhaps these findings show only that some investors are good at anticipating significant new public information. It is impossible to say one way or the other.

MARKET EFFICIENCY AND ANOMALIES

anomaly

A situation that appears to violate the traditional view of market efficiency.

In recent years, many so-called **anomalies** have been identified. Anomalies are situations that appear to violate the traditional view of market efficiency, suggesting that it may be possible for careful investors to earn higher risk-adjusted returns.

Some of the better-known anomalies are listed in Table 7.2. Most of the anomalies listed revolve around four themes:

1. Investors tend to overreact to new information, both positive and negative.
2. Value investing is contrarian in nature and is often profitable because investors tend to overreact.
3. The market consistently ignores certain stocks, especially small stocks.
4. All things being equal, it is sometimes more advantageous to buy stocks, and at other times it is better to avoid stocks.

Let's examine some of the major anomalies, why they exist, and what they mean for investors and the concept of market efficiency.

Do Investors Overreact?

One of the most intriguing issues to emerge in the past few years is the notion of market overreaction to new information, whether positive or negative. For years, many investment professionals insisted that markets do overreact. One momentous event some point to as perhaps an extreme example of investor overreaction is the 1987 market break. The Investment History box on page 170 recounts "Meltdown Monday."

Recent statistical evidence for both the market as a whole and individual securities shows errors in security prices that are systematic and therefore fairly predictable. Overreactions are sometimes called reversals. Stocks that perform poorly in one period suddenly reverse direction and start performing well in a subsequent period, and vice versa.

For example, Merck was one of the poorest-performing stocks among the Dow 30 during 1993, only to reverse direction and become among the top performers during 1994. In 1997 DuPont was among the best-performing stocks in the Dow 30. DuPont then reversed direction in 1998 and finished close to the bottom of Dow 30 in terms of total performance.

Anecdotal Evidence of Market Overreaction After the market closed on July 19, 1999, software giant Microsoft announced its quarterly earnings. On the surface the company's earnings were impressive. Earnings grew by more than 60%, compared with the same quarter in 1998, beating analyst forecasts by 5 cents

		TABLE 7.2
Low Price-Earnings Ratio	Stocks that are selling at price-earnings rations that are low relative to the market	Some Stock Market Anomalies
Low Price-Sales Ratio	Stocks that have price-to-sales ratios that are lower compared with other stocks in the same industry or with the overall market	
Low Price-to-Book Value Ratio	Stocks whose stock prices are less than their respective book values	
High Dividend Yield	Stocks that pay high dividends relative to their respective share prices	
Small Companies	Stocks of companies whose market capitalization is less than $100 million	
Neglected Stocks	Stocks followed by only a few analysts and/or stocks with low percentages of institutional ownership	
Stocks with High Relative Strength	Stocks whose prices have risen faster relative to the overall market	
January Effect	Stocks do better during January than during any other month of the year	
Day of the Week	Stocks do poorer during Monday than during other days of the week	

Source: *"Picking Stocks: Techniques That Stand the Test of Time,"* American Association of Individual Investors, 1994. Available at www.aaii.org (accessed December 2, 2002).

per share. Yet when stock opened for trading the following day, the price fell by more than 5%. Why? Apparently many investors were spooked by comments made by Microsoft's CFO forecasting a slowdown in future revenue growth. Most analysts immediately concluded that the market overreacted. They noted that even with a slowdown in revenue growth, Microsoft's earnings would continue to grow at an impressive rate due to lower costs and higher margins. Several investment firms reiterated buy recommendations on stock. Within a few days, Microsoft's stock had recovered from the July 20 selloff. This kind of anecdotal evidence of market overreaction can be found almost daily.

Scientific Evidence of Market Overreaction In addition to widespread anecdotal evidence of market overreaction, researchers continue to compile a considerable amount of scientific evidence of reversals. Several studies found that stock returns over longer time horizons (in excess of one year) display significant negative serial correlation. This finding means that high returns in one time period tend to be followed by low returns in the next period, and vice versa.

Others studies tested for market overreaction by forming portfolios of winners and losers based on performance over a specific time period and then measuring the performance of these portfolios over subsequent periods of time. One study, for example, found that over the subsequent year a portfolio of "losers" earned about 15% more than a portfolio of "winners."[8]

---

[8]See Werner DeBondt and Richard Thaler, "Does the Stock Market Overreact?" *Journal of Finance,* July 1985, p. 800.

INVESTMENT HISTORY

The 1987 Market Break: Meltdown Monday

On October 19, 1987, stocks suffered their worst one-day decline in history. The Dow Jones Industrial Average lost more than 500 points that day. In percentage terms, the Dow's decline on October 19, 1987, was far greater than its decline on October 29, 1929 (23% versus 12%). The S&P 500 dropped more than 50 points, a decline of 20%. Even relatively stable utilities dropped sharply. The S&P utilities index, for example, fell by more than 19 points (18%) on that single day.

Much has already been written about the causes of the 1987 market break. Some argued that it was the result of rampant speculation in stocks; others blamed the break on program trading; still others blamed it on simple investor panic. In our view, all three factors probably contributed to what became known as Meltdown Monday. Did it mark the end of a period of speculative frenzy similar to that of the 1920s, or was it a simple, albeit extreme, case of overreaction? Perhaps both.

The accompanying table puts the 1987 market break into some perspective. Stocks had risen rapidly throughout 1987, before the break. The S&P 500 added more than 90 points (about 38%) between the end of 1986 and August 25, when the index peaked at 336.8. Many individual stocks did much better. Ford, for example, more than doubled between the end of 1986 and its high in the summer of 1987.

Stock/Index	Opening (1987)	High (1987)	Closing Price (10/19/87)	High (1989)
Ford	28.125	56.375	34.50	56.625
General Electric	43.00	66.375	41.875	64.75
Microsoft	24.125	39.625	22.625	44.625
Wal-Mart Stores	23.25	42.875	26.625	44.875
S&P 500	242.20	336.80	224.80	359.80
Dow 30	1,895.95	2,722.42	1,738.74	2,791.41
Nasdaq Composite	348.83	455.26	291.88	485.73

During the late summer and early fall of 1987, some investors began to worry that stocks were becoming overvalued. The average price/earnings ratio of the S&P 500 stocks had risen from 16.7 to 21.1. Interest rates were also rising. The yield on long-term Treasury bonds, for example, had risen 1.5% between January and August. Stocks started to drift lower throughout September and the first week of October. The S&P 500 lost about 30 points between August 25 and October 14.

Then, things got serious. Several bad economic reports were released, fueling fears of inflation and recession. Also, interest rates continued to climb; the yield on long-term Treasury bonds crossed a psychological barrier at 10% several days before the market break. Friday, October 16, was a bad day for stocks. The S&P 500 lost more than 16 points (about 5%), and trading volume was heavy.

Over the weekend, many investors apparently hit the panic button. By the time the U.S. markets opened Monday morning, thousands of sell orders were waiting. (Markets in Asia and Europe had already experienced sharp selloffs.) Prices tumbled from the opening bell. Falling prices triggered sell commands in computer trading programs, driving prices even lower. By the time the dust settled, the S&P 500 had lost more than 58 points, or about 21% of its value. The stocks shown in the table below all took big hits. Ford, for example, dropped 15 points, to 34. NYSE trading volume on October 19, 1987, set a record, exceeding 600 million shares.

Following many anxious days after Meltdown Monday, the markets stabilized by the end of the year. The Federal Reserve quickly intervened to prevent any liquidity crisis. No major banks or brokerage firms failed. Interest rates started to fall (the yield on the long-term Treasury bond was down to about 9% by the end of 1987), and no recession materialized. Unlike the 1929 crash, which ushered in a prolonged bear market, the 1987 market break turned out to be only a temporary setback. The S&P 500 crossed the 300-point mark again on April 14, 1989, and broke its earlier 1987 record on July 26, 1989. The individual stocks listed in the table all recovered from Meltdown Monday by 1989. In retrospect, Meltdown Monday presented investors with a historic buying opportunity.

Questions for Critical Thinking

1. In retrospect, why do many classify the 1987 market break as an extreme example of investor overreaction?

2. Some contend that the 1987 market break was an example of a bubble breaking, not a case of market overreaction. Did the behavior of the market up to the 1987 market break exhibit the characteristics of a classic speculative bubble?

Reversals and Other Anomalies Market overreaction may offer the best explanation for several of the anomalies listed in Table 7.2. For example, low price/earnings ratio (P/E) stocks may be analogous to the losers just described, or they may simply be stocks that are out of favor with investors. However, high P/E stocks may be the current investor favorites, or winners. As the market demonstrates almost daily, today's favorite stocks can fall from grace and reverse direction quickly.

Why Do Investors Overreact? Behavioral finance is a fast-growing, relatively new field of study that considers the influence of psychology on investor behavior.[9] Behavioral finance explains investor overreaction in the context of representativeness—judgments based on stereotypes. In an investment context, some argue that representativeness leads investors to become overly optimistic about past winners while becoming overly pessimistic about past losers. Therefore, the price of past winners tend to get too high relative to their fundamental value, while the price of past losers tend to get too low relative to their fundamental value. Eventually, though the mispricing corrects itself and losers outperform winners over subsequent periods of time.

representativeness

Judgments based on stereotypes.

Profiting from Reversals

Market overreaction and reversals suggest several possible investment strategies that may product abnormal profits for investors. Some possibilities include buying last year's worst-performing stocks, avoiding stocks with higher-than-average P/E ratios, or buying stocks on bad news. At the risk of oversimplifying, any investment strategy based on market overreaction represents a contrarian, or value approach to investing—buying what appears to be out of favor with the majority of investors. The Investment Insight box on page 172 describes one well-known contrarian approach to picking stocks, the so-called Dow 10.

contrarian (or value) investing

Buying what is out of favor with most investors.

Contrarian, or value investing has several strong proponents in the investment community. Respected professionals such as Warren Buffet, Mario Gabelli, the late Benjamin Graham, Peter Lynch, and John Templeton all embrace aspects of contrarian/value investing. But does value investing work? Can an investor consistently earn higher risk-adjusted returns by following the popular value-oriented strategies, such as those listed in Table 7.2?

A considerable amount of evidence suggests that answer to both questions may indeed be yes. The results of one study of value investing is shown in Table 7.3 on page 173. The study was conducted by respected investment professional James O'Shaughnessy. He compared the records of dozens of stock selection methods using data from 1952 through 1997. O'Shaughnessy's results generally support the notion that contrarian/value investing may indeed work. He found that buying stocks with low price-to-sales ratios, low price-to-book ratios, or low P/E ratios produced returns that were higher, on average, than those from the overall market, even after adjusting for higher transactions costs and differences in risk. For example, a strategy in which an investor buys a set number of stocks with the

---

[9]A good, readable guide to behavioral finance is Hersh Shefrin, *Beyond Greed and Fear: Understanding Behavioral Finance and the Psychology of Investing* (Boston: Harvard Business School Press, 2000).

INVESTMENT INSIGHT

The Dow Dividend Strategy

One popular investment strategy is clearly based on contrarian or value investing. It is called the Dow dividend strategy. This simple strategy consists of just three steps:

1. At the end of the year rank the Dow 30 stocks from highest to lowest based on dividend yield. Dividend yield equals dividends divided by price per share, so a stock with a dividend of $1.50 a share an a price of $50 per share has a dividend yield of 5%.
2. Buy equal dollar amounts of the 10 Dow stocks with the highest dividend yields.
3. Hold the portfolio for one year; at the end of the following year repeat the first two steps (rank the Dow by dividend yield and buy—or keep—the 10 stocks with the highest dividend yields).

The Dow dividend strategy is often considered to be a value-oriented investment strategy. The question is: Does it work? According to Jeremy Siegel, the answer is a smashing yes. Take a look at the accompanying table. It shows the average annual performance of Dow 10, compared to the overall Dow 30 and S&P 500 (both buy and hold) over varying periods of time.

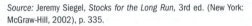

Time Period	Dow 10 Stocks	Dow 30	S&P 500
1928–2001	12.9%	11.4%	10.7%
1940–2001	15.5	12.7	12.7
1970–2001	16.3	13.0	12.4

Source: Jeremy Siegel, *Stocks for the Long Run,* 3rd ed. (New York: McGraw-Hill, 2002), p. 335.

Before you invest next year's tuition money into the Dow's highest dividend yielding stocks, consider a couple of things. For one, the Dow dividend strategy is extremely tax inefficient. By buying and selling more frequently than you would if you buy and hold, you end up losing more of your profits to taxes. It also requires you to pay more in transactions costs.

Questions for Critical Thinking

1. Why is the Dow dividend strategy an example of value investing?
2. In addition to taxes and transactions costs, what is another factor to consider when evaluating the Dow dividend strategy?

lowest price-to-sales ratios produced an average annual compound return of 13.7% between 1952 and 1997. In comparison, a buy-and-hold strategy produced an average annual compound return of 11.5% over the sample period.[10]

Some Caveats About Contrarian/Value Investing

Although value investing appears quite attractive, it requires several caveats. First, it is important to remember that good fundamental reasons may be driving reversals. Reversing prices may be a response more to new information than the correction of an overreaction.

Second, stocks with low P/E ratios are not necessarily cheap, nor are stocks with high P/E ratios necessarily expensive. The inverse relationship between value and P/E ratios (or other measures such as price-to-book ratios) is far from perfect. Some stocks may have low (or high) P/E ratios for good reasons. Further, value is definitely in the eye of the beholder. Ford, for instance, recently had a P/E ratio of

---

[10]Even though 2.2% per year may not seem like much, compounded over 55 years it adds up to a huge difference in wealth. An investment of $1,000 in a value portfolio based on low price-to-sales— was worth almost $1.2 million by the end of 1997. An investment of $1,000 in a buy-and-hold portfolio in 1952 was worth *only* $398,000 by the end 1997.

Strategy	Average Annual Return (1952–1997)	TABLE 7.3
		What Appears to Work for Investors
High relative strength	14.28%	
Low price-to-book value	14.30	
Low price-to-cash flow	14.02	
Low price-to-sales	13.67	
Low price/earnings ratio	13.61	
Buy-and-hold (S&P 500)	11.51	

Source: James O'Shaughnessy, *What Works on Wall Street,* 2nd ed. (New York: McGraw-Hill, 1998).

about 7. In spite of the low P/E, most analysts had "sell" or "hold" recommendations on the stock.

Third, although some evidence supports overreactions and reversals, other evidence indicates that stocks occasionally get stuck on one-way streets, meaning that poor, or good performance persists for long periods of time. One study found evidence of significant positive serial correlation in security returns.[11] O'Shaughnessy's findings also bear out these results. Even though investment strategies-based value measures outperformed the overall market, he found that a strategy based on buying last year's winners beat all the value-oriented strategies.[12]

Finally, past success never guarantees future success. Think about what would happen if every investor suddenly became a contrarian. If contrarian investing really does offer consistently higher investment returns, it would not be unreasonable to expect the wise investors to exploit these opportunities aggressively. Abnormal returns would eventually disappear and value investing would no longer work. On the other hand, according to behavioral finance most people have a difficult time becoming contrarian investors due to two behavioral phenomena: regret and hindsight bias.[13]

Calendar-Based Anomalies

Are there better times than others to own stocks? Should you avoid stocks on certain days? The evidence seems to suggest that several calendar-based anomalies exist. The two best known, and widely documented, are the weekend effect and the January effect.

Weekend Effect Studies of daily returns began with the goal of testing whether the markets operate on calendar time or trading time. In other words, are returns for Mondays—which is actually the Friday-to-Monday period—different from

---

[11]Andrew Lo and A. Craig MacKinlay, "Stock Prices Do Not Follow Random Walks," *Review of Financial Studies,* Spring 1988, pp. 41–66.

[12]O'Shaughnessy used a common measure of something called *relative strength* to identify winners and losers. (We talk more about relative strength and market momentum in the next chapter.) He found that buying the stocks with the highest relative strength produced an average annual compound return of 14.3% between 1952 and 1997. Interestingly, O'Shaughnessy also found that combining relative strength with various value measures greatly improved performance.

[13]See Shefrin, *Beyond Greed and Fear,* pp. 84–86.

other day-of-the week returns? Some studies concluded that the answer was indeed yes.[14] One study found that returns on Mondays were substantially less than returns for any other day of the week.

Seasonal Patterns Some evidence shows that stock returns often exhibit seasonal return patterns, meaning that returns are systematically higher in some months than in others. Historically, small stock returns have been much higher in January than in other months. Between the end of 1925 and the end of 2001, the average return on small stocks in January was 6.5% (more than 112%, annualized). By contrast, the average return on the S&P 500 in January was about 1.7%.[15]

One widely accepted explanation for the January effect is tax-loss selling by investors at the end of December. Because this selling pressure depresses prices at the end of the year, it would be reasonable to expect a bounce-back in prices during January. Small stocks, the argument goes, are more susceptible to the January effect because their prices are more volatile, and institutional investors (many of whom are tax-exempt) are less likely to invest in shares of small companies.

If January is a good month to own small stocks, September is a lousy month to own large stocks. In fact, historically the average monthly return in September for large stocks is negative. For the other 11 months, historical average returns are all positive. Each dollar invested in the Dow Jones Industrial average starting in 1885 would have been worth $394 by the end of 2001 (excluding dividends). This return increases to more than $1,500 simply by avoiding Septembers.[16]

Calendar-Based Trading Strategies

Both seasonal and day-of-the-week effects are inconsistent with market efficiency because both suggest that historical information can generate abnormal profits. As with all anomalies, however, a more important issue is whether seasonal or day-of-the-week effects can create profit opportunities for investors. Should you, for example, always buy stocks at the close of trading on Mondays and sell them at the close of trading on Wednesdays?

Although differences in daily returns appear impressive, they are probably much too small to offset transaction costs. The daily mean return on Wednesdays, for example, is only 0.097%. A purchase at the end of trading on Tuesday followed by a sale at the end of trading on Wednesday, based on the mean Wednesday return, would earn only about $9.70 on a $10,000 investment, a profit that would be gobbled up by commissions. Even E*TRADE charges about $15 per trade.

The **January effect** appears to have far more profit potential. For example, the average January return suggests that buying a portfolio of small stocks at the end of December and selling them at the end of January will produce an extra profit of about $679 per $10,000 invested, probably more than enough to offset the added transactions cost.

If this method sounds too good to be true, it is because it probably is. The average 6.5% January return from small stocks is a historical average. It hides

January effect

A phenomenon in which stock returns are higher in January than during other months of the year.

[14]See Burton Malkiel, *A Random Walk Down Wall Street,* rev. ed. (New York: W. W. Norton, 1999), pp. 247–249; and Jeremy Siegel, *Stocks for the Long Run,* pp. 264–266.
[15]Jeremy Siegel, *Stocks for the Long Run,* p. 300.
[16]*Ibid.,* pp. 308–309.

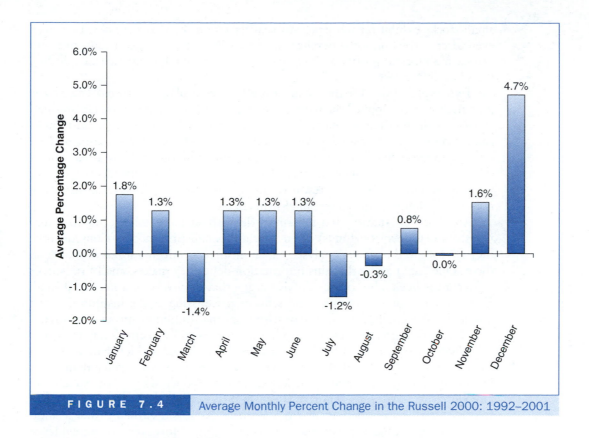

FIGURE 7.4   Average Monthly Percent Change in the Russell 2000: 1992–2001

substantial year-to-year variation in January returns. In January 1990, for example, small stocks produced a total return of −7.6%. Remember, past performance never guarantees future performance.

Another reason we are skeptical that an investor can exploit the January effect to produce abnormal profits goes back to a point made over and over again in this chapter: Once profitable investment strategies are recognized, it is reasonable to expect other investors to aggressively exploit them, eventually eliminating the profit potential. This phenomenon may be happening to the January effect. Entire books published about this widely recognized anomaly may be contributing to its disappearance. For example, Figure 7.4 shows average monthly percentage change in the Russell 2000—a popular index of small stocks—between 1992 and 2001. Even though January was still a good month to own small stocks, the index rose an average of 1.8% during January, December was a far better month to have owned small stocks. The index rose on average by 4.7% during December. This result suggests that investors are now aware of the January effect and adjust their buying and selling behavior accordingly.

The Small-Firm Effect

Historically, small stocks outperformed large stocks by a wide margin. Each dollar invested in large stocks at the end of 1925 was worth around $2,000 at the end of 2001. By contrast, a dollar invested in small stocks at the end of 1925 was worth in excess of $6,600 at the end of 2001. Of course, history also shows that small stocks exhibit far more year-to-year variation than large stocks. However, even after correcting for differences in risk, some studies suggest that investors can earn abnormal profits by investing in shares of small companies, exploiting the small-firm effect.

Two explanations for the small-firm effect seem plausible to us. The first is that analysts have applied the wrong risk measures to evaluate returns from small stocks. Small stocks may well be riskier than these traditional risk measures indicate. If proper risk measures were used, the argument goes, the small-firm effect might disappear. Small-firm stocks may not generate larger risk-adjusted returns than large stocks. Although the risk of small stocks may not be adequately captured by standard risk measures, it is difficult to believe that better measures of risk would eliminate the entire small-firm effect.

Another explanation for the small-firm effect is that large institutional investors (e.g., pension funds) often overlook small firm stocks. Consequently, they are followed by fewer analysts, which means less information is available on them. One could argue that this information deficiency makes small firm stocks riskier investments, but one could also argue that discovery of a neglected small firm stock by the institutions could send its price rising as the institutions start buying it. The small-firm effect may arise from the continuous process of discovery of neglected small firm stocks leading to purchases by institutional investors.

Whatever the explanation, small firm stocks, although riskier than large firm stocks, historically provided substantial returns to investors, higher than those produced by large firm stocks. However, history also shows that the small-firm effect is closely tied to the January effect. In fact, excluding Januarys, large stock returns actually exceeded small stock returns. As noted earlier, evidence indicates that the January effect may be disappearing. Moreover, strong evidence shows a link between value investing and the small-firm effect. For instance, between 1963 and 2000, the average annual return from small value stocks was about 23.3%, substantially higher than the average annual return from large value stocks (13.6%). By contrast, the average annual return from small growth stocks was only 6.4%, far less than the average annual return from large growth stocks (10.3%).

Performance of Investment Professionals

As demonstrated, both in the prior chapter and in this one, investments professionals such as pension fund managers or mutual fund managers seem to have a difficult time beating the overall market. We know that the performance of the average mutual fund lagged the market over the past 10 years, for example.

Of course, this figure represents an average. In a particular year, some professionals will beat the market, whereas others will not. The key question is whether some professionals can consistently outperform the market. Some evidence suggests that the answer to this question may be yes.

The Value Line Enigma The performance of investment advisory services has been closely examined. The well-known investment advisory firm Value Line gives each of the 1,700 or so stocks it follows a timeliness rating of 1 to 5 (1 being the highest). Several studies examined the predictive value of the Value Line ranking system.[17] These studies found that an investor who bought stocks with Value Line rankings of 1, while avoiding or selling stocks with rankings of 5, would have earned abnormal returns. Financial columnist Mark Hulbert found that the Value Line system produced an average return about 4.5% higher than that of the overall stock market.

Playing Hot Hands Several studies show that the past performance of mutual fund and pension fund managers is a good predictor of their future performance. For example, a comprehensive study of mutual fund performance found that the past performance of stock mutual funds was strongly, and positively, related to subsequent performance.[18] A study of pension fund managers found that more than 65% of the top-ranked managers, based on past performance, ranked above average in performance over subsequent periods.[19]

SO, ARE THE MARKETS EFFICIENT?

Today, it is fashionable, both in academia and on Wall Street, to discuss the pending demise of the old EMH. Well, we are not quite yet ready to bury it, but a considerable amount of evidence does contradict it, and more evidence seems to emerge daily. However, a considerable amount of evidence still supports the concept of market efficiency.[20] Even if the markets are not efficient in an academic sense, they may be efficient in a more practical sense. In most parts of the world, the financial markets are well-functioning, competitive institutions in which consistent abnormal profits based on public or historical information are rare.

In an often-repeated joke, a Wall Street trader and a finance professor are walking down the street. The trader notices a $100 bill lying on the street and stops to pick it up. "Why bother?" the finance professor says, "If it had really been a $100 bill, someone would already have grabbed it."

In one sense, this joke sums up the debate over market efficiency. An unquestioning acceptance of the EMH, and subsequent rejection of all investment analysis and research as worthless, can leave a lot of money lying on the street for someone else. Real-world situations and investor psychology defy a strict view of market efficiency often enough to justify the careful search for undervalued (and overvalued) securities. However, one should always be skeptical of someone who claims to have a clever system or special insight to consistently beat the market. Not too many $100 bills are lying on the sidewalk, waiting to be picked up. Finally, to reiterate one more time, past performance never guarantees future

---

[17]See, for example, Thomas Copeland and David Myers, "The Value Line Enigma," *Journal of Financial Economics*, November 1982, pp. 289–321.
[18]James Philpot, "Performance Related Characteristics of Mutual Funds," Ph.D. dissertation, University of Arkansas, Fayetteville, AR, 1994.
[19]Josef Lakonishok et al., "The Structure and Performance of the Money Management Industry," *Brookings Papers on Economic Activity* (Washington, DC: Brookings Institute), pp. 339–379.
[20]See, for example, Eugene Fama, "Efficiency Survives the Attack of the Anomalies," *Alumni Bulletin*, Graduate School of Business, University of Chicago, Winter 1998, pp. 14–16.

performance. James O'Shaughnessy puts it this way, "Finding exploitable investment opportunities does not mean it's easy to make money."[21]

SUMMARY

1. What is the efficient markets hypothesis?

The efficient markets hypothesis (EMH) states that security prices fully reflect all available information, making it impossible to earn above-average returns by using this information. Price changes may appear to follow a random walk. The source of market efficiency may be competition, thousands of investors constantly searching for the best investments. The efficient markets hypothesis raises a number of questions concerning the value of the two techniques used by many professional investors: technical and fundamental analysis. Further, the efficient markets hypothesis suggests that passive investing is superior to active investing.

2. What are the three traditional forms of market efficiency?

Efficient markets hypothesis takes three traditional forms. The weak form says that security prices fully reflect all historical information and using historical information to make buy and sell decisions will not produce abnormal profits. The semi-strong form states that prices reflect all historical information and react quickly to new public information. The strong form states that prices fully reflect all historical, public, and private information.

3. How is the efficient markets hypothesis tested?

The efficient markets hypothesis can be tested directly by assessing the success of various trading rules and investment strategies. It can also be tested indirectly by examining the statistical properties of security returns. Numerous issues arise when it comes to testing the efficient markets hypothesis, including the type of test used, the establishment of a benchmark, and the time period used to test the EMH. In addition, investors have a strong incentive to keep profitable trading strategies to themselves.

4. What evidence supports the efficient markets hypothesis?

Considerable evidence exists that supports at least the weak and semi-strong forms of the EMH. Numerous tests suggest that past prices are of little value when it comes to predicting future prices. Evidence also shows that security prices adjust quickly to new public information. Other evidence indicates that private information has value.

5. Can investors profit from anomalies?

An anomaly is a situation that appears to contradict the efficient markets hypothesis. Of the numerous anomalies identified, many are based on the observation that investors overreact. Thus, a value or contrarian approach to investing can be profitable. Other anomalies include calendar-based effects and the small-firm effect. In addition, the fact that some professional investors—mutual fund and pension fund managers, for example— appear to consistently beat the market can also be considered an anomaly.

REVIEW EXERCISES

1. Define the term *random walk*. Does a random walk imply that stock prices will be independent of each other?
2. If a series follows a random walk, what is the best forecast of tomorrow's price? Why?
3. How does competition produce an efficient market? What does competition imply about the future success of trading rules?

---

[21] James O'Shaughnessy, *What Works on Wall Street*, p. 5.

4. What are the implications of market efficiency for technical and fundamental analysis? Why, in an efficient market, is a passive approach to investing superior to an active approach?

5. Distinguish between the weak, semi-strong, and strong forms of market efficiency. What is meant by *all available information?*

6. Explain the difference between a direct test of market efficiency and an indirect test. What major issues affect the selection of methods to test the EMH?

7. What is meant by *sample selection bias?* How does sample selection bias apply to tests of market efficiency?

8. Define the term *serial correlation?* If security returns follow a random walk, what results should you obtain from a serial correlation test?

9. Compute the number of runs in the following series of 20 daily stock prices. Do the price changes appear to be random?

Day	Price	Day	Price
1	$30.25	11	$33.00
2	30.50	12	33.25
3	30.75	13	33.00
4	32.25	14	33.50
5	31.75	15	33.75
6	31.25	16	33.50
7	32.00	17	34.00
8	32.25	18	34.25
9	32.00	19	34.75
10	32.75	20	35.00

10. What is a filter rule? Describe how you would go about testing a filter rule.

11. Explain how you would go about testing how rapidly security prices respond to new public information. What would you look for?

12. What is meant by the term *reversal?* Explain how an investor might profit from a reversal.

13. Discuss an investment strategy that you would classify as contrarian. What are some the issues regarding contrarian/value investing?

14. What is the January effect? How are the January and small-firm effects related?

15. Discuss the small-firm effect. What causes it?

CRITICAL THINKING EXERCISES

1. This exercise requires computer work. Open the Index worksheet in the Data Workbook. The worksheet lists daily values for the Nasdaq Composite Index over a recent two-year period. Use the data to perform the following exercises and answer the following questions.

   a. Compute the daily percentage change. Plot both the index and the percentage change against time.

   b. Compute the daily change in the index value. Plot the changes. Do they appear to be random? Explain your answer.

   c. Design a filter rule. Set your filter no lower than 0.5% and no higher than 2.5%.

   d. Identify when the filter says to buy or sell.

   e. Evaluate how well your filter worked. In other words, did your filter give you correct buy and sell signals?

   f. If you had simply bought the Nasdaq Composite at the beginning of the period and held it until the end of the period, how well would you have done? Is the performance of the buy-and-hold approach better or worse than the performance of your filter? (Ignore dividends.)

2. This exercise requires both computer work and library/Internet research. Open the Dow worksheet in the Data Workbook available at the *Contemporary Investments* Web site (http://hearth.swlearning.com). The worksheet contains end-of-year dividend yields and annual total returns for the Dow 30 stocks between 1991 and 2001.
   a. Rank the stocks by dividend yield.
   b. Using library sources or a computer database, collect annual data on sales, earnings, dividends, and year-end prices for each of the Dow 30 stocks for the period 1992 and 2001.
   c. Calculate the price/earnings, sales-to-price, and market-to-book value ratios for each stock for each year. Also, calculate the change in price from year to year. Rank the stocks by each measure.
   d. Compare the rankings for one year with the total returns for the next. Do you see any patterns? For example, do stocks with low market-to-book value ratios consistently outperform stocks with high market-to-book value ratios?
   e. Discuss your findings with respect to the market anomalies described in the chapter.

THE INTERNET INVESTOR

1. Visit one of the major online book sellers (www.amazon.com or www.bn.com). Search the available titles and identify those dealing with value or contrarian investing. Read the synopsis of each title and prepare a brief report, including whether you would recommend the title to a novice investor.
2. Review the recent financial news and identify an announcement that appears to be significant new information. Look at a chart of the stock price for several days around the announcement. (A variety of investment-oriented Web sites provide charts including www.quote.yahoo.com and www.investor.msn.com.) Using the information you collected, answer the following questions:
   a. How did the company's stock react to the announcement?
   b. How rapidly did the stock price react to the announcement?
   c. Can you detect any leakage of new information before the announcement date? Why or why not?
   d. Would you classify the stock price reaction as an overreaction? Explain your answer.
3. The efficient markets hypothesis is not widely popular among many on Wall Street, yet almost every investment firm attempts to explain the EMH to investors. Visit www.vanguard.com and www.fidelity.com, and go to each site's investor education section. Read their descriptions of the EMH and prepare a report comparing and contrasting each description.

8

Technical and Fundamental Analysis: How the Pros Make Investment Decisions

| PREVIOUSLY . . . | IN THIS CHAPTER . . . | TO COME . . . |

We examined the efficient markets hypothesis, the notion that security prices reflect all available information. We reviewed implications of the EMH, the evidence supporting it, and the evidence against it.

Part II ends with a discussion of technical and fundamental analysis—the two techniques by which most professional investors make decisions. We describe each technique, give some reasons why it might work, and review how well each technique works in actual practice.

We move on to a detailed examination of one of the major investment alternatives, fixed income securities. We describe how fixed income securities are priced and the major risks facing bond investors.

CHAPTER OBJECTIVES

After reading Chapter 8, you should be able to answer the following questions:

1. How do technical and fundamental analysis differ?

2. What are some technical indicators?

3. How well does technical analysis work?

4. What is the process of fundamental analysis?

5. How well does fundamental analysis work?

In Chapter 4 we made the point that, on average, mutual funds rarely outperform the overall market. These funds, actively managed by investment professionals, often fail to match the performance of an unmanaged portfolio of stocks. For instance, the average stock fund beat the S&P 500 in only 9 out of the last 30 years. Between the end of 1971 and the end of 2001, stock funds produced an average annual return of 10.7%. By comparison, the S&P 500 produced an average annual return of 12.4% over the same period.

This example is not an isolated one. In late August 1996, a well-known market technician finally turned bullish on stocks.[1] He had recommended avoiding stocks since April 1994. Anyone who followed his advice missed out on a substantial increase in stock prices; between April 1994 and August 1996, the S&P 500 added more than 250 points, a 50% increase. Moreover, many stock analysts retained "buy" ratings on Enron during 2001 even as the company's finances unraveled and it headed for bankruptcy. Because professional investment advice is rarely free— managers of stock mutual funds collect an average fee of about 1% per year and an annual subscription to a technician's newsletter can costs several hundred dollars— one can legitimately ask: Is professional investment advice worth the cost?

We are not prepared to answer that question unambiguously in this chapter, though based on discussions in prior chapters we argued that all investors should approach investment advice with a healthy degree of skepticism. Rather, we present a critical examination of the two techniques by which most professional investors make their investment recommendations and decisions. Most rely on either technical or fundamental analysis, or some combination of the two, to make decisions. Our discussion of fundamental analysis will be fairly general in this chapter. The process of fundamental analysis will be covered in depth in Part 4 (Chapters 11–14).

TECHNICAL VS. FUNDAMENTAL ANALYSIS

In the prior chapter we broadly defined both technical and fundamental analysis. Now, let's be more specific. Technical analysis refers to a broad group of indicators, all based on the belief that past patterns in security prices can reliably predict future price patterns. Technical analysts believe that these patterns reflect the changing attitudes of investors to a variety of economic, political, and psychological factors. Technical analysis has been applied to stock indexes, individual stocks, bonds, foreign currencies, and many other investments. Those who believe in, or at least pay attention to, technical analysis are much more interested in a stock's past price record than how much the company is really worth.

Fundamental analysis, however, is based on the notion that every security has an intrinsic value. For common stocks, that value is based on the company's expected future earnings and dividend payments, the expected growth rate of those earnings and dividends, and the degree of uncertainty surrounding these forecasts. Fundamental analysts, or fundamentalists, believe that the intrinsic value of a security can be estimated and that it must eventually sell for this intrinsic value. Fundamentalists search for undervalued or overvalued securities, secu-

---

[1] Mark Hulbert, "Long-Term Bear Turns Bullish," *Forbes*, September 23, 1996, p. 238.

rities whose prices are out of line with their intrinsic values, hoping to profit from the price correction.

Both technical and fundamental analysts believe that security prices depend on the interaction of supply and demand. They simply look at different factors to evaluate supply and demand. Fundamentalists believe that supply and demand are determined, at least in the long run, by such factors as the growth rate in earnings and dividends. Although technicians agree that intrinsic value plays a role in determining supply and demand, they argue that a wide range of other rational and irrational factors (e.g., investor emotions) governs these relationships. As a result, a technician would not hesitate to recommend a stock with indications of good technical strength, even if the stock appeared to be selling for more than its intrinsic value. In the technician's view, a favorable market supply-and-demand relationship is all that matters. Likewise, if the technician thought that a stock had poor supply-and-demand characteristics, he or she would probably not recommend the stock regardless of the relationship of its current price to its intrinsic value.

UNDERSTANDING TECHNICAL ANALYSIS

Double bottoms, head-and-shoulder formations, resistance levels, trendlines, and relative strength are all part of the sometimes strange language of technical analysis. No subject in investments has as many critics as technical analysis. At the same time, however, technical analysis has a core of almost fanatical believers.

Technicians have developed literally dozens of technical indicators. It may seem at times that technical analysis has more indicators than technicians. Often technicians cannot agree as to how a particular indicator is calculated or interpreted. Given space constraints, we review just a few of the better-known indicators, divided into the following, somewhat rough and arbitrary, categories: charts, investor sentiment measures, and measures of market momentum.[2]

Charting

Perhaps the best-known form of technical analysis is charting. Charting involves simply plotting the past price history of a security or index and then examining the chart for patterns that suggest shifts in the underlying supply-and-demand relationship, indicating shifts in investor attitudes. Anyone can draw a chart—similar to the one shown in Figure 8.1. In fact, most investment-oriented Web sites offer excellent charting capabilities.

Although it may not be difficult to generate a chart, interpreting it is another matter. Because a technician believes that historical price patterns accurately predict the future, the key lies in recognizing the patterns and understanding what they mean. The history of charting can be traced back to a series of writings by

---

[2]Several fairly easy-to-read guides explain technical analysis. One of the better is Martin Pring, *Technical Analysis Explained,* 3rd ed. (New York: McGraw-Hill, 1991).

3M Stock Price

| FIGURE 8.1 | Daily Closing Prices for 3M: September 2000–November 2002 |

Charles Dow in the late 1800s. These writings formed the basis for the so-called Dow Theory.[3]

Dow Theory The Dow Theory is based on the assumption that a demonstrated trend in stock prices will continue until a reversal in investor attitudes—from bullish to bearish, or from bearish to bullish—occurs. The theory identifies three types of moves in stock prices: primary, secondary, and minor. The *primary movement* is the major or overall trend in prices. The primary movement can be toward either rising prices (bull market) or falling prices (bear market). Within each primary move, prices can show secondary and minor movements. Secondary moves are defined as large changes (33% to 67% of the primary change) in the opposite direction from the primary move; secondary movements bring declines in bull markets or advances in bear markets. Minor movements are small advances or declines that last only for a short period of time. Dow Theory

---

[3]Charles Dow was the founding editor of *The Wall Street Journal*. Dow himself never used the term *Dow Theory* to describe his approach to investing. The term came later in writings by William Hamilton-who succeeded Dow as *The Wall Street Journal* editor-and Charles Rhea. Both men expanded and formalized Dow's original approach.

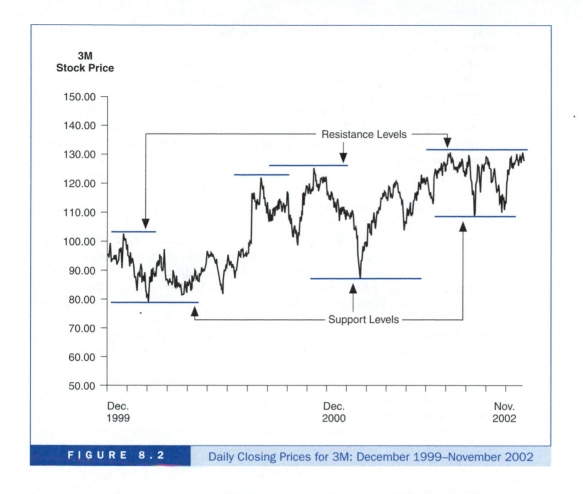

FIGURE 8.2 Daily Closing Prices for 3M: December 1999–November 2002

adherents believe minor moves can usually be ignored. The objective is to determine changes in the primary movement of stock prices. In other words, the theory attempts to ascertain when a secondary move is about to become a change in the primary direction of prices. One approach is to look at a price chart and establish **support levels**, below which prices tend not to fall, and **resistance levels**, above which prices tend not to rise.

Support and Resistance Levels Figure 8.2 shows a price chart of the daily closing values of 3M over a recent three-year period. Notice that the overall trend in 3M's stock price is positive; it rose from about $90 a share to more than $130 a share. Note also, however, that the chart shows lots of ups and downs along the road. Initially, 3M's stock price moved up sharply and established a resistance level at about $125 per share. 3M then retreated to about $100, a support level, before rising again. It again approached the resistance level at $125, but failed to break through it—possibly a sign that the primary up move was over. The stock price again fell, breaking through the old support level of $100, before establishing another support level at $85 per share. Again, a technician might take this event as further evidence that the primary up move was over. However, prices did not continue to fall; rather they generally rose. Prices never again approached the $85 support level. Further, toward the end of the period shown,

support level

A level prices should not drop below.

resistance level

A level prices should not rise above.

3M's stock price finally broke through the $125 resistance level. Overall, this pattern is mildly bullish.

Different technicians believe in support and resistance levels for different specific reasons, but they generally agree on the following explanation. As prices approach a support level, investors who failed to buy at the prior low begin buying, pushing prices back upward. Similarly, when prices start to approach a resistance level, investors who failed to sell at the prior high begin doing so, pushing prices back downward. Prices that break through either a support or resistance level suggest a substantial change in investor attitude—from bullish to bearish (when a support level is breached) or from bearish to bullish (when a resistance level is breached).

More Complex Price Patterns Beyond simple support and resistance levels, technicians may look for a variety of specific price patterns in their charts, many with colorful names. Some examples include fulcrum, compound fulcrum, head and shoulders, duplex horizontal, and inverse saucer. All of these more complex price patterns, we argue, are merely variations, modifications, or extensions of the basic notion of support and resistance levels, and attempt to predict a coming change in the primary direction of prices.

Trendlines A trendline is simply a line that connects secondary highs (upper trendline) or secondary lows (lower trendline). A movement in both trendlines upward (downward) tends to confirm a bull (bear) market. However, trendlines moving together—called a narrowing formation—might indicate that the bull market (if the trend is up) or the bear market (if the trend is down) will continue. One explanation for this conclusion states that plenty of buyers (sellers) will still be waiting for any price decline (increase) to buy (sell). However, trendlines that are moving apart—called a broadening formation—it might suggest that the market is about to reverse direction.

Moving Averages Another type of charting uses moving averages—averages of prices over a specified number of days (or weeks or months) that move over time. Each day (or week or month), the technician adds the most recent price and deletes the most distant price from the average. An example of a moving average is presented in Figure 8.3, showing the daily closing price of 3M along with its 200-day moving average.

Because a moving average smoothes the variations in any time series, technicians argue that a moving average can better represent support and resistance levels. Prices that break below or above the moving average may indicate a breach in a support or resistance level, which would signal that prices are heading even lower or higher. For instance, in about the middle of the period shown, 3M's stock price broke above its 200-day moving average. As expected, its stock price generally continued to increase.

Investor Sentiment Indicators

Many technicians move beyond studying charts to looking at indicators that, they argue, measure investor sentiment. They seek to gauge whether investors are optimistic (bullish) or pessimistic (bearish). Some of these investor sentiment indicators are based on contrary opinion, whereas others are based on following the

---

moving average

An average price over a specified period of time that moves over time.

investor sentiment

Technical indicators that measure whether investors are optimistic or pessimistic.

FIGURE 8.3   Daily Closing Prices for 3M versus 200 Day Moving Average: Sept. 2000–Nov. 2002

so-called smart money. Most technicians chart these indicators, often in conjunction with various price charts.

Contrary Opinion Theory The notion behind contrary opinion theory is quite simple. As the market approaches a peak (i.e., the primary upward move in prices is about over), the consensus among investors tends to be bullish. Likewise, as the market approaches a trough, the consensus among investors tends to be bearish. Two indicators that technicians believe measure contrary opinion are the odd-lot sales ratio and the cash positions of mutual funds.

The odd-lot sales ratio is defined as odd-lot sales volume divided by odd-lot buying volume, in which volume is usually measured in number of shares. (An odd lot is a trade involving less than a round lot, or 100 shares.) The rationale behind this indicator is simply that small investors, who are much more likely to trade in odd lots, are generally less sophisticated and more conservative. As a result, technicians argue, small investors tend to sell toward the end of a bear market (i.e., just before the primary downward move stops) and they tend to buy toward the end of a bull market (i.e., just before the market peaks). Thus, a declining odd-lot sales ratio, indicating increasing margins of odd-lot purchases over sales, tells technicians that the bull market has about run its course, so they consider selling.

The cash positions of mutual funds provide another contrary opinion indicator. Every mutual fund holds a percentage of its assets in cash or cash equivalent securities (such as Treasury bills). Mutual funds can affect stock prices significantly by moving cash in and out of stocks. Some technicians see a sign of an impending market top if the cash positions of mutual funds are shrinking or are near historic lows (say, less than 5% of total assets). In other words, they fear that demand for stocks is about to drop. However, if mutual funds have as much as 15% or so of their assets in cash, technicians may conclude that stocks are likely to enter, or continue, a primary bull market because the demand for stocks is likely to increase.

Smart Money Indicators Other indicators of investor sentiment are based on the notion that investors should follow the smart money, investors who are more astute than average and, the argument goes, should lead bull and bear markets. Two examples of smart money indicators are short sales by specialists and the level of debit balances in brokerage accounts.

Specialists on the New York Stock Exchange (NYSE), as part of their market-making function, often engage in short selling. Specialists are also allowed, with certain restrictions, to sell stocks short for their own accounts. Technicians believe that specialists may have access to better, more timely information, giving them a better feel for the future direction of prices compared with average investors. Therefore, if technicians see specialists engaged in heavy short selling, they take this behavior as a bearish signal. Likewise, if short selling by specialists is relatively light, technicians take it as a sign of an impending bull market. To make this determination, technicians usually look at the ratio of specialist short sales to total short sales. This ratio is typically about 40%. If it rises above, say, 50%, technicians may conclude that specialists are selling short more heavily, and the market is about to fall.

Finally, technicians often look at the debit balances in brokerage accounts (i.e., total margin debt). This indicator is based on the notion that only more sophisticated investors use margin debt. Thus, if the amount of margin debt in brokerage accounts is rising, these investors are buying. In fact, these supposedly more astute investors are borrowing to buy stocks. Technicians see this behavior as a bullish indicator.

Market Momentum Indicators

The final group of technical indicators we review is based on a concept known as **market momentum**. Those who believe in market momentum equate the market for stocks (or any security) to a freight train: it takes a long time to get going (either upward or downward), and it takes a long time to stop (or change directions) once it gets going. Usually, measures of market momentum are plotted on charts along with prices.

market momentum

Technical indicators that measure how much energy is behind the current trend.

Technicians use many other indicators to measure market momentum, the most obvious of which is simply trading volume. A technician sees a rising market on low, or perhaps, even falling, volume as a sign of an impending peak because it indicates weak upward momentum. However, a rising market on increasing volume is a sign that the market has strong momentum and that, therefore, prices are likely to go higher before peaking. As well-known technician Martin Zweig likes to say, "The trend is your friend."

Advance/Decline Ratio Another simple indicator of market momentum is the relationship between advancing and declining stocks, called the diffusion index. The diffusion index is often calculated as the number of advancing stocks plus one-half the number of unchanged stocks divided by the total number of stocks trading. A rising diffusion index is usually interpreted as a bullish signal, a signal that a primary upward move in the market has substantial momentum behind it. By contrast, if the diffusion index is falling as the market rises, technicians see it as a sign that the bull market is losing its momentum and approaching a peak.

A variation of an advance/decline ratio is to determine the number of stocks that are selling above or below their respective moving averages. For example, assume that 90% of the stocks that make up the S&P 500 are selling at prices above their 13-week moving averages. Many technicians would argue that it strongly suggests a trend has enough momentum to carry the overall market higher in the coming months.

Relative Strength Indicators Another example of technical indicators that purport to measure market momentum are relative strength indicators. As noted in the prior chapter, a simple measure of relative strength is a stock's price change. Another, somewhat more sophisticated, measure of relative strength divides the price of stock (or group of stocks) by a broad market average and then creates an index.[4]

Figure 8.4 shows the relative strength of 3M and Disney over a recent three-year period. Notice that the during the period shown, the relative strength of 3M generally rose while the relative strength of Disney fell. Rising relative strength is bullish whereas declining relative strength is bearish. Relative strength that starts to show signs of declining after rising for a period of time may indicate that the stock has topped out. However, relative strength that starts to show signs of rising after a sustained period of decline might indicate it is time to buy the stock.

ASSESSMENT OF TECHNICAL ANALYSIS

We described technical analysis and a few of the better-known technical indicators. Many technical indicators are simple to calculate, and their interpretations seem straightforward and full of common sense. For investors, however, the most important question is, how well does technical analysis work? This question evokes more than a little controversy. Many investors sincerely believe that technical analysis works, or least gives them an edge. Even though technical analysis has attracted some individuals who can best be described as crackpots, even charlatans, the field also includes some serious, almost scholarly professionals who carefully examine their technical indicators. Some of these individuals built impressive track records.

On the other hand, critics regard technical analysis in much the same way astronomers view astrology. They argue that technical analysis simply does not work consistently. Burton Malkiel, one of the more articulate critics of technical analysis states flatly, "I, personally, have never known as successful technician, but I have seen the wrecks of several unsuccessful ones."[5] Malkiel adds, "With large numbers of technicians predicting the market, there were always be some

---

[4]You could use the following formula to calculate relative strength: $RS_t = [(S_t/I_t)/(S_{t-1}/I_{t-1})](RS_{t-1})$, where S is the stock price, I is the index value, and RS is the relative strength measure. RS_0 is set at an arbitrary value, most commonly 100.

[5]Burton Malkiel, *A Random Walk Down Wall Street* (New York: W.W. Norton, 1999), p. 139.

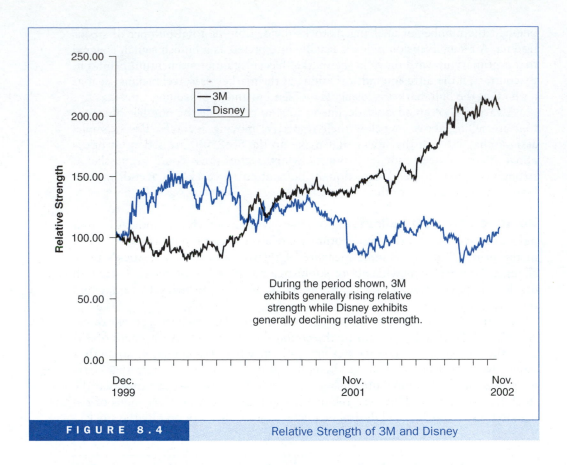

FIGURE 8.4   Relative Strength of 3M and Disney

who called the last turn, or the last few turns, but none will consistently be accurate."[6] Indeed history is full of market gurus—such as Elaine Garzarelli—who make one famous call—her call was accurately forecasting the 1987 market break—and then are never heard from again.

Although we cannot hope to resolve the controversy over the value of technical analysis, we would like to provide some basic insight into the question of how well it works. We begin with a discussion of some of the reasons technical analysis might work, and some reasons why it might not work.

Why Technical Analysis Might Work

In describing technical indicators, we explained some of the basic rationales behind them, in other words, why they might work. For example, recall that the basic rationale for the Dow Theory is that investors who held back from buying a stock at its prior low (or support level) will be anxious to buy as the stock approaches that price level again. Other reasons why technical analysis might work, or at least appear to work, deal with the inadequacies of fundamental information.

It is quite possible that not all investors have equal access to fundamental information. Also, some investors might have access to relevant information

---
[6]Malkiel, *A Random Walk Down Wall Street*, p. 159.

before other investors. This lag suggests a separation between the initial dissemination of information and the stock market reaction. Therefore, some investors may miss out on major moves if they wait for the fundamental information to reach them. Perhaps following the smart money (investors who presumably have better and more timely access to information) could produce higher returns than the general market over the long run.

Technical analysis might also work if fundamental information is incomplete or misleading. As discussed in Chapter 13, accounting information can be manipulated to represent a situation as something other than what it really is. In addition, fundamental information reveals little about nonquantitative factors such as employee morale. Past stock price patterns might provide better insight into these nonquantitative factors, technicians argue.

Beyond the inadequacies of fundamental information, technical analysis might work because investor emotions can impose a major impact on stock prices. Because people make investment decisions, human psychology affects prices. It is one of the important lessons of speculative bubbles, remember. Behavioral finance argues that human psychology leads investors to make the same mistakes over and over again, creating the possibility of recurrent and predictable patterns in security prices.

Aside from these reasons, technical analysis might appear to work through the effects of a self-fulfilling prophecy. For example, assume that a significant number of investors believes in and follows moving averages. These investors abandon the market if a stock market index breaks below its moving average. Assume that the S&P 500's 200-day moving average is 1,000 and the index closes at 1,005. Many of these investors are likely to sell. As a result, stock prices are likely to drop farther, at least in the short run. Does this result mean that the indicator works? One could argue that the answer is both yes and no.

For all the arguments supporting why technical might work, several strong arguments also give reasons that it might not work. Essentially critics attack technical analysis on two points. First, critics label most of technicians' recurrent patterns in short-term security prices as mere illusions. As an example, take a look at the chart shown in Figure 8.5. (It may look familiar; it's the same as Figure 7.1.) One of the series is the S&P 500; the other is a random walk. Random walks can produce price series that appear to show trends, recurring patterns, resistance levels, support levels, and so forth. It is easy to be fooled into seeing something where there is nothing.[7] Second, even if security prices followed recurrent and predictable patterns, many other investors would quickly recognize the patterns. Once that happened, any trading rule based on those patterns would rapidly self-destruct.

As an example of the second point, assume that a trading rule based on some historical price pattern indicates that a specific stock is about to rise from $50 to $55 a share. A technician who believes in the indicator would immediately buy the stock, as would other investors who recognize the price pattern. The price would jump almost instantaneously from $50 to $55 under the pressure of many

---

[7]Burton Malkiel likes to tell the following story: "One of the charts showed a beautiful upward breakout from an inverted head and shoulders (a bullish formation). I showed it to a chartist friend of mine who practically jumped out of his skin. 'What is the company?' he exclaimed. 'We've got to buy immediately.' He did not respond kindly when I told him the chart had been produced by flipping a coin." Malkiel, *A Random Walk Down Wall Street*, pp. 143–144.

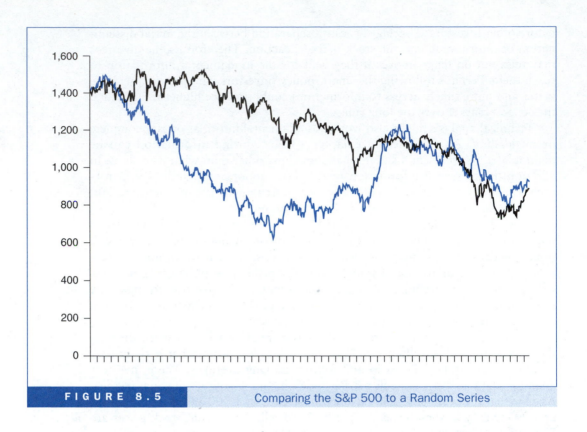

FIGURE 8.5   Comparing the S&P 500 to a Random Series

buyers and no one willing to sell the stock at a price less than $55. (Remember, every buyer must find a seller.) In fact, some investors might buy the stock in *anticipation* of the pattern. In any event, the trading rule would no longer produce an abnormal profit.

How Well Do Technical Indicators Really Work?

We have examined some reasons why technical analysis might work and some reasons why it might fail. To resolve some of the controversy, we evaluate the track record of systems based on one popular technical indicator (moving averages). Again, our discussion does not attempt to be comprehensive.

Before we get to the question of how well moving average systems work, however, we need to define how to determine whether technical analysis does or does not work. It is not enough to say that technical analysis works if it correctly predicts an event—say, a bull market. One can say that technical analysis works only if it consistently produces above-average returns for investors who follow its signals. Above-average returns must exceed the returns that the investor would have earned by simply buying and holding a similar investment over the same period. Adjustments for differences in risk, transaction costs, and taxes should also be made.

We also note a problem with testing how well technical analysis works: The interpretation of many technical indicators is often ambiguous. In addition, most market technicians examine several indicators when making their forecasts. This use of multiple indicators can make it quite difficult to scientifically evaluate the fore-

Period	Passive Strategy	Active Strategy	
		Before Transactions Costs	After Transactions Costs
1886–2001	9.8%	10.4%	8.9%
1886–1925	9.1	9.8	8.1
1926–1945	6.3	11.1	9.4
1946–2001	11.5	10.7	9.3
1990–2001	14.1	7.4	5.2

TABLE 8.1

Performance of a Dow Moving Average Strategy (average annualized returns)

Source: Jeremy Siegel, *Stocks for the Long Run,* 3rd ed. (New York: McGraw-Hill, 2002), p. 293.

casts. Most technicians admit that interpreting technical indicators is subjective—more of an art than a science. Consequently, it is not unheard of for one technician to argue that a particular indicator is giving a bullish signal while another, looking at the same data, concludes that the indicator is really giving a bearish signal.

As mentioned earlier, moving averages are another way of finding support and resistance levels. Breaking below the 200-day moving average is analogous to breaking below a support level (a bearish signal), while breaking above the 200-day moving average is the same as breaking through a resistance level (a bullish signal). So, how well do moving averages work? According to critics, not very well. Substantial scientific evidence suggests that moving averages, as well as other technical indicators, fail to produce above-average returns consistently.[8]

However, recently emerging evidence suggests it may not be time to put away your charts yet. A recent scientific study found fairly strong support for moving average systems.[9] The study found that breaking through resistance and support levels produced good buy and sell signals, respectively.

Jeremy Siegel, in his book *Stocks for the Long Run,* back-tested the moving average strategy using a series of daily values of the Dow Industrials starting in 1885. He assumed that investors bought the Dow when the index crossed above its 200-day moving average, and left the market when the index fell below its 200-day moving average. Siegel assumed investors reinvested dividends—when in the market—and earned interest—when not in the market. Table 8.1 summarizes Siegel's findings.

At first glance, Siegel's results seem to suggest a mixed track record for moving average systems. The active strategy produced higher average returns than a passive buy-and-hold strategy *only* if you ignore transactions costs. After adjusting for transaction costs, the performance of the passive strategy either matched or, in some cases, exceeded the performance of the active strategy. During the most recent subperiod, 1990–2001, the passive strategy beat the active strategy by a wide margin.

The one exception was the 1926–1945 time period. Even after adjusting for transactions costs, the active strategy beat the passive strategy by an average of more than 4% per year. According to Siegel, this difference is due to the fact that the moving average strategy would have gotten an investor out of the market prior to the 1929 crash, and kept the investor out of the market for most of the

---

[8]Many of these studies are listed in Malkiel, *A Random Walk Down Wall Street,* pp. 432–435.
[9]William Brock, Blake LeBaron, and Josef Lakonishok, "Simple Technical Trading Rules and the Stochastic Properties of Stock Returns," *Journal of Finance,* December 1992, pp. 1731–1764.

TABLE 8.2			Active Strategy	
Performance of a Nasdaq Moving Average Strategy (average annualized returns)	Period	Passive Strategy	Before Transactions Costs	After Transactions Costs
	1972–2001	11.9%	16.7%	15.2%
	1990–2001	13.7	17.5	15.8

Source: Jeremy Siegel, *Stocks for the Long Run,* 3rd ed. (New York: McGraw-Hill, 2002), p. 295.

early 1930s—a dismal period for stock investors.[10] This caveat raises another important point about Siegel's findings. Although a moving average system does not appear to improve performance, it does appear to reduce risk, especially helping investors avoid large losses (such as 1929–1932). In fact the standard deviation of returns from the active strategy is 20% lower than the standard deviation of returns from the passive buy-and-hold strategy.

Siegel also tested the moving average strategy using the Nasdaq Composite Index. His findings are shown in Table 8.2. Notice that the active strategy produced, on average, considerably higher returns than the passive strategy. Between 1990 and 2001, for instance, the annual return from the active strategy averaged about 2% more than the return from the passive strategy, even after adjusting for transactions costs.

Siegel's overall assessment of moving averages and technical analysis, in general, gives a cautious endorsement as long as transactions costs are not too high. However, he notes that throughout history actions of investors affect future returns. Indeed his findings suggest that the moving average strategy may be breaking down, at least for the Dow stocks. In other words, profitable trading strategies often disappear, something we discussed in the prior chapter. Siegel concludes his assessment of technical analysis by quoting Benjamin Graham: ". . . chartists admit that continued success is dependent upon keeping the successful method known to only a few people."[11]

WHAT IS FUNDAMENTAL ANALYSIS?

In one sense, technicians focus exclusively on a stock's current and past price patterns. Intrinsic value, what the stock really should be worth, plays only a supporting role. Fundamental analysts, however, try to determine the true value of a stock under the belief that all stocks, in the long run, will sell for their fundamental values. Therefore, fundamentalists are not as interested in passing effects, such as investor sentiment, as in, say, the company's five-year projected growth rate in earnings.

Benjamin Graham and David Dodd are considered to be the fathers of modern security analysis. The first edition of their seminal work, *Security Analysis,* argued that common stocks were not wildly speculative investments, but rather belonged

---

[10]Unlike the 1987 market break where stock prices bounced back fairly quickly, the 1929 Crash was only the beginning of a brutal bear market. Between the 1929 peak, which was reached in early September—and the eventual bottom—reached in 1932, the Dow Industrials lost nearly 90% of their value. It took more than 25 years for the Dow to fully recover from the 1929 crash.

[11]Jeremy Siegel, *Stocks for the Long Run,* 3rd ed. (New York: McGraw-Hill, 2002), p. 297.

Benjamin Graham

The father of modern security analysis, Benjamin Graham once remarked, "An astonishingly large portion of those trading common stocks don't appear to know—in polite terms—one part of their anatomy from another." In the early 1930s, Graham, a money manager and part-time instructor at Columbia University, set out to prove that all stocks had a fundamental value, and that this value could be estimated. The fundamental value of a stock, Graham believed, could be quite different from its market price. In fact, he likened the stock market an emotional "voting machine" where stock prices varied from day to day, independent of their real values. The goal of security analysis was to find a stock that was selling for less the true value of the business. The key to achieving that goal, Graham believed, was the realization that a share of stock represents a share of a real business. Co-authored with David Dodd, Graham's book *Security Analysis* effectively created the field of modern security analysis. *Security Analysis* is an even a more remarkable accomplishment considering it was written and published during the height of the Great Depression when common stocks were being shunned by most investors. Graham's work inspired a legion of famous investors, including one of his students from the early 1950s, Warren Buffet.

in the portfolios of all prudent long-term investors.[12] Graham and Dodd presented a methodology often referred to as the Graham and Dodd approach to analyzing and valuing common stocks. What is remarkable about *Security Analysis* is that it was initially published during the depths of the Great Depression when interest in common stocks was weak. Graham and Dodd showed a great deal of faith in the long-run future of the capital markets and the U.S. economy.

The Process of Fundamental Analysis

Fundamental analysis is usually completed in a three-stage process, beginning with economic and aggregate market analysis and proceeding to industry analysis and then company analysis. The four major variables that generally drive stock prices are (1) current earnings and dividends, (2) the future growth rate in earnings and dividends, (3) the uncertainty surrounding the growth rate, and (4) interest rates. One cannot forecast future earnings and dividends without some idea of such things as the company's future sales, operating expenses, capital investment, and financing requirements.

We devote four chapters to a detailed description of the process of fundamental analysis (Chapters 11–14). Chapter 11 describes economic and industry analysis, and Chapters 12 and 13 deal with company analysis. Chapter 14 ties fundamental analysis together by presenting several stock valuation models.

An Example of Fundamental Analysis in Action

To give you an idea of how the process of fundamental analysis is used in practice, let's look at an example, Peter Lynch's 1994 analysis of Johnson & Johnson.[13] Lynch is strongly devoted to fundamental analysis. He also has an excellent track

---

[12]Benjamin Graham and David Dodd, *Security Analysis* (New York: McGraw-Hill, 1934).
[13]Peter Lynch and John Rothchild, *Learn to Earn* (New York: Simon & Schuster, 1995), pp. 166–169.

record. Until 1989, Lynch ran Fidelity's Magellan Fund, making his investment decisions on the basis of fundamental analysis. Instead of looking at charts, he read company annual reports and listened for stories he liked. Lynch and his associates must have done something right; Magellan has one of the best performance records of any mutual fund since 1980. After retiring from Magellan, Lynch continued to be active in the investments game, publicly recommending stocks.

In late 1993, Lynch noticed that the price of Johnson & Johnson's stock had been falling since early 1992, losing almost one-third of its value. Lynch was puzzled, thinking something might be wrong with the company. Looking through its annual report, Lynch discovered that Johnson & Johnson's earnings had risen every year for the previous 10 years (more than doubling), that the company had raised dividends each year for the past 32 years, and the company was becoming more efficient. He also noticed that the company had almost $1 billion in cash, $5.5 billion in equity, and only $1.5 billion in long-term debt. Lynch also observed that Johnson & Johnson had excellent products in the pipeline. In short, Johnson & Johnson had solid fundamentals. So, why was its stock not responding?

Lynch believed that the answer lay in the market's reaction to proposals for health care reform. The market was worried that these proposals might have a negative impact on the earnings of health care companies. Consequently, all health care companies saw their stocks take beatings. Yet, Lynch concluded, that even if the proposals became law, Johnson & Johnson would be less affected than most health care companies. One-half of its profits came from international sales and another 20% came from the sale of consumer products such as shampoo. Lynch decided that at about $5 a share (adjusted for subsequent stock splits), Johnson & Johnson was one of the great bargains of the decade. He recommended the stock publicly in the spring of 1994.

Lynch turned out to be right. Johnson & Johnson's stock price rose almost steadily since the middle of 1994, trading at more than $60 a share today. Johnson & Johnson continue to raise its dividend each year since 1994. In the bear market that began in 2000, Johnson & Johnson is one of the few bright stars.

ASSESSING FUNDAMENTAL ANALYSIS

Before we get to an assessment of fundamental analysis, we need to point out that investment opinions by fundamental analysts can have a dramatic impact on stock prices. For instance, on December 2, 2002, an analyst at Lehman Brothers raised his rating on two chips stocks, Advanced Micro Devices and Intel, citing stronger demand for personal computers. Both stocks rose sharply in response to these positive comments.

Track Records of Fundamental Analysts: Some Examples

A great deal of evidence, both anecdotal and scientific, lays out the records of fundamental analysts. This record appears somewhat mixed. Consider mutual funds, for example. As noted, the average stock mutual fund underperformed the overall market over the past 10 years. Most of these funds are managed by individuals who rely primarily on fundamental analysts.

However, unlike critics of technical analysis, even the most severe detractors of fundamental analysis criticize not the process or technique but rather its execution. Critics often still find a great deal of value for investors in analyst commentaries on the overall market, or specific industries and companies. We have more to say about this topic in Part IV, but let's look at some examples of the successes and failures of fundamental analysis.

Forecasting Earnings One of the more important tasks of an analyst is to forecast earnings. However, some evidence suggests that analysts have a less-than-stellar record when it comes to forecasting earnings.[14] One study found that a naïve model assuming that next year's earnings will equal this year's earnings produced better forecasts than those of professional security analysts. Another study found that the average forecast error of next year's earnings made by professional analysts exceeded 30%.

Blown Calls As a group, security analysts have a long, somewhat dubious history of blowing calls. In one story, an analyst kept recommending America West Airlines in the early 1990s even as the stock was losing more than 70% of its value. The airline eventually filed for bankruptcy. Another story involves Sunbeam's first quarter 1998 earnings. Sunbeam had been touted by most analysts for its remarkable turnaround under "Chainsaw Al" Dunlap. The company had returned to profitability, and growth prospects appeared strong. Most analysts had "strong buy" or "buy" recommendations on the stock, even though it had more than doubled since Dunlap took over in 1996. As it turned out, Sunbeam stunned many on Wall Street by announcing a loss for the first quarter of 1998. Moreover sales actually declined by 5%. Red-faced analysts immediately cut their ratings on Sunbeam and investors stampeded for the exits. By the summer of 1998, the stock had dropped by more than 80% and Dunlap was out as CEO. Consider also that most analysts maintained at least "hold" ratings on Enron, even as the company was collapsing.

Success Stories For every story of a failure of fundamental analysis, at least one story can be told of fundamental analysis success. Beyond Peter Lynch, many other pros with impressive track records rely on fundamental analysis. Bill Gross is considered the "guru of bonds." Gross manages several PIMCO bond funds, including the PIMCO Total Return fund with its more than $66 billion in assets. (It recently became the largest mutual fund in the United States.) Gross relies on interest rate forecasts and other fundamental techniques when managing his bond portfolios. One his funds had a recent five-year return that averaged 7.37% per year more than the average taxable bond fund.

Abby Joseph Cohen of Goldman Sachs is another star among analysts. Cohen is more of a market strategist than a securities analyst, meaning she spends most of her time trying to forecast the overall market rather than the fortunes of individual companies. Her market forecasts have generally been right on the mark; she correctly called the great bull market of the 1990s. Cohen does not rely on charts, but rather on sophisticated economic analysis of the domestic economy.

---

[14]For citations, see Malkiel, *A Random Walk Down Wall Street,* pp. 435–437.

Her accurate prediction of noninflationary growth led to her successful forecast of the stock market.

Why Fundamental Analysis Might Fail to Work

What makes fundamental analysis so difficult? Why do analysts "blow" calls? Essentially, we see two primary reasons: institutional factors and the nature of the task itself.

One institutional factor revolves around the behavior of analysts. According to psychologists, a normal human reaction in the face of uncertainty is the tendency to stick together and follow the crowd. Analysts whose recommendations stick out from the pack expose themselves to risk, which can cost both themselves and their firms if they are wrong. Being wrong is a lot easier to take when all of your professional colleagues were also wrong. The following remark has been attributed to legendary economist John Maynard Keynes: "Worldly wisdom teaches that it is better for reputation to fail conventionally than to succeed unconventionally."[15]

However, more nefarious institutional factors are also present. Until recently, analysts almost always had positive, or at least neutral opinions about the stocks they followed. Negative opinions were rare. One study, for example, found that over a 15-year period, analyst "buy" recommendations exceeded "sell" recommendations by more than seven to one.[16]

To understand why analysts generally had positive opinions, you have to understand the nature of the research function on Wall Street. Simply put, at most investment firms, research is an expense, not a source of revenue. Brokerage commissions and especially investment banking fees pay the bills. Negative reports do not help to sell stocks or bring in investment banking business. Because of this reality, critics contend, analysts face a certain amount of pressure to say positive things about the stocks they follow. The wall separating the research function from the brokerage and banking functions, critics suggest, has always been porous.

A recent 10-month investigation by New York State Attorney General Eliot Spitzer uncovered some alarming cases of research being manipulated at many of the nation's largest investment firms. Analysts at Merrill Lynch publicly recommended Internet stocks that, privately, they considered to be "junk." They did so out of a fear of losing lucrative investment banking business. In another case, a top energy analyst at Merrill Lynch was allegedly forced to resign after he refused to alter a slightly negative report on Enron. A telecom analyst at Salomon Smith Barney, a division of Citigroup, may have changed his rating on AT&T in the hope of obtaining assistance to get his children into a prestigious preschool.

These, and other, revelations lead investors, investment firms, and government regulators to reexamine the role of investment research. Some firms erected stronger barriers between research analysts and investment bankers. Sell recommendations are much more common today than they were in years past. The Investment Insight box on page 199 further explores the future of investment research.

Aside from the institutional reasons, fundamental analysis often breaks down simply because it is a difficult task. Analysts must attempt to forecast the future

---

[15]Quoted in Malkiel, *A Random Walk Down Wall Street*, p. 176.
[16]Womack, "Do Analyst Recommendations Have Investment Value?" *Journal of Finance*, March 1996, pp. 137–167.

INVESTMENT INSIGHT

The Future of Investment Research

Recent revelations of the extent to which some investment firms manipulated research in order to support their brokerage and investment banking business caused some speculation about the future of investment research. Two conclusions from the various investigations seem obvious: First, investment banking fees, and to a lesser extent brokerage commissions, were of paramount importance to investment firms; and second, research reports were tailored to assist the investment banking and brokerage businesses. Although neither conclusion comes as much of a surprise to many Wall Street observers, they create the impression that some investment firms view ordinary investors as suckers waiting to be fleeced.

Consequently, many argue that new laws and regulations are needed. Research analysts, they argue, need to independently evaluate stocks, free of pressure from investment bankers and brokers. Analysts need to be able to produce unbiased reports that provide value to investors. Valid reports would help to restore investor trust. One proposal would require investment firms to offer research reports to their clients prepared by independent firms. Another proposal would essentially force investment firms to create semiautonomous research units.

The problem with many of these reform proposals is cost, and who will pay that cost. Investment firms already spend hundreds of millions of dollars each year on research, and many reform proposals will only add to these expenses. Firms will likely pass these higher costs along to consumers. Some firms may even decide to get rid of their research departments entirely, rather than allow the new independent analysts to potentially harm their investment banking business. Brokers would stop giving advice to clients and just execute orders. Small investors will then be left scrambling for new sources of information and advice. Research from independent firms—those not supported by investment banking fees—is quite expensive. Large investors, who can better afford to pay for independent research, may gain the advantage over small investors.

Questions for Critical Thinking

1. Can investment firms really totally separate the investment banking and research functions? Will investors pay for truly independent investment research and advice?
2. Some suggest that the entire controversy over independent investment research is much ado about nothing, because most investment research is of little value. Explain why you agree or disagree.

---

stream of earnings and dividends using data that are often incomplete and ambiguous. Financial data reported by companies can be misleading, occasionally made deliberately so by the companies themselves. In several recently well-publicized cases, including WorldCom and Qwest, companies were forced to admit that some of their previously released financial reports were wrong. Analysts must also try to anticipate changes to key macroeconomic variables and overall industry conditions—random events that can cloud even the best crystal ball. Needless to say, accurately forecasting earnings in such an uncertain environment can be quite daunting. Let's look at a classic, albeit somewhat extreme example.

Delta Airlines' 1991 Earnings In July 1990, the airline analyst for Standard & Poor's estimated that Delta Airlines would earn about $7.00 a share for the fiscal year ending on June 30, 1991, a healthy increase from its 1990 earnings of $5.79 per share. The analyst cited several reasons for the rosy forecast: moderate overall growth in airline passenger traffic due to continued economic expansion, an increase in average fare yields due to fewer price wars, and stable or perhaps even falling fuel prices. Then, Iraq invaded Kuwait on August 2, 1990.

Perhaps the most significant of the initial impacts of the Iraqi invasion, for the airline industry, was a sharp increase in oil, and thus jet fuel prices. The price index for crude petroleum was at 46.3 in July 1990 (1982 = 100); it shot up to 118.0 by October 1990, an increase of about 155%. The average July price of jet fuel of 56 cents per gallon (excluding taxes) increased to 114.4 cents per gallon by October. This increase significantly cut into airline operating margins, and thus earnings. By the end of September, S&P had cut its estimate of Delta's 1991 earnings from $7.00 per share to $2.75 per share.

The sharp increase in oil prices, and overall war fears, also helped push the U.S. economy into recession. Typically, passenger traffic slows during economic downturns, forcing airlines to reduce fares, which further depresses operating margins and earnings. Thus, by December 1990, even with slightly lower jet fuel prices (90.1 cents per gallon), S&P projected that Delta would lose $5.10 per share for the 1991 fiscal year.

After the Gulf War began in January 1991, oil prices rose sharply again, but then they started to fall after it became apparent that the United States and its allies would defeat Iraq without disrupting oil supplies. The crude petroleum price index fell from 87.9 in January to 54.1 in March. Jet fuel prices fell, as well, from 82.2 cents per gallon in January to 62.2 cents per gallon in March. Unfortunately for the airlines, passenger traffic also fell, as economic recession and fears of terrorism kept many travelers home. In fact, U.S. passenger traffic fell 7.7% for the first three months of 1991, compared with the same period in 1990. Even heavy price discounting and the end of the war failed to help much. The U.S. economy started to grow again toward the summer of 1991, but only slowly, and passenger traffic continued to be sluggish. By May 1991, S&P revised its forecast and said that Delta would lose about $6.00 per share for the 1991 fiscal year. As it turned out, even that forecast was somewhat optimistic; Delta ended up losing $7.73 per share for the 1991 fiscal year. Comparing the July 1990 forecast with the actual result, S&P overestimated Delta's 1991 earnings by almost $15.00 per share. As an airline analyst, how could you have predicted all those events when making your initial prediction?

IMPLICATIONS FOR INVESTORS

Both technical and fundamental analysis show mixed track records. Following technicians or fundamental analysts sometimes produces good returns and sometimes produces poor returns. Some go so far as to argue that an investor who buys and holds a well-diversified portfolio of stocks will do as well as, and perhaps even better than someone who follows the advice of investment professionals over long periods of time. The Investment Insight box on page 201 raises another interesting point about the value of professional investment advice. Most professionals, whether technicians or fundamental analysts, are overwhelmed by their human nature and base their forecasts in large part on qualitative and intuitive methods. Yet ample evidence shows that actuarial, or quantitative, forecasts are usually better. Perhaps it is no fluke that unmanaged index funds often beat actively managed mutual funds.

Critics often deride technicians as sellers of some modern-day snake oil. They argue that their methods are patently false and simply do not work. We looked at some of the evidence—both in this chapter and the prior one. Even though we agree that some technicians are flakes and perhaps even charlatans, we are not

---

INVESTMENT INSIGHT

The Limits of Human Judgment

Although it may seem like hearsay to some on Wall Street, professional money manager and investment analyst James O'Shaughnessy suggests that human judgment—or as he says "the unreliable experts"—may be the biggest obstacle to outstanding investment performance. In his book, *What Works on Wall Street,* O'Shaughnessy contends that models that don't require subjective judgments consistently beat intuitive models.

Why are "experts" unreliable? According to O'Shaughnessy, "Successful investing runs contrary to human nature. "We make the simple complex, follow the crowd, fall in love with the story, let our emotions dictate decisions, buy and sell on tips and hunches, and approach each investment decision on a case-by-case basis" (pp. 17–18). The following all contribute to the limits of human judgment:

- *People often ignore the information contained in base rates.* Base rates are like averages—they tell you what to expect from a group, but say nothing about each individual within the group. People tend to ignore the information contained in the base rate in favor of their "feel" for an individual in the group. Here's an example. Say you flip a fair coin five times and come up with five heads in a row. If you flip the coin for the sixth time, what's your prediction? Because it is a fair coin and each flip is independent of the others, the base rate says the odds are 50% that the sixth flip will be a heads and 50% that it will be a tail. According to psychologists who have conducted similar experiments, however, most people will answer tails. Why? Because they "feel" a tails is due given the run of five heads. In other words, they ignore the base rate and substitute their intuition, which has no real basis in fact.

    Here's an investments example. After several years of above-average returns in the stock market, it is not uncommon to hear market strategists predict at least a couple of years of below-average returns. Why? Sometimes their predictions are based on factors such as the outlook for interest rates and corporate profits, but more often than not they make predictions on the observation that the market has to regress back to its mean. However, objectively reviewing past market history—the base rate—no evidence shows that a series of above-average years is necessarily followed by several below-average years, or vice versa.

- *Personal experience is preferred.* People place more weight on their personal experience, than on the base rate, and as a result are overconfident. For example, the data show that most initial public offerings underperform the overall market and disappoints investors. However, an investor who made money on the last IPO he or she bought—personal experience—is likely to ignore the facts of the base rate—as well as any other objective financial data. The fact that the investor picked a winner last time is the main factor driving the decision to buy the next IPO.

- *Simple vs. complex.* Psychologists argue that human nature makes people prefer the complex to the simple. This tendency leads people to believe that successful investing requires the mastery of a wide of range of complicated variables. Yet that assumption is not often the case. Simple investing strategies, such as buying the Dow stocks with the highest dividend yields or lowest price-to-sales ratios, usually produce higher, more consistent returns than complicated investment strategies. One of the most important axioms of modern science is something called Occam's razor: Most often the simplest theory is the best.

- *The herd instinct.* When confronted with uncertainty and incomplete information, people will imitate each other's behavior. Investing obviously involves a great deal of uncertainty. Many resolve this uncertainty by assuming that, for example, if others are buying an investment, they should be also. If you think everyone around you is getting rich by investing in something, you may feel like a fool if you do not invest.

Questions for Critical Thinking

1. Does the unreliability of experts help to explain the persistence of speculative bubbles?
2. If mechanical trading rules work so much better than those based on human judgment, why don't all investors adopt them?

prepared to dismiss technical analysis entirely. Some technicians have impressive track records that cannot be chalked up merely to luck. Investors may well gain something of value by listening to what the serious technicians have to say about both where they think the market is going and why.

Likewise, it is easy to pick on fundamental analysts for their blown calls, sometimes quite badly blown. Nevertheless, analysts still have much to contribute to the investment analysis and selection process. You may not want to bet your financial future on their earnings forecasts, but analysts often have insightful and valuable comments concerning a company's current situation and its prospects for the future. Just remember who they are working for. It is up to each investor to adapt his or her behavior to the inherent optimism of analysts.

In conclusion, we argue that some, although certainly not all, professional investment advice is worth your attention. Is professional investment advice worth the cost? Every investor must answer that question individually. All investors should follow these steps: ask questions, think for yourself, be skeptical of anyone who claims to have a system that beats the market consistently, and remember the past never guarantees the future. Good luck!

SUMMARY

1.   How do technical and fundamental analysis differ?

Technical analysis is based on the notion that past price patterns predict future price. Fundamental analysis is based on the belief that stocks have a fundamental or intrinsic value. The analyst seeks stocks selling for prices above or below their respective fundamental values.

2.   What are some technical indicators?

Technical indicators can be grouped into broad categories: charting, measures of investor sentiment, and measures of market momentum. Charting includes the notion of support and resistance levels, trendlines, and moving averages. Investor sentiment measures include contrary opinion indicators and smart money indicators. Market momentum measures include trading volume and relative strength indicators.

3.   How well does technical analysis work?

Some good reasons explain why technical analysis might work as well as why it might not work. Interpreting technical indicators can be more of an art than a science, making it difficult to assess how well it works. The evidence is mixed, though recent scientific studies suggest that charting and moving averages are useful market timing devices.

4.   What is the process of fundamental analysis?

Fundamental analysis attempts to determine how much a stock should be worth. Fundamental analysis is usually completed in a three-stage process beginning with economic and aggregate market analysis, and proceeding to industry analysis and then company analysis. The most important determinant of the fundamental value of a stock is its future stream of earnings and dividends.

5.   How well does fundamental analysis work?

The track record of fundamental analysis is mixed, although stock prices do react to analyst comments. Analysts have a poor record of forecasting earnings and occasionally blow calls. However, many fundamental analysts have excellent track records. Forecasting is made difficult due to institutional reasons and by the nature of the task itself.

REVIEW EXERCISES

1. What major assumptions underlie technical analysis? What role does supply and demand play?
2. Define the terms *support level* and *resistance level*. What signals are given if prices break through support and resistance levels?
3. What is a trendline? Is the closing gap between upper and lower trendlines in a bull market suggestive of a continuing bull market?
4. The following table lists 20 weekly stock prices. Find the four-week moving average. Plot both the moving average and the raw stock prices. Why is the moving average considered to be a better indicator of a trend than the raw data?

Week	Stock Price	Week	Stock Price
1	35.875	11	41.625
2	36.625	12	41.500
3	38.000	13	40.750
4	39.000	14	40.375
5	40.125	15	40.875
6	39.250	16	40.750
7	38.000	17	40.375
8	39.250	18	40.000
9	40.500	19	40.375
10	42.500	20	41.000

5. Define what technicians mean by investor sentiment. Give an example of an indicator that supposedly measures investor sentiment.
6. Why is trading volume considered to be an indicator of market momentum? Give an example of another market momentum indicator.
7. List some of the reasons why technical analysis might work. List and explain some of the reasons why it might not work.
8. Why is it so hard to determine whether technical analysis really works? What standard should be used to test the effectiveness of technical analysis?
9. How does fundamental analysis differ from technical analysis? Why is intrinsic value so important to fundamental analysis?
10. Explain the three-step process of fundamental analysis. What are the four variables that, in general, determine stock prices?
11. Why might fundamental analysis fail to work? Why is the criticism of fundamental analysis different from the criticism of technical analysis?
12. Why are analysts as a group optimistic? Explain the herd instinct.

CRITICAL THINKING EXERCISES

1. This exercise requires computer work. Open the Nasdaq worksheet in the Data Workbook available on the text Web site (http://hearth.swlearning.com). The worksheet contains daily values for the Nasdaq Composite index. Use the data to complete the following activities.
   a. Graph the original value with time as the x variable and the index value as the y variable.
   b. Compute the 10- and 200-day moving averages. Graph the moving averages and the original data against time.

     c. On the first graph, find the support and resistance levels. When did the Nasdaq Composite index break through a support or resistance level? Did stock prices behave as expected after breaking through support/resistance levels (e.g., continue to drop after breaking through a support level)?

     d. On the second graph, determine when moving averages gave buy and sell signals. Did these signals coincide with the signals given by the first chart.

     e. Discuss what this exercise illustrates about the nature of technical analysis.

2. This exercise requires computer work. Open the Relative Strength worksheet in the Data Workbook available on the text Web site. The worksheet contains daily price data for three stocks along with daily data for the S&P 500. Use the data to answer the following questions.

     a. Compute relative strength measures for each company using the formula given in the text.

     b. What do the relative strength measures tells you about these companies? Do they indicate rising or falling momentum?

     c. Describe how you might use the relative strength measures to develop buy and sell signals.

3. This exercise requires library/Internet research. Quarterly earnings announcements are available from a variety of sources. Most sources also identify earnings surprises—situations in which a firm's actual earnings were either higher or lower than analyst expectations.

     a. Go back over a recent month's announcements and identify the five largest earnings surprises on both the upside and downside. (Earnings announcements are concentrated in February, April, July, and October.)

     b. How much did the actual numbers differ from what analysts were expecting?

     c. Do you see any correlation between the number of analysts following a stock and the size of the error?

     d. Pick one company from each list. Why were the analysts wrong? What did they miss?

 THE INTERNET INVESTOR

1. Visit the MSN Investor Web site (*http://moneycentral.msn.com*) and click on the section entitled "Super Models." The section explains the approaches used by various investment professionals to pick stocks. Read two or three "Super Models" and prepare a report summarizing the approach used by the pro (technical, fundamental, or both) along with some recent recommendations.

2. Pick a stock you are interested in buying. Using your Web browser to find out as much as you can about the stock, including analyst opinions. Make sure to visit some of the following investment-oriented Web sites:
   http://www.quicken.com
   http://www.morningstar.com
   http://investor.msn.com
   http://www.fidelity.com
   http://quote.yahoo.com

3. Visit the Morningstar Web site (http://www.morningstar.com). It contains a section entitled "University." Read the section on technical analysis. Prepare a brief report on what you learned.

PART 3

Fixed Income Securities

To this point, we provided a general discussion of investment alternatives. It is now time to discuss these investment choices in greater detail, beginning with fixed income securities or bonds. There are good reasons to invest in bonds, and bonds make up a large percentage of many investors' portfolios. However, bond investing is not without its pitfalls and risks. The next two chapters take a closer look at the investment characteristics and potential of bonds.

9

Fixed Income Securities: Valuation and Risks

PREVIOUSLY . . .

We concluded the section on financial markets and investment selection by discussion how the pros make investment decisions for various investment alternatives.

IN THIS CHAPTER . . .

Our discussion of fixed income securities begins with an outline of the basic principles of bond valuation. We then move on to a description of the two major risks faced by bond investors: interest rate risk and credit risk. We see that, regardless of the quality of the bond issuer, all investors are exposed to interest rate risk.

TO COME . . .

We continue our discussion of bond investing by describing both active and passive bond management strategies.

CHAPTER OBJECTIVES
After reading Chapter 9, you should be able to answer the following questions:

1. Why are bonds viable investment alternatives?

2. What are the risks faced by bond investors?

3. How are bonds priced?

4. What are the basic bond pricing theorems?

5. How can interest rate risk be measured?

6. How can credit risk be evaluated?

7. How are bond risk and required return related?

In Chapter 3, we described many different types of fixed income securities. The U.S. government issues bonds and notes through the Treasury Department and various federal agencies; state and local governments issue municipal bonds; and domestic corporations, foreign governments, and foreign corporations all issue their own bonds. Mortgage pass-through securities and preferred stock issues are also considered to be fixed income securities.

The market offers literally thousands of different bonds.[1] The U.S. Treasury, for example, currently has more than 200 different bond and note issues outstanding. Billions of dollars' worth of new bonds are issued each year by a variety of corporations and governments.

At first glance, bonds may seem to be relatively simple securities, at least compared with common stocks. A bond represents a debtor/creditor relationship: the investor is the creditor and the issuer is the debtor. Most investors purchase bonds primarily for current income rather than capital appreciation. A bondholder collects interest payments, usually twice a year, and then the issuer returns the principal—or par value—when the bond matures. In the process, the bondholder earns a fixed rate of return. Bonds seem like simple securities, right? Well, in the real world, bond investing can get quite complicated.

In this chapter, we concentrate on two basic issues: bond valuation and the major risks associated with investing in bonds (interest rate risk and credit risk). Before discussing how bonds are valued, we begin by answering what seems like a simple question: Why invest in bonds at all?

WHY BONDS?

Even though bond trading makes up a substantial portion of total trading volume in the world's financial markets, bonds have a reputation as being rather dull, conservative investments. Others argue that bonds offer poor risk/return trade-offs when compared with stocks. Even legendary investment guru Peter Lynch said less-than-kind things about investing in bonds: "In stocks you've got the company's growth on your side," he writes, "you're a partner in a prosperous and expanding business. When you lend money [buy bonds], the best you can hope for is to get it back, plus interest."[2] Lynch then recites a list of all the things that can go wrong if one buys bonds and concludes that bond prices fluctuate as wildly these days as stock prices.

Although some of what Lynch and others have to say about bonds is probably true, we regret the attitude that bonds generally are dull and/or poor investments. In fact, after the implosion of the stock market bubble, investors showed a renewed enthusiasm for the bond market. As investors demand for bonds increased, coupled with declining interest rates in 2001 and early 2002, bond returns exceeded stock returns. In 2001, bond returns were in excess of 6% while the S&P 500 Index lost approximately 13% in 2001 and 20% in 2002.

For many investors, both individuals and institutions, bonds are a viable and important investment option. What do bonds offer investors?

---

[1]From this point on, we use the generic term *bond* to refer to all fixed income securities.
[2]Peter Lynch, *One Up on Wall Street* (New York: Penguin Books, 1989), p. 57.

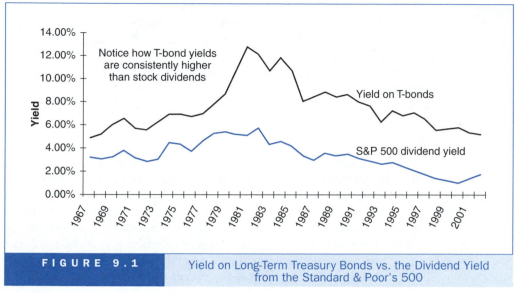

FIGURE 9.1   Yield on Long-Term Treasury Bonds vs. the Dividend Yield
from the Standard & Poor's 500

Source: Standard & Poor's Security Price Index Record (*various issues*).

Income

Investors who want predictable regular income buy bonds. Although many common stocks do pay cash dividends and these dividends often increase regularly, few common stocks have dividend yields that exceed the current yield on bonds. This comparison is illustrated in Figure 9.1, which shows the Standard & Poor's (S&P) 500 dividend yield and the average yield on Treasury bonds (T-bonds) between 1967 and 2002. Notice that the dividend yield on the S&P 500 has generally been about half the current yield on long-term T-bonds.

In addition, the financial trauma associated with reducing cash dividends on common stocks is much less than the trauma associated with suspending interest payments on bonds (which, of course, constitutes default). A source of reliable regular income can also improve the liquidity of any well-diversified portfolio.

Potential for Capital Gains

The data on historical returns presented in Chapter 3 refute the argument that bonds have been dull investments in recent years. For example, during a three-year period from the beginning of 1991 through the end of 1993, bonds (both corporate and government) produced average annual compound returns that exceeded the average annual return on common stocks. In 1982, long-term T-bonds produced an annual return in excess of 40%. In periods of falling interest rates, bonds can produce spectacular returns. In 2002, some bond funds produced a 10% return during periods of declining interest rates and outperformed the average annual return on stocks.

Paper vs. Real Losses

Of course, rising interest rates can also clobber bond prices. In 1994, for example, T-bonds produced a total return of −7.8%. Still, it is important to remember that rising interest rates produce only paper losses, not real losses, unless the investor

TABLE 9.1		Large Stocks	Small Stocks	Treasury Bonds	Treasury Bills
Correlations of Historical Returns Between Stocks and Bonds	Large stocks	1.00			
	Small stocks	0.79	1.00		
	Treasury bonds	0.20	0.03	1.00	
	Treasury bills	−0.03	−0.10	0.25	1.00

sells the bond at the depressed price. Assume that someone buys a bond for its face value of $1,000 and rising interest rates drop the bond's price to $900. This loss is only a paper loss, unless the bondholder turns around and sells the bond. Furthermore, holding the bond to maturity guarantees return of the $1,000 (assuming that the issuer does not default). Now, if someone buys a stock at $50 per share and it declines to $40 per share, the investor suffers only a paper loss, not a real loss, of $10 per share. However, unlike a bond, the stock provides no guarantee that it will *ever* get back to $50 per share, regardless of how long it is held.

Diversification

Bonds may expand the risk/return opportunities available to investors by further diversifying a portfolio of common stocks. Table 9.1 shows the correlation coefficients between stock and bond returns. Later when you study common stocks, you will learn that any correlation coefficient less than 1.0 between two sets of returns indicates some diversification potential (or a potential to reduce risk). Correlation coefficients between stock and bond returns are generally quite small, ranging from −0.10 to 0.20.

Tax Advantages

The Tax Reform Act of 1986 eliminated many popular tax shelters. One that remained was the tax treatment of municipal bond interest; interest received from municipal bonds remains exempt from individual federal income taxes. Municipal bonds are one of the few tax shelters still available to a wide range of individual investors.

RISKS ASSOCIATED WITH INVESTING IN BONDS

Although bonds have much to offer investors, buying bonds is not without risk. Further, some bonds expose investors to more risk than other bonds. U.S. government bonds, for example, do not have any default risk but still expose investors to other risks.

credit risk

The possibility that the issuer of a bond will not make interest and principal payments when due.

default

The technical name for credit risk.

Credit Risk

Whenever anyone lends money, the biggest concern is getting it back. Essentially, **credit risk** involves the possibility that the bond's issuer will not make interest and principal payments when due. (The technical term is **default**.) As discussed in

Chapter 3, bonds' levels of credit risk vary widely. Some bonds, such as those issued by the U. S. Treasury, have no credit risk, whereas other bonds have much greater probabilities of default. Generally, we would expect to see a positive relationship between credit risk and expected returns. We have a lot more to say about credit risk later in this chapter.

Interest Rate Risk

As interest rates rise, bond prices fall, and vice versa. If an investor were forced to sell a bond when rates were high, he or she could suffer a capital loss. Even if the investor does not sell before maturity, rising interest rates also create an opportunity cost. For example, if someone buys a bond with a coupon rate of 8% and rates rise to, say, 10%, the bondholder loses the opportunity to get the higher rate because the bond is locked in at 8%. All bonds expose investors to interest rate risk, but as we will see, some bonds have more interest rate risk than others. We also discover, in the next chapter, that investors can manage, and perhaps almost eliminate, interest rate risk.

Reinvestment Risk

If a bond promises a return (referred to as yield to maturity) of 8%, when it matures, assuming that the issuer does not default, will its actual rate of return equal 8%? Not necessarily because part of the actual return from owning a bond comes from reinvesting the intermediate cash flows (i.e., the coupon payments). Reinvesting the coupon payments at a rate higher than the bond's yield to maturity could raise the actual rate of return above the promised return when the bond was initially purchased. Note that interest rate risk and reinvestment risk tend to offset each other to some extent. The immunization techniques discussed in the next chapter are based on this offsetting effect.

Purchasing Power Risk

Purchasing power risk deals with the impact of future rates of inflation on cash flows. If a bond has a coupon rate of 6% when inflation is raging at 8%, the purchasing power of the invested money actually declines. Purchasing power risk hurts a bond investor if actual inflation exceeds the rate the investor expected when he or she first purchased the bond. Second, purchasing power risk and interest rate risk are closely related. As we know, rising expected inflation leads to higher interest rates.

purchasing power risk
The impact of inflation on a bond's cash flows.

Call Risk

In Chapter 3, we pointed out that many bonds (especially corporate and municipal bonds) are *callable*. A call provision gives the issuer the option of buying the bond back from the investor at a specified price during a specified period of time, before maturity. Why should bond investors care about this call risk? An issuer is most likely to call a bond when interest rates are low or have fallen substantially from when the bond was initially issued. To replace the called bond in

call risk
The possibility of a bond being called back before maturity.

call protection

Period during which a bond is not callable.

such an environment, the investor would probably have to accept a lower coupon rate. A bond may offer investors a period of **call protection** during which the bond is not callable.

Liquidity Risk

liquidity risk

The possibility of not being able to sell a bond before maturity at a price approaching the bond's true value.

As discussed in Chapter 5, some bonds trade in poor secondary markets, so the spreads between their respective bid prices and ask prices (prices at which a dealer would buy or sell the bond, respectively, in response to a customer order) could be quite high. It may be difficult for investors to sell certain bonds before maturity for anything approaching their true values. **Liquidity risk** is a special problem for small municipal bond issues.

Foreign Exchange Risk

In recent years, many U.S. investors have been attracted to bonds issued by foreign governments and corporations; many foreign issuers' bonds have offered yields well above those offered by domestic bonds. Many foreign bonds are denominated in foreign currencies, however, so their returns depend on both interest rates and foreign exchange rates. For example, a bond denominated in British pounds (£) may have a par value of £1,000 and a coupon rate of 10%. (It pays annual interest of £100.) If the exchange rate between the dollar and the pound ($/£) when the bond is purchased is $1.50 per pound, the bond would cost $1,500 and pay $150 per year in interest. However, if the dollar were to gain strength relative to the pound and the $/£ exchange rate declines to $1.20 per pound, the bond's £100 in annual interest would translate into only $120. Even if all other factors remain the same, the bondholder loses $30 a year merely due to the U.S. dollar's increasing strength relative to the British pound. This uncertainty is known as foreign exchange risk.

BOND VALUATION

So far, we examined the reasons for buying bonds as well as the general risks investors take when they buy bonds. In this section, we turn to a detailed discussion of bond valuation. An understanding of bond valuation is critical to an understanding of the general risk/return profile of bonds, as well as how to select and evaluate individual bonds.

face value

Amount paid at maturity; also called the par value.

coupon rate

Amount of interest paid each year.

time to maturity

The number of periods before the bond matures; also called term to maturity.

promised return

The interest rate used to discount a bond's cash flows.

Basics of Bond Pricing

The price of a bond depends on the values of four variables: (1) **face value** (F, also called *par value*), (2) **coupon rate** (CR), (3) **time to maturity** (T), and (4) **promised return**. For a noncallable, default-free bond, the first three variables are fixed at issue. These first three variables also determine the cash flows associated with a bond. The fourth variable, the promised return, is also the bond's required rate of return, the interest rate used to discount its cash flows to determine its present value. Given these four variables, we can calculate the present value of the bond's cash flows, which, added up, equals the bond's price, P_b.

For example, a 10-year bond ($T = 10$) has a 6% coupon rate (CR) and a $1,000 face value, F. The promised, or required, return (r) equals 8% per annum. The bond's price can be calculated in two steps.

Step 1 Calculate cash flows. The coupon payment (or interest payment per year in dollars), C, equals

$$C = (CR)(F) \tag{9.1}$$

In our example, 6% times $1,000 equals $60. The final cash flow at maturity equals $1,000, the face value, which is repaid in ten years.

Step 2 Calculate the present value of these cash flows to find bond value, P_b.

$$
\begin{aligned}
P_b &= \text{PV of coupon payments} + \text{PV of face value} \\
&= \$60(P/A;8\%;10) + \$1{,}000(P/F;8\%;10) \\
&= \$60(6.7101) + \$1{,}000(0.4632) \\
&= \$865.81 \text{ (rounded to the nearest penny)}^3
\end{aligned} \tag{9.2}
$$

Semiannual Coupons Equation 9.2 assumes that the bond pays coupon interest once a year, or annually. The vast majority of bonds actually make coupon payments every six months. To accommodate the semiannual coupon, the bond pricing equation (Equation 9.2) needs three modifications. The first is to divide the annual coupon by 2. This represents the coupon payment per six-month period. The second change is to divide the required rate of return by 2, and the third is to multiply the time to maturity by 2. For the preceding example, Equation 9.2 becomes

$$
\begin{aligned}
P_t &= \$30(P/A;4.0\%;20) + \$1{,}000(P/F;4.0\%;20) \\
&= \$30(13.5903) + \$1{,}000(0.4564) \\
&= \$864.11 \text{ (rounded)}^4
\end{aligned} \tag{9.3}
$$

Accrued Interest Someone who buys a bond between coupon payment dates must pay the seller, in addition to the bond's price, the **accrued interest** since the last coupon payment date. When the bond makes its next coupon payment, the new owner receives the entire amount. Virtually all bonds accrue interest daily and pay every six months.

accrued interest

Amount of interest between the last coupon payment date and today, paid by the buyer to the seller.

---

[3]From now on, the following notation will be used: (P/A; r percent; T) represents the present value of an annuity, received for T periods and discounted at r percent. (P/F; r percent; T) represents the present value of a single sum, received in T periods and discounted at r percent. Mathematically,

$$(P/A;r;T) = \frac{1}{r} - \frac{1}{r(1+r)^t} \quad \text{and} \quad (P/F;r;T) = \frac{1}{(1+r)^t}$$

[4]Some argue that merely dividing the yield to maturity by 2 when adjusting semiannual coupon payments is not technically correct, because you are actually discounting cash flows at an effective rate higher than the stated yield to maturity, thus understating the "true" price of the bond. This issue has been analyzed and debated in detail elsewhere. See, for example, Frank Fabozzi, *Bond Markets, Analysis and Strategies*, 3rd ed. (Upper Saddle River, NJ: Prentice Hall, 1996), pp. 39–42; and especially, James Lindley et al., "A Measurement of the Errors in Intra-period Compounding and Bond Valuation," *The Financial Review*, February 1987, pp. 33–51.

Say, for example, that a bond with an 8% coupon pays coupon interest on February 1 and August 1. Assuming a 360-day year and a face value of $1,000, this bond accrues about $0.22 per day ($80/360 days per year) in interest. Someone who buys this bond on May 1, 90 days after its last coupon payment, must pay the seller $20.00 in accrued interest ($0.22 times 90). When the bond makes its next coupon payment, on August 1, the new owner receives the entire six-month (180-day) coupon of $40.

Accrued interest may seem like a trivial issue, but it does affect the prices of bonds slightly. One reason goes back to a basic rule of present value. Continuing the preceding example, the new owner pays $20.00 today (May 1) and gets the $20.00 back in three months (on August 1, when the bond makes its next coupon payment). Because this money has a time value, the $20.00 received on August 1 is worth less than the $20.00 paid on the purchase date. Furthermore, buying the bond on May 1, instead of on its last coupon payment date (February 1), entitles the new owner to receive the first coupon payment in three months rather than six months.

Adding accrued interest, the basic bond valuation equation, assuming semi-annual coupons, becomes

$$P_b = \frac{c}{2} \sum_{t=1}^{2T} \frac{1}{(1 + r/2)^v(1 + r/2)^{t-1}} + \frac{F}{(1 + r/2)^v(1 + r/2)^{2T-1}} \tag{9.4}$$

where v is the days until the next coupon divided by the number of days in the six-month period, and $r/2$ is the appropriate semiannual rate of interest. Accrued interest is then added to the bond's price. Although Equation 9.4 looks confusing, it is not as bad as it seems. Let's look at an example.

Maintaining the same example bond we have been using throughout this section (face value of $1,000, term of 10 years, 6% annual coupon, and 8% annual required rate of return, or 4.0% per six months), assume someone buys the bond exactly three months after its last coupon payment and exactly three months before it makes its next coupon payment (so, $v = 0.5$). Now, compare the prices of the bond with and without accrued interest. The relevant numbers are summarized here:

	Without Accrued Interest	With Accrued Interest
Maturity	Exactly 10 years	9 years, 9 months
Number of coupons	20	20
First coupon received	In exactly 6 months	In 3 months
Price of bond	$864.11	$881.22

The new owner still receives 20 coupon payments of $30, but now the bond matures in nine years and nine months. The bond's price now equals $881.22 (*plus* $15 in accrued interest). Two reasons explain why the bond's price is about $17 higher than it is without accrued interest. First, the bond matures three months sooner, and second, the owner receives the first coupon payment in three months rather than six months.

Yield to Maturity We can interpret the continuing bond example as follows: What rate of return would an investor earn by buying a bond today for $864.11, receiving $30 every six months for 10 years (a total of 20 payments), and receiving the bond's face value, $1,000, at the end of 10 years? The answer is 8% per annum. The return on a bond, held to maturity, is referred to as the yield to maturity. This new name refers to the promised return, discussed earlier.

A bond's **yield to maturity** represents the market's current assessment of the rate the bond ought to pay given current market conditions. However, the coupon rate represents the market's assessment of the rate the bond should pay at the time of issue. As a result, yield to maturity can be higher or lower than the coupon rate and will change over time as market conditions change.

From another perspective, the yield to maturity is the interest rate that equates the present value of a bond's cash flows to its current price. Technically, a bond's price determines its yield to maturity, not vice versa. Based on the price of a bond and its coupon rate, face value, and maturity, we can compute its yield to maturity. Let's consider a simple example. The market offers a bond today for $1,100. It has a coupon rate of 7.0% and a face value of $1,000, and it matures in 20 years. Assume semiannual coupons and that the bond made a coupon payment today (eliminating accrued interest). The bond pricing equation is

$$\$1,100 = \$35(P/A;r/2;40) + \$1,000(P/F;r/2;40)$$

Find $r/2$ (the semiannual discount rate) and r (the effective annual rate or yield to maturity). In the dark ages when the authors went to school, this calculation used to be a fairly tedious task, using present value tables and trial and error. These days, financial calculators and PCs have taken over this work. Still, you need to understand what the yield to maturity means, and why it is an important number.

Relationship Between Coupon Rate and Yield to Maturity The relationship between a bond's coupon rate (CR) and yield to maturity (YTM) can be stated as follows:

1. If $P_b = F$, then YTM = CR.
2. If $P_b < F$, then YTM > CR.
3. If $P_b > F$, then YTM < CR.

Let's get an intuitive understanding of the relationship between CR and YTM. If the bond's price, P_b, equals its face value of $1,000, F, then YTM equals CR. Why? Because the bond price already equals its face value (a known cash flow at maturity, assuming a default-free bond), its only return comes in the form of coupon payments. Thus, the yield on this investment if held to maturity (YTM) must exactly equal the return generated from the coupon payments, which is, of course, the coupon rate (CR).

A bond selling below its face value of $1,000 is called a **discount bond**. The total return on a discount bond comes from two cash flows: the coupon payments and the certain payment of the bond's face value at maturity. Thus, yield to maturity is greater than coupon rate because the bond's price appreciation will add value over and above the return generated by the coupon payments.

A bond selling for more than its face value is called a **premium bond**. For a premium bond, the relationship between yield to maturity and coupon rate is the exact opposite of a discount bond. In this case, the certain depreciation of the bond price to its face value reduces the yield to maturity below the coupon rate.

yield to maturity
Another name for the promised return on a bond.

discount bond
A bond selling for less than its face value.

premium bond
A bond selling for more than its face value.

current yield

Coupon rate divided by the bond's price.

Current Yield Quotes of a bond price printed in the financial press (as discussed in Appendix A) often state the **current yield** on the bond. The current yield is simply the coupon rate divided by the bond's price (stated as a percentage of face value). For example, the bond we have been using has a price of $864.11 (or 86.411% of par) and a coupon rate of 6%. Therefore, this bond has a current yield of about 6.9% (6% divided by 0.86411). Notice that the current yield is more than the yield to maturity.

yield to call

Return on a bond if called.

Yield to Call A call provision may lead a bond investor to calculate another measure of return, the **yield to call**. Basically, this analysis asks the following question: If a bond bought today is called by the issuer at some point in the future, before maturity, what return should the owner expect to earn? An answer to this question requires two modifications to the basic bond pricing equation. First, substitute the call price for the bond's face value, and second, substitute the call date for the maturity date. Assume a 20-year bond with a current price of $975, a coupon rate of 6.5%, and a face value of $1,000. Also, assume the bond is callable in 15 years at a price of $1,065. Ignoring any accrued interest, the yield to call would be the discount rate that equates $975 to the present value of $65 per year (or $32.50 per six months) for 15 years, plus $1,065 received at the end of 15 years. Not surprisingly, the yield to call exceeds the yield to maturity, in this example (7.02% versus 6.73%).

Actual Return vs. Yield to Maturity

Suppose that someone buys the bond discussed in the prior section (6% coupon, annual coupon payments, 10-year maturity, face value of $1,000, current price of $865.81, and yield to maturity of 8%).[5] The owner holds the bond for the entire 10-year period, and the issuer pays all interest and principal when due. This investment actually earns 8% per annum, right? Not always! Even if an investor holds a bond until maturity and the issuer does not default, his or her actual rate of return may differ from the promised return (the yield to maturity) when the bond was first purchased. We referred to this variation earlier in the chapter as reinvestment risk. The yield to maturity, or promised rate of return, assumes reinvestment of the coupon payments at the yield to maturity. If the reinvested coupon payments earn a rate other than the yield to maturity, then the investor's actual return differs from the promised return.

Having bought the example bond for $865.81 (again, ignoring accrued interest), the owner holds it to maturity, spending the coupon payments when received. How much cash did the bond actually pay over its 10-year life? The bondholder received $1,600 (10 coupon payments of $60 each plus the face value of $1,000). Because the coupon payments were not reinvested, the future value of all the cash received from the bond at maturity (after five years) also equals $1,600. Remember from the basic time value of money discussion, if we know the present and future values of an investment, and the length of time it is held,

actual rate of return

The rate that is effectively or actually earned on the bond investment.

we can calculate the **actual rate of return** using the following formula:

$$\text{ARR} = \left(\frac{\text{FV}}{\text{PV}} \right)^{1/n} - 1 \tag{9.5}$$

---

[5]This example assumes no accrued interest.

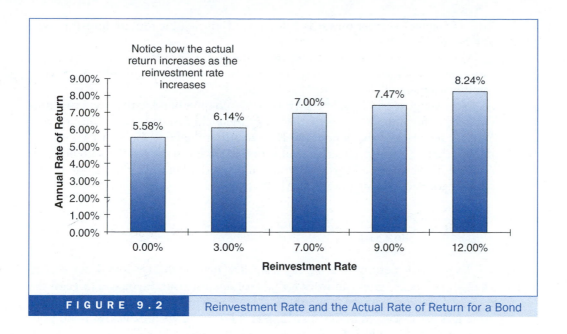

FIGURE 9.2   Reinvestment Rate and the Actual Rate of Return for a Bond

where ARR is the actual rate of return, FV is the future value of all cash flows on the liquidation date, PV is the present value (or price), and n is the length of time the investment is held. Using our example, FV = $1,600, PV = $865.81, and $r = 10$. Substituting these values into Equation 9.5 gives an actual rate return of 6.33%. (This return rate is also called the *effective annual rate*.) This rate is less than the yield to maturity (and a promised rate of return of 8%).

Now, change the example slightly. Assume that, instead of spending the coupon payments, the bondholder deposits them in a bank account that pays 3% per annum. The new value of the bond investment at the end of 10 years equals $1,687.83; the extra $87.83 is interest earned on interest (the return from the reinvested coupons). Equation 9.5 gives an actual rate of return of 6.90% (effective annual rate). It is still less than the yield to maturity but higher than not reinvesting coupons at all (for a reinvestment rate of 0%).

Now, assume that the bondholder can reinvest the bond's coupons in an account that pays 9% per annum. Under this assumption, the future value of cash flows in 10 years equals $1,911.58 and the actual rate of return equals 8.24%.

By now it should be clear: Reinvesting a bond's coupon payments at a higher rate increases the bond's actual rate of return. If the coupons are reinvested at a rate lower (or higher) than the yield to maturity, the actual rate of return will be lower (or higher) than the yield to maturity, or promised rate of return. Of course, this calculation still assumes that the bond is held to maturity and the issuer does not default. Figure 9.2 illustrates the relationship between the reinvestment rate and the actual rate of return for the example bond. Notice that the actual rate of return equals the promised rate of return only when the reinvestment rate equals the yield to maturity.

The relationship between reinvestment rates and actual rates of return illustrate that bond investors can be hurt by falling interest rates as well as rising interest rates. Interest rate risk, therefore, reflects the risks associated with interest rates changing (whether upward or downward) during the time an investor owns any bond.

We have more to say about this topic later in Chapter 10, but here is a simple example that shows how changes in interest rate can dramatically affect your bond investment.

Now suppose you bought the 10-year 6% coupon bond with a yield to maturity of 8% for $865.81. Shortly thereafter the yield to maturity declines to 6%. What is the price of the bond now? Knowing that the bond $CR = YTM$, we can deduce that P_b must equal its face value or $1,000 given the relationship between CR and YTM discussed earlier. If you could sell the bond for the $1,000 today, what is your actual rate of return (ARR)? It is

$$\text{ARR} = \left[\frac{\$1060}{\$865.81} \right]^{1/1} - 1 = 22.4\%$$

Twenty-two percent is a far cry from 8% or 6%! As we found out earlier, changes in interest rates can work for you (or against you). If you can forecast the correct directional change in interest rates, it can work for you. (These and other strategies are discussed in the next chapter.) For now, we present five bond pricing theorems that will help you understand the impact of yield to maturity and coupon on bond prices.

RECAP **RECAP**

Let's review what we have learned about bond valuation up to this point. The price of a bond is the present value of future cash flows—called coupon payments—plus the present value of the amount received at maturity—called the par value—discounted at the required rate of return—called the yield to maturity.

Consider a seven-year bond, with a 7% coupon and a face value of $1,000. This bond has a yield to maturity of 10.0% and no accrued interest.

1. Find the bond's price assuming annual coupon payments.
2. Find the bond's price assuming semiannual coupon payments.
3. Find the bond's price assuming it matures in six years and nine months and coupons are paid semiannually.
4. Find the bond's yield to call assuming it can be called in exactly five years at a price of $1,070 (assume annual coupons).

FIVE BOND PRICING THEOREMS

In this section, we review five well-known bond pricing theorems that attempt to explain various mathematical relationships between bond prices and interest rates. These theorems are important for understanding bond investing. They also provide an important link between understanding bond valuation and interest rate risk.

Before we get to the bond pricing theorems, two things need to be made clear. First, if interest rates are generally rising (or falling), the yield to maturity on every existing bond will rise (or fall). Think about it this way, if the yield on a newly issued five-year Treasury note increased from 3% to 3.5%, what would happen to the yield on already-issued Treasury securities that mature in five years? Obviously, market forces would push their yields upward, as well, probably to about 3.5%.

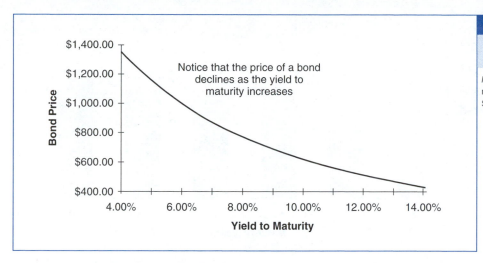

FIGURE 9.3

Bond Price vs.
Yield to Maturity

Note: The bond has a coupon rate of 6%, a maturity of 30 years, and a face value of $1,000.

Second, yields on short-term and long-term bonds can move in different directions for short periods of time. For example, during the summer of 1993, the yield on Treasury bills (T-bills), (which are essentially short-term bonds, rose slightly, whereas the yield on long-term T-bonds fell substantially. With these preliminaries out of the way, let's look at the five bond pricing theorems.

1. Bond Prices Move Inversely to Changes in Interest Rates

This first theorem comes from basic valuation principles: as interest rates rise, bond prices fall, and vice versa. The reason, of course, is that bond investors discount fixed future cash flows at higher interest rates, and higher discount rates give lower present values. This relationship is shown in Figure 9.3, which illustrates the various prices of a bond with a 30-year maturity and a 6% coupon, assuming a yield to maturity between 4% and 12%. For example, at a yield to maturity of 4% per annum, the bond has a price of $1,347.61. To increase the bond's yield to maturity to 7%, the market would drive its price down to $875.28.

2. Longer Maturity Makes a Bond Price More Sensitive to Interest Rates

The best way to illustrate this pricing relationship is with an example. Consider several bonds, each of which has a coupon rate of 8%, a current yield to maturity of 8%, and a face value of $1,000. One bond matures in 5 years, another in 10 years, still another in 15 years, and so forth. How much will the price of each bond change if the market yield to maturity falls from 8% to 6%? The answer indicates each bond's price sensitivity. We already know that the price of each bond will rise, but will they all rise by the same amount? The answer is no. Figure 9.4 shows the percentage price changes for all the bonds. Clearly, longer maturities bring greater percentage price increases. (Remember, other than maturity, all the bonds are identical, with initial prices of $1,000.) For example, the 5-year bond increases in price from $1,000 to $1,085, or about 8.5%. By contrast, the 30-year bond increases in price from $1,000 to $1,277, or about 27.7%.

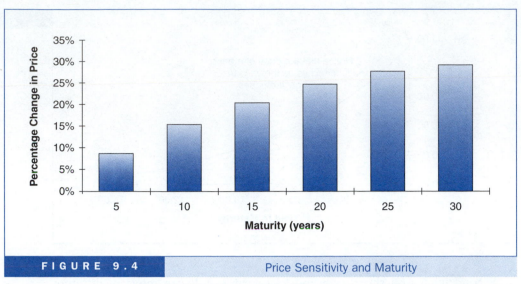

FIGURE 9.4	Price Sensitivity and Maturity

Note: All bonds have coupon rates of 8% and face values of $1,000; price changes assume a drop in the yield to maturity from 8% to 6%.

3. Price Sensitivity Increases with Maturity at a Decreasing Rate

Take another look at Figure 9.4. When the yield to maturity on the bonds falls from 8% to 6%, the 5-year bond increases in price by about $85, the 10-year bond increases in price by about $149, and the 15-year bond increases in price by about $196. The 10-year bond is more price sensitive than the 5-year bond, and the 15-year bond is more price sensitive than the 10-year bond. However, the difference in sensitivity between the 15-year and 10-year bonds is *less* than the difference in price sensitivity between the 10-year and 5-year bonds ($47 versus $64).

4. Lower Coupon Rates Increase Price Sensitivity

Again, this theorem is easiest to illustrate using an example. Assume a series of bonds each having a 10-year maturity, face values of $1,000, and current yields to maturity of 8%. The bonds differ only in their coupon rates. One bond has a coupon rate of 4%, another has a coupon rate of 6%, another has a coupon rate of 8%, and so forth. Let's assume the yield to maturity on all the bonds falls from 8% to 6%. Figure 9.5 shows that the prices of all the bonds rise, with the low-coupon bonds rising the most. For example, the price of the 4% bond increases from $728 to $851 (16.9%) whereas the price of the 12% bond increases from $1,272 to $1,446 (13.7%).

5. A Price Increase Caused by a Yield Decrease Exceeds a Price Decrease Caused by a Similar Yield Increase

Consider a bond with a coupon rate of 8%, a maturity of 10 years, a face value of $1,000, and a current yield to maturity of 8%. Basic bond valuation confirms that because the yield to maturity equals the coupon rate, the bond is currently selling for its face value. What would happen to the bond's price if its yield to maturity were to fall from 8% to 6% or rise from 8% to 10%? The results are

FIGURE 9.5 Price Sensitivity and Coupon Rate

Note: All bonds have maturities of 10 years, and face values of $1,000; price changes assume a drop in yield to maturity from 8% to 6%.

shown in Figure 9.6. If the bond's yield increases from 8% to 10%, its price falls by about 12.5%. By contrast, if the bond's yield decreases from 8% to 6%, its price increases by about 14.9%.

ASSESSING INTEREST RATE RISK

So far, we discussed bonds' investment characteristics, including the general risks investors take when they buy bonds and how bonds are valued. In this section, we take a more detailed look at how to evaluate the most important risk to a bondholder: interest rate risk. Much of this material flows directly from the bond valuation principles we examined in the prior section.

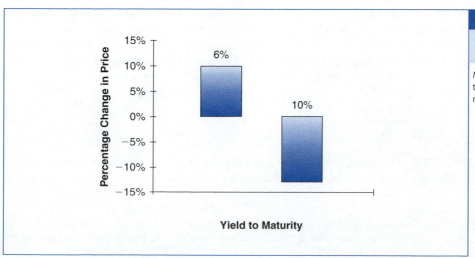

FIGURE 9.6

Price Changes for Increase and Decrease in Yield

Note: Bonds have coupon rates of 8%, a maturity of 10 years, and initially yield to maturity is 8%.

At this point, it might be useful to summarize what we already know about interest rate risk. As interest rates move up and down, the prices of all bonds change as well. Furthermore, some bonds are more price sensitive than others. Bonds with low coupon rates, for example, are more price sensitive than similar bonds with high coupon rates. Therefore, some bonds expose investors to more interest rate risk (i.e., are more price sensitive) than other bonds.

Although the bond pricing theorems are important for understanding bond investing, each assumes that various factors remain constant while only the one under examination varies. When trying to compare various bonds' price sensitivity levels, these theorems may provide only limited insight. Consider the following two bonds:

Bond A: Coupon = 10%, maturity = 20 years
Bond B: Coupon = 6%, maturity = 10 years

Assume that both bonds have the same yield to maturity and face value. Which bond is more price sensitive? So far, we really cannot say. Bond A has the longer maturity, which, according to theorem 2, makes it more price sensitive. However, bond A also has a higher coupon, which, according to theorem 4, makes it less price sensitive. Some sort of a measure is needed to compare the price sensitivity of various bonds, regardless of individual coupons and maturities. This measure is called **duration**.

duration

Amount of time before the "average" dollar is repaid; a measure of interest rate risk.

Duration

The concept of bond duration was formalized by Frederick Macaulay in 1938.[6] Duration provides a measure of price sensitivity, and thus interest rate risk, that takes into account three important factors: coupon rate, time to maturity, and yield to maturity. A longer duration characterizes a more price-sensitive bond.

Technically, duration summarizes the effective maturity of a bond, measuring when an investor receives the average promised cash flow from the bond. More intuitively, duration measures the number of periods it takes to *recover* the bond's price. As an example, consider a zero coupon bond with a maturity of five years. Because it pays only one cash flow, at maturity in five years, the average cash flow is received in five years. Therefore, the bond has a duration of five years.

Finding the duration for a bond with a coupon rate not equal to zero is somewhat more complicated. For any bond, duration (D) is calculated as follows:

$$D = \frac{\sum_{t=1}^{T} \frac{t(CF_t)}{(1 + r)^t}}{P_b} \tag{9.6}$$

where CF_t is the cash flow received in period t, T is the number of periods, and r is the appropriate yield to maturity (also adjusted for semiannual coupons if

---

[6]Frederick Macaulay, *Some Theoretical Problems Suggested by the Movements of Interest Rates, Bond Yields, and Stock Prices in the United States Since 1856* (New York: Columbia University Press, 1938).

TABLE 9.2

Example of Duration Calculation

Basic Information

Coupon	6%
Maturity	10 years
Face value	$1,000
YTM	8%
Bond price	$864.11

Col. 1 Period (t)	Col. 2 Cash Flow	Col. 3 (t) × CF	Col. 4 PV Factor	Col. 5 Col. 3 × Col. 4
1	$30	30	0.9615	28.85
2	$30	60	0.9246	55.48
3	$30	90	0.8890	80.01
4	$30	120	0.8548	102.58
5	$30	150	0.8219	123.29
6	$30	180	0.7903	142.25
7	$30	210	0.7599	159.58
8	$30	240	0.7307	175.37
9	$30	270	0.7026	189.70
10	$30	300	0.6756	202.68
11	$30	330	0.6496	214.37
12	$30	360	0.6246	224.86
13	$30	390	0.6006	234.23
14	$30	420	0.5775	242.55
15	$30	450	0.5553	249.89
16	$30	480	0.5339	256.27
17	$30	510	0.5134	261.83
18	$30	540	0.4936	266.54
19	$30	570	0.4746	270.52
20	$1030	20,600	0.4564	9,401.84

			Sum	12,882.68
			Sum/Bond price	14.909
			Duration	7.45 years

needed). If the bond pays interest semiannually, Equation 9.6 will state D in half-year periods. To restate duration in years, divide D by 2. Let's look at an example.

Table 9.2 details the duration calculation for the familiar bond with a face value of $1,000, a coupon rate of 6%, a term of 10 years, a yield to maturity of 8% (4.0% per half-year), and a price of $864.11. The process to calculate duration consists of five steps:

Step 1. List the cash flow received in each period (t), which appears in column 2 in Table 9.2.

Step 2. Multiply the cash flow (column 2) by the period (the number in column 1). The result, $t(CF_t)$, is shown in column 3.

Step 3. Find the present value of the amount in column 3, by multiplying column 3 by the present value factors shown in column 4. The result is shown in column 5.

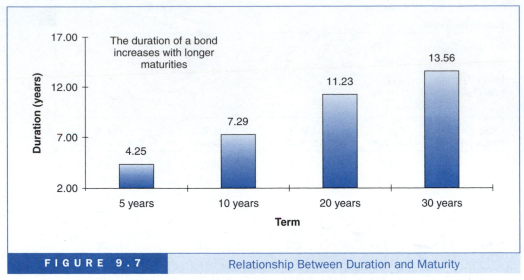

FIGURE 9.7   Relationship Between Duration and Maturity

Note: All bonds have coupon rates of 8% and yields to maturity of 6%.

Step 4. Sum column 5. In Table 9.2, the sum of column 5 is 12,882.68.

Step 5. Divide the sum by the bond's current price. In the example, 12,882.68 is divided by $864.11, which results in the duration of the bond in half-years. Dividing by 2 gives the duration of the bond in years, 7.45.

An investor would receive the bond's average cash flow in about 7 years. It should come as no surprise that the duration is relatively close to the bond's maturity, 10 years, because the single largest cash flow, the face value, and the final six months' interest ($1,030) arrive when the bond matures.

modified duration

Duration divided by the yield to maturity; approximate percentage change in price for a given change in yield to maturity.

Investors often look at the ratio $D/(1 + r)$. This measure is referred to as **modified duration**. The above bond's modified duration is equal to 7.45/1.08 = 6.90. Modified duration reflects the approximate percentage change in price for a given change in yield to maturity.

As mentioned earlier, duration takes into account three important bond pricing factors (maturity, coupon rate, and yield to maturity). The relationship of duration to all three is summed up in three general statements:

1. A longer maturity gives a longer duration, holding the other two factors constant.
2. A higher coupon rate gives a shorter duration, holding the other two factors constant.
3. A higher yield to maturity gives a shorter duration, holding the other two factors constant.

The first two statements are fairly intuitive. Bonds with longer maturities spread out their periodic cash flows over longer periods of time. In addition, they take longer to return their face values to investors. Bonds with higher coupon rates have larger intermediate cash flows (those prior to maturity), so it takes less time to get back the average dollar.

Figures 9.7 and 9.8 illustrate the relationships between duration, maturity, and coupon rates. Figure 9.7 shows the durations of four bonds, all with coupon rates of 8% and yields to maturity of 6%; the bonds have maturities of 5, 10, 20,

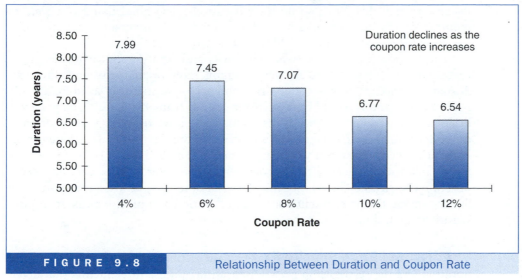

FIGURE 9.8   Relationship Between Duration and Coupon Rate

Note: All bonds have terms of 10 years and yields to maturity of 8%.

and 30 years. The positive relationship between duration and maturity is shown clearly. For example, the 10-year bond has a duration of 7.29 years, whereas the 30-year bond has a duration of 13.56 years.

Figure 9.8 shows the negative relationship between coupon rate and duration. All five bonds have maturities of 10 years and yields to maturity of 8%. Notice that the 4% coupon bond has a duration of almost 8 years whereas the 12% coupon bond has a duration of about 6.5 years.

The relationship between duration and yield to maturity is illustrated in Figure 9.9. All the bonds have equal coupon rates (8%) and maturities (10 years).

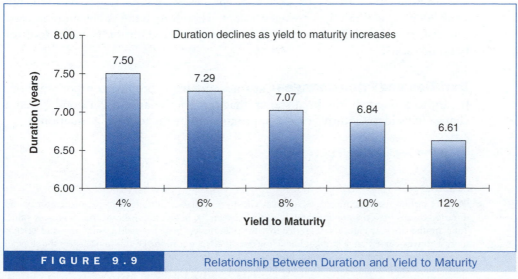

FIGURE 9.9   Relationship Between Duration and Yield to Maturity

Note: All bonds have terms of 10 years and coupon rates of 8%.

Because their yields differ, so do their durations. The bond that has a yield to maturity of 4%, for example, has a duration of 7.5 years compared with about 6.6 years for the bond with a yield to maturity of 12%.

The relationship between yield to maturity and duration is probably less intuitive than the relationships between coupon rates or maturity and duration. Assume a bond has an 8% coupon rate and a 10 year maturity as in Figure 9.9. A dramatic example would be if interest rates rise from 4% to 12%, its price will decline. Because you pay less for the bond, the relative recovery years shorten as the coupon that is recovered becomes relatively more significant. To restate: As the bond prices decline, current yields rise from 6% ($80/$1324) to 10% ($80/$774). So the relative significance of coupon increases as interest rates rise, and hence duration decreases.[7] The relationship between duration and yield is important to understanding the uses, and limitations, of duration as a precise measure of price sensitivity and, thus, interest rate risk.

Duration and Price Sensitivity The prior section explained how to compute duration and the relationship between duration and the three factors that determine bond prices. These discussions lead to an obvious conclusion: a longer duration indicates greater price sensitivity, for a given change in yield. This suggests one use of duration: to compare the price sensitivity levels of two bonds regardless of their individual coupon rates and maturities.

As an example, reconsider the two bonds that we tried to compare earlier:

Bond A: Coupon rate = 10%, maturity = 20 years, YTM = 8%
Bond B: Coupon rate = 6%, maturity = 10 years, YTM = 8%

Before the concept of duration was introduced, analysts had no way to say, unequivocally, that one bond was more price sensitive than the other. Duration more accurately measures this important relationship. The duration of bond A is 9.87 years and the duration of bond B is 7.45 years. Therefore, if yields rise by a given amount (say, from 8% to 8.5%), the prices of both bonds will fall, but bond A's price will fall by a greater amount. Therefore, bond A has more interest rate risk than bond B. This feature, by itself, makes duration a useful tool for bond investors.

Duration and Price Changes Can this comparison become any more specific? It can, to a point. It has been shown that the price change for a bond, given a change in yield to maturity, can be approximated by the following equation:

$$\Delta P \approx -D[\Delta(1 + r)/(1 + r)]P_b \tag{9.7}$$

[7]A more technical explanation is as follows: The inverse relationship between yield to maturity and duration results from the nonlinear relationship between the bond's interest rate and its present value. Take another look at Figure 9.3. Notice that the relationship between yield to maturity and price is more a convex curve than a straight line. How does it affect duration? Duration measures the slope of a straight line tangent to each point along that curve. As a bond moves up or down the curve, the slope of the line changes. For example, moving down the curve (i.e., as yield to maturity increases), the slope of the line decreases.

INVESTMENT INSIGHT

Understanding the Importance of Duration

Morningstar classifies more than 100 mutual funds as intermediate-term government bond funds, meaning they invest primarily in U.S. Treasury and agency securities with maturities of 10 years or less. In the world of mutual funds, you would think that this group would be fairly homogenous and show little variation in performance among these funds. Yet, reviewing performance figures for 2002 does show more variation from fund to fund that you might initially expect.

For instance, the Vanguard Intermediate U.S. Government fund had a total return for 2002 of 14.2%. The Vanguard fund beat the group average by about 5% and the market index (the Lehman Brothers Aggregate Bond index) by almost 4%. By contrast, the Strong Government Securities fund had a total return for 2002 of 10.2%, only slightly more than the group average and index. Even more interesting is the breakdown in each fund's total return between income and capital appreciation (change in the fund's net asset value). Both funds had income returns of about 7%. On the other hand, the Vanguard fund's capital appreciation return was about twice that of the Strong fund's capital appreciation return.

Given that the two funds state similar investment objectives and invest in similar types of securities, what explains the difference in returns? The answer is duration. The Vanguard fund's duration was longer than the Strong fund's duration. This difference means that as interest rates fell throughout much of 2002, the value of the Vanguard fund's portfolio rose by more than the value of the Strong fund's portfolio. Duration is one of the least understood, yet most important considerations when choosing a bond fund.

Technically duration measures the number of years of cash flows required to recover the initial price of a bond. It can also be used to link changes in market interest rates to bond price changes. As such, duration is a good measure of bond volatility. Suppose a bond fund has a duration of 4.5 years. A 1% decrease in the market interest rate will lead to approximately a 4.5% increase in the fund's net asset value. Similarly, a 1% increase in the market interest rate will lead to approximately a 4.5% decrease in the fund's net asset value. Because of the Vanguard fund's longer duration, its net asset value increased by a greater amount than the Strong fund as market interest rates fell during 2002.

Most investors realize that longer-term bonds are more price sensitive than shorter term bonds, but maturity alone doesn't determine price sensitivity. The bond's coupon rate and market interest rates also affect price sensitivity. Duration takes all three factors into account and allows the investor to quantify the approximate gain, or loss, due to interest rate changes. Consequently, investors should pay more attention to duration than average maturity when choosing a bond fund.

Questions for Critical Thinking

1. If you believe that market interest rates are about to rise, what changes should you make to the average duration of your bond portfolio? Why?

2. The formula for finding duration looks complicated. How would you explain it in nontechnical terms to an investor? Use examples to illustrate your explanation.

where ΔP is the change in price, D is the bond's duration, $\Delta(1 + r)/(1 + r)$ is the percentage change in the yield to maturity, and P_b is the current price of the bond. Consider the preceding example of two bonds, A and B, and assume the yield to maturity on both increases from 8% to 8.5%. Their approximate price changes can be calculated as follows:

Bond A: $\Delta P \approx -9.87[(0.005/(1 + .08)]($119.79)$
  $\approx -$5.47$ **(per $100 face value)**

Bond B: $\Delta P \approx -7.45[(0.005/1 + .08)]($86.41)$
  ≈ -2.98 **(per $100 face value)**

Why are these results only approximate price changes? The reason goes back to our discussion in the prior section: as a bond's yield to maturity changes, so does its duration. Duration is a measure of price sensitivity but only a *point* measure. A greater change in yield to maturity gives a less precise statement of price change calculated using duration, sometimes referred to as duration tracking error.

Even if duration only gives approximate price changes, it is still a useful measure of interest rate risk. Duration is a key consideration when it comes to assessing the safety of a bond mutual fund.

Let's try to recap what we learned about interest rate risk. First, interest rate risk can be described as the price sensitivity of a bond to a change in its yield to maturity. Second, we determined that all bonds expose investors to interest rate risk, although some have more than others. Third, the usefulness of a summary measure of price sensitivity (duration) was demonstrated. Consider a bond with a coupon rate of 7%, a maturity of five years, a face value of $1,000, and a yield to maturity of 7% (assume annual coupon payments and no accrued interest).

5. Find the bond's duration and modified duration.
6. Find the approximate price change if the bond's yield to maturity falls from 7% to 6.5%.

CREDIT RISK

In this section, we examine the other major risk to which bond investors are exposed, the risk of not receiving promised cash flows in a timely fashion credit, or default risk. Although all bonds feature interest rate risk, some expose investors to zero credit risk. These are bonds issued by the U.S. Treasury. (Remember, because the Treasury owns the only legal financial printing press, it can always print money to pay its bills.) Bonds issued by corporations and municipalities all have varying degrees of credit risk. Some of these bonds are almost as safe as Treasuries, whereas others are far more speculative. In this section, we discuss how to evaluate credit risk. We also take a detailed look at an actual bond default to see how it affected issuers and investors. First, let's take a detailed look at **bond ratings**—perhaps the most common tool for assessing credit risk.

bond ratings

Independent assessments of bond credit risk.

Bond Ratings

Most, although not all, publicly traded corporate and municipal bonds are rated by independent investment information services. The two best-known rating agencies are Moody's and S&P. Table 9.3 presents a brief description of Moody's and S&P bond ratings. In addition to those letter ratings, Moody's occasionally assigns a number to a bond rating to indicate where a bond ranks within its rating category. For example, a bond with a rating of A1 is considered to be of slightly higher quality than a bond with a rating of A3. S&P sometimes adds a plus (+) or minus (−) to a letter rating to show relative standing within a rating category.

Moody's and S&P rate bonds similarly. Both rate bonds primarily on the issuers' ability to make required principal and interest payments in a timely fashion. Bonds that receive the highest rating (Aaa or AAA), for example, are considered to have virtually no credit risk, regardless of the economic environment. An issuer whose bond receives a middle rating (say, Baa or BBB) is considered to have adequate capacity to

Description of Potential Credit Risk	Standard & Poor's Rating	Moody's Rating	TABLE 9.3
Capacity to pay interest and repay principal is extremely strong	AAA	Aaa	General Description of Bond Ratings
Very strong capacity to pay interest and repay principal; only slightly less safe than debt rated triple A	AA	Aa	
Strong capacity to pay interest and repay principal, though somewhat susceptible to adverse changes in economic and financial conditions	A	A	
Speculative; faces ongoing uncertainties or exposure to adverse conditions, which could lead to the inability to pay interest or repay principal	BB	Ba	
Vulnerable to default, but currently has the capacity to meet interest and principal obligations	B	B	
Currently identifiable vulnerability to default and is dependent on favorable conditions to meet obligations	CCC	Caa	
More vulnerable to default and highly speculative	CC	Ca	
Extremely speculative, poor prospects for attaining any real investment standing	C	C	
Currently in default	DDD or below	—	

make interest and principal payments, but that capacity may be adversely affected by deteriorating economic conditions. Both Moody's and S&P divide bonds into two general categories based on their ratings: **investment-grade bonds** (Baa/BBB-rated issues, or above) and speculative-grade bonds (Ba/BB-rated issues, or below). Speculative-grade bonds are commonly referred to as **junk bonds.**[8]

Moody's and S&P rate newly issued bonds and update their ratings on existing bonds. Both companies publish lists of bonds whose ratings are under review. S&P's publication, for example, is called *Credit Watch*.

Determinants of Bond Ratings Why do some bonds receive higher ratings than other bonds? As we indicated, Moody's and S&P base a bond rating primarily on the ability of the issuer to make required principal and interest payments in a timely fashion. Not surprisingly, the financial characteristics of issuers that receive high ratings differ from those that receive lower ratings. For example, a corporate issuer that receives an Aaa/AAA rating should be stronger financially than a corporation that receives a Baa/BBB rating. This distinction is illustrated in Table 9.4, which breaks down three-year median values of selected financial ratios by S&P rating category. (These data refer to corporate issuers only.) The data show that higher-rated corporations are, on average, less levered and more profitable, and they have greater capacity to cover fixed financial charges, when compared with lower-rated corporations.

In addition to the issuer's financial characteristics, both Moody's and S&P examine other factors when determining bond ratings. These include the nature

investment-grade bonds

Bonds with ratings of BBB or greater.

speculative-grade bonds

Bonds with ratings below BBB; also known as junk bonds.

---
[8]Some institutional investors are prohibited from buying speculative-grade bonds.

TABLE 9.4				
Median Financial Ratios by S&P Rating Category Three-Year (1999–2001) Medians	**Rating Category**	**EBIT Interest Coverage**	**Cash Flow/ Total Debt**	**Long-Term Debt to Capital**
	AAA	23.1%	97.3%	4.4%
	AA	11.4	27.6	23.0
	A	6.2	17.5	33.3
	BBB	3.8	9.3	41.5
	BB	2.2	4.3	56.4

Source: Standard & Poor's, Adjusted Key U.S. Industrial Financial Ratios, Aug. 13, 2002.

of the bond, its specific provisions, and the protection it affords creditors in the event of bankruptcy. S&P, for example, assigns a rating of BB to a corporation's subordinated debt if its senior debt has a BBB rating. As another example, a municipal bond that is insured will generally receive an Aaa/AAA rating regardless of other characteristics.

Bond Ratings and Default Rates Bond ratings raise several important questions. Perhaps the most important is whether bond ratings predict default reasonably well. In other words, has the historical default rate been higher for bonds with lower ratings? Available evidence appears to answer this question with a yes. For example, Table 9.5 lists 1-year and 10-year default rates for corporate bonds between 1970 and 1990, broken down by original bond ratings.

Less than 0.5% of bonds originally rated Aaa defaulted within 10 years of issue. (None defaulted within 1 year of issue.) By contrast, slightly more than 8% of bonds originally rated B defaulted within 1 year of issue, and almost one-quarter defaulted within 10 years of issue. In addition, notice the dramatic difference in the historical default rates between investment-grade bonds (Baa and above) and speculative-grade, or junk, bonds (Ba and B). For example, the 10-year default rate for bonds rated Baa was less than 4% compared with a 10-year default rate of more than 11% for bonds rated Ba.

Another way of assessing the effectiveness of bond ratings is to see whether (and how) they have changed prior to default. We would expect to see bond ratings falling well before issuers actually defaulted, as issuers' financial conditions

TABLE 9.5		Default Rates	
Historical Default Rates for Corporate Bonds, 1970–1990	**Original Rating**	**1 Year from Issue**	**10 Years from Issue**
	AAA	0.00%	0.37%
	Aa	0.04	0.65
	A	0.01	0.99
	Baa	0.17	3.78
	Ba	1.80	11.29
	B	8.08	24.17

Source: J. S. Fons and A. E. Kimball, "Corporate Bond Defaults and Default Rates," *Journal of Fixed Income*, June 1991, pp. 36–47.

	Rating Prior to Reaching Default Status		
Rating Category	**Rating When Issued**	**One Year Prior to Default**	**Six Months Prior to Default**
AAA	0.9%	0.0%	0.0%
AA	3.4	0.0	0.0
A	10.8	0.4	0.4
BBB	11.2	9.3	7.3
BB	10.6	9.8	5.9
B	47.8	49.4	40.4
CCC	14.6	28.4	40.2
CC	0.7	2.1	5.1
C	0.0	0.6	0.6

TABLE 9.6

S&P Rating Distributions of Defaulting Bond Issues

Note: The table shows the distribution of bond ratings at the time issued, one year prior to default, and six months prior to default. For example, almost 48% of bonds that eventually defaulted were rated B when issued; almost half of bonds that eventually defaulted were rated B one year prior to reaching default status.

Source: E. I. Altman, "Revisiting the High-Yield Bond Market," *Financial Management,* Summer 1992, p. 85. With permission from Dr. Edward Altman, Professor of Finance, NYU Stern School of Business.

deteriorate. This expectation appears to be the case. Table 9.6 lists the distribution of original ratings on 556 corporate bond issues that eventually defaulted between 1970 and 1991, as well as the rating distributions one year and six months before actual default.

Only about one-quarter of the 556 corporate issues that actually defaulted between 1970 and 1991 were originally classified as investment grade. (Five bonds were even initially rated AAA.) The rest were originally classified as junk bonds. The most common original bond rating was B. The data suggest that as default approached, the average rating did indeed decline. One year before default, more than half the bonds were rated B, CCC, or CC, whereas less than 10% were still classified as investment grade. Finally, six months before reaching default status, less than 8% of the bonds carried investment-grade ratings whereas almost 90% were rated B or below.

Graham and Dodd on Credit Risk and Bond Selection

Although bond ratings are useful tools for assessing credit risk, they are not perfect predictors. Further, many bonds are not even rated. Investors often need to look beyond bond ratings to evaluate the specific characteristics of issues and issuers when selecting bonds. In addition to being the fathers of modern stock analysis, Graham and Dodd also had a lot to say about bond investing.[9]

Graham and Dodd argued that bond investors should focus primarily on avoiding losses. Therefore, bond selection is "primarily a negative art. . . . [I]t is a process of exclusion and rejection, rather than [of] search and acceptance."[10] To meet this objective, Graham and Dodd established a set of qualitative and

---

[9]See S. Cottle et al., *Graham & Dodd's Security Analysis,* 5th ed. (New York: McGraw-Hill, 1998), pp. 480–482.
[10]*Ibid.,* p. 441.

TABLE 9.7	1. Retained earnings equal to 40% of assets, except in capital-intensive businesses where 25% may be adequate.
Graham and Dodd's Standards for Safety: Investment Grade Bonds	2. Positive trends in growth and profitability relative to trends in the economy and in the company's industry.
	3. Reasonable stability of earning power, with no or infrequent loss years.
	4. A minimum size of $50 million as measured by the five-year average market value of the borrower's net worth.
	5. Reasonable protection against excessive dilution of the priority of claim on earning power.
	6. Net current assets equal to 100% of total long-term debt.
	7. A working capital ratio of at least 1.75:1.
	8. A quick ratio of 1:1.
	9. An equity cushion of 200% of total debt as measured by the five-year average of the market value of the borrower's net worth.
	10. Interest charges earned an average of five times before taxes for industrials and three times for public utilities, with a poorest-year minimum of twice.
	11. Total debt service coverage averaging twice and not below once in the poorest year.

Source: S. Cottle et al., *Graham and Dodd's Security Analysis,* 5th ed. (New York: McGraw-Hill, 1988), p. 465. Reproduced with permission of the McGraw-Hill Companies.

quantitative standards of safety. After reviewing these standards, it is probably reasonable to say that Graham and Dodd would not be big fans of junk bonds.

Graham and Dodd's qualitative standards include stability, issuer size, and issue terms. They argue that more-stable companies with better interest coverage ratios and profitability over several business cycles are better credit risks. For example, a company whose interest coverage ratio stays near 3.03 over several business cycles is a better credit risk than one whose interest coverage ranges from, say, 1.5 to 4.5, depending on the economic environment. Larger issuers, according to Graham and Dodd, are safer than smaller issuers. Indeed, the historical default rate is higher for smaller issuers (measured in terms of total assets) than the rate for larger issuers. Finally, the terms of the issue are also important. Shorter maturities, more secure types of securities (e.g., mortgage bonds), and protective provisions make for safer bonds. For example, Graham and Dodd believed that bonds with sinking funds are better, safer investments compared to bonds without sinking funds.[11]

In addition to these qualitative standards, Graham and Dodd also list 11 minimum quantitative standards for investment-grade bonds. They believed, for example, that issuers of investment-grade bonds should have net total current assets (current assets minus current liabilities) equal to at least 100% of outstanding long-term debt. We reprint this list in Table 9.7. Unfortunately, Graham and Dodd provide no information on how they came up with these standards. In addition, these standards are quite strict; many companies with investment-grade bond ratings probably do not meet them.

---

[11]A sinking fund is a provision that requires the issuer to retire—by calling—a fixed percentage of bonds each year, over a specified period, before maturity. In essence, a sinking fund shortens the effective maturity of a bond issue and also stretches the repayment of principal over several years. Bonds with sinking funds tend to have a lower yields compared with similar bonds without sinking funds.

INVESTMENT HISTORY

Anatomy of a Default

On July 23, 1983, the Washington Public Power Supply System (often referred to in the press as "Whoops") defaulted on more than $2 billion in bonds. Even today, 20 years later, it remains the largest municipal bond default in history—more than twice the size of the next largest, the 1994 default by Orange County, California. The Whoops default was caused by problems associated with two partially completed nuclear power plants in Washington state. Financial and other problems led to project cancellation and bond default.

Even though some rumors circulated prior to the default, the announcement took the financial markets somewhat by surprise. The default caused the price of Whoops bonds to collapse. Within a few weeks, some of the bonds were trading for as little as 8.5 cents per dollar. In response to the default, several class action federal lawsuits were filed on behalf of bond investors.

More than five years later, in late 1988, the plaintiffs and defendants (the State of Washington, more than 100 utilities, plant contractors, and several securities firms) reached a preliminary settlement. The settlement called for payment of approximately $750 million to the plaintiffs. A federal court approved the allocation of these funds to individual bondholders, and final payment was made in September 1992, almost 10 years after Whoops defaulted. Bondholders received about 45 cents on the dollar, considered by most standards to be generous.

Investors can learn many important lessons from the Whoops default. One of the most important is that large, well-known bond issues can go into default. The Whoops bonds were originally rated single A by both Standard & Poor's and Moody's, a solid investment-grade rating. Even 18 months before default, the Whoops bonds still carried an A rating. Not until about eight months before default did Standard & Poor's downgrade the Whoops bonds to junk status.

Another important lesson to be learned is that default is costly to bond investors. Although, they settled the lawsuit for a record amount and recovered far more than most investors do in a default, investors still received less than half the face value of their bonds. In addition, almost a decade passed between default and settlement, during which investors received nothing. The bottom line of the Whoops story is that bond investors ignore credit risk at their peril.

Questions for Critical Thinking

1. Why didn't Washington State use tax revenues to pay off the bondholders after the Whoops default?
2. Does the Whoops saga suggest that investors should ignore ratings and evaluate the creditworthiness of a bond issuer themselves?

RISK AND REQUIRED RETURNS FOR BONDS

Throughout this text, we discuss the notion that risk and return are related; riskier investments must promise higher returns. Therefore, we would expect to see bond investors demanding higher promised returns on higher-risk bonds. Given that bonds expose investors to several different types of risk, we can relate the promised (required or expected) return on a bond to several factors, as follows:

$$r = f(i, \Delta p, ir, rr, dr, cr, lr, fxr) \tag{9.8}$$

where i is the **real rate of interest**, Δp is the expected rate of inflation over the bond's term, ir is interest rate risk, rr is reinvestment risk, dr is default (credit) risk, cr is call risk, lr is liquidity risk, and fxr is foreign exchange risk. As each risk factor rises (or falls), the promised return on a bond also rises (or falls).

real rate of interest

The rate of interest in the absence of inflation or any risk premium.

The first two factors in Equation 9.8 (i and Δp) make up the required return on a risk-free bond. (The closest thing to a truly risk-free security is a short-term T-bill.) The other seven factors can be thought of as compensation (or risk premiums) for investing in bonds that expose investors to various types of risk. For some bonds, certain risk premiums may be zero, or close to zero. For example, T-bonds have no credit risk, thus investors can demand no risk premium to the bonds' required returns to compensate investors for credit risk. However, T-bonds do expose investors to other types of risk (e.g., interest rate risk), and thus those risk premiums will be added to the bonds' promised returns.

Equation 9.8 represents only a general model of the determinants of bond yields and is difficult to quantify. Nevertheless, the model can give some insight into the determinants of bond yields. Let's now take a more detailed look at the relationship between bond yields and two important factors: maturity and credit risk.

Bond Yields and Maturity

term structure of interest rate

The relationship between maturity and bond yields, also known as the yield curve.

The relationship between bond yields and maturity is often referred to as the **term structure of interest rates**, or **yield curve**. The yield curve shows the relationship between yield and maturity for a group of bonds that are similar in other respects. U.S. Treasury securities are often used to represent the yield curve because all are free of default risk and have excellent secondary markets.

Although the yield curve raises several important and interesting questions, for our purposes in this chapter we need to examine only two: What is the expected shape of the yield curve? Does the shape of the yield curve change over time?

Based on our discussion in this chapter, one could argue that the normal shape of the yield curve should be upward sloping. In other words, as the term to maturity increases, so should the yield. Several reasons lead to this expectation. We have seen that a longer-maturity bond exposes the investor to greater interest rate risk (holding other factors constant). Also, as one holds a bond longer, the probability of unfavorable changes in interest rates rises. Thus, one could argue that longer-term bonds expose investors to greater amounts of reinvestment risk. Furthermore, longer-term bonds also expose investors to greater amounts of purchasing power risk. After all, it is easier to forecast inflation for next year than to forecast inflation for the next 30 years. Investors who bought bonds back in the 1950s never expected the inflation of the 1970s.

Adding up all these factors suggests that, all things being equal, investors would rather own short-term bonds than long-term bonds; investors require inducements in the form of higher yields to purchase longer-term bonds. Therefore, the normal shape of the yield curve should be positive. The evidence does indeed suggest that the yield curve is normally upward sloping. But is it always upward sloping? The answer is no.

Figure 9.10 shows the general shape of the Treasury yield curve between 1966 and 2002. To simplify the shape, the figure shows the yield spread between three-month T-bills and long-term T-bonds (with at least 10 years to maturity). A yield spread is just the difference in yield between the two instruments. For example, if the yield on three-month T-bills is 4.3% and the yield on long-term T-bonds is 7%, then the yield spread (bonds minus bills) is 2.7%. If the yield

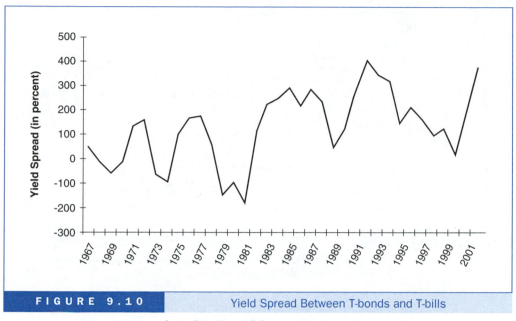

| **FIGURE 9.10** | Yield Spread Between T-bonds and T-bills |

Source: *Federal Reserve Bulletin* and *Federal Reserve Statistical Release* (various issues).

spread is positive, then the yield curve is upward sloping. Notice that the shape of the yield curve has changed from time to time.

The yield spread between three-month bills and long-term bonds has generally been positive over this time period (indicating an upward-sloping yield curve). However, the slope has been much steeper in some years than other years. In 1992, for example, the spread was over 4% compared with 1990 when it was 1.24%. In some years, the yield spread has been virtually zero. In 1970, for example, the yield spread was about 0.10%. A yield spread close to zero defines a flat yield curve. Finally, in other years, yields on T-bills actually exceeded yields on long-term T-bonds. In 1981, for example, T-bills were yielding almost 2% more than long-term bonds. A negative yield spread defines an inverted (i.e., downward-sloping) yield curve.

What do differently shaped yield curves mean? We discuss several interesting theories of the yield curve, along with several implications for active and passive bond portfolio management strategies in the next chapter. We discuss these in Chapter 10 as well.

Bond Yields and Credit Risk

Just as interest rates have a term structure, one can also define a risk structure of interest rates, which takes into account differences in bond yields across bonds with different degrees of credit risk. In general, of course, bonds with higher credit risk always have higher yields. However, the yield spreads between bonds of varying credit risk do not remain constant over time. The risk structure of interest rates changes from time to time. As an example, look at Figure 9.11. It shows two yield spreads (Aaa corporates minus long-term T-bonds, and Baa corporates minus Aaa corporates) between 1968 and 2002.

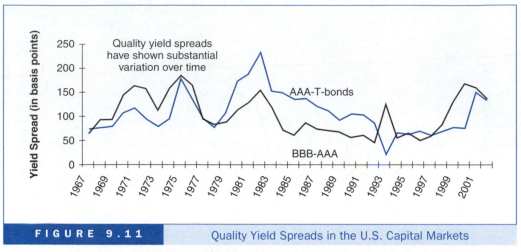

FIGURE 9.11   Quality Yield Spreads in the U.S. Capital Markets

Source: *Federal Reserve Bulletin* and *Federal Reserve Statistical Release* (various issues).

Both yield spreads were positive throughout this 30-year period; the yield spread between Aaa corporates and T-bonds, as well as the spread between Baa corporates and Aaa corporates, averaged about 1%. However, both spreads show a good deal of variation around their averages. In 1992, for example, the spread between Aaa corporates and long-term T-bonds was 0.48%. By contrast, in 1985 the spread was almost 2%. During this 30-year period, the yield spread between Baa and Aaa corporates has been as low as 0.38% (1968) and as high as 2.32% (1982).

Several theories try to explain the risk structure of interest rates. One popular theory suggests that yield spreads widen and narrow in response to economic expectations. If investors are pessimistic about the economy, yield spreads widen; if investors are optimistic, spreads narrow. Apparently, the argument goes, investors are more quality conscious in a poor economic environment than they are in a good environment. Investors are willing to hold lower-quality bonds in a poor economy but require higher credit risk premiums.

We learned quite a bit about bonds in this chapter. We know how to value bonds, measure interest rate risk, and assess credit risk. In the next chapter, we examine passive and active bond management strategies.

SUMMARY

1. Why are bonds viable investment alternatives?

Bonds are viable investment alternatives because they provide the best source of consistent income. Bonds can also help to diversify a stock portfolio and have the potential for producing substantial capital gains. Some bonds offer tax advantages as well.

2. What are the risks faced by bond investors?

Investing in bonds is not without risk. Bond investors are exposed to interest rate risk, credit risk, purchasing power risk, reinvestment risk, liquidity risk, and foreign exchange risk. Bonds vary substantially in terms of risk, and some bonds do not expose investors to every type of risk. T-bonds, for example, have no credit risk.

3. How are bonds priced?

The price of a bond is the present value of future coupon payments plus the present value of the amount to be returned at maturity, called the par or face value, discounted at the yield to maturity. If the bond pays coupon interest twice a year—which most bonds do—an adjustment is necessary to find the price of the bond. If the bond is purchased between the dates coupon interest is paid, the buyer owes the seller accrued interest. Purchase timing also affects the bond's price. If coupon payments are reinvested at a rate other than the yield to maturity, the actual return on the bond will differ from the bond's yield to maturity.

4. What are the basic bond pricing theorems?

Five basic theorems explain bond pricing. First, bond prices move inversely within interest rates. Second, the price sensitivity of bonds, with respect to changes in interest rates, increases as maturity increases. Third, the price sensitivity of bonds with respect to maturity increases at a decreasing rate. Fourth, bonds with lower coupon rates are more price sensitive compared with bonds with higher coupon rates. Fifth, a price increase caused by a yield decrease exceeds a price decrease caused by a similar yield increase.

5. How can interest rate risk be measured?

Interest rate risk is defined as the price sensitivity of a bond to a given change in interest rates. The most widely used summary measure of interest rate risk is duration. Duration is defined as the length of time before the average dollar is repaid to the investor. The longer the duration of a bond, the more price sensitive. The duration of a bond is positively related to a bond's maturity but is negatively related to a bond's coupon rate and yield to maturity.

6. How can credit risk be evaluated?

Bonds vary widely in terms of credit risk from very little to substantially more. One way of assessing credit risk is to look at the bond's rating. Most corporate and municipal bonds are rated by S&P and Moody's. The higher the rating, the lower the amount of credit risk. Although not perfect, bond ratings are fairly accurate predictors of credit risk. Graham and Dodd suggested some qualitative and quantitative standards for evaluating credit risk, arguing that safety of principal was the most important consideration.

7. How are bond risk and required return related?

The expected, or promised, return on a bond is a function of the real rate of interest plus compensation for the expected rate of inflation. To this real rate, investors add a risk premium reflecting, when applicable, credit risk, interest rate risk, liquidity risk, and foreign exchange risk. The yield curve—the relationship between long- and short-term bond yields—has generally been upward sloping. However, at times the yield curve has been flat or even downward sloping. Likewise, the yield spreads between bonds of varying credit risk have varied substantially over time.

MINI CASE

The purpose of this mini case is to provide opportunities to practice basic principles of bond valuation. Use the following bond data to answer the following questions:

Coupon rate = 4%
Yield to maturity = 6%
Face value = $1,000
Maturity = 5 years

1. Assuming annual coupon payments, and maturity in exactly five years, find the price of this bond.
2. Assuming semiannual coupon payments, maturity in exactly five years, and a yield to maturity of 6%, find the price of this bond.

3. Why do the prices you found in Questions 1 and 2 differ?
4. Now, assume that the bond matures in exactly four years and three months. (Also, assume semiannual coupons and an effective annual yield to maturity of 6%.) Find the bond's price. How much accrued interest could a buyer owe?
5. Go back to the assumptions in Question 2. If someone were to buy the bond today and hold it until maturity and the issuer did not default, would the actual annual rate of return always be equal to 6%? What would the actual rate of return be if the owner were simply to spend the coupon payments?

REVIEW EXERCISES

1. List some of the reasons investors should consider buying bonds. Elaborate on one of the reasons you listed.
2. What are the risks associated with investing in bonds? To which type(s) of risk are all bond investors exposed?
3. List the variables you need to know to find the price of a bond. What does *yield to maturity* mean?
4. Determine the price of a bond with a 4% coupon rate maturing in 10 years with a $1,000 face value, and a yield to maturity of 6%.
   a. Assume annual interest payments and no accrued interest.
   b. Assume semiannual interest payments and no accrued interest.
5. Find the price of a bond with a 6% coupon rate maturing in 10 years with a $1,000 face value, and yielding 8%.
   a. Assume annual interest payments and no accrued interest.
   b. Assume semiannual interest payment and no accrued interest.
6. Determine the price of a bond with a 5% coupon rate maturing in five years with a $1,000 face value, and a yield to maturity of 4%.
   a. Assume annual interest payments and no accrued interest.
   b. Assume semiannual interest payments and no accrued interest.
7. Find the price of a bond with zero coupon payments maturing in 10 years with a $1,000 face value, and a yield to maturity of 6%.
   a. Assume annual interest payments.
   b. Assume semiannual interest payments.
8. Find the price of a zero coupon bond maturing in 20 years with a $1,000 face value, and a yield to maturity of 8%.
   a. Assume annual interest payments.
   b. Assume semiannual interest payments.
9. Define *accrued interest* and how it affects the bond price.
10. Find the price of a 4% coupon bond that pays semiannual interest, and interest is accrued. It matures in exactly four years and nine months, and yields 6%.
11. What is the price of a three-year, 6% coupon bond yielding 6% if the bond matures in two years eight months and interest is accrued and paid semiannually?
12. What is the price of a three-year, 4% coupon bond yielding 6% if the bond matures in two years 8 months and interest is accrued and paid semiannually?
13. What is the price of a 6% coupon, five-year bond yielding 8% if the bond matures in four years 10 months and interest is accrued and paid semiannually?
14. Assume a bond has a current price of $1,100, a face value of $1,000, a coupon rate of 8%, and exactly 10 years to maturity (assume annual coupon payments). Find the bond's yield to maturity. If this bond is callable in exactly eight years at $1,080, what is the yield to call?

15. A 10-year bond is priced at $851.25 and its coupon rate equals 4% per annum. Assuming semiannual coupon payments and a $1,000 face value, what is its yield to maturity?

16. A bond matures in 20 years and is priced at $548.60. Its annual coupon rate equals 6% paid semiannually with a face value of $1,000. What is its yield to maturity?

17. A zero coupon bond matures in 10 years and is priced at $508.34. If it has a $1,000 face value, what is its yield to maturity?

18. If you were to buy a 10-year, 7% coupon bond today for its face value of $1,000, what would your actual rate of return be if you reinvested the coupon payments at 8%? Assume you would hold the bond to maturity and the bond would pay interest once a year.

19. Why is the actual rate of return always equal to the yield to maturity for a zero coupon bond (assuming it is held to maturity and the issuer does not default)?

20. A 6% coupon bond has five years to maturity. If coupon is paid annually and reinvested at 7% over the five years, what is the actual rate of return?

21. A 4% coupon bond matures in 10 years and its yield to maturity is 7%. If coupon is paid annually and the coupons are reinvested at 5% for the next 10 years, what is the actual rate of return?

22. Suppose you purchased a 10-year, 5% coupon bond with a yield of 7%.
    a. What is the bond price?
    b. Two years later, its market yield declines to 6%. What is its price 2 years later?
    c. If you collect two coupon payments that are reinvested at 6% and then sell the bond, what is your actual rate of return?

23. Suppose you purchased a 15-year, 3% coupon bond with a yield of 5%.
    a. What is the bond price?
    b. Two years later, its market yield rises to 6%. What is its price two years later?
    c. If you collect two coupon payments that are reinvested at 6% and then sell the bond, what is your actual rate of return?

24. List the five basic bond pricing theorems. How do these theorems relate to interest rate risk?

25. Define *duration*. How does duration relate to interest rate risk?

26. Calculate the duration of a 6% coupon, three-year bond yielding 6% and interest is paid annually with no accrued interest.

27. Find the duration of a 2% coupon, three-year bond yielding 6% and interest is paid annually with no accrued interest.

28. Calculate the duration of a 2% coupon, three-year bond yielding 4% and interest is paid annually with no accrued interest. Discuss the difference in duration between the results of Questions 27 and 28.

29. Assume a bond has a duration of 4.5 years, a current price of $1,000, and a yield to maturity of 7%. If the bond's yield to maturity declines from 7% to 6.5%, how much will the price of the bond increase? What will happen to the bond's duration?

30. Suppose a bond has a duration of 7.62 years with a current price of $865.806 and a 8% yield to maturity. If the bond's yield increases to 8.3%, how much will the bond price decrease? What will happen to its duration?

31. What is a duration tracking error? What causes it?

32. What are the major issues associated with the use of bond ratings? How well do bond ratings predict actual default rates?

33. According to Graham and Dodd, what should the investor's most important criterion be in selecting bonds? What types of things did they look at when assessing the risk of a bond?

34. Explain the relationship between risk and required return for a bond. Why do bonds generally show positive relationships between maturity and required return?

35. Define *risk structure of interest rates*. Has it remained constant over time? Why or why not?

CRITICAL THINKING EXERCISES

1. This exercise requires computer work. Open the Bond 1 worksheet in the Data.xls file on the Data Workbook. It contains the data you will need to answer the following questions. You can do this problem by hand, but it is easier to set it up on a spreadsheet.
   a. Find the bond's duration.
   b. Assume that the bond's yield to maturity increases from 7.25% to 7.75%. Find the estimated price change using duration.
   c. Assume that the bond's yield to maturity decreases from 7.25% to 6.5%. What will happen to the bond's duration? Why?
   d. If this bond had a coupon rate of 8.0% (not 6.5%), a maturity of 10 years, a yield to maturity of 7.25%, and a face value of $1,000, find the duration.

2. This exercise requires computer work and library/Internet research. Open the Wal-Mart worksheet in the Data Workbook. The worksheet contains financial information on Wal-Mart Stores, Inc. In addition, obtain Wal-Mart's most recent annual report. Your library may have a copy; if not, Wal-Mart's most recent annual report may be obtained from Wal-Mart's Web site (www.wal-mart.com) or from the SEC's Edgar database (www.sec.gov/edgar).
   a. How many of the Graham and Dodd standards for investment-grade bonds listed in Table 9.7 does Wal-Mart appear to meet? Would Graham and Dodd, if they were alive, consider Wal-Mart's bonds to be "investment grade"?
   b. Table 9.4 lists median financial ratios by S&P rating category. Based on these medians, what rating would you assign Wal-Mart's bonds? What are the bonds actually rated? What might account for any differences?

10

Managing Bond Portfolios

PREVIOUSLY . . .

We discussed how bonds are valued and how to assess the two major risks facing bond investors, interest rate risk and credit risk.

IN THIS CHAPTER . . .

We continue our examination of bonds with discussions of bond market volatility and the term structure of interest rates. We then describe passive and active bond management strategies as well as interest rate swaps.

TO COME. . . .

In the next chapter, we move beyond stocks and bonds to more exotic investments, derivative securities, beginning with options.

CHAPTER OBJECTIVES

After reading Chapter 10, you should be able to answer the following questions:

1. What has happened to the volatility of bond prices?

2. How does the term structure of interest rates affect bond investors?

3. What are some active bond management strategies?

4. How can bond portfolios be managed passively?

5. What are interest rate swaps?

Bond investors had a wild ride during the first half of the 1980s. In 1979, yields on long-term U.S. Treasury bonds (T-bonds) broke the 10% psychological barrier for the first time in history. Even though rates had been rising almost steadily for several years, the bond market was not especially volatile. Day-to-day (or month-to-month) swings in bond prices and yields were not that extreme. During 1978, for example, the range between the highest and lowest yields on long-term T-bonds was less than 1%. That consistency changed abruptly in late 1979.

Between September 1979 and March 1980, yields on T-bonds shot up from about 9% to more than 12%. Bond yields then changed direction and proceeded to fall by more than 2% between March and June 1980. Just as quickly, bond yields reversed direction again and rose sharply, peaking at just more than 15% in September 1981. Bond yields then fell sharply again, falling as low as 10% in 1982. T-bond yields then started up again, reaching almost 14% in June 1984, only to fall sharply again for about the next two years, dropping to as low as 7.3% in late 1986. However, again in 1987, T-bond yields increased and hit a high of 8.9% in 1988. Shortly, thereafter, yields fell in the early 1990s by approximately 1% per year to a low of 5.9% in 1993. In 1994, inflation expectations drove yields up to 7.1%. Since that peak, yields fell precipitously from 1994 to 2002. By late 2002, T-bond yields fell to a historic low of 3.9%.

This volatility shattered, perhaps for many years, the image of bonds as staid conservative securities that investors could safely buy and hold. The major lesson of the volatile bond market of the last two decades, we believe, is the importance of bond portfolio management. Careful management is essential. The investor wants to take advantage of anticipated changes in interest rates to boost returns or to protect the value of the portfolio from adverse changes in interest rates.

In Chapter 9, we discussed bond valuation principles and the major risks facing bond investors, especially interest rate risk and credit risk. Although investors must never disregard credit risk, always carefully evaluating the creditworthiness of individual bond issuers and issues, the major risk to which *all* bond investors are exposed is changing interest rates. This chapter explores bond portfolio management techniques, building on the material we discussed in Chapter 9.

BRIEF HISTORY OF BOND MARKET VOLATILITY

As we noted, 25 years ago, bonds were considered to be dull, almost boring, securities. Investors bought bonds for regular income, usually with the intention of holding them to maturity. Investors worried about credit risk, of course, but the risk of not receiving interest and principal when due could be minimized by careful selection and analysis of individual issuers. It was an era when interest rates, and thus bond prices, changed little from month to month. In fact, interest rates often changed little from year to year.

Figure 10.1 illustrates this stability. It shows the annual range of yields on long-term U.S. T-bonds (those with maturities in excess of 10 years) between 1948 and 1993. Notice that from 1948 to the early 1970s, the annual difference, or range, between the high and low yields on T-bonds was generally quite small. Between 1948 and 1972, it averaged less than 0.6% and exceeded 1% in only 4 of the 25 years. During the last 26 years shown in Figure 10.1 (1977–2002),

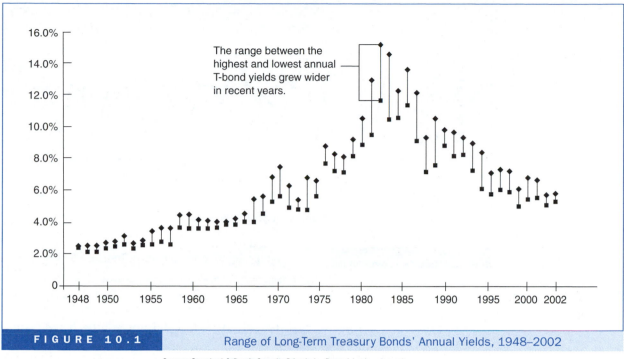

FIGURE 10.1   Range of Long-Term Treasury Bonds' Annual Yields, 1948–2002

Source: Standard & Poor's Security Price Index Record (various issues).

however, the range between the annual high and low yields on T-bonds averaged more than 1.8%. The range exceeded 1% in 17 of the 26 years, and in 7 of the 26 years, it exceeded 2%.

As interest rates become more volatile, so too do bond returns. This connection seems reasonable because bond prices and interest rates are inversely related; as interest rates move up, bond prices fall, and vice versa. Bond holding period returns, therefore, are also inversely related to changes in interest rates.

Generally, month-to-month bond returns were relatively stable until the late 1960s. By the late 1970s and early 1980s, substantial swings in month-to-month bond returns became common, and continued into the next 20 years. Figure 10.2 shows month-by-month total returns on long-term T-bonds between August 1999 and June 2002. The figure vividly illustrates the increasing volatility of bond returns over time.

Comparing Stock Market and Bond Market Volatility

The increase in bond market volatility over the past 20 years raises the question of how bond market volatility compares with that of the stock market. Figure 10.3 shows the annualized standard deviations of monthly returns by year for stocks and T-bonds between 1926 and 2002.

Stocks were clearly volatile during the beginning of the period, especially before 1940. The stock market settled down somewhat during the 1940s and 1950s, and although volatility increased somewhat after the mid-1970s, with the

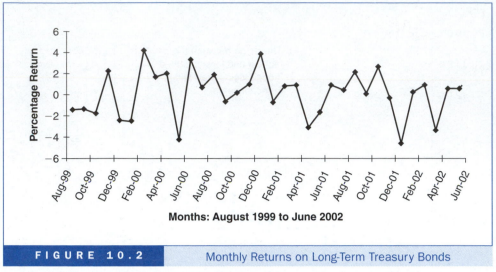

FIGURE 10.2   Monthly Returns on Long-Term Treasury Bonds

Source: Standard & Poor's Security Price Index Record (various issues).

exception of a few years (most notably, 1987), it did not approach the frantic variability of the 1920s and 1930s.

However, Figure 10.3 confirms prior evidence on increasing bond market volatility. Further, since the mid-1960s, the bond market frequently changed almost as erratically as the stock market. In the early 1980s, bond market volatility briefly exceeded stock market volatility.

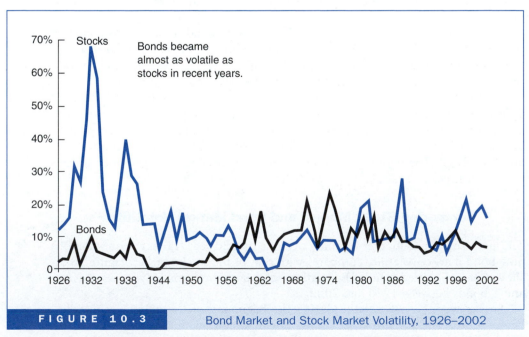

FIGURE 10.3   Bond Market and Stock Market Volatility, 1926–2002

Source: Standard & Poor's Security Price Index Record (various issues).

Impact of Bond Market Volatility on Investors

It is difficult to know exactly what caused the bond market to become more volatile during the past 20 years. Both inflation and institutional changes in the bond market probably contributed. Further, although some evidence suggests that the bond market regained some of its former stability during the past couple of years, questions still cloud any prediction of how volatile the bond market will be in the future. Whatever the causes of volatility swings, and whatever the outlook, bond market volatility affects both active and passive investors.

The most obvious impact of increased volatility in the bond market is the potential to profit from anticipated changes in interest rates by actively managing a bond portfolio. Volatility also increases the potential for losses, however. We assess the potential to increase risk-adjusted profits by actively managing a bond portfolio later in this chapter.

How does volatility affect passive investors? Remember from Chapter 9 that bonds have set face (or par) values. Barring default, a bond will eventually mature and return its par value, regardless of its price in the secondary market before maturity. Why should a passive (buy-and-hold) bond investor care about volatility, because the bond will return the investment at maturity? The short answer is that increased volatility increases the various risks associated with changes in interest rates, and these risks affect *all* bond investors. For example, increased volatility makes it more difficult to accurately predict an actual rate of return when purchasing a bond. Increased volatility in the bond market, therefore, increases the importance of strategies designed to minimize the risks associated with changes in interest rates. We discuss some of these strategies later in this chapter.

ANALYZING THE YIELD CURVE

To structure a sound bond portfolio, passive and active investors alike must understand the relationship between yield and maturity. This knowledge helps the portfolio manager determine the appropriate mix of bond durations in a portfolio. Understanding the relationship between yield and maturity can also indicate when to adjust the average duration of the portfolio. As discussed in Chapter 9, adjusting the average duration of the bond portfolio alters its sensitivity to changes in interest rates. Making the correct adjustments can dramatically improve the risk and return characteristics of any bond portfolio.

The term structure of interest rates, or yield curve, is an important tool for evaluating the relationship between yield and maturity; a great deal of important information about interest rates lies embedded in the yield curve. To better comprehend this information, the investor must understand the nature of the term structure of interest rates, and this understanding begins with a review of the various theories of the yield curve.

What Is the Yield Curve?

In Chapter 9, we briefly defined the yield curve when discussing the historical relationship between yield and maturity. Recall that the yield curve graphs the relationship between maturity and yield for a group of bonds that are similar in

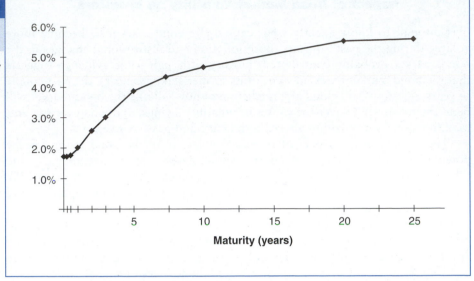

FIGURE 10.4

U.S. Treasury Securities
Yield Curve

Source: Federal Reserve Statistical Release,
August 19, 2002.

every respect other than maturity. Because Treasury securities all have similar default risk, call provisions, and tax status, they are typically used to construct the market term structure of interest rates. Further, yields on Treasury securities often serve as benchmarks for determining yields on non-T-bonds. Therefore, analysis of the Treasury yield curve can provide insight into the relationship between yield and maturity of non-T-bonds, as well.

Figure 10.4 shows a T-bond yield curve based on yields as of the end of 2002. Notice the classic upward slope, which indicates that yields on short-term Treasuries are lower than yields on long-term Treasuries. As we discussed in Chapter 9, short-term yields are generally lower than long-term yields, but not always. Variations in this relationship give yield curves a variety of shapes. Occasionally, as in June 2000, the yield curve is flat, meaning that short-term and long-term yields are roughly the same. At other times, the yield curve forms a hump, as in late 1989 and early 1990, which means that, as maturities increase, yields rise and then fall. In a few cases (most notably, the last half of 2000), the yield curve is actually inverted; long-term Treasuries yield less than short-term Treasuries.

Changes in the yield curve's slope, and even its shape, over short periods of time give rise to several questions. What do the different shapes mean? Does the yield curve contain information about future interest rates? The various theories of the yield curve, which we discuss shortly, address these questions. To fully understand these theories, however, one must understand *forward rates* and how to calculate them.

spot rate

Prevailing yield on a bond with a
particular maturity today.

forward rate

Expected rate on a bond with a
particular maturity at some point
in the future.

Implied Forward Rates

A **spot rate** of interest is today's prevailing annual yield on a bond with a particular maturity; a **forward rate** is the expected rate on a bond with a particular maturity at some point in the future (i.e., tomorrow's projected spot rate). For example, the current yield on a one-year bond is a spot rate; the expected rate on a one-year bond, one year from today is a forward rate. If forward rates are *implied* by current spot rates, then knowing current spot rates would allow the bond investor to calculate forward rates.

Suppose that someone wants to make a two-year bond investment. This investor must choose between two alternatives:

Alternative A: Buy a two-year Treasury security.
Alternative B: Buy a one-year Treasury security today and another one-year security one year from today.

Further, assume indifference between the two alternatives if they produce the same expected dollar return. The one that could produce a higher dollar return would, of course, be preferred. The spot rates are the current market yields on one-year and two-year Treasuries. Knowing these spot rates, can one find the forward rate on a one-year Treasury, one year from today (i.e., the rate that would make one indifferent between alternatives A and B)?

The answer depends partially on the timing of interest payments. The example assumes that all the example bonds are pure discount, or zero coupon bonds. Coupon payments would not change the basic relationships we are about to discuss, but they would complicate the mathematics of the relationships between spot and forward rates.

Given the assumption that all bonds are pure discount bonds, we can express the relationship between the two alternatives mathematically. To be indifferent between alternatives A and B, the following relationship must hold:

$$(1 + R_2)^2 = (1 + R_1)(1 + {}_1r_1) \qquad\qquad (10.1)$$

where R_2 is the spot rate on a two-year bond, R_1 is the spot rate on a one-year bond, and ${}_1r_r$ is the forward rate on a one-year bond, one year from today.[1] To solve for the forward rate implied by the spot rates, manipulate Equation 10.1 as follows:

$$ {}_1r_1 = \frac{(1 + R_2)^2}{(1 + R_1)} - 1 \qquad\qquad (10.2)$$

For example, if the spot rate on a one-year bond is 4.50% and the spot rate on a two-year bond is 4.75%, then the implied forward rate on a one-year bond one year from today is

$$(1.0475)^2/(1.0450) - 1 = 5.00\%$$

We can also write this relationship as

$$(1.0475)^2 = (1.0450)(1.0500)$$

Thus, buying two consecutive one-year bonds with spot rates of 4.5% and 5% would produce the same total return as buying a single two-year bond at 4.75% per annum.

---

[1] In general, R_n is the spot rate on an *n*-year bond, and ${}_tr_n$ is the forward rate on an *n*-year bond *t* years from today.

TABLE 10.1		
Alternative		**Expected Return Formula**
One three-year bond		$(1 + R_3)^3$
Three one-year bonds		$(1 + R_1)(1 + {}_1r_1)(1 + {}_2r_1)$
One two-year bond and one one-year bond		$(1 + R_2)^2(1 + {}_2r_1)$
One one-year bond and one two-year bond		$(1 + R_1)^1)1 + {}_1r_2)^2$

Alternative Three-Year
Investments

Note: ${}_1r_1$ is the forward rate on a one-year bond, one year from today; ${}_2r_1$ is the forward rate on a one-year bond, two years from today; ${}_1r_2$ is the forward rate on a two-year bond, one year from today.

Now, let's extend the example to a three-year investment. Four alternative investment combinations are listed, along with their expected return formulas, in Table 10.1. To be indifferent between these four alternatives, all four would have to have the same expected return. Therefore, we can find the forward rates implied by the spot rates calculated from Table 10.1.

To illustrate this, assume that the spot rate on a one-year bond is 4.5%, the spot rate on a two-year bond is 4.75%, and the spot rate on a three-year bond is 5%. As before, assume that all bonds are pure discount bonds. The formula for finding an implied forward rate (the general form of Equation 10.2) is

$$_tr_n = \left[\frac{(1 + R_{n+t})^{n+t}}{(1 + R_t)^t}\right]^{1/n} - 1 \tag{10.3}$$

where t is the number of years from today and n is the bond's time to maturity.

Plugging the assumed spot rates into Equation 10.3 gives the implied forward rates shown:

$$_1r_1 = (1.0475)^2/(1.045) - 1 \quad = 5.00\%$$
$$_2r_1 = (1.05)^3/(1.0475)^2 - 1 \quad = 5.50\%$$
$$_1r_2 = [(1.05)^3/(1.045)]^{1/2} - 1 = 5.25\%$$

Locking in Future Returns Computing forward rates from spot rates implies that investors can lock in future rates of return. To illustrate, compute the market values of discount T-bonds with one-year and two-year maturities. Using the spot rates from the prior example, their prices would be

One-year bond price (per $100) = $100/(1.045)   = $95.69
Two-year bond price (per $100) = $100/(1.0475)² = $91.14

To lock in the return on a one-year bond one year from today, an investor would sell short the one-year bond today and purchase some multiple of the two-year bond today to return the initial cash outlay to zero. Table 10.2 details the effects of this strategy. If these bonds are risk-free, this strategy locks in a 5% return on a one-year bond one year from today.[2]

---

[2]We should note that borrowing the present value of $100 would be equivalent to a short sale if the loan's interest rate matched the yield on a one-year T-bond. Obviously, it would be difficult for most small, individual investors to sell T-bonds short. However, some large institutional investors and most government bond dealers routinely sell T-bonds short. These investors can also borrow money at rates close to what the government pays.

TABLE 10.2

Locking in a Future Return

	Cash Flow		
	Year 0	Year 1	Year 2
1. Short a single one-year bond	+$95.69	($100)	—
2. Buy 1.05 two-year bonds	($95.69)	—	+$105
Total cash flow	$0.00	($100)	+$105
One-year return, one year from today = ($105 − $100)/$100 = 5%			

The potential to lock in future rates suggests a close interrelationship between spot rates and implied forward rates with a yield curve of any shape. One can then think of all market interest rates as consisting of explicitly known spot rates, as well as implied forward rates.[3] The interrelationship between spot and forward rates suggests a potential to use implied forward rates to *forecast* future spot rates. Thus, the shape of the yield curve may indeed give clues about the future direction of interest rates. This basic issue is addressed by the various theories of the yield curve, as discussed in the next section.

Theories of the Yield Curve

Three general theories seek to explain the shape of the yield curve: the pure expectations theory, the liquidity preference theory, and the market segmentation theory. Each theory draws different conclusions about the interrelationships between spot and forward rates and, as a result, the amount of information contained in the yield curve. We describe each theory and then look at some empirical evidence.

Pure Expectations Theory The **pure expectations theory** holds that forward rates are unbiased estimates of expected future spot rates.[4] It is based on the assumption that many, if not all, investors are indifferent between various combinations of maturities that add up to the same term. Investors choose the combination that offers the highest expected return, eliminating any differences in returns between combinations. Going back to the investments shown in Table 10.1, the pure expectations theory says that investors are indifferent between any of those three-year investment combinations. The theory states that all four combinations must offer the same expected rate of return.

If the pure expectations theory is correct, then the shape of the current yield curve reveals investors' expectations for the future direction of interest rates. An upward-sloping curve indicates that investors expect rates to rise. In other words, they think that the spot rate on a one-year bond will be higher one year

pure expectations theory

States that forward rates are unbiased estimates of expected future spot rates.

---

[3] We can think of a discount bond's yield to maturity as being equal to the geometric average of many shorter-term implied forward rates. For example, the spot rate, R_n, equals

$$R_n = [(1 + R_1)(1 + {}_1r_1)(1 + {}_2r_1)(1 + {}_{n-1}r_1)]^{1/n} - 1$$

[4] The pure expectations theory does not imply that forward rates always perfectly forecast future spot rates, only that they give unbiased forecasts, which means that forecasts are not consistently too high or too low.

from today than it is today. However, a flat curve suggests that investors expect rates to remain about the same. An inverted curve indicates that investors expect rates to fall.

In addition to the shape of the yield curve, changes in its slope are also important indicators of the market's expectations concerning future spot rates, according to the pure expectations theory. For example, if the slope of the yield curve becomes less steep, the theory says that investors expect smaller magnitudes for future interest rate changes, whether upward or downward.

Liquidity Preference Theory

liquidity preference theory

States that forward rates are not unbiased projections of future spot rates because, all things being equal, investors prefer short-term bonds to long-term bonds.

The liquidity preference theory holds that forward rates are good predictors of future rates, but they do not provide unbiased projections because, all things being equal, investors prefer short-term bonds to long-term bonds. Investors will hold longer-term bonds only in exchange for a liquidity premium.

Going back to the alternative three-year investment combinations in Table 10.1, the liquidity preference theory states that investors would rather hold three one-year bonds than one three-year bond. Therefore, the expected return from three one-year bonds should be lower than the return from one three-year bond. In equation form, the following would suggest a liquidity preference:

$$(1 + R_3)^3 > (1 + R_1)(1 + {}_1r_1)(1 + {}_2r_1)$$

If the liquidity preference theory is correct, the yield curve should generally slope upward. Further, according to the liquidity preference theory, forward rates should consistently overestimate future spot rates. That is, if the yield curve is upward-sloping, the forward rate on a one-year bond one year from today will be, on average, higher than the current spot rate on a one-year bond. However, depending on the size of the liquidity preference, the actual spot rate on a one-year bond one year from today may be the same, or even lower, than the current spot rate on a one-year bond.

Market Segmentation Theory

market segmentation theory

States that forward rates are essentially unrelated to future spot rates because bonds with different maturities are not substitutes for each other.

The market segmentation theory argues that forward rates have essentially no relationship with future spot rates. The reason, according to the theory, is that bonds with different maturities are not substitutes for each other. Some issuers wish to borrow short term and some wish to borrow long term. Short-term borrowers will not borrow long-term, and vice versa. Similarly, some investors prefer short-term bonds, and some prefer long-term bonds. Long-term investors do not see short-term bonds as substitutes, and vice versa. Going back to Table 10.1, market segmentation theory denies that the four alternative three-year investment combinations are substitutes for each other, regardless of their expected returns. One group of investors will buy one-year bonds and a different group of investors will buy three-year bonds.

The market segmentation theory argues that spot rates for different bonds are determined solely by interactions of supply and demand with maturity categories. If the market segmentation theory is correct, the shape and slope of the yield curve reveal nothing about the future direction of interest rates. This theory sees implied forward rates as poor forecasts of future spot rates. If, for example, the upward slope of the yield curve becomes steeper, the change means only that supply and demand conditions in either the short or long ends of the bond market have changed.

Empirical Evidence of Yield Curve Relationships

Some evidence, both anecdotal and scientific, supports all three theories of the yield curve.[5] Some evidence suggests, for example, that implied forward rates forecast future spot rates reasonably well, supporting the pure expectations theory. Supporters of the pure expectations theory note that inverted yield curves generally occur during recessions, when current interest rates are high, but declining future interest rates are likely. However, a great deal of evidence finds that forward rates contribute little value as forecasts of future spot rates. Upward-sloping yield curves are common, but they do not necessarily give way to rising interest rates. For example, in June 2001 the yield curve sloped sharply upward, yet interest rates continued to generally decline throughout the rest of 2001 and much of 2002.

Evidence also gives somewhat ambiguous signals about liquidity preference theory. The typical upward slope of the yield curve is often cited as evidence of a liquidity preference that leads investors, as a group, to prefer short-term bonds to long-term bonds. Average annual yields on Treasury bills (T-bills), for example, have exceeded yields on long-term T-bonds only seven times since 1948. Yet other scientific evidence implies that if a liquidity premium exists, it is not large and probably limited to short-term bonds.

Evidence of Market Segmentation The market segmentation theory is difficult to believe in its purest form. Can the markets for long-term bonds and short-term bonds be *completely* separate from one another? Corporations and governments issue both long-term and short-term bonds. Further, many investors seem willing to own varying mixes of maturities, adjusting the average maturities of their bond portfolios as market conditions change. In addition, if the bond market were segmented enough to sever any relationship between current spot rates, forward rates, and future spot rates, the differences could create substantial arbitrage opportunities.

Nevertheless, some evidence supports the contention that shifts in supply and demand conditions can affect the shape and slope of the yield curve. For example, in the early 1980s the municipal yield curve was far steeper than the Treasury yield curve. One study attributed this difference, in large part, to a supply-and-demand imbalance in the municipal bond market.[6] In the early 1980s, tax-exempt money market funds grew rapidly. As a result of this heavy demand, the study concluded, yields on tax-exempt money market instruments were "artificially" depressed.

Anecdotal evidence of market segmentation can also be seen in the slope of the Treasury yield curve during the early 2001. Beginning in January 2001, the Federal Reserve cut short-term interest rates 11 times—and by a total of 4.75%—in an attempt to stimulate the economy. The federal funds rate, for example, fell from 6.5% to 1.75% between January 2001 and August 2002. The effect of this change on the Treasury yield curve appears in Figure 10.5. It shows the spread between three-month T-bills and 10-year T-bonds at various points in time between June 2000 and August 2002.

---

[5]This evidence is reviewed in several sources. See, for example, James Van Horne, *Financial Market Rates and Flows* (Upper Saddle River, NJ: Prentice Hall, 1993), pp. 108–116.
[6]See David Kidwell and Timothy Koch, "Market Segmentation and the Term Structure of Municipal Yields," *Journal of Money, Credit & Banking*, Spring 1983, pp. 40–55.

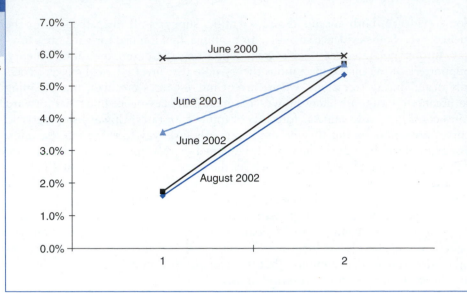

FIGURE 10.5

Slope of the Treasury
Yield Curve: June 2000–
August 2002

Source: Federal Reserve Bulletin (various issues).

In June 2000, this Treasury yield curve was essentially flat; the spread between 10-year bonds and three-month bills was only 0.07%. As the Fed pushed short-term rates downward, the yield on T-bills fell rapidly from 5.86% in June 2000 to 3.57% in June 2001 and to 1.75% in June 2002. By August 2002, T-bill yield equaled 1.62%. The yield on 10-year Treasuries also fell but not nearly as far, from 5.93% in June 2000 to 5.66% in June 2002. The difference in changes between long-term and short-term rates made the yield curve steeper. The spread between short-term and long-term Treasuries increased from 0.07% to 3.94%. By August 2002, the spread between 10-year T-bonds and T-bills was 3.72%, slightly lower than in June.

One explanation for this behavior, where T-bills declined significantly while T-bonds did not, is that investors kept long-term rates high due to worries about a double-dip recession. Investors worried that the slow recovery of the economy and the federal budget deficit would cause heavy demand for funds by the Treasury. These factors could alter supply and demand factors in the long-term portion of the bond market, influencing the slope of the Treasury yield curve from 2001 to 2002. Is this effect evidence of market segmentation? It is difficult to say, but in any case, actions by the Federal Reserve to lower interest rates in 2001 took an unusually long time to affect the long-term portion of the bond market.

RECAPRECAP

Up to this point, we discussed the slope and shape of the yield curve and important information it may contain for all types of bond investors. These effects are critical regardless of whether the pure expectations, liquidity preference, or market segmentation theory (or a combination of the three) best explains the yield curve. Changes in the slope and shape of the yield curve may forecast future spot interest rates, changes in the size of the liquidity premium, and changes in supply-and-demand conditions in various segments of the bond market. All bond investors should pay close attention to these implications of the yield curve.

1. Assume that the one-year spot rate is 5.3%, the two-year spot rate is 5.97%, and the three-year spot rate is 6.1%. Calculate the forward rate on a one-year bond one year from today. Calculate the forward rate on a two-year bond one year from today.

2. Show how an investor could theoretically "lock in" the rate on a one-year bond two years from today.

ACTIVELY MANAGING BOND PORTFOLIOS

Investors can manage their portfolios actively or passively or use strategies that have both passive and active elements. All active strategies require the investor to specify expectations about variables that determine the performance of the assets in the portfolio. For a stock portfolio, important variables include such things as company earnings, dividends, and risk. For a bond portfolio, the investor must estimate interest rates, interest rate volatility, yield curves, and yield spreads. (An estimate of foreign exchange rates should guide any transaction in bonds denominated in a foreign currency.)

Most active bond strategies involve swaps in which the investor buys one set of bonds with certain characteristics while selling another set of bonds with different characteristics. Swaps are based on expectations regarding future interest rates, yield spreads, and so forth. Passive portfolio strategies, by contrast, require little attention to expectations. They make no real attempt to forecast the variables that determine the performance of a portfolio's assets. These strategies generally follow buy-and-hold decision rules. The investor buys a well-diversified portfolio and holds those securities, making few if any changes regardless of either current or expected market conditions. In one popular passive portfolio strategy, indexing, the investor tries simply to replicate the performance of a well-known predetermined market index.

In this section, we examine several active bond portfolio strategies. (More passive strategies are discussed in the next section.) We also try to assess how well active bond management strategies actually work. Active strategies can be classified in the following ways:

- Interest rate expectations strategies
- Yield curve strategies
- Yield spread strategies
- Foreign exchange strategies
- Individual bond selection strategies

Of course, specific strategies can span these categories. For example, we observed in the last chapter that changes in interest rates and changes in yield spreads are often interrelated. Therefore, bond strategies based on expected changes in interest rates may also evaluate expected changes in yield spreads.

Interest Rate Expectations Strategies

We know that as interest rates rise (or fall), bond prices fall (or rise). We also know that certain bonds are more price-sensitive than others and that duration measures the relative price sensitivity of bonds. These premises suggest a fairly

Duration, Convexity, and Yield Curve Changes

As noted in the chapter, many active bond management strategies are based on expected shifts in the yield curve. The yield curve may be expected to experience a parallel shift (up or down) or a non-parallel shift (the yield curve gets steeper or flatter). In general, one would expect that two bonds with the same duration would have the same performance, regardless of how the yield curve changed. Not necessarily. We also have to consider the convexity of each bond.

In the prior chapter, we noted that duration measures the sensitivity of a bond's price to a change in its yield to maturity. The longer the duration of a bond, the more price sensitive. In essence, convexity measures the sensitivity of a bond's duration to a change in the bond's yield to maturity. All other things being equal, it is better to have more convexity than less. As an example, take a look at the two bonds listed in the following table.

	Bond A	Bond B
Maturity (years)	15	10
Coupon rate	8%	0%
Yield to maturity	4.98%	4.98%
Price	$131.34[1]	$61.49
Duration	10 years	10 years
Convexity	123.39	99.80

[1]Assumes annual coupon payments and no accrued interest.

Both bonds have the same yield to maturity and duration, but Bond A has more convexity than Bond B. Convexity is a desirable property in a bond. To illustrate this, assume we form two portfolios. The first portfolio consists of 1,000 Bond As. The second portfolio consists of approximately 2,136 Bond Bs. (We do this to equalize the initial dollar investment.) Assume we hold each portfolio for one year and compute the one year holding period return.

As the following table shows, regardless of whether the yield curve shifts up or down, the return from the first portfolio (consisting of Bond A) is always higher than the return from the second portfolio (consisting of Bond B). Notice that the greater the shift in the yield curve—either up or down—the greater the difference in performance between the two portfolios.

Change in Yield to Maturity	New Yield to Maturity	Holding Period Return Portfolio 1 (Bond A)	Holding Period Return Portfolio 2 Bond B)
1.50%	6.48%	−7.36%	−7.60%
1.00%	5.98%	−3.49%	−3.60%
0.50%	5.48%	0.62%	.59%
0.00%	4.98%	4.98%	4.98%
−0.50%	4.48%	9.63%	9.59%
−1.00%	3.98%	14.56%	14.43%
−1.50%	3.48%	19.82%	19.50%

Questions for Critical Thinking

1. Because convexity is a desirable property in a bond, how would differences in convexity be reflected in bond prices?
2. How could two bonds have the same duration, yet different amounts of convexity?

basic bond portfolio strategy: lengthen or shorten the average duration of the bond portfolio based on expectations for future interest rates. If rates are expected to fall (or rise), try to lengthen (or shorten) the average duration of the portfolio. One can increase the duration of a bond portfolio by swapping bonds with high coupon rates and short maturities for bonds with low coupon rates and longer maturities. Of course, the opposite swap would shorten the portfolio's duration.

As an example, assume that a bond portfolio has a current market value of $500,000, an average coupon rate of 7%, an average yield to maturity of 7%, and an average maturity of 10 years. These characteristics give the bond portfolio an average duration of about 7.36 years. Suppose that interest rates are about to fall, dropping the average yield to maturity of the bonds in the portfolio from 7% to 6%. Table 10.3 shows that, without any adjustment to the portfolio's duration, its market value would increase by approximately $34,393 (or 6.88%). However, lengthening the duration of the portfolio would cause a larger increase in the

Basic Data

Average coupon rate = 7%
Average maturity = 10 years
Current average yield to maturity = 7%
Current market value = $500,000
Current duration = 7.36 years
New yield to maturity = 6%

Duration	Approximate Price Change	Percentage Change
7.36	$34,393	6.88%
7.50	35,047	7.01
8.00	37,383	7.48
8.50	39,720	7.94
9.00	42,056	8.41

portfolio's value. If the portfolio's duration could be increased from 7.36 years to, say, 8.00 years, the portfolio would increase in value by approximately $37,383 (or 7.48%). The change in duration caused about a $3,000 difference in return. If the duration could be increased to 9.00 years, the portfolio's value would increase by approximately $42,056 (or 8.41%). Of course, this strategy brings the risk of inaccurate expectations. If interest rates rise as the duration of the portfolio becomes longer, the price decline will be greater than if no change had been made.

Riding the Yield Curve (Horizon Analysis) Another strategy based on interest rate expectations is sometimes called riding the yield curve. If the yield curve is upward-sloping and expectations predict that neither the shape nor the slope of the yield curve will change over the investment horizon, then yields on specific bonds will fall as they ride the yield curve downward (i.e., as they approach maturity).

As an example, assume that the current yield on a one-year bond is 4.5% and the yield on a two-year bond is 5%. If both bonds are discount bonds, the price of a one-year bond is $95.69 and the price of the two-year bond is $90.70. An investor with a one-year investment horizon could buy the one-year bond and earn 4.5%. Expectations for stable rates in a year could lead the investor to ride the yield curve by buying the two-year bond and selling it after one year, when it would have one year left to maturity and be priced as a one-year bond. If rates remained unchanged, the two-year bond would sell for $95.69, generating a one-year return of 5.5% [($95.69 − $90.70)/$90.70].

Someone who rides the yield curve hopes, of course, that a rising yield curve does not portend rising interest rates, as predicted by the pure expectations theory. If the pure expectations theory is correct, the one-year return from the strategy we just described would be only 4.5%.[7] Riding the yield curve should not produce

---

[7] If the spot rate on a one-year bond is 4.5% and the spot rate on a two-year bond is 5%, then the forward rate on a one-year bond one year from today would be 5.5%. According to the pure expectations theory, it is the best unbiased forecast of the spot rate on a one-year bond one year from now. If the rate in one year on a one-year bond did equal 5.5%, the price of the original two-year bond would be $94.78 in one year. The one-year return would then equal 4.5%.

consistently higher returns, therefore, if the pure expectations theory is correct (i.e., forward rates are reasonably accurate predictors of future spot rates).

Yield Curve Strategies

As we observed earlier in this chapter, historically both the shape and slope of the yield curve have shifted over time. Changes in the shape and slope of the yield curve create several possible trading strategies.[8]

Before we review some yield curve strategies, let's describe the types of changes to the yield curve that have been observed historically. Figure 10.6 illustrates three types of changes:

1. *Parallel shifts.* Yields rise or fall over all maturities. The slope of the yield curve remains essentially unchanged as the entire curve moves either up or down.
2. *Changes in slope.* The slope of the yield curve gets either flatter or steeper. A flatter yield curve means that short-term yields rise more than intermediate-term yields, which in turn rise more than long-term yields. A steeper yield curve means the exact opposite; short-term yields decline by more than intermediate-term yields, which decline by more than long-term yields.
3. *Butterfly shifts.* This change in the "humpedness" of the yield curve can be positive or negative. In a positive butterfly shift, long-term and short-term yields rise more than intermediate-term yields. In a negative butterfly shift, long-term and short-term yields fall more than intermediate-term yields.

Historically, parallel shifts and changes in slope are responsible for the vast majority of observed changes to the yield curve. Furthermore, history shows a high degree of correlation between parallel shifts and changes in slope. Rising yields are often associated with flatter slopes, and falling yields often accompany steeper slopes.

Optimal Yield Curve Strategies An expected parallel shift in the yield curve, with no other changes, implies probable success for a simple strategy of adjusting the average duration of the portfolio in the opposite direction of the expected change in interest rates. However, a parallel shift combined with some sort of change in slope implies somewhat more complex bond portfolio strategies. Let's look at an example.

Table 10.4 lists yields and prices on three hypothetical discount securities: one short-term, one intermediate-term, and one long-term assuming a flat yield curve. Based on these inputs, the table outlines optimal yield curve strategies for four scenarios of different parallel shifts and changes in slope. The table states one-year holding period returns, given each scenario's relative yield curve change. The optimal strategy is the one that produces the highest one-year holding period return. In scenario 1, the yield curve has a parallel downward shift of 0.50%, but at the same time, the slope gets steeper by the same amount. The optimal bond to own is the intermediate-term bond, which produces the highest one-year holding period return, 9.05%. In scenario 2, the yield curve shifts upward 0.5% while the slope gets steeper

---

[8]These strategies are discussed in detail in Frank Fabozzi, *Bond Markets, Analysis & Strategies,* 2nd ed. (Upper Saddle River, NJ: Prentice Hall, 1993), pp. 490–495; or Frank Jones, "Yield Curve Strategies," *Journal of Fixed Income,* September 1991, pp. 43–51.

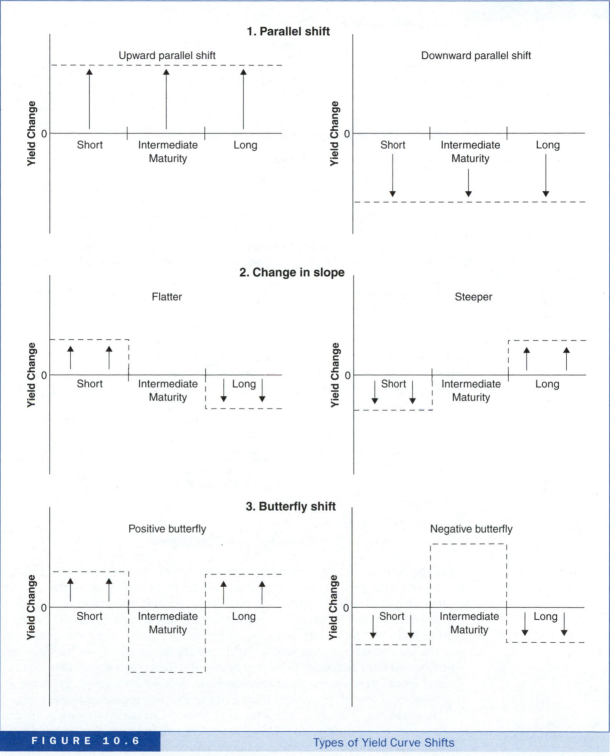

FIGURE 10.6 Types of Yield Curve Shifts

Source: Frank Fabozzi, *Bond Markets, Analysis & Strategies,* 2nd ed. (Upper Saddle River, NJ: Prentice Hall, 1993), p. 496. Adapted by permission of Prentice-Hall, Inc.

TABLE 10.4
Examples of Optimal Yield Curve Strategies

A. Price and Yield Data

Bond	Maturity	Yield	Price
Short-term	2 years	6.00%	$89.00
Intermediate-term	7 years	6.00	66.51
Long-term	15 years	6.00	41.73

B. Optimal One-Year Strategies, Given Expected Yield Curve Changes

Scenario	Parallel Shift	Change in Slope	Optimal Bond to Hold	Yield in One Year	Price in One Year	One-Year Return
1	Down	Steeper	Intermediate-term	5.50%	$72.52	9.05%
2	Up	Steeper	Short-term	6.00	94.34	6.00
3	Down	Flatter	Long-term	5.00	50.51	21.04
4	Up	Flatter	Long-term	6.00	44.23	6.00

Note: All bonds are assumed to be zero coupon bonds. Both parallel shifts and slope changes are ±50 basis points (0.5%). The new short-term yield is 6% + parallel shift − slope change. The new intermediate-term yield is 6% + parallel shift. The new long-term bond yield is 6% + parallel shift + slope change.

by the same amount. In this case, the short-term bond produces the highest one-year return of the three, 6%. If the yield curve shifts downward by 0.5% and the slope gets flatter by the same amount (scenario 3), the long-term bond is optimal, producing a one-year holding period return of 21.04%. Finally, if the yield curve has an upward, parallel shift of 0.5%, while the slope gets flatter (scenario 4), the long-term bond again produces the highest one-year holding period return of the three, 6%.

Depending on the relative change in the yield curve, the optimal strategy is sometimes to hold a short-term bond, sometimes to hold an intermediate-term bond, and sometimes to hold a long-term bond. The optimal yield curve strategies are summarized in Table 10.5.

Yield Spread Strategies

Yield spread strategies involve altering the contents of the bond portfolio to capitalize on existing yield spreads or expected changes in yield spreads. As discussed in Chapter 9, a yield spread measures the difference in yields between bonds of different qualities. We also observed in the prior chapter that quality-based yield spreads become wider and more narrow at various points in time. Further, yield spreads are often related to interest rate levels. Yield spreads tend to increase (or decrease) when interest rates are rising (or falling) and tend to be at their maximums (or minimums) when interest rates are historically high (or low). As a result, expectations regarding yield spreads are closely related to expectations regarding interest rates.

However, rising interest rates may also foreshadow an improving economy. As the economy improves, investors may see less risk in lower-quality bonds and become more willing to buy them. Consequently, yield spreads may continue to narrow even as interest rates, in general, rise.

A simple yield spread strategy is often referred to as a **pure yield pickup swap**. In this strategy, the bond investor swaps lower-yielding bonds for higher-yielding

pure yield pickup swap

Swapping lower-yielding bonds for higher-yielding bonds with roughly similar maturities to earn a higher return.

Change in the Slope of the Yield Curve	Parallel Shift in the Yield Curve		
	Decrease	**No Change**	**Increase**
Steeper	Long-term or intermediate-term bonds (a less-steep curve relative to the yield decrease favors long-term bonds)	Intermediate-term bonds	Short-term bonds
None	Long-term bonds	Long-term bonds	Short-term bonds
Flatter	Long-term bonds	Long-term bonds	Short-term or long-term bonds (a flatter curve relative to the yield increase favors long-term bonds)

TABLE 10.5

Optimal Yield Curve Strategies for Parallel Shift and Change in Slope of the Yield Curve

Source: Adapted from Frank Fabozzi, *Bond Markets, Analysis & Strategies,* 2nd ed. (Upper Saddle River, NJ: Prentice Hall, 1993), Exhibit 20-6, p. 499.

bonds with roughly similar maturities to earn a higher return. At the end of 1996, for example, AA-rated corporate bonds were yielding more than 0.5% more than long-term T-bonds (7.29% versus 6.75%). Someone might swap Treasuries for AAA corporates in an attempt to earn the higher term premium associated with the higher-yielding bonds. This strategy implicitly assumes that neither interest rates nor yield spreads will change significantly over the expected holding period.

Other yield spread strategies are designed to capitalize on expected changes in yield spreads. As we observed in Chapter 9, yield spreads between bonds with varying quality levels tend to be at their maximums when interest rates are at their maximums. This wide spread tends to occur right after a peak in economic activity. The usual explanation for this phenomenon is that the risk of default rises in a declining economy. Consequently, investors demand higher premiums to hold non-T-bonds. The reverse is true during an economic expansion. Therefore, as the economic outlook improves, the yield spread between T-bonds and non-T-bonds should start to narrow. In such a situation, the optimal strategy is to swap high-quality bonds for lower-quality bonds if interest rates are expected to remain the same, or even decline, with narrowing yield spreads.

Table 10.6 details a hypothetical example. Assume the current yield on 15-year Treasuries is 7.5% and the yield on 10-year AAA corporates is 8.75% (giving us yield spread of 1.25%). As interest rates generally decline over the next year, the yield spread between Treasuries and AAA corporates should decline to about 0.75%. Both bonds are expected to earn impressive one-year returns, but the AAA corporate bond is expected to earn a higher return (39.6% compared with 29.8%) due to the decline in the yield spread between Treasuries and AAA corporates.

Another scenario involves narrowing yield spreads during a general rise in interest rates. As we noted earlier, interest rates could rise due to an improving economy, even as yield spreads continue to narrow. In this scenario, an investor might consider making two changes to a bond portfolio: swapping Treasuries

TABLE 10.6		Treasury	AAA Corporate
Illustration of a Yield Spread Strategy	Term (years)	15	15
	Initial yield	7.50%	8.75%
	Initial price	$33.80	$28.42
	Expected yield	6.50%	7.00%
	Expected price	$41.41	$38.78
	Holding period return	22.51%	36.45%

Note: Both bonds are assumed to be zero coupon bonds.

and other high-quality bonds for lower-quality bonds, and at the same time reducing the portfolio's average duration.

Tax Swaps Market forces create yield spreads based on other characteristics besides quality level. One of these spreads compares the yield on taxable bonds to that on tax-exempt bonds. Over the past 30 years, high-quality (AAA-rated or AA-rated) municipal bonds yielded about 86% of the yield on T-bonds with similar maturities on average. (The difference arises because the interest from municipal bonds is exempt from federal income taxes.) That ratio varies substantially, though. For example, it was more than 90% in 1986 and less than 80% in the late 1970s. A taxable investor who thinks that the ratio between municipal and Treasury yields is too high might switch from Treasuries to municipals, and vice versa. Further, if an investor's marginal federal tax rate goes up (or down), the attractiveness of municipal bonds relative to T-bonds goes up (or down).

Consider, for example, an investor in a 28% federal marginal tax bracket. (This person pays $0.28 in additional taxes on every additional dollar of income.) Also, assume that AAA-rated corporate bonds are currently yielding 7% and AAA-rated municipal bonds with similar durations are yielding 4.8%. To compare these yields, one must adjust for the fact that interest from municipal bonds is not subject to federal income tax. The municipal bond's taxable equivalent yield of 6.67% [4.8% divided by (1 − 28%)] is less than the yield on corporate bonds. If all other factors are the same, the investor is better off holding corporate bonds rather than municipal bonds. Now, assume that interest rates are generally declining; AAA corporates are now yielding 6% and AAA municipals are yielding 4.5%. The marginal tax rate remains at 28%, but the investor is now better off holding municipal bonds because they have a higher taxable equivalent yield than corporate bonds (6.25% versus 6%).

Foreign Exchange Strategies

As discussed in Chapter 9, bonds denominated in foreign currencies expose investors to foreign exchange risk, because the coupon payments are necessarily translated back into dollars. Expected changes in foreign interest or exchange rates create some possible bond trading strategies. Several of these strategies are illustrated in Table 10.7.

One simple strategy is based on the expectation of no significant changes in foreign exchange rates. Investors switch to bonds denominated in foreign currencies if they offer higher yields, illustrated in scenario A in Table 10.7. The investor

TABLE 10.7

Foreign Exchange Strategies

Basic Information (Canadian Government Bond)

Term (year)	10
Initial yield	7.75%
Price (C$)	47.41
Initial FX rate (US$/C$)	0.775
Price (US$)	36.74

One Year Hence	Scenario				
	A	B	C	D	E
Yield	7.75%	7.25%	7.75%	7.25%	7.25%
Price (C$)	51.08	53.26	51.08	53.26	53.26
One-year return (C$)	7.75%	12.36%	7.75%	12.36%	12.36%
FX rate (US$/C$)	0.775	0.775	0.800	0.800	0.750
Price (US$)	39.59	41.28	40.86	42.61	39.95
One-year return (US$)	7.75%	12.36%	11.23%	15.98%	8.73%

Note: The Canadian government bond is assumed to be a zero coupon bond. Assume a 10-year U.S. government bond is yielding 6.75%

buys the Canadian government bond because of its higher yield compared with the U.S. government bond.

Another profitable opportunity is created if the investor expects Canadian interest rates to decline, with no change in the exchange rate. In scenario B, Canadian rates decline by 50 basis points to 7.25%. The one-year return, in U.S. dollars, is about 12.4%.

More complicated strategies are based on expected changes in the exchange rate between Canadian and U.S. dollars. If the investor expects the Canadian dollar to get stronger relative to the U.S. dollar (rising from, say, US$/C$50.75 to US$/C$50.80), the one-year return is larger when measured in U.S. dollars than in Canadian dollars (scenario C). The best of all possible worlds for the U.S. investor would be scenario D in which Canadian interest rates decline and the Canadian dollar strengthens relative to the U.S. dollar.

Strategies based on foreign exchange rates can be tricky, however. They can also be risky. The main reason is that interest rates are a major determinant of foreign exchange rates. If Canadian interest rates decline, relative to U.S. interest rates, then it is also possible that the Canadian dollar will actually lose value relative to the U.S. dollar. Take a look at scenario E in Table 10.7. Notice that the decline in the value of the Canadian dollar creates a situation in which the one-year return measured in U.S. dollars is substantially less than the one-year return measured in Canadian dollars.

Individual Bond Selection Strategies

Individual bond selection strategies seek to uncover individual bonds that are undervalued for some reason. Once the market recognizes that these bonds are undervalued, their prices should rise (as their yields decline), providing a high rate of return. Individual bond selection techniques really look for one of two situations: (1) a bond with a higher yield than other similar bonds (e.g., those with the same maturity or bond rating), and (2) a bond for which credit analysis suggests that its rating will improve. Let's look at an example.

In the early 1990s, Chrysler was struggling financially. Some observers even speculated about whether the company could survive. As its financial woes mounted, Chrysler's bond rating fell. In July 1990, Standard & Poor's (S&P) and Moody's dropped Chrysler's bond rating below investment grade. Chrysler bonds fell sharply in price as a result of the downgrade, but some investors thought that the market overreacted. They may have been right. As Chrysler's fortunes improved, so did the prices of Chrysler bonds. Between August 1990 and December 1993, for example, the price of Chrysler's 10.95%, 2017 debentures rose from 86% of par value to more than 120% of par value, an increase of more than 41%.

Guilt by Association We refer to a situation in which an entire class of securities is affected by problems of a few individual securities in the class as guilt by association. One can argue that this is another case in which the market overreacts. A good example of this affected high-yield corporate bonds (junk bonds) from 1989 through 1991.

As indicated earlier, junk bonds are bonds rated below investment grade (below BBB or Baa). These issues became popular during the 1980s to finance acquisitions, leveraged buyouts, and so forth. By the end of the 1980s, many junk bond issuers faced financial trouble. Several major defaults rocked the junk bond market (notably, the 1990 defaults of Campeau Corporation and Southland Corporation). As a result, prices of all junk bonds were mauled. By April 1990, the average yield on B-rated corporate bonds was more than 8% higher than the average yield on T-bonds, setting a record.

Some analysts thought that the market punished all junk bonds too severely, especially those that carried only moderate credit risk. They started to recommend selected junk bonds.[9] Prices of higher-quality junk bonds soon started to recover. In fact, over the three-year period ending on December 31, 1993, mutual funds that invested in junk bonds had an average annual return of 24.2%, compared with 11.7% for all taxable bond funds.

PASSIVELY MANAGING BOND PORTFOLIOS

Active bond portfolio management strategies attempt to profit from anticipated changes in such variables as interest rates and yield spreads by buying and selling bonds. Passive strategies are more concerned with controlling the risk of a bond portfolio. Passive bond management strategies fall into two broad categories. Indexing strategies are designed to replicate the performance of broad market indexes. The second type of strategies, commonly referred to as immunization, are designed to reduce the risks associated with fluctuations in interest rates.

indexing strategies

Strategies designed to replicate the performance of broad market indexes.

immunization strategies

Strategies designed to reduce the risks associated with fluctuations in interest rates.

---

[9]See, for example, "Why You Should Buy Junk Now," *Forbes*, April 30, 1990, pp. 440–441.

Indexing Bond Portfolios

As discussed before, indexing is perhaps the ultimate passive investment strategy. Indexing grew in popularity among bond investors in recent years.[10] The amount of pension money currently invested in bond index funds is more than $100 billion. The Vanguard Bond fund, an indexed bond mutual fund, currently has more than $5 billion in net assets.

Investors follow two basic rationales for indexing bond portfolios. First, indexing tacitly recognizes the extreme difficulty of an active bond investor consistently outperforming the overall market. Second, indexing reduces transaction costs and management expenses compared with actively managed portfolios. For example, a typical pension fund pays advisory fees between 0.15% and 0.50% per year for active management of a bond portfolio compared with between 0.01% and 0.20% for an index fund.

Indexing does, however, involve some drawbacks. For one thing, indexing restricts the investor to the sectors of the bond market that the index tracks, even though attractive opportunities may exist in other sectors. Further, indexing does not ensure that sufficient funds will be available at a specific point in time to meet a predetermined liability. This problem is common for institutional investors such as life insurance companies and pension funds. Other passive bond management strategies are designed to ensure that future liabilities are fully funded.

Choosing an Index One of the most important decisions to make when indexing a portfolio is choosing the appropriate index. The most popular index for stock index funds is the S&P 500, although some index funds track broader indexes such as the Wilshire 5000. Bond index funds may try to replicate the domestic taxable bond market by tracking one of three indexes: the Salomon BIG Index, the Lehman Brothers Aggregate Index, or the Merrill Lynch Domestic Master Index. Each index contains more than 4,500 different bond issues, with a total market value in excess of $3 trillion. Investors who wish to replicate the performance of a specific sector of the bond market (e.g., Treasuries, municipals, or foreign bond markets) can choose among several indexes. Examples include the Moody's Bond Buyer Index, a municipal bond index, and the Salomon World Government Bond Index.

Three criteria should guide the choice of an index. First, the index should match the investor's risk tolerance. For example, an investor who wants to eliminate any exposure to credit risk should avoid indexes that include corporate bonds. The second criterion is the investor's set of objectives and goals. An investor who has a short-term investment horizon may find some indexes more appropriate than others. The final criterion is regulatory constraints. Some institutional investors are restricted to investment-grade bonds. These investors would have to avoid any indexes that included below-investment-grade bonds.

Indexing Methodologies Indexing methodologies are more difficult for bond portfolios than for stocks. For one thing, bond indexes contain thousands of individual bond issues. Purchasing each individual bond in proportion to its market

---

[10]The issues associated with indexing bond portfolios are discussed in detail in Sharmin Mosavar-Rahmani, *Bond Index Funds* (Chicago: Probus Publishing, 1991).

TABLE 10.8	Type of Security			
Stratification of Treasury Securities into Cells	**Maturity**	**Notes**	**Bonds**	**Total Percentages**
	1 to 5 years	99%	1%	57%
	5 to 10 years	94	6	19
	10 to 20 years	0	100	5
	More than 20 years	0	100	19
	Total percentages	78	22	100

Note: Composition of the market as of June 30, 1996; excludes Treasury bills and other Treasury securities with times to maturity of less than one year.

value may be extremely difficult, especially because many bonds are thinly traded. In addition, rebalancing presents more of a problem with bond index funds than with stock index funds. Most indexes drop individual bonds once their times to maturity fall below six months or one year. Thus, new bonds are constantly being added to the index, and the index fund must be rebalanced each time. Also, the portfolio manager must decide what to do with all the interest income when it is received.

Several indexing methodologies can be used. The most common, the stratified sampling or cell approach, stratifies the bond market into several subclasses based on criteria such as credit risk, maturity, and issuer.[11] The resulting cells are considered to consist of reasonably homogeneous groups, from which the index selects a sample.

Let's illustrate this approach using a simple example. To design a bond portfolio that is tied to a Treasury index consisting of all U.S. Treasury securities with times to maturity in excess of one year, first divide the Treasury market by maturity. Next, stratify each maturity class by type of security, bonds or notes. As you may recall from Chapter 3, the only difference between bonds and notes, other than maturity when issued, is the fact that some bonds are callable starting five years from their maturity dates. The resulting cells are shown in Table 10.8.

The bottom row shows the breakdown between notes and bonds. Because 78% of outstanding Treasuries with more than one year remaining before maturity are notes and 22% are bonds, 78% of the entire portfolio should consist of notes and 22% should consist of bonds. The last column shows the general breakdown of the portfolio by maturity. For example, 19% of the portfolio should consist of Treasuries with maturities between 5 and 10 years. The other cells show the breakdown between notes and bonds within each maturity group. The group of securities with maturities between 5 and 10 years should be broken down as 94% notes and 6% bonds.

tracking error

One way of assessing how well an index fund replicates the performance of its benchmark index.

Tracking Error Tracking error is one way of assessing how well an index fund replicates the performance of its benchmark index. Tracking error simply measures the difference between the total return of the portfolio and that of the index. This measure is usually calculated monthly. A Salomon Brothers study found that portfolios indexed to broad bond market indexes (e.g., Salomon's BIG Index) had the lowest tracking errors.[12] Portfolios indexed to specific sectors of

[11]Other indexing methodologies are discussed in Fabozzi, *Bond Markets,* pp. 518–522.
[12]Reported in Fabozzi, *Bond Markets,* pp. 522–523.

TABLE 10.9

Three Bonds for Funding
a Future Liability

Bond	Term (year)	Coupon Rate	Yield to Maturity	Duration (year)	Price (per $100 par value)
A	10	10.0%	6.9%	7.08	$121.87
B	16	7.5	6.9	10.00	105.71
C	25	5.0	6.9	13.40	77.66

Note: Bonds pay interest annually.

the bond market (e.g., corporate bonds) had the highest tracking errors. Further, indexing a larger portfolio generally leads to smaller tracking error.

Immunization

In contrast to indexing, immunization is an attempt by a bond investor to reduce a portfolio's exposure to the risks associated with changing interest rates. As discussed in Chapter 9, bond investors are exposed to both interest rate and reinvestment risk. As interest rates rise, bond prices fall. At the same time, however, bond investors can reinvest coupon payments at higher rates, earning more interest on interest. When interest rates fall, bond prices rise, but investors are forced to reinvest coupon payments at lower rates. Therefore, both rising and falling interest rates can hurt bond investors.

Although it is probably impossible to totally eliminate these risks, careful immunization can substantially reduce them. The specific immunization strategy used by an investor will depend on the risk from which the portfolio needs protection.[13] Let's examine three immunization strategies.

Target Date Immunization Target date immunization seeks to ensure that an investor has sufficient funds available at a point in time to meet a single liability. It does so by setting the duration of the bond portfolio equal to the horizon date (i.e., the point in time when the single liability will fall due). This duration matching protects the future value of the portfolio from fluctuations in interest rates between the current date and the horizon date. Let's illustrate target date immunization with a simple example. A pension fund manager determines that the fund will need $10 million in 10 years to meet obligations to retiring employees. The current yield to maturity on 10-year bonds is 6.9%. Therefore, to have $10 million in 10 years, the pension fund needs to invest $5,131,247 (the present value of $10 million discounted at 6.9% for 10 years). The pension fund manager decides to invest the money in bonds, leaving the three choices listed in Table 10.9. For simplicity, assume that all three bonds have the same yield to maturity, pay interest annually, and are free of credit and call risk.

Does it matter which bond the pension fund buys? Absolutely! Table 10.10 shows the future values of the cash flows after 10 years for the bonds under three different interest rate scenarios. The future value of each cash flow is made up of the

target date immunization

Technique designed to ensure that an investor has sufficient funds available at a point in time to meet a single liability.

[13]In practice, immunization strategies can get more complicated than what we are about to describe. See, for example, Fabozzi, *Bond Markets,* pp. 511–549. Furthermore, financial futures can reduce interest rate risk, as discussed in Chapter 16.

TABLE 10.10							
Target Date Immunization	Rate of Interest	Future Value of Cash Flow in 10 Years (per bond)			Value of Bonds in 10 Years ($ millions)		
		Bond A	Bond B	Bond C	Bond A	Bond B	Bond C
	5.90%	$231.19	$206.29	$156.80	$ 9.73	$10.01	$10.36
	6.90	237.51	206.00	151.34	10.00	10.00	10.00
	7.90	244.18	206.28	147.11	10.38	10.01	9.72

Details of Calculations of Future Value of Cash Flows in 10 Years for Bond B

Interest Rate	Coupon Payments	Interest on Coupon Payments	Price in 10 Years	Total Cash Flow (per bond)
5.90%	$75.00	$23.39	$107.89	$206.29
6.90	75.00	28.14	102.87	206.00
7.90	75.00	33.13	98.15	206.28

Notes: Number of bonds purchased with initial investment of $5,131,247 are 42,103 (bond A), 48,543 (bond B), and 66,076 (bond C). Future value of cash flows equals coupon payments, interest on coupons (reinvested at the rate of interest shown), and the face value of bonds (bond A) or the prices of the bonds (bonds B and C).

price of the bond after 10 years (in the case of bonds B and C) or the face value (in the case of bond A), the coupon payments, and interest on the coupon payments.

The optimum choice depends on what happens to interest rates. If rates stay exactly the same (6.9%), then all three bond alternatives will produce exactly $10 million in 10 years. However, if rates fall from 6.9% to 5.9%, bond A fails to produce sufficient cash flows. If rates rise from 6.9% to 7.9%, bond C fails to produce sufficient cash flows. The durations of bonds A and C are either longer or shorter than 10 years. Only bond B, which has a duration close to the horizon date of 10 years, produces about $10 million regardless of whether interest rates rise or fall. Table 10.10 details the calculation of the future value of bond B's cash flows. If rates fall, the decline in interest on coupon income is exactly offset by a higher price in Year 10, and rising interest on interest compensates exactly for a lower price if rates rise. To summarize, then, if interest rates fall and the average duration of the bond portfolio fails to reach the target date, the portfolio will fail to produce the needed cash flow. However, if interest rates rise and the average duration of the bond portfolio runs past the target date, the portfolio will fail to produce the needed cash flow. Only if the duration of the portfolio is equal to the period before the target date will the portfolio produce the needed cash flow.

Two comments should be made about target date immunization. First, buying a zero coupon bond that matures on the horizon date will produce sufficient cash flows regardless of interest rates. Remember, the duration of a zero coupon bond equals its maturity. In practice, however, such a zero coupon bond may not be available. Second, duration changes as interest rates change, as you may recall from Chapter 9. As a result, if interest rates change significantly, it may be necessary to rebalance the bond portfolio to bring the duration back into line with the horizon date.

Cash Flow Matching and Multiperiod Immunization Many investors need to fund a series of obligations over a period of time. One multiperiod strategy is to purchase a series of bonds (either zero coupon or coupon bonds)

	Year	Beginning Obligation	Cash Flow from Bonds	Remaining Obligation
Step 1				
Bond A	1	$ 5,000,000	$ 500,000	$4,500,000
	2	5,000,000	500,000	4,500,000
	3	10,000,000	500,000	9,500,000
	4	10,000,000	500,000	9,500,000
	5	10,500,000	10,500,000	0
Step 2				
Bond B	1	$ 4,500,000	$ 452,381	$4,047,619
	2	4,500,000	452,381	4,047,619
	3	9,500,000	9,500,000	9,047,619
	4	9,500,000	9,500,000	0
Step 3				
Bond C	1	$ 4,047,619	$ 430,829	$3,616,780
	2	4,047,619	430,839	$3,616,780
	3	9,047,619	9,047,619	0
Step 4				
Bond D	1	$ 3,616,780	$ 172,228	$3,444,552
	2	$ 3,616,780	3,616,780	0
Step 5				
Bond E	1	$ 3,444,552	$3,444,552	0

Summary

Bond	Amount Purchased	Maturity
A	$10,000,000	5 years
B	9,047,619	4 years
C	8,616,780	3 years
D	3,444,552	2 years
E	3,280,526	1 year

TABLE 10.11

Illustration of a Dedicated Portfolio

Note: All bonds have coupon rates of 5%, sell at par, and pay interest annually.

with durations equal to the horizon date of each obligation. In essence, this strategy extends target date immunization.

An alternative strategy is to construct a **dedicated portfolio**. Such a portfolio is designed to generate sufficient cash flow in each period to match the series of obligations faced by the investor. A bond is selected with a maturity that matches the last liability and produces sufficient cash flow at maturity to meet this obligation. The coupons from this bond, paid prior to maturity, reduce the other obligations. Next, a second bond is selected with a maturity equal to the next to last obligation that produces sufficient cash flow at maturity to meet this reduced obligation. The portfolio manager continues to go backward in time until all periodic obligations are fully funded. An example of a dedicated portfolio is shown in Table 10.11.

dedicated portfolio

Portfolio designed to generate sufficient cash flow each period to match a series of obligations faced by an investor.

TABLE 10.12			Average Interest Rate	Duration (years)
Net Worth Immunization		Amount ($000)		
Original balance sheet	Assets	$10,000	6.5%	7.5
	Liabilities	9,000	5.50	1.5
	Net worth	$ 1,000		
		New Amount	Change	
Rates rise by 2.0%	Assets	$8,592	($1,408)	
	Liabilities	8,744	(256)	
	Net worth	$ (153)	(1,153)	
		Amount ($000)	Average Interest Rate	Duration (years)
Net worth immunization	Assets	$10,000	6.5%	4.5
	Liabilities	9,000	5.50	5.0
	Net worth	1,000		
		New Amount	Change	
Rates rise by 2.0%	Assets	$9,155	($845)	
	Liabilities	8,147	(853)	
	Net worth	$1,008	8	

Net Worth Immunization Many depository institutions, such as commercial banks, must compensate for natural mismatches between the average durations of their assets (loans and securities) and the average durations of their liabilities (mainly deposits). Because the average duration of assets is longer than the average duration of liabilities for the typical bank, when interest rates rise, the market value of its assets will fall by more than the market value of its liabilities. As a result, the bank's net worth will fall.[14]

This situation is illustrated in Table 10.12. The hypothetical bank has total assets of $10 million, total liabilities of $9 million, and a net worth of $1 million. The average duration of the bank's assets is 7.5 years whereas the average duration of its liabilities is 1.5 years. Notice what happens if interest rates rise by 2%; the bank's net worth drops from $1 million to $153,000. **Net worth immunization** is an attempt to narrow the gap between the average duration of a depository institution's assets and the average duration of its liabilities. (We discuss a way a bank can do this in the next section.) If the average durations of the bank's assets and liabilities could be equated to one another, then the institution's net worth would be immunized from increases in interest rates.[15] This scenario is also

net worth immunization

Process designed to narrow the gap between the average duration of a depository institution's assets and the average duration of its liabilities.

[14]A bank's net worth is commonly referred to as *capital*. The typical bank has capital equal to between 5% and 10% of its assets.
[15]Unless the value of the bank's assets equals the value of its liabilities, the average duration of assets should be less than the average duration of liabilities for new worth to be immunized. Durations

illustrated in Table 10.12. Notice that if the average duration of the bank's assets is 4.5 years and the average duration of its liabilities is 5.0 years, then a 2% increase in interest rates has no material effect on the bank's net worth because the decrease in the value of the bank's assets is offset by the decrease in the value of its liabilities.

INTEREST RATE SWAPS

In an **interest rate swap**, two parties agree to exchange a series of interest payments. Interest rate swaps first emerged in the early 1980s as a way of controlling interest rate and foreign exchange risk. Although the exact size of the swap market is hard to determine precisely, some estimates place the total value of these transactions as high as $2.5 *trillion*. The typical interest rate swap involves two parties that face opposite types of interest rate risk or foreign exchange risk. A third party, a large bank or investment banking firm, usually acts as an intermediary between the two parties. Let's look at an example of a simple interest rate swap.

interest rate swap

Agreement between two parties to exchange a series of interest payments over a specified period of time.

Example of an Interest Rate Swap

Assume that a bank has $100 million in 10-year loans outstanding that carry an average annual interest rate of 8%. The loans charge simple interest only, so the borrowers make annual interest payments of $8 million. The bank finances these loans by issuing one-year certificates of deposit that pay interest equal to the yield on one-year T-bills plus 0.5%. On the other side, assume that an insurance company has sold $100 million worth of 6.5% annuities. The insurance company pays simple interest on the annuities once a year, and it invests the proceeds from the sale of the annuities in a floating rate security. The security's rate is adjusted annually to equal the yield on one-year T-bills plus 1%. The bank and the insurance company face opposite types of interest rate risk. If rates rise, the bank suffers; if rates fall, the insurance company suffers. As discussed in the prior section, the duration of the bank's assets is greater than that of its liabilities. Therefore, if rates rise, the value of the bank's assets falls by more than the value of its liabilities.

To manage their respective risks, the bank and the insurance company decide to do an interest rate swap, with a third party acting as the intermediary. The bank agrees to pay 6.6% annually in exchange for the yield on a one-year T-bill. The insurance company agrees to pay the yield on a one-year T-bill in exchange for a set payment of 6.3%. The annual cash flows for both parties are shown here:

	Receives	Pays	Net
Bank	1. 8%	1. T-bill yield plus 0.5%	0.9%
	2. One-year T-bill yield	2. 6.6%	
Insurance company	1. T-bill yield plus 1%	1. 6.5%	0.8%
	2. 6.3%	2. T-bill yield	

---

should be equated as follows. Let A be the value of the bank's assets, L be the value of its liabilities, D_A be the duration of its assets, and D_L be the duration of its liabilities. To immunize the bank's net worth, AD_A should be set equal to AD_L.

		Bank			Insurance Company		
TABLE 10.13							
Year	**One Year T-Bill Yield**	**Receive**	**Pay**	**Net (%)**	**Receive**	**Pay**	**Net (%)**
1	4.5%	12.5%	11.6%	0.9%	11.8%	11.0%	0.8%
2	5.0	13.0	12.1	0.9	12.3	11.5	0.8
3	5.5	13.5	12.6	0.9	12.8	12.0	0.8
4	6.0	14.0	13.1	0.9	13.3	12.5	0.8
5	5.0	13.0	12.1	0.9	12.3	11.5	0.8
6	4.0	12.0	11.1	0.9	11.3	10.5	0.8
7	3.0	11.0	10.1	0.9	10.3	9.5	0.8
8	4.0	12.0	11.1	0.9	11.3	10.5	0.8
9	4.0	12.0	11.1	0.9	11.3	10.5	0.8
10	4.0	12.0	11.1	0.9	11.3	10.5	0.8

TABLE 10.13 Effects of an Interest Rate Swap

Note: Each year the bank receives 8% and the one-year T-bill yield, and pays the one-year T-bill yield plus 0.5% and 6.5%. Each year the insurance company receives the one-year T-bill yield plus 1% and 6.3%, and pays 6.5% and the one-year T-bill yield.

The swap, in effect, pays both parties the same spread each year regardless of whether interest rates rise or fall. The results of this swap are illustrated in Table 10.13. The table assumes that interest rates first rise and then fall. Notice that the bank makes 0.9% each year and the insurance company makes 0.8% each year, regardless of what happens to interest rates.

SUMMARY

1. What has happened to the volatility of bond prices?
Over the past few years, the volatility of bond prices increased sharply. Changes in interest rates are more frequent and more pronounced today than they were 20 years ago. In fact, over the past 20 years or so, bond volatility on occasion even exceeded stock price volatility. Volatility in the bond market creates opportunities for active bond investors and increases the importance of strategies used by passive bond investors to minimize the risks associated with changes in interest rates.

2. How does the term structure of interest rates affect bond investors?
The term structure of interest rates shows the relationship between yield and maturity for a similar class of bonds—usually T-bonds are used to construct the term structure. Theorists who explored the possibility that future spot rates are implied by current spot rates and the possibility of locking in future returns developed three major theories of the yield curve: the pure expectations theory, the liquidity preference theory, and the market segmentation theory. Changes in the slope and shape of the yield curve may forecast future spot rates, changes in the liquidity premium, and changes in supply and demand conditions.

3. What are some active bond management strategies?
Most active bond management strategies involve swaps: buying one set of bonds with one set of characteristics, such as long durations, while selling another set of bonds with the opposite characteristics. Some examples of active strategies include those based on interest rate expectations, those based on expected changes in the yield curve, strategies based on changes in yield spreads, those based on changes in foreign exchange rates, and individual bond selection strategies.

4. How can bond portfolios be managed passively?
Passive bond management strategies are concerned with controlling the risk of a bond portfolio. Examples of passive strategies include indexing, in which a bond portfolio is

designed merely to replicate the performance of a broad bond index, and immunization, in which the investor attempts to reduce the amount of interest rate risk to which the portfolio is exposed. Two immunization techniques are target date immunization and cash flow matching. In both cases, the portfolio produces desired future cash flows regardless of changes in interest rates. Financial institutions attempt to immunize their net worth by matching the duration of assets with the duration of liabilities.

5. What are interest rate swaps?

An interest rate swap is an agreement by which two parties agree to exchange a series of interest payments. Interest rate swaps are designed to control interest rate and foreign exchange risks. The typical interest rate swap involves two parties that face opposite types of interest rate or foreign exchange risk. If a swap is done correctly, both parties are guaranteed certain cash flows over a period of time.

MINI CASE 1

The purpose of this mini case is to practice computing implied forward rates from actual spot rates and to further understand the various theories of the yield curve. The following yields were quoted on pure discount U.S. Treasury securities.

Term	Yield
3-month	5.20%
6-month	5.33
1-year	5.55
2-year	5.90
3-year	6.06
4-year	6.13
5-year	6.22
6-year	6.30
7-year	6.36

1. Compute as many implied forward rates from these spot rates as you can.
2. How would each of the three theories of the yield curve interpret the relationship between the forward rates calculated in Question 1 and the current spot rates?
3. Show what is meant by *riding the yield curve*. Show why riding the yield curve would not work if the pure expectations hypothesis were correct.

MINI CASE 2

Use the following information to put together a dedicated bond portfolio. Assume that no zero coupon bonds are available and that all bonds listed sell at par, pay interest once a year, and are free of default and call risks. Round to the nearest dollar.

Year (maturity)	Obligation	Coupon Rate on Bond
1	$20,000,000	4.5%
2	25,000,000	5.0
3	25,000,000	5.5
4	40,000,000	6.0
5	53,000,000	6.0

1. Explain why all bond investors should be concerned about increased bond market volatility. Cite some specific examples of how bond investors can respond to increased volatility in the market.

2. Define the *term structure of interest rates*. Why are Treasury securities often used to measure the term structure?

3. Assume that a one-year discount bond currently yields 4% and a two-year discount bond currently yields 4.25%. Find the implied forward rate on a one-year bond one year from today. Show how to lock in that rate today.

4. Assume that a one-year discount bond currently yields 5% and a two-year discount bond currently yields 5.5%. Find the implied forward rate on a one-year bond one year from today. Show how to lock in that rate today.

5. Explain the differences between the pure expectations theory, the liquidity preference theory, and the market segmentation theory. What would constitute evidence of market segmentation?

6. What is the basic goal of active bond portfolio management strategies? List several categories of active bond strategies.

7. What is meant by *riding the yield curve?* Would riding the yield curve work if the pure expectations theory of the yield curve were correct?

8. List the three types of changes in the yield curve that have been observed historically. For each kind of shift, what is the optimal yield curve strategy?

9. What is the general idea behind yield spread strategies? Why are yield spread strategies and interest rate strategies often interrelated ?

10. Assume the current yield on a BBB 10-year is 8.5% and the current yield on a 10-year T-bond is 6.5% (assume both bonds are pure discount bonds and have face values of $1,000). Also, assume you believe that the yield on the T-bond will fall to 6% over the next year and the yield spread between the BBB bond and the T-bond will narrow from 2% to 1.5%. Calculate the one-year holding period return for both bonds, assuming your expectations are correct. What type of strategy did you use?

11. Assume that Congress just cut the top marginal tax rate on individuals. What would you expect to happen to the yield spread between taxable and tax-exempt bonds? Why?

12. Give two examples of foreign exchange strategies. Why are foreign exchange strategies so potentially risky?

13. Assume that one year ago you purchased a five-year British government bond (denominated in British pounds, has a face value of £1,000, and is a pure discount bond). At that time, the bond had a yield of 6% and the exchange rate ($ per £) was $1.20. Today, one year later, you sold the bond. The yield fell to 5.5% and the exchange rate is now $1.10. Compute your one-year holding period return in both pounds and dollars. Why are the two different?

14. Why has bond indexing become so popular? What are some of the important decisions an investor has to make when indexing a bond portfolio?

15. What is *rebalancing?* Why is rebalancing more difficult with bond portfolios than with stock portfolios?

16. What is *target date immunization?* Show how zero coupon bonds can solve target date immunization problems.

Use the data in the following table to answer Questions 17–26.

You just won a $30 million lottery and are considering investing the funds in bonds. You consider hedging using target immunization or maximizing your return. You will invest for 4.54 years then liquidate to move to Tahiti. You narrow your investment choices to the following four bonds.

Bond	Coupon Rate	Yield to Maturity	Term (years)	Duration (years)
E	5%	5%	7	6.07
F	5	5	2	
G	5	5	5	4.54
H	0	5	4.54	

Note: Assume that interest payments are made annually and ignore accrued interest. Conduct analysis on one bond even though you will be investing $30 million.

17. What is Bond F's duration?

18. What is Bond H's duration?

19. What is the price of Bond H?

20. If you decide to hedge using target immunization, will Bond E achieve it? Explain your answer by including a discussion on the type of risk that will be greater if immunization is not achieved.

21. If you decide to hedge using target immunization, will Bond F achieve it? Explain your answer by including a discussion on the type of risk that will be greater if immunization is not achieved.

22. If you decide to hedge using target immunization, will Bond G achieve it? Explain your answer by including a discussion on the type of risk that will be greater if immunization is not achieved.

23. If you decide to hedge using target immunization, will Bond H achieve it? Explain your answer by including a discussion on the type of risk that will be greater if immunization is not achieved.

24. Suppose instead of hedging using target immunization, you decide to maximize your return. If you anticipate an increase in market interest rates from the current 5% to 6%, which bond is most desirable? Explain your choice.

25. If interest rates do increase from 5% to 6% one month after you invest, what is the impact on the Bond F's price?

26. Calculate the annual rate of return (ARR) over the 4.54-year investment period for Bond F. Assume that you will purchase a 6% coupon 4-year bond selling at par value when Bond F matures.

27. How can an investor solve a multiperiod immunization problem? Explain how a dedicated portfolio works.

28. Assume that a bank currently has $50 million in assets (with an average duration of five years and an average interest rate of 7.5%) and $45 million in liabilities (with an average duration of one year and an average interest rate of 5%). If interest rates rise by 2%, to what risk are the bank's shareholders exposed? How could the bank immunize the shareholders' investment from adverse changes in interest rates?

29. Two British companies each want to borrow £20 million for five years. Company A has been offered a 9% fixed-rate loan or a variable-rate loan with the interest rate equal to LIBOR plus 0.5%. Company B has been offered either an 8% fixed-rate loan or a variable-rate loan with the interest rate equal to LIBOR plus 0.5%. Due to the composition of their assets, Company A would prefer a fixed-rate loan whereas Company B would prefer a variable-rate loan. Construct an interest rate swap that benefits both parties.

30. Two Japanese companies each want to borrow 100 million yen for five years. Company J has been offered a 5% fixed-rate loan or a variable-rate loan with the interest rate equal to LIBOR plus 0.5%. Company K has been offered either an 4% fixed-rate loan or a variable-rate loan with the interest rate equal to LIBOR plus 0.5%. Due to the composition of their assets, Company J would prefer a fixed-rate loan whereas Company K would prefer a variable-rate loan. Construct an interest rate swap that benefits both parties.

CRITICAL THINKING EXERCISES

1. This exercise requires computer work. Open Bond 2 worksheet in the Data Workbook. It gives yields and prices for pure discount bonds with maturities of 1, 7, and 20 years. Classify the 1-year bond as a short-term bond, the 7-year bond as an intermediate-term bond, and the 20-year bond as a long-term bond. The anticipated holding period is 1 year. Given the following scenarios, determine which bond is optimal.
    a. All yields remain constant.
    b. All yields rise by 1%.
    c. All yields fall by 1%.
    d. Yields on long-term bonds fall by 1.5%, yields on intermediate-term bonds fall by 0.75%, and yields on short-term bonds fall by 0.25%.
    e. Yields on long-term bonds rise by 1%, yields in intermediate-term bonds rise by 1.25%, and yields on short-term bonds rise by 1.5%.
    f. Yields on long-term bonds fall by 1%, yields on intermediate-term bonds fall by 1.5%, and yields on short-term bonds fall by 2%.

2. This exercise requires computer work. Open the Bond 3 worksheet in the Data Workbook and use the data provided to answer the following questions:
    a. A pension fund will need $10 million in exactly five years. Given current yields, how much will the pension fund have to invest today?
    b. Given the choices available, which bond should the pension fund buy? Why?
    c. Would your answer to part (b) change if the fund manager believed that interest rates might rise or fall during the next five years?
    d. Show what would happen if (1) interest rates were to rise immediately by 1.5% after the bonds were purchased and remain at that level for the rest of the five-year period, or (2) interest rates were to fall immediately by 1.5% after the bonds were purchased and remain at that level for the rest of the five-year period.
    e. Should the pension fund make any changes to the bond portfolio if rates were either to rise or fall during the five-year period?

3. This exercise requires library research. Find five bonds that have been upgraded by the rating agencies recently (either corporate or municipal bonds). Obtain price and yield information for the bonds six months before the upgrade and six months after it. In addition, obtain yield information from some relevant index for either corporate or municipal bonds.

    What happened to the bond prices and yields before and after the upgrade announcement? How did the spreads between the yields for your sample bonds and the index yield change? Did they widen or narrow?

    Had you purchased these bonds six months before the upgrade announcement, approximately how much higher would your return have been compared with the performance of the broad market index? (*Hint:* S&P's monthly *Bond Guide* is a good source of upgrade, price, and yield information.)

Principles of Security Analysis

Part 4 is devoted to a detailed discussion of the fundamental analysis and valuation of common stocks—commonly referred to security analysis. The goal of security analysis is to determine whether the price of a common stock reflects its intrinsic value. The process of security analysis has often been described as a sort of inverted triangle, as the analysis moves from the general to the specific. We start with economic analysis, then move to industry analysis, then to company analysis. Next we consider several stock valuation models which tie the process together. The purpose of Part 4 is to illustrate how analysts arrive at estimates of the variables that appear to determine the value of common stock. We will see that the analyst must consider both quantifiable and non-quantifiable variables and issues, and must make both subjective and objective judgments concerning the intrinsic value of a stock.

11

Economic and Industry Analysis

PREVIOUSLY . . .

In the prior two chapters, we described the investment characteristics of fixed income securities and some strategies involving bonds.

IN THIS CHAPTER . . .

We examine the two macro components of security analysis: economic and industry analysis. All stocks are to some extent affected by these macro factors. Stock prices, in general, and interest rates are strongly related to the business cycle. Economic variables also affect the fortunes of industries. Regardless of the overall market, variation in the performance of industries should be expected.

TO COME . . .

In the next two chapters, we discuss company analysis, beginning with qualitative factors and historical financial data.

CHAPTER OBJECTIVES

After reading Chapter 11, you should be able to answer the following questions:

1. Why are economic and industry analyses important?

2. How are investment decisions related to the business cycle?

3. How are economic forecasts made?

4. How are industries classified?

5. What are the important components of industry analysis?

6. What is the framework and some of the techniques used in industry analysis?

In Chapter 8, we briefly discussed the basic steps for analyzing a common stock. Security analysis, or fundamental analysis, can be thought of as a three-step process described as an inverted triangle, with the analyst moving from the general to the specific. He or she begins with economic analysis and tries to determine where the domestic and international economies appear to be headed (expansion or recession), as well as the outlook for important economic variables such as inflation and interest rates. Among other things, the analyst considers whether the overall economic outlook appears favorable or unfavorable for stocks.

After assessing the economic environment, the analyst completes an industry analysis. Is the company's industry in a growth phase or a mature phase? Is the industry subject to rapid technological change? Are demographic trends favorable or unfavorable for the industry? Are industry production costs rising more quickly or more slowly than the overall inflation rate? Is the industry subject to substantial government regulation? These questions are examples of the issues an analyst might rise when examining a company's industry.

Following a review of economic and industry factors, the analyst examines the specific company in detail, looking at both quantitative and qualitative issues. We begin our detailed look at security analysis in this chapter with an examination of economic and industry analysis to assess the company's macro environment, which strongly influences common stock valuation.

THE IMPORTANCE OF ECONOMIC AND INDUSTRY ANALYSIS

We begin our look at the macro analysis of securities by asking a simple question: How important are economic and industry factors in the valuation of individual common stocks? We believe that both are critical, although neither economic or industry analysis can substitute for a careful examination of a specific company. History is replete with examples of poor stock performance despite favorable economic environments for stocks and good industry characteristics. The reverse situation (a good stock in poor economic and industry conditions) occasionally occurs as well. Economic and industry analysis should complement and enhance the analyst's examination of a specific company, not replace it.

Economic analysis is important, for one reason, simply because stock prices demonstrate a strong positive relationship with overall economic performance. Since 1949, according to the National Bureau of Economic Research, the U.S. economy passed through nine economic expansions and eight recessions. During the eight expansions, stock prices, as measured by the Standard & Poor's (S&P) 500, rose an average of almost 100%. By contrast, during the eight recessions, stock prices *fell* by an average of 18.2%. Not surprisingly, a stronger expansion (or contraction) in economic activity generally produces a larger increase (or decrease) in stock prices. We have more to say about the relationship between stock prices and economic activity later in the chapter.

The same positive relationship between economic performance and stock prices exists in other countries as well. For example, Britain experienced a recession between mid-1990 and late 1991; its real gross domestic product (GDP stated in constant dollars, removing the effects of inflation) declined by approximately 2.6%. The associated decline in British stock prices (measured by the Financial Times 100 index) was slightly more than 16%.

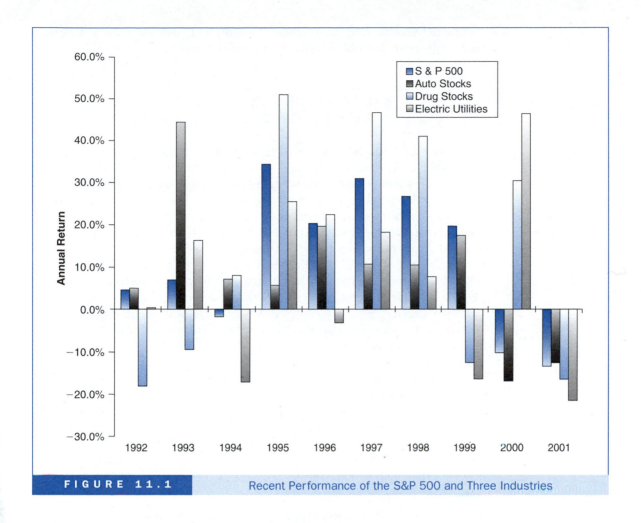

FIGURE 11.1 Recent Performance of the S&P 500 and Three Industries

It is important to note that over the duration of a bull or bear market, performance levels among various industry groups often show substantial differences. Figure 11.1 illustrates that, regardless of how well the overall market performs, we can expect to see disparate performance among various industry groups. In 1995, for instance, the S&P 500 had a total return of over 34%. By contrast, the total return from auto stocks was only 5.6%. Overall, 2000 was a poor year for stocks—the total return for the S&P 500 was −10.1%. Yet, some industries did well. Drug stocks, for one, had a total return in excess of 30%. So, even if the economic outlook for stocks in general is favorable or unfavorable, the outlook for some industry groups may be different. Therefore, the analyst must examine the industry as well as the economy.

Macro analysis is also important because it is naive to assume that the fortunes of individual companies, and thus the performance levels of their stocks, are not somehow tied to the prospects for the overall economy and the industries within which those companies operate. No company operates in a vacuum. For example, as we noted in Chapter 9, one variable that determines the intrinsic value of a common stock is the expected growth in earnings. Without any economic or industry information, could you come up with a reasonable estimate of the expected growth rate in earnings? Probably not, because most companies' future earnings are heavily influenced by economic and industry conditions.

BUSINESS CYCLES AND INVESTMENT DECISIONS

Having established the importance of an examination of economic and industry factors in the evaluation of individual stocks, we now turn to a discussion of the relationship between business cycles and investment decisions. First of all, what is a **business cycle**? Long-term economic growth in the United States (and in other developed market-oriented countries) exhibited nonperiodic but recurrent sequences of expansions and contractions (recessions) around the long-term, secular trend. Economists refer to these sequences as business cycles.

Since the end of World War II, the United States experienced eight complete business cycles (measured from trough to trough). By comparison, Canada experienced 12 complete business cycles since 1948, and Britain, France, Germany, and Japan each experienced seven complete business cycles during the same period. The average business cycle in the United States since 1949 lasted 62 months (slightly more than five years).

It is important to note, however, that no two business cycles are exactly alike. The longest complete postwar business cycle lasted 120 months (March 1991 to March 2001) whereas the shortest lasted only 28 months (between July 1980 and November 1982). During the postwar era, U.S. expansions ranged from 12 to 110 months long, whereas contractions ranged between 6 and 16 months.[1] During the average postwar expansion, real GDP increased by about 5% per year, with a range between 4% and 7.3%. The average contraction saw real GDP decline by about 2.5% per year, with a range between −0.1% and −4.4% per year.

Business Cycles and Stock Prices

As we discussed earlier, stock prices and economic activity are closely related; economic expansions are generally associated with rising stock prices, and contractions are usually associated with falling stock prices. However, stock prices and economic activity are not *coincident;* they do not occur at the same time. Rather, stock prices tend to lead overall economic activity, typically by several months, in all developed market-oriented economies. Stock prices could fall even when the economy was still expanding, and they could rise in a recession.

Table 11.1 illustrates the leading relationship between stock prices and economic activity in the United States. During expansions, stocks prices (measured by the S&P 500) peaked almost six months before economic activity, on average. Stock prices, on average, bottomed out roughly five months before the ends of recessions. Note, however, that the leading relationship between stock prices and economic activity has been far from consistent. Stock prices peaked anywhere

---

business cycle

Nonperiodic recurrent sequences of expansions and contractions around long-term economic growth.

---

[1]The longest economic expansion in postwar history began in November 1990 and didn't end until March 2001.

S&P	GDP	Lead (months)
A. Peaks		
January 1953	July 1953	6
July 1956	August 1957	13
July 1959	April 1960	9
December 1968	December 1969	12
December 1972	November 1973	11
February 1980	January 1980	21
April 1981	July 1981	3
June 1990	July 1990	1
August 2000	March 2001	7
Average		**5.9**
B. Troughs		
June 1949	October 1949	4
September 1953	May 1954	8
December 1957	April 1958	4
October 1960	February 1961	4
June 1970	November 1970	5
September 1974	March 1975	5
April 1980	July 1980	3
July 1982	December 1982	5
October 1990	March 1991	5
Average		**4.8**

TABLE 11.1

Turning Points in the Business Cycle and U.S. Stock Prices

Source: Survey of Current Business, various issues.

between 1 and 13 months before peaks in economic activity. In 1980, stock prices did not actually peak until *after* the economic contraction began.

To further complicate the relationship, many large declines in stock prices do not led into recessions. One of the best examples is the 1987 market break. Between August and December of 1987, the S&P 500 dropped by more than 27%, yet no recession followed in either 1988 or 1989. In fact, real U.S. GDP grew by more than 7% during both years. However, in far fewer cases, large increases in stock prices failed to presage economic expansions.

Why do stock prices tend to lead economic activity? One explanation is that an increase or decrease in stock prices is a self-fulfilling prophecy. Some economists argue that stock price reversals affect consumer and business confidence, and thus spending decisions. A sharp decline in stock prices, for example, may lead to less consumer spending, depressing economic activity. Other economists dismiss the notion that major stock price reversals are the main cause of changes in the direction of economic activity. The Investment History box on page 282 tries to answer the question: Did the 1929 Stock Market Crash *Cause* the Great Depression? Contrary to popular belief, the answer appears to be no.

Another explanation is that the variables that drive stock prices (such things as earnings, dividends, and interest rates) are based more on *expected* business

INVESTMENT HISTORY

Did the 1929 Great Stock Market Crash Cause the Great Depression?

In the history of the twentieth century, two of the most significant events were the great stock market crash of 1929, which ended one of the great stock market bubbles in history, and the Great Depression, which lasted from the end of the 1920s to the beginning of World War II. Popular history suggests that the stock market crash was a cause of the depression. But was it really? Before we answer the question, let's review the Great Crash of 1929.

Stock prices, measured by the Dow Jones Industrial Average, almost tripled between the end of 1920 and the end of 1927. This increase could be characterized as more a standard bull market than a speculative bubble. The increase was generally orderly and backed by favorable economic fundamentals (inflation, interest rates, and corporate profits).

Sometime during 1928, however, the bull market became a true speculative bubble. After a fairly quiet winter, during which prices actually fell slightly, stock prices began to rise and rise sharply. During the second half of 1928 alone, the Dow increased about 42% as trading volume soared. By the end of 1928, the frenzy was in full force.

By almost any measure, 1929 is perhaps the most remarkable and infamous year in stock market history. The Dow added another 27% between the beginning of January and September 3, when the bubble finally reached its zenith. Trading was often frantic with wild daily price swings—both up and down. Trading volume set records almost every day, even during the normally slow summer months.

Finally the end came. On September 5, 1929, respected financial advisor Roger Babson, repeated a prediction that a stock market crash was coming. Stocks suffered a sharp selloff that day, known as the *Babson Break.* Stocks recovered somewhat and then started to drift over the next few weeks, experiencing more down days than up days. The bubble finally ruptured on October 28 and 29. Stock prices dropped in almost a linear fashion. Prices of some individual stocks fell by $5 to $10 per share on each subsequent trade. The Dow lost more than 23%, and the dreams of many, along with billions of dollars, were suddenly wiped out.

The 1929 crash was only the beginning of a prolonged slide in stock prices. The next three years, 1930, 1931, and 1932, were among the worst in history for stocks. The Dow lost almost 90% of its value between September 3, 1929, and July 8, 1932. Trading volume also evaporated as stocks were shunned. It took the Dow more than 25 years to recover from the Great Crash. The record estimated on September 3, 1929, wasn't broken until November 23, 1954.

Back to the original question: Did the Great Crash cause the Great Depression? According to many economists and historians, probably not. They note that fewer than 3 million Americans out of a population of more than 110 million owned any stocks whatsoever in 1929. Further, a substantial amount of evidence shows that the U.S. economy was already well into a recession by fall of 1929. Industrial production was falling, interest rates were rising, and corporate profits were declining. In fact, according to historians, the weather actually played a bigger role than the stock market. Several years of severe drought in the Midwest devastated the farm economy—a much more significant part of the U.S. economy then than it is now. Farmers couldn't repay loans to banks, leading to bank runs and eventually to a general banking panic. Depositors lost billions of dollars as banks failed. The collapse of the banking system pushed an already weakening economy into a depression. So, in the end, it appears that the Great Crash was more *caused by* the coming Depression, rather than a *cause of* the Depression.

Questions for Critical Thinking

1. Historians believe that one factor that contributed to the severity of the 1929 stock market crash was low margin requirements (margin requirements as little as 10% were common). Explain how low margin requirements can contribute to a stock market crash.

2. In terms of the magnitude of the price drop, the 1987 market break was worse than the 1929 crash. Why didn't the U.S. economy fall into depression, or at least a severe recession, following the 1987 market break?

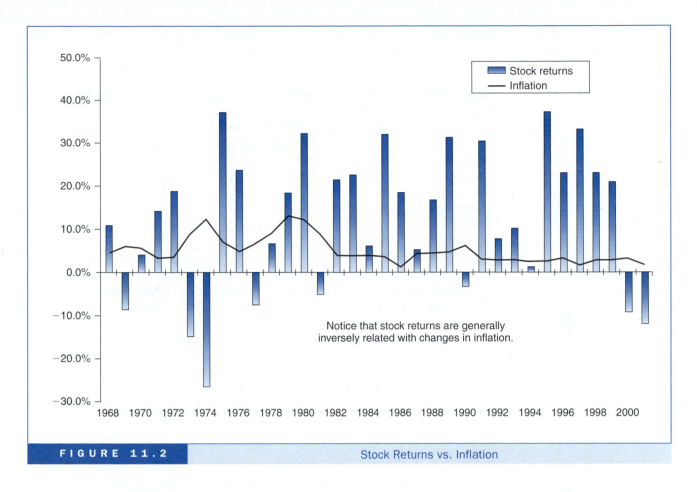

| FIGURE 11.2 | Stock Returns vs. Inflation |

conditions than on current conditions. Stock investors may be responding to what they think is going to happen, rather than what is currently happening. Further, some of the fundamental factors that determine stock prices, such as companies' profit margins and earnings, also tend to lead overall economic activity.

Stock Prices and Inflation Stock investors constantly watch for signs of a change in the rate of inflation. Any increase in inflation, actual or expected, is considered to be bad for the overall stock market. (The reverse is also true; lower inflation lifts stocks.) For one thing, rising inflation normally means rising interest rates. Rising interest rates, in turn, tend to depress stock prices, because the required rate of return on a stock moves up and down with general market interest rates.

Figure 11.2 shows the relationship between stock returns and inflation. The annual total return from the S&P 500 is shown along with the annual inflation rate between 1968 and 2001. Although the data indicate a generally inverse relationship between stock returns and inflation, it appears that changes in inflation, rather than a particular inflation rate, are more strongly associated with stock market performance.

Caution is important, of course, when interpreting the relationship between stock prices and inflation. Inflation tends to be at its highest around economic peaks and at its lowest around economic troughs. Because stock prices generally lead economic activity, it is not surprising to see falling stock prices and rising inflation in anticipation of an economic peak and subsequent contraction.

Overall Market and the Performance Levels of Industry Groups If the overall stock market tends to lead economic activity, what relationship do specific industry groups have with the economy? The evidence suggests that certain industry groups tend do better during the early phases of bull markets, whereas other groups often do better during the later stages. Historical data suggest that cyclical stocks of credit and consumer goods firms (e.g., home-building companies and automobile manufacturers) generally outperform the overall market early in bull markets. Energy stocks, defensive consumer goods stocks (e.g., food companies), and utilities exhibit the market's best relative performance late in bear markets. Growth stocks of consumer goods companies (e.g., cosmetics, soft drinks, and drug stocks) often outperform the market late in bull markets. Remember, interpret these generalizations and all other studies of past performance with caution: just because these relationships were true historically does not mean that they will be true in the future.

Business Cycles and Interest Rates

Even though no two business cycles are alike, interest rates and business cycles are unquestionably related. Generally, interest rates rise during economic expansions and fall during economic contractions. During the 1975–1980 economic expansion, for example, the yield on three-month Treasury bills (T-bills) rose 634 basis points. In comparison, during the 1981–1982 recession, yields on three-month T-bills fell by 654 basis points.

One reason for the relationship between business cycles and interest rates, of course, is inflation. Actual and expected future rates of inflation tend to rise during economic expansions and fall during economic contractions. As actual inflation and inflationary expectations rise, so do interest rates.

In past business cycles, however, both inflation rates and interest rates tended to rise (and fall) more sharply in the later stages of economic expansions (and contractions). For example, during the first two quarters of the 1975–1979 expansion (April through September 1975), the annual rate of inflation was about 7.3%. T-bill yields increased by about 80 basis points between April and October 1975. By contrast, during the last two quarters of the expansion (July through December 1979), the annual rate of inflation was more than 12.5%, and T-bill yields increased by more than 300 basis points.

In addition, both inflation and interest rates often continued to increase or decline for several additional quarters following turning points in economic activity. For example, the rate of inflation remained essentially constant during the first 2.5 years of the 1983–1990 expansion.

Aside from inflation, interest rate changes are related to economic activity in another way. The demand for loanable funds by businesses and households rises during expansions and falls during recessions. To illustrate this relationship, Table 11.2 shows the change in a real rate of interest before and during postwar recessions.

As expected, the real rate of interest rose, with one exception, during the four quarters preceding each peak in economic activity. During all postwar recessions,

Recession	Prerecession Period[b]	During Recession
1953–1954	−0.55%	−0.99%
1957–1958	+1.05	−0.30
1960–1961	+1.90	−0.03
1969–1970	+1.82	−1.50
1973–1975	+0.64	−1.50
1980	+4.57	−5.68
1981–1982	+7.96	−3.69
1990–1991	+0.75	−2.99
2001–	+0.025	N/A

TABLE 11.2

Changes in Real Rates of Interest Before and During Recessions[a]

[a]Figures are changes in real interest rates over the designed intervals. Real interest rates are defined as the rate on 90-day commercial paper minus a four-quarter average of current and past inflation as measured by the GDP deflator.

[b]The four quarters preceding the peak in economic activity.

Source: Survey of Current Business, various issues.

real interest rates declined. Prior to the 1990–1991 recession, for example, the real rate of interest rose by 75 basis points. During the recession itself, real interest rates dropped by almost 300 basis points.

Business Cycles and Yield Spreads As noted in the prior section on bonds, a yield spread is the difference in yield between any two fixed income securities. Evidence from past business cycles suggests that yield spreads (based on both credit risk and maturity) often widen and narrow in response to changes in economic activity.

This relationship is illustrated in Figure 11.3, which shows the relationship between turning points in economic activity (both peaks and troughs) and the yield spreads between BBB-rated corporate bonds and Treasury bonds (T-bonds) and between T-bonds and T-bills. The spread between T-bonds and T-bills forms part of what is known as the yield curve.

The data show that the yield spread between BBB-rated corporate bonds and T-bonds tends to be wider at the ends of contractions and narrower at the ends of expansions. This tendency suggests that bond investors become more quality-conscious during recessions. Investors may be worried that corporations are more likely to default on bonds during economic contractions.

The data presented in Figure 11.3 show that the spread between T-bonds and T-bills is generally narrower at peaks in economic activity and wider at troughs. Notice that at some economic peaks, the yield on T-bills actually exceeded the yield on T-bonds. (This occurrence is referred to as an inverted yield curve.) One explanation for this pattern is that at economic peaks (or troughs), investors expect interest rates to fall (or rise). Another explanation suggests that short-term rates are influenced by expected short-term inflation whereas long-term rates are influenced by expected long-term inflation. Inverted yield curves normally coincided with high rates of both inflation and interest. Investors may believe, therefore, that the *average* rate of inflation may be higher in the short run than in the long run.

FIGURE 11.3

Turning Points in the U.S. Economy and Yield Spreads

Date	Turning Point	Yield Spreads			
		BBB, Absolute	BBB, Relative	T-Bonds, Absolute	T-Bonds, Relative
October 1949	Trough	120	0.55	114	1.09
July 1953	Peak	88	0.29	88	0.42
May 1954	Trough	101	0.40	173	2.21
August 1957	Peak	143	0.39	28	0.08
April 1958	Trough	203	0.73	166	1.48
April 1960	Peak	117	0.28	93	0.29
February 1961	Trough	144	0.38	137	0.57
December 1969	Peak	181	0.26	−86	−0.11
November 1970	Trough	287	0.44	122	0.23
November 1973	Peak	262	0.44	−195	−0.25
March 1975	Trough	144	0.18	236	0.41
January 1980	Peak	158	0.15	−151	−0.13
July 1980	Trough	190	0.19	208	0.26
July 1981	Peak	237	0.18	−119	−0.08
December 1982	Trough	276	0.26	251	0.31
July 1990	Peak	173	0.20	98	0.13
March 1991	Trough	164	0.19	257	0.43
March 2001	Peak	250	0.47	92	0.22

Note: BBB refers to BBB rated corporate bonds: T-Bond refers to Treasury bonds with maturities in excess of 15 years; T-Bill refers to 90-day Treasury bills. Absolute yield spreads are stated in basis points. Relative yield spreads are equal to absolute yield spreads divided by the yields on T-bonds (or T-bills).

Source: Survey of Current Business, various issues.

Investment Timing Implications

The relationships between business cycles, stocks prices, and interest rates discussed in the past few pages have several possible implications for investment timing. The Investment Insight box on page 287 provides some general investment advice for both stock and bond investors at various points in the business cycle. For example, in anticipation of an economic upturn, and the related increase in stock prices, a stock investor should generally allocate a greater share of a portfolio to cyclical stocks, especially those with high betas. (The higher the beta, the more a stock should increase relative to the overall market.) On the other hand, a bond investor should continue to lengthen the maturity of the bonds within the portfolio and should shift some funds from high-quality bonds (e.g., T-bonds) to lower-quality bonds given that the yield spread between high-quality and lower-quality bonds is beginning to narrow.

ECONOMIC FORECASTING

The discussion in the prior section strongly suggests that an ability to forecast economic activity several months ahead may improve the ability to forecast the general levels of stock prices and interest rates. Further, reasonable forecasts of

INVESTMENT INSIGHT

Business Cycles and Investment Timing

Stage of the Business Cycle	Stock Investors	Bond Investors
Late recession to trough	1. End of bear market, beginning of bull market 2. Begin to shift portfolio toward high-quality cyclical stocks.	1. Interest rates falling, yield spreads at their at their widest 2. Continue to lengthen the average maturity (or duration) of a bond portfolio; switch some funds into lower-quality bonds.
Early expansion	1. Early-to-middle bull market 2. Continue to move funds into cyclical growth stocks; buy other cyclical stocks and stock with high betas.	1. Yield spreads beginning to narrow, interest rates still falling. 2. Continue to lengthen the average maturity of the portfolio and switch to lower-quality bonds.
Middle expansion	1. Middle-to-late bull market 2. Slowly lower the portfolio's beta and build cash reserves by taking profits.	1. Interest rates bottoming out and may begin rising, yield spreads continuing to narrow. 2. Start to decrease the average maturity of the portfolio; continue the movement into lower-quality bonds.
Late expansion to peak	1. End of bull market, beginning of bear market 2. Take profits in cyclical stocks, build cash reserves, and reduce portfolio beta; slowly begin buying defensive stocks and utilities.	1. Interest rates rising, yield spreads at their narrowest. 2. Start to move funds toward quality bonds; continue to reduce the average maturity of the portfolio.
Early recession	1. Early-to-middle bear market 2. Begin to shift cash into defense stocks, utilities, and high-quality, noncyclical growth stocks.	1. Yield spreads widening, interest rates still rising 2. Hold short-term, high-quality bonds.
Middle recession	1. Middle-to-late bear market 2. Start to take profits in utilities and defensive stocks.	1. Interest rates peaking, and may begin falling, yield spreads continuing to widen. 2. Begin to lengthen the average maturity of the portfolio.

Questions for Critical Thinking

1. Why should a stock investor switch from low beta to high beta stocks during the early part of an economic expansion? Similarly, why should an investor lower the beta of his or her portfolio as the economic expansion matures?

2. What is the reasoning behind bond investors lengthening the average duration of their portfolios and switching from high- to low-quality bonds right around the trough in economic activity?

future conditions in most industries depend on assumptions concerning future economic activity.

Economic forecasting has two general objectives. The first is to foresee turning points in the business cycle (peaks and troughs), and the second is to provide estimates of specific economic variables, such as the growth rate in real GDP, inflation, interest rates, unemployment, and personal income. Even if no recession is on the horizon, an investor still needs an idea about whether the economy is likely to grow slowly or rapidly.

Two general approaches can be taken in economic forecasting. They can be roughly classified as qualitative and quantitative forecasting. In a qualitative forecast, the economist looks at a variety of economic data and then makes a subjective assessment about the economic outlook. A quantitative forecast is derived from econometric models. Of course, these two perspectives are not mutually exclusive. Many experienced economic forecasters blend the two approaches.

Qualitative Forecasts

As mentioned, a qualitative forecast results from subjective analysis of economic data. For example, an economist might observe an increase in the number of new household formations in the United States. She might conclude that this increase is a good sign for future economic growth, because it is likely that an increase in household formations will boost consumer spending on such things as new homes, appliances, and furniture. Qualitative forecasts often rely on two techniques: leading indicators and anticipation surveys.

Leading Indicators A fairly simple approach to economic forecasting is to follow the behavior of specific variables that historically have been indicators, or barometers, of future economic activity. Some economists, for example, carefully examine monetary indicators, such as money supply data, because they believe future economic growth is more a function of monetary conditions than anything else. Sometimes, economists combine several indicators into a leading indicator index, the best known of which is the **index of leading indicators**, published by the Conference Board.

index of leading indicators

Well-known combination of 10 economic measures, all of which tend to indicate overall economic activity.

The index combines 10 economic measures, all of which historically led overall economic activity. Each month the index rises, falls, or remains unchanged. Analysts look for any clear reversal in the *direction* of the index. If the index reaches a certain level and then clearly declines, it is a signal of an impending peak in economic activity (and subsequent recession). However, if the index falls to a certain level and then starts to increase, it is a signal of an impending trough in economic activity (and subsequent expansion).

The index of leading indicators currently contains 10 components, listed in Table 11.3 along with the expected direction (up or down) of each component preceding an economic peak or trough. Note that the S&P 500 is one of the components of the leading index. As described previously, it should rise before an economic trough and fall before an economic peak. Because stock prices are a component of the index of leading indicators, any use of the index to forecast stock prices based on future economic activity can cause conflicts. Changes in stock prices may be driving changes in the overall index, so you might be using changes in stock prices to forecast changes in stock prices!

Components	Direction Prior to *Trough* in Economic Activity	Direction Prior to *Peak* in Economic Activity
1. Average weekly hours, manufacturing	Up	Down
2. Average weekly initial claims for unemployment insurance	Down	Up
3. Manufacturers' new orders for consumer goods and materials	Up	Down
4. Vendor performance (slower deliveries index)	Down	Up
5. Contracts and orders for plant and equipment (constant dollars)	Up	Down
6. New, private housing units authorized by local building permits (index)	Up	Down
7. Stock prices (S&P 500 index)	Up	Down
8. Money supply (M2)	Up	Down
9. Consumer expectations (index)	Up	Down
10. Yield spread between 10-year Treasury Bond to Federal Funds	Up	Down

TABLE 11.3

Components of the Index of Leading Indicators

Anticipation Surveys Another qualitative economic forecasting method examines surveys that attempt to measure the future economic behavior of businesses, consumers, and government agencies. These surveys are commonly referred to as **anticipation surveys**.

Because consumer spending is such a large component of U.S. GDP (comprising approximately 67%), many economists examine surveys that measure consumer confidence. This connection is based on the notion that the more confident consumers are about their current and future economic situation, the more money they will spend, especially on big ticket items such as homes and automobiles. The more consumers spend, the faster the economy grows. You may have noticed that the Consumer Expectations Index—widely followed anticipation survey—is one component of the index of leading indicators. It is worth noting that the major difference between anticipation surveys and other leading indicators is that anticipation surveys measure *planned* activity whereas other leading indicators, such as building permits and unemployment claims, measure actual activity. Higher consumer confidence does not always translate into increased consumer spending and increased economic activity, however.

anticipation surveys

Surveys that attempt to measure the future economic behavior of business and consumers.

Econometric Model Building

Econometric models apply mathematical and statistical techniques to economic forecasting. These models are the principal tools of the quantitative economist. Although anticipation surveys and leading indicators provide fairly simple forecasts, econometric models provide perhaps the most complex. This most scientific approach to economic forecasting requires the user to specify the precise interrelationships among a variety of economic variables to come up with a model.

Econometric models predict not only the direction of future economic activity but its duration and magnitude as well. Instead of a general forecast (e.g., sluggish

econometric models

Applications of mathematical and statistical techniques to economic forecasting.

growth in real GDP), an econometric model yields a precise number (e.g., next year real GDP will grow by 2.5%). The accuracy of this precise forecast depends, of course, on the quality of the input data and validity of the assumptions made by the model builder.

A variety of private and public organizations build econometric models and use them to produce econometric forecasts. Several of the better-known models were developed by Chase Econometrics, Data Resources (DRI), General Electric, the University of Michigan, and the University of Pennsylvania (Wharton School of Business). All these models are extremely complex, containing many equations and dozens of variables. Their forecasts are widely reported in the financial press.

Implications for Investors

It may come as no surprise that economic forecasters, as a group, are not revered for their accuracy. One study looked at the track records of 111 forecasters over 20 years in predicting the following year's change in real gross national product (GNP).[2] The group, on average, overestimated the change in real GNP in 8 of the 20 years by an average error of 0.5%. They underestimated the following year's growth rate in 9 of the 20 years by an average error of 1.2%. In three years, the group missed turning points by an average error of 2.8%. This group of forecasters was especially bad at predicting recessions.

Why Is Economic Forecasting Difficult? If economists do not have a great record forecasting future economic activity, the next question is, why? In Chapter 8, we saw that security analysts do not have a great track record forecasting future earnings of companies, and we discussed some reasons. Many of the same explanations apply to economic forecasts. First, all forecasting is difficult, and forecasting economic activity is probably more difficult than forecasting earnings. For one thing, it is difficult to obtain good, accurate, and timely data on the U.S. economy. Government economic statistics are constantly being revised, and many are considered to be misleading if not downright inaccurate. Aside from data problems, the U.S. economy is an extremely complex system that is interrelated with an even more complex system, the global economy.

Second, the impact of random shocks on economic activity, such as severe weather events, can be as significant as they are unpredictable. For example, a colder-than-normal winter can affect everything from oil prices to retail sales. Third, most economic forecasting models are derived from historic data, which give few clues about major structural or secular changes in the economy (e.g., the impact of technology on productivity and corporate profits).

Critics argue that economic forecasters tend to respect momentum too much and believe that the next business cycle will look like the last business cycle, when, in fact, it may not due to major secular changes. Finally, human psychology may play a role. Economic forecasters, like securities analysts, may be reluctant to forecast bad news and to make a forecast that differs substantially from those made by colleagues. Remember, in the face of uncertainty, the "herd instinct" plays a major role in human behavior.

---

[2]Victor Zarnowitz, *Business Cycles* (Chicago: University of Chicago Press, 1992).

Using Economic Forecasts In the light of their poor record of accuracy, how should investors use economic forecasts? The flip answer is that investors should take what economic forecasters have to say with a grain of salt. However, even if specific numbers are not particularly accurate, the commentary behind the numbers may be valuable. How did economists come up with their forecasts? What variables did they consider? *Why* forecasters think that the economy will grow slowly next year, for example, could be useful to investors. Investors should ask why economists believe that inflation and interest rates are likely to rise or fall or why the dollar is likely to grow stronger against most other currencies. A good economic forecast will address these types of questions, and the answers deserve attention by investors. Like securities analysts, the general directions implied by economist forecasts may provide much more insight than their forecasts of specific values, such as next year's GDP growth rate or inflation.

For example, let's say that you follow the auto industry or are interested in one of the auto stocks. As you would probably expect, auto sales are strongly related to personal income. Higher personal income usually means higher auto sales. Assume an economist tells you that he believes that the growth in disposable personal income will accelerate over the next few years.[3] If his reasoning makes sense to you, this information is valuable because it suggests a good environment for increasing auto sales. Whether his specific forecast of personal income growth turns out to be 0.5% too high or too low is much less important.

INDUSTRY ANALYSIS

Having completed an economic analysis, an investor should turn to the next step in the security analysis process: industry analysis. We begin with a discussion of how to define and classify industries, because industry statistics are based upon these classifications.

Defining and Classifying Industries

In a broad sense, an industry might be considered a community that shares common interests that distinguish it from other communities. The dictionary defines an industry as "a distinct group of productive or profit-making enterprises." At first glance, this definition seems pretty straightforward. However, in practice, classifying industries can be difficult and the results somewhat ambiguous. Further, assigning specific companies to particular industries is sometimes no easy task.

Classifying industries can be done in several simple ways. One obvious method is to classify industries by product or service (e.g., the chemical industry, the airline industry, or the restaurant industry). Another simple way of classifying industries is based on their reactions to the business cycle. A **cyclical industry** is one whose performance tends to be positively related to economic activity. Examples of cyclical industries include auto makers, home builders, and paper companies. A **defensive industry** is one whose performance tends to be relatively insensitive to economic activity, despite some cyclical ups and downs. Examples of defensive industries include electric and gas utilities and the drug industry. A

cyclical industry

Industry whose performance tends to be positively related to economic activity.

defensive industry

Industry whose performance tends to be relatively insensitive to economic activity.

---

[3]Disposal personal income is personal income after taxes.

growth industry

Industry characterized by rapid growth in sales, often independent of the business cycle.

growth industry is characterized by rapid growth in sales and earnings, often independent of the business cycle. Examples of growth industries during the 1990s include biotechnology and semiconductors.

Several nongovernment organizations use industrial classification systems based on product (good or service) and business cycle characteristics. Two examples are Dow Jones and Standard & Poor's. Both divide companies initially into major industry groups, as Table 11.4 shows. They then subdivide each major industry group into secondary groups. As you can see, Dow Jones divides companies into nine major groups, whereas S&P divides them initially into 24 major groups. Table 11.4 also breaks down the Dow Jones energy group and the S&P fuel group into their various subdivisions. The two systems differ substantially. Dow Jones, for example, includes pipeline companies as part of its energy industry, whereas S&P includes them as part of its utility industry. Investors should be aware of such differences in industry classifications.

These classification systems often define industries by grouping firms that are not homogeneous. Take the airline industry as an example. Both Dow Jones and S&P put all airlines into one subgroup. Although each company in the industry provides the same service, flying people from point A to point B, grouping them masks differences among domestic airlines with both domestic and international routes (e.g., Delta), domestic airlines with only domestic routes (e.g., Southwest), and foreign airlines (e.g., British Airways). Obviously, all the companies in this industry are affected by some of the same general factors (e.g., the price of jet fuel), but it is still a diverse group.

North American Industrial Classification System Recently, the United States, Canada, and Mexico adopted the North American Industrial Classification System (NAICS) for classifying industries. The six-digit NAICS codes reflect changes in business such as new technology, as well as new kinds of services industries, such as warehouse clubs. The NAICS codes are a result of the adoption by the three nations of the North American Free Trade Agreement (NAFTA), and they replace the older four-digit Standard Industrial Classification System (SIC) codes. The first five digits of NAICS codes are set for the three NAFTA nations. The final digit can vary from country to country.

Although most experts consider the NAICS codes to be a major improvement over the old SIC codes, the NAICS classification system can still cause confusion and

	Dow Jones	Standard & Poor's
A. Major Groups	1. Basic materials	1. Aerospace
	2. Conglomerates	2. Automotive
	3. Consumer cyclical	3. Banks
	4. Consumer noncyclical	4. Chemicals
	5. Energy	5. Conglomerates
	6. Financial services	6. Consumer products
	7. Industrial	7. Containers and packaging
	8. Technology	8. Discount and fashion retailers
	9. Utilities	9. Electrical and electronics
		10. Food
		11. Fuel
		12. Health care
		13. Housing and real estate
		14. Leisure-time industries
		15. Manufacturing
		16. Metals and mining
		17. Nonbank financial
		18. Office equipment and computers
		19. Paper and forest products
		20. Publishing and broadcasting
		21. Service industries
		22. Telecommunications
		23. Transportation
		24. Utilities and power
	Group 5 (Energy)	**Group 11 (Fuel)**
B. Subdivision	a. Coal	a. Coal
	b. Oil (drilling)	b. Oil and gas
	c. Oil (integrated majors)	c. Petroleum services
	d. Oil (secondary)	
	e. Oilfield equipment	
	f. Pipelines[a]	

TABLE 11.4

Industry Classification Systems

[a] In S&P's classification system, most pipeline companies are included in utilities and power (major group), oil and gas transmission (secondary group).

Source: Dow Jones & Company; Standard & Poor's.

result in very heterogonous industries. The point is, be careful when looking at any industry classification system. Otherwise, the quality of analysis may suffer. It is not difficult, for example, to inadvertently compare a specific company's data with averages for the wrong industry. We consider this issue further in the next chapter.

Components of Industry Analysis

In a nutshell, industry analysis focuses on two general objectives: to determine the long-term secular trend of the industry, and to ascertain the industry's cyclical pattern around its long-term secular trend. To meet these general objectives, a thorough industry analysis needs to consider several issues, both quantitative and qualitative. The following list includes brief discussions of eight of the most pertinent issues. The more qualitative issues are listed first.

1. *Competitive Structure of the Industry.* The analyst begins by listing all the companies that operate in the industry (both domestically and globally, if appropriate). It may also be useful to determine how many are publicly traded, how many are privately owned or owned by other companies, and perhaps, how many are government owned. The analyst then considers some questions: Which companies have the largest market shares? Have their market shares been rising or falling (i.e., has the industry become more or less concentrated) during the past few years? Has the number of competitors been rising or falling in recent years?

2. *Permanence.* In this age of rapid changes in technology and major demographic trends, the permanence of an industry becomes an important issue. Could technological changes, for example, make the industry obsolete in a short period of time? A single technological change, the electric refrigerator introduced in 1927 by GE, doomed the ice companies. Ice companies were among the most established and profitable companies in the United States at that time.

3. *Vulnerability to External Shocks.* How vulnerable is the profitability and performance of an industry to some dramatic economic, political, or natural event? As an example, consider what happened to the airline industry during the Persian Gulf crisis of 1990 to 1991. When Iraq invaded Kuwait on August 2, 1990, fear gripped the world oil market. The price of crude oil soared, and along with it, the price of jet fuel. Between July and October 1990, the price of jet fuel more than doubled (from 55.3 cents to 115.8 cents per gallon). Because each penny increase in the price of jet fuel costs U.S. airlines something like $150 million per year, this increase devastated airlines' profitability. During the second quarter of 1990, U.S. airlines had an after-tax profit of $503 million; the industry lost $218 million in the third quarter, and $3,647 million in the fourth quarter. If airlines want to continue operating, they have little choice but to pay the going rate for jet fuel, over which they have little control.

4. *Regulatory and Tax Conditions: Government Relations.* The analyst needs to determine whether an industry is subject to any special or unusual government regulation at either the federal or state level. The electric utility industry, for example, is subject to much more government regulation than the typical industry. Some industries' foreign operations are subject to more regulation by other countries' governments than the U.S. government imposes. Tax issues must also be considered. The key question is whether the industry is subject to any special tax treatment with either positive or negative effects. The oil and gas industry, for example, has traditionally been subject to special tax treatment compared with most industries, ranging from oil depletion allowances to windfall profits taxes. The analyst should also keep an eye on emerging federal legislation that may have a special impact on an industry.

5. *Labor Conditions.* The key questions concerning labor conditions deal mostly with unions, including the percentage of the workforce that is unionized and whether that percentage is rising or falling. The industry's overall relationship with the unions is important as well. Further, even if the industry's workforce is not heavily unionized, the analyst still needs to check for unusual labor conditions. For example, does the industry have a difficult time finding and retaining workers? Does it have an unusually high number of

workers' compensation claims? The airline industry has been historically troubled by labor problems (both union and nonunion).

6. *Historical Record of Revenue, Earnings, and Dividends.* The analyst should compile a historical record of industry revenue, earnings, and dividends over at least two complete business cycles. This review can reveal obvious patterns and trends. Do industry revenue and earnings grow at above-average rates? Do industry earnings grow more quickly or slowly than industry revenues? Do patterns in revenue and earnings suggest that the industry is cyclical? What percentage of industry earnings are paid in dividends? Did this percentage change over time? The historical record can help answer these types of questions.

    The analyst should also examine the industry's cost structure. Obviously, if earnings rose faster than revenue, the industry's costs, as a percentage of revenue, fell. However, the analyst needs to determine the relationship between fixed and variable costs (operating leverage) as well. High operating leverage means that a given increase in revenue can translate to a still larger increase in operating profits. The airline industry has a high fixed-cost component; it costs about the same for an airline to operate regardless of whether its load factor (the percentage of seats filled with paying passengers) is 50% or 80%.

7. *Financial and Financing Issues.* What does the industry's balance sheet look like, and how has it changed over the past couple of years? The analyst should evaluate how much leverage is common in the industry, how asset intensive its operations are (the ratio of revenues to assets), and so forth. If an industry needs to make substantial capital investments in the near future, how much of the needed funds will it have to raise externally?

8. *Industry Stock Price Valuation.* Finally, the analyst needs to consider how investors have historically valued the industry's stocks, although, once again, the past is no guarantee of the future. For example, does the industry price/earnings (P/E) ratio typically exceed that of the overall market? Has the industry's P/E ratio changed in recent years? How does the P/E ratio compare with the growth rate in industry earnings? A stock's P/E multiple should generally show a positive relationship with its expected earnings growth rate. However, historically some industries sold for higher P/E multiples than other industries, which could not be explained by differences in their expected earnings growth rates. Current investor favorites often exhibit higher than-average P/E ratios.

The analyst should also examine how industry stocks performed, measured by price appreciation as well as total returns, relative to an appropriate broad market average. As indicated in Figure 11.1, substantial variation in price performance among various industry groups exists regardless of the overall direction of the market.

Industry Life Cycles

The **industry life cycle theory** provides a framework in which to understand many of the pertinent issues discussed here. This theory argues that every industry goes through a life cycle consisting of four stages: birth, growth, mature growth, and stabilization/decline. These stages are illustrated in Figure 11.4. Gauging an industry's position in its life cycle may help the analyst gain some important insight into the industry's investment potential.

industry life cycle theory

Theory that posits that all industries go through a life cycle consisting of birth, growth, mature growth, and stabilization phases.

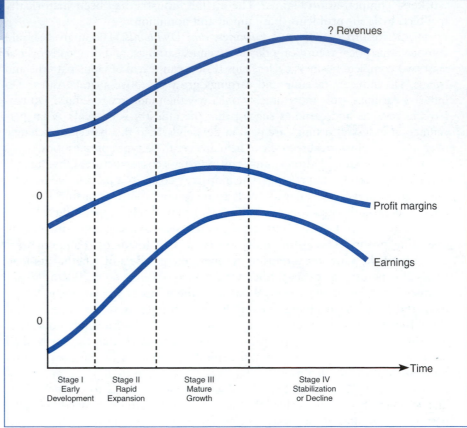

FIGURE 11.4

Industry Life Cycle

Source: Cohen et al., *Investment Analysis and Portfolio Management,* Fifth Ed. Irwin © 1987, p. 376.

Before we briefly describe each phase of the industry life cycle, remember that the theory is a general one and the life cycles of specific industries differ substantially. For one thing, the speed at which industries move from phase to phase varies. Some industries, for example, stay in a mature growth phase much longer than other industries. Industries even appear to have skipped entire phases. Further, the transition from phase to phase may be subtle and gradual. Also, technological changes can sometimes cause a mature industry to revert back to a growth industry. In the early 1900s, for example, the oil industry was considered to be a mature, perhaps even declining, industry. Oil was used primarily to light lamps, and the development of electric lighting was eroding the demand for oil. The development of the automobile and the internal combustion engine suddenly launched the oil industry into a major new growth phase.

The oil industry example also illustrates that the industry life cycle is not always a one-way progression. Industries can go backward as well as forward in their life cycles. For another example, consider the aluminum industry. In the 1930s, aluminum was considered to be a dying industry; production was falling rapidly, both in absolute terms and relative to overall industrial production. During the early 1940s, to supply the burgeoning aircraft industry during World War II, aluminum production rose much faster than overall industrial production. Between 1939 and 1945, U.S. industrial production rose 60% while aluminum production rose 110%.

The growth in aircraft production slowed after the end of World War II, and aluminum production actually started to fall. The aluminum industry then entered another phase of rapid growth between 1950 and 1974. The index of aluminum production rose more than 579% compared with a 170% increase in the index of overall industrial production. Since 1974, the aluminum industry exhibited characteristics of a mature industry and grew at about the same rate as the overall economy. With these comments in mind, let's look at each phase in the industry life cycle.

Birth Phase Industries are often born to exploit a major technical advancement or the invention of some new product. The development of the internal combustion engine, for example, helped give birth to the automobile industry. Infant industries often exhibit several important characteristics. Costs are high, product quality is uneven, sales growth is erratic, and profitability is low. (The industry may actually lose money for most, if not all, of the birth phase.) Birth-phase industries are often highly competitive and dynamic, with many companies entering and exiting.

The birth phase is perhaps the riskiest stage for stock investors, although the rewards can be substantial. A stock investor in an infant industry bets on two things: that the industry and its new good or service will survive infancy (some do not) and that a specific company will be among the survivors.

Growth Phase An industry's growth phase is often characterized by a faster sales growth rate than the overall economy. Further, industry sales may be less vulnerable to a cyclical downturn in the overall economy compared with more mature industries. As the industry is growing, the quality of its product (either a good or a service) usually improves. Prices often fall, either in absolute or relative terms.[4] Costs tend to fall as production becomes more efficient and capital investment requirements decline. Industry profitability improves as well. During the growth phase, more companies exit the industry than enter it. A few companies tend to grab the lion's share of the industry's growth.

Many analysts consider the growth phase to be the best time to invest in an industry. The product has proven itself, and profits are growing rapidly. Stock investors should generally stick with industry leaders, because they are more likely to prosper. Also, investors should not expect substantial cash dividends. Further, some industries failed to make the transition from a short period of rapid growth to a longer period of slower, more sustainable growth to reach the next phase.[5]

Mature Growth Phase During the mature growth phase, the sales growth rate starts to slow and industry performance may become more cyclical. Product demand starts to near its saturation point, and the industry may begin to face inroads from newer products competing for the same basic market. The competitive structure of the industry is generally quite stable; few companies either enter or exit the industry. In addition, large barriers to entry may develop. As the industry matures, it becomes more difficult to increase demand by reducing prices or improving quality. Companies put more effort into gaining market share in mature industries. Capital

---

[4]A relative price decline could mean one of two things: either the price of the product or service doesn't rise as fast as the rate of inflation or the quality of the product improves relative to the price increase.
[5]According to economists, one common reason some growth industries burn out is the failure of the industry to develop follow-up goods or services that build naturally on the success of the initial good or service.

investment requirements fall to relatively low levels, and profits tend to be high. This stage is often the most profitable in the industry life cycle.

This phase imposes lower risk on investors than the rapid growth phase, especially if investors stick to the industry leaders. Even though growth is slowing, profits are high and dividend yields are likely to be above average. Investors should not become complacent, however. If growth slows too much, for example, future profits could diminish as competitors start to aggressively cut prices to boost their market shares.

Stabilization or Decline Phase A mature growth phase can last for a long time, and an industry nearing the end of its mature growth phase may begin to grow more rapidly due to technological or demographic changes. Emerging global markets may help to pump more life into mature industries. Barring those changes, however, a typical industry eventually reaches a stabilization or decline phase.

Conditions in this last phase are difficult to generalize. In the stabilization or decline phase, industry sales may continue to grow, but more slowly than the overall economy. Alternatively, sales may stabilize to meet replacement demand, which neither increases nor decreases. However, sales may actually start to fall in absolute terms and the industry may eventually disappear. Profitability generally follows the trend in sales.

This phase can be difficult for investors. If the industry is stable, some companies may be good investments. These stocks may have less risk and pay higher dividends than the average stock. However, as a general rule, most investors should probably avoid declining industries. These companies often have falling profits and deteriorating balance sheets. Further, companies in declining industries face strong temptations to embark on ill-conceived, poorly planned diversification efforts to restore growth. These ventures often end up hurting shareholders even more. However, analysts should always carefully monitor declining industries for, as history shows, their fortunes can rapidly improve due to external factors. (Remember what the automobile did for the oil industry and what growth spurts in aircraft production did for the aluminum industry.)

ANALYZING INDUSTRY DATA

So far in our examination of industry analysis, we discussed what the analyst ought to look for and what type of information he or she should obtain concerning the industry. At this point, we turn our attention to ways investors can analyze this information to further evaluate an industry.

End-Use Analysis

end-use analysis

Technique that attempts to identify the source(s) of demand for an industry's products or services.

An important tool is **end-use**, or product-demand, **analysis**, in which the analyst attempts to identify the source of demand for the industry's product and, in the process, to uncover relationships that help to explain demand. Understanding these relationships will likely help the analyst make more accurate forecasts of future industry revenues and earnings. One way to increase accuracy is to analyze who uses the industry's product and how the demand for the product is likely to change for each user.

As an example, let's briefly look at the semiconductor industry. Who uses semiconductors? Obviously the major user is the personal computer industry (about 40% of semiconductors go into personal computers), but the telecommunications, electronics, defense, and automotive industries use semiconductors as well. As the demand for personal computers, gaming systems, and cell phones rose sharply during the late 1990s, semiconductor sales soared. The industry reported record sales of more than $200 billion in 2000. However, the demand for PCs and many other electronic devices fell sharply in 2001. Semiconductor sales slumped to about $155 billion in 2001. What does the future hold?

According to industry experts, demand for personal computers, especially by businesses, is expected to rise somewhat during the 2003–2005 period. In addition, sales of the next generation of cordless phones and cell phones are expected to increase sharply over the next couple of years. The result, according to the experts, is a healthy rise in semiconductor sales over current levels to about $200 billion by 2005. Moreover, the industry appears to be growing less dependent on personal computer sales. By 2005, only an estimated one-third of semiconductors will go into PCs.

Ratio Analysis

Ratio analysis with industries involves dividing industry data by aggregate economic data over a period of time. The movement, or lack of movement, in a ratio may suggest some important characteristics of the industry. Let's look at two examples.

ratio analysis
Dividing industry data by aggregate economic data over a period of time and examining the result for trends.

Figure 11.5 illustrates the ratio of the auto production index to the overall industrial production index between 1968 and 2001. A ratio equal to 100 would mean that the two production indexes were the same. A rising ratio over time would suggest growth in the auto industry. However, a falling ratio over time would suggest decline. Figure 11.5 shows no obvious upward or downward trend, suggesting that the auto industry is a mature cyclical industry. Notice, however, that the ratio between auto production and overall industrial production falls sharply before and during recessions (the shaded areas in the chart) and rises sharply early in economic expansions. This pattern suggests that, although the auto industry is cyclical in nature, it is more volatile than the overall economy, especially around turning points in economic activity.

Another example is shown in Figure 11.6. It shows the ratio of the growth rates in semiconductor sales and auto sales, both relative to the growth rate in GDP. (As with Figure 11.5, a ratio of 100 would suggest a cyclical or mature industry.) The chart clearly shows that the semiconductor industry is a growth industry; between 1988 and 2001 the growth in semiconductor sales was more than four times overall economic growth, even factoring in the sharp decline in semiconductor sales that occurred in 2001. However, the auto industry is more of a cyclical/mature industry. Auto sales rose only slightly relative to overall economic activity.

Regression and Correlation Analysis

Statistics offers two useful and fairly simple techniques for analyzing demand and other industry data: correlation analysis and regression analysis.[6] For one thing,

regression analysis
A statistical technique that can determine the relationship between two or more variables.

---

[6]A multitude of technical issues surround the use of correlation and regression analyses, which are beyond the scope of our text. We suggest that you consult a standard statistics or econometrics textbook.

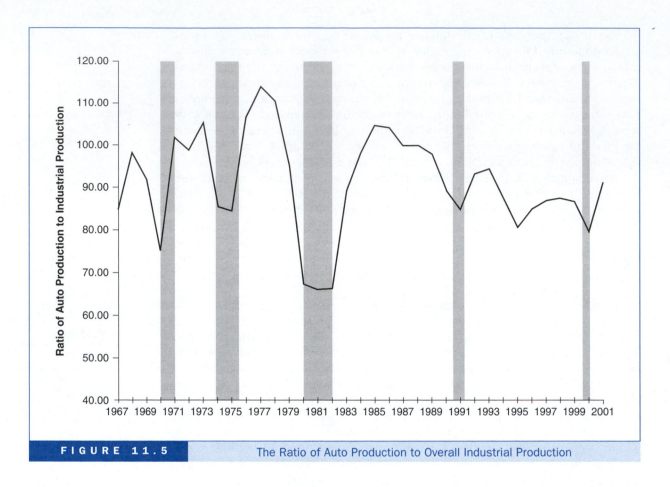

FIGURE 11.5   The Ratio of Auto Production to Overall Industrial Production

these techniques help to quantify many important relationships. As you may remember from statistics, bivariate regression (regression with two variables) is a mathematical process that fits a line to a series of points on an XY scatter diagram. Y is the dependent variable, and X is the independent variable. The model states that Y is a function of X (e.g., the level of industry sales is a function of GDP). Correlation analysis evaluates the strength of the relationship between X and Y.

Figure 11.7 shows an XY scatter diagram. The X axis measures disposable personal income whereas the Y axis measures auto sales. The regression line is also shown. In equation form, the regression line can be expressed as

Auto sales = 11.68 + 0.41(Personal income), R^2 = .973

The value of Y on the regression line is the predicted value of Y, for a given level of X.

The regression equation helps the analyst to forecast next year's auto sales, based on the expected growth in personal income. Assume, for example, that personal income next year is expected to increase to \$6,900 billion. Based on the regression equation, auto sales should equal: 11.68 + .041(6,900) = \$296 billion.

Notice that most of the dots in Figure 11.7 fall close to the regression line, meaning that the actual and predicted values for annual auto sales match fairly closely.

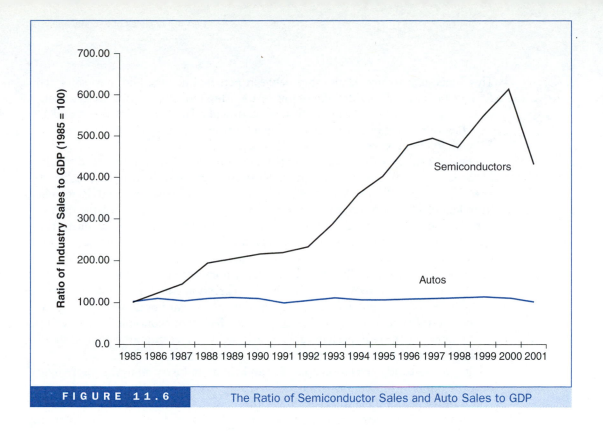

FIGURE 11.6 The Ratio of Semiconductor Sales and Auto Sales to GDP

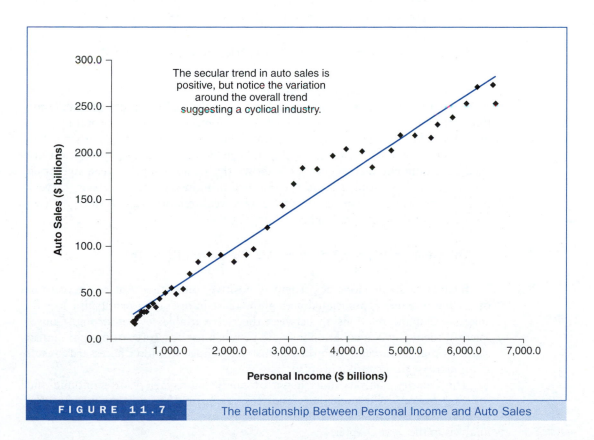

The secular trend in auto sales is positive, but notice the variation around the overall trend suggesting a cyclical industry.

FIGURE 11.7 The Relationship Between Personal Income and Auto Sales

This suggests a strong relationship between personal income and auto sales. The R^2 statistic measures the strength of this relationship more precisely. It ranges from 0 to 1. An R^2 close to 1 indicates a stronger statistical relationship between X and Y.

Does this strong historical relationship allow the analyst to rely on the forecast of $296 billion for next year's auto sales? The answer to the question is both yes and no.

Figure 11.7 shows the secular trend in auto sales in relation to the trend in GDP. Both increased at about the same rate as the overall economy. Notice that Figure 11.7 also shows the cyclical variation of auto sales around the secular trend. Remember from Figure 11.5, however, that the auto industry tends to be more volatile than the overall economy. Therefore, auto sales tend to be above the secular trend during periods of strong economic growth, especially when the economy is coming out of a recession. Auto sales also tend to be below the secular trend during periods of slow economic growth, especially when the economy is entering a recession.

As a result, the forecast produced by the regression equation is a good starting point. The analyst might want to adjust the forecast upward or downward, depending on several factors. For example, if he or she feels that economic growth will be below normal next year, perhaps giving early signs of recession, the analyst should probably lower his or her forecast below the secular trend.

Regression and correlation analysis can help an industry analyst explore many other relationships. One important relationship is that between industry revenue and industry profits. Figure 11.8 shows another XY scatter diagram for the electric utility industry for a recent 25-year period. The X axis measures operating revenue, and the Y axis measures operating profits. A strong positive relationship is evident between industry revenue and profits. The regression equation is

$$\text{Operating profits} = -747.773 + 0.112(\text{Revenues}), R^2 = 0.970$$

As before, the regression equation can help the analyst forecast. For example, assume that utility revenues are expected to be $230 billion next year. Using the regression equation, we can come up with a forecast of industry operating profits of about $25 billion. The high R^2 indicates that the forecast may be fairly reliable.

Finally, let's look at a relationship in which regression and correlation are used in a different way. Figure 11.9 shows the relationship between operating revenues and operating profits for the airline industry over a recent 43-year period. The diagram appears to show only a weak relationship between the two series. The estimated regression equation is

$$\text{Operating profits} = -176.90 + .033(\text{Revenues}), R^2 = .161$$

Even though the slope coefficient is positive, indicating that an increase in operating revenues is associated with an increase in operating profits, the low R^2 suggests that the relationship between the two variables is not strong. Consequently, the regression equation may not be much use as a forecasting tool. It also suggests that an increase in airline industry revenues wouldn't necessarily result in an increase in operating profits.

The security analysts must begin by analyzing a variety of economic and industry factors. Although these analyses can provide important insights, the process must continue with a thorough company analysis. We turn to company analysis in the next chapter.

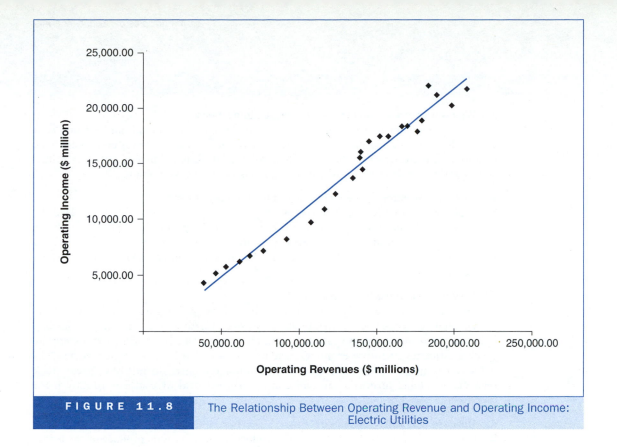

FIGURE 11.8 The Relationship Between Operating Revenue and Operating Income: Electric Utilities

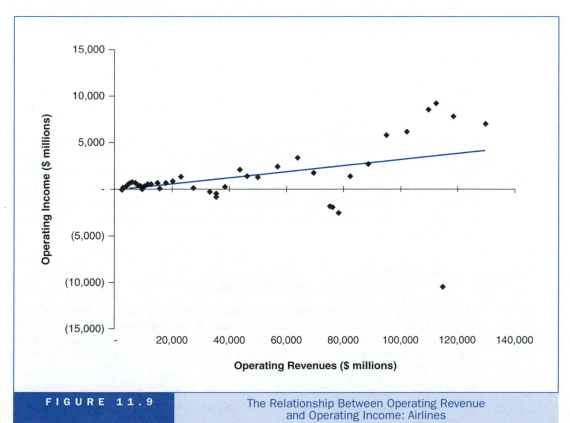

FIGURE 11.9 The Relationship Between Operating Revenue and Operating Income: Airlines

SUMMARY

1. Why are economic and industry analyses important?

No stock can be valued in a vacuum; all stocks are affected by economic and industry conditions. Stock prices and interest rates are closely related to the business cycle. Economic conditions can greatly affect industries. Regardless of the general direction of stock prices, substantial variation in performance among industry groups is common.

2. How are investment decisions related to the business cycle?

Stock prices are positively related to economic growth. Historically, stock prices lead the business cycle. In addition, certain industries tend to perform best during different phases of the business cycle. Interest rates are also positively related to the business cycle. Yield spreads tend to be at their highest right before a recession and narrowest right before an expansion.

3. How are economic forecasts made?

Economists make qualitative and quantitative forecasts of future economic activity. Qualitative forecasts are general and descriptive in nature, and often rely on leading indicators and sentiment indicators. Quantitative forecasts are designed to determine specific estimates of future economic activity and are based on mathematical models. Although economic forecasting is difficult, and economists do not have great track records, economic forecasts can still contain a great deal of useful information for investors.

4. How are industries classified?

Industries can be classified in terms of the products or services they produce or their relationship to the business cycle. Several governmental and nongovernmental organizations classify industries. Industry classifications, however, are arbitrary and can be misleading. Further, it can be difficult to place a specific company within a particular industry.

5. What are the important components of industry analysis?

The analyst should consider the competitive structure of the industry, its permanence, its vulnerability to external shocks, regulatory and tax considerations, labor conditions, its record of earnings and dividends, various financial and financing issues, and how the industry stocks have been historically valued.

6. What are the framework and some of the techniques used in industry analysis?

The industry life cycle approach provides a framework for understanding many of the important issues with respect to industry analysis. The life cycle approach says that industries go through phases (birth, rapid growth, mature growth, and stabilization). Phases can be repeated due to technological or external changes. Some of the major techniques used in industry analysis include end-use analysis, ratio analysis, correlation analysis, and regression analysis.

MINI CASE

The objective of the mini case is to practice interpreting actual industry data. Open the Electric Utility worksheet in the Data Workbook available at the text Web site (http://hearth.swlearning.com). The worksheet contains annual operating and financial data for the electric utility industry. Using these data and some of the techniques discussed in the chapter, answer the following questions.

1. Compute the ratio of electric utility production to overall industrial production for each year given and graph the result. Compare this graph with the one shown in

Figure 11.8. What conclusions concerning the utility industry can you draw from this exercise?

2. Graph the relationship between industry revenue and GDP. Regress industry revenue onto GDP (treat industry revenue as the Y variable and GDP as the X variable). How strong is the relationship between GDP and industry revenue?

3. Assume you have a forecast that nominal GDP will grow by 6% next year. Using the regression equation you just estimated, forecast industry revenue. Based on your results, would you modify this forecast? Why or why not?

4. Assume you are satisfied with the forecast of industry revenue you obtained in the prior question. Can you now come up with a reasonable estimate of industry profits for next year?

REVIEW EXERCISES

1. In general terms, why are economic and industry analyses important when evaluating specific common stocks? Do economic and industry conditions influence some stocks more than others?

2. Why does inflation typically increase toward the end of an economic expansion and fall toward the end of a contraction? How does inflation affect stock prices?

3. Why do stock prices lead the business cycle? Cite an example of where a large decline in stock prices was not followed by a recession.

4. What factors explain the relationship between interest rates and the business cycle? When, during the business cycle, have the sharpest declines in interest rates occurred?

5. Define the *yield spread*. Why do yield spreads based on maturity and quality tend to rise and fall during the business cycle?

6. Why is economic forecasting important? What are the two objectives of economic forecasts?

7. What are the two general approaches to economic forecasting? How do the forecasts of future economic activity produced by the two approaches differ?

8. What is an anticipation survey? Why is consumer confidence considered to be such an important leading indicator of future economic activity?

9. List three components of the index of leading indicators. Give the direction in each indicator prior to a peak in economic activity.

10. Discuss the various ways industries can be classified. What issues affect an analyst's use of industry classifications?

11. List the major components of an industry analysis. What is meant by the term *permanence?*

12. What are the four stages (or phases) of the industry life cycle? Give several examples of industries that experienced renewed growth due to external changes.

13. What are some characteristics of the mature growth phase? Why is this phase generally the most profitable for investors?

14. Define end-use analysis and ratio analysis. If the ratio of an industry's production index to the overall index of industrial production remained constant over time, what kind of industry is it?

15. Assume you regress industry sales onto GDP. You come up with following estimated regression equation:

$$\text{Sales (\$ billions)} = 1.753 + 0.014\text{GDP (\$ billions)}, R^2 = 0.98$$

What kind of industry do you think it is? If GDP next year is expected to be $8,250 billion, forecast industry sales. How much confidence do you have in this forecast?

CRITICAL THINKING EXERCISE

This exercise requires both computer work and library research. Open the Industry worksheet in the Data Workbook available at the course Web site (http://hearth.swlearning.com). The worksheet contains data for four industries—chemicals, department stores, drugs, and railroads—along with some economic data. Using the data and the techniques described in the chapter, determine the life cycle phase of each industry. Which of these industries appear to be cyclical, if any? Assuming you had a good forecast for next year's GDP, for which industry could you come up with the best forecast?

Go the library and read the most recent Standard & Poor's or Value Line report on each industry. How does S&P and Value Line classify each industry? Other than GDP, what economic and other external factors do you think affect the prospects for each industry?

THE INTERNET INVESTOR

1. As a service to clients, discount broker Charles Schwab offers commentary from various experts on a different industry each week. Visit the Schwab Web site (www.schwab.com) and read this week's industry commentary. Write a brief report summarizing the expert's opinion of the industry.
2. Each week Merrill Lynch posts on its Web site economic commentary from members of its staff (www.ml.com). Read the current economic commentary. Which events does Merrill Lynch feel will have the biggest impact on investors? Does the commentary reflect qualitative or quantitative economic forecasting?
3. Using one of the various Internet search engines, such as Yahoo! (www.yahoo.com) or Google (www.google.com), find sites that are sources of economic data (both historical and current) for the United States and other countries. Visit several of the sites and prepare a brief report.

12

Company Analysis:
The Historical Record

PREVIOUSLY . . .	IN THIS CHAPTER . . .	TO COME . . .
We described economic and industry analysis, the two macro factors in security analysis.	We review the components of company analysis and discuss how to evaluate the historical record including the quality of the company's management, its competitive position, and its financial statements.	We describe how to forecast a company's future earnings and how to assess the investment potential of its common stock.

CHAPTER OBJECTIVES

After reading Chapter 12, you should be able to answer the following questions:

1. What are the components of a company analysis report?

2. How do analysts evaluate the quality of a company's management?

3. How is the competitive position of a company within its industry evaluated?

4. What is financial statement analysis?

Sunbeam is a maker of small household appliances. In the summer of 1996 the company hired "Chainsaw" Al Dunlap as its new CEO. Dunlap, a noted turn-around specialist, immediately began slashing costs, revamping product lines, and firing hundreds of workers. Dunlap's magic appeared to work. In 1996 Sunbeam reported a net loss in excess of $228 million. The next year, 1997, it reported a profit of more than $109 million. Sunbeam's stock price soared from nearly $12 a share when Dunlap was hired as CEO to more than $50 a share by the end of 1997. Quite a turnaround for Sunbeam. Or was it?

Although most investors and analysts cheered the news of Sunbeam's apparent dramatic turnaround, a few uncovered some troubling signs by more closely analyzing Sunbeam's financial statements. For example, while sales rose by 19% between 1996 and 1997, accounts receivable rose by 36% and inventory rose by 58%. Accounts receivable and inventory turnover both slowed dramatically. Big buildups of both accounts receivable and especially inventory can suggest potential problems. Another area of concern was the company's cash flow. Sunbeam's actual cash flow—the actual cash the company's operations were generating—fell from $14.2 million in 1996 to *minus* 8.2 million in 1997. In other words, the company spent more cash during 1997 than it collected.

Then, Sunbeam released its first quarter results for 1998 and stunned many on Wall Street by reporting a loss. Not only that but sales actually fell by 5% from what they were during the first quarter of 1997. However, accounts receivable soared by 90% and inventory more than doubled. On the other side of the balance sheet, accounts payable, mostly to vendors, rose by a staggering 94%. One analyst concluded that Sunbeam appeared to be stuck with lots of inventory it couldn't sell, receivables it hadn't collected, and bills it wouldn't pay. Some speculated that Sunbeam secretly encouraged speed-up purchases by big customers to lift its 1997 results. Analysts immediately cut their ratings and investors headed for the exits. By August 1998, Sunbeam's once high-flying stock had lost more than 80% of its value, and Dunlap was out as CEO.

As it turned out, the story was far from over. The SEC began an investigation into Sunbeam's accounting practices and several shareholder lawsuits were filed. It became apparent that the company may have been cooking its books and it was forced to restate several years' worth of financial statements. The SEC then filed a civil complaint against Dunlap. The agency and Dunlap reached a settlement in the fall of 2002 that, among other provisions, bars Dunlap from serving as the CEO of any publicly traded company.

The Sunbeam saga illustrates some of the kinds of information that a careful analysis of a company's historical record, specifically its financial statements can yield. This chapter is the first of two devoted to company analysis and describes how to assess a company's historical record, both qualitative and quantitative factors.

OVERVIEW OF COMPANY ANALYSIS

Investors buy common stock hoping to earn a satisfactory rate of return in relationship to the risk they assume when buying the stock. One key to determining whether a stock can produce the desired rate of return is its current price. A stock's attractiveness depends on the answer to the question: Is the stock correctly priced today? As we see more formally in Chapter 14, the correct price of a stock is essentially the present value of expected future cash flows—dividends and expected future prices. Because no one knows either the timing or the level of these future cash flows with certainty, investors must rely on estimates.

Future earnings are probably the most important determinant of a company's future dividend stream and stock price. Because it pays dividends from earnings, higher future earnings often translate into higher future dividends. In addition, independent of the impact on future dividends, higher future earnings usually mean higher future stock prices. In a nutshell then, the major goal of company analysis is to forecast the quantity and quality of future earnings. Any item that may materially affect future earnings should be considered in a company analysis report.

According to the fathers of modern security analysis, Benjamin Graham and David Dodd, the typical company analysis report is divided into four parts:

1. A description of the company's business and properties, including some historical data and details about senior management
2. Financial material including capitalization, a record of earnings and dividends for several complete business cycles, a flow of funds analysis, and an analysis of recent balance sheets and income statements
3. Past stock price history and volume data
4. Prospects for the company in the form of projected future financial statements and analysis of the investment merits of the security[1]

To give you an idea what a real company analysis report looks like, from a real investment firm, we include a report on Kohl's Corporation from an A.G. Edwards analyst. The report contains most of the elements listed by Graham and Dodd and is available on the text Web site (http://hearth.swlearning.com).

In summary, the example analysis on Kohl's and guidance from Graham and Dodd suggest four general issues that a security analysis report should address: (1) the quality of the company's management, (2) the competitive position of the company within its industry, (3) an analysis of the company's financial statements, and (4) its future financial prospects. The first three issues will be considered in this chapter; the fourth issue, which is probably the most difficult, will be left to Chapter 13.

ASSESSING THE QUALITY OF MANAGEMENT

Some experts believe that the quality of a company's management may be the single most important influence on its future profitability and overall success. A company can have strong financial statements, for example, and yet be overly bureaucratic and incapable of responding quickly to changing business conditions. It is also important to note that management announcements can also significantly affect stock prices. As an example, look at Figure 12.1. It shows the daily trading range and trading volume for Sunbeam between the beginning of

---

[1]Benjamin Graham and David Dodd, *Security Analysis*, 5th ed. (New York: McGraw-Hill, 1988).

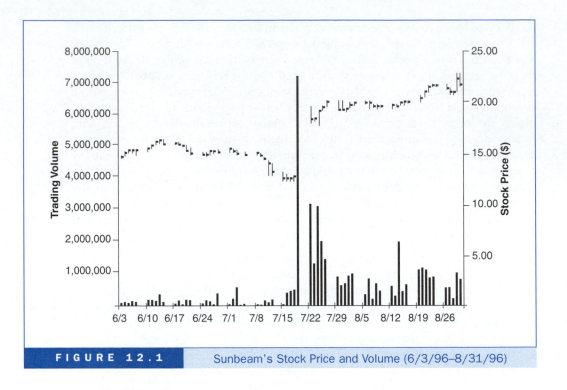

| **FIGURE 12.1** | Sunbeam's Stock Price and Volume (6/3/96–8/31/96) |

June and the end of August 1996. Your eye probably goes to the middle of the chart (July 7). On that day Sunbeam announced the hiring of Al Dunlap as its new CEO. The stock price rose more than 50% on heavy volume (almost 8 million shares).

How then do you tell if a company is well run? In order to assess management quality, the analyst must first understand the nature of management.

The Nature of Management

One leading expert defines management as follows:

Management is the attainment of organizational goals in an effective and efficient manner through planning, organizing, leading, and controlling organizational resources.[2]

The general definition of management conveys two important ideas. First, managers are responsible for the attainment of various organizational objectives both effectively and efficiently. Second, management includes four basic functions: planning, organizing, leading, and controlling. The management process of deploying resources to achieve organizational objectives (i.e., promoting organizational performance) within the context of the four basic functions is illustrated in Figure 12.2. Let's elaborate on both parts of the definition.

_____

[2]Richard Daft, *Management,* 5th ed. (Ft. Worth, TX: Harcourt, Inc., 2000), p. 8.

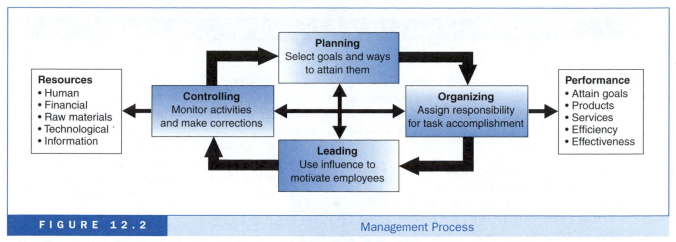

FIGURE 12.2 Management Process

Source: Figure from Richard L. Daft, Management, 4th ed., © 1997, 1994, 1991, 1988, Dryden Press, reproduced by permission of the publisher.

The first part of the definition of management deals with **organizational performance**. Managers are ultimately responsible for applying company resources effectively and efficiently to accomplish the company's goals. *Effectiveness* is defined as the degree to which the company achieves its goals; *efficiency* is defined as the amount of resources required to produce a certain level of output of a good or service.

The second part of the general definition lists four functions. The **planning function** involves setting goals for the organization and then identifying the tasks and resources necessary to obtain those goals. The **organizing function** assigns tasks to various parts of the organization and allocates resources within the organization. The **leading function** involves the motivation of employees to achieve the goals of the organization. The **controlling function** is concerned with monitoring performance, keeping the organization moving toward its goals, and correcting deficiencies.

To carry out the management function, what kinds of skills must managers possess? Experts identify three essential types of managerial skills: technical, conceptual, and human skills. Technical skills involve knowledge and mastery of such disciplines as engineering, manufacturing, computer information systems, or finance. Conceptual skills involve the ability to think and plan, to see the company as a whole as well as the relationships among its parts. Finally, human skills involve the ability to work with and through other people. Some important human skills include leadership, motivation, communication, and conflict resolution.

Evaluating Management

Determining the quality of management is neither easy nor totally objective. In a nutshell, the fundamental issue is how well the company's management performs the four basic functions. Of course, this analysis cannot stop with an assessment of how well management performed in the past; it must extend to their likely future performance, as well.

---

organizational performance

Application of company resources effectively and efficiently to achieve company goals.

planning function

Setting future goals for the organization and determining the resources needed to meet these goals.

organizing function

Assigning tasks to the various parts of the organization and allocating resources within the organization.

leading function

Motivating employees to achieve the goals of the organization.

controlling function

Monitoring performance, keeping the organization moving toward its goals, and correcting deficiencies.

INVESTMENT INSIGHT

Warren Buffet on Management

The highest complement legendary investor Warren Buffett can pay the management of a company is to say that they always act as though they were owners, not just managers. To help Buffet assess the quality of a company's management, he starts by asking three simple questions:

1. *Is management rational?* According to Buffet rational managers never lose sight of the fact that their primary goal is to increase shareholder value. Consider a company that is in the mature phase of its life cycle. The company's operations are generating positive cash flow, but if reinvested the excess cash earns below-average returns. Management can do three things with the excess cash. It can reinvest it (and continue to earn below-average returns), it can buy growth (in the form of an acquisition), or it can return the excess cash to shareholders. Buffett argues that the rational thing for managers to do is to return cash to shareholders.

2. *Is management candid?* Candor on the part of managers means reporting financial results clearly and completely, and not hiding behind legal, though somewhat dubious, account-

ing rules. He admires managers who are willing to discuss mistakes and other failures honestly and openly.

3. *Does management resist the institutional imperative?* The institutional imperative, according to Buffet, is the lemming-like tendency of managers to imitate the behavior of their peers, even if their peers are making irrational, even stupid, decisions. Evidence of an institutional imperative include resisting any changes in the company's current direction; spending excess cash on any project or acquisition that comes along, regardless of its merits; adopting any business craving of the CEO; and mindlessly following the behavior of peer companies in such areas are acquisitions, divestitures, or executive compensation, whether or not the behavior makes any sense.

Questions for Critical Thinking

1. What are some recent examples of companies in which management failed to resist the institutional imperative? Why are shareholder responses generally so muted?

2. Some argue that excessive executive compensation is one of the major problems with today's corporations. Do you agree or disagree?

Although many experienced investors have trouble defining *good management*, they often know it when they see it. The basic tenants used by legendary investor Warren Buffett to evaluate management are described in the Investment Insight box on this page. To give you an idea of how investors can assess the quality of management, here are some questions to ask:

1. *What are the age and experience characteristics of senior management?* Information on senior management appears in the company's annual report. These descriptions generally include ages, current titles, and brief biographical sketches of each individual. Experts look for a senior management group that appears to have some depth of experience. At the same time, the group should exhibit some diversity in terms of age, length of service with the company, and background. Homogeneity of senior management may have been a source of some of GM's management problems during the 1980s.[3] It is also important to consider likely successors to current leaders, especially if the company bears the stamp of one or two individuals. When Jack Welch announced in 1999 his intention to retire as CEO of General Electric in

---

[3]Maryann Keller, *Rude Awakening* (New York: Morrow, 1989).

2001, the stock price dropped by more than 5% as nervous investors wondered who would replace him.[4]

2. *How effective is the company's strategic planning?* Management experts suggest that strategic planning may be the single most important function of senior management because success or failure of this work determines much of the future prosperity of the company. Therefore, the effectiveness of the company's strategic planning efforts can reveal a great deal about the overall quality of a company's management. Some questions to ask about a company's strategic planning include whether the strategy is identifiable, consistent, and feasible. Johnson & Johnson is often cited as an example of a company with excellent strategic planning.

3. *Has the company developed and followed a sound marketing strategy?* An investor's analysis should not discount the importance of a clear, well-planned marketing strategy. To prosper, every company must satisfy the demands of consumers. An investor should evaluate how well the company delineates its target market (or markets) and then combines the four marketing mix variables (distribution, price, product, and promotion).

4. *Has the company effectively and nimbly adapted to changes in the external environment?* The contemporary business environment is marked by rapid and sometimes unpredictable changes. How well a company anticipates and reacts to changes in its external business environment depends on the quality of its management. Think of the Internet. Which retailers understood the growing importance of the Internet and adapted their business strategies accordingly?

5. *Has management maintained, or improved, the company's overall competitive position?* We discuss this topic in greater depth in the next section, but at least maintaining, and hopefully improving, a company's competitive position is a prime responsibility of management. Well-run companies strive to maintain or improve the competitive positions of their various business units.

6. *Has the company grown in an organized, sustainable manner?* History is replete with examples of companies that grew too quickly, outstripping their financial and managerial resources.

7. *Has the company been financed adequately and appropriately?* The quality of management is often reflected in the company's financial statements. As a general rule, better-run companies have better-looking financials than poorly run companies.

8. *Does the company have good relations with employees?* Managers cannot achieve goals by themselves; they must be able to motivate and lead employees. As a general rule, well-run companies maintain better employee relationships than poorly run companies.

9. *What is the company's public image?* Does a company's public image convey a positive or negative image? Well-run companies understand the importance of public image, though management should never neglect other responsibilities while cultivating a positive public image.

10. *How effective is the company's board of directors?* Well-run companies have effective boards of directors. One result of the wave of recent corporate

---

[4]Welch ended up staying as CEO until 2001. Though GE lost two key executives during the transition from Welch to new CEO Jeffrey Immelt, the transition itself was considered fairly smooth.

scandals has been efforts to strengthen corporate boards. As noted in Chapter 6, the New York Stock Exchange developed a new set of rules on corporate boards, especially the increased role of independent directors, that will apply to all listed firms.

THE COMPETITIVE POSITION OF A COMPANY

One task of the industry analyst must be to determine the competitive structure of the industry, as we saw in Chapter 11. For one thing, knowing the structure will shed some light on the industry's position in its life cycle. Having evaluated the competitive structure of the industry, the company analyst must then assess the competitive position of the specific company within the industry. Initially, this assessment requires answers to two questions.

First, why is the company's competitive position important? One factor that clearly influences the future quality (or riskiness) and quantity of earnings of a firm is its competitive position in its industry. Simply put, a leading or dominant company in an industry should produce higher and more consistent future earnings than a company in a weak competitive position. This generalization should be true for any stage of the industry life cycle. For example, if the industry is starting to show signs of stabilization, or even decline, the leading companies may be the only ones that survive for any length of time. Further, how well a company maintains its competitive position over time may reveal a great deal about the quality of its management.

The second question that drives analysis of competitive position asks, should one *always* restrict investment choices to industry leaders? This question is difficult to answer. One theme we emphasize throughout this text, remember, is that investors can rely on few absolutes. An industry may seem attractive, but a company other than the industry leaders may have the most attractive valuation (e.g., price/earnings ratio). This fact, coupled with others, may confirm the decision to invest in the nonleading company.

Nevertheless, *all other things being equal,* leading companies offer lower-risk investment prospects than nonleading companies. Companies that established dominant positions in their respective industries proved that they can meet the competition. They built high market shares for their products and services and demonstrated the ability to lead their industries. Further, these companies demonstrated the ability to make money; they could not have achieved their dominant positions without operating profitably.

This generalization requires another important caveat: *never* assume that a company will maintain its competitive position within its industry in the future. Although many companies establish dominance and leadership and never lose them, history provides many examples of leading companies that lost their dominant positions for a variety of reasons.

Evaluating a Company's Competitive Position

The discussion of the importance of the company's competitive position raises the question of how to ascertain whether a specific company enjoys a strong competitive position within its industry. In some cases, this task could be fairly straightforward, even easy. In others, it is more arduous.

Many companies operate in several different industries. Johnson & Johnson, for example, makes hundreds of different products, from prescription drugs to disposable contact lenses to baby shampoo. Giant General Electric manufactures everything from lightbulbs to home appliances to jet engines. It also has a huge consumer and corporate financing subsidiary. Should the analyst evaluate the competitive position of the company in *every* industry in which it operates? Probably, but experienced analysts concentrate their efforts on the industries that provide the largest shares of overall company revenue and earnings. With respect for these complexities, let's now review the forces that determine the competitive position of a company. (One of the critical thinking exercises at the end of the chapter asks you to assess the competitive position of an actual company.)

Revenues or Sales In general, size is a good guide to competitive position. Higher annual sales or revenue often comes from success at meeting the competition; at least this generalization has been true historically. Size alone does not guarantee continuing dominance in the future, however. A better indicator may be the *growth rate* in sales, relative to the industry. The leading company may not necessarily be the largest, but the one that is growing the fastest compared with its competitors.

Profitability How profitable is the company, especially when compared with industry averages? Analysts measure profitability not just in dollars but also by such variables as profit margin and return on equity. This analysis should also determine whether the company is becoming relatively more or less profitable compared with the industry. As a general rule, a more profitable company, especially one that is becoming relatively more profitable compared with the industry, has a better competitive position.

Product Line A longer and broader product line, compared with the industry, generally indicates a more competitive position. (The term *product* includes both goods and services.) Strong marketing and financial reasons drive a company to increase the length and breadth of its product line, including expanding growth opportunities, optimizing company resources, increasing the importance of the company in the market, and exploiting the product life cycle. Failure to increase the length and breadth of a company's product mix can have severe negative consequences.

New Products and Product Innovation Another sign of a competitively strong company is its ability to introduce new products (or improved versions of existing products) more rapidly than its competitors, to take advantage of changes in demand or technology.

Operating Efficiency Industry leaders, especially those that will be dominant in the future, usually produce goods and services more efficiently than their competitors. Companies that are low-cost producers—able to produce the same quality good or service more cheaply than competitors—are considered to be more efficient. These firms are more likely to build strong competitive positions within their respective industries.

price leader
Ability to set prices in an industry.

Pricing Pricing is an important component of any marketing strategy. Dominant companies tend to follow certain pricing practices, depending on the industry. For example, a **price leader** may hold the dominant competitive position, especially in a mature growth industry. A simple example will illustrate the meaning of price leadership. If company A is the price leader in its industry, all its competitors match its decision to raise (or lower) its prices. However, if a competitor raises (or lowers) its prices, competition will correct the price change unless A makes the same change. Pricing and operating efficiency are often related. A company that is a price leader is often a low-cost producer, as well. Airlines such as Southwest and JetBlue are considered to be price leaders; they also have operating costs that are well below the industry average.

Patents and Technology Many companies establish dominant positions in various industries by exploiting patents or proprietary technology. Once the patent expires or the technology evolves, however, the company's dominant position in the industry becomes less secure.

ANALYZING FINANCIAL STATEMENTS

After evaluating the competitive position of a company within its industry, the next part of a company analysis report requires a detailed analysis of the company's financial statements. As you probably remember from your introductory accounting and finance classes, accounting practices create three major financial statements: the balance sheet, the income statement, and the statement of cash flows. Examples of all three statements are shown in Figure 12.3.[5] Public companies are required to periodically disclose their financial statements. Independent auditors review and affirm the statements.

One issue investors confront when analyzing financial statements is whether the numbers are reliable. (We touched on this issue briefly in Chapter 9 when discussing why analysts occasionally blow calls.) For the majority of companies, financial statements do reasonably represent financial position and performance, but the numbers can be manipulated to make the company's financial position appear better. Further, accounting rules give managers wide latitude in some cases as to how certain activities are reported. Remember also that some financial statement numbers don't represent cash flows.

In several well-publicized cases recently, however, companies went beyond proper boundaries and presented financial statements that were, at best, misleading and, at worst, fraudulent. Examples of companies accused of accounting wrongdoing include Sunbeam, Enron, Global Crossing, Qwest, Tyco International, and WorldCom. You would be wrong if you concluded that accounting shenanigans are a recent development—they aren't. Cooking the books has, unfortunately, a long and colorful history. The Investment History box on page 319 provides some historical perspective.

---

[5]If you feel as though you need to review the major financial statements, and how they are related to one another, consult any basic accounting textbook. A prepared review of financial statements is available from your instructor.

FIGURE 12.3

Sample Financial Statements

Kohl's Corporation
Income Statement ($ millions)

	Fiscal Year ending January 31		
	2002	2001	2000
Sales	7,488.7	6,152.0	4,557.10
Cost of goods sold	4,913.6	4,049.9	3,013.8
Gross profit	2,575.1	2,102.1	1,543.3
Operating expenses	1,558.0	1,317.6	1,006.2
Operating income	1,017.1	784.5	537.1
Depreciation & amortization	167.0	133.3	88.8
EBIT	850.1	651.2	448.3
Other income (net)	7.2	3.1	2.3
Interest	57.4	49.3	29.5
Earnings before taxes	799.9	605.0	421.1
Taxes	304.2	233.0	163.0
Net income	495.7	372.0	258.1
Earnings per share	1.48	1.13	0.80
Dividends per share	0.00	0.00	0.00
Stock price (year-end)	67.67	65.91	37.91

	Fiscal Year Ending January 31		
Balance Sheet ($ millions)	2002	2001	2000
Current Assets			
Cash and equivalents	106.7	123.6	12.6
Receivables	835.9	681.3	501.2
Inventories	1,198.3	1,003.3	794.4
Other Current Assets	323.1	113.7	58.3
Total Current Assets	2,464.0	1,921.9	1,366.5
Non-Current Assets			
Net Fixed Assets	2,199.5	1,726.5	1,353.0
Intangibles	9.3	14.5	152.8
Other Non-Current Assets	256.7	192.3	42.4
Total Non-Current Assets	2,465.5	1,933.3	1,548.2
Total Assets	4,929.6	3,855.2	2,914.7
Liabilities & Equity			
Current Liabilities			
Accounts payable	478.9	399.9	330.1
Short-term debt	16.4	21.6	96.6
Other Current Liabilities	384.7	301.8	207.7
Total Current Liabilities	880.0	723.3	634.4
Non-Current Liabilities			
Long-Term Debt	1,095.4	803.1	495.0
Deferred Income Taxes	114.2	84.3	66.5
Other Non-Current Liabilities	48.6	41.9	33.3
Total Non-Current Liabilities	1,258.2	929.3	594.8
Total Liabilities	2,138.2	1,652.6	1,229.2
Shareholders' Equity	2,791.4	2,202.6	1,685.5
Total Liabilities & Equity	4,929.6	3,855.2	2,914.7
Shares Outstanding	335.1	332.2	326.1

FIGURE 12.3				
(continued)		**Fiscal Year Ending January 31**		
	Annual Cash Flow ($ millions)	**2002**	**2001**	**2000**
	Cash Flow from Operating Activities			
	Net Income	495.7	372.1	258.1
	Depreciation and Amortization	167.0	133.3	88.8
	Deferred Income Taxes	17.2	0.4	4.9
	Operating (Gains) Losses	0.0	99.1	0.0
	Change in Working Capital			
	Increase in receivables	(154.7)	(176.2)	(230.5)
	Increase in inventory	(195.0)	(208.9)	(177.1)
	Increase in other current assets	(15.8)	(4.4)	(1.3)
	Increase in accounts payable	78.9	63.5	117.2
	Increase in other current liabilities	143.7	88.5	46.4
	Other Non-Cash Items	4.8	4.6	3.5
	Net cash flow from operating activities	541.8	372.1	110.2
	Cash Flow from Investing Activities			
	Cash Flow Provided by:			
	Sale of fixed assets	0.0	0.0	4.4
	Cash Used by:			
	Purchase of fixed assets	(662.0)	(481.0)	(625.4)
	Purchase of investments	(180.8)	(21.1)	(0.8)
	Other Investing Changes, Net	(28.5)	(25.0)	(20.2)
	Net cash flow from investing activities	(871.3)	(527.1)	(642.0)
	Cash Flow from Financing Activities			
	Cash Flow Provided by:			
	Issuance of debt	299.5	319.4	282.3
	Issuance of capital stock	36.1	45.9	264.6
	Cash Used for:			
	Repayment of debt	(23.0)	(92.1)	(3.2)
	Repurchase of capital stock	0.0	0.0	0.0
	Payment of cash dividends	0.0	0.0	0.0
	Other Financing Charges, Net	0.0	(7.1)	(2.2)
	Net cash flow from financing activities	312.6	266.1	541.5
	Change in Cash	(16.9)	111.0	9.8

Financial Ratios

Financial ratios provide one of the most widely used tools for analyzing a company's financial statements. Ratios are designed to show relationships between, or within, financial statements. Financial ratios are used to identify a company's strengths or weaknesses, or highlight areas in need of further investigation.

In your introductory finance class you likely discussed how the various financial ratios are calculated. Even though we want to concentrate more on how to interpret financial ratios, let's briefly review them. Financial ratios for companies are typically divided into five general categories: liquidity ratios, asset efficiency

INVESTMENT HISTORY

Cooking the Books

As we've discussed, one explanation for why security analysts have such a difficult time forecasting earnings is the impact of creative accounting practices. History is full of examples of companies that used creative accounting to produce dubious earnings reports.

One classic example, detailed by Andrew Tobias in his book *The Funny Money Game,* was National Student Marketing. Never heard of it? Well, investors back in the late 1960s knew all about National Student Marketing, one of the great concept stocks of all time. National Student Marketing (NSM) was started by flashy entrepreneur Cortess Randell as a company that would market services to college-age students. NSM grew primarily by acquisition; buying up small companies that sold everything from records to airfare discount cards. Randell was something of a showman and held Wall Street spellbound as he promoted the company almost nonstop. Investors believed his increasingly optimistic earnings projections. After all, youth was in, and this company would soon have a huge share of the youth-oriented market. At its peak in 1969, NSM was selling for a lofty 110 times reported earnings.

The trouble for investors was that what NSM was reporting as earnings was the result of substantial manipulation. For example, in 1969 the company made generous use of something called "deferred new product development and start-up costs." These are monies the company actually spent during the year but were not charged against 1969 revenues. Even more amazing, NSM also counted *unearned* revenues. It included almost $4 million in the form of earnings from companies

who had generally agreed to be acquired by NSM, but whose acquisitions had yet to be completed.

Like all financial houses of cards, NSM eventually collapsed. A brief bear market in 1970 took care of NSM, as well as several other notable concept companies. A series of investigations by security regulators didn't help. By the end of 1970, NSM had lost more than 98% of its value. Cortess Randell pleaded guilty to stock fraud and served several months in prison.

Earnings manipulation continues today. One of the most egregious cases in recent years is MCI WorldCom. Starting in the mid-1990s, WorldCom routinely capitalized billions of dollars of ordinary operating expenses. In other words, instead of charging off the entire amount in the year it occurred, which accounting rules require, the firm spread out the expenses over several years. The end result was that firm was substantially inflating its actual earnings. WorldCom finally admitted wrongdoing in 2002 and filed for bankruptcy. The firm is in the process of restating several years worth of financial statements. Several former company executives are facing civil and criminal charges.

Questions for Critical Thinking

1. What are some other ways companies can use creative accounting to manipulate their earnings?
2. Why is so easy to fool investors with accounting gimmicks? What can investors do to protect themselves from accounting frauds such as National Student Marketing and WorldCom?

(or activity) ratios, leverage and coverage ratios, profitability ratios, and ratios based on market values. Figure 12.4 lists the major financial ratios and shows how each is calculated.[6]

Liquidity Ratios Liquidity ratios are designed to measure a company's *liquidity*—whether it has sufficient liquid assets to meet its short-term obligations. A liquid asset is defined as an asset that can be quickly converted into cash at a price close to the asset's true value. Short-term obligations are normally defined as current liabilities. Three liquidity ratios are the current ratio, the quick ratio, and the cash ratio.

liquidity ratios

Ratios that measure a company's ability to meet its short-term obligations.

Activity Ratios The second group of ratios, activity or asset management ratios, are designed to measure how effectively and efficiently a company is using its assets to generate revenues or sales. In general, the more efficiently and effectively a company uses its assets, the stronger it is financially. Four principal

activity (asset management) ratios

Ratios that measure how effectively and efficiently a company is using its assets.

---

[6]It is not uncommon to see some small differences in how certain analysts calculate particular ratios. The key, however, is consistency.

	How Calculated	**Kohl's (2002 fiscal year)**
I. Liquidity Ratios		
Current ratio	Current assets divided by current liabilities	$\dfrac{2{,}464.0}{880.0} = 2.80$
Quick ratio	Current assets minus inventory divided by current liabilities	$\dfrac{(2{,}464.0 - 1{,}198.3)}{880.0} = 1.44$
Cash ratio	Cash and marketable securities divided by current liabilities	$\dfrac{106.7}{880.0} = 0.12$
II. Activity Ratios		
Inventory turnover	Sales divided by average inventory	$\dfrac{7{,}488.7}{\left[\dfrac{1{,}198.3 + 1{,}003.3}{2}\right]} = 6.80$
Accounts receivable turnover	Sales divided by average accounts receivable	$\dfrac{7{,}488.7}{\left[\dfrac{(835.9 + 681.3)}{2}\right]} = 6.48$
Fixed asset turnover	Sales divided by average net fixed assets	$\dfrac{7{,}488.7}{\left[\dfrac{(2{,}199 + 1{,}726.5)}{2}\right]} = 3.81$
Total asset turnover	Sales divided by average total assets	$\dfrac{7{,}488.7}{\left[\dfrac{(4{,}929 + 3{,}855.2)}{2}\right]} = 1.70$
III. Leverage & Coverage Ratios		
Debt ratio	Total liabilities divided by total assets	$\dfrac{2{,}138.2}{4{,}929.6} = 43.4\%$
Long-term debt to equity	Long-term debt divided by shareholders' equity	$\dfrac{1{,}095.4}{2{,}791.4} = 39.2\%$
Times interest earned	Earnings before interest and taxes divided by interest	$\dfrac{850.1}{57.4} = 14.8$
IV. Profitability Ratios		
Gross profit margin	Gross profit divided by sales	$\dfrac{2{,}571.1}{7{,}488.7} = 34.4\%$
Operating profit margin	Operating profit divided by sales	$\dfrac{1{,}017.1}{7{,}488.7} = 13.6\%$
Net profit margin	Net income divided by sales	$\dfrac{495.7}{7{,}488.7} = 6.6\%$
Return on assets	Net income divided by average total assets	$\dfrac{495.7}{\left[\dfrac{(4{,}929.6 + 3{,}855.2)}{2}\right]} = 11.3\%$
Return on equity	Net income divided by average shareholders' equity	$\dfrac{495.7}{\left[\dfrac{(2{,}791.4 + 2{,}202.6)}{2}\right]} = 19.9\%$

FIGURE 12.4   Major Financial Ratios

	How Calculated	Kohl's (2002 fiscal year)
IV. Profitability Ratios (*continued*)		
Earnings growth rate	Percent change in earnings per share	$\left(\dfrac{1.48}{1.13}\right) - 1 = 31.0\%$
Retention rate	One minus dividends per share divided by earnings per share	$1 - \left(\dfrac{0.00}{1.48}\right) = 100\%$
V. Market Value Ratios		
Price-to-earnings ratio	Market price divided by earnings per share	$\dfrac{67.67}{1.48} = 45.7$
Market-to-book value ratio	Market price divided by book value per share	$\dfrac{67.67}{\left[\dfrac{2{,}791}{335.1}\right]} = 8.1$
Dividend yield	Dividends per share divided by price per share	$\dfrac{0.00}{67.67} = 0.0\%$

FIGURE 12.4   (*continued*)

activity ratios are inventory turnover, accounts receivable turnover, fixed asset turnover, and total asset turnover.

Leverage and Coverage Ratios Leverage ratios measure the extent to which companies rely on borrowed funds to finance their operations. Coverage ratios measure the ability of a company to pay its debts. Companies that rely more on borrowed funds are said to be more leveraged. Now, the effect of leverage can be both positive and negative. Debt financing is a way for companies to raise capital without existing shareholders giving away some of their control. Debt financing is also cheaper than equity financing, because interest is tax deductible. Further, leverage can magnify a small increase in operating income into a larger return to shareholders.

Although some leverage can be beneficial, too much leverage can be dangerous. Leverage not only magnifies increases in operating income into larger returns to shareholders, it also magnifies *decreases* in operating income into smaller returns to shareholders. In extreme cases, too much leverage can lead to financial distress and even bankruptcy. The major leverage and coverage ratios are the debt ratio, the ratio of long-term debt to liabilities, and times interest earned.

leverage ratios
Measures of the extend to which a company relies on borrowed money.

coverage ratios
Measures of the ability of a company to repay its debts.

leveraged
The degree to which a company uses borrowed money.

Profitability Ratios Profitability ratios measure what the name implies, how much money a company is making. One of the two groups of profitability ratios consists of profit margins; the other group consists of returns. The principal profitability ratios are gross profit margin, operating profit margin, net profit margin, return on assets, return on equity, earnings growth rate, and the retention rate.

profitability ratios
Measures of how much money the company is making.

Market Value Ratios Most ratios are based solely on book values, meaning based on numbers that come directly from a company's financial reports. Ratios based on market values give some indication of what investors think of a company, both how it has performed historically as well as its future prospects.

Some market value-based ratios include the price-to-earnings ratio, the price-to-book value ratio, the dividend yield, and the total return to shareholders.

Interrelationship Among Ratios As you perhaps already observed, many of the financial ratios are interrelated with one another. Companies with lots of inventory, for example, may have relatively high current ratios, yet low inventory turnover and total asset turnover ratios. A company with a relatively great amount of financial leverage will likely have a high debt ratio and a low times interest earned ratio. Interrelationships are especially important when it comes to a company's profitability. A company's profitability is affected by liquidity, asset efficiency, and leverage.

Breaking Down ROE: The DuPont Formula

Several years ago, analysts working for DuPont devised a method of breaking down return on equity into various components. By separating the factors, analyst could determine which ones drive profitability. Breaking down return on equity (ROE) also allows the analyst to better identify strengths, weaknesses, and areas in need of further investigation.

DuPont formula

A way of breaking down return on equity into its various components.

As a first step, the DuPont formula breaks ROE into the following three components:

$$\text{Return on equity} = \frac{\text{Net income}}{\text{Average equity}}$$

$$= \frac{\text{Sales}}{\text{Average assets}} \times \frac{\text{Net income}}{\text{Sales}} \times \frac{\text{Assets}}{\text{Average equity}}$$

You should recognize the first two components: asset turnover and the net profit margin. If you multiply them together, you get return on assets (net income divided by average assets), or ROA.

The third component of the DuPont formula, assets divided by average equity, is merely another measure of leverage. The higher the ratio, also called the *equity multiplier,* the more levered the company. If the company has any liabilities at all, then the equity multiplier will be greater than one. Therefore, ROE—the return to shareholders—will be greater than return on assets. For example, if the equity multiplier is 2, and return on assets is 8%, ROE will be 16%. This result indicates the effect of leverage on a company's profitability.

Interpreting Financial Ratios

By themselves, financial ratios are little more than just a bunch of numbers. To be meaningful, ratios must be compared to some sort of benchmark. A benchmark can be established by looking at the same ratio over a number of years or by comparing a company's ratios to industry (or competitor) averages. In the first case, you are looking for obvious trends, while in the second you are looking for company ratios that appear to be out of line with industry (or competitor) averages. Once the analyst uncovers a trend in a particular ratio, or a ratio that appears out of line with industry (or competitor) averages, the analyst must then dig further to determine the underlying cause.

Financial Ratios	Fiscal Year Ending January 31					TABLE 12.1
	2002	2001	2000	1999	1998	Selected Financial Ratios for Kohl's Corporation
Current ratio	2.80	2.66	2.15	2.47	2.84	
Quick ratio	1.44	1.27	0.90	0.85	1.03	
Cash ratio	0.12	0.17	0.02	0.01	0.15	
Inventory turnover	6.80	6.84	6.46	6.50	6.52	
Accounts receivable turnover	6.48	6.85	7.81	9.59	17.08	
Fixed asset turnover	3.81	4.00	3.99	4.38	4.55	
Total asset turnover	1.70	1.82	1.88	2.07	2.23	
Total debt to total assets	43.4%	42.9%	42.2%	39.9%	41.1%	
Long-term debt to equity	39.2%	36.5%	29.4%	26.7%	32.5%	
Gross profit margin	34.4%	34.2%	33.9%	33.5%	33.1%	
Operating profit margin	13.6%	12.8%	11.8%	11.1%	10.3%	
Net profit margin	6.6%	6.0%	5.7%	5.2%	4.6%	
Return on assets	11.3%	11.0%	10.6%	10.8%	10.3%	
Return on equity	19.9%	19.1%	18.1%	18.2%	19.2%	
Earnings growth rate	31.0%	41.3%	31.1%	29.8%	34.3%	
Price/Earnings ratio	45.7	58.3	47.4	56.6	42.7	
Market to book value	8.1	9.9	7.3	9.4	6.6	
Retention rate	100%	100%	100%	100%	100%	
ROE Breakdown						
Sales/Average assets	1.70	1.82	1.88	2.07	2.23	
Net income/Sales	6.6%	6.0%	5.7%	5.2%	4.6%	
Average assets/Average equity	1.76	1.74	1.70	1.68	1.86	
ROE	19.9%	19.1%	18.1%	18.2%	19.2%	

Trend Analysis

The purpose of examining the same set of ratios over a number of years is to look for obvious trends. If a trend is identified, the next step is to determine the cause (or causes) of the trend and whether the trend suggests a strength or weakness. Let's look at three examples.

Kohl's Table 12.1 lists financial ratios for Kohl's for a recent five-year period. Analysis of these data suggest the following:

- Overall, liquidity appears to remain unchanged during the period shown. As with most retailers, inventory makes up the largest portion of Kohl's Corporation's current assets. Consequently, the firm's quick ratio and cash ratio are substantially less than the firm's current ratio.
- Inventory turnover improved slightly while fixed asset turnover declined slightly. Total asset turnover also declined.
- Overall, leverage appears to remain about the same. However, the ratios suggest that Kohl's relies slightly more on long-term debt relative to short-term debt.
- Profitability improved. Both the gross profit margin and net profit margin rose steadily throughout the period shown. In relative terms, the net margin

TABLE 12.2		**2001**	**2000**	**1999**	**1998**	**1997**
ROE Breakdown for Johnson & Johnson	Sales/Average assets	0.95	0.96	0.99	0.99	0.99
	× Net income/Sales	17.2%	16.5%	15.2%	12.9%	14.6%
	× Average assets/Average equity	1.59	1.67	1.80	1.93	1.74
	= ROE	25.9%	26.4%	27.0%	24.7%	25.1%

increased by more than the gross margin. As the ROE breakdown shown at the bottom of Table 12.1 suggests, the improving net profit margin is primarily responsible for the increase in the firms' return on equity.

- The company's earnings grew rapidly. Investors responded by pushing the stock price higher. The P/E ratio is relatively high.
- Not surprisingly, given its rapid growth, Kohl's retains all of its earnings.

ROE Breakdown for Johnson & Johnson Table 12.2 presents an ROE breakdown for Johnson & Johnson over a recent five-year period. Notice that the firm's ROE fluctuated only slightly on a year-to-year basis. The key drivers, however, changed. Asset turnover remained constant but leverage decreased. At the same time, Johnson & Johnson's net margin rose. The increase in the net profit margin offset the decline in leverage.

Sunbeam Finally, let's revisit Sunbeam briefly. As we noted, two trends that alarmed a few analysts prior to the bombshell Sunbeam dropped in 1998 were a steady decline in both receivables and inventory turnover. The chart in Figure 12.5 shows the company's quarterly receivables and inventory turnover over the five quarters preceding the first quarter of 1998. As you can see, both ratios, especially the inventory turnover, declined sharply. Inventory turnover fell from a respectable 1.7 times per quarter (6.8 times per year) to 0.4 times per quarter (1.6 times per year).

Industry Comparisons

Trends in ratios can yield some information about a company, but comparing a company's ratios to industry averages may provide additional insight into the company being analyzed. One year's worth of comparisons are rarely sufficient. Good financial analysis rules of thumb suggest that the analyst compare the company's ratios over several years to the industry averages over the same period of time. Before proceeding, however, three points need to be made about industry comparisons:

First, different industries experience significantly different average ratios. Table 12.3 lists several additional ratios for five companies in five different industries. Substantial differences are evident. Take leverage ratios, for example. First Energy has more than $1.50 in long-term debt for each dollar in equity. By contrast, Nike has less than 17 cents in long-term debt for each dollar in equity. Electric and gas utilities, like First Energy, rely much more heavily on long-term debt as a source of capital than do most industries.

Another obvious difference between industries is asset turnover. Wal-Mart generates $2.70 in sales for each dollar invested in assets. By contrast, Southwest Airlines generates only 71 cents in revenue for each dollar invested in assets. This

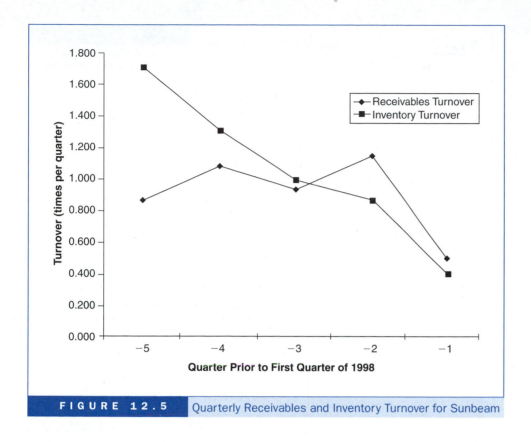

FIGURE 12.5   Quarterly Receivables and Inventory Turnover for Sunbeam

difference shouldn't surprise you. Airlines are an asset-intensive business and aircraft are expensive assets.

Second, many industries are far from homogeneous. Take retailing, for example. A retailer such as the Gap is distinctly different from a retailer such as Albertson's. Not surprisingly, some of their financial ratios are quite different, as shown in Table 12.4. The Gap has higher liquidity ratios (current and quick) and higher profit margins (both gross and net). On the other hand, Albertson's turns its inventory much faster and has a higher total asset turnover. None of these

TABLE 12.3

Industry Differences in Selected Financial Ratios

	Company				
Ratio	3M	First Energy	Nike	Southwest Airlines	Wal-Mart
Current ratio	1.40	0.54	2.26	1.13	1.04
Fixed asset turnover	2.86	0.64	6.13	0.86	4.76
Asset turnover	1.10	0.29	1.61	0.71	2.70
Debt ratio	42.0%	81.0%	40.0%	55.0%	58.0%
Long-term debt to equity	25.0%	161.7%	16.3%	33.1%	53.4%
Net profit margin	8.9%	9.1%	6.8%	9.2%	3.1%
Return on equity	23.5%	8.9%	17.4%	13.7%	19.0%

Ratio	Albertson's	Gap Stores
Current ratio	1.28	1.85
Quick ratio	0.25	1.11
Inventory turnover	11.23 times	8.88 times
Total asset turnover	2.80 times	1.95 times
Debt to total assets	54.0%	52.5%
Long-term debt to equity	46.7%	33.7%
Gross profit margin	28.7%	38.3%
Net profit margin	3.5%	8.2%

TABLE 12.4

Comparing the Ratios
of Two Retailers

differences should come as a surprise; the Gap sells primarily casual clothing while Albertson's sells mostly grocery items.

Finally, many companies operate in several different industries. Giant General Electric makes everything from lightbulbs to jet engines. The company also owns a broadcasting network (NBC) and has a huge financial services division. For a company such as GE, the results of any industry comparison may be of more limited value than for a company that operates in one, well-defined industry.

With all of these factors in mind, let's do two comparisons of pairs of companies that operate in similar industries. We compare Kohl's to Target, and Merck to Pfizer (both large pharmaceutical companies).

Kohl's vs. Target Before we begin, we should note that Kohl's and Target are similar in some ways, but different in others. Kohl's is a discount department store chain. Target owns several more upscale department store chains such as Marshall Fields, though its Target division accounts for a majority of the firm's overall sales. In addition, Target is more of a general retailer while Kohl's generates the majority of its sales from clothing. With these differences in mind, let's compare the two companies financial ratios presented in Table 12.5.

• Kohl's turns its inventory slightly faster than Target does. Moreover, inventory turnover at Kohl's is improving while it is remaining about the same at Target. On the other hand, Target generates more sales for each dollar invested in assets.
• Kohl's is the more profitable company. It has higher profit margins, and its margins are rising. By contrast, Target's profit margins remain flat. Kohl's also has a higher ROE due to its higher net profit margin.
• Target is more levered. It has about 33 cents in equity for each dollar in assets. On the other hand, Kohl's has approximately 55 cents in equity for each dollar in assets. Further, Target relies much more heavily on long-term debt than Kohl's does. Target has about $1.03 in long-term debt for each dollar in equity; Kohl's has less than 40 cents in long-term debt for each dollar in equity.

Merck vs. Pfizer Table 12.6 lists financial ratios for Merck and Pfizer for a recent three-year period. Both companies generally show good-looking numbers, but also some interesting differences are evident. One is leverage. Merck is more levered and relies much more on long-term debt compared with Pfizer, though neither company is highly levered. Merck has almost 30 cents in long-term debt for each dollar in equity. By contrast, Pfizer has less than 15 cents in long-term

Ratio	2002 Fiscal Year		2001 Fiscal Year		2000 Fiscal Year	
	Kohl's	Target	Kohl's	Target	Kohl's	Target
Current ratio	2.80	1.37	2.66	1.16	2.15	1.11
Quick ratio	1.44	0.61	1.27	0.36	0.90	0.35
Inventory turnover	6.80	6.27	6.84	6.29	6.46	6.33
Fixed asset turnover	3.81	2.95	4.00	3.23	3.99	3.40
Total asset turnover	1.70	1.83	1.82	2.01	1.88	2.05
Debt ratio	43.4%	67.0%	42.9%	66.5%	42.2%	66.0%
Long-term debt to equity	39.2%	102.9%	36.5%	86.4%	29.4%	77.1%
Gross profit margin	34.4%	31.7%	34.2%	31.5%	33.9%	31.7%
Net profit margin	6.6%	3.4%	6.0%	3.4%	5.7%	3.5%
Return on assets	11.3%	5.7%	11.0%	6.5%	10.6%	6.8%
Return on equity	19.9%	17.5%	19.1%	19.4%	18.1%	19.9%

TABLE 12.5

Kohl's vs. Target

Note: Both companies' fiscal year ends on January 31.

Ratio	2001		2000		1999	
	Merck	Pfizer	Merck	Pfizer	Merck	Pfizer
Current ratio	1.12	1.35	1.38	1.43	1.29	1.22
Inventory turnover	8.45	1.50	7.34	1.86	6.13	1.01
Accounts receivable turnover	9.33	5.71	8.86	6.06	8.77	4.50
Total asset turnover	1.14	0.88	1.07	1.09	0.97	0.83
Debt ratio	64.0%	53.0%	63.0%	51.5%	63.0%	57.0%
Long-term debt to equity	29.9%	14.3%	24.3%	6.7%	23.7%	5.9%
Operating profit margin	23.4%	36.9%	25.6%	32.6%	26.5%	32.9%
Net profit margin	15.3%	24.2%	16.9%	12.6%	18.0%	19.7%
Return on equity	45.4%	42.3%	46.0%	23.1%	44.5%	36.0%

TABLE 12.6

Merck vs. Pfizer

Note: Both companies' fiscal year ends on December 31.

debt for each dollar in equity. On the other hand, Pfizer has higher profit margins. Further, its margins showed some improvement, while Merck's declined slightly. However, because Merck is more levered and turns its assets faster, the company's ROE is higher than Pfizer's.

A review of the historical record of a company—both financial and nonfinancial—is an important component of a company analysis report. We are not finished with company analysis, however, for we still have to forecast future financial performance in order to fully assess the investment potential of a company's common stock.

SUMMARY

1. What are the components of a company analysis report?

The major goal of company analysis is to forecast the quality and quantity of future earnings. Four general issues are addressed: (1) the quality of management; (2) the company's competitive position within its industry; (3) the strength and weaknesses of the company's financial statements; and (4) the company's future financial performance.

2. How do analysts evaluate the quality of a company's management?

Management is defined as the effective and efficient attainment of organizational goals. Management consists of four functions: planning, organizing, leading, and controlling. Assessing management quality can be both difficult and subjective. Some things to look for include an experienced management team, good strategic planning and marketing, appropriate financing, sustainable growth, a good public image, and an effective board of directors.

3. How is the competitive position of a company within its industry evaluated?

Leading companies have several important characteristics. They are usually among the largest companies in an industry and are growing faster than the industry as a whole. Leading companies are more profitable or are becoming more profitable than the industry. A longer and broader product line often indicates a more competitive position, as does the company's ability to introduce new products faster than competitors. Leading companies are also usually the most efficient, exhibit price leadership, and may have the advantage of proprietary technology or patents.

4. What is financial statement analysis?

Financial statement analysis involves a careful evaluation of a company's financial statements. Financial ratios are one of the most important tools for assessing the strengths and weaknesses of a company. The five categories of ratios include: liquidity, activity, leverage and coverage, profitability, and ratios based on market values. In and of themselves ratios are just numbers. To be meaningful they must be compared across time or to industry averages, or both.

MINI CASE

This mini case will provide you with practice in calculating and interpreting financial ratios. Open the Wal-Mart Stores worksheet in the Data Workbook, available on the textbook Web site (http://swlearning.hearth.com). Using the data, perform the following exercises:

1. Calculate all the ratios listed in Figure 12.4.
2. Break down return on equity into its three components. From where does Wal-Mart's high ROE come?
3. List any major trends revealed by the ratios and the ROE breakdown.

REVIEW EXERCISES

1. What is the major goal of company analysis? What type of information does the typical company report contain?
2. The general definition of management contains two important ideas. What are they? Give an example of each idea in practice.
3. What are the four functions of management? Give a brief example of each function.
4. List some of the important questions to ask when evaluating management. When looking at the characteristics of senior management, what do you want to see?
5. List some of the things you might examine when analyzing the competitive position of a company. Should an investor always limit his or her investments to leading companies?
6. What are the five categories of financial ratios?
7. Use the following ratios to fill in the balance sheet and income statement. (All dollar values are in millions.)

Current ratio	1.75
Quick ratio	1.00
Gross profit margin	30%
Net profit margin	5%
Accounts receivable turnover	10x
Long-term debt to equity	50%
Total asset turnover	1.50
Times interest earned	5.00
Return on equity	15%

Cash and equivalents	$20.0	Current liabilities	_____
Accounts receivable	_____	Long-term debt	_____
Inventory	_____	Equity	_____
Total current assets	_____	Total liabilities & equity	_____
Net fixed assets	_____		
Total assets	_____		

Sales	_____
Cost of goods sold	_____
Selling, administrative, and general expenses	_____
Depreciation	$15.0
Interest	_____
Earnings before taxes	_____
Income taxes	$5.0
Net income	$15.0

8. A company has a current ratio of 2.00 and a quick ratio of 1.50. If the company has current liabilities of $25 million, how much inventory does it have?

9. A company's return on equity is 30% and its net profit margin is 5%. It has $300 million in assets and $150 million in equity. What is the company's return on assets and asset turnover? What are the company's total sales?

10. Using the information provided in the prior question, break down the company's return on equity into its three components. Which of the three appears to be driving ROE?

11. Assume the company would like to reduce its assets to equity ratio from 2 to 1.75. What would have to happen to asset turnover or net profit margin if the company is to maintain the same ROE?

12. Why must the analyst establish benchmarks when interpreting financial ratios? Why is it often so difficult to compare a company's ratios to industry averages?

13. Assume you observed that a company's gross profit margin has been declining steadily for the last few quarters while its net profit margin remained about the same. Explain how these two trends could occur simultaneously.

14. You observe that a company's current ratio has been declining steadily. Before you conclude that the company's liquidity is deteriorating, what other data should you examine?

15. Two companies that operate in the same industry provided the following data. Break down ROE for each company. How are the two companies different? What would you want to investigate next?

(in $ millions)	Total Assets	Shareholders' Equity	Sales	Net Income
Company A	$ 350	$ 150	$1,200	$ 40
Company B	5,500	2,500	6,500	375

CRITICAL THINKING EXERCISES

1. This exercise requires computer work. Open the Airline worksheet in the Data Workbook. The worksheet contains financial and operating data for Southwest Airlines and the airline industry. Use the data to answer the following questions:
   a. What is your overall assessment of the competitive position of Southwest? On what do you base your conclusion?
   b. What information other than that presented in the worksheet, would you like to have to further assess the various airlines' competitive positions?

2. This exercise requires library and Internet research. According to retail analysts, investors need to ask some relevant questions concerning the corporate strategy of any retailer. Considering these questions, read what Value Line, Standard & Poor's, and other investment firms have to say about the following retailers: Home Depot, Kohl's, Nordstrom's, and Wal-Mart. Based on what you know about each retailer, do you agree with the investment firms? Why or why not?
   a. Has the retailer stayed on top of major demographic and economic trends?
   b. What category of retailing is the company in? Does it appear to be diversified?
   c. Where are the company's key regional markets? Are those markets strong or weak economically?
   d. How strong is the competition relative to the company?
   e. How does the company position itself in terms of price, value, quality, and service? Where does it make trade-offs between price, value, quality, and service?
   f. How many stores does the company plan to open? Has its past growth been orderly and well managed?

3. This exercise requires computer work. Open the Sneaker worksheet in the Data Workbook available on the textbook Web site. The worksheet contains financial data for Nike and Reebok over a recent six-year period. Use the data to perform the following exercises:
   a. Calculate all the ratios listed in Figure 12.4 for both Nike and Reebok for the last five years.
   b. Break down ROE for both companies for the last five years.
   c. Discuss you findings. Answer questions such as what drives ROE for both companies, and which company appears to be the strongest financially.

THE INTERNET INVESTOR

1. Pick a company whose stock is publicly traded. Using one of the major search engines, as well as some of the major investment-oriented Web sites, find out as much as you can about the company's senior management, including information on the composition of the board of directors and executive compensation.

2. Visit the Web site www.sec.gov/edgar. Look around the site and then prepare a brief report as to the financial information the site contains.

3. Most companies now include recent financial reports as part of their Web sites. Visit these three Web sites: www.southwest.com, www.johnsonandjohnson.com, and www.microsoft.com. Review their financial reports. From the prospective of an investor, which site did you prefer and why?

13

Company Analysis:
Looking Forward

PREVIOUSLY . . .

We listed the elements contained in a company analysis report and considered how to assess and analyze a company's current financial position.

IN THIS CHAPTER . . .

We describe various methods for forecasting future earnings, including simple models and well as more complex ones. We also consider estimating some of the other variables important in determining the intrinsic value of a common stock.

TO COME . . .

Our discussion of security analysis concludes in the next chapter with a description of the major stock valuation models.

CHAPTER OBJECTIVES

After reading Chapter 13, you should be able to answer the following questions:

1. Is there a long-term relationship between earnings and stock prices?

2. How are earnings calculated?

3. What are the simple quantitative methods for forecasting earnings?

4. How are business models used to forecast earnings?

5. What are some of the other financial variables the analyst needs to estimate?

After the market closed on December 3, 2002, the Walt Disney Company announced that its fiscal fourth quarter earnings would be 9 cents per share, rather than the 11 cents previously reported. The following day, the stock lost 8% of its value on heavy volume. Less than two weeks later, on December 12, 2002, Amgen, the world's largest biotechnology company, said that its 2003 earnings would be between $1.70 and $1.80 per share, surpassing the consensus Wall Street forecast of $1.65 per share. The stock promptly rose by more than 7% on the news.

These two announcements, and the stock price reactions to them, are not uncommon. Announced earnings are often higher or lower than analyst expectations. Further, considerable evidence—both anecdotal and scientific—show that stock prices react significantly to current earnings and expected future earnings. Consequently, the ability to forecast earnings and the factors that drive earnings can greatly improve the security analysis process.

In this chapter we examine how analysts forecast the future. We review some of the evidence concerning the relationship between earnings and stock prices, the major forecasting techniques, including business models, and some of the other variables the analyst needs to estimate. In the next chapter, we present several stock valuation models, which try to find the intrinsic value of a stock.

EARNINGS AND STOCK PRICES

As noted in Chapter 3, in the long run stock prices tend to follow earnings. Let's revisit this issue in more detail. Anecdotal evidence abounds. For example, between 1959 and 2002 stock prices, as measured by the S&P 500, rose by more than 1,400%. During the same period, corporate profits rose by about 1,360%. A long-term relationship between earnings and stock prices exists for individual stocks as well. Over the past 10 years, the share price and earnings of retail giant Wal-Mart Stores have both risen in excess of 300%. Figure 13.1 shows the relationship between stock prices and earnings for Johnson & Johnson. Generally, during the period shown, as earnings rose, so did the value of Johnson & Johnson's stock.

Scientific evidence also shows a strong relationship between stock prices and earnings.[1] Early studies arrayed stocks by both earnings and prices over varying periods of time. These studies found a strong association between the two arrays. The strength of the association increased over longer and longer time periods. More recent studies found that perfect earnings forecasts—in other words, knowing actual earnings at the beginning of a period—results in substantial returns. All in all, most research concluded that earnings, and earnings growth rates, explain much of the variation in stock returns over time.

Other research focused on the relationship between earnings announcements and stock price reactions.[2] Generally, these studies find that announcements of actual earnings that are higher (lower) than expected earnings, result in significant positive (negative) returns around the announcement date. It's interesting to

---

[1] This research is detailed in Samuel Stewart, "Forecasting Corporation Earnings," in *The Financial Analyst's Handbook,* 2nd ed. Sumner Levine, ed. (Homewood, IL: Richard D. Irwin, 1989), pp. 532–564.
[2] *Ibid.*

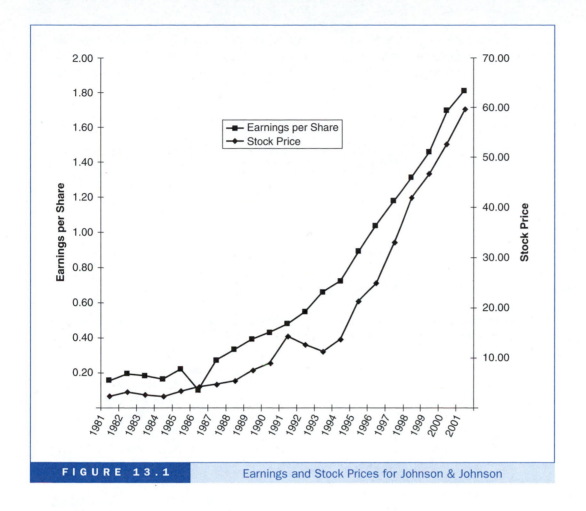

FIGURE 13.1   Earnings and Stock Prices for Johnson & Johnson

note that many of these studies also find that the positive (negative) reaction continues for several months following the announcement.

The evidence shows a strong relationship, at least in the long run, between earnings and stock prices, but history is replete with situations where stock prices got well ahead of earnings. Many of these situations resulted in speculative bubbles. The Nifty Fifty bubble of the early 1970s is one such example. The Investment History box on page 334 discusses another, the bubble in technology stocks of the late 1990s. Arguably, it may have been the most spectacular speculative bubble of all time.

WHAT ARE EARNINGS AND EARNINGS FORECASTS?

Having established the importance of earnings, we now must consider what exactly are earnings and earnings forecasts. As you remember from accounting, earnings per share (or EPS) equal a company's net income divided by the number of outstanding shares. Alas, for many real companies, it's not that simple.

The Greatest Bubble of Them All?

As we noted, the speculative bubbles are part of the history of investments. Usually during a speculative bubble earnings and stock prices diverge sharply as prices shoot skyward only to eventually come crashing back to earth. New issues involving companies in hot new industries or technologies are especially bubble prone. Take the Internet, for instance.

During the late 1990s, anything that dealt with the Internet was white hot. To give you an idea of how white hot, take a look at the following table. It contains some mind-blowing numbers.

Stock	Stock Price (year-end 1997)	Stock Price (2000 peak)	Change (1998–2000)	P/E Ratio (at peak)	Market Value ($ billions at peak)
Cisco Systems	$ 10.50	$ 78.75	650%	131	$559.1
JDS Uniphase	5.17	131.81	2449	N/A	123.1
PMC Sierra	7.00	245.25	3404	409	33.6
QualComm	5.80	161.75	2689	190	120.9
Sun Microsystems	4.73	63.47	1242	115	203.1
Yahoo!	8.00	237.50	2869	1,979	126.6
Nasdaq Composite	1,523.00	5,046.00	231%		

From the end to 1997 to its peak in early 2000, the tech-heavy Nasdaq Composite index rose by 231%. Many individual stocks did even better. Cisco Systems soared by 650%. At its peak, the stock was selling for more than 130 times earnings. It had the highest market value of any stock, anywhere in the world. Internet portal and search engine Yahoo! did even better, rocketing from $8.00 a share to more than $237 a share. At its peak, Yahoo! had a market value in excess of $125 billion. Not bad for a company with less than $600 million in annual sales.

Could these stocks continue to defy the laws of financial gravity? Of course not. In the previous edition of this book, published during the height of the mania, we wrote:

There is no question that the Internet is becoming a big deal and many of these companies are well positioned to exploit the explosive growth of the Internet. In the process, they're likely going to earn a great deal of money. Trouble is, not all these companies are going to make it in what is an incredibly competitive environment. And even for the ones who do survive, it will take years and years before their earnings can catch up with their current stock valuations. While the past is never a guarantee of the future, the current situation with Internet stocks looks an awful lot like a classic speculative bubble. And bubbles have always eventually broken.

As it turns out, that prediction was pretty prophetic. The Internet bubble did indeed break sometime in early 2000. As with all bubbles, once a few investors finally figured out that these stratospheric valuations simply couldn't be sustained, the bubble collapsed. Evidence of a weakening econ-

omy didn't help matters. Technology and Internet stocks came plunging back to earth.

The following table recounts some of the damage. All of the formally high-flying stocks listed crashed, many losing 90%, or more, of their value. Even giant Cisco Systems, a market leader with an excellent balance sheet, lost more than 80% of its value. The Nasdaq Composite dropped by more than 70% in slightly more than two years. You would have to go back to the late 1920s and early 1930s to find a similar decline in a broad stock market index.

Stock	Stock Price (late 2002)	Percent Change (2000–2002)
Cisco Systems	$ 14.25	−82%
JDS Uniphase	3.40	−97
PMC Sierra	6.00	−98
QualComm	37.60	−77
Sun Microsystems	3.52	−94
Yahoo!	18.40	−92
Nasdaq Composite	1,367.00	−73%

Questions for Critical Thinking

1. If bubbles are so obvious, why do investors seem to constantly fall into the bubble trap? Are stock market bubbles inevitable?
2. Are stocks with high price/earnings ratios always expensive? Similarity, are stocks with low price/ earnings ratios always cheap? Why or why not?

	Fiscal Year (ending December 31)				
	2001	**2000**	**1999**	**1998**	**1997**
Basic EPS from Continuing Operations	1.30	2.08	2.10	1.83	1.61
Basic EPS from Discontinued Operations	1.40	0.32	0.00	0.00	0.00
Basic EPS from Total Operations	2.70	2.40	2.10	1.83	1.61
Diluted EPS from Continuing Operations	1.29	2.05	2.06	1.79	1.57
Diluted EPS from Discontinued Operations	1.38	0.31	0.00	0.00	0.00
Diluted EPS from Total Operations	2.67	2.36	2.06	1.79	1.57

TABLE 13.1

Earnings per Share Measures for Bristol Myers Squibb Corporation

Source: MSN Money, available at http://moneycentral.msn.com (accessed December 20, 2002). Reprinted with permission from Microsoft Corporation.

Measuring Earnings per Share

Table 13.1 shows several measures of earnings per share (EPS) for Bristol Myers Squibb Corporation for a recent five-year period. Why are these measures different? It's because each measure of earnings per share has a different numerator or denominator. Let's define each measure shown in the table.

Each of the first three measures of earnings per share have the same denominator but different numerators. **Basic earnings per share from total operations** equals net income divided the number of shares outstanding.[3] **Basic earnings per share from continuing operations** equals net income from continuing operations only divided by the number of outstanding shares. **Basic earnings per share from discontinued operations** only divided by the number of outstanding shares. Companies undergoing substantial restructurings often report large (both positive and negative) EPS from discontinued operations. For example, in 2001, Bristol Myers Squibb reported basic EPS from continuing operations of $1.30. At the same time, it reported basic EPS from discontinued operations of $1.40. Thus the company reported a profit for the year of $2.70 per share.

The next three measures have the same numerator as their basic counterpart, but a different denominator. So-called **diluted measures** of earnings per share use a figure for the number of outstanding shares—assuming employee stock options, convertibles, and warrants—are converted into new shares of common stock.[4] Because the number of outstanding shares on a fully diluted basis is more than the basic number of shares outstanding, diluted measures of earnings per share are always lower than basic measures of earnings per share. In 2001, for instance, Bristol Myers Squibb reported diluted earnings of $2.67 per share— 3 cents less than basic earnings per share.

Depending on the company, the difference between diluted and basic earnings can be quite substantial. For example, for the fiscal year ending June 30, 1999, Microsoft reported basic earnings per share of $1.54. By contrast, diluted earnings per share were only $1.42 almost 10% lower than basic EPS. Over the

basic EPS from total operations

Net income divided by the number of outstanding shares.

basic EPS from continuing operations

Net income from continuing operations only divided by the number of outstanding shares.

basic EPS from discontinued operations

Net income from discontinued operations only divided by the number of outstanding shares.

diluted measures

Calculations of EPS that use a figure from the number of outstanding shares—assuming employee stock options, warrants, and convertibles are converted into new shares of common stock.

---

[3]The number of outstanding shares is calculated using a weighting procedure established by the Financial Accounting Standards. The weighting procedure takes into account the number of shares issued or redeemed during the fiscal year.

[4]The exact method used to find the number of outstanding shares on a fully diluted basis is complicated. We suggest you consult an intermediate accounting text if you would like additional details.

TABLE 13.2		Quarter (ending)				
Actual and Forecast Quarterly Earnings for Bristol Myers Squibb	**Earnings**	**9/02**	**6/02**	**3/02**	**12/01**	**9/01**
	Actual	$0.26	$0.23	$0.45	$0.59	$0.6%
	Estimate	0.27	0.30	0.48	0.59	0.62
	Difference	−0.01	−0.07	−0.03	0.00	0.01
	Percent	−3.7%	−23.3%	−6.3%	0.0%	1.6%

Source: MSN Money, available at http://moneycentral.msn.com (accessed December 20, 2002). Reprinted with permission from Microsoft Corporation.

years, Microsoft relied on stock options as an important component of total employee compensation.

Earnings Forecasts

Most large Wall Street brokerage and investment firms employ analysts who follow specific stocks. One of their jobs is to forecast earnings. Several investment information services—such as First Call, IBES, and Zach's compile earnings forecasts made by analysts. They then come up with a **consensus forecasts** for individual stocks, which is essentially the forecast average, as well the range of forecasts made by the analysts.

consensus forecast

Average of forecasts made by analysts following a stock.

Consensus Forecasts Twenty-four analysts follow Bristol Myers Squibb and make earnings forecasts for the company. For the fiscal year ending December 31, 2003, the forecasts range from $1.45 per share up to $1.80 per share. The average, or consensus forecast is $1.63 per share. We should note that the range of earnings forecasts is often a measure of the degree of uncertainty surrounding forecasts.

earnings surprise

Actual earnings that are higher or lower than the consensus forecast.

Earnings Surprises Investment information services also report so-called **earnings surprises** earnings that turn out to be higher or lower than analyst forecasts. Table 13.2 compares actual earnings for Bristol Myers Squibb to the consensus forecasts for several recent quarters. Note that only once did the analysts accurately forecast quarterly earnings. For the other quarters, the forecast was either too high or too low. Most of the forecast errors were small, though in one quarter the analysts overestimated actual earnings by more than 23%. As we briefly discussed in Chapter 8, some studies concluded that analysts have little forecasting ability. On the other hand, other studies concluded that analyst forecasts are reasonably accurate.[5]

Management Forecasts In addition to forecasts made by analysts, forecasts are also made by management. Given that management has access to information not generally available to outside analysts, it is not surprising that the accuracy of management forecasts is higher than the accuracy of analyst forecasts. Critics contend that companies make selective disclosures of management earnings forecasts, often to favored analysts.

_____

[5]Samuel Stewart, "Forecasting Corporate Earnings," pp. 535–536.

As we noted in an earlier chapter, the SEC recently adopted a regulation—Regulation FD—that prohibits companies from selectively disclosing earnings forecasts. Companies must now either say nothing or disclose the forecasts to everyone, at the same time. Some companies responded to Regulation FD by refusing to provide any earnings guidance at all, while others make extensive public disclosure of management earnings forecasts at regular intervals.

FORECASTING EARNINGS

Having discussed the relationship between stock prices and earnings, how earnings are measured, and earnings forecasts made by analysts and management, we now turn to a discussion of the techniques used to forecasts earnings. We start by distinguishing between the various approaches to forecasting earnings.

Approaches to Forecasting Earnings

In Chapter 11 we described the difference between qualitative and quantitative economic forecasts. The same difference applies to earnings forecasts. Quantitative forecasts rely on an explicit statistical or mathematical model. On the other hand, qualitative forecasts rely on subjective judgments made by the analyst without direct reference to any statistical or mathematical model. Some earnings forecasts made by analysts and management are more qualitative in nature, while others are more quantitative in nature. In reality, however, most forecasters mix the two techniques. They may use a quantitative model to arrive at a preliminary earnings forecast that is then "tweaked" using the analysts' judgment.

Another distinction we can draw is between **bottom-up forecasts** and **top-down forecasts**. In a bottom-up forecast, the analyst starts by studying the relationship between earnings and firm-specific variables. For example, the analyst might ask whether earnings are rising or falling relative to sales. In a top-down forecast, the analyst begins by studying the relationship between earnings, and various economic and industry variables. For example, the analyst might consider the relationship between oil prices and earnings.

Top-down forecasts may work better than bottom-up forecasting for certain companies in particular industries. For instance, top-down forecasting may be more appropriate for companies that operate in cyclical industries, such as auto makers and home builders, than bottom-up forecasts. On the other hand, for other companies and industries, bottom-up forecasting may work better. Even though top-down and bottom-up forecasts are not mutually exclusive, most analysts tend to focus on one approach over the other. Warren Buffet and Peter Lynch, for example, both use primarily a bottom-up approach to forecasting earnings and picking stocks.

bottom-up forecast

A forecast in which the analyst begins by studying the relationship between earnings and firm-specific variables such as sales.

top-down forecast

A forecast in which the analyst begins by studying the relationship between earnings and economic or industry variables.

Trend-Based Forecasts

Having reviewed the different approaches to forecasting, let's now turn our attention to some of the simple techniques used to forecast earnings. Perhaps the simplest forecasting technique is one that merely extrapolates a trend in the data. The chart in Figure 13.2 shows Kohl's Corporation's earnings for the prior 11 fiscal years

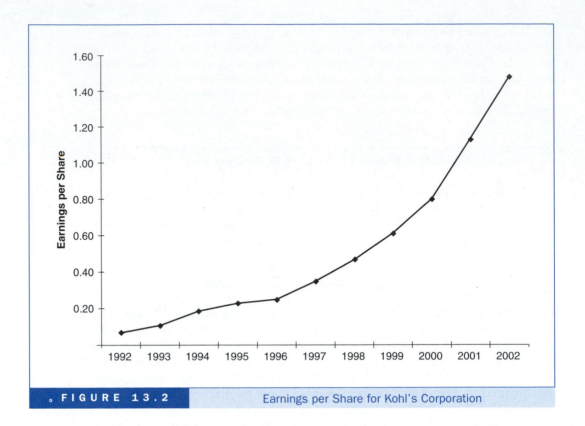

∘ FIGURE 13.2   Earnings per Share for Kohl's Corporation

(1992 through 2002). Let's use these data to extrapolate the trend and come up with an earnings forecast for the 2003 fiscal year.

You can extrapolate a trend in one of two ways. First, you can find the average compound growth rate. Second, you can estimate a simple regression model.

Finding the average compound growth rate involves solving the following equation:

$$g = \left(\frac{EPS_n}{EPS_0}\right)^{1/n} - 1$$

where EPS_n is earnings at the end of the period, EPS_0 is earnings at the beginning of the period, and n is the number of years. In our example, Southwest earned $0.12 per share in 1988 and $0.87 per share in 1998. From the end of 1988 to the end of 1998 is 10 years. Thus, the average compound growth rate is

$$g = (\$1.48/\$0.07)^{1/10} - 1 = 35.7\%$$

If Kohl's earnings grow at 35.7% in fiscal 2003, its fiscal 2003 earnings will equal

$$\$1.48(1.375) = \$2.01$$

The other method for extrapolating a trend is to estimate the following simple regression equation:

$$EPS_t = a + b(Year_t)$$

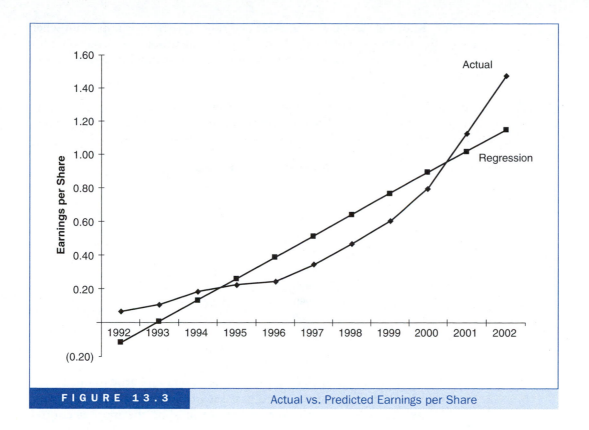

FIGURE 13.3   Actual vs. Predicted Earnings per Share

So earnings are the dependent variable and year is the independent variable. The parameters *a* and *b* are the estimated intercept and slope. Using the data shown in Figure 13.2, we come up with this regression equation:

$$EPS_t = -252.557 + 0.127(Year_t)$$

Plugging in 2003 as our year, we get the following estimate of earnings:

$$EPS_{2003} = -252.557 + 0.127(2003) = \$1.28$$

Comparing the two trend-based forecasts reveals two obvious points. First, the two forecasts are different. The forecast that uses the compound growth rate is quite a bit higher than the regression forecast ($2.01 versus $1.28). Second, the regression forecast of 2003 earnings is actually less than the actual earnings for fiscal 2002. So the regression forecast is not likely to be particularly accurate.

You can see the problem with the regression forecast by looking at the chart shown in Figure 13.3. Notice that even though earnings generally increased, they didn't increase in a linear fashion. The regression fits a line to the data. As a result, in this example the regression line underestimates earnings during the beginning and end of the period while overestimating earnings during the middle of the period.

In some cases, trend-based forecasts are very accurate, but they tell the analyst little about how a company makes money, and what causes its earnings to rise or fall. Knowing the answers to these and other questions is important when assessing the investment potential of a stock. Consequently, analysts rely on more sophisticated techniques when estimating earnings. Most build business models, which we discuss in the next section.

So far we discussed two techniques for estimating earnings, which involve extrapolating the historical trend. The following data show 11 years' worth of earnings for a company. Use these data to answer the following questions:

Fiscal Year	Earnings
1992	0.508
1993	0.630
1994	0.760
1995	0.915
1996	1.060
1997	0.935
1998	1.190
1999	1.350
2000	1.600
2001	1.915
2002	2.205

1. Estimate 2003 earnings by finding the average compound growth rate.
2. Estimate 2003 earnings using a trend-based regression equation.
3. Of the two forecasts, which do you believe may be the more accurate? Explain your answer.

Business Models

business model

A model of how a company operates and makes money.

A **business model** is merely a model of how a company operates and makes money. A business model generates a pro forma income statement and an estimate of earnings, but it also can provide much more detailed insight for the analyst. A business model breaks revenues and expenses down into greater detail and identifies the key drivers of profitability. This additional detail helps the analyst fine-tune the forecast and adjust it to changes in the company's operating and financial environment. The typical business model consists of both qualitative and quantitative elements. The model can take a top-down approach, a bottom-up approach, or a combination of the two approaches.

The easiest way to understand how to build and use a business model is to go through an example. We will build a business model for Kohl's Corporation. Our purpose is not to make you an expert on either the retailing industry or Kohl's, but rather to give you a feel for the kinds of information analysts need to understand to properly do their jobs.

For this business model example we refer frequently to Figure 13.4, which presents five years' worth of income statements and operating statistics for Kohl's.

Understanding the Business In order to build a business model you must first have a broad understanding of the business. Retailing is a fairly simple business, and Kohl's is fairly simple retailer. Retailers sell a variety of merchandise

Income Statement ($ millions)	Fiscal Year (ending January 31)				
	2002	2001	2000	1999	1998
Sales	7,488.7	6,152.0	4,557.1	3,681.8	3,060.1
Cost of goods sold	4,913.6	4,049.9	3,013.8	2,447.3	2,046.5
Gross profit	2,575.1	2,102.1	1,543.3	1,234.5	1,013.6
Operating expenses	1,558.0	1,317.6	1,006.2	826.6	697.4
Operating income	1,017.1	784.5	537.1	407.9	316.2
Depreciation	167.0	133.3	88.8	70.2	57.7
EBIT	850.1	651.2	448.3	337.7	258.5
Other income (net)	7.2	3.1	2.3	1.8	0.8
Interest	57.4	49.3	29.5	22.7	24.3
Earnings before taxes	799.9	605.0	421.1	316.8	235.0
Taxes	304.2	233.0	163.0	124.5	93.8
Net income	495.7	372.0	258.1	192.3	141.2
Earnings per share	1.48	1.13	0.80	0.61	0.47
Dividends per share	0.00	0.00	0.00	0.00	0.00
Stock price (year-end)	67.67	65.91	37.91	34.50	20.05
Number of stores (year-end)	382	320	259	213	182
Same store sales growth	6.8%	9.0%	7.9%	7.9%	10.0%
Percent of Sales	**2002**	**2001**	**2000**	**1999**	**1998**
Sales	100.0%	100.0%	100.0%	100.0%	100.0%
Cost of goods sold	65.6%	65.8%	66.1%	66.5%	66.9%
Gross profit	34.4%	34.2%	33.9%	33.5%	33.1%
Operating expenses	20.8%	21.4%	22.1%	22.5%	22.8%
Operating income	13.6%	12.8%	11.8%	11.1%	10.3%
Depreciation	2.2%	2.2%	1.9%	1.9%	1.9%
EBIT	11.4%	10.6%	9.8%	9.2%	8.4%
Other income (net)	0.1%	0.1%	0.1%	0.0%	0.0%
Interest	0.8%	0.8%	0.6%	0.6%	0.8%
Earnings before taxes	10.7%	9.8%	9.2%	8.6%	7.7%
Taxes	4.1%	3.8%	3.6%	3.4%	3.1%
Net income	6.6%	6.0%	5.7%	5.2%	4.6%

FIGURE 13.4

Income Statements and Operating Statistics for Kohl's Corporation

that they, in turn, purchase from suppliers. Kohl's has only one type of store. Its stores are not located in enclosed malls; they are freestanding, and all are about the same size and carry the same mix of merchandise. As you can see from Figure 13.4, Kohl's expanded rapidly by adding dozens of new stores each year. Although Kohl's does sell merchandise online, only a tiny portion of its sales come from channels other than its retail stores.

Sales Armed with some general knowledge of the retailing industry and Kohl's, we can now attempt to estimate sales for the 2003 fiscal year. Sales come from two primary sources: existing stores (stores open the entire year) and new stores

(stores open for less than the entire year). Kohl's ended the 2002 fiscal year with 382 stores. Let's assume that it open 60 new stores during the 2003 fiscal year and will open them at a constant rate during the year. Therefore, the company will have an average of 412 stores open the entire year (382 plus one-half of 60).

Now, we need to estimate sales per store for the 2003 fiscal year. During the 2002 fiscal year, Kohl's added 62 new stores. If we also assume that these stores were opened at a constant rate during the year, the firm had an average of 351 stores open the entire 2002 fiscal year. Dividing 351 into its 2002 fiscal year sales, $7,488.7 million, gives us sales per store of $21.34 million. Same-store sales growth—sales for stores open for at least one year—ranged between 6.8% and 10% over the past five years. If we assume that same-store sales growth will fall slightly to 6.7% for the 2003 fiscal year, sales per store will equal $22.76 million [($21.34)(1.067)]. Given that Kohl's will have 412 stores open the entire year, our estimate of 2003 fiscal year sales equals $9,379.1 million [(412)($22.76)].

Gross Profit The major expense for any retailer is the cost of the merchandise it sells. According to the income statements shown in Figure 13.4, the cost of goods sold, as a percentage of sales, ranged between 66.9% and 65.6%. The trend suggests that this percentage decreased (i.e., the gross profit margin rose). Let's assume that for the 2003 fiscal year, the cost of goods sold will equal 65.5%. Consequently, we estimate the company's gross profit at $3,235.8 million (34.5% of sales).

Taxable Income After estimating gross profit, we need to estimate some other expenses in order to get to taxable income. Next to the cost of goods sold, the most significant expenses for a retailer are operating expenses, which include everything from employee wages to the cost of utilities. Aside from operating expenses, other expenses include depreciation and interest.

Over the five years shown in Figure 13.4, operating expenses, depreciation, and interest equaled 25.4% to 23.7% of sales (including a small adjustment for "other" income). The trend for this percentage is clearly falling. It was 25.4% in fiscal year 1998 and 23.7% in fiscal year 2002. Let's assume it continues to fall, albeit slightly, for the 2003 fiscal year to 23.6%. Multiplying this percentage by our sales estimate, $9,379.1 million, and subtracting the result, $2,213.5 million, from gross profit gives us an estimate of taxable income: $1,022.3 million

Net Income and Earnings per Share Assuming taxes remain at 4.1% of sales, which they were in fiscal year 2002, taxes for the 2003 fiscal year will equal $384.5 million. Subtracting taxes from taxable income gives us an estimate of net income: $637.8 million.

At the end of the 2002 fiscal year, Kohl's had about 334.9 million shares of common stock outstanding. Dividing 334.9 million into $637.8 million equals an estimate of earnings per share for fiscal year 2003 of $1.90. This forecast represents an increase of about 29% over fiscal year 2002 earnings of $1.48 per share. The increase results from a combination of strong sales growth, 25%, coupled with a slight increase in the net profit margin from 6.6% to 6.8%.

The text covered a lot of ground coming up with the earnings forecast. The steps are summarized in Figure 13.5.

Step 1: Estimate 2003 fiscal year sales

Number of stores (2002 year end)	382
Number of new stores (2003)	60
Average number of stores	412
Sales per store (2002)	$21.34 million
Same-store sales growth	6.7%
Sales per store (2003)	$22.76 million
Sales estimate (2003)	$9,379.1 million

Step 2: Estimate 2003 fiscal year gross profit margin

Sales estimate (2003)	$9,379.1 million
Estimated gross profit margin	34.5%
Gross profit (2003)	$3,235.8 million

Step 3: Estimate 2003 fiscal year taxable income

Gross profit (2003)	$3,235.8 million
Operating and other expenses (% of sales)	23.6%
Operating and other expenses (2003)	$2,213.5 million
Taxable income (2003)	$1,022.3 million

Step 4: Estimate 2003 fiscal year net income and earnings per share

Taxable income (2003)	$1,022.3 million
Taxes (% of sales)	4.1%
Taxes (2003)	$384.5 million
Net income (2003)	$637.8 million
Number of shares outstanding	335.68 million
Earnings per share (2003)	$1.90

FIGURE 13.5

Summary of Earnings Forecast for Kohl's Corporation

Sensitivity Analysis

sensitivity analysis

A technique for testing the assumptions of a forecast.

The business model forecast of fiscal year 2003 earnings of $1.90 per share is on the high end of analyst forecasts (they range from $1.81 per share to $1.91 per share). What could go wrong with the $1.90 forecast? Well, lots of things. For one thing, we made more than a few assumptions, and those assumptions may turn out to be wrong.

Consequently, it is useful to test the sensitivity of a forecast to changes in assumptions. By doing this type of test you identify the key drivers in your forecast. These variables are the factors to which you should pay close attention. If key drivers show evidence of changing more or less than expected, you can adjust your forecast appropriately.

Sensitivity analysis is one technique for identifying the key drivers. It requires a listing of each of your variables, which are then change one at a time by some fixed percentage, keeping the other variables constant, to see which has the greatest impact on your forecast.

As an example, let's go back to our Kohl's Corporation earnings forecast and see how sensitive it is to changes in three assumptions: same-store sales growth, gross profit margin, and operating and other expenses as a percentage of sales. For the following original estimates and the revised estimates, note that all of the revised estimates are 5% higher or lower than the original estimate, and are revised in such a way as to lower earnings per share.

Variable	Original Estimate	Revised Estimate
Same-store sales growth	6.7%	6.3%
Gross profit margin	34.5%	32.8%
Operating and other expenses (% of sales)	23.6%	24.8%

The results of the sensitivity analysis follow. As you can see, the sensitivity of the earnings forecasts varies substantially from variable to variable. For example, a five percent decrease in same-store sales growth (from 6.7% to about 6.3%), results in a change in earnings per share of less than a penny. On the other hand, if the gross profit margin falls to 32.8% (from 34.5%), earning per share falls to $1.43 per share. An increase in operating and other expenses (as a percentage of sales) also results in a material decline in earnings.

Original forecast	$1.90
Slower same-store sales growth	$1.90
Lower gross profit margin	$1.43
Higher operating and other expenses	$1.57

So, what can we conclude? For one thing, it would take a major change in same-store sales growth, up or down, to have a significant impact on earnings. On the other hand, any change in profit margin will result in a material change in earnings. Heavy discounting in response to a weak economy, increased competition, or both will negatively affect earnings, even if sales increase. An analyst following Kohl's and other retailers would be well advised to pay close attention to costs and profit margins.

RECAP RECAP

Use the Kohl's business model to reestimate 2003 earnings, assuming the following. (Use original estimates for other variables.)

4. Same-store sales growth increases to 8.5% and gross profit margin falls to 33.5%.

FORECASTING OTHER FINANCIAL VARIABLES

In addition to earnings, the analyst may wish to forecast several other financial variables. Three of these include common stock dividends, after tax cash flow, and the required rate of return.

Dividends

Once the analyst arrives at a forecast of earnings, forecasting dividends is relatively straightforward. Although not all companies follow reasonably predictable dividend policies, companies that pay dividends often aim to pay out a certain

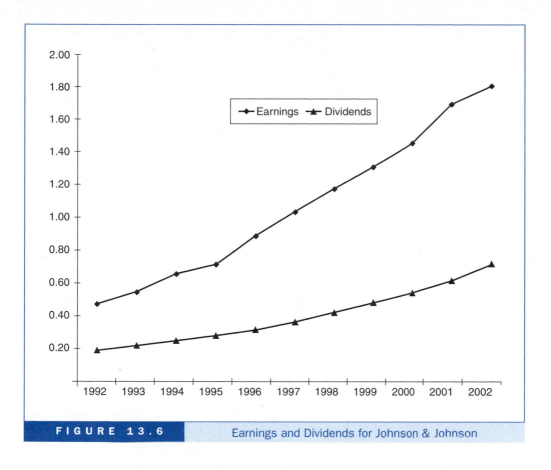

| FIGURE 13.6 | Earnings and Dividends for Johnson & Johnson |

percentage of earnings in dividends, so as earnings increase, dividends will tend to increase as well. If you covered dividend policy in your introductory finance class you may remember that dividends are much more stable from year to year than earnings, and most companies are reluctant to cut dividends, even if earnings decline.

In the case of Kohl's, estimating dividends is easy. The company has never paid a common stock dividend since it went public in the early 1990s. A zero payout policy is not uncommon for rapidly growing firms. We project that Kohl's will continue to grow rapidly Consequently, it is likely that Kohl's will continue its zero payout policy for the foreseeable future.

As another example, let's turn to Johnson & Johnson. Unlike Kohl's, Johnson & Johnson paid common stock dividends for many years. Moreover, as Figure 13.6 illustrates, dividends rose along with earnings. In fact, over the past 10 years, dividends increased by about 14% per year. The current dividend is 72 cents per share, so a reasonable forecast for next year's dividend would be 14% higher, or around 82 cents per share.

Cash Flow

Some analysts believe that a better measure of profitability is after-tax cash flow rather than earnings. To these analysts, a pattern of rising cash flow is more interesting than a pattern of rising earnings. After all, the company uses cash, not earnings, to pay bills, buy back shares, or make capital investments. As you no doubt remember from accounting, and something we touched on briefly in the prior chapter, on a year-to-year basis, earnings and cash flow can be quite different. Two main reasons explain the differences: accounting rules give companies some leeway when it comes to reporting incomes and expenses; and certain expenses—most notably depreciation—do not represent real bills to be paid. So, how do you calculate after-tax cash flow?

Although various methods are used for calculating after-tax cash flow, the conventional measure of cash flow takes net income, subtracts preferred stock dividends (if any), and then adds depreciation and other noncash expenses (as given in the income statement). Dividing after-tax cash flow by the number of outstanding shares gives you cash flow per share.

free cash flow

Cash flow from operations minus common stock dividends, minus capital expenditures.

You will also run across the term *free cash flow*. Free cash flow is generally defined as cash flow from operations (as reported in the statement of cash flows) minus capital expenditures minus common stock dividends.[6] Opinions differ, however, as to whether free cash flow is any more meaningful than more conventional measures of cash flow when it comes to measuring how much money a company is really making. Common stock dividends are optional and most companies can survive reduced capital spending, at least for a short period of time.

Regardless of which measure of cash flow you use, estimating cash flow requires that you first estimate earnings. You then need, depending on the cash flow measure you use, to estimate depreciation, the change in working capital, cash dividends, and capital expenditures.

Let's return to the Kohl's example. We estimated its fiscal 2003 earnings at $637.8 million. Adding back the estimated depreciation expense gives us one measure of cash flow. Going back to Figure 13.4, you notice that depreciation historically was about 2% of sales. Given our estimate of fiscal 2003 sales, $9,379.1 million, a reasonable estimate of fiscal 2003 depreciation is $187.6 million [($9,379.1)(.02)]. Adding depreciation to our estimate of earnings gives us an estimate of after-tax cash flow: $825.4 million.

Required Return

A final variable analysts often estimate is the required return on a stock. One of the foundations of finance is that risk and return are positively related—higher risk investments must offer higher expected returns. As discussed in Chapter 2, the required return on any investment equals the nominal return on a risk-free investment (a combination of the real return and compensation for expected inflation) plus a risk premium.

For common stocks, one method of estimating the required return is to use the so-called capital asset pricing model (or CAPM). It states that the required return on a stock equals:

Risk-free rate + Beta(Market risk premium)

---

[6]Cash flow from operations generally equals net income plus depreciation (and other noncash expenses) minus the change in working capital. An increase in working capital is considered to be a use of cash, while a decrease in working capital is considered to be a source of cash.

INVESTMENT INSIGHT

Are Stocks Really Riskier Than Bonds?

Conventional wisdom says that stocks are riskier investments than bonds. Consequently, in order to get investors to buy stocks, instead of bonds, stocks have to promise higher returns. As a result, a so-called risk premium should be built into the required return on stocks.

Although still a minority, a number of academics and professionals—let's call them "revisionists"—now question conventional wisdom regarding the risk of stocks relative to that of bonds. Some even go so far as to argue that stocks are in reality no riskier than bonds, and in fact may actually be less risky. We may not be quite ready to fully endorse the revisionist viewpoint, but it is important to understand their argument. So, on what do they base their argument?

Essentially revisionists argue that conventional wisdom is based on the short-term volatility of stocks. Undeniably, over short periods of time, stock prices are highly volatile—a fact even the most casual observer of the financial markets knows. For example, if you reviewed the monthly returns from stocks since the mid-1920s, you would observe that stocks returns were positive only about 53% of the time. You would also note that on an annual basis, the standard deviation of stock returns is more than twice the standard deviation of bond returns. Therefore, based on these observations, a substantial risk premium needs to be offered to induce investors to buy stocks. In fact, since the mid-1920s stock returns exceeded bond returns by about 7% per year. Conventional wisdom concludes that 7%, or thereabouts, is the "proper" equity risk premium.

According to the revisionists an equity risk premium of about 7% is too high because stocks are much less risky if one looks beyond short-term volatility. Again, examining historical returns you would observe that much of the short-term volatility in stock returns disappears over longer and longer holding periods. Since the mid-1920s, stocks rose in only about three out of four years, so investors stood a one-in-four chance of losing money. Not great odds. On the other hand, over rolling five-year periods since the mid-1920s, stock investors made money 90% of the time. Over rolling 20-year periods, stocks made money each and every time. Further, as the length of the holding period increases, the annualized standard deviation of stock returns falls sharply. In fact, for holding periods of 10 years or longer, the annualized standard deviation of stock returns is actually less than the annualized standard deviation of bond returns. By taking a longer-term perspective, revisionists argue, stocks are not any riskier than bonds. Therefore, the equity risk premium ought to be closer to zero.

What does all the fuss over the correct size of the equity risk premium mean to investors? It could mean a great deal. It could mean that a historic buying opportunity in stocks awaits, especially given the recent decline in stock prices. If the "correct" risk premium is close to zero, stocks are substantially undervalued. Are the revisionists right? It is a question each and every investor must answer for him or herself.

Questions for Critical Thinking

1. What are the problems with using historical averages to estimate variables such as the market risk premium?
2. Why does much of the volatility in stock prices disappear over longer holding periods? What are some of the practical implications for investors?

Beta is a measure of a stock's risk—the higher a stock's beta, the greater the risk. By definition the overall stock market has a beta of 1.00. The market risk premium is the required return on the overall market minus the risk-free rate.

CAPM comes from modern portfolio theory, which we discussed briefly in Chapter 2 and will discuss in more depth starting in Chapter 17. For now a simple example of how use CAPM will suffice. We need to estimate three variables: beta, the risk-free rate, and the market risk premium. According to Standard & Poor's, Kohl's has a beta of 1.11. The current yield on long-term Treasury securities—a proxy for the risk-free rate—is about 4%. Historically, stocks managed an average annual return about 7% higher than the average annual return from long-term Treasury bonds. As the Investment Insight box discusses, some believe that stocks really are not that much riskier than bonds. Thus, the correct size of the market risk premium is much less than 7%. For now, however, we use 7% as a proxy for the market risk premium.

Putting it all together then, the required return for Kohl's is equal to:

$$4\% + 1.11(7\%) = 11.8\%$$

How the required return is actually used to value stocks is explained in the next chapter.

In this chapter we discussed the importance of estimating earnings when analyzing the investment potential of common stocks. We also described several methods for estimating earnings. The next chapter presents stock valuation models and ties together all the material on security analysis.

SUMMARY

1. Is there a long-term relationship between earnings and stock prices?
The evidence strongly suggests that, in the long run, a positive relationship exists between earnings and stock prices. Most research concludes that earnings, and the growth rate in earnings, explain much of the variation in stock returns over time. Further, studies show that announcements of actual earnings that are higher (lower) than expected result in significant positive (negative) returns around the announcement date.

2. How are earnings calculated?
Several measures are used to calculate earnings per share, including basic earnings from total operations, basic earnings from continuing operations, and basic earnings from discontinued operations. In addition, companies report diluted measures of earnings—assuming convertibles, warrants, and employee stock options are converted into new shares of common stock. Most large Wall Street brokerage and investment firms employ analysts who follow specific stocks and forecast earnings. Consensus forecasts are the forecast average. The range of earnings forecasts is often a measure of the degree uncertainty surrounding forecasts.

3. What are the simple quantitative methods for forecasting earnings?
Several approaches can be taken to earnings forecasting. Quantitative forecasts rely on an explicit statistical or mathematical model. Qualitative forecasts rely on subjective judgments made by the analyst without direct reference to any statistical or mathematical model. Bottom-up forecasts begin by determining the relationship between earnings and firm-specific variables. Top-down forecasts begin by determining the relationship between earnings and economic and industry variables. Some simple quantitative methods for forecasting earnings involve extrapolating the trend in historical earnings. Two methods work by calculating the average growth rate or by estimating a trend-based regression.

4. How are business models used to forecast earnings?
Most analysts forecast earnings by building a business model of the company. A business model is merely a model of how a company operates and makes money. A business model will generate a pro forma income statement and an estimate of earnings. At the same time, however, a business model provides much more insight into both revenues and expenses, and helps the analyst identify the key drivers of profitability. The analyst can fine-tune his or her forecast and adjust it to changes in a company's operating and financial environment.

5. What are some of the other financial variables the analyst needs to estimate?

In addition to earnings, three other financial variables are estimated by analysts: dividends, after-tax cash flow, and the required rate of return. Dividend forecasts are often derived from earnings forecasts. Forecasting dividends is less daunting a task than forecasting earnings because companies tend to follow identifiable dividend policies that rarely change from year to year. Some analysts believe cash flow, not earnings, is the better measure of how much money a company is really making. The most conventional measure of cash flow is to take net income, subtract preferred stock dividends (if any), and then add back depreciation (and any other non-cash expenses). The required rate of return is the return a stock should earn, given its risk. A common way of estimating the required rate of return is to use the capital asset pricing model.

REVIEW EXERCISES

1. What is the general relationship between earnings and stock prices? Research concluded that what two variables explain major portions of the variation in stock returns?
2. Explain the difference between basic earnings per share and diluted measures of earnings per share. Why is one never lower than the other?
3. What is meant by a *consensus earnings forecast?* Is the range of earnings forecasts of any interest?
4. What is the difference between a top-down and a bottom-up approach to earnings? Give some examples of industries where a top-down approach might be more appropriate than a bottom-up approach.
5. What is a trend-based earnings forecast? What are the limitations of trend-based forecasts?
6. The following data show 11 years' worth of earnings for Home Depot. Using these data, find the average compound growth rate and an estimate of earnings for next year.

Year	Earnings
1	0.07
2	0.11
3	0.15
4	0.20
5	0.27
6	0.34
7	0.44
8	0.51
9	0.65
10	0.80
11	1.10

7. Using the data given in Question 6, estimate a simple regression where earnings is the dependent variable and time is the independent variable. Use the regression to forecast earnings for next year.
8. Explain a business model. Why do most analysts build business models when forecasting earnings?
9. Why do some analysts feel cash flow is a better measure than earnings of a company's true profitability? Explain the difference between the conventional measure of cash flow and so-called free cash flow.
10. What is a company's required rate of return. If a company has a beta of .95, and the risk-free rate is 5% and the market risk premium is 8%, what is the company's required rate of return?

CRITICAL THINKING EXERCISES

1. This exercise requires computer work. Open the Home Depot worksheet in the Data Workbook available on the text Web site (http://hearth.swlearning.com). The worksheet contains 11 years of financial and operating data for the company. Use the data to answer the following questions:
   a. Estimate fiscal 2004 earnings by extrapolating the trend in the data. Critique your forecasts. In other words, are they of any value?
   b. Build a business model for Home Depot and use the model to estimate 2004 earnings. Clearly state and justify your assumptions.
   c. Test the sensitivity of your business model-based earnings forecast. What appear to be the key drivers to profitability?
2. This exercise requires both computer work and library/Internet research. In the chapter we built a business model for Kohl's Corporation and used the model to estimate fiscal 2003 earnings. Research actual fiscal 2003 earnings (you will need to compile both financial and operating statistics) and compare our forecast to the actual earnings. Where did we go wrong?
3. The exercise requires both computer work and library/Internet research. Use the business model we built for Kohl's in the chapter to forecast fiscal 2004 earnings. Clearly state and justify your assumptions.

THE INTERNET INVESTOR

1. Search one of the investment-oriented Web sites (such as finance.yahoo.com or www.quicken.com) for a recent major earnings surprise, one where the difference between the actual and consensus forecast was at least 10%. What did the analysts appear to miss?
2. Go to the following Web site: investor.msn.com. Click on the section entitled Analyst Info. Look up information on consensus forecasts for next year's earnings, the range of forecasts, and earnings surprises for the following companies: American Express, Boeing, Dell Computer, First Energy, and Procter & Gamble.
   a. Which company showed the most agreement by the analysts over forecasts for next year's earnings? The least agreement? Can you explain why agreement was high for one company but much less for another?
   b. Which company experienced the most earnings surprises in recent quarters? Were the surprises positive or negative?
   c. Click on the section entitled Ratings. Do the earnings forecasts correspond with how analysts rate the stocks (strong buy, buy, hold, etc.)? Why or why not?
3. Management often provides an earnings forecast in the annual report to shareholders. Today most companies place copies of their annual reports on their Web sites. Pick a well-known company and visit its Web site. Read the most recent annual report, specifically the opinion of management concerning future earnings. Compare management's forecast to analyst forecasts.

Fundamentals of Common Stock Valuation

PREVIOUSLY . . .	IN THIS CHAPTER . . .	TO COME . . .
We discussed how to analyze various financial aspects of a company with the general expectation that a financially sound company is a "good" investment. The chapter included many factors that may help an investor assess the value of a company and how it may affect its common stock.	We describe methods to value common stocks so that you can make better investment decisions. By understanding the underlying process, investors can better estimate a stock's fundamental value and then determine whether it is a good investment. The chapter gives conceptual and practical discussions and a step-by-step process to estimate a fundamental value for Lone Star Steakhouse, a casual dining establishment known for its Texas-style fare.	As you gain experience in common stock investing, you may become interested in another avenue of investment—derivative securities. We discuss the risks and rewards associated with these speculative investment securities known as options and futures.

CHAPTER OBJECTIVES
After reading Chapter 14, you should be able to answer the following questions:

1. What is intrinsic value?

2. What is the dividend discount model (DDM)?

3. What is the earnings model (EM)?

4. How does an investor conduct fundamental analysis on a company stock?

5. How can an investor value a stock with nonconstant growth?

6. How is the market-to-book ratio used for investment purposes?

7. What are the pros and cons of using the price/earnings multiple, or P/E ratio?

How does an investor determine a common stock's fundamental value? Suppose we call the fundamental value a stock's true value. How would you determine it? To illustrate how difficult it may be to estimate a common stock's true value, let's consider IBM, a company whose stock price changed significantly after its restructuring in 1993.

In late 1993, under the helm of a new CEO, Louis Gerstner, IBM underwent a major restructuring to increase its stock price from its historical low of about $40 per share. Since the restructuring, many analysts and investors alike, believed that IBM's value improved and they invested in IBM's common stock. By 1996, its stock traded in the $83 to $135 per share range. Although everyone following the news seem to agree that its true value rose from its low, it brings up an important question about the true value of IBM. What is IBM's true value? Is it less than or more than $100 per share now? If it is more, how much more? By December 1999, IBM stock was trading about $400 (adjusted for two 2-for-1 stock splits, one in 1997 and another in 1999); not a bad investment if you bought IBM between 1993 and 1999. However, by 2002, with the tech bust and the economy in a recession, IBM was trading in the $60s ($240 adjusted for stock splits).

Although this history may be an unusual example of a company making drastic changes and thereby increasing its value, it illustrates that the company's true value can be an elusive number. Therefore, it is helpful to develop an understanding of it. Perhaps we can determine what IBM's true value may be.

The true value of a stock is called its intrinsic value. Intrinsic value is important because the investor can base a relatively simple strategy on it. The investor would buy the stock if its market price fell below its intrinsic value and sell it, or sell it short, if its market price rose above its intrinsic value. In an efficient market, the market price should eventually match the intrinsic value, so an investor can profit by buying stocks selling at less than their intrinsic values. Conversely, selling short stocks whose market prices exceed their intrinsic values should generate profits as the market prices fall to the intrinsic values. This basic strategy focuses on finding securities whose prices are out of line with their intrinsic values.

We start this chapter with an intuitive discussion of intrinsic value, then we discuss quantitative models by which the analyst can determine intrinsic values. We begin with the basic dividend discount model (DDM), which implies that a stock's value is simply the present value of its expected future dividends. Next, we turn to the earnings model (EM), which posits that stock prices are a function, not only of expected future dividends but also of the growth of earnings due to companies' investment opportunities. The earnings model allows us to closely examine the real meanings of the widely used terms *growth company* and *growth stock*. Some stocks may be incorrectly labeled growth stocks. Finally, we review two common measures of stocks' values: the market-to-book ratio (MV/BV) and the price/earnings ratio (P/E) ratio. This discussion highlights possible pitfalls of buying only stocks that appear to be cheap.

INTRINSIC VALUE

Back in Chapter 8, we described the major differences between technical and fundamental analysis. Briefly, technical analysis is based on the belief that past patterns in security prices can be used to reliably predict future price patterns. By contrast, fundamental analysis is based on the notion that every security has an intrinsic value determined by future expectations about the company.

Our earlier characterization of an intrinsic value as the true value of a security gives little insight into estimating it. The **intrinsic value** of a stock is defined as the fundamental economic value of the issuing company's equity.[1] A simple intuitive generalization of what creates value of a stock can clarify our definition.

A company produces goods and services, which it sells. We refer to these products as *projects* or *investment opportunities* of the company. For example, Ford's projects produce goods such as cars and trucks, and Walt Disney's projects provide services such as entertainment and relaxation from its films and theme parks. Both firms undertake their projects to generate sales. After paying taxes and other expenses from sales revenues, the remaining amount is the company's net profits or earnings. These earnings are the cash returns to the stockholders for investing in the equity of the company. Conceptually, then, the fundamental economic value of a stock is the economic value of these projects, or the present value of the cash returns to stockholders who invest in the company's equity.

Although we admit that this definition ignores other aspects of company operations, a fundamental quantifiable economic value (or intrinsic value) is in essence the present value of the expected future earnings that its investment opportunities will generate. Based on some assumptions we discuss later, the intrinsic value of a common stock also equals the present value of the company's future dividends.

In this chapter, we present four models by which to estimate the intrinsic value of a common stock. At the outset, we should point out that these models are simplified generalizations and may be difficult to apply to all common stocks. However, although the model might yield only a rough estimate in some cases, the process still builds important insights into the factors that determine stock prices in the real world.

intrinsic value

Fundamental economic value of issuing company's equity; rationally reflects all relevant publicly available information and, perhaps, privately available information.

DIVIDEND DISCOUNT MODEL (DDM)

If any generalization is safe, we can surely say that most investors purchase common stocks with expectations of making profits from their investments. More specifically, though, profits come in two forms: periodic cash dividend payments and capital appreciation from selling the stock at a price higher than the purchase price. How can an investor evaluate the expected profit from an investment? Even when investors do not bother to formally determine values systematically, most make at least an informal assessment of intrinsic value. Suppose for a moment that someone can travel forward 20 years (to Year 20) and find that a common stock will sell for $18.00 per share and pay an annual dividend of $1.00 per share. If that person requires a 16% return on the stock (i.e., if the required rate of return on stock, ER_s, is 0.16), in Year 19, that investor would be willing to pay

$$V_{s19} = \frac{\$1.00 + \$18.00}{(1 + 0.16)} = \$16.38$$

where V_{s19} is defined as the intrinsic value of the stock in Year 19.

---

[1]Economic value is calculated as the present value of a series of cash flows. Shortly, we review the sources of the cash flows.

In symbols, this looks like

$$V_{s19} = \frac{\text{DIV}_{20} + V_{s20}}{(1 + ER_s)} \tag{14.1}$$

In Year 19, the intrinsic price of the stock just equals the present value of its Year 20 cash flow, $16.38 at a 16% required return. Stated differently, if someone pays $16.38 for the stock in Year 19 expecting cash flows over the next year of $19.00, then the investment will earn an expected return, ER_s, of 16% (0.16).

Suppose that this time traveler decides to invest in Year 18, instead, to earn cash flows equal to the sum of Year 19 and Year 20 dividends (DIV_{19} and DIV_{20}) plus the selling price of the stock in Year 20 (V_{s20}). This investor would be willing to pay

$$V_{s18} = \frac{\text{DIV}_{19}}{(1 + ER_s)} + \frac{\text{DIV}_{20} + V_{s20}}{(1 + ER_s)^2} \tag{14.2}$$

Assuming dividends in Years 19 and 20 equal to $1.00 and an expected Year 20 price of $18.00,

$$V_{s18} = \frac{\$1.00}{(1 + 0.16)} + \frac{\$1.00 + \$18.00}{(1 + 0.16)^2} = \$14.98$$

The stock's present value in Year 18 is less than its value in Year 19. Although it pays an extra dollar in dividends in Year 19, the cash flow from the dividend and expected selling price ($19.00) occurs a year later, in Year 20, and the present value of $19.00 is less two years earlier, in Year 18, than one year earlier, in Year 19.

This pattern continues as the traveler returns back from Year 17 through Year 1, and finally, to Year 0, today. To invest at Year 0, using the same logic, the investor would be willing to pay

$$V_{s0} = \frac{\text{DIV}_1}{(1 + ER_s)} + \frac{\text{DIV}_2}{(1 + ER_s)^2} + \cdots + \frac{\text{DIV}_{19}}{(1 + ER_s)^{19}} + \frac{\text{DIV}_{20} + V_{s20}}{(1 + ER_s)^{20}} \tag{14.3}$$

Inserting values for expected dividends of $1 per year from Year 1 to Year 20, a Year 20 selling price of $18.00, and a required return of 16%, the value of the stock today equals

$$V_{s0} = \frac{\$1.00}{(1 + 0.16)} + \frac{\$1.00}{(1 + 0.16)^2} + \cdots + \frac{\$1.00}{(1 + 0.16)^{19}} + \frac{\$1.00 + \$18.00}{(1 + 0.16)^{20}} = \$6.85$$

Would the Year 18 valuation of $V_{s18} = \$14.98$ give the same value, V_{s0}, today? Yes, it would! Recall that V_{s18} is the present value of cash flows from Year 19 and Year 20 (Equation 14.2). So, you are just substituting V_{s18} ($14.98) for the present value of DIV_{19}, DIV_{20}, plus V_{20}.

$$V_{s0} = \frac{\$1.00}{(1 + 0.16)} + \frac{\$1.00}{(1 + 0.16)^2} + \cdots + \frac{\$1.00}{(1 + 0.16)^{17}} + \frac{\$1.00 + \$14.98}{(1 + 0.16)^{18}} = \$6.85$$

Two Implications

Two major implications stem from these numerical examples.

Implication 1 The Year 18 price, V_{s18}, in the preceding example is a present value of the Year 19 and Year 20 future dividends and future price, V_{s20}. It implies that the investment holding period is irrelevant for determining the intrinsic value. If you sell it in Year 20 or Year 18, its intrinsic value today still equals $6.85.

Implication 2 The present value of a selling price far in the future, such as Year 20 (V_{s20} = $18.00), is small. (The present value of $18.00 in Year 20 equals only $0.925.) This implication allows us to ignore the future price (which is virtually impossible to predict) because its impact on the intrinsic value is negligible.

General Dividend Discount Model

Now, suppose the investor travels past Year 20 to an indefinite point in the future, Year N. The general **dividend discount model (DDM)** formula equals

$$V_{s0} = \sum_{t=1}^{N} \frac{\text{DIV}_t}{(1 + ER_s)^t} + \frac{V_{sN}}{(1 + ER_s)^N} \tag{14.4}$$

dividend discount model (DDM)

Method of evaluating the intrinsic value of a stock based on the present value of expected dividends.

Remember from Implication 2 that the present value of the price in Year N, V_{sN}, can be ignored because it is virtually equal to zero. This implication allows the model to approximate the preceding equation by

$$V_{s0} \approx \sum_{t=1}^{N} \frac{\text{DIV}_t}{(1 + ER_s)^t} \tag{14.5}$$

If the dividends remain at $1 per year, the present value calculation is simple using a table of the present value of an annuity. However, if the expected dividends differ for each year, it can be a horrendous task (although it is much easier with a financial calculator). Fortunately, a simpler formula can accommodate dividends that are expected to grow at a constant rate, g.

Let's define the future dividend stream relative to the current dividend as follows:

$$\text{DIV}_1 = \text{DIV}_0(1 + g)$$
$$\text{DIV}_2 = \text{DIV}_0(1 + g)^2$$
$$\vdots$$
$$\text{DIV}_N = \text{DIV}_0(1 + g)^N$$

The general formula of Equation 14.5 can be rewritten to allow for growth in the dividends at a constant rate, g:

$$V_{s0} = \frac{\text{DIV}_0(1 + g)}{(1 + ER_s)} + \frac{\text{DIV}_0(1 + g)^2}{(1 + ER_s)^2} + \cdots + \frac{\text{DIV}_0(1 + g)^N}{(1 + ER_s)^N} \tag{14.6}$$

A constant growth sequence such as Equation 14.6 converges to

$$V_{s0} = \frac{DIV_0(1 + g)}{(ER_s - g)} \quad \text{or} \quad \frac{DIV_1}{(ER_s - g)} \tag{14.7}$$

This DDM assumes a constant growth rate and that $ER_s > g$. For practical purposes, we use Equation 14.7 exclusively because it is difficult, if not impossible, to accurately estimate future dividends for every year. We almost always assume that a firms' dividends will grow at a constant rate.

Let's go through an example for Lone Star Steakhouse (STAR), an international casual dining establishment that serves Texas-style fare.[2] Suppose that STAR pays a current annual dividend of $0.60 per share, which should grow at a constant annual rate of 8% indefinitely. Also, analysts estimate the company's required return, ER_s, at 10%. Using Equation 14.7, STAR's intrinsic value is approximately $32.

$$V_{s0} = \frac{\$0.60(1 + 0.08)}{(0.10 - 0.08)} = \$32.40$$

How does a fundamental analyst use this information? To compare the intrinsic value, V_{s0}, with the stock's market price, suppose that STAR is currently trading at about $21 in September 2002. Comparing the intrinsic value of $32.40 with the market price of $20.96, STAR appears to be undervalued. It is a bargain to buy at $21 because it is likely to increase to the fundamental economic value near $32.

The general rules for fundamental analysis prescribe trading strategies when a stock's market price differs from its intrinsic value. The two diagrams in Figure 14.1 depict the two possibilities. The horizontal line represents the intrinsic value ($32) and the Xs indicate market prices greater than or less than the intrinsic value. A market price less than the intrinsic value (V_{s0}) indicates an **undervalued** security. A market price greater than the intrinsic value indicates an **overvalued** security.

The development of the DDM implies that stock prices are valued by the dividends of the company alone, which seemed implicit in Implication 1. Yet, how can an analyst value stocks that pay no dividends? We can accommodate this situation later when we discuss the P/E ratio. First, however, let's discuss the earnings model because it provides important implications about valuing a stock's intrinsic value, whether it pays dividends or not.

undervalued

When the market price of a stock is less than the intrinsic value, the stock should be purchased.

overvalued

When the market price of a stock is greater than the intrinsic value, the stock should be sold or not purchased.

EARNINGS MODEL

earnings model (EM)

Method of estimating intrinsic value of common stock by estimating the present value of earnings for future investment opportunities generated by reinvesting earnings, or retained earnings.

The **earnings model (EM)** is another way to estimate the intrinsic value of a common stock. It derives the intrinsic value by dividing the earnings generated by the firm's future investment opportunities into two parts: (1) earnings that the firm pays out as cash dividends, and (2) earnings that it reinvests to fund future

---

[2]Here we provide the numbers and go through the calculation. In a later section we explain how to estimate each variable.

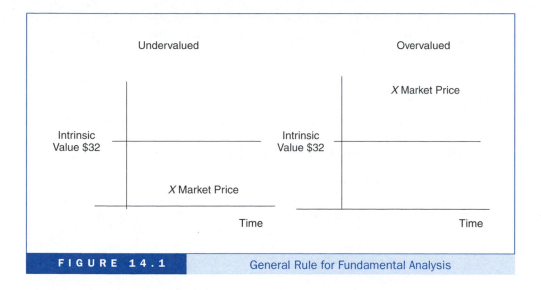

FIGURE 14.1 General Rule for Fundamental Analysis

investment opportunities. It also serves two purposes other than estimating an intrinsic value.

1. It can identify the underlying factors for a growth company's success.
2. It can contrast a growth company with a growth stock.

In fact, we could argue that future dividends are part of future earnings. Generally speaking, investors value expected dividend streams because those payments represent the return on their investments, but future dividend streams stem from future earnings, or profits, of the company. The EM takes this notion further, demonstrating that future earnings exist only because of investment opportunities, and increases in future earnings will exist if future investment opportunities exist. Also the EM adds another dimension to the analysis by clarifying the concept of growth companies; it provides five implications about growth companies and then contrasts a growth company and a growth stock. Through the EM, we hope to shed some light on these elusive terms.

Earnings Model Formula

The general formula for the EM is

$$V_{s0} = \frac{EPS_1}{ER_s} + \frac{EPS_1}{ER_s}\left[\frac{g - ER_s(b)}{ER_s - g}\right] \tag{14.8}$$

where EPS_1 is the expected earnings per share, ER_s is the required rate of return or the expected return, g is the expected constant annual growth rate, and b is the retention rate, or $(1 - \text{dividend payout ratio})$.

Equation 14.8 can be viewed as having two parts: the no-growth term defined by EPS_1/ER_s and the growth term defined by

$$\frac{EPS_1}{ER_s}\left[\frac{g - ER_s(b)}{ER_s - g}\right]$$

The no-growth term represents the present value of the company's flagship product, whereas the growth term represents the present values of the firm's other future investment opportunities. These growth opportunities are expected to grow at a constant rate, g.

Perhaps it is easiest to get an intuitive feel for the model by going through an example and then tying it to the formula. We use data from STAR to show how the model works.

Lone Star Steakhouse (STAR): An Earnings Model Example

No-Growth Term STAR's beginning was Texas-style mesquite grilled steaks, ribs, chicken, and fish in Texas. The founders are expecting earnings per share (EPS_1) to be $1.95 next year, and it anticipates no growth as it continues to serve at the Texas restaurant, promising shareholders all the profits.[3] The last condition sets the company's dividends per share equal to its earnings per share ($DIV_1 = EPS_1 = $1.95 per share). If STAR's profits remain at $1.95 per share forever and the shareholders require a return of 10% (ER_s), then the present value (PV) of the stock equals $1.95 times the present value of an annuity factor for 10% in perpetuity.[4] This calculation gives the present value of the stock as $19.50 per share. It is the amount that investors should pay for STAR's stock if its future growth rate equals zero.

This value can also be calculated by the no-growth term of the EM:

$$\text{PV of no growth term} = \frac{EPS_1}{ER_s} = \frac{\$1.95}{0.10} = \$19.50$$

Now suppose that the company begins innovative new projects that it expects to fuel growth at a constant rate. Let's explore how to determine the value of the constant growth term.

Constant Growth Term Now, suppose that STAR decides to branch out from casual dining to upscale steakhouses such as DelFrisco and Sullivan's Steakhouse. Investors expect these investments to return 11.5% to stockholders (or return on equity, ROE_1 is 11.5%) and STAR chooses to invest some of the company's current earnings for the new venture. STAR expects to pay $0.65 per share ($DIV_1$) as dividends and to retain $1.30 per share (or retained earnings, RE_1). The company will pay 33% of its earnings as dividends (0.65/1.95), which is its **dividend payout ratio**. Conversely, STAR's retention ratio, b, is 67% (1.30/1.95). This drop in dividends may seem disturbing, but actually STAR is reinvesting 67% of its current earnings in investments that will benefit current stockholders to earn greater future earnings.

We can use this idea to define the growth rate, g, as

$$g = ROE_1(b) \qquad\qquad (14.9)$$

where ROE_1 is the *expected* **return on equity** and b is the retention rate. (Remember that the ROE_1 should be the firm's *expected* return on equity in the future,

dividend payout ratio

Portion of earnings paid as dividends or defined as dividends per share/earnings per share.

rentention ratio (b)

Portion of earnings retained in the company or defined as retained earnings/earnings per share.

return on equity (ROE)

Return on investment for equity or common stockholders, defined as net profits after taxes/common stockholder equity.

---

[3]Assume these numbers are given to you by your assistant. We discuss where to find them later.
[4]The PV of annuity factor at interest rate i for perpetuity equals $1/i$. For this example, it is $1/0.10 = 10$.

not a historical value based on past projects.)[5] Equation 14.9 gives the company's growth rate because the additional earnings plowed back into the company are expected to generate a return on the stockholders' investment equal to ROE_1. So, if additional investments are made with retained earnings (b) and these investments earn a 11.5% return, then the stockholders' future earnings will increase by 11.5% of the retained earnings invested, or 0.115 of b. Because b equals 67%, STAR's earnings will grow at the rate equal to 11.5% of 67%, or 7.7% (rounded to 8%), which explains why the general formula for the growth rate is $ROE_1(b)$.

Now, let's return to STAR's new venture. STAR retains $1.30 per share and expands into upscale steakhouses. Assuming that its sales generate an expected return of 11.5% (ROE_1), the venture's earnings per share come to $0.1495, or 11.5%($1.30). At the company's required return of 10%, the net present value (NPV) of this venture to stockholders is $0.195 per share.[6] This calculation says that the upscale steakhouses should add $0.195 to the stock price in Year 1. We must discount this Year 1 value to find its Year 0 or current value:

$$NPV_1/(1 + ER_s) = \$0.195/(1 + 0.10) = \$0.177$$

This return from the upscale restaurant business is also reflected in STAR's earnings per share in Year 2. STAR's Year 1 earnings will increase to $2.0995 (rounded to $2.10) per share ($1.95 from the casual dining restaurants and $0.1495 from the upscale restaurants).

Now suppose this growth orientation continues in Year 2. Instead of being satisfied with these restaurants, STAR decides to expand to Australia. Again, it will retain 67% of Year 2 earnings: 0.67($2.10), or $1.407 per share, and invest these funds in expanding its restaurant in Australia. At the same 11.5% return on this investment, it increases the value of the stock by $0.213 per share in Year 2; this amount is the net present value for the expansion in Australia in Year 2.[7] Again, to determine the Year 0 value, we must discount the Year 2 value:

$$NPV_2/(1 + ER_s)^2 = \$0.213/(1 + 1.10)^2 = \$0.176$$

The second term back in Equation 14.8 summarizes the present values of all the firm's future growth opportunities (PVGO) or the NPVs of all the future expansions in other countries as well as more upscale restaurants. PVGO is defined to equal the sum of the NPVs of each investment opportunity over the years, or

$$PVGO = \frac{NPV_1}{(1 + ER_s)} + \frac{NPV_2}{(1 + ER_s)^2} + \frac{NPV_3}{(1 + ER_s)^3} + \cdots$$

Because each NPV follows a sequence of constant growth rate equaled to g, it can be rewritten to resemble the growth term in Equation 14.8 or

$$PVGO = \frac{EPS_1}{ER_s} \left[\frac{g - ER_s(b)}{ER_s - g} \right]$$

---

[5]Other caveats are discussed later in the discussion of fundamental analysis.
[6]$NPV_1 = [\$0.1495/0.10] - \$1.30 = \$0.195$
[7]Retained earnings from Year 2 equals $1.407, and the investment is expected to provide a 11.5% return, so the cash flow per year is (0.115)($1.407) = $0.162. Assuming the investment will continue to perpetuity, the PV of annuity factor is 1/0.10 and $NPV_2 = [\$0.162/0.10] - \$1.407 = \$0.213$.

TABLE 14.1	
Summary of the Lone Star Steakhouse Example	$EPS_1 = \$1.95$ $DIV_1 = \$.65$ Dividend Payout Ratio = $\$0.65/\$1.95 = 33\%$ $RE_1 = \$1.30$ Retention Ratio $= b = \$1.30/\$1.95 = 67\%$ $ER_s = 0.10$

No-Growth Company Value

Value of STAR if growth equals zero and all earnings are paid out as dividends:

$PV = \$1.95/0.10 = \$19.50$

Present Value of Growth Opportunities (PVGO)

$ROE_1 = 0.115$
Growth rate, $g = ROE_1(b) = 0.115(0.67) = 7.7\% \approx 8\%$
$NPV_1 = (\$0.1495/0.10) - \$1.30 = \$0.195$
$PV(NPV_1) = \$0.195/(1 + 0.10) = \$0.177$
$NPV_2 = (\$0.162/0.10) - \$1.407 = \$0.213$
$PV(NPV_2) = \$0.213/(1 + 0.10)^2 = \$0.176$

Intrinsic Value

$$V_{s0} = \frac{\$1.95}{0.10}\left[1 + \left(\frac{0.08 - (0.10)(0.67)}{0.10 - 0.08}\right)\right] = \$32.175$$

Now combining the present value of the firm's continuing growth opportunities, PVGO, with its no-growth term, we have Equation 14.8

$$V_{s0} = \frac{EPS_1}{ER_s} + \frac{EPS_1}{ER_s}\left[\frac{g - ER_s(b)}{ER_s - g}\right]$$

Equation 14.8 can be further simplified to

$$V_{s0} = \frac{EPS_1}{ER_s}\left[1 + \left(\frac{g - ER_s(b)}{ER_s - g}\right)\right] \tag{14.10}$$

Using Equation 14.10, STAR's intrinsic value equals

$$V_{s0} = \frac{\$1.95}{0.10}\left[1 + \left(\frac{0.08 - (0.10)(0.67)}{0.10 - 0.08}\right)\right] = \$32.18$$

Table 14.1 summarizes the results. If STAR can continuously find other investment opportunities that earn 11.5%, it can sustain this 8% growth rate per year and its intrinsic value of its stock should equal around $32 or the low $30s.

Figure 14.2 depicts the cash STAR generates and the marginal value of its stock as it accepts positive NPV investments. The figure begins with the no-growth case, which features constant earnings of $1.95 and a NPV of $19.50. Notice that each subsequent investment opportunity adds value to the company's common stock. For example, the upscale restaurant expansion opportunity adds $0.177 per share to the stock price today, and the Australian expansion adds

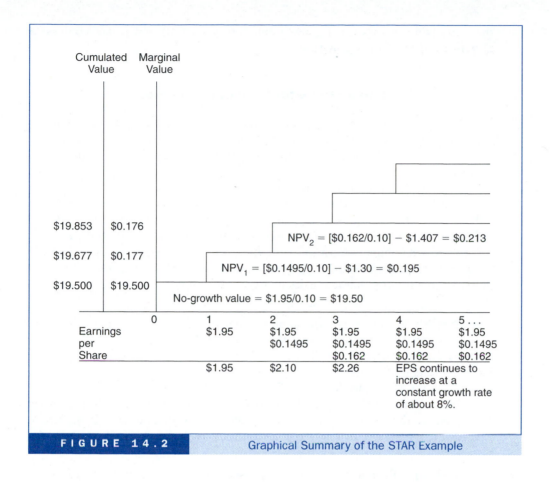

Cumulated   Marginal
  Value   Value

$19.853 $0.176

                $NPV_2 = [\$0.162/0.10] - \$1.407 = \$0.213$

$19.677 $0.177

                $NPV_1 = [\$0.1495/0.10] - \$1.30 = \$0.195$

$19.500 $19.500

            No-growth value = $1.95/0.10 = $19.50

	0	1	2	3	4	5 ...
Earnings per Share		$1.95	$1.95	$1.95	$1.95	$1.95
			$0.1495	$0.1495	$0.1495	$0.1495
				$0.162	$0.162	$0.162
		$1.95	$2.10	$2.26	EPS continues to increase at a constant growth rate of about 8%.	

FIGURE 14.2   Graphical Summary of the STAR Example

another $0.176 per share to the current stock value. Additionally, each invest-ment adds to the firm's earnings per share, which increases at a constant growth rate of 8%, or $1.95 to $2.10 to $2.26, and so forth. One vertical axis indicates the marginal value each investment adds to STAR's stock price. Each horizontal step indicates another marginal investment, and the steps climb indefinitely into the future at a constant growth rate, g, or 8%. Each year, new projects increase the stock's value by 8% from $0.195 ($NPV_1$) to $0.213 ($NPV_2$), and so forth, indefinitely.[8] Notice that both the earnings per share and the marginal value of the stock increase at the constant rate of 8%. These growth opportunities, PVGO, plus the no-growth term, $[EPS_1/ER_s]$ equals around $32 for STAR.

Now we can conduct our fundamental analysis, as we did with the DDM. The rule is the same: if intrinsic value exceeds the market price, the stock is undervalued; if intrinsic value falls to less than the market price, it is overvalued. Given that STAR's intrinsic value equals $32 and it has a market price of approxi-mately $21, the stock is undervalued, and we would invest.

Recall that at the beginning of the section on the EM, we stated that the model serves two purposes other than intrinsic value estimations. It can identify

---

[8] The numbers may differ slightly from equation results due to rounding.

the underlying factors for a growth company's success, and it can contrast a growth company with a growth stock.

Implications for Growth Companies

The EM example showed that generally company earnings growth leads to an increasing intrinsic value. Given that general case, let's spend some time discussing how a **growth company** earns a higher intrinsic value so it could be a potentially good investment.

growth company

Company whose net present value of future investment opportunities are greater than zero, or PVGO > 0.

Focus on the second term, or the growth term, of Equation 14.8. Because EPS_1 and ER_s are expected to be positive, notice that the growth term is positive only if $[g - ER_s(b)]$ is positive.[9] It means that g must be greater than $ER_s(b)$. Because g equals ROE_1 times b, $ROE_1(b)$ exceeds $ER_s(b)$ only if ROE_1 exceeds ER_s. A growth company must therefore have a return on equity greater than the return required by stockholders.[10] Five implications of this relationship can help investors identify the characteristics of a growth company.

Implication 1 Not every expanding company is a growth company. Suppose that a stockbroker informs you that General Motors (GM) is expanding extensively, building new warehouses and factories. Is GM a growth company? Its accounting data show growth in the form of increasing fixed assets. However, an astute investor should ask: "What is the company's return on these investments?" Expanding assets do not necessarily constitute growth; the return generated by the increased asset investment is critical, and only if its return exceeds the required return does it constitute a growth company.

Implication 2 Even if the company's investments earn an overall rate of return equal to the return required by stockholders, it is not a growth company. Earning positive returns is not enough! Again, it must exceed the required return, or 10% for STAR.

Implication 3 If the company's investments earn a positive overall rate of return less than the required rate of return, then it is not a positive growth company but a *negative* growth company. In fact, if g is less than $ER_s(b)$, then the stock has a negative growth rate. The stock's PVGO will be negative, indicating that company projects decrease the stock's value instead of adding value.

Implication 4 Retaining profits ($b > 0$) by itself does not constitute growth. Again, the return generated by the invested funds determines whether a firm is a growth company.

---

[9]The growth term can be negative if g is less than $ER_s(b)$. See Implication 3.
[10]Actually, an economically more meaningful term for ROE_1 is the internal rate of return, IRR, or the rate of return on investment. If we substitute IRR for ROE_1, we have $IRR > ER_s$. It is simply the IRR decision rule for evaluating capital budgeting projects in corporate finance.

Implication 5 If a company cannot find any investments with returns (ROE_1) greater than the return that stockholders require (ER_s), then it can maximize stockholder value by increasing cash dividends instead of retaining earnings to finance negative NPV projects.

Now that we understand what constitutes a growth company, let's determine the difference between a growth company and a growth stock. Although these terms seem synonymous, they are not.

Contrasting a Growth Company with a Growth Stock

As previously defined, a growth company is a company that undertakes positive NPV projects that increase its stock value. Generally, a growth company's stock tends to appreciate as shown by the EM example, with some exceptions. For example, if investors overestimate growth opportunities for a company and bid up its stock's market price based on these rosy expectations, even a growth company may become overvalued. Technical analysts may also bid up market prices based on some perceived buy signal. As investors realize that they possibly overestimated the company's opportunities, its excessive market price will decline. It does not mean that the market was wrong; the investors are simply adjusting to the economic value of the company as new information emerges.

Perhaps the best example is the tech bubble of the late 1990s. The market and many technology companies were convinced that the way of the future was through the Internet. Cisco and other technology companies believed that the economy was in a super growth phase to connect the world through the Internet, and all the believers coined the phrase, "the new economy." Cisco became the darling of Wall Street as its stock soared to $82, and its market value reached $550 billion, surpassing Microsoft and GE. The huge appreciation gave Cisco a skyrocketing P/E ratio of about 400 times. A cover of *Fortune* magazine pictured Cisco's CEO, John Chambers, with a title, "Is he the best CEO in the world?"[11] At this point, Cisco was a growth company with promising investment opportunities or positive PVGO. However, perhaps, the investors were overly optimistic of the "new economy" and its sustainable growth. Many tech stocks including Cisco, became overvalued or no longer a growth stock, as the excessive market price incorporated these high unsustainable growth rates. The Internet bubble started to fizzle in 2000; and Cisco stock suffered along with all technology stocks, bringing its market price to the low teens by the end of 2002.

A **growth stock** is a stock that is currently undervalued enough to drive its return above those of other stocks at the same risk level. Shares in a growth company do not necessarily constitute a growth stock. For example, a company can be a growth company because its PVGO > 0, but it could be overpriced so it is not a growth stock.

Alternatively, a stock can be a growth stock although the company is not a growth company. Investors may ignore a stable unglamorous company, undervaluing its stock to the point that it offers superior returns relative to other stocks

growth stock

An undervalued stock; when market price is less than its intrinsic value; expected to earn superior returns compared with other stocks with similar risk.

---

[11]"Is He the Best CEO in the World?" *Fortune,* April 17, 2000.

at the same risk level, assuming that the efficient market eventually recognizes its intrinsic value.

In most cases, however, we expect a growth company to be a growth stock. Going back to our STAR example, it is a good example of a growth company that is also a growth stock, because its positive PVGO and the stock is currently under-valued. These factors say that the stock is a growth company and a good invest-ment; the value of the investment still depends on how much it costs and returns! Someone who buys STAR at $21 will earn a higher return than other stocks with the same risk because its market price should rise to its economic value of about $32. Watch out, though, because not all stocks are both a growth company and a growth stock like STAR. The moral of this discussion may be that the difference between real and false growth stocks often is not obvious. Even if growth compa-nies may be growth stocks, never assume it! Instead of assuming that a company with a positive PVGO (a growth company) is a good investment, always take that last step and compare the stock's intrinsic value with its market price to make sure it is undervalued before chasing those abnormal profits! (Recall we discussed this relationship in Chapter 11 when we discuss company analysis.)

The two stock valuation models, the DDM and the EM, are simply more formal ways of evaluating common stocks relative to their trading prices. An investor may suggest that STAR is a good investment with ample growth opportunities as STAR may discover many more dining opportunities and hence it is currently undervalued. This investor is informally assessing the economic value relative to its traded price.

RECAPRECAP

Most investors believe that a stock has an intrinsic value and that, in an efficient market, the stock price will converge to that value. We described two models, the DDM and the EM, by which to determine a stock's intrinsic value. A sound investment decision should be based on a careful study of a company's financials (as discussed in Chapter 13), investment growth opportunities, and an estimate of its intrinsic value. Finally, compare the stock's intrinsic value with its market price to identify any undervalued (or growth) stocks. This step is important because no one should ever assume that a growth company is always a growth stock.

1. Suppose Coca-Cola (KO) expects dividends to equal $0.80 next year and its earnings per share is expected to be $1.84. If KO's growth rate is estimated to be 7.5% and its required return is 9%, what is KO's intrinsic value using DDM? Reestimate KO's intrinsic value using EM.
2. KO is currently trading for $48.49. Is KO an overvalued or undervalued stock? Explain.
3. If KO's expected ROE equals 13%, is KO a growth company? Explain why.
4. Is KO a growth stock? Explain why.

FUNDAMENTAL ANALYSIS IN PRACTICE

Value Line is one of many sources of information on which to base an estimate of an intrinsic value for STAR. We used many numbers to explain the two valuation models; we now go back to illustrate the calculation of those numbers.

Figure 14.3 reprints the one-page Value Line summary on STAR. Given these data, we assume that today is December 31, 2002, and that STAR's earnings, and

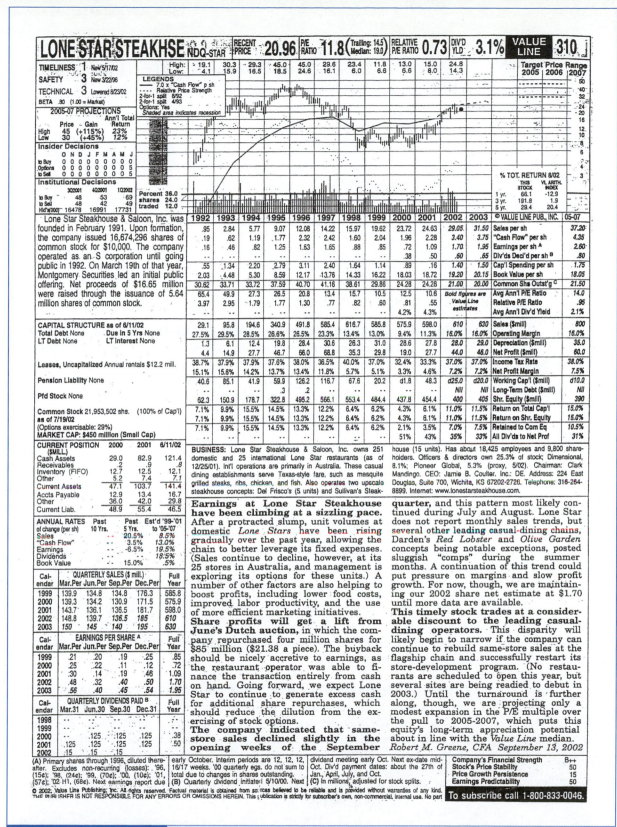

FIGURE 14.3 Value Line Report for Lone Star Steakhouse (STAR)

Reprinted with the permission of Value Line Publishing, Inc.

therefore its future dividend streams, can be estimated by a constant growth rate, g. Recall the DDM formula from Equation 14.7:

$$V_{s0} = \frac{DIV_0(1 + g)}{ER_s - g}$$

Three basic steps are required in the process to estimate the intrinsic value of a common stock.

Step 1: Estimate Growth, g

Three ways to estimate a firm's growth rate are described next. Because the growth rate is such an important component of the estimate of intrinsic value, we use all three methods to gather as much information as possible. At the end, however, we must settle on one growth estimate.

Estimate a Historical Growth Trend for Dividends per Share Using some historical time period that best illustrates the stock's expected growth in dividends, estimate an average growth rate. The analyst must, of course, decide which period best represents *future* earnings for STAR—not an easy task. No magic formula is available, but once a historical trend is designated as the best representation of future earnings, the analysis proceeds to estimate STAR's geometric average growth rate, g.

STAR started paying dividends in 2000, therefore we assume that dividend growth between December 31, 2000, to December 31, 2002, best represents the company's expected future dividend growth. Dividends declared per share (Value Line abbreviates it as "Div'ds Dec'd per sh") were $0.38 in 2000 and $0.60 in 2002. Find the growth rate, g, using a compounded future value formula that would make $0.38 compound over two years to equal $0.60:

$$\$0.38(1 + g)^2 = \$0.60$$
$$(1 + g)^2 = 1.5789$$
$$g = (1.5789)^{1/2} - 1$$
$$g = 25.66\%$$

Extrapolating from the historical dividend growth trend, the future growth rate should equals only 25.66%.

Estimate a Historical Growth Trend for Earnings per Share Using the same method, but over a longer period to determine the long-run growth rate. Let's assume that the earnings per share growth from 1998 to 2002 represents our future expectations for STAR. It means the EPS would grow from $0.88 in 1998 to $1.70 in 2002. Thus, g equals

$$\$0.88(1 + g)^4 = \$1.70$$
$$(1 + g)^4 = 1.9318$$
$$g = (1.9318)^{1/4} - 1$$
$$g = 17.89\%$$

Extrapolating from STAR's historical earnings trend, its estimated growth rate equals about 18%. This rate seems a little high to sustain long term given our weak economy, though possible if the economy recovers.

Earnings Model Growth Definition Finally, the growth definition in the EM (Equation 14.9) can give an estimate of STAR's growth rate. ROE_1 can be obtained from Value Line under the definition of "Return on Shr. Equity" for the next year (2003), which equals 11.5%.

The common stock dividend payout ratio is also obtained from the last row of the Value Line sheet, called "All Div'ds to Net Prof," and it equals 33%.

Now, STAR's growth, using Equation 14.9, is

$$g = ROE_1(b)$$
$$= ROE_1(1 - \text{Dividend payout ratio})$$
$$= 0.115(1 - .33)$$
$$= 7.7\% \text{ rounded to } 8\%$$

This definition of growth gives an estimate of the expected growth rate equal to 8.0%. Given the economic period of 2002, it may be the most realistic estimate of the future growth rate.

Step 2: Estimate ER_s

Using the capital asset pricing model (CAPM), we can estimate the required return on STAR stock.[12] The CAPM states

$$ER_s = RF + \beta(ER_M - RF) \tag{14.11}$$

The risk-free rate, RF, is found in *The Wall Street Journal* quotes for Treasury bond yields to be 3% annually. The yield spread for the market return [the $(ER_M - RF)$ term] is estimated at approximately 8.6% by using the results of historical spreads documented by Ibbotson Associates. Beta, a relative risk measure, can be found in Value Line, and it equals 0.80 for STAR. Based on these numbers, STAR's expected return equals

$$ER_s = 0.03 + 0.80(.086) = 0.0988 \cong 10\%$$

Step 3: Estimate DIV_1 or DIV_0 (1 + g)

Multiply STAR's dividends per share declared for the current year-end by $(1 + g)$ to obtain DIV_1. An alternative method is to multiply EPS_1 by the dividend payout ratio.

---

[12]The CAPM is discussed in detail in Chapter 18. The equation attempts to measure an investor's required rate of return for a given beta risk of the stock relative to the overall market risk.

To find DIV_1 in this way, we need to set a growth rate that is appropriate for STAR. Because Equation 14.9 attempts to capture expected growth (instead of historical growth), it probably gives the best estimate. Therefore, DIV_1 equals

$$DIV_1 = DIV_0(1 + g) = \$0.60(1 + 0.08) = \$0.648$$

Given the estimates from the three steps and using Equation 14.7,

$$V_{s0} = \frac{DIV_0(1 + g)}{ER_s - g} = \frac{\$0.60(1 + 0.08)}{0.10 - 0.08} = \$32.40$$

Alternatively, using EM (Equation 14.10) to estimate STAR's intrinsic value, we have

$$V_{s0} = \frac{\$1.95}{0.10}\left[1 + \left(\frac{0.08 - (0.10)(0.67)}{0.10 - 0.08}\right)\right] = \$32.175$$

These estimates indicate that STAR's intrinsic value is approximately in the low \$30s per share. Compared with the recent price of about \$21, the fundamental analyst would say that the stock is undervalued and recommend purchasing it.

Given reasonably efficient markets, and assuming that other market participants agree with our assessment and assumptions, STAR should increase to the low \$30s range. Before you call your broker, however, some caveats must be considered.

Caveats for the Dividend Discount Model

homogeneous expectations

Assumption about the investors in the market having the same future expectations about a stock.

"Assuming that other market participants agree with our assessment" expresses an important assumption called **homogeneous expectations**. Without this condition, we cannot guarantee that the stock price will converge to the intrinsic value. If other investors have different expectations about STAR, then they should arrive at different intrinsic values and different investment decisions, even if they use the same DDM formula.

Further, the DDM is highly sensitive to the estimates of the growth rate and the required return on stock ER_s. For example, decreasing the estimate of STAR's growth rate by 1% to 7% would drop the stock's intrinsic value to \$21.40 instead of \$32. That \$10.60 difference comes from a one percentage point difference in the growth estimate. This change would make STAR trading at its true value, and not undervalued.

Another variable is equally difficult to estimate: the yield spread between the market portfolio and the risk-free rate, or $(ER_M - RF)$. Ibbotson Associates estimates the yield spread for common stocks between 1926 to 1993 at 8.6%, but a yield spread estimate over a shorter period would fall to between 5% and 6%. Using a 6% yield spread and an 8% growth rate results in an intrinsic value estimate for STAR of $-\$324$. This result leads to our third caveat: be wary of unreasonable numbers. An intrinsic value can never be negative! It does not make sense to estimate that STAR has negative economic value. In fact, when $g > ER_s$, stop and use the P/E method, discussed later in this chapter, to calculate intrinsic value because the constant growth assumption is violated!

This warning ties in with the earlier problem with the growth variable. Besides being sensitive to the growth estimate, the DDM uses an ROE_1 value in the growth estimate that comes from accounting relationships, not a market value or an economic value. This value may not accurately reflect the stock's true expected return on investment. A more meaningful number may be the internal rate of return (IRR) on the firm's investment projects, but that number is not publicly available. (Review footnote 10.) Use ROE_1 only with great caution. Again, if the final intrinsic value estimate is unreasonable, be suspicious of ROE_1 or the growth estimate.

A final caveat: If a company does not pay dividends, it does not mean its intrinsic value equals zero as the DDM seems to suggest. Unfortunately, the EM cannot be used to estimate an intrinsic value for a company that pays no dividends. In a later section where P/E ratios are discussed, a modified method is introduced to overcome the zero dividend problem. This alternative method also works well for stocks with $g > ER_s$.

These caveats also apply to the EM, and the moral is the same. An investor needs to carefully study a company's investment opportunities before attempting to estimate its intrinsic value to determine whether the stock might be overvalued or undervalued.

RECAP We analyzed STAR's intrinsic value using the DDM and the EM. Once we determined an intrinsic value, we compared it with the stock's market price. If market price is less than the intrinsic value, the stock is considered to be undervalued. If market price is greater than the intrinsic value, the stock is overvalued. In this way, fundamental analysis provides a decision rule to buy or sell. Suppose a fast-food company's financial data are as follows.

	1998	2002	Est. 2003
EPS	$1.13	$1.93	$2.10
DIV	0.64	1.10	1.20
ROE			0.116
Dividend payout			0.57
Beta		0.70	
Market price		$35	

5. Estimate the historical growth trend for dividends per share for the four-year period from 1998 to 2002.
6. Estimate the historical growth trend for earnings per share for the four-year period from 1998 to 2002.
7. Estimate growth rate using Equation 14.9, $g = ROE_1(1 - \text{dividend payout ratio})$.
8. Estimate ER_s via the CAPM or Equation 14.11, if the risk-free rate equals 0.02 and the market risk premium equals 0.086.
9. Estimate the company's intrinsic value using the growth rate calculated by using Equation 14.9 and DDM.
10. Is the stock overvalued or undervalued? Explain.

Fundamental analysis clarifies the old adage, "Buy low, sell high." The analysis answers the equally old question, how low is low? When market price is less than the intrinsic value, it is low enough and time to buy. How high is high?

When market price is greater than the intrinsic value, it is high enough to sell. The decision rule is an old one, but the process to find intrinsic value in a rational, logical way adds credibility to fundamental analysis.

This process works when dividends or earnings grow at nearly a constant rate, g. Suppose, however, that dividends and earnings do not follow a constant growth rate. Even worse, what if growth is greater than the required return on a stock? Notice in Equation 14.7 that V_{s0} is negative if g is greater than ER_s, but in a rational world, stocks can never have negative values.[13] The next section discusses a nonconstant growth model that allows for variation in the growth rate, even to exceed the required return in some years.

NONCONSTANT GROWTH MODEL

This section shows how to modify the DDM to apply it to stocks with different growth rates over various years, including growth rates that exceed expected returns. First, let's discuss whether a stock's growth rate *can* be greater than its required rate of return. Suppose a stock's expected growth rate is 20% and the return required by stockholders, ER_s, equals 15%. Corporate finance often defines the required rate of return as

$$ER_s = \text{Dividend yield} + \text{Growth rate}$$

assuming a constant growth rate. Based on the formula, a stock cannot grow at a constant rate higher than ER_s for an indefinite period because growth is a component of the expected, or required, rate of return, ER_s. Constant higher growth would, therefore, drive the expected return higher as well. Eventually, then, the growth rate must be less than the required rate of return. Stated differently, growth cannot exceed the required return forever (i.e., the growth rate must be nonconstant). This statement implies that two growth phases must exist: (1) a phase with a nonconstant growth rate, g, higher than the required return, and (2) a phase with a constant growth rate, g, less than the required return. Let's see how we can apply a model with a two-phase growth rate.

Step 1: Determine the Value for the Nonconstant Growth Phase

Suppose that a company is expected to grow at a nonconstant rate of 20% for four years and then to grow at a lower rate of 10% indefinitely. If the current dividend per share is $2.00, then we can determine the future dividend stream up to Year 4 in the following way:

Year	Dividend per Share
1	$2.00(1 + 0.20) = $2.40
2	$2.00(1 + 0.20)^2 = $2.88
3	$2.00(1 + 0.20)^3 = $3.46
4	$2.00(1 + 0.20)^4 = $4.15

---

[13]A negative value says that you would pay me to take the stock from you. Rarely does someone pay to give up something, except for garbage, perhaps.

Because the stock's intrinsic value is the present value of its future dividend stream, we can find the present value of each dividend for the nonconstant growth period. If stockholders' required rate of return equals 15%, then each of these future dividends has the following present value:

Year	Dividend per Share	Present Value Factor at 15%	Present Value
1	$2.40	0.8696	$2.087
2	2.88	0.7561	2.178
3	3.46	0.6575	2.275
4	4.15	0.5718	2.373
Total present value of nonconstant growth dividend stream			$8.913

A timeline illustrates the cash flows from the nonconstant growth phase, each cash flow's present value, and the sum of those present values.[14]

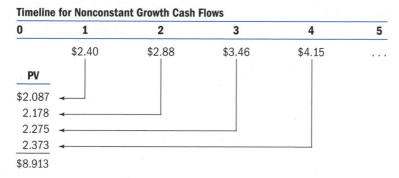

Timeline for Nonconstant Growth Cash Flows

Therefore, the present value of the stock in its nonconstant growth phase equals $8.913.

Step 2: Determine the Value for the Constant Growth Phase

Now, let's examine the second phase when the stock's growth falls back to a constant rate. For a moment, suppose we jump forward to Year 4, after which the stock is expected to grow at 10% annually with a required rate of return of 15%; using the DDM, we can estimate a value for the stock during this period. Treating Year 4 as Year 0, DIV_4 ($4.15) replaces DIV_0 and

$$V_{s4} = \frac{DIV_4(1 + g)}{ER_s - g} = \frac{\$4.15(1 + 0.10)}{0.15 - 0.10} = \$91.30$$

Recall that this value is a Year 4 value. To really find the present value of this future value at Year 0, we need to multiply the future value by the present value factor for 15%:

$$\$91.30/(1 + 0.15)^4 = \$91.30(0.5718) = \$52.205$$

---

[14]Timelines are often used in corporate finance to display present value problems. See, for example, Eugene Brigham, *Fundamentals of Financial Management*, 8th ed. (Fort Worth, TX: Dryden Press, 1998).

The following timeline illustrates how the present value of each constant growth cash flow at Year 4 becomes one cash flow, V_{s4}, for which we find the present value at Year 0:

Timeline of Constant Growth Cash Flows

0	1	2	3	4	5	6	...
				$4.15	$4.15(1 + g)	$4.15(1 + g)^2	...
				0	1	2	...

$$V_{s4} = \frac{DIV_0(1 + g)}{ER_s - g}$$

$$V_{s4} = \frac{\$4.15(1 + 0.10)}{0.15 - 0.10}$$

$$V_{s4} = \$91.30$$

$$\text{PV of Constant Growth Phase} = \frac{V_{s4}}{(1 + ER_s)^4}$$

$$= \frac{\$91.30}{(1 + 0.15)^4}$$

$$= \$52.205$$

Therefore, the value of the stock in its constant growth rate phase equals $52.205.

Step 3: Calculate the Intrinsic Value of the Two-Phase Nonconstant Growth Stock

Finally, combine the present value of future dividends from the nonconstant growth phase with the present value of future dividends from the constant growth phase:

$$V_{s0} = (\text{PV of nonconstant growth phase}) + (\text{PV of constant growth phase})$$
$$= \quad\quad\quad \$8.913 \quad\quad\quad + \quad\quad\quad \$52.205$$
$$= \$61.12$$

General Formula for the Nonconstant Growth Model

The general formula for the two-phase growth model assumes that the constant phase growth rate remains the same indefinitely and that it is less than the required rate of return, ER_s:

$$V_{s0} = \sum_{t=1}^{T} \frac{DIV_0(1 + g_n)^t}{(1 + ER_s)^t} + \frac{DIV_0(1 + g_n)^T(1 + g_c)}{ER_s - g_c}\left[\frac{1}{(1 + ER_s)^T}\right]$$

where DIV_0 is the current dividend per share, g_n is the nonconstant growth rate, g_c is the constant growth rate when g_n is less than ER_s, ER_s is the required rate of return, and T is the number of years that the stock grows at the nonconstant growth rate.

The model can be extended to three or more phases as long as the last phase is a constant growth phase. The following example shows how to extend it to three different growth rates.

Three-Phase Nonconstant Growth Model

Suppose that a firm's current dividend of $2.00 is expected to grow at 20% for the first two years, then to decline to 10% for the next three years, and finally to settle at an 8% constant rate thereafter. The following timeline illustrates the process, which closely resembles the two-phase model:

Timeline for Three-Phase Cash Flows

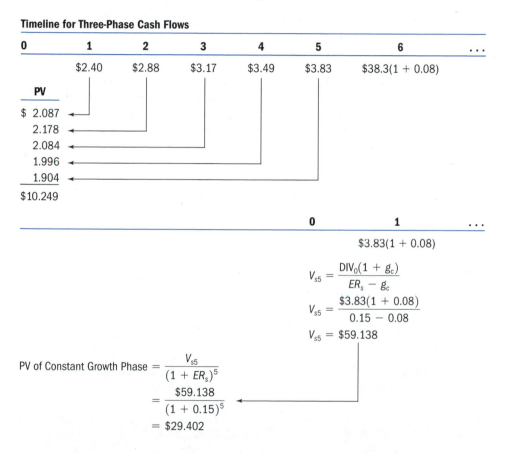

First, the timeline shows the present value of the nonconstant growth phase, including both the 20% growth phase and the 10% growth phase (step 1), which equals $10.249. It then shows the present value of the constant growth phase (step 2), or $29.402. Finally, it combines the two nonconstant growth phase values with the constant growth phase value to find the intrinsic value: $10.249 + $29.402 = $39.651.

Notice that it does not matter how many different nonconstant growth rates a stock has. This process finds the present value of each cash flow separately in step 1.

Estimating the Nonconstant and Constant Growth Rates

Now, let's briefly discuss how we can estimate these growth rates. The nonconstant growth rate for Year 1 can be estimated using Equation 14.9:

$$g = \text{ROE}_1(b)$$

Value Line reports usually provide estimates of companies' return on equity and dividend payout ratios for the following year in bold type. Remember, the retention rate, b, $= 1 -$ dividend payout ratio. How long will the company grow at the super growth rate? Again, it is difficult to estimate, but four to five years is a good approximation.

Value Line can provide data for next year, but how do you estimate a constant growth rate for a stock several years from today? This task is more difficult. One suggestion is to enter an industry average ROE into Equation 14.9 and assume that the stock will approximate the return of the average industry firm when it can no longer grow at a nonconstant rate. Value Line provides industry data, as do other sources.[15]

The two-phase model may more accurately value a high-growth company than a constant growth DDM could. For example, Dole Foods Co., Inc., the well-known pineapple and fruit juice company, is expected to grow at 19.6% based on its ROE_1 and its retention rate 23%(0.85); however, Value Line expects the foods industry overall to grow at 10%. It would be quite difficult for Dole Foods to sustain a 19.6% growth rate indefinitely while its industry was growing at 10%. The two-phase model should give a better value for a high-growth company such as Dole Foods.

RECAP RECAP

We examine a valuation process for a nonconstant growth stock when growth is greater than required rate of return. We apply a modified, two-phase DDM with two growth rates, a nonconstant growth rate, g_n, that was greater than the required rate of return and a constant growth rate, g_c, that was less than the required rate of return.

11. Suppose that Dole Foods is expected to grow at 20% for five years, then its growth rate will decline to a constant rate of 10%. If Dole Foods' current dividends per share are $0.70 and its required return is 12%, what is its intrinsic value?

Now, we turn to a third method that investors use to find undervalued stocks. It has become increasingly popular due to recommendations by some researchers.[16]

MARKET-TO-BOOK RATIO

market-to-book ratio (MV/BV)

Market price per share/book value per share; a low MV/BV (MV/BV < 1.0) is considered a good potential investments.

Another valuation method based on the **market-to-book ratio (MV/BV)** has become popular in recent years as a way to find undervalued stocks. The ratio is defined as

$$\text{MV/BV} = \frac{\text{Total market value of common stock}}{\text{Total assets} - \text{Total debt} - \text{Preferred stock}} \tag{14.13}$$

---

[15]Other sources are the Standard & Poor's Industry Survey and the Standard & Poor's Statistical Service.
[16]Eugene Fama and Kenneth French, "The Cross-Section of Expected Stock Returns," *Journal of Finance*, June 1992, pp. 427–466.

where MV, the total market value of the stock, equals the stock's market price per share multiplied by the number of shares outstanding, and BV, the company's total assets minus total debt minus preferred stock, measures the book value of common equity or common stock.

If the company does absolutely nothing to generate sales, the market value of its stock should approximately equal its book value. Book value measures the equity value of the firm if it were to sell all its assets and pay off all its debts and preferred stock at the values on its balance sheet. Book value presumably gives the company's value, assuming it were to stop operating and liquidate. When the company does nothing, market value equals book value and the ratio MV/BV equals 1.0.

Therefore, if MV/BV is less than 1.0, then someone could profit by buying enough shares of the stock to gain a controlling interest in the company and sell its assets for book value. For example, suppose that a company has a ratio of MV/BV equal to 0.8. This ratio says that the stock is selling for $0.80 per share for every $1.00 of its equity's book value. Someone might buy up all the shares at $0.80, then take control of the company, and then liquidate it for $1.00 per share, making $0.20 per share on the investment, a 20% return. During the merger mania of the 1980s, corporate raiders such as T. Boone Pickens became well known doing this type of thing.

An investor who has smaller financial means could still reason that the stock was undervalued because its shares should be worth at least its book value. In an efficient market, investors would force management to take action so that the ratio becomes closer to 1.0. The stockholders may even replace the old management with a more efficient group or create incentives for them to make better investment decisions (positive net present value investments).

Based on this kind of scenario, the MV/BV ratio strategy directs investors to buy stocks of firms that have low MV/BV ratios. A company turnaround should, it is hoped, raise the stock's market value at least to its book value.

What type of stock has an MV/BV ratio greater than 1.0, or market value greater than book value? They could be the growth companies discussed in the section on the EM. Investors may bid up market value above book value because the value generated by the firm's investment opportunities is greater than its liquidated value. The ratio above 1.0 suggests that the firm is actually earning positive returns on its investments (positive net present values), raising its value above that of a similar company doing nothing (which would be worth its book value).

Remember from the discussion of the EM, however, that shares in growth companies do not necessarily represent growth stocks. To invest in growth stocks, one must find stocks that are undervalued (with market values less than their intrinsic values) to earn returns superior to those of other stocks with the same risk level.

Beware of MV/BV

Unfortunately, the MV/BV ratio cannot distinguish between the overvalued stocks with MV/BV greater than 1.0 and undervalued growth stocks with MV/BV greater than 1.0. Stated differently, because market value is the market price, not intrinsic value, MV/BV can be greater than 1.0 in two cases: (1) MV/BV greater than 1.0 with market value greater than intrinsic value (an overvalued stock), and

(2) MV/BV greater than 1.0 with market value less than intrinsic value (undervalued growth stock). Investors want to find the second type, not the first.

Another danger with MV/BV is that the book value may differ from the company's true liquidation value. Even if market value is less than book value, liquidation may not generate cash equal to book value. Book value is just an accounting number and may not reflect all the market forces that determine the firm's liquidation value.

For example, Value Line reported STAR's book value per share as $19.20 in 2002, when its stock was trading for approximately $21 (MV/BV equals 1.09). Because MV/BV is greater than 1.0, STAR is considered to be a growth company. We also found it to be a growth stock, because it was undervalued when we compared its market value with its intrinsic value. Again, do not lose sight of the importance of examining the stock to determine the company's investment opportunities and the returns they may generate in the future, rather than blindly applying a ratio-based decision rule that seemed to work in the past. After careful analysis, compare the stock's market price with its estimated intrinsic value to determine whether it is undervalued. The MV/BV ratio may be part of a good initial sorting process to find potential good investments. Do not stop there; do the fundamental analysis.

Besides the MV/BV ratio, another ratio is popular with investors who hunt for undervalued stocks. It is called the P/E ratio.

PRICE/EARNINGS RATIO

price/earnings ratio (P/E)

Market price per share/earnings per share. Some investors buy low P/E stocks because they believe low P/E stocks are cheap; while others buy high P/E stocks because they believe these stocks are popular.

The **price/earnings ratio**, more often referred to as the P/E ratio, is a commonly used measure to which investors refer when searching for potential investments. However, many pitfalls complicate fundamental valuation using the P/E ratio. This section starts with a discussion of how an investor may view the P/E ratio, and then it delves into some of the underlying problems. The P/E ratio is defined as

$$P/E \text{ ratio} = \frac{\text{Market price per share}}{\text{Earnings per share}} \qquad (14.14)$$

Interpreting P/E Ratios

Given the preceding definition, how would an investor interpret P/E to make an investment decision? Suppose two firms, Apple and IBM, have P/E ratios of 10 times and 15 times. An investor might interpret the P/E of 10 as indicating that the stock is selling for 10 times the company's earnings; that is, the stock price per share is 10 times the company's earnings per share (usually written as 10X). They often view the ratios as a unit-pricing scale. Apple's P/E of 10X means that the market values the stock at $10 per $1 of company earnings, whereas it values IBM at $15 per $1 of earnings. This comparison resembles grocery shopping, in which ground chuck may sell for $2.50 per pound whereas sirloin steak sells for $3.75 per pound. Both IBM and sirloin steak appear to be more expensive.[17] An

---

[17]Our intent here is *not* to imply that Apple is analogous to ground chuck and IBM to sirloin steak.

Holding Period Return (HPR) from September 1986 to September 1996

Low P/E Stock	P/E	HPR	High P/E Stock	P/E	HPR
1. Storage Technology	3.7	37.1%	1. VICORP Restaurant	89.5	−17.6%
2. Long Island Lighting	4.2	151.4	2. Handy & Harman	85.0	30.4
3. DeBeers Consolidated	4.6	506.5	3. MCI Communications	85.0	212.4
4. McDermott International	4.7	53.0	4. Rouse Company	66.7	72.9
5. Chrysler	5.1	195.4	5. Butler International	63.3	150.0
6. Ford Motors	5.6	465.8	6. Lamson & Sessions	62.0	180.0
7. United Illuminating	6.2	75.4	7. Coherent Inc.	60.0	166.7
8. CalFed Bancorp	6.3	−74.9	8. Comcast Corp.	60.0	493.6
9. GlenFed Inc.	6.4	449.0	9. Homestake Mining	60.0	48.4
10. Great Western Financial	6.7	146.7	10. Hudson's Bay Company	59.5	2.1
			S&P 500 Index	−	246.5

Holding Period Return (HPR) from September 1991 to September 1996

Low P/E Stock	P/E	HPR	High P/E Stock	P/E	HPR
1. Salomon	4.3	95.1%	1. Noranda	90.0	113.3%
2. KLM Dutch	4.6	72.4	2. Media General	84.0	838.7
3. Travelers	4.7	732.0	3. LADD Furniture	73.3	−4.3
4. Telefoia Eso	5.9	165.3	4. Fieldcrest Cannon	64.0	93.4
5. Provident Life	5.5	147.5	5. Coherent Inc.	63.6	164.3
6. Paine Webber	6.0	211.5	6. Telephone & Data	63.3	186.0
7. Safeguard Scientific	6.0	1500.0	7. ALZA Corp 'A'	62.9	63.6
8. Aetna	6.2	264.6	8. New York Times	62.9	262.1
9. Fremont General	6.3	201.8	9. Playboy Enterprises	61.7	252.5
10. Pioneer Financial Services	6.6	303.2	10. Ampco-Pittsburgh	61.0	134.0
			S&P 500 Index	−	77.7

TABLE 14.2 Holding Period Return for Low P/E and High P/E Stocks, 1986–1996 and 1991–1996 Period

investor may reason that Apple can provide the same dollar of earnings more cheaply than IBM, hence the stock may appear more attractive. This investor believes that the low P/E stock pays a greater return because it cost less for the same $1 of earnings.

Another investor may reason that the market values IBM's $1 in earnings at $15 whereas it values Apple's $1 at only $10; therefore the market considers IBM to be more valuable and more likely to rise in price. This investor may purchase IBM stock. As Table 14.2 indicates, both types of investors are right. Unfortunately, not all stocks beat the Standard & Poor's (S&P) 500 Index or the market benchmark all the time.

Table 14.2 shows a sample of low P/E and high P/E stocks, in which the P/E ratios were calculated in 1986 and 1991, respectively. The stocks were tracked until 1996, and the table shows the results of the total holding period returns for the low P/E and high P/E stocks. Several firms with low P/E ratios earned handsome returns over the 1986–1996 and also over the 1991–1996 period; however, many did not earn as much as the S&P 500 Index over the same period. Firms such as DeBeers Consolidated, the diamond company, earned a 506.5% return in 10 years. Also, Ford Motors (465.8%) and Glendale Federal Inc. (449.0%) both have tremendous returns over the 10-year period; however, several companies did not exceed the S&P 500 Index return of 246.5%. The 5-year period had 9 out of 10 stocks outperform the S&P 500 Index return of 77.7%. Of the 9 stocks, Safeguard Scientific (1500.0%) and Travelers (732.0%) had the highest returns followed by Pioneer Financial Services (303.2%), Aetna Insurance Company (264.6%), Paine Webber (211.5%), and Fremont General (201.8%).

How did the high P/E stocks fare? Again, the results show that high P/E stocks did not always outperform the market (S&P 500 Index). Only one company, Comcast Corp., outperformed the S&P, with a 493.6% return, whereas the rest fell short of the market performance. During the five-year period, high P/E stocks fared better. Noranda (113.3 %), Media General (838.7%), Fieldcrest Cannon (93.4%), Coherent Inc. (164.3%), Telephone & Data (186.0%), New York Times (262.1%), Playboy Enterprises (252.5%), and Ampco-Pittsburgh (134.0%) outperformed the S&P 500 Index return.

The table suggests that buyers of high P/E stocks may be buying glamour stocks that are in high demand. Unfortunately, glamour stocks of today may be unglamorous in the future. Further, buying at a stock's peak price increases the danger of buying overvalued investments. The message from this example is simply that investors should not choose stocks solely on the basis of P/Es. The P/E ratio may have other uses, though. Can we use P/E to conduct fundamental analysis?

Determining Value from P/E

A quick and crude way of determining a stock's value is to multiply its P/E ratio by its expected earnings per share, EPS_1:

$$V_{s0} = (\text{P/E ratio})(\text{EPS}_1) \qquad (14.15)$$

For STAR, this calculation would be

$$V_{s0} = 11.8(\$1.95) = \$23.01$$

Does this quick estimate approximate STAR's intrinsic value? It does not because the P/E ratio (called the practical P/E) was calculated using market price per share, just like the MV/BV ratio. Therefore, a value based on a P/E ratio may ignore many factors that an intrinsic value estimate must incorporate.

Practical P/E vs. Theoretical P/E Let's carefully examine some of the factors that P/E-based fundamental analysis may ignore. First, the DDM can give a theoretical definition of P/E:

$$V_{s0} = \frac{DIV_1}{ER_s - g}$$

Dividing both sides of the equation by EPS_1 gives

$$\text{P/E ratio} = V_{s0}/EPS_1 = \frac{DIV_1/EPS_1}{ER_s - g} \tag{14.16}$$

This equation is a theoretical definition of the P/E ratio (called the theoretical P/E), substituting intrinsic value for price. It implies that the P/E ratio consists of three components:

1. DIV_1/EPS_1, the dividend payout ratio for next year's dividends and earnings
2. ER_s, the required rate of return by investors
3. g, the expected growth rate

Now, let's examine the effects of these components on the P/E ratio. Suppose that someone believes that a high P/E indicates a better investment selection, devising a strategy to buy common stocks with high P/E ratios. What factors might this person look for to assure he or she has made a sound investment decision when using P/E?

1. Suppose the practical P/E is high because the company truly has exceptional growth opportunities (as shown in the theoretical P/E, a high expected g leads to a high P/E). If P/E is high due to strong growth opportunities, then the stock may be a reasonable investment. This situation is analogous to a growth company with a high intrinsic value based on high expected growth.
2. Suppose the practical P/E ratio is high because the analysis ignored the level of risk inherent in ER_s. Notice that the practical P/E does not incorporate risk as does the theoretical P/E. The future stream of expected earnings per share of IBM is probably less risky than the future stream of expected earnings per share for Apple. In this case, practical P/E could be high only because the novice ignored the fact that Apple's expected earnings stream are more uncertain (or riskier) than IBM's. By using the practical P/E to compare Apple and IBM, the investor is assuming that the two computer firms have similar required rates of return. Ignoring the riskiness of the expected earnings of a firm would lead the practical P/E ratio to overstate the true theoretical P/E.
3. Most analysts calculate a P/E ratio by dividing a stock's price per share by the firm's current earnings per share (EPS_0). As the theoretical P/E formula shows, the calculation should instead reflect expected earnings per share (EPS_1). For a firm with rising earnings, a P/E based on current earnings per share will overstate the true P/E ratio.
4. Finally, an expected earnings per share close to zero can give a large calculated P/E ratio. In fact, as expected EPS approaches zero, the P/E ratio approaches infinity. As an example, if a company estimates expected earnings per share of $0.01 and a price per share of only $1.00, its P/E ratio equals 100 times.

After examining each component separately, we can draw the following conclusion: if P/E is high because of exceptional growth potential, then it may be a good reason to invest; if P/E is high because the calculation included the wrong expected return for the company's risk level, then it cannot support a decision to invest. P/E can also deceive the investor if it fails to reflect expected earnings or if it reflects small earnings per share.

What About Low P/E Stocks?

Many of the problems we discussed for high P/E stocks also apply to low P/E stocks, too. However, proponents of the low P/E investment strategy believe that such stocks are the best investments because they are cheap. For example, Graham and Dodd suggest that one should never buy a stock with a P/E higher than 12 for "value" investing.

This strategy resembles contrarian investing (discussed in Chapter 7), which advocates buying last year's worst-performing stocks. Contrarians look for P/Es that are low because other investors shunned the stocks, believing that low P/Es indicate likely candidates for undervalued stocks. Recall that Chapter 7 discussed results from several studies that examined low P/E stocks. Generally, these stocks seemed to earn excess returns in the past, and the studies seem to support the view that they earn superior returns. However, researchers are still looking for answers as to why low P/Es seem to indicate consistently strong performance. The relationship has been linked to the small-firm effect, which implies strong growth in companies with low market values, and the January effect, because much of the performance advantage of small firms occurred in January. Still, no final judgment has been passed. Like the MV/BV ratio, P/E analysis may be a good initial sorting method to identify candidates for more thorough fundamental analysis. A sound investment decision still requires detailed research about the company.

Implications for Investors on P/E

The foremost problem with P/E analysis arises from basing fundamental analysis on Equation 14.14 (practical P/E) because it uses the market value to calculate price. Instead, Equation 14.16 (theoretical P/E) gives a more accurate representation of company value. The best use of P/E comes from comparing values calculated by Equations 14.14 and 14.16 rather than comparing P/Es of different companies. This point helps clarify three problems with P/E-based investing.

1. It is dangerous to compare two companies' P/Es. Instead, one should compare a company's intrinsic value to its market value. Comparing P/Es of two firms could ignore critical differences between them.
2. Some investors avoid high P/E stocks because the statistic makes them look too expensive. A high P/E does not always mean that a stock is too expensive. Again, compare a company's practical P/E calculated from its market price (Equation 14.14) to that calculated from its intrinsic value or the theoretical P/E (Equation 14.16). This comparison may make a high P/E stock look like a bargain!
3. Similarly, some investors believe that all low P/E stocks are cheap and likely to be undervalued. Wise investors do not rely on this likelihood; they make direct comparisons of market prices with intrinsic values. The proper comparison may reveal that a lower P/E stock is not so cheap.

At the risk of sounding like a broken record, if a company's investment opportunities offer solid potential, it is a growth company and its shares may indicate a growth stock. Identify a growth stock by comparing practical P/E with the theoretical P/E. If the P/E ratio is used correctly, it leads to the same investment decisions as the EM or the DDM. Given the potential of P/Es to mislead, most investors should use the EM or the DDM to perform a fundamental analysis. It is the same analysis and gives much more straightforward results.

Two Alternative Ways to Use P/E

Holt's Alternative Use of P/E Those who must use P/E ratio as a way to make investment decisions could try Charles Holt's approach. He developed a formula that provides a different perspective on the use of P/E ratios.[18] Instead of calculating a P/E ratio and investing based on whether it is low or high, Holt's method analyzes the stock's current growth rate and its stated P/E ratio. His formula determines the number of years the stock must grow at its current growth rate to justify the stated P/E ratio.

For example, suppose that a stock's practical P/E is 50 times and its current growth rate is 40% whereas the stock market's growth rate is 15%. If Equation 14.17 yields 10, it says that the stock must grow at 40% for 10 years to justify the 50X P/E. Could this stock really grow at 40% for 10 years when the general market is growing at 15%? An alternate interpretation suggests that someone who pays 50 times the stock's earnings must hold it for 9 years to recover the investment. This method puts the company's P/E ratio in a different perspective.

The formula is

$$t(\text{in years}) = \frac{\ln\left[(P/E_g)/(P/E_s)\right]}{\ln\left[\dfrac{(1 + g_g + d_g)}{(1 + g_s + d_s)}\right]} \tag{14.17}$$

where P/E_g is the P/E ratio for a growth stock, P/E_s is the P/E ratio for a stock market index (e.g., the S&P 500), g_g is the growth rate of a growth stock, g_s is the growth rate of a stock market index, d_g is the dividend yield of a growth stock, and d_s is the dividend yield of a stock market index.

We illustrate Holt's alternative P/E method by applying it to Krispy Kreme Doughnuts, KKD, a popular doughnut company that started in Winston-Salem, North Carolina, in 1937. KKD went IPO in April 2000 at $21 per share issuing 13,800,000 shares. It had two 2-for-1 stock splits in 2001.

Let's use the appropriate numbers provided in Table 14.3 for Krispy Kreme (g) and the S&P500 Index (s) to find the number of years (t) Krispy Kreme must grow at 40% to justify its current P/E of 50 times.

$$t(\text{in years}) = \frac{\ln\left[50/14\right]}{\ln\left[\dfrac{(1 + 0.40 + 0.0)}{(1 + 0.15 + 0.02)}\right]} = 7.1 \text{ years}$$

Interpreting Holt's method of P/E, Krispy Kreme must grow at the rate of 40% for more than seven years to justify a P/E ratio of 50 times. What are the chances that any company can maintain a growth rate of 40% per year for seven

---

[18]Charles Holt, "The Influence of Growth Duration on Share Price," *Journal of Finance*, September 1962.

Company	P/E Ratio	Growth Rate (g)	Dividend Yield (d)	TABLE 14.3
Krispy Kreme (g)	50X	40%	0%	Effect of P/E Ratio When Measured in t Years
S&P 500 Index (s)	14X	15%	2%	

years when the stock market is growing at 15%? If this kind of growth rate seems unlikely, it raises questions about the reasonableness of the P/E ratio. Perhaps the P/E ratio is high because the calculation ignores risk. Perhaps the stock is simply overvalued.

The Investment Insight on page 383 confirms the dangers of investing in stocks with high P/E or glamour stocks. At its height, three stocks showed P/Es exceeding 100 and JDS Uniphase and Yahoo! were close to 100. Notice that the five-year required earnings growth rate are high for all the stocks, and they exceed the historical as well as the estimated five-year growth rate. This means that an investor would probably overpay for the stocks at its current P/E.

Firms That Pay No Dividends, or When $g > ER_s$ A second alternative use of P/E is to value companies that currently do not pay dividends. Most high-technology companies, though not as popular after the bursting of the tech bubble, fall under this category. The method follows the general valuation technique by calculating the present value of a future cash flows. Except in the case of firms that pay no dividends, their only future cash flow is the expected stock appreciation, say in Year 3 or P_3. A company's price, P_3, can be calculated by multiplying its forecasted earnings per share in Year 3 (EPS_3) and P/E forecasted for Year 3 (P/E_3), usually provided by analysts and in investment reports. Notice that by multiplying (EPS_3) by (P/E_3), the earnings cancel and the product equals P_3. To estimate an intrinsic value, V_{s0}, calculate the present value of P_3 using a risk-adjusted required return, ER_s. (ER_s can be calculated using CAPM or Equation 14.11). The intrinsic value, V_{s0}, of a stock that pays no dividends is calculated as follows:

$$V_{s0} = \frac{P_3}{(1 + ER_s)^3}$$

(14.18)

This method allows us to incorporate risk (ER_s) and expectations about the company's future earnings. For example, Value Line forecasts Krispy Kreme (KKD), the doughnut company, earnings to be $1.85 per share three years from today (2005) and its P/E ratio to be 40 times.[19] It gives a $74 (40 times $1.85) price for 2005 or P_3. Discounting at KKD's required return ($ER_s = .14$), its intrinsic value is estimated at about $50. Now, you can decide whether Krispy Kreme is undervalued or overvalued by comparing its intrinsic value with Krispy Kreme's market price (it was $34.28 in late 2002).

Another way to use this P/E method is to estimate the "implied EPS growth rate" for Krispy Kreme using its current market price of $34.28. If we assume

---

[19]Value Line Investment Survey, October 2002.

INVESTMENT INSIGHT
Stock Valuations and P/E Ratios

One of the most important lessons for investors to learn from the bubble in technology stocks that broke in early 2000 is to pay attention to the stock price/earnings ratio, and its relationship to historical and projected earnings growth rates. As a general rule, investors should be wary of stocks that are selling for P/E ratios that are substantially larger than earnings growth rates. It could be a sign that the stock is overvalued, perhaps even part of a bubble that is about to break.

Consider the five stocks listed in the following table. All five were among the darlings of the "new economy" and, by early March 2000, had risen substantially in price. Cisco Systems, for instance, almost tripled in price between March 1999 and March 2000. With a market value of about $452 billion, Cisco had the second-highest market value of any stock traded in the United States. In addition to Cisco, the other four stocks all had P/E ratios in March 2000 that exceeded 100. Two, JDS Uniphase and Yahoo!, were selling in excess of 600 times earnings.

Stock	Market Value March 2000 ($ billions)	P/E Ratio	Five-Year Earnings Growth Rates (per year)		
			Historical	Estimated	Required*
Cisco Systems	452	148	38%	30%	69%
JDS Uniphase	99	668	57	44	129
Oracle	211	153	28	25	70
Sun Microsystems	149	119	29	21	62
Yahoo!	90	623	444	56	126

*The annual earnings growth rate required to justify the stock's P/E ratio in relationship to the market's P/E ratio and the expected growth rate in overall corporate profits.

The table also lists the required annual growth rate in earnings over the next five years to justify the stock's P/E ratio. The required earnings growth rate was found by using the formula presented in the chapter. The formula includes the market's P/E ratio (which was 28 in March of 2000), the stock's dividend yield (all five paid no dividends), the market's dividend yield (1.14%), and the expected annual growth rate in corporate earnings (approximately 20%).

Notice that the required five-year earnings growth rates are substantially higher than the estimated five-year earnings growth rates—in some cases three times higher. With the exception of Yahoo!, the required five-year earnings growth rates are at least twice as high as the historical five-year earnings growth rates. In short, by this measure all five appear substantially overvalued.

What happened is well known. The bubble in technology stocks broke in the early spring of 2000, and the prices of all five fell. The following table shows their valuations three years later. Notice that each declined by at least 70%; two declined by more than 90%.

Stock	Market Value February 2003 ($ billions)	Percent Change
Cisco Systems	104	−77%
JDS Uniphase	4	−96
Oracle	63	−70
Sun Microsystems	11	−93
Yahoo!	12	−87

Even though an economic slowdown certainly contributed to the fall in these and other high-flying stocks, so too did a realization on the part of investors in early 2000 that the companies simply couldn't make enough money to justify their stratospheric valuations.

Questions for Critical Thinking
1. Under what circumstances would an investor be justified in ignoring a stock's high P/E ratio?
2. Do you feel as though any of these stocks are now undervalued? In other words, have investors overreacted?

that the forecasted P/E and ER_s are relatively stable, we can find the EPS_3 for the given market price. For Krispy Kreme, it is

$$\frac{40(EPS_3)}{(1 + .14)^3} = \$34.28$$

We can solve for EPS_3 to equal $1.27. We know that today's EPS (EPS_0) is $0.65, so the annual EPS growth rate for KKD is 25%. This result says that if you pay $34.28 for KKD, you are paying for EPS to grow at 25% per year. To estimate the growth rate, use the growth trend equation, $\$0.65(1 + g)^3 = \$1.27$. Effectively an investor has prepaid $34.28 for a promise of EPS to grow at 25% per year. Now you need to explore whether KKD's PV of growth opportunities offers a minimum growth rate of 25%. If so, you would buy the stock, otherwise you would not.

RECAPRECAP

If the shoe fits, wear it. All kinds of investors, novices and money managers alike, follow this advice and use the MV/BV and P/E ratios to make investment decisions simply because they seem to work. Research studies show that stocks with low MV/BV and low P/E ratios tend to earn superior returns, and practical investors say, If it works, use it.

12. Wendy's International (WEN), the well-known fast-food company, has a market price of $35, and its expected earnings per share equals $2.10. What is WEN's P/E ratio?

13. If WEN's book value per share equals $11.00, what is its MV/BV ratio at a market price of $35?

14. The Cheesecake Factory's (CAKE) expected EPS in Year 3 equals $2.35 ($EPS_3$) and its expected P/E ratio in Year 3 is 26X (P/E_3). If the Cheesecake Factory's required return via CAPM equals 11%, what is its intrinsic value using Equation 14.18? If its market price is $32.71, is it a good investment?

15. What is CAKE's implied EPS growth rate at the market price of $32.71 and EPS_0 of $0.60? Is that growth rate reasonable?

Many money managers use criteria such as P/Es less than 14 times, MV/BV ratios less than 1.5 times, and price/sales per share ratios less than 1.0 as bargain stocks. These money managers used terms similar to ours. They used low P/E and MV/BV ratios as part of initial sorting processes to find stocks likely to be undervalued, but they do not stop there. Most money managers continue to examine the fundamentals and the growth opportunities for these companies to see whether the stocks still look undervalued based on those assessments. When they use terms such as *dirt cheap* or *a little expensive* or *realistic target,* they seem to have estimated intrinsic values for these stocks and compared them with market prices before making investment decisions.

IMPLICATIONS FOR INVESTORS USING FUNDAMENTAL ANALYSIS

We learned some ways to determine whether to invest in certain stocks. One way is to calculate an intrinsic value. If the company had and will continue to show relatively constant earnings growth, then use either the DDM or the EM. If the company is currently experiencing extraordinarily high growth, then use the non-constant growth model. Finally, if a company pays no dividends, use the P/E method. If a company is a new issue (an IPO) or shows declining earnings, an investor cannot rely on these methods but must dig deeply into qualitative information about the company's future investment opportunities. Remember the implications pointed out in the EM section; that is, the return on investment must exceed the required return, ER_s, before it adds value to the company stock. Once the intrinsic value is estimated, an investor must compare this value with the stock's market price. If the intrinsic value is greater than the market price, the stock is undervalued and an attractive investment. If the intrinsic value is less than the market price, the stock is overvalued, suggesting a decision to sell any currently owned shares or perhaps to sell short. Of course this final decision is made after considering all other factors and growth opportunities for the company as described in Chapters 11 through 13 as well as in this chapter. Fundamental analysis is a combination of intrinsic valuation and company analysis in the context of the economy and industry.

Investors use shortcut methods for fundamental analysis. Two popular ones are based on MV/BV and P/E ratios. These two ratios are subject to some conceptual shortcomings, but offer effectiveness as analytical tools. These ratios can underlie a very effective initial sorting process to identify stocks that are likely to be undervalued. The ratio-based strategy calls for buying stocks with low MV/BV or low P/E ratios because they tend to be undervalued, relatively cheap issues. The analysis should not stop with just finding low P/E stocks or low MV/BV stocks. Based on the DDM or the EM, further analysis should compare a stock's intrinsic value with its market price to make sure it is undervalued. Analyzing and studying a company's future investment opportunities increase the odds of finding undervalued, or growth, stocks. This analysis of the company's fundamental economic value must evaluate *future* opportunities and separate true growth opportunities from fluff.

The next section explores an even more exciting area of investment—derivative securities, better known as options and futures. With excitement usually comes greater risk. The chapters in the next section discuss the risks involved in derivative securities. Once you develop a better understanding of the risks, you will find that options and futures can be used for hedging as well as speculative purposes. Studying Chapters 15 and 16 may open up other investment avenues.

SUMMARY

1. What is intrinsic value?
The intrinsic value of a common stock is its fundamental economic value. Fundamental analysts try to determine the intrinsic value of a stock by evaluating the future dividend payments and growth opportunities of the company. This chapter discusses the methods by which an investor may estimate an intrinsic value for a company's common stock.

2. What is the dividend discount model?
The DDM is one method by which to estimate an intrinsic value of a common stock. The model defines common stock value as the present value of the stock's future dividend stream and its future value. A constant dividend growth model can be used if company dividends are estimated to grow at an average constant rate, g.

3. What is the earnings model?

The EM is another method by which to estimate an intrinsic value for a common stock. The model assumes that a company's earnings grow at a constant rate, g, and defines common stock value as the present value of the future earnings stream of the company. It also shows that the future earnings stream is generated by the firm's future growth opportunities. We discussed some implications stemming from the EM, and we differentiated a growth company from a growth stock.

4. How does an investor conduct fundamental analysis on a company stock?

Once an intrinsic value is calculated via the models described, the analyst can assess whether the stock is an attractive investment. Intrinsic value is a benchmark value to which the analyst compares the stock's market price. If the market price is less than the intrinsic value, the stock is undervalued and an attractive investment; if the traded price is greater than the intrinsic value, the stock is overvalued and should be avoided.

5. How can an investor analyze a stock with nonconstant growth?

When growth is greater than required rate of return, the DDM and EM breaks down. Nonconstant growth stocks, with growth greater than required rate of return, require a modified two-phase DDM. It combines an estimate of a nonconstant growth rate and a constant growth rate to calculate the present value of dividends using the appropriate growth rates for each period of time.

6. How is the MV/BV ratio used for investment purposes?

The MV/BV ratio, defined as the market value of the stock divided by its book value, is another way to determine whether a stock is undervalued. The market value of a stock should at least equal its book value, which indicates the value of the firm's assets after it satisfies its liabilities. If the MV/BV ratio equals 1.0, then market value equals book value. If the ratio is less than 1.0, then the stock's price is depressed below the book value, and it may be undervalued because, by liquidating the company (selling the assets and paying off the liabilities), an investor may make an excess positive return. Stocks with low MV/BV ratios fulfill a popular investment criterion.

7. What are the pros and cons of using the price/earnings multiple, or P/E ratio?

Four components make up the P/E ratio used with the DDM. Whatever the P/E, only if the firm has solid growth opportunities is the stock a good investment. However, P/E ratios do not account for the risk of the stock, can be misleading if earnings per share is close to zero, and generally are improperly calculated using the current earnings per share instead of the forecasted earnings per share. The DDM or EM could provide the same conclusion, without the potential problems of P/E. The chapter offers an alternative use of P/E that may not be as misleading.

MINI CASE 1

The purpose of this mini case is to practice applying fundamental analysis on a company. Table 14.4 provides financial information for Company WWX. Suppose at the end of 2002, you are estimating WWX's intrinsic value.

1. Estimate WWX's expected long-run growth rate using the dividend trend, the earnings trend, and Equation 14.9. Assume that the historical trend from 1997 to 2002 estimates the future growth rate.
2. Estimated WWX's required rate of return using the CAPM, with the risk-free rate at 2% and the market risk premium estimated to be 8.6%.
3. Estimate DIV_1, using equation $DIV_0(1 + g)$.
4. Estimate WWX's intrinsic value using the DDM.
5. Estimate WWX's intrinsic value using the EM.

	1997	2002
DIV	$0.85	$1.17
EPS	$1.18	$1.80

WWX has no preferred stock issue. Beta equals 0.75.
WWX market price today is $53.

	2003
Return on share equity	18.6%
All dividends to net profits	65%

TABLE 14.4

Company WWX Data Sheet

6. Is WWX overvalued or undervalued if its market price is about $53? What investment decision would you make on WWX?
7. What other information would you consider before making this investment decision? (*Hint:* Review Chapters 11 through 13).

MINI CASE 2

The purpose of this mini case is to apply the alternative P/E method from Equation 14.17 and learn to interpret it. These data apply to Cisco during its height in 2000.

	P/E Ratio	Growth Rate	Dividend Yield
Cisco	400X	40.0%	0%
S&P 500 Index	25X	15.0%	5.0%

1. Apply Holt's model (Equation 14.17) and interpret the results.
2. What is Cisco's stock today? Does the price confirm the results as given here? Explain.

REVIEW EXERCISES

1. What is a stock's intrinsic value, and how do fundamental analysts use this figure?
2. Suppose that a stock's expected dividends are $1.50 per year for the next 10 years, and its expected price in Year 10 is $65.00. The required rate of return equals 0.12.
   a. What is the price of the stock in Year 5?
   b. What is the price of the stock today using the future value of $65.00?
   c. Determine the price of the stock today based on the stock price for Year 5.
   d. What can you conclude about your answers in Questions (b) and (c)? Explain.
3. Suppose that a stock's expected dividends are $2.00 per year for the next 10 years, and its expected price in Year 10 is $85.00. The required rate of return equals 0.17.
   a. What is the price of the stock in Year 3?
   b. What is the price of the stock today using the future value of $85.00?
   c. Determine the price of the stock today based on the stock price for Year 3.
   d. What can you conclude about your answers in questions b and c? Explain.
4. Suppose that a stock's expected dividends are $1.00 per year for the next 15 years, and its expected price in Year 15 is $125.00. The required rate of return equals 0.14.
   a. What is the price of the stock in Year 10?
   b. What is the price of the stock today using the future value of $125.00?
   c. Determine the price of the stock today based on the stock price for Year 10.
   d. What can you conclude about your answers in Questions (b) and (c)? Explain.

5. Suppose that stock A's current dividends per share are $1.55 and you expect it to grow at a 15% annual rate for the next five years. Also, you speculate that it will sell for $95.00 five years from now. You would like to earn 18% on this investment.
   a. How much are you willing to pay for the stock today?
   b. Suppose it is selling for $42.50 today. Would you buy the stock? Explain.
6. Suppose PepsiCo's expected price in Year 2006 is $50 and the company expects to pay dividends of $2.25 in 2004, $2.50 in 2005, and $2.75 in 2006.
   a. If today is the year-end of 2003, what is PepsiCo's intrinsic value if ER_S equals 15%?
   b. If PepsiCo is selling for $45 today, is it undervalued or overvalued based on its intrinsic value? Would you invest in Pepsi's stock?
7. Suppose Coca-Cola's expected price in 2006 is $75, and the company expects to pay dividends of $.92 in 2004, $1.10 in 2005, and $1.30 in 2006.
   a. If today is the year-end of 2003, what is Coke's intrinsic value if ER_S equals 16%?
   b. Using fundamental analysis on Coca-Cola, would you invest in its stock if it is selling for $65 today? Explain.
8. Suppose that stock W's expected dividends equal $1.65, and it is expected to grow annually at 9% for an indefinite period.
   a. If the required rate of return is 12%, what is the stock's intrinsic value?
   b. If stock W's price today were $56.50, would you invest? Explain.
9. Suppose that stock Z's expected dividends equal $2.50, and it is expected to grow annually at 12% for an indefinite period.
   a. If the required rate of return is 16%, what is the stock's intrinsic value?
   b. If stock Z's price today were $55.00, would you invest? Explain.
10. Stock X is currently trading at $29.50. Its current dividends per share equal $1.25, and this amount is expected to double in 10 years.
    a. What is stock X's growth rate?
    b. If you have a 12% required return on stock X, what is its intrinsic value?
    c. Is it overvalued or undervalued? Explain.
11. Stock ABC is currently trading at $32.50. Its current dividends per share equal $0.50, and this amount is expected to triple in 10 years.
    a. What is stock ABC's growth rate?
    b. If required return on stock ABC equals 0.13, what is its intrinsic value?
    c. Is it overvalued or undervalued? Explain.
12. Stock DOG is currently trading at $35.00. Its current dividends per share equal $2.50, and this amount is expected to triple in 15 years.
    a. What is stock DOG's growth rate?
    b. If required return on the stock equals 0.18, what is its intrinsic value?
    c. Is it overvalued or undervalued? Explain.
13. Gunhoe Company is expecting its return on equity to equal 25% and expects to pay 40% of profits as dividends. Its current dividends are $2.00, and the investors require an 18% return.
    a. What is Gunhoe's expected growth rate?
    b. What is Gunhoe's intrinsic value?
    c. If its market price is $73.50, would you invest in Gunhoe stock? Explain.
14. Why is it incorrect to say that a stock's intrinsic value is equal to the present value of its earnings per share?
15. State the equation for an intrinsic value based on the EM. Based on the EM, how does one define the term *growth company*? (*Hint:* When is present value of growth opportunities positive?)
16. Using the concept developed in the EM, comment on the following statement made by a tipster: "WXY Corp is purchasing a lot ($250 million) of machines and warehouses right now. They must be expanding and so they must be a growth stock. I would strongly recommend that you buy 200,000 shares today."

17. General Form invested in several projects last month, but the stock price did not move at all. A puzzled stockbroker asks, "Is the market stupid?" Explain the possible reasons for the stable stock price by referring to the EM.

18. For what reasons can a company's P/E ratio be high? Why is this ratio not an accurate measure of a good investment?

19. Explain how a low MV/BV ratio could contribute to a good investment strategy.

20. Corie Kobb plans to invest in common stocks for a period of 12 years, after which she will sell out, buy a lifetime room-and-board membership in a retirement home, and retire. She feels that Odell Mines is currently, but temporarily, undervalued by the market. Kobb expects Odell Mines' current earnings per share and dividend to double in the next 12 years. Odell Mines' last dividend was $2.00, and its stock currently sells for $45 a share.
    a. To estimate Odell Mines' expected return, Kobb finds that the U.S. Treasury bill rate is at 4% whereas the S&P 500 Index has a 14% rate of return. Also, the stock's beta estimate is found to be 0.6. Estimate Odell Mines' required rate of return.
    b. If Corie wants to earn a 10% return, would she buy the stock?
    c. If Corie purchases Odell Mines for $45 per share, what rate will she earn?

21. MaDonna plans to invest in common stocks for a period of 15 years, after which she will sell out, buy a lifetime room-and-board membership in a retirement home, and retire. She feels that stock XYZ is currently, but temporarily, undervalued by the market. MaDonna expects XYZ's current earnings per share of $5.00 to increase to $35.69 in the next 15 years. XYZ's current dividend was $1.25, and its stock currently sells for $50 a share.
    a. To estimate XYZ's expected return, MaDonna finds that the U.S. Treasury bill rate is at 5% whereas the S&P 500 Index has a 14% expected rate of return. Also, the stock's beta estimate is found to be 1.3. Estimate XYZ's required return.
    b. If MaDonna wants to earn a 16.7% return, would she buy the stock?
    c. If MaDonna purchases XYZ for $50 per share, what rate will she earn?

22. Stock ABC is considered to be a growth stock with a nonconstant growth rate of 25% for the next five years, followed by 15% sustainable annual growth thereafter. ABC's current dividends per share are $1.10, and its required rate of return is 18%. Calculate its intrinsic value.

23. Stock CAT is considered to be a growth stock with a nonconstant growth rate of 20% for the next five years, followed by 14% sustainable annual growth thereafter. CAT's current dividends per share are $2.00, and its required rate of return is 16%. Calculate its intrinsic value.

24. Boston Chicken (ticker symbol BOST) went public in 1993 and pays no dividends to its stockholders. An analyst forecasts its earnings per share to equal $2.60 in three years with a P/E ratio of 25 times.
    a. Estimate Boston Chicken's forecasted price three years from now, given that the analysts' forecasts are accurate.
    b. If the market risk premium equals 0.086, the U.S. Treasury bill yields 5%, and the analyst estimates BOST's beta to be 1.55, what is Boston Chicken's required return?
    c. What is Boston Chicken's intrinsic value?
    d. If Boston Chicken is currently selling for $35 per share, is it a good investment? Explain.

25. Cisco Systems went public in 1990 and pays no dividends to its stockholders. Analysts' forecasts estimate that Cisco's earnings per share will equal $1.25 in three years, and its expected P/E ratio will be 23 times.
    a. Estimate Cisco's forecasted price three years from now if the analysts' forecasts are accurate.
    b. If the market risk premium equals 0.086, the U.S. Treasury bill yields 5%, and the analysts estimate Cisco's beta to equal 1.65, what is Cisco's required return?

    c. What is Cisco's intrinsic value?

    d. If Cisco is currently trading for $14 per share, is it a good investment? Explain.

26. Papa John International (ticker symbol PIZZA) went public in 1993 at $13 per share, and the stock currently pays no dividends. Analysts' forecasts estimate that Papa John's earnings per share will equal $2.10 in three years, and its expected P/E ratio will be 30 times.

    a. What product does Papa John produce and sell?

    b. Estimate Papa John's forecasted price three years from now if the analysts' forecasts are accurate.

    c. If the market risk premium equals 0.086, the U.S. Treasury bill yields 5%, and the analysts estimate Papa John's beta to equal 1.80, what is PIZZA's required return?

    d. What is Papa John's intrinsic value?

    e. If Papa John is currently trading for $37 per share, is it a good investment? Explain.

27. Go-Tek Company is expecting its return on equity to equal 15% and expects to pay 20% of profits as dividends. Its current dividends are $1.00, and the investors require a 16% return.

    a. What is Go-Tek's expected growth rate?

    b. What is Go-Tek's intrinsic value?

    c. If its market price is $30.00, would you invest in Go-Tek stock? Explain.

    d. What is Go-Tek's earnings per share if the dividend payout ratio is currently 20%?

    e. What is Go-Tek's intrinsic value if it pays all the company's earnings per share as dividends?

    f. Assuming that the return on equity remains constant at 15%, what should the management do to increase the intrinsic value?

28. Silly-Con Valley Company is expecting its return on equity to equal 18% and expects to pay 10% of profits as dividends. Its current dividends are $2.00, and the investors require a 20% return.

    a. What is Silly-Con's expected growth rate?

    b. What is Silly-Con's intrinsic value?

    c. If its market price is $60.00, would you invest in Silly-Con stock? Explain.

    d. What are Silly-Con's earnings per share if the dividend payout ratio is currently 10%?

    e. What is Silly-Con's intrinsic value if it pays all the company's earnings per share as dividends?

    f. Assuming that the return on equity remains constant at 18%, what should the management do to increase the intrinsic value?

    g. What conclusion about dividend policy can you draw from this problem?

29. ZAP Inc.'s expected dividends are $2.50 per share, and its expected earnings per share are $10.00. The required rate of return, ER_s, for ZAP equals 0.18, and the expected return on equity is 0.20.

    a. What is the ZAP's growth rate?

    b. Calculate the intrinsic value of the stock using the EM.

    c. Suppose *The Wall Street Journal* reports that ZAP is trading at $75. Using the fundamental analysis, would you buy the stock? Why?

    d. Using the EM and the present value of growth opportunities term, determine whether the stock is a growth company.

    e. Is stock ZAP a growth stock?

30. SpiderWeb, an Internet company, expects dividends to equal $1.50 per share, and its expected earnings per share are $5.00. The required rate of return for the stock equals 0.13, and the expected return on equity is 0.12.

    a. What is SpiderWeb's growth rate?

    b. Calculate the intrinsic value of the stock using the EM.

   c.   Suppose *The Wall Street Journal* reports that the stock is trading at $35. Using the fundamental analysis, would you buy the stock? Why?

   d.   Using the EM and the present value of growth opportunities term, determine whether the stock is a growth company.

   e.   Suppose your client comments that this stock has a growth rate that is greater than zero, so it should be a growth stock. Is he or she right? If so, how would you support his or her comment, and if not, how would you explain his or her error?

31. HPT's current dividends are $1.00 per share, and it is expected to increase to $3.7072 in 10 years. The required rate of return for the stock equals 0.16, and the expected dividend payout ratio equals 20%.

   a.   Calculate HPT's growth rate.

   b.   What is HPT's current earnings per share?

   c.   Calculate the intrinsic value of HPT using the EM.

   d.   Suppose *The Wall Street Journal* reports that the stock is trading at $55. Using the fundamental analysis, would you buy the stock? Why?

   e.   Using the EM and the present value of growth opportunities term, determine whether the stock is a growth company.

32. MICK, an entertainment company, reported that current earnings per share equal $10.00, and it expects earnings to double in 10 years. It currently pays 25% of earnings as dividends. The required rate of return for the stock equals 0.10.

   a.   What is MICK's growth rate?

   b.   What is MICK's return on equity?

   c.   Calculate the intrinsic value of the stock using the EM for MICK.

   d.   Suppose *The Wall Street Journal* reports that the stock is trading at $85. Using the fundamental analysis, would you buy the stock? Why?

   e.   Is MICK a growth company? Explain.

   f.   Is MICK a growth stock? Explain.

   g.   How can a firm be a growth stock, but not a growth company? Explain.

33. Zoom, Inc., a laser company, expects earnings per share to be $20.00 next year, and shareholder equity per share equals $87. The company is expected to pay $5.00 in dividends next year. The required rate of return for the stock equals 0.19.

   a.   What is Zoom, Inc.'s return on equity?

   b.   What is Zoom, Inc.'s growth rate?

   c.   Calculate the intrinsic value of Zoom, Inc. using the EM.

   d.   Suppose The Wall Street Journal reports that the stock is trading at $295. Using the fundamental analysis, would you buy the stock? Why?

   e.   Is it a growth company?

   f.   How can a firm be a growth company, but not a growth stock? Explain.

CRITICAL THINKING EXERCISES

1. At the library, find information on McDonald's, the fast-food restaurant chain, and conduct a fundamental analysis. If necessary, use the nonconstant growth model instead of the DDM. Is McDonald's stock overvalued or undervalued? Carefully justify your answer with information to back your analysis.

2. Repeat the fundamental analysis conducted in the Lone Star Steakhouse (STAR) with more recent Value Line data. Do you concur with the analysis conducted in the chapter? Justify your answer.

3. Using Value Line or a similar source, find the 10 stocks with the highest P/E ratios and the 10 with the lowest P/E ratios as listed in Value Line's Index. Also, find their stock prices as recorded by Value Line. Find today's stock prices for these 20 stocks.

Calculate returns for the 10 low P/E stocks and the 10 high P/E stocks. (Remember to include dividends paid during the holding period.) Next, calculate an arithmetic mean return for each group of low P/Es and high P/Es. Does this return confirm or refute the contention that low P/E stocks outperform high P/E stocks?

4. Using Value Line's list again, find the 10 stocks with the highest and lowest MV/BV ratios. Find today's stock prices for these 20 stocks. Repeat the same process of calculating returns for each group, low MV/BV and high MV/BV ratios. Discuss your results. What is your conclusion?

THE INTERNET INVESTOR

1. Visit a Web site of a brokerage firm that offers news about a firm that just announced its earnings (for either the quarter or the year). Determine the effect of any difference between forecasted earnings and actual earnings on the stock price. Discuss factors that may affect the difference in forecasted and actual earnings.

2. Visit a Web site of a brokerage firm or security analysis firm and find a company analysis report conducted by an analyst. What factors does the analyst mention that are consistent with the models discussed in this chapter? What factors aren't consistent with the factors mentioned in the models discussed in this chapter? Discuss which factors are important and why.

3. Find a stock that interests you and follow its news releases from one of the Internet sites. Usually a brokerage firm Web site will provide news releases that may affect the firm. Find the intraday prices for the day and determine whether the stock prices react appropriately to the news releases. Does the stock movement lag or lead the news release?

Derivative Securities

In the next two chapters, we describe so-called derivative securities:

options and futures. They are called derivative securities because the

value of options and futures derive from other securities. Even if you

never participate in the options and futures markets, it is important to

understand the basics of derivative securities. For one thing, options

and futures are closely linked to the stock and bond markets.

15

Fundamentals of Options

PREVIOUSLY . . .

In the prior three chapters, we described the investment characteristics of common stock and some strategies involving stock investing. Security analysis taught us that by understanding and analyzing the company, we could make a sound investment decision in the company's common stock.

IN THIS CHAPTER . . .

We discuss the fundamentals of options, one of two major types of derivative securities. The pricing of options and investment strategies using options are described. In addition, we examine other securities that involve options.

TO COME . . .

In the next chapter, we continue our coverage of derivative securities by examining futures contracts.

CHAPTER OBJECTIVES

After reading Chapter 15, you should be able to answer the following questions:

1. What are the basic characteristics of option contracts?

2. What is the value of an option at expiration?

3. What are some common option trading strategies?

4. How are options valued?

5. What other securities resemble options?

Assume that a few years ago you bought shares Wal-Mart for $40. Today, Wal-Mart is selling for about $52. You are still optimistic about the company's long-run prospects but worry about a short-term price decline. You wonder whether you could find a way to protect most of your profits while still holding on to your stock.

Here is another situation to consider. Let's assume you determine that Bank of America's stock price will rise sharply over the next few months. The trouble is that at $66 a share, you are not sure you want to commit $6,600 to buy 100 shares. Can you find a way of making money in Bank of America stock without having to buy the stock?

Finally, you watched shares of Intel stock slide sharply as the sales in the semiconductor industry remain down. You decide that Intel will be volatile in the short run, and expect its stock price to continue declining. You could sell Intel stock short to take advantage of your expectation, but you believe short sales are just too risky. You wish you could find another way to profit if Intel's stock price does fall.

By trading options, you can accomplish all three of these investment objectives. You could buy a put option to protect your Wal-Mart profits; buy a call option to profit if B of A's stock takes off; and buy a put option to profit if Intel's stock price falls.

In this chapter, we discuss the fundamentals of options. Options are different from more traditional investments, such as stocks and bonds, and confront investors with a unique set of risks. At the same time, however, options offer investors unique opportunities, examples of which we just outlined. Options are not for everyone, but they still play an important role in the contemporary investment world.

BASIC CHARACTERISTICS OF OPTION CONTRACTS

exercise (or strike) price

Price at which stock is bought or sold if an option is exercised.

expiration date

Date the option expires; usually the third Friday of the month indicated.

call option

An option to buy.

put option

An option to sell.

in the money

If the stock price exceeds the exercise price of a call option.

out of the money

If the stock price is less than the call option's exercise price.

An option contract gives the buyer, or holder, the right but not the obligation to buy or sell a stated number of shares of common stock (usually 100 shares) at a specified price (called the **exercise or strike price**) until a specified point in time (called the **expiration date**).[1] An option to buy stock is a **call option**; an option to sell is a **put option**. Let's look at an example of each.

On September 30, 2002, a call option on General Electric (GE) stock with an exercise price of $25 that would expire in October 2002 was selling for $1.05. On the same day, a put option on GE with the same exercise price and expiration date was selling for $1.45. Owning the call option gives the holder the right to buy 100 shares of GE at $25 per share until October 18, 2002. Owning the put option gives holder the right to sell 100 shares of GE at $25 per share until October 18, 2002. The price of the call option contract was $105 ($1.05 times 100 shares) and the put option cost $145 ($1.45 times 100 shares). GE stock closed on September 30, 2002, at $24.46 per share. If a call option's stock price higher than the exercise price, it is said to be **in the money**. If a call option's stock price is less than the exercise price, it is said to be **out of the money**. If a put option's stock price is less than the exercise price, the put is in the money. If the put option's stock price is greater than the exercise price, the put is out of the

---

[1]Almost all options are protected from stock splits and stock dividends. If the underlying stock splits, say, 2 for 1, the exercise price of the options will automatically be halved.

money. If, by chance, the exercise price of an option, either a call or a put, is equal to the stock price, the option is said to be **at the money**. Notice that the GE call is out of the money (stock price equals $24.47 and exercise price is $25), while the GE put is in the money.

An option is considered to be a **derivative security** because its value derives from another security (i.e., the underlying stock). Because a call is an option to buy at a set price, holding all other factors constant, its price should move in the same direction as the price of the stock; the price of a put, because it is an option to sell, should move in the opposite direction from the price of the stock.

Call options are generally bought by investors who expect the price of a particular stock, such as GE, to rise over a short period of time. However, put options are generally bought by investors who believe that the price of the underlying stock will fall over a short period of time. A buyer can decide whether the option is worthwhile by calculating the premium on the option. The **premium** can be defined as the "break-even" dollar increase (or decrease) in the stock price for the option to be profitable.

The premium on a call option is defined as the call price minus the stock price plus the exercise price. For the 25 October GE call, the premium equals

$$\$1.05 - \$24.47 + \$25 = \$1.58$$

This premium of $1.58 reflects the $0.53 ($24.47 − $25) deficit in the GE call—meaning it is out of the money by $0.53—plus the market price on the call contract, which cost $1.05. So, for the buyer of the call to begin making a profit, GE stock must increase by $1.58, or that is the "break-even" point.

The premium on a put option is defined as the put price minus the exercise price plus the stock price. For the 25 October GE put, the premium equals

$$\$1.45 - \$25 + \$24.47 = \$0.92$$

Again, this premium indicates the dollar amount that GE stock must decrease by before the buyer of the put can begin making a profit. Because the put is in the money by $0.53, it reduces the "break-even" point by that amount. However, the buyer paid $0.92 more than the profits that can accrue from the put option, making $0.92 the premium beyond the put option value.

Options create some tricky situations. The holder of the option has the right to buy or sell stock at a set price for a set period of time. The holder of the option is said to have a **long position**. If the option is exercised (i.e., if the holder actually buys or sells the stock), from whom does he or she buy the stock or to whom does he or she sell it? The answer is the person who sold the option that the holder bought. In other words, someone who sells a call option agrees to sell stock at a fixed price for a fixed period of time to someone else at the buyer's discretion. Likewise, someone who sells a put option agrees to buy stock at a fixed price for a fixed period of time from someone else, again at that buyer's discretion. Selling an option is often referred to as **writing an option**; the option writer is said to have a **short position**. It is important to remember that every long position in options *must* be offset by a short position.

Why would anyone write an option and accept an uncertain obligation? The writer takes this position in exchange for the price of the call. The writer of the call receives the amount paid by the buyer of the call and agreeing to assume the risk

---

at the money

If the stock price equals the call option's exercise price.

derivative security

Security whose value derives from another security.

premium

Call price minus the current stock price plus the exercise price.

long position

Position held by the buyer of the option.

writing an option

Selling an option.

short position

Position held by the writer of the option.

of delivering the stock when "called." The writer of the put also receives the price of the put, which is paid by the buyer of the put. The writer then assumes the risk of taking the stock from the buyer when the stock is "put" on him or her.

Options traders often use the terms *intrinsic value* and *time value* when referring to options. The intrinsic value of a call option equals either zero if the option is out of the money or the difference between the stock price and exercise price if the option is in the money. The intrinsic value of a put option equals either zero if the option is out of the money or the difference between the exercise price and stock price if the option is in the money. The time value of an option is defined as the difference between the price of the option and its intrinsic value. If the option is in the money, the time value equals the premium. The use of the term *time value* is unfortunate because the difference between an option's price and intrinsic value, like the size of the option's premium, is a function of more than the time until expiration. This issue is explored in more depth later in the chapter when we discuss option pricing models.

The general reason an investor writes an option is to capture the price of the option. In other words, someone might write the call option in the previous example expecting that GE's stock would not rise much between early October and mid-October. Similarly, someone might write the put option, betting that GE's stock would not fall too far over the same period. In the ideal situation for an option writer, the option expires unexercised. The buyer of the GE call option would allow it to expire unexercised if GE were trading at less than $25 per share on October 18. The buyer of the GE put option would allow it to expire unexercised if the stock were trading at more than $25 per share on October 18. Table 15.1 summarizes the rights and obligations of the long and short positions for the GE call and put option contracts.

After defining option contracts and explaining the rights and obligations of both parties, we now discuss how option contracts are traded.

Option Trading

An investor can trade options much like stocks and bonds, by giving a market order or a limit order for a specific option to a broker. The broker then transmits the order to the exchange where the option is traded and the order is executed. Note, however, that most brokerage firms have restrictions on option trading by clients. Most, for example, handle option trades only for clients who have large holdings of cash, or other liquid assets, in their accounts.

Before 1973, options were traded only on the over-the-counter (OTC) markets. The OTC markets allowed investors to determine the terms of each contract, such as the strike price, expiration date, and number of shares. Transaction costs for these individualized contracts were quite high, and trades were infrequent after the initial transaction.

In 1973, the Chicago Board Options Exchange (CBOE) was formed as the first organized option exchange. Since then, most options trading occurred on organized exchanges. By 1989, options were traded on five U.S. exchanges, including the CBOE, American Stock Exchange (AMEX), Philadelphia Stock Exchange (PB), Pacific Stock Exchange (PC), and New York Stock Exchange (NYSE).

Options are also actively traded on several foreign stock exchanges. Three of the largest option markets outside the United States are located in London,

Type of Option	Long Position (Buyer)	Short Position (Writer)
25 October call	Has the right but no obligation to buy 100 shares of GE stock at $25 per share until October 18, 2002	Is obligated to sell 100 shares of GE stock at $25 per share until October 18, 2002, if the option is exercised
25 October put	Has the right but no obligation to sell 100 shares of GE at $25 per share until October 18, 2002	Is obligated to buy 100 shares of of GE stock at $25 until October 18, 2002, if the option is exercised

Tokyo, and Toronto. The organized exchanges provide significant advantages over OTC option trading. Five important ones are as follows:

1. *Standardized contracts.* The strike price on a modern option is standardized, as is the expiration date (the close of business on the third Friday of the stated month). Strike prices usually are stated in $5 increments, although larger increments are likely for stocks priced at more than $100 and increments as low as $2.50 are possible for stocks priced at less than $30 per share. New call option contracts with new strike prices are written as a stock's price exceeds currently available strike prices.
2. *Increased liquidity.* Trading on organized exchanges allows buyers and sellers to exchange option contracts at any time.
3. *More comprehensive disclosure and surveillance rules.* Organized exchanges impose relatively strict trading, disclosure, and monitoring procedures. They also keep a market flowing smoothly.
4. *Guaranteed clearing of contracts.* The Option Clearing Corporation (OCC), the clearinghouse for options trading, is jointly owned by the exchanges where options are traded. The OCC basically acts as a guarantor of each options trade to ensure that all parties meet their contractual obligations. Because option traders need not be concerned with the creditworthiness of other participants, the OCC helps create liquidity in the options market. The OCC acts as an agent between the buyer and the seller (or writer) of an option. Once the buyer and seller agree on a price (through orders executed by their brokers), the OCC writes and sells to the option buyer while it buys the contract from the seller. Because all options investors contract with the OCC, it guarantees that all contracts are fulfilled. Also, the OCC is responsible to fulfill any exercised options contract. If a call option is exercised, the OCC arranges for a member firm to randomly select a client who has written (or sold) a call to deliver 100 shares of the specified common stock at the strike price. If a put option is exercised, the OCC arranges for a member firm to randomly select a client who has written a put to purchase 100 shares of the specified common stock at the strike price.
5. *Lower transaction costs.* Brokerage fees for options traded on organized exchanges are substantially less than fees required for OTC trading. The lower costs reflect increased trading activity (which simplifies making a market), and the OCC relieves brokers of many functions, as already discussed.

Option Price Quotations Figure 15.1 provides a listing of option price quotes from *The Wall Street Journal* for September 30, 2002. Let's examine GE call and put options. Some GE options expire in October, November, December, and March. At each expiration date, the strike prices for individual option contracts, range from $20 to $37.50.

In *The Wall Street Journal* quotes, the first column provides the company name with its closing stock price for that day under it. The second column lists options' strike prices, and the third column lists expiration months. (Remember, all options technically expire on the third Saturday of the month; however, because no trading occurs on Saturday, for all practical purposes, it expires when the market closes on Friday.) The next two columns list the volume of call options traded and the last transacted price per share. (Multiply by 100 to get the dollar price of the option contract.) The last two columns list the volume of put options traded and the last transacted price for the put. A dotted line means that no such option contract exists or none was traded.

As you look through option price quotations in *The Wall Street Journal* or other financial publications, two questions may come to mind. First, why do some stocks underlie more options with different strike prices and expiration dates than others? Second, why do some option prices seem out of line, either too high or too low? The answer to the first question is rather simple. The exchange, such as the CBOE, determines the number of option contracts available. Its decision is based on investor interest and the volatility of the stock. In general, more investor interest in a stock and a more volatile price lead the exchange to create more options.

To answer the question about the relationship of the option price to the underlying stock price, remember that each price printed reflects the price of the last transaction; it is not a current bid or ask price. The fact that a call option last traded for $1.05 does not mean that anyone could buy or sell for $1.05 now if the stock price has changed substantially. Also, keep in mind that many options listed are not actively traded. (Look at the volume figures.)

Options on Other Securities

During the 1980s, many exchanges began to offer options on stock indexes such as the Standard & Poor's (S&P) 100 and Value Line Index. Options on industry indexes, foreign currencies, and commodity and financial futures also became available. We discuss the index options and foreign currency options here, leaving options on financial futures for Chapter 16.

index option

Call or put option based on a stock market index.

Index Options An index option is a call or put based on a stock market index such as the S&P 100, S&P 500, Value Line Index, or Major Market Index. The S&P 100 Index is a value-weighted average of the 100 largest stocks in the S&P 500. The Major Market Index is an average, weighted by price, of 20 large-firm stocks, most of which are also included in the Dow Jones Industrial Average sample. The Value Line Index is an arithmetic (equally weighted) average of approximately 1,700 stocks. Examples of index option price quotations appear in Figure 15.2.

Unlike stock options, exercise of an index option does not require the writer to deliver the securities that comprise the index; instead, a cash settlement takes

FIGURE 15.1

Option Price Quotes from The Wall Street Journal

Source: The Wall Street Journal, September 30, 2002, p. C11. Copyright © 2002 Dow Jones & Co. Reprinted by permission of the publisher, Dow Jones & Co., via Copyright Clearance Center.

OPTION/STRIKE		EXP	-CALL- VOL	LAST	-PUT- VOL	LAST
AMR	5	Oct	792	0.35	6	1.15
AOL TW	10	Nov	78	2.60	1597	0.50
12.12	12.50	Oct	3932	0.55	1097	0.90
12.12	12.50	Nov	1051	0.95	150	1.45
12.12	12.50	Jan	1125	1.75	321	1.95
12.12	15	Oct	614	0.10	24	2.80
12.12	15	Jan	1029	0.75	48	3.60
A S A	27.50	Oct	...	...	1000	0.35
Abbt L	37.50	Nov	...	...	734	1.50
AdvAuto	55	Dec	727	3.90	5	4.30
AdvFibCm	12.50	Oct	32	1.10	3067	0.90
Alcoa	22.50	Oct	1005	0.20	502	3.30
Amazon	17.50	Oct	1409	0.80	257	1.30
17.01	20	Oct	1271	0.15	200	3
AmExpr	30	Oct	21	2.75	1252	0.95
AmIntGp	75	Nov	751	0.10	...	...
Amercrd	7.50	Oct	1625	1.45	859	0.50
8.50	7.50	Nov	1429	2	565	0.95
8.50	10	Oct	639	0.30	188	1.85
8.50	10	Nov	417	0.85	3728	2.35
Amgen	40	Oct	153	3.30	609	1.30
42.00	42.50	Oct	519	1.80	1797	2.35
42.00	45	Oct	859	0.70	3587	3.60
Aon Cp	22.50	Oct	735	0.50	...	...
AppleC	12.50	Oct	1000	2.50	...	...
AppldMat	10	Oct	603	2.10	814	0.30
11.82	12.50	Oct	2438	0.50	1885	1.25
AstrZen	30	Nov	...	...	693	1.70
BakrHu	27.50	Oct	2500	2.40	...	...
BancOne	40	Oct	251	0.55	750	3.10
Biogen	30	Oct	80	2	1219	2.50
Block	45	Oct	83	1.45	884	4.80
41.63	50	Oct	722	0.35	...	...
BrMySq	25	Nov	1403	1.15	5	1.50
24.49	27.50	Nov	1186	0.60	...	...
Broadcom	12.50	Oct	1155	0.60	374	2.05
10.95	15	Oct	314	0.15	692	4.10
Brocade	5	Apr	...	...	1359	1.25
7.83	7.50	Oct	1224	1.15	4585	0.85
7.83	7.50	Nov	195	1.60	1777	1.30
7.83	10	Oct	5120	0.35	95	2.45
C S X	30	Oct	700	0.30	...	...
CV Thera	22.50	Oct	931	0.50	360	2.20
Cablvision	5	Mar	...	...	3135	0.75
CabotMc	40	Jan	2021	6.30	...	...
CarolinaGr	17.50	Nov	752	1.40	20	1
Caterp	40	Oct	210	0.70	1634	3.20
37.50	45	Oct	10	0.05	1000	7.40
Cendant	10	Nov	62	2	838	1
11.00	12.50	Nov	131	0.65	2897	2.10
11.00	15	Nov	1745	0.15	7074	4.10
11.00	17.50	Nov	1300	0.15	...	...
Cephln	40	Oct	158	2.85	1464	3.20
39.62	45	Oct	595	0.85	53	5.90
ChkPoint	20	Oct	866	0.10	20	5.70
ChevrnTex	75	Oct	641	0.75	3	3.60
ChildPlc	15	Oct	20	0.05	899	3.90
Cisco	10	Oct	216	1.50	2328	0.30
11.23	12.50	Oct	1190	0.25	943	1.50
11.23	12.50	Nov	604	0.65	133	1.80
11.23	12.50	Jan	6243	1.10	346	2.30
11.23	12.50	Apr	8577	1.80	99	2.60
Citigrp	22.50	Oct	444	2.60	1869	1.10
29.02	22.50	Nov	213	3.40	782	1.75
29.02	25	Oct	13	4.30	1502	0.30
29.02	30	Oct	1601	1.10	1374	2.25
29.02	32.50	Oct	1495	0.45	373	3.8
Gen El	20	Oct	133	4.70	763	0.20
24.47	22.50	Oct	659	2.65	1947	0.60
24.47	22.50	Nov	120	3.20	2759	1.05
24.47	22.50	Dec	135	3.70	2947	1.50
24.47	25	Oct	5809	1.05	3328	1.45
24.47	25	Nov	1376	1.65	1388	2.10
24.47	25	Dec	713	2.10	784	2.50
24.47	27.50	Oct	8012	0.20	1829	3.10
24.47	27.50	Dec	1463	1.05	70	3.90
24.47	30	Oct	936	0.10	249	5.60
24.47	30	Nov	1330	0.25	10	5.70
24.47	30	Dec	1228	0.45	170	5.80
24.47	30	Mar	898	1	22	6.70
24.47	37.50	Dec	174	0.10	811	12.80
GnMills	40	Oct	22	4.60	2252	0.45
GenMotrs	42.50	Oct	125	1.10	681	3.80
GM H	12.50	Dec	1381	0.50	...	...
Gillet	30	Dec	13	1.95	3463	2
GlobalSFe	22.50	Jan	1173	2.75	...	...
GoldmnS	60	Oct	1	8.30	3511	0.90
66.13	65	Oct	342	3.30	3040	2.20
66.13	65	Nov	5400	4.80	...	...
66.13	65	Jan	11278	6.60	146	5.20
66.13	70	Jan	1018	1	307	4.70
Gucci	80	Jan	125	9.70	1108	3.80
84.77	85	Oct	...	...	675	1.75
HewlettPk	15	Nov	670	0.20	10	2.95
HomeDp	27.50	Nov	1024	1.95	300	2.40
26.76	30	Oct	834	0.35	146	3.40
IDEC	40	Nov	970	5.90	52	2.80
42.22	45	Oct	911	1.45	222	4
42.22	45	Nov	660	3.10	15	4.90
IGEN Int	35	Oct	796	0.60	...	...
iShSm600	85	Feb	...	...	2000	3.50
Intel	12.50	Nov	6	3.10	5061	0.60
14.62	15	Oct	2154	0.85	2358	1.15
14.62	15	Jan	854	1.85	508	2.20
14.62	17.50	Oct	4450	0.20	1503	3
14.62	17.50	Nov	719	0.40	107	2.85
14.62	17.50	Jan	421	0.95	1191	3.80
14.62	20	Oct	1240	0.10	16	4.80
InterMune	35	Apr	600	5.30	...	...
I B M	55	Oct	84	7	1105	1.25
60.36	60	Oct	917	3.50	2832	3.20
60.36	65	Oct	2374	1.45	1324	6
60.36	70	Oct	1529	0.55	202	10.30
60.36	70	Nov	293	1.15	1676	10.80
60.36	70	Jan	3565	2.75	39	12
60.36	75	Oct	1273	0.20	87	13.90
JPMorgCh	17.50	Oct	629	1.50	893	0.95
18.34	20	Oct	1124	0.45	501	2.40
18.34	22.50	Oct	1079	0.15	78	4.70
18.34	22.50	Dec	2048	0.70	26	5
JHFnSrv	30	Oct	...	...	1000	2.35
JohnJn	30	Jan	...	...	1060	0.30
55.10	50	Jan	117	7.20	1542	2.25
55.10	55	Oct	853	1.65	727	1.60
55.10	60	Oct	655	0.20	117	5
55.10	60	Nov	5120	0.60	123	0.70
55.10	60	Jan	710	1.60	17	6.40
JnprNtw	5	Oct	624	0.35	123	0.75
KLA Tnc	30	Oct	2045	1.65	3273	2.95
KindME	32.50	Dec	950	2.05	350	2.25
Kohls	60	Oct	54	5.90	642	2
64.09	70	Oct	602	0.70	198	6.50

FIGURE 15.2

Price Quotes
for Index Options

Source: The Wall Street Journal, October 16, 2002, p. C14. Copyright © 2002 Dow Jones & Co. Reprinted by permission of the publisher, Dow Jones & Co., via Copyright Clearance Center.

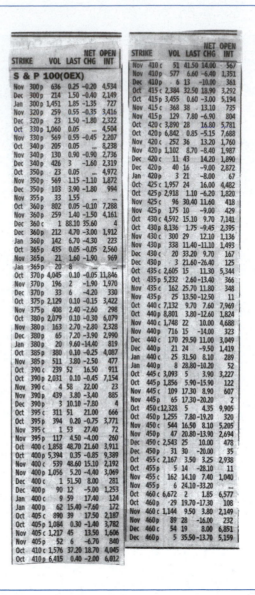

place. The writer pays, in cash, the difference between the strike price of the option and the value of the index at the time of exercise, multiplied by a fixed number. The multiplier for S&P 100 options is 100. For example, suppose that someone were to write a call option on the S&P 100 Index with a October 18, 2002, expiration and a strike price of 390. Now, assume that the buyer exercised the option when the index equaled 400. The writer would owe the buyer of the option $1,000, composed of 400 (the index value when the option was exercised) minus 390 (the option's exercise price) multiplied by 100. More recently, foreign stock index options have been introduced into U.S. options markets. Options are available on such foreign stock indexes as the Financial Times 100 and the Japan Index (a composite index of most major Japanese stocks).

Foreign Currency Options A currency option gives the holder the right to buy or sell a specified quantity of foreign currency for a specified amount of U.S. dollars. Contracts are quoted in cents or fractions of a cent per unit of foreign currency. Foreign currency options are traded on the PB and the CBOE.

Long-Term Options In 1994, the CBOE initiated trading in long-term options, called LEAPS. These long-term call and put options are similar to standard call and put options except that they have expiration dates of up to two years from the date of issue. LEAPS are available on both individual stocks and major stock indexes.

OPTION VALUE AT EXPIRATION

In this section, we discuss how to find the values of call and put options at expiration. This calculation allows the investor to determine the profit or loss, at expiration, from the four basic option trades (buying a call option, writing a call option, buying a put option, and writing a put option). Before we get to this discussion, however, we need to define some symbols.

The value, or price, of a call option at a point in time is denoted by C_T. The value of a put option is denoted by P_T. The value of the underlying stock is denoted by S. We define the exercise price of the option as E and the time left until the option's expiration as T. At the expiration date, T equals 0.

Valuing Calls and Puts at Expiration

Let's assume that a time traveler can return to a point in time right before the October 2002 GE options expired. It would be a few minutes before the markets closed on October 18, 2002. How much would this person expect the October call and put options to be worth? (Remember the exercise price is $25, so E equals 25) The answer, of course, depends on the price of GE's stock. Let's start with the call option.

Call Option Value at Expiration Assume GE's common stock was trading for $30 per share moments before the market closed on October 18, 2002. How much would the 25 October call be worth? The answer is $5. To see why, consider what would happen if the option were selling for $2. One could then buy the option contract for $200, exercise it immediately to buy GE for $25 per share, and then sell the GE shares on the NYSE for $30 per share. The profit, ignoring commissions, would be $300, and this return would be risk-free. This scenario is an example of arbitrage, the simultaneous purchase and sale of two different securities to make a guaranteed profit.

Now, what would happen if GE's stock were trading for $20 per share moments before the 25 October call was about to expire? The call would be worthless ($C = 0$). After all, would you pay *anything* for an option to immediately buy a stock at $25 per share when it was selling for $20 in the stock market?

These examples illustrate that valuing a call option at expiration is fairly simple. It is equal to zero if the option is about to expire out of the money ($S \leq E$); the value of the call is equal to the stock price minus the exercise price ($S - E$) if the call is about to expire in the money. More formally, the value of a call option at expiration is calculated as follows:

$$C_T = \text{Max}(0, S - E), \text{ where } T = 0$$
$$C_T = 0, \text{ if } S \leq E \qquad\qquad (15.1)$$
$$C_T = (S - E), \text{ if } S > E$$

Put Option Value at Expiration Similar logic leads to a value for a put option at expiration. Let's use the 25 October GE put option. Right before the put option expires on October 18, 2002, suppose that GE's common stock is selling for either $30 per share or $20 per share.

If GE were selling for $30 per share, the put option would be worthless; it would be about to expire out of the money. No one would pay anything for an option that would allow the holder to immediately sell GE at $25 per share when one could get $30 per share in the stock market.

However, if GE were trading at $20 per share right before the put option expired, it would have a value of $5. If it were selling for less than $5, arbitrageurs could buy the option, buy the stock, and then exercise the option (in essence selling the stock at $25 when its market price was $20).

Putting the example into a more general form, the value of a put option at expiration is equal to zero if the option is about to expire out of the money $(S \geq E)$ or $E - S$ if the put option is about to expire in the money $(S < E)$. More formally, the value of a put option at expiration is calculated as follows:

$$P_T = \text{Max}(0, E - S), \text{ where } T = 0$$
$$P_T = 0, \text{ if } S \geq E \qquad\qquad (15.2)$$
$$P_T = (E - S), \text{ if } S < E$$

Calculating the Profit and Loss from an Option

Knowing the value of call and put options at expiration allows one to calculate the profit or loss from the four basic option trades (buying a call, writing a call, buying a put, and writing a put). Example calculations will use the two familiar GE options; the 25 October call was selling for $1.05 (the buyer paid $105 to the writer) about three weeks before expiration, and the 25 October put was selling for $1.45 (the buyer paid $145 to the writer) three weeks before expiration in October 2002.

Buying a Call Option The profit from buying the call option depends, of course, on the price of GE's stock at expiration. Table 15.2 shows the profit or loss from buying the 25 October call, with a purchase price of $105, for various stock prices. The data are shown graphically in Figure 15.3. At a stock price of $25 or below, the call expires out of the money and worthless; the buyer loses $105. However, at a stock price greater than $25, the buyer's profit or loss is calculated as follows:

$$[(S - E) - 1.05] \times 100$$

For example, at a stock price of $30, the buyer's profit is

$$[(\$30 - \$25) - \$1.05] \times 100 = \$395$$

TABLE 15.2

Profit (Loss) from Buying or Writing a 25 GE Call Option

Stock Price at Expiration ($T = 0$)	Value of Call Option	Profit (Loss)	
		Buyer	Writer (Seller)
5	$ 0.00	$(105)	$ 105
10	0.00	(105)	105
15	0.00	(105)	105
20	0.00	(105)	105
$E = 25$	0.00	(105)	105
30	5.00	395	(395)
35	10.00	895	(895)
40	15.00	1,395	(1,395)
45	20.00	1,895	(1,895)

Note: Price of the option is $105 and the exercise price (E) equals $25.

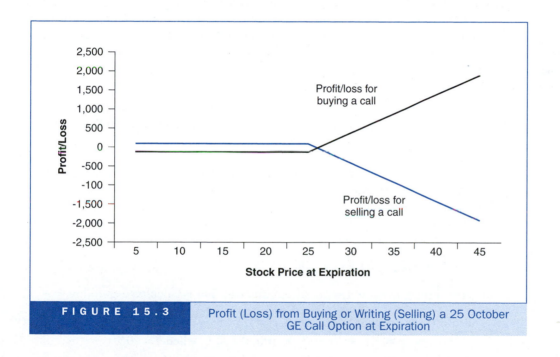

| FIGURE 15.3 | Profit (Loss) from Buying or Writing (Selling) a 25 October GE Call Option at Expiration |

In general, then, the profit or loss from buying a call option is

$$\textbf{Profit (Loss)} = C, \text{ if } S \leq E, \text{ when } T = 0$$
$$= [(S - E) - C] \times 100, \text{ if } S > E, \text{ when } T = 0$$

where C is the price paid for the call option.[2]

___

[2]Now that you understand how call profits are calculated, it's easy to remember it as $(S - E - C)$.

Before we go any further, we should make two additional points. First, in reality, most option buyers do not exercise their options when they decide to take profits in cash unless they actually want to buy or sell the underlying stock. Buyers simply sell their options on the appropriate markets. Exercising an option entails additional transactions, and thus additional transaction costs. For example, exercising a call to cash in option profits requires the holder to sell the shares of stock acquired by exercising the option. The profit from selling the option will be the same, before transaction costs, as that from exercising the option and then selling the stock, simply because many investors in the market pay virtually no transaction costs. Their low-cost trades help to eliminate any arbitrage profits.

Second, the example shown in Table 15.2 illustrates the derivative nature of options. Options derive their values from the values of the underlying stocks (GE in the example). Notice how the value of the call option at expiration increases exactly as much as the stock price once the call option is in the money ($S > E$).

Writing a Call Option The profit or loss from writing the 25 October GE call is also shown in Table 15.2 for various stock prices. Figure 15.3 shows clearly that the profit or loss for the option writer is the exact opposite of the profit or loss for the option buyer. This characteristic is the essence of option trading: it is a **zero-sum game**—for someone to make a dollar, someone else must lose a dollar. In the example, at a stock price of $25, the option buyer loses $105 and the writer of the option makes $105.

zero-sum game
Investment in which, for someone to make a dollar, someone else must lose a dollar.

Buying a Put Option Table 15.3 shows the profit or loss from buying the 25 GE October put at $145 for various stock prices at expiration. (The data are shown graphically in Figure 15.4.) If GE stock is selling for $25 or higher just before the put option expires, the option is worthless. (It is about to expire out of the money.) The buyer of the option loses $145. However, if GE is selling for less than $25 just before the put option expires, it is about to expire in the money. The profit or loss equals the difference between the exercise price ($E = 25$) and the stock price, minus $145, multiplied by 100. For example, at a stock price of $20, the profit from the put option is

$$[(\$25 - \$20) - \$1.45] \times 100 = \$355$$

In general then, the profit or loss from buying a put is calculated as follows:

Profit (Loss) = P, if $S \geq E$, when $T = 0$
= $[(E - S) - P] \times 100$, if $S < E$, when $T = 0$

where P is the price paid for the put option.[3]

Writing a Put Option The profit or loss from writing the 25 October GE put for $145 is also shown in Figure 15.4 for various stock prices at expiration. Table 15.3 illustrates that the profit or loss from writing the put is the exact opposite of the profit or loss from buying the same put option. Put option trading is also a zero-sum game. If GE is trading for $20 per share right before the 25 October put option expires, the buyer of the option makes $355 and the writer of the option loses $355.

[3]Again, after developing an understanding of the profits, it's easy to remember it as $(E - S - P)$.

TABLE 15.3

Profit (Loss) from Buying or Writing a 25 October GE Put Option

Stock Price at Expiration ($T = 0$)	Profit (Loss)		
	Value of Call Option	Buyer	Writer (Seller)
$ 5	$20.00	$1855	$(1855)
10	15.00	1355	(1355)
15	10.00	855	(855)
20	5.00	355	(355)
$E = 25$	0.00	(145)	145
30	0.00	(145)	145
35	0.00	(145)	145
40	0.00	(145)	145
45	0.00	(145)	145

Note: Price of put is $145 and the exercise price (E) equals $25.

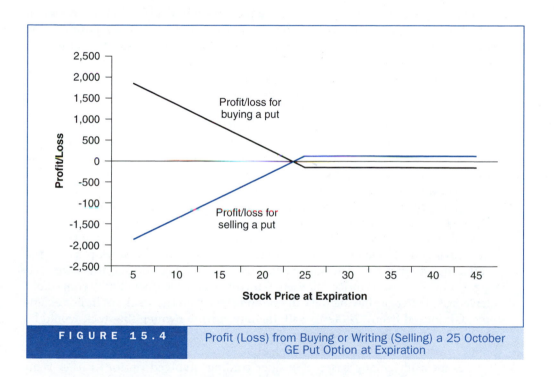

FIGURE 15.4   Profit (Loss) from Buying or Writing (Selling) a 25 October GE Put Option at Expiration

COMMON OPTION TRADING STRATEGIES

In this section, we review some of the unique risks and opportunities of options along with common option trading strategies.[4] Some of these strategies involve positions in options alone (either calls or puts), whereas others combine option

[4]Traders use many more option strategies than we discuss in this section. See, for example, Don Chance, *An Introduction to Options & Futures*, 3rd ed. (Fort Worth, TX: The Dryden Press, 1995), pp. 197–236.

positions with positions in the underlying stocks. Throughout this discussion, we illustrate these strategies using various October 2002 GE options and GE's common stock. The options, their prices, and the stock price are shown here:

Security	Price
GE common stock	$24.47
22.50 October call	2.65
25 October call	1.05
22.50 October put	0.60
25 October put	1.45

Note: Quotes are from *The Wall Street Journal*, September 30, 2002.

Some Unique Risks and Opportunities of Options

Option trading offers investors some unique opportunities. Options, as we see in the next section, can be used to hedge, or reduce the risk of, stock positions. At the same time, however, option trading exposes investors to substantial unique risks. An obvious risk of options is the need to be right—not only about the direction of a move in a stock's price but also about its timing. Someone who believes the S&P 100 is going to decline by a certain percentage over the next few months may buy a put option that expires in three months. Even if that person is right and stocks do decline, he or she may still be wrong about when. The decline may begin in four months, after the three-month put option expires. Another risk unique to options is the fact that options trading is a zero-sum game; for someone to make money, someone else has to lose the same amount. Still, options do offer investors attractive features.

One of the most potentially attractive features of call options is their inherent leverage. Buying a call option is similar to buying a stock on margin. To illustrate this inherent leverage, compare the holding period returns from buying GE stock and buying the 25 October call. The returns, assuming various stock prices at the call option's expiration date, are shown graphically in Figure 15.5. If you guessed right and GE rose in price between September and October 2002, you would have been better off buying the call option rather than the stock itself. For example, GE moved from $24.47 to $30, the return from owning the stock would be about 22.6% (ignoring transaction costs). However, owning the 25 October call option would give a return of more than 376%.

As an aside, many cases of insider trading involved options rather than stocks. Some famous insider trading cases—individuals convicted of violating insider trading laws in the 1980s—more often than not involved those buying call options. The reason comes from the inherent leverage of call options. Those who knew that the price of a stock was going to rise could generate far higher profits from the same dollar investment in the options market than in the stock market.

The trouble with leverage, of course, is that it is a double-edged sword. Take another look at Figure 15.5. If GE's stock stayed at about $24.47 or even fell, the call option owner would be worse off than the stockholder. For example, if GE's stock remained constant at about $24 between September and October 2002, the

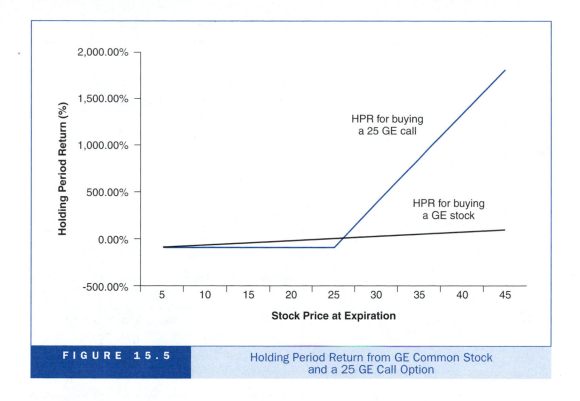

| FIGURE 15.5 | Holding Period Return from GE Common Stock and a 25 GE Call Option |

stock's return would be about 0%. However, the option's return would be −100%. The option would expire out of the money and be worthless.

Put options offer investors unique opportunities as well. They give investors the opportunity to speculate on the prices of specific stocks or on specific stock indexes, declining over short periods of time. Remember, as we discussed in Chapter 3, investors can sell a stock short (selling borrowed shares and buying them back later, it is hoped at a lower price). Short sellers often face restrictions. An investor may find it easier to speculate on price declines using put options rather than short sales.

Finally, consider the unique risk associated with writing options; the potential gain is limited whereas the potential loss is almost unlimited. Examine Figure 15.3 for a moment. The maximum gain from writing the 25 October call would be the price on the option, $105. However, if GE's stock had soared over the next four weeks, the potential loss would be much higher. If GE traded at $30 per share in mid-October, the call option writer would lose $395 per option contract. Only experienced option traders who can afford to risk substantial capital should consider writing options.

Strategies Involving Just One Option Contract

We already looked at the profit and loss associated with buying and writing call and put options. (Review Figures 15.3 through 15.5.) By now, you should have a pretty good idea what investors are expecting when they buy and write call and put options; they buy call options to speculate on the price of a stock rising over a short period of time, and they buy put options to speculate on the price of a

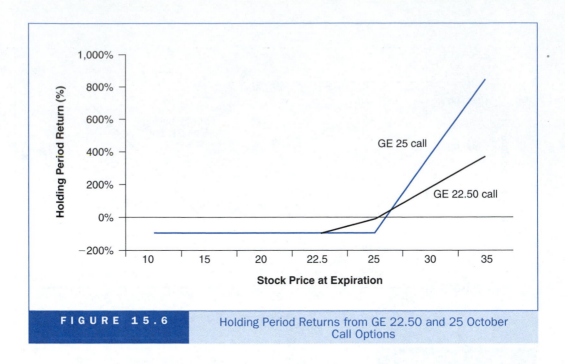

FIGURE 15.6   Holding Period Returns from GE 22.50 and 25 October Call Options

stock falling over a short period of time. An investor who writes an option attempts to capture the option's price, hoping that it expires out of the money.

Buying and writing call and put options involves more than just choosing an underlying stock on which to trade options. One must also decide which call or put to buy or write. Go back to Figures 15.1 and 15.2 for a moment; take a look at all the options available for specific stocks or indexes. Deciding which option to buy or write often depends on a trade-off between risk and return. Generally, an option further out of the money or with a shorter time until expiration has a greater potential return and greater risk for the option buyer. The option writer takes more risk on an option with a strike price close to the stock's price or with a longer time until expiration. Let's illustrate this with an example.

Someone may believe that GE's stock price would rise sharply between early October and mid-October 2002. This belief would support a decision to buy a October call option. The next question is, which strike price should the option have? The inherent risk/return trade-off is shown in Figure 15.6. The figure shows the holding period return for the 22.50 October call and the 25 October call between early October and the options' expiration date in mid-October.

The call option with the higher exercise price would cost less ($1.05 versus $2.65), and its leverage potential would be greater. For example, if the price of GE were to rise to $27 at about the options' expiration date, the 25 call would produce a return in excess of 90% whereas the 22.50 call would produce a return of about 70%. (This and all the examples that follow ignore transaction costs.) At the same time, however, the 25 call is riskier than the 22.50 call. Assume that GE's stock rises only slightly between early October and mid-October from $24.47 to $26. The 22.50 call would produce a return of about 32%. The 25 call, however,

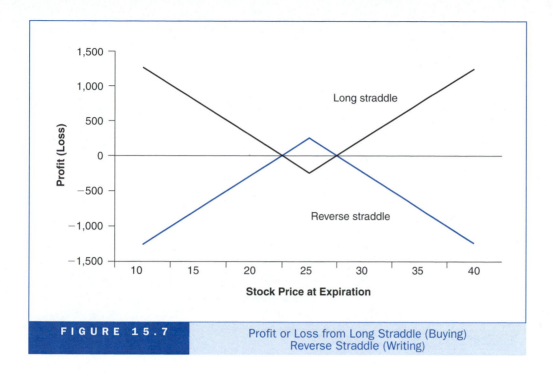

F I G U R E 1 5 . 7	Profit or Loss from Long Straddle (Buying) Reverse Straddle (Writing)

would produce a *negative* 5% return. Hence the returns for the 25 call are more volatile than the 22.50 call.

Straddles

A **straddle** involves buying both a call and a put with the same exercise price and the same expiration date. A straddle is essentially a bet on the volatility of the underlying stock. However, a *reverse straddle* involves writing both a call and a put with the same exercise price and the same expiration date. Not surprisingly, a reverse straddle is a bet against volatility in the underlying stock.

Assume that someone believed in early October 2002 that one of two things was going to happen to GE by mid-October: either the stock would rise sharply as blue chip stocks rallied in early October or would fall sharply due to a possible war with Iraq. In a straddle, the trader would buy both the 25 October call (for $1.05) and the 25 October put (for $1.45). The profit or loss from this straddle is illustrated in Figure 15.7.

For the straddle to be profitable, the stock price would have to move substantially in one direction or the other. At the expiration date, a stock price of about $22.50 and less, or about $27.50 and more, would result in a profitable straddle. The straddle buyer would suffer if GE remained at about $25 through mid-October.

Figure 15.7 also illustrates the profit and loss from a reverse straddle (or a short straddle). This trade combines writing the 25 October call and 25 October put. The strategy works if GE's common stock remains at about $25 until mid-October. Like writing a call or a put individually, a wrong guess exposes the option writer to an almost unlimited potential loss.

straddle

Buying both a call and a put with the same exercise price and the same expiration date.

FIGURE 15.8   Profit or Loss from a Bull Spread or Bear Spread.

Spreads

spread

Buying one option and writing another on the same underlying stock.

A **spread** involves purchasing one option and writing another on the same underlying stock. The options differ only in terms of one parameter, usually either exercise price or expiration date. The most common type of spread is a money spread.[5]

Money Spreads A money spread involves the purchase of one call or put option and the sale of another. The options have the same expiration date but different exercise prices. Money spreads are often referred to as either *bull spreads* or *bear spreads,* because they constitute bets on whether underlying stocks' prices will rise or fall over a short period of time.

Figure 15.8 illustrates both a bull spread and a bear spread. In the bull spread, one buys the 22.50 October call and writes the 25 October call. In general, a bull spread involves buying the call with the lower exercise price, E_1, while writing the call with the higher exercise price, E_2. In the bear spread, one writes the 22.50 October call and buys the 25 October call. Notice the limits on how much one can make or lose with either spread. The bear spread, for example, has a maximum profit of $120 and a maximum loss of $160.

Bull and bear spreads can also be constructed with put options. A bear spread would involve buying the put with the higher exercise price, E_2, while writing the put with the lower exercise price, E_1. A bull spread would combine writing the put with the higher exercise price, E_2, while buying the put with the lower exercise price, E_1.

[5]In addition to money spreads, option traders can construct calendar spreads, butterfly spreads, and box spreads. See Chance, *Introduction to Options,* pp. 208–217.

Why Trade Spreads? As you probably already guessed, a bull spread using call options is a substitute for simply buying a call option, whereas a bear spread using call options is a substitute for writing a call option. The advantage of a bull spread over buying a call option is that smaller upward movements in the price of the underlying stock will produce higher profits. For example, if GE had moved from about $24.47 in December to $25 in mid-October, the bull spread shown in Figure 15.8 would produce a profit of $90. By contrast, simply buying the 22.50 October call would produce a loss of $15 because of the bigger price of the 22.50 call ($2.65). By selling the 25 call, you defray the cost of the 22.50 call. The disadvantage of the bull spread is that it limits the maximum profit to $90, regardless of how high GE's stock price climbs.

The advantage of a bear spread over simply writing a call option is obvious: limited downside risk. Remember, simply writing a call option exposes one to unlimited potential loss. The bear spread shown in Figure 15.8 limits the potential loss to $90, regardless of how high GE's stock price climbs. Although a bear spread does sacrifice some upside potential, most experienced option traders speculate on price declines by using spreads rather than simply writing individual call options.

Combining Option and Stock Positions

Another common use of options is to combine them with positions in underlying stocks. These combined positions are often called *hedges;* the option is used to reduce the risk of the stock position. Let's look at three common techniques that combine options and stock: writing covered calls, buying protective puts, and covering short sales.

Writing Covered Calls Writing a covered call involves writing a call option on a stock already owned by the investor. Investors write covered calls for two basic reasons: to increase income from the stock (because the writer of an option receives the option premium) and to reduce the downside risk of the stock. Optimism about a stock's long-term prospects does not eliminate worry about it in the short term.

Assume someone bought GE at $25 and, at the same time, wrote a 25 October call option, perhaps thinking that GE's stock price should increase in the long run, despite concern that it may not rise over the short term due to anticipated war and the weak economy. The profit and loss from this combination is shown in Table 15.4. Note that this position is unusual. In reality, few investors would buy a stock and immediately write a call option on it. They are more likely to write call options on stocks they have owned for some time.

As shown in Table 15.4, if GE's stock declined slightly from $25 to $24 between early October and mid-October 2002, the covered call would be more profitable than simply owning the stock. At the same time, if GE declined in price, the profit from writing the call would offset some of the loss from the stock position. (The losses in the stock are only paper losses, of course; they become real cash losses only if the stock is actually sold.)

Protective Puts A protective put is another common combined stock option position in which an investor buys put options on stock he or she already owns. The rationale for a protective put is straightforward: it reduces some of the

covered call

Writing a call option on stock the investor already owns.

protective put

Buying a put option on stock the investor already owns.

TABLE 15.4	Stock Price at Expiration ($T = 0$)	Profit (Loss)		
Profit (Loss) from a Covered Call on GE		Write a October 25 Call	Buy a GE Stock at $25	Covered Call
	$20	$105	$(500)	$(395)
	21	105	(400)	(295)
	22	105	(300)	(195)
	23	105	(200)	(95)
	24	105	(100)	5
	$E = 25$	105	0	105
	26	5	100	105
	27	(95)	200	105
	28	(195)	300	105
	29	(295)	400	105
	30	(395)	500	105

Note: Price of call is $105 and the exercise price (E) is $25. Assume that the stock was purchased at $25.

downside risk associated with owning stocks, either by guaranteeing a sale price or offsetting losses on the stock with profits on the put. Protective puts can be thought of as a kind of insurance.

Table 15.5 assumes that an investor purchased 100 shares of GE stock in August 2002 for $22 a share and then watched the stock rise sharply in price. The investor worries about the stock falling in the near term. So, he or she decides to protect some of the profit by buying a 25 October put for $145. Notice that even if GE's stock price collapses, the investor has "locked in" a profit of $155.

Buying a protective put requires careful attention to the strike price of the option. A higher strike price lowers the risk, but at the same time, a higher strike price also increases the cost of the put. This decision resembles the choice of a deductible on auto insurance: a higher deductible reduces the cost of the auto insurance, but it increases the loss from an accident.

covered short sale

Buying a call option on stock the investor has shorted.

Covered Short Sales A covered short sale is similar to a protective put: the option provides insurance. In a covered short sale, the investor combines a short position in a stock with a long position in a call option. Remember, a short sale represents a bet on a drop in the price of a stock, allowing the investor to buy back borrowed shares at a lower price. The risk of a short sale is the potential loss if the stock price does not drop. The call option reduces some of this risk.

For example, assume that in early October 2002, due to the weak economy, you are convinced GE's stock is going to fall sharply over the next few weeks. So, you decide to short the stock at $25 and, at the same time, buy the 25 October call for 1.05 in September 2002. The results are shown in Table 15.6.

The table shows clearly how owning the call option greatly reduces the risk of the short sale. For example, if GE soared to $30 per share by mid-October, the combined position would lose only $105, compared with a $1,000 loss for a simple short sale without the call option. Of course, like all insurance, buying the call reduces some of the short sale's profits if GE were to fall in price.

Stock Price at Expiration ($T = 0$)	Profit (Loss)		
	Buy a October 25 Put	Bought Stock at $22, 2 months ago	Protective Put
$20	$355	$(200)	$155
21	255	(100)	155
22	155	0	155
23	55	100	155
24	(45)	200	155
$E = 25$	(145)	300	155
26	(145)	400	255
27	(145)	500	355
28	(145)	600	455
29	(145)	700	555
30	(145)	800	655

TABLE 15.5

Profit (Loss) from Buying a Protective Put on GE Stock

Note: Price of put is $145 and the exercise price (*E*) is $25. Assume that the stock was purchased at $22, two months ago.

Stock Price at Expiration ($T = 0$)	Profit (Loss)		
	Buy a October 25 Call	Sell Short on the Stock at $25	Covered Short Sale
$20	$(105)	$500	$395
21	(105)	400	295
22	(105)	300	195
23	(105)	200	95
24	(105)	100	(5)
$E = 25$	(105)	0	(105)
26	(5)	(100)	(105)
27	95	(200)	(105)
28	195	(300)	(105)
29	295	(400)	(105)
30	395	(500)	(105)

TABLE 15.6

Profit (Loss) from a Covered Short Sale on GE

Note: Price of call is $105 and the exercise price (*E*) is $25. Assume that the stock was sold short at $25.

PRICING OPTIONS

Up to now, we discussed how to determine the value of an option at expiration, and we used this knowledge to examine the profit and loss potentials of several common option trading strategies. This section explores the factors that affect the value of an option before expiration. These factors help explain why some options are worth more than others and why option prices rise and fall. They also help us to understand the most widely used option pricing model.

Determinants of Option Values

The fundamental value of an option before expiration is affected by six factors: (1) the price of the underlying stock, (2) the exercise price, (3) the length of time until expiration, (4) the volatility of the underlying stock, (5) the level of interest rates, and (6) the amount of dividends the underlying stock pays between now and the expiration date. Let's discuss each of these factors.

Price of the Underlying Stock As already discussed, as the price of the underlying stock rises (or falls), the value of a call option rises (or falls). The reverse is true for a put option; the value of a put rises (or falls) as the stock falls (or rises) in price.

Exercise Price Because a call is an option to buy, a higher exercise price implies a lower value. A put is an option to sell, so a higher exercise price implies a higher value. To verify these relationships, go back to Figure 15.1 for a moment. Notice that the 22.50 October call on GE sold for $2.65 whereas the 25 October call sold for $1.05. The 22.50 October put sold for $0.60 whereas the 25 October put sold for $1.45.

Time Until Expiration Referring again to Figure 15.1, what relationship do you see between the value of GE options and their times until expiration? The relationship, for both calls and puts, is positive; a longer time until expiration implies a higher price. For example, the 25 November 2002 call traded for $1.65 whereas the 25 October 2002 call traded for $1.05.

Why do we see this positive relationship between option price and time until expiration? The answer is simply that a longer time until expiration increases the probability that an option will be in the money before it expires.

Earlier in this chapter, we defined an option's premium. For a call, the premium is equal to the price of the option plus the exercise price minus the current stock price. For a put, the premium equals the price of the option plus the current stock price minus the exercise price. If the price of the underlying stock remains constant, the option's premium diminishes as the expiration date gets closer.

Volatility of the Underlying Stock An option buyer's loss is limited to the price of the option. However, the potential profit is almost unlimited. As a result, the stock price at expiration is irrelevant if the option expires out of the money. For example, someone who bought the 22.50 October call for $2.65 would not care whether GE sold for $20 or $15 in mid-October. In both cases, the option expired out of the money and the owner lost $265. However, GE's stock price becomes critical if the option is about to expire in the money.

More volatility in the underlying stock makes an option more valuable. Increased volatility increases the odds that the option will expire in the money. This generalization is true for both call and put options.

One way of gauging the volatility of the underlying stock is to compare the premiums investors are willing to pay for options on particular stocks. For example, recently Johnson & Johnson was trading for $55.10. At the same time,

	Impact on the Value of		
Variable	**Direction of Change**	**Call Option**	**Put Option**
1. Price of underlying stock	Higher	Increases	Decreases
2. Exercise price	Higher	Decrease	Increases
3. Time until expiration	Longer	Increases	Increases
4. Volatility of underlying stock	Higher	Increases	Increases
5. Interest rates	Higher	Increases	Decreases
6. Dividends	Larger	Decreases	Increases

TABLE 15.7

Six Factors That Affect
the Value of Options
Before Expiration

a 55 October 2002 call option was trading for 1.65. The option premium is calculate as $1.65 - 55.10 + 55 = \$1.55$. On the same day, IBM was trading for $60.36 while a 60 October 2002 call was trading for 3.50. The IBM option premium is calculated as $3.50 - 60.36 + 60 = \$3.14$. Given the technology slump, conventional wisdom suggests that IBM's common stock is more volatile in price than is Johnson & Johnson's common stock.

Level of Interest Rates As interest rates rise, the value of a call option increases, while the value of a put option decreases. This relationship may initially seem puzzling, but the reason is quite straightforward. As interest rates rise, the present value of the exercise price falls. To exercise a call option, the owner must pay something (the exercise price); therefore, as the present value of this price falls, the value of the call option should rise. The reverse, of course, is true for a put option.

Dividends We mentioned earlier that options are protected from stock splits and stock dividends. If a stock splits 2 for 1, for example, the exercise price of all options will automatically be halved. Options are not, however, protected from cash dividends. Now, you may also remember that when a stock goes ex-dividend, its price falls because the buyer is no longer entitled to the current dividend. A larger cash dividend (as apercentage of the stock price) implies a greater price decline. What does this event mean for the price of an option?

   If the underlying stock pays dividends between the option's purchase and its expiration date, the dividend payment and the resulting price drop on the ex-dividend date tend to decrease the value of a call option and increase the value of a put option. A larger dividend causes a greater price decrease (or increase) in a call (or put) option.

   Table 15.7 summarizes the relationships between these six factors and the value of an option before expiration. Although the material that follows is somewhat more difficult than what was covered up to this point, even if you read no further in this section, understanding the relationships summarized in the table will help you understand why some options are worth more than others and why option prices increase or decrease over time. This knowledge is essential if you wish to successfully trade options.

Black-Scholes Option Pricing Model[6]

An option pricing model developed by Fischer Black and Myron Scholes in 1973 is probably the best-known option pricing model and is widely used by option traders.[7] The model was developed for so-called European call options. European options are identical to so-called American options except that they can be exercised only on the expiration date.[8] All options traded throughout the world are American options.

The Black-Scholes model makes several important assumptions. It assumes that the risk-free rate and the underlying stock's price volatility remain constant over the life of the option and that the underlying stock pays no dividends. Given these assumptions, the fundamental value of a European call is calculated as follows:

$$C = S[N(d_1)] - Ee^{-rT}[N(d_2)] \tag{15.3}$$

$$d_1 = \frac{\ln(S/E) + \left(r + \frac{\sigma^2}{2} \right)T}{\sigma\sqrt{T}}$$

$$d_2 = d_1 - \sigma\sqrt{T}$$

where C is the fundamental value of the option, S is the current price of the underlying stock, E is the exercise price, T is the time until expiration stated in years (for an option that expires in six months, $T = 0.5$), r is the risk-free rate of interest, σ is the standard deviation of the underlying stock (a measure of volatility), $\ln(S/E)$ is the natural log of S/E, e equals 2.71828 (the base of the natural log function), and $N(d)$ is the probability that a random draw from a standard normal distribution function will be less than d. The term Ee^{-rT} is the present value of the exercise price, assuming continuous compounding.

With a little math, the Black-Scholes model, Equation 15.3, can be modified to price European put options.

Loose Interpretation of the Black-Scholes Model Although the formula looks horrendous, it is not as bad as you think if you take it step by step. If the price of the stock when the option expires is known pretty much with certainty, assuming that $S > E$, the two $N(d)$ terms will be close to 1, making Equation 15.3 approach

$$C = S - Ee^{-rT}$$

In English, the call price equals the current stock price minus the present value of the exercise price.

---

[6]This section may be skipped without any loss of continuity.
[7]Fischer Black and Myron Scholes, "The Pricing of Options and Corporate Liabilities," *Journal of Political Economy,* May/June 1973, pp. 637–659.
[8]Mathematically, European options are much simpler to value than American options. However, it can be shown that a rational investor will never exercise a call option before expiration, choosing instead to sell the option. See Chance, *Introduction to Options,* pp. 80–83 and 94–95.

At the other extreme, with virtually no chance of the option expiring in the money, the two $N(d)$ terms approach zero. The value of the option also approaches zero.

For all the probabilities in between, the Black-Scholes option pricing model can be loosely interpreted as saying that the value of a call is equal to the expected stock price at expiration minus the present value of the exercise price, both weighted by the probability of the option expiring in the money.

Determinants of the Fundamental Value of an Option Table 15.7 lists the six variables that appear to affect the value of an option. The Black-Scholes model incorporates five of the six. (Remember that it assumes that the underlying stock pays no dividends.) Adjusting the values of these five factors individually in the model increases or decreases the value of the call, exactly as shown in Table 15.7.

For example, increasing the underlying stock's standard deviation, σ in Equation 15.3, while holding all the other variables constant increases the value of the call option. Familiar information about the intrinsic value of a call option confirms the validity of the Black-Scholes model (which is always a good feeling).

Applying the Black-Scholes Model Let's apply the Black-Scholes model to one of the GE options we used in the previous examples, the 25 October call option. One appealing characteristic of the model is that all its variables but one are easily available from a source such as *The Wall Street Journal*. The current stock price (S), the exercise price (E), the risk-free rate (r), and the time to expiration (T) can be obtained from the financial press. The only variable that must be estimated is the standard deviation of the underlying stock. Usually, historical stock returns (continuously compounded) are used to estimate the standard deviation.

In early October 2002, we obtained the following information for estimating the value of the 25 October GE call option: $S = 24.47$, $E = 25$, $T = 18/365 = 0.0493$, and $r = 1.75\%$. Annualizing the standard deviation of monthly returns from GE stock for the past 60 months gives us an estimate of $\sigma = .6753$.

The first step is to calculate d_1 and d_2. Based on our inputs, $d_1 = 0.2236$ and $d_2 = 0.0737$. The next step is to find the probability that a random draw from a standard normal distribution $N(d_1)$ and $N(d_2)$ with a mean of 0 and a standard deviation of 1.0, will be less than 0.2236 and 0.0737, respectively. The answers are $N(d_1) = 0.5885$ and $N(d_2) = 0.5294$. The final step is to fill in the values in Equation 15.3:

$$C = (\$24.47)(0.5885) - (\$25)(e^{-0.493(0.0175)})(0.5294)$$
$$= \$1.177$$

Note that we rounded these numbers, so you may obtain an answer that is a penny or two different.

The Black-Scholes model gives a price for the call option of $1.177. Its actual market price, as of December 15,1999, was $1.05. The Black-Scholes model's estimate is pretty close to the market price of the 25 October GE call. Remember, though, that the prices quoted in the press are past trade prices, not current bid or ask prices.

Arbitrage Strategy Using the Black-Scholes Model Someone who believes the Black-Scholes model's estimate of the fundamental value of a call option may be able to use a simple arbitrage trading strategy. The Black-Scholes model gave a fundamental value for the GE call of $1.177. Assuming that its market price is $1.05, the Black-Scholes model estimates that the call is underpriced.

An arbitrageur could profit from the underpriced call by selling short GE stock and buying the GE 25 call. If the Black-Scholes model's price is correct, the call is underpriced, then when the market corrects this mistake, the arbitrageur makes money regardless of whether the stock price rises or falls. How many shares does the arbitrageur buy for every call written—assuming one call controls one share of stock? The answer is 0.5885, the value of $N(d_1)$.[9] Because each call contract is associated with 100 shares of the stock, we multiply the hedge ratio, $N(d_1)$, by 100, or $0.5885 \times 100 = 58.85$ shares per contract.

Let's illustrate with an example. Suppose the market price of a 25 October call is $2 and its fundamental value from the Black-Scholes model is $1.63. Also the hedge ratio, $N(d_1)$ is calculated to equal 0.55 and the stock is trading at $25. In the sample trade, buying 550 shares at $25 costs $13,750; writing 1,000 calls at $2.00 generates income of $2,000. The net investment is $11,750. Now, assume that the price either rises to $26 or falls to $24.

If the price rises to $26, the position makes $550 on the stock (550 shares times $1); if the price falls to $24, the stock's value falls by $550. What about the option? The term $N(d_1)$ indicates the change in the price of the option, given a $1 change in the price of the stock. This option price change is not a change in the market price but only a change in the option's fundamental value. Given that $N(d_1)$ is 0.55, if the stock rises to $26, the price of the option should be $1.63 + $0.55 = $2.18. Therefore, the option position will lose only $180 in value (1,000 times $0.18). The net profit from the combined option/stock position is $370.

If the stock falls to $24, the new option price should be $1.63 − $0.55 = $1.08, giving profit on the option position of $920 (1,000 times $0.92). The net profit, should the stock decline in price from the combined option/stock position, is $370 ($920 − $550), the same profit as the price increase. Remember, this assumes that the market eventually recognizes the fact that the option is priced above its fundamental value and corrects this overpricing.

This example is but one of how the Black-Scholes model could be used in the real world of option trading. Before investing your tuition money for next year based on the Black-Scholes model, note a few caveats about the model:

1. The Black-Scholes model does not consider dividend payments that accrue while the hedged position remains outstanding. Recall from the previous section that a dividend payout decreases a call's price.
2. The model assumes that the risk-free rate, r, and the standard deviation of the stock return are constant over time; they may well vary.
3. The model also assumes that stock prices are continuous and no sudden extreme jumps occur. From the GE example, we know that the market can give no guarantee of continuous pricing as new information becomes available.

---

[9]$N(d_1)$ is referred to as the "hedge ratio," meaning that one could construct a risk-free portfolio combining the option and the stock—either buying the option and shorting the stock or writing the option and buying the stock. This portfolio would earn the risk-free rate regardless of whether the stock moved up or down in price.

4. The model also assumes that the hedging process is continuously managed so that hedges remain continuously perfect. Unfortunately, the trades necessary to guarantee this would quickly erode any profits through commission costs.

Like all mathematical models, the Black-Scholes formula approximates the real world and it requires caution. Nevertheless, the model opens a way to price options and other securities that resemble them. The model is widely used by option traders to identify potentially over- and underpriced options.

OTHER SECURITIES THAT RESEMBLE OPTIONS

Several securities exhibit features like those of options, allowing investors to buy or sell something at fixed prices for fixed periods of time. Many of the same pricing rules discussed up to this point apply to these securities as well. The most common securities with option-like features are convertibles and warrants.

Convertible Securities

A convertible security, either a bond or a preferred stock issue, gives the holder the right to convert the security for a specified number of shares of common stock in the same company that issued the convertible. The prescribed number of shares obtained when the bond or preferred share is tendered for conversion, referred to as the conversion ratio, though normally fixed for the life of the convertible, can change as specified in the firm's indenture agreement. For example, a conversion ratio of 20 says that a convertible bond can be exchanged for 20 shares of the company's common stock.

To see how a convertible security resembles a call option, let's look at an example. Reebok International, Ltd., currently has a convertible bond issue outstanding. The convertible has a conversion ratio of 25.93 (meaning that each bond can be exchanged for 25.93 shares of Reebok's common stock), a face value of $1,000, a coupon rate of 4.25%, and a maturity date of 2021. This bond gives its owner the right to buy 25.93 shares of Reebok's stock (by exchanging the bond) at a *conversion price* of $38.56 per share ($1,000 divided by the conversion ratio) until the bond matures in 2021. Until the owner exercises the option and converts the bond, it pays $42.50 per year in coupon interest.

Valuing a Convertible Security To value a convertible security, let's consider Reebok convertible bond, which had a market price of $980. At the same time, Reebok's common stock was trading at $24.46 per share. Multiplying the current stock price ($24.46) by the conversion ratio (25.93) gives the conversion value of the bond, $635 (rounded to the nearest dollar). In other words, the owner of the convertible could exchange the bond for common stock worth about $635.

In option terminology, the Reebok convertible bond is out of the money because the stock price, $24.46, is less than the conversion price, equivalent to an option's exercise price, of $38.56. However, the convertible is selling at a premium above its conversion value ($980 versus $635). Why? As we discussed, one factor that makes some call options more valuable is the volatility of their underlying stocks. Reebok has been a volatile stock historically, ranging in stock price from $42.50 to $25.38 in 2002.

convertible security

A bond or preferred stock that gives the owner the right to convert the security for a specified number of shares of common stock.

conversion ratio

Number of shares of common stock received if the conversion feature is exercised.

conversion value

Current stock price multiplied by the conversion ratio.

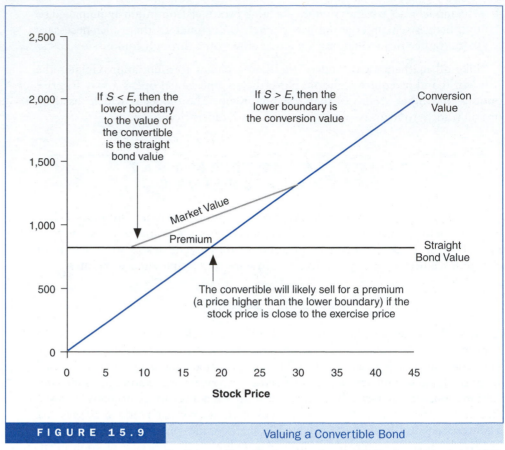

FIGURE 15.9   Valuing a Convertible Bond

Note: The convertible used here has a conversion ratio of 25.93 and a straight bond value of $669.

The conversion value, of course, shows a linear relationship with the stock price, as Figure 15.9 illustrates. Will the conversion value always form the lower boundary to the value of a convertible, regardless of the stock price? The answer is no. If the Reebok convertible did not have the conversion option, it would simply be a corporate bond with a maturity in 2021 and a coupon rate of 4.25%. Presumably, it would be valued as such, which is referred to as the convertible's *straight bond value,* the value of the convertible without the conversion feature.

To estimate the straight bond value, find the price of the bond at the same yield to maturity common for straight bonds with similar maturity and quality characteristics. Straight bonds similar to the Reebok's convertible bond (with Baa rating) had average yields of about 7.6%. Therefore, the bond pricing equation developed in Chapter 9 gives the Reebok convertible a straight bond value of about $669 per $1,000 of par value. The straight bond value is also shown in Figure 15.9.

To summarize, the straight bond value is the lower boundary for the value of a convertible if $S < E$. If $S > E$, the lower boundary becomes the conversion value. Will the convertible always sell for a premium over its straight bond value? The answer is not necessarily; it depends on the relationship between the stock price and bond's conversion price. If the convertible is deeply out of the money, then it will likely sell for close to its straight bond value. However, if the convertible is deeply in the money, it will likely sell for close to its conversion value. For values in between, the convertible will sell for a premium, perhaps a large one, above its straight bond value.

Why Buy Convertibles? Convertibles can offer investors attractive combinations of the best of both bonds and stocks. They have more upside potential than bonds; as the stock price increases, so does the value of the convertible. However, at the same time, convertibles provide more downside protection than stocks; they can always be valued as straight bonds. Furthermore, the coupon rate on a convertible usually exceeds the stock's dividend yield by a substantial amount. The Reebok convertible has a coupon rate of 4.25%; Reebok common stock pays no cash dividends.

Convertibles are not perfect securities, however. For one thing, they tend to be rated lower than straight bonds. (The Reebok convertible is rated Baa3.) For another, because of the conversion feature, convertibles have lower coupon rates than similar straight bonds. The investor must give up some current income in exchange for the conversion feature. As a result, when considering a convertible, an investor needs to evaluate the prospects for the company's common stock.

Another risk is unique to convertibles: almost all convertibles are callable. Issuers may use the call provision to essentially force conversion. Would you, assuming you are a rational investor—and we hope at this point that you are— ever exercise the conversion feature before maturity? No! You would exercise the conversion option only if the convertible were in the money. If it is in the money, its value will increase dollar for dollar as the stock price increases, while still offering the downside protection of a bond and the higher current income from the coupon payments. When the issuing company wants the convertible bond converted into common stock, if it is deeply in the money and the call price is well below the market price, the firm will call the bond. Rather than allowing the company to call the bond in exchange for its par value, you would either convert the bond into common stock or sell the bond to someone else who would.

Warrants

A **warrant** is simply a long-term call option issued by a company. It allows the holder to buy a fixed number of shares of stock (usually one warrant buys one share) from the issuing company at a fixed price for a fixed period of time. It is often issued with stocks as an inducement to investors. Warrants usually have lives between 5 and 10 years when issued. They are often attached to other securities, such as bonds. Most warrants can be detached and sold in the secondary market. Warrants typically trade, along with the company's stock, on one of the major stock exchanges.

Though warrant issues are not as popular as they use to be, Inco's warrant expiring on August 21, 2006 serves as an example. The warrant allows the owner to buy one share of Inco common stock for $30.00 Canadian dollars. Assuming an exchange rate of $.70 US$/Can$, the exercise price equals $21.00 US dollars. In March 2003, the warrants were selling for $5.80 while Inco's common stock was selling for $19.85. This means that the Inco warrant is out of the money (S < E).

Valuing a warrant is similar to valuing a call option. The Inco warrant is selling for a premium of $6.95 ($5.80 − $19.85 + $21.00 = $6.95). That may seem high, but remember that Inco can be a volatile stock.

warrant

A long-term call option issued by a company giving its owner the right to buy a fixed number of shares of stock at a fixed price for a fixed period of time.

INVESTMENT INSIGHT

Confederate Cotton Bonds of 1863

The history of options is long. The famous Dutch tulip bubble of the early seventeenth century was reportedly fueled by the use of options. Dealers would buy call options—giving them the right, but not the obligation, to buy tulip bulbs at fixed prices—protecting them from skyrocketing prices. Growers, on the other hand, purchased put options to protect themselves from falling prices.

In the United States, options history is also long. Traders began buying and selling call and put options soon after the Buttonwood Tree Agreement was signed in 1792, establishing what eventually became the New York Stock Exchange. In his fascinating book, *Against the Gods: The Remarkable Story of Risk,* Peter Bernstein tells the story of the Confederate cotton bonds. It is example of the many uses of options.

In early 1863 the Confederate States of America was desperate for capital. It needed hard foreign currency to purchase weapons from Europe. At the same time, the Confederacy needed legitimacy in the eyes of the European powers. If these governments were given a financial stake in the survival of the Confederacy, they might create enough pressure to force the Union into negotiating a peace treaty. Selling bonds denominated in Confederate dollars was not a realistic alternative because Confederate dollars had little appeal to foreign investors. Offering exorbitant interest rates would have been necessary to entice European investors to buy Confederate dollar-denominated bonds. Enter the cotton bonds.

Interest and principal on the bonds was payable in either Confederate dollars or one of the two major European currencies, British pounds or French francs, at the *option* of the bondholder. European investors need not travel to Richmond, Virginia—a somewhat risky journey—to collect interest and principal payments. They could be collected in one of four European cities—London, Paris, Amsterdam, or Frankfurt. Moreover, the bondholder had the option of converting the obligation into cotton, effectively buying cotton for about one-quarter of its current market price.

The buyers of these bonds, therefore, acquired several options. Each of these options helped to control risk. The option of repayment in British or French currency eliminated the risk associated with the further devaluation of the Confederate dollar. The option of converting the bond into cotton, provided a hedge against inflation and the ravages of war. In return for these options, European investors were willing to lend the Confederacy money at an annual rate of 7%, only 1% more than Union was paying for long-term money at the time. This rate was probably less than half what the money would have cost the Confederacy without the options.

Approximately £3 million worth of cotton bonds were sold in 1863, sometimes even at prices slightly above face value. The Confederacy met its obligations due in 1863 and 1864, but paid nothing after the Confederacy collapsed in 1865. Only about £370,000 worth of the bonds were converted into cotton. The Confederate cotton bonds of 1863 remain an interesting example of the many uses of derivatives.

Questions for Critical Thinking

1. It is said that the introduction of an option transforms a transaction into one in which uncertainty is an integral part. Why is uncertainty such an important part of a transaction involving an option?

2. Peter Bernstein suggests that options "bear a strong family resemblance to insurance policies and are often bought and sold for the same reasons." Further, if insurance policies were converted into securities, they would be priced exactly as options are priced. Explain Bernstein's reasoning.

Source: Some material adapted from Peter Bernstein, *Against the Gods: The Remarkable Story of Risk* (New York: John Wiley & Sons, 1998).

Trading strategies for warrants are similar to those for call options. Warrants, like call options, provide inherent leverage that allows individuals to speculate on the price of a specific stock moving up over the next few months or years. Warrants can also be used to cover, or hedge, a short sale. The downside of warrants is that they are available on only a limited number of stocks, and they are often not actively traded.

The Investment Insight on this page discuss the long history of securities that resemble options. It gives a historical account of how the Confederates used cotton bonds to finance the Civil War. They enticed European investors to accept interest and principal payments on the bond with an *option* to accept payment in Confederate dollars or one of the two major European currencies, British pounds or French francs. They even had the option of converting the obligation into cotton, giving them the right to buy cotton for about one-quarter of its current market price.

SUMMARY

1. What are the basic characteristics of option contracts?
A call option gives the owner the right, but not obligation, to buy shares of stock at a fixed price for a fixed period of time. The owner of a put option has the right, but not obligation, to sell shares of stock at a fixed price for a fixed period of time. Every option bought must have a seller. The seller—or writer—of a call option may be obligated to sell stock at a fixed price; the writer of a put option may be obligated to buy stock at a fixed price.

2. What is the value of an option at expiration?
The value of a call option, at expiration, is equal to the maximum of zero or the difference between the stock price and the exercise price. At expiration, the value of a put option is equal to the maximum of zero or the difference between the exercise price and the stock price.

3. What are some common option trading strategies?
Investors buy options as a way of speculating on short-term price movements in stock or stock indexes. If you believe a stock will rise (fall) in price, you might buy a call (put) option. Many option traders trade several options at the same time. A straddle involves buying a call and a put option with the same expiration date and exercise price. It is a bet that the stock price will move substantially in one direction or the other. Another common option trade is a spread, say, buying one call option while selling another with a different exercise price. Spreads are less risky than buying or selling just one option. Options can also be used to reduce the risk of a position in the underlying stock.

4. How are options valued?
The intrinsic value of an option is a function of six variables: the price of the underlying stock, the exercise price, the time until expiration, the level of short-term interest rates, the volatility of the underlying stock, and the amount of dividends the stock pays before expiration. The Black-Scholes option pricing model explicitly includes five of these six variables—the model assumes the underlying stock pays no dividends.

5. What other securities resemble options?
A convertible security is a bond or preferred stock that can be converted into common stock, at a fixed price, for a fixed period of time. In essence, a convertible contains a call option and can be valued as such. A warrant is a long-term call option issued by corporations. Warrants are often attached to other security issues. Warrants often trade in the stock markets.

MINI CASE 1

This mini case allows you to practice finding prices, premiums, values at expiration, and profits (losses) for S&P 100 (OEX) options. The October 16, 2002, quotes for the S&P100 options are listed here.

Strike Price	Expiration	Call or Put	Price
440	November 2002	Call	22
440	November 2002	Put	15
440	December 2002	Call	29.50

Strike Price	Expiration	Call or Put	Price
440	December 2002	Put	24
440	January 2003	Call	31.50
440	January 2003	Put	28.80
450	December 2002	Call	25
450	December 2002	Put	30

1. When do the options expire? What rights do they give their buyers?
2. Which option(s) is (are) in the money? Find the options' premiums. What does *premium* mean?
3. What will the call and put options be worth when they expire?
4. Construct profit and loss graphs for a call option's buyer and writer (you choose the call option).
5. Construct profit and loss graphs for a put option's buyer and writer (you choose the put option).
6. Assume you believed the OEX was going to rise sharply during the next few days. Use the options to construct a bull spread.

MINI CASE 2

The purpose of this mini case is to learn to apply the Black-Scholes option pricing model to an actual call option.

Stock: IBM
Stock price: $60.36
Exercise price: $60
Risk-free rate of interest: 1.75%
Expiration: 18 days
Standard deviation of stock returns: 0.674
Market price of call: $3.50

1. Is the IBM call option in the money? What is its intrinsic value? What is its time value?
2. Use the given information and the Black-Scholes model to find the fundamental value of this option.
3. If the fundamental value of the option differs from its market price, explain how to take advantage of this difference.

REVIEW EXERCISES

1. What is a derivative security? Why are options considered to be derivative securities?
2. What rights and obligations does the buyer of an option have? How do these differ from the rights and obligations of the writer of the option?
3. Explain cash settlement of index options. Give a numerical example.
4. If a put option has a price of $5 and an exercise price of $50 while the underlying stock is selling for $48, is the put option in the money? What is its premium?
5. For the put option described in Question 4, calculate the profit and loss from holding the option to expiration. How much would the price of the stock have to change for the option buyer to break even?
6. What does it mean when we say call options have inherent leverage? What other risks are unique to options?

7. From the option prices shown in Figure 15.1, construct a bull spread using IBM 60 and 65 October call options. Create a profit/loss table if the stock price equals $45, $50, $55, $60, $65, $70, or $75 at expiration. What is the purpose of a bull spread?

8. From the option prices shown in Figure 15.1, construct a bull spread using IBM 60 and 65 October put options. Create a profit/loss table if the stock price equals $45, $50, $55, $60, $65, $70, or $75 at expiration. What are the advantage of using the puts versus the calls to create a bull spread?

9. Using the options quotes shown in Figure 15.1, construct a straddle using Cisco 12.50 November options. Create a profit/loss table if the stock price equals $5, $10, $12.50, $15, or $20 at expiration. What is the purpose of a straddle?

10. Using the option prices shown in Figure 15.1, create a money spread using GE 22.50 and 25 December call options to reflect the expectation that the price of GE stock will decline. Create a profit/loss table if the stock price equals $10, $15, $20, $22.50, $25, $30, $35, or $40 at expiration.

11. Using the option prices shown in Figure 15.1, create a money spread using GE 22.50 and 25 December put options to reflect the expectation that the price of GE stock will increase. Create a profit/loss table assuming the stock price equals $10, $15, $20, $22.50, $25, $30, $35, or $40 at expiration.

12. Suppose you bought an Intel stock at $10 a month ago, and the stock price today is close to $15. Assume you want to hold the stock until January 2003 for tax purposes, but you are afraid the stock may decline between mid-December and January 2003. How can you protect your profits using a put from the quotes in Figure 15.1? Create a profit/loss table assuming that the stock price equals $5, $10, $15, $20, $25, or $30 at expiration.

13. Using Figure 15.1 find the intrinsic value of Home Depot (HomeDp) 27.50 October call? Is it in the money? Explain. What are its time value and its premium?

14. Using Figure 15.1, find the intrinsic value of Home Depot (HomeDp) 27.50 October put? Is it in the money? Explain. What are its time value and its premium?

15. Suppose you bought an Intel stock at $10 a month ago, and the stock price today is about $15. You decide to write a covered call on the Intel stock using the 15 January call. Create a profit/loss table for a covered call assuming that the stock price equals $5, $10, $15, $20, $25, $30, or $35 at expiration.

16. Discuss the six factors that affect the value of a call option before expiration. How do these relationships change for the value of a put option before expiration?

17. Give a loose interpretation of the Black-Scholes option pricing model. How realistic are the assumptions made by the model?

18. Assume a convertible bond with a $1,000 face value is convertible into 25 shares of stock. What is the conversion price? If the stock price is currently $50, how much is the conversion value?

19. What are the major investment advantages of convertibles? What are their drawbacks?

20. Why is a warrant just a long-term call option? Why might an investor buy a warrant as opposed to the underlying stock?

CRITICAL THINKING EXERCISES

1. This exercise requires computer work. Contained in the America Online (AOL) worksheet in the Data Workbook are recent prices for AOL options. Using the information in the file, perform the following calculations and answer the following questions:
   a. Calculate each option's premium. Why are some premiums larger than others?
   b. Construct a straddle and a reverse straddle using the options that are closest to being at the money. Calculate the profit and loss from both at expiration.

c.   Assume that someone believes that the AOL will rise over the next few weeks. Describe some option trades that would take advantage of this anticipated rise in prices. Which would be the most risky? The least risky?

d.   Assume you already own AOL. Describe two option strategies that can reduce the risk associated with your stock position.

2.   This exercise requires both computer work and library research. In the Black-Scholes worksheet in the Data Workbook are returns for five stocks. Use these returns to compute standard deviations for the series. Using a recent issue of *The Wall Street Journal* or a similar publication, find one call option on each of these five stocks.

a.   Using the standard computed deviations, along with the other input variables from the financial press, calculate the Black-Scholes model's intrinsic value for each.

b.   Comparing the Black-Scholes values to the options' market prices, indicate whether either option is correctly valued. What could explain differences between the Black-Scholes prices and the market prices?

c.   Assume you believe the Black-Scholes model finds the "correct" intrinsic value for call options. Describe some option/stock trades you could execute to take advantage of your belief.

3.   This exercise requires library research. Potomac Electric Power has a convertible bond issue outstanding that matures in 2015 with a coupon rate of 7%. Answer the following questions about this bond:

a.   What are the bond's conversion ratio and conversion price?

b.   What is the bond's current conversion value? Is the convertible currently in the money or out of the money?

c.   If this bond were not convertible, for what price would it sell? (What is its straight bond value?)

d.   What is the bond's current market price?

e.   How much of a premium is included in the bond's current price? Why does this premium seem relatively small?

THE INTERNET INVESTOR

1.   Find a stock with several options written on it. Using a Web site that provides stock price quotes and options quotes, chart the daily stock prices, one call option contract close to being at the money and one put option contract with the same expiration and exercise over a one-month period. What observations can you make from the relationship between stock price, call price and put price? What seems to be investor expectations about the stock in question?

2.   Using a Web site that provides options quotes, track the call option quotes for a non-technology firm and call options quotes for a technology firm. Use at the money calls and same expiration dates. What factors described in Table 15.7 are observed from the data.

3.   Using a Web site that provides options quotes, chart two call option quotes for a technology stock. Find two calls with the same exercise but different expirations. What can you conclude from the data? Find two calls with the same expiration but different exercise prices. What can you conclude from these data?

16

Futures Contracts

| PREVIOUSLY . . . | IN THIS CHAPTER . . . | TO COME . . . |

We discussed options as the first major type of derivative security. We described not only stock options but other securities that contain options.

We continue our coverage of derivative securities by examining futures contracts. These contracts call for the future delivery of an asset at a price agreed on today. Futures are traded in a variety of underlying assets, everything from corn to stock indexes. They share some characteristics of options but have some important differences.

We conclude our journey into the world of investments by discussing modern portfolio theory and diversification, one of the most popular investment processes today. All professional investment advisers, technical and fundamental, agree that diversification is the best way to reduce risk.

CHAPTER OBJECTIVES
After reading Chapter 16, you should be able to answer the following questions:

1. What are futures contracts?

2. How can futures contracts be valued?

3. How do traders use futures?

4. What are financial futures?

5. What are options on futures?

Suppose you are in the market for a new car. You visit the local dealer who is selling this year's hottest new model. At the dealership, the dealer does not have a car to sell you right now. The dealer will have the model you want in one month. Waiting a month for delivery is actually better for you, because you would like to sell your old car to raise money for the down payment. You and the dealer might enter into a binding contract in which you agree to take delivery of the car in one month at a specified price, and the dealer agrees to deliver the car in one month at the same price. This kind of agreement is commonly called a **forward contract**.

forward contract

Contract calling for the future delivery of an asset at a price agreed on today.

Most economic transactions occur in the spot, or cash, market, in which the buyer takes delivery of the asset from the seller immediately. As the preceding example illustrates, however, the buyer and seller may agree to complete the transaction at some future date. For these individuals, forward contracts offer a way of locking in the price of the asset today and guaranteeing that the transaction will be completed at a future date.

If a forward contract is an agreement between a buyer and seller that stipulates the future delivery of some asset, at a specified price, what is a futures contract? A **futures contract** is simply a highly standardized version of a forward contract. Futures contracts specify standard amounts, delivery dates, and so forth. Unlike forward contracts, futures contracts are marketable and trade on organized exchanges, subject to specific rules.

futures contract

Highly standardized version of a forward contract.

In this chapter, we examine futures contracts, through which people take positions in such assets as Treasury bonds (T-bonds), Japanese yen, soybeans, pork bellies, orange juice, gold, and crude oil. Like options, which we discussed in Chapter 15, futures are considered derivative securities, which means that their values derive from underlying assets. Also like options, futures are considered speculative in nature; options and futures are inherently more risky than more traditional financial assets such as stocks and bonds. However, as we saw in Chapter 15 and discuss in this chapter, traders use both options and futures to *reduce* the risks associated with stock and bond positions.

WHAT ARE FUTURES?

A *futures contract* is a binding legal contract that calls for the future delivery of an asset. The contract specifies the asset to be delivered, the delivery location, the amount to be delivered, the delivery date, and the price. A futures contract has two parties, or *positions:* the long position and the short position. The person who holds the **long position** agrees to accept delivery of the asset, at the terms specified by the contract, and the person who holds the **short position** agrees to deliver the asset, again at the terms specified by the contract. Someone who goes long in July corn at $2.50 per bushel agrees to accept delivery of 5,000 bushels (the size of one corn contract) in July at a price of $2.50 per bushel. It is important to note that for every long position there *must* be a short position.

long position

Person agreeing to take delivery of the asset.

short position

Person agreeing to deliver the asset.

Trading in futures, like that in options, is considered a zero-sum game. If someone makes a dollar in a futures position, the person who holds the opposite position must lose a dollar. If the price of a futures contract rises by a certain amount, the wealth of the long position increases by that amount, and the short position's wealth declines by that amount.

Must the holder of the long position take delivery of the corn? Yes, if the position remains open until the delivery date. However, before the actual delivery

Size	$1,000,000 face value U.S. Treasury bonds	**TABLE 16.1**
Deliverable grade	U.S. Treasury bonds maturing at least 15 years from date of delivery, if not callable; if callable, not so for at least 15 years from the first day of the delivery month; coupon based on an 8% standard	Contract Highlights: U.S. Treasury Bond futures
Price quotation	In points ($1,000) and thirty-seconds of a point; for example, 92-16 equals 92 16/32	
Minimum price fluctuation	One thirty-second of a point, or $31.25 (one tick) per contract	
Daily trading limits	3 points ($3,000) per contract above or below the previous day's settlement price	
Months traded	March, June, September, and December	
Trading hours	7:20 A.M. to 2 P.M. (Chicago time), Monday through Friday; Evening trading hours from 5:20 to 8:05 P.M. (Central Standard Time) or 6:20 to 9:05 P.M. (Daylight Saving Time), Sunday through Thursday*	
Ticker symbol	US	
Last trading day	Seven business days prior to the last business day of the month	
Last delivery day	Last business day of the month	
Delivery method	Federal Reserve book entry wire transfer system	

*Project A afternoon session hours are 2:30 to 4:30 P.M. (Chicago time), Monday through Thursday; and Project A overnight session hours are from 10 P.M. to 6 A.M., Sunday through Thursday.

Source: Chicago Board of Trade, *1997 Specifications.* Content reprinted by permission of the Board of Trade of the City of Chicago, Inc.

date he or she can close out the position merely by taking the opposite position in the same contract. For example, someone who is long in July corn can close out the position by going short in July corn. Most futures traders have no intention of taking delivery, or delivering, the assets they trade; the majority close out their positions before the delivery dates.

An example of a futures contract summary appears in Table 16.1. The table shows the highlights of the futures contract on U.S. T-bonds—one of the most actively traded futures contract. The contract sets specific terms for elements such as size ($100,000 face value), deliverable grade (any T-bond with at least 15 years remaining to call), delivery months (March, June, September, and December), and delivery method (Federal Reserve book entry wire transfer system).

Evolution of Modern Futures Markets

The historical origins of forward and futures contracts go back to ancient civilizations. Evidence indicates that the Greeks and Romans actively traded instruments that we would recognize today as forward contracts. Roman emperors are said to have engaged in active forward contracting to ensure that grain was available during winter.

The origins of modern futures exchanges can be traced to the establishment, in 1848, of the Chicago Board of Trade (CBOT, or CBT in financial quotes and listings). In the mid-1800s, Chicago was rapidly becoming a major transportation and distribution center for agricultural products, especially grains such as corn and wheat. Farmers shipped their grain to Chicago for sale and distribution eastward along rail and water shipping channels. The problem, of course, is that grain production in the Midwest is seasonal in nature. At harvest time, supplies would soar, often overwhelming the city's storage facilities, and prices would plunge. As supplies diminished through the winter and spring, prices would soar.

To alleviate some of the problems associated with the seasonal nature of grain production, the newly formed CBT began to offer farmers what were known as *to arrive contracts*. These contracts allowed farmers to deliver their grain at predetermined future dates at prices set in advance of delivery. Financiers soon discovered that these contracts allowed them to speculate on grain prices without having to worry about taking delivery of the grain and storing it. Modern futures trading had begun.

In late 1874, a second futures exchange was established in Chicago. Initially named the Chicago Produce Exchange, it concentrated on futures contracts in meat and livestock. In 1898, the exchange was renamed the Chicago Mercantile Exchange (CME). Also in the late 1800s, the Coffee, Sugar & Cocoa Exchange and the New York Cotton Exchange were formed in New York. Other futures exchanges, both in the United States and the rest of the world, soon followed.

Development of Financial Futures Before 1972, futures trading was limited to physical commodities such as grains, cotton, and metals. In 1972, the International Monetary Market (IMM), a subsidiary of the CME, was created in response to the 1971 decision by most Western nations to allow their currency exchange rates to fluctuate. The IMM offered futures contracts on foreign currencies—the first financial futures. Then in 1975, the CBT introduced the first futures contract on an interest-bearing financial instrument, the GNMA mortgage pass-through security. In 1976, the IMM introduced a futures contract on 90-day Treasury bills (T-bills), and in 1977, the CBT introduced a futures contract on long-term T-bonds that soon became the most successful new contract of all time.

The early 1980s saw the emergence of stock index futures contracts. In 1982, the Kansas City Board of Trade launched a futures contract based on the Value Line Index. It was followed a few months later by the CME's introduction of a futures contract based on the Standard & Poor's (S&P) 500. By the mid-1980s, trading in financial futures exceeded trading in commodity futures.

Today's Futures Exchanges Approximately 14 exchanges handle futures trading in the United States today. In addition, another 11 major futures exchanges operate in other parts of the world. The two largest futures exchanges are still the two oldest: the CBT and the CME. Today, these two exchanges account for approximately 40% of all futures trading worldwide. Several of the fastest-growing futures exchanges, however, are located outside the United States. The Singapore International Monetary Exchange, established only in 1984, emerged in recent years as a major trading center for financial futures, especially currency futures.

One characteristic of today's futures exchanges, especially those in the United States, is exchange specialization. One exchange tends to dominate trading in a specific asset. Virtually all trading in T-bond and T-note futures, for example, takes place on the CBT. The New York Mercantile Exchange dominates trading in petroleum futures. The exchanges compete intensely to introduce new contracts. Once a successful new contract is introduced, the exchange that introduced it will likely develop a near monopoly in trading in that contract.

Contract	Exchange	Contract	Exchange	Contract	Exchange
Grains and Oilseeds		**Metals & Petroleum**		**Stock Index**	
Corn	CBT	Copper	COMEX	Nikkei 225	CME
Oats	CBT	Crude oil	NYMEX	Major Market Index	CBT
Soybeans	CBT	Gold	COMEX	NYSE Index	NYFE
Soybean meal	CBT	Heating oil	NYMEX	S&P 500	CME
Soybean oil	CBT	Natural gas	NYMEX		
Wheat	CBT	Palladium	NYMEX	**Interest Rate**	
		Platinum	NYMEX	Eurodollar	CME
Livestock and Meat		Propane	NYMEX	Municipal bond index	CBT
Feeder cattle	CME	Silver	COMEX	Treasury bills	CME
Hogs	CME	Unleaded gasoline	NYMEX	Treasury bonds	CBT
Live cattle	CME			Treasury notes (10 yr.)	CBT
Pork bellies		**Foreign Currency**		Treasury notes (5 yr.)	CBT
		Australian dollar	CME	Treasury notes (2 yr.)	CBT
Food and Fiber		British pound	CME		
Cocoa	CSCE	Canadian dollar	CME		
Coffee	CSCE	German mark	CME		
Cotton	NYCTN	Japanese yen	CME		
Domestic sugar	CSCE	Swiss franc	CME		
Orange juice	NYCTN				
Rice	CRCE				
World sugar	CSCE				

TABLE 16.2	Major Futures Contracts Listed on U.S. Exchanges

Notes: CBT is the Chicago Board of Trade; CME is the Chicago Mercantile Exchange (or one of its subsidiaries); COMEX is the Commodity Exchange; CRCE is the Chicago Rice and Coffee Exchange; CSCE is the Coffee, Sugar & Cocoa Exchange; NYCTN is the New York Cotton Exchange; NYFE is the New York Futures Exchange; and NYMEX is the New York Mercantile Exchange.

In the United States, futures trading is regulated by the Commodity Futures Trading Commission (CFTC), rather than the Securities and Exchange Commission (SEC). The CFTC regulates even futures on stocks and bonds. Several bills introduced in Congress in recent years would eliminate the CFTC and give regulatory power over futures trading to the SEC.

Types of Contracts

We can initially divide futures contracts into those based on physical commodities and those based on financial instruments. We can divide physical commodities contracts into those based on agricultural products (grains and oilseeds, livestock and meat, and food and fiber) and those based on nonagricultural products (lumber, metals, and petroleum). Financial futures can be divided into three more specific categories: currency futures, stock index futures, and interest rate futures. The major futures contracts traded on U.S. futures exchanges, along with the dominant exchange for each, are listed in Table 16.2.

Requirements for a Viable Futures Market

An asset that develops a viable futures market must have five characteristics: (1) the ability to be standardized, (2) active demand, (3) the ability to be stored for a period of time, (4) relatively high value in proportion to bulk, and (5) relatively high value in proportion to storage and other carrying costs. As an example, consider gold. Gold can be standardized (for example, by purity grades). It is subject to active demand; some 20 million ounces of gold are bought and sold each year. Gold can be stored; it does not deteriorate over time. It is valuable in proportion to its bulk; one pound of gold is worth almost $6,000. Finally, the cost of storing and carrying gold for a period of time is probably less than 5% of its value.

Mechanics of Futures Trading

As with the world's stock exchanges, futures exchanges are becoming more and more automated. Some foreign futures markets conduct all trading via computer systems; in some cases, no trading takes place on the floor of the exchange (similar to trading on the Nasdaq system or the London Stock Exchange).

In the United States, futures markets, particularly the two largest, the CBT and the CME, still retain much of the traditional futures trading system. In this *open outcry system*, trading takes place on the floor of the exchange, where traders stand in trading pits (each contract is assigned to one pit) and bid against one another. They shout out buy and sell bids and use hand signals to communicate to other traders. Every trader standing in the pit has, at least in theory, an equal chance of trading. Unlike the New York Stock Exchange (NYSE) or Nasdaq, futures exchanges have no specialists or market makers as such. Generally, all traders are allowed to trade all contracts listed on the exchange, although many traders choose to specialize in particular futures contracts.

Who Are the Traders? All traders must be either members of the exchange or employees of members. Some people trade on the floor by leasing trading privileges from a member. The CBT, for example, currently has about 3,600 members. Like NYSE seats, memberships are bought and sold. Recently, a CBT membership sold for about $450,000.

Traders can be grouped into three general categories: commission brokers trade strictly for others; local traders trade strictly for their own or their firms' accounts; and dual traders perform both functions, sometimes acting as brokers and sometimes trading for their own accounts.

We can also classify local and dual traders in terms of trading style. Scalpers attempt to profit from small changes in the contract prices; they rarely hold positions open for more than a few minutes. Day traders also attempt to profit from short-term market movements. Although they hold positions much longer than scalpers, they do not hold positions overnight. Finally, position traders hold positions open over much longer periods of time and attempt to profit from longer-term market movements.

Placing an Order Placing an order to buy or sell a futures contract (go long or go short) is similar to placing an order to buy or sell stocks or bonds. In response to the order, the broker contacts the firm's trading desk on the floor of the exchange. The order is relayed for execution to the firm's floor broker or to a dual trader who handles the firm's orders. After execution, the same chain returns confirmation of the trade. Futures traders can place the same types of orders discussed in Chapter 3 (market orders, stop-loss orders, limit orders, good till canceled orders, and day orders). Commissions on futures trades vary widely from firm to firm. Some brokerage firms offer no futures trading services for their customers.

Role of the Clearinghouse A feature unique to the options and futures markets is the clearinghouse, or clearing corporation. Each futures market operates a clearinghouse as a nonprofit corporation owned by members of the exchange. The clearinghouse acts as both an intermediary and guarantor to every trade. The first clearinghouse was organized by the CBT in 1925.

Any futures trade, as already noted, requires a short position for every long position, and vice versa. Both parties promise to fulfill certain contractual obligations (deliver or take delivery of the asset at the agreed-on price at the agreed-on time). Without a clearinghouse, each party would have to depend on the other party to fulfill his or her contractual obligations. If one party failed to meet obligations, the other party would be left with a worthless claim. The clearinghouse guarantees that both parties fulfill their contractual obligations by acting as a counterparty in each trade. Let's say Trader W decides to go long in July corn. To take this position, Trader W must find someone to go short (Trader X). The clearinghouse would establish a short position in July corn with Trader W, who wants to go long in July corn. At the same time, the clearinghouse would establish a long position in July corn with Trader X.

Margins and Daily Price Limits In a futures transactions, both parties must post margin deposits (either in cash or, in some cases, T-bills).[1] After satisfying this initial margin requirement, they must also meet maintenance margin requirements. The margin, a percentage of the contract's value, acts as a good-faith security deposit. At the end of each trading day, a committee of traders and clearinghouse officials meets to establish a **settlement price** for each contract. Based on that settlement price, each open account is **marked to market** daily. Depending on whether a trader is long or short and whether the current settlement price is higher or lower than the previous day's settlement price, that trader's margin will either rise or fall. Margin transactions are best illustrated with an example.

Assume you take a long position in March crude oil at $24.50 per barrel on February 3. You must post an initial margin of $2,970 and maintain a maintenance margin of $2,200.[2] Suppose the position remains open until February 14. Table 16.3 shows the settlement prices and transactions for the margin account during the period between February 3 and February 14. Notice how losses are subtracted from your account, whereas gains are added to the account.[3] Also

settlement price

Price established at the end of each trading day used to calculate trader's margins.

marked to market

Adjusting each trader's margin account by the change in the settlement price.

---

[1] In stock trading, remember, *margin* is the amount of your money you put up to buy a stock; you borrow the rest. Futures traders do not borrow money.

[2] These figures are the minimum margins on crude oil futures set by the exchange where they are traded. In reality, most traders would be required to post higher margins, depending on their futures brokerage firm.

[3] Some firms might allow you to withdraw "surplus" margin from the account, that is, the amount above the initial margin.

On February 3, a trader went long in March crude oil at $24.15 per barrel (1,000 barrel contract). The position remained open until February 14. The trader is required to post an initial margin of $2,970 and maintain a margin of $2,200.

Date	Settlement Price	Daily Mark to Market	Initial Margin Account Balance	Deposit or (Withdrawal)	Ending Margin Account Balance
Feb. 3	$24,150		$ 0	$2,970	$2,970
Feb. 4	24,250	100	3,070	0	3,070
Feb. 5	24,250	0	3,070	0	3,070
Feb. 6	23,750	(500)	2,570	0	2,570
Feb. 7	23,000	(750)	1,820	1,150	2,970
Feb. 10	22,750	(250)	2,720	0	2,720
Feb. 11	23,500	750	3,470	0	3,470
Feb. 12	23,750	250	3,720	0	3,720
Feb. 13	24,500	750	4,470	0	4,470
Feb. 14	25,000	500	4,970	(4,970)	0

note that on February 7, the balance in your margin account falls below the maintenance requirement, $2,200. You must deposit another $1,150 into the account to bring the balance back up to the initial requirement. On February 14, you close out your position by going short in March crude oil at $25 per barrel. You withdraw the amount in the margin account, $4,970. You end up making $850 ($4,970 − $2,970 − $1,150).

Partly because a trader must post only a small percentage of the contract's value as margin, many contracts limit the maximum daily price change (crude oil futures generally have a daily limit of $1.50 per barrel). If the contract price moves up or down by the maximum amount, the contract is said to be **limit up** or **limit down**. Normally, no trading can take place at prices outside the daily price limits. However, the exchanges can, under certain circumstances, increase daily price limits to help ensure orderly markets.

limit up (limit down)

The maximum amounts, high and low, by which the futures price can change during a particular trading day.

Delivery Procedure As noted earlier, most traders have no intention of taking delivery, or delivering, the asset on which they trade futures. However, exceptions arise; delivery actually occurs in about 3% of T-bond and T-note contracts, for example. Should a trader actually wish to take delivery, or deliver, the asset, he or she must follow the delivery procedure specified by the contract. In all cases, the short initiates the delivery procedure.

FUTURES PRICING PRIMER

In this section we review the pricing of futures contracts, covering two theories of futures pricing. One theory suggests that futures prices and expected spot prices are related, whereas the other theory denies any relationship between futures prices and expected spot prices. Before we discuss these two theories, let's consider several important pricing concepts, beginning with a discussion of how to read futures price quotations in the financial press.

Future Price Quotations

Figure 16.1 reproduces a sample set of futures price quotations for one trading day. For example, the first quote refers to a contract on corn futures traded on the CBT. Prices are quoted in cents per bushel, which means 255.75 cents is equal to $2.5575 per bushel. Delivery dates range from December 2002 to July 2004. The December 2002 contract settled on October 1, 2002, for 255.75 per bushel; it previously traded as high as 256.50 per bushel and as low as 250 per bushel.

Open Interest Open interest refers to to the number of contracts outstanding at any point in time. Remember, each contract must have both a long and a short position. As of October 1, 2002, traders had taken approximately 282,422 long positions and 282,422 short positions in the December 2002 corn futures. Open interest changes constantly as contracts are traded. To see how transactions affect open interest, take a look at the hypothetical example shown in Table 16.4.

The table's hypothetical futures market has five trading days and five participants. During the first day, A goes long in 10 contracts; B takes the short position. Open interest increases by 10 contracts. During the second trading day, C goes long in 10 contracts; D takes the short position. Open interest increases again by 10 contracts. Notice what happens, however, on days 3 and 4. Trader B, who went short on day 1, closes out the position by going long in 10 contracts; E takes the short position. This situation is considered a trade of existing contracts (E replaces B) and does not effect open interest. The same thing is true on day 4 when D, who went short on day 2, closes out the position (F replaces D). On the last day, E closes out a short position by going long. In the same trade, A also closes out a long position by going short. This trade *decreases* open interest by 10 contracts. At the end of the five-day trading period, only C and F still have open positions, so total open interest equals 10 contracts. As you would expect, open interest increases as the time until delivery gets shorter. Open interest typically peaks a few weeks before the first delivery date and then declines sharply. By the time the first delivery date arrives, open interest is close to zero for some contracts.

open interest

Number of contracts outstanding at any point in time.

Basis and Spreads

The terms *basis* and *spread* receive a great deal of attention in futures markets. Both are important concepts for understanding futures pricing. In addition, many trading strategies, which we discuss later in the chapter, rely on expected changes to basis or spread, or both. Let's discuss basis first.

Basis is merely the difference between the cash price, or spot price, of an asset and the futures contract price. Basis can be either negative or positive. Basis also can change for futures contracts with different delivery dates. The cash price of an asset can differ depending on location and grade. A properly measured basis should compare the cash price of an asset that matches the specific delivery characteristics of the futures contract as closely as possible.

Figure 16.2 shows an example of basis for T-bond futures. The cash price of T-bonds is the price of the 8% bond that matures in November 2021. This bond can be delivered in any of the contracts shown in Figure 16.2.

Notice that the T-bond basis gets larger (more positive) as the time to delivery lengthens. It indicates that the spot price of T-bonds is higher than the futures price.

basis

Difference between the cash price of an asset and the future price.

Grain and Oilseed Futures

	OPEN	HIGH	LOW	SETTLE	CHG	LIFETIME HIGH	LIFETIME LOW	OPEN INT
Corn (CBT)-5,000 bu.; cents per bu.								
Dec	251.75	256.50	250.00	255.75	4.25	296.00	215.00	282,422
Mr03	259.00	263.25	258.25	262.50	3.50	301.50	224.00	109,179
May	263.50	266.75	262.00	266.00	2.75	301.00	229.25	29,572
July	264.50	268.00	263.00	266.75	2.75	297.25	233.75	33,505
Sept	252.50	255.00	252.25	254.00	2.50	276.00	233.00	7,833
Dec	243.00	245.50	243.00	244.50	1.25	269.00	235.00	25,728
Jl04	250.25	251.50	250.25	251.50	1.25	264.50	247.75	598
Est vol 72,133; vol Mon 109,746; open int 491,830, −7,105.								
Oats (CBT)-5,000 bu.; cents per bu.								
Dec	209.00	215.50	206.50	214.50	2.75	215.50	123.00	7,384
Mr03	206.50	209.50	206.50	209.00	4.00	209.50	130.00	2,383
May	201.00	202.00	200.00	201.50	2.50	202.00	167.00	404
Est vol 971; vol Mon 1,233; open int 10,174, +100.								
Soybeans (CBT)-5,000 bu.; cents per bu.								
Nov	545.75	547.75	539.50	542.00	−3.75	591.00	428.50	95,952
Ja03	550.00	552.00	544.00	546.00	−4.75	593.50	445.00	31,092
Mar	552.50	554.25	546.00	548.50	−4.75	593.00	449.00	26,701
May	551.50	553.00	546.00	548.50	−4.25	588.00	461.00	30,887
July	552.00	552.50	546.00	548.50	−3.75	586.50	450.00	14,172
Aug	544.00	545.00	542.00	543.00	−2.00	580.00	510.00	935
Nov	510.00	510.50	506.00	508.00	−.25	543.00	484.00	6,624
Est vol 53,989; vol Mon 74,042; open int 206,661, −611.								
Soybean Meal (CBT)-100 tons; $ per ton.								
Oct	170.50	170.90	167.50	168.30	−2.00	189.80	141.50	8,709
Dec	172.80	173.00	169.80	171.00	−1.20	189.30	142.70	67,866
Ja03	172.70	173.10	170.50	172.00	−.70	188.30	143.50	13,174
Mar	172.80	173.70	171.00	172.80	−.50	187.20	145.50	11,982
May	172.20	173.10	170.80	171.50	−.90	185.50	146.00	14,867
July	172.20	173.30	170.80	171.50	−.80	184.50	147.00	10,030
Aug	172.00	172.00	169.50	169.70	−.80	181.30	148.00	2,339
Sept	169.50	169.50	166.50	167.20	−1.30	178.00	148.00	1,961
Oct	161.10	161.50	161.00	161.00	.50	170.00	148.10	1,214
Dec	161.10	161.50	160.50	161.20	.20	168.50	148.00	3,150
Est vol 41,893; vol Mon 43,630; open int 135,294, −4,038.								
Soybean Oil (CBT)-60,000 lbs.; cents per lb.								
Oct	19.64	19.85	19.64	19.65	−.09	21.38	15.15	5,401
Dec	19.85	19.92	19.67	19.68	−.15	21.43	16.10	78,856
Ja03	19.93	19.97	19.71	19.72	−.16	21.40	16.35	15,919
Mar	20.01	20.02	19.78	19.79	−.17	21.35	16.70	15,930
May	20.04	20.05	19.83	19.82	−.20	21.33	16.80	10,816
July	20.00	20.00	19.82	19.84	−.20	21.35	16.95	6,352
Aug	19.85	19.85	19.75	19.70	−.16	20.90	19.75	1,301
Sept	19.65	19.65	19.55	19.50	−.15	20.88	19.55	684
Oct	19.20	19.25	19.20	19.25	−.10	20.50	19.20	1,016
Dec	19.20	19.20	19.15	19.20	−.10	21.00	19.15	4,297
Est vol 20,871; vol Mon 24,017; open int 140,724, −1,203.								
Wheat (CBT)-5,000 bu.; cents per bu.								
Dec	397.25	401.50	390.00	396.50	...	440.00	283.50	83,272
Mr03	400.00	404.50	394.00	399.75	−.25	448.50	288.50	23,433
May	379.00	382.00	375.00	376.00	−2.00	422.00	287.00	2,143
July	351.00	352.00	345.00	346.75	−5.25	380.00	280.50	13,409
Sept	354.50	354.50	348.50	349.00	−7.00	382.00	321.50	872
Dec	358.00	358.00	356.00	357.00	−5.00	385.00	291.00	2,249
Est vol 23,773; vol Mon 34,565; open int 125,433, −428.								
Wheat (KC)-5,000 bu.; cents per bu.								
Dec	475.50	485.00	475.50	481.50	6.25	494.25	293.00	46,035
Mr03	461.00	468.00	460.00	466.00	6.50	486.50	297.50	19,820
May	430.50	436.00	428.00	434.00	7.00	458.25	299.50	2,020
July	382.00	387.00	381.50	385.75	3.00	408.00	302.00	7,352
Sept	385.00	387.00	383.00	386.50	3.50	405.00	349.00	315
Est vol 11,829; vol Mon 12,215; open int 75,989, −793.								
Wheat (MPLS)-5,000 bu.; cents per bu.								
Dec	507.50	517.25	507.00	515.25	9.00	521.50	305.00	19,531
Mr03	502.50	511.00	502.00	509.25	7.00	522.00	311.00	8,228
May	481.00	488.50	480.00	486.00	7.00	489.00	313.00	1,733
July	448.00	456.00	446.00	451.00	6.00	458.75	314.50	1,572
Est vol na; vol Mon 9,394; open int 32,671, +1,120.								

Petroleum Futures

	OPEN	HIGH	LOW	SETTLE	CHG	LIFETIME HIGH	LIFETIME LOW	OPEN INT
Crude Oil, Light Sweet (NYM)-1,000 bbls.; $ per bbl.								
Nov	30.45	31.18	30.45	30.83	0.38	31.39	19.55	171,721
Dec	30.30	30.85	30.21	30.48	0.27	31.02	15.50	84,937
Ja03	29.85	30.25	29.71	29.97	0.22	30.42	19.90	45,922
Feb	29.27	29.65	29.20	29.34	0.18	29.65	19.70	19,394
Mar	28.53	28.83	28.49	28.61	0.15	28.83	20.05	19,665
Apr	27.81	28.05	27.77	27.89	0.15	28.05	20.55	25,174
May	27.10	27.30	27.06	27.19	0.14	27.50	20.70	14,806
June	26.49	26.70	26.49	26.54	0.13	27.25	19.82	27,711
July	25.86	26.05	25.86	25.99	0.12	26.70	20.76	8,911
Aug	25.63	25.63	25.63	25.56	0.11	26.39	21.16	5,178
Oct	24.95	24.95	24.84	24.87	0.10	25.61	20.55	4,177
Nov	24.55	24.66	24.55	24.59	0.10	25.35	20.70	5,199
Dec	24.35	24.45	24.15	24.36	0.10	25.20	15.92	36,839
Ja04	24.23	24.23	24.23	24.17	0.10	25.00	20.35	5,245
Feb	24.05	24.05	24.05	23.99	0.10	24.82	20.35	1,757
Mar	23.80	23.80	23.74	23.81	0.10	24.73	20.35	1,113
June	23.31	23.34	23.23	23.36	0.10	24.40	20.53	6,373
Dec	23.00	23.00	22.90	22.99	0.10	24.00	16.35	17,181
Dc06	22.00	22.00	22.02	22.10	0.12	22.80	19.10	4,364
Est vol 203,153; vol Mon 145,243; open int 540,085, +4,134.								
Heating Oil No. 2 (NYM)-42,000 gal.; $ per gal.								
Nov	.8100	.8295	.8100	.8204	.0127	.8295	.5570	60,355
Dec	.8170	.8340	.8170	.8259	.0122	.8340	.5660	26,222
Ja03	.8220	.8345	.8220	.8269	.0117	.8345	.5680	15,918
Feb	.8070	.8180	.8070	.8109	.0107	.8180	.5710	11,081
Mar	.7875	.7875	.7800	.7799	.0097	.7875	.5640	8,187
Apr	.7530	.7530	.7500	.7454	.0092	.7530	.5500	5,364
May	.7180	.7180	.7110	.7114	.0092	.7210	.5450	3,207
June	.6990	.6990	.6960	.6924	.0092	.7050	.5600	3,641
July	.6910	.6910	.6910	.6834	.0087	.6990	.5625	2,371
Aug	.6890	.6890	.6820	.6814	.0082	.7010	.5705	1,381
Sept	.6930	.6930	.6930	.6844	.0082	.6990	.6215	711
Oct	.6955	.6955	.6955	.6874	.0082	.7030	.6290	452
Nov	.6990	.6990	.6990	.6904	.0077	.7000	.6750	713
Ja04	.6950	.6950	.6950	.6939	.0077	.7000	.6810	682
Est vol 38,519; vol Mon 42,775; open int 149,997, −3,208.								
Gasoline-NY Unleaded (NYM)-42,000 gal.; $ per gal.								
Nov	.8110	.8335	.8105	.8271	.0217	.8335	.5523	47,252
Dec	.7970	.8140	.7970	.8096	.0157	.8140	.5700	16,621
Ja03	.7990	.8020	.7990	.7989	.0132	.8020	.5775	9,490
Feb	.7960	.7960	.7950	.7947	.0120	.7965	.6010	3,202
Mar	.7950	.7970	.7950	.7945	.0120	.7970	.6510	3,091
Apr	.8400	.8400	.8400	.8410	.0115	.8430	.7670	3,781
May	.8310	.8320	.8310	.8350	.0110	.8380	.7710	3,368
Est vol 46,658; vol Mon 42,521; open int 91,458, −5,794.								
Natural Gas (NYM)-10,000 MMBtu.; $ per MMBtu								
Nov	4.140	4.250	4.000	4.067	−.071	4.900	2.630	59,151
Dec	4.330	4.395	4.190	4.240	−.083	5.010	2.720	36,366
Ja03	4.409	4.470	4.330	4.330	−.073	5.049	2.730	34,070
Feb	4.300	4.347	4.195	4.222	−.071	4.874	2.700	21,317
Mar	4.140	4.170	4.030	4.053	−.071	4.710	2.710	28,590
Apr	3.945	3.980	3.850	3.870	−.065	4.520	2.610	17,288
May	3.900	3.925	3.800	3.830	−.065	4.490	2.630	12,550
June	3.890	3.940	3.840	3.848	−.065	4.400	2.610	19,820
July	3.890	3.960	3.865	3.870	−.065	4.530	2.550	14,582
Aug	3.965	3.970	3.890	3.885	−.065	4.535	2.890	9,730
Sept	3.948	3.970	3.900	3.880	−.066	4.445	2.880	12,080
Oct	3.965	3.980	3.890	3.890	−.070	4.455	2.910	12,117
Nov	4.130	4.140	4.050	4.063	−.067	4.673	3.050	9,268
Dec	4.273	4.278	4.185	4.206	−.067	4.820	3.250	10,119
Ja04	4.318	4.320	4.230	4.256	−.062	4.880	3.300	10,617
Feb	4.220	4.220	4.160	4.136	−.062	4.760	3.260	6,031
Mar	4.020	4.020	3.960	3.958	−.060	4.510	3.150	9,454
Apr	3.760	3.760	3.760	3.713	−.055	4.190	2.970	8,681
July	3.718	3.718	3.718	3.668	−.050	3.990	3.040	4,077
Aug	3.720	3.720	3.710	3.678	−.045	4.120	3.120	5,158
Sept	3.710	3.710	3.620	3.658	−.045	3.880	3.100	2,517
Oct	3.655	3.655	3.655	3.673	−.050	3.962	3.100	4,559
Dec	4.085	4.085	4.085	4.036	−.050	4.300	3.460	6,379
Est vol 96,225; vol Mon 67,529; open int 403,756, −10,702.								
Brent Crude (IPE)-1,000 net bbls.; $ per bbl.								
Nov	28.85	29.39	28.70	29.01	0.26	29.88	19.04	75,115
Dec	28.79	29.25	28.68	28.91	0.25	29.59	18.50	73,812
Ja03	28.56	28.97	28.45	28.66	0.20	29.29	19.15	24,386
Feb	28.08	28.52	28.08	28.20	0.20	28.85	19.20	14,071
Mar	27.38	27.75	27.38	27.45	0.20	28.10	19.22	13,549
Apr	26.74	26.92	26.74	26.70	0.17	26.95	23.03	9,677
May	26.00	26.31	26.00	25.98	0.15	26.43	23.28	8,234
June	25.40	25.70	25.40	25.31	0.11	26.10	19.45	19,542
Sept	24.34	24.34	24.34	24.05	0.11	25.21	20.21	4,484
Dec	23.35	23.60	23.35	23.31	0.11	24.47	18.65	29,068
Ju04	22.43	22.43	22.43	22.32	0.03	23.30	20.90	1,999
Dec	22.10	22.10	22.10	21.91	−0.04	23.06	19.85	3,409
Est vol 110,000; vol Mon 77,516; open int 292,619, +2,054.								

FIGURE 16.1 Price Quotes for Futures

Source: The Wall Street Journal, October 2, 2002, p. C14. Copyright © 2002 Dow Jones & Co. Reprinted by permission of the publisher, Dow Jones & Co., via Copyright Clearance Center.

TABLE 16.4

How Trading Affects
Open Interest

Trading Day	Number of Contracts Traded	Long Position	Short Position	Change in Open Interest
Day 1	10	Trader A	Trader B	+10
Day 2	10	Trader C	Trader D	+10
Day 3	10	Trader B	Trader E	None
Day 4	10	Trader D	Trader F	None
Day 5	10	Trader E	Trader A	−10

Open interest after Day 5:

	Long Position	Short Position
Trader A	0	0
Trader B	0	0
Trader C	10	0
Trader D	0	0
Trader E	0	0
Trader F	0	10

Total open interest = 10 contracts

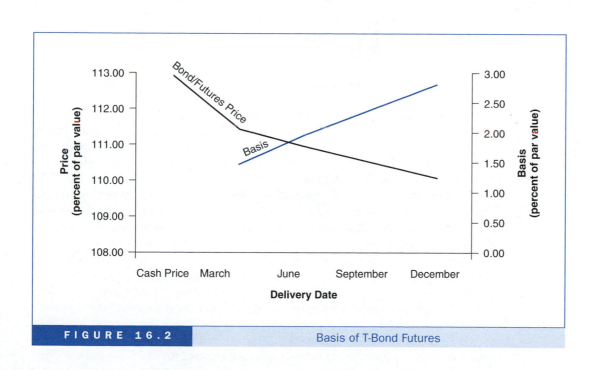

FIGURE 16.2 Basis of T-Bond Futures

Does this larger basis mean that the futures market expects interest rates to rise and the price of T-bonds to fall? As we see when we discuss the two general theories of futures pricing a little later, the answer to this question could be either yes or no.

Convergence As the delivery date approaches, it seems natural to expect basis to approach zero. In other words, spot prices and futures prices should show convergence as the time until delivery approaches zero. Will basis always equal zero on the delivery date? The answer is yes, with a couple of qualifications: If the spot and futures prices are for *exactly* the same grade of asset, the same delivery location, and the same delivery size, the basis should be zero on the delivery date.

Spreads A spread is the difference between the prices of two different futures contracts. Traders watch two major types of spreads. An **intracommodity spread** measures the difference in price between two futures contracts on the same asset but with different delivery dates; an example would be the spread between March and June crude oil contracts. An **intercommodity spread** measures the difference in price between two futures contracts on different assets but with the same delivery date. Traders are most interested in intercommodity spreads that involve related, but different, assets. Examples of related assets include heating oil and unleaded gas, corn and soybeans, gold and silver, and T-bills and T-bonds.

Spreads are important because of the likelihood of strong economic relationships between them. Spreads that become either too narrow or too large may create some profitable trading opportunities. Many of the speculative trading strategies that we review later in the chapter involve trading spreads (that is, buying one contract while selling another).

Futures Prices and Expected Future Spot Prices

With terms defined and a foundation established, we can build two models of futures contract prices. The first general theory of futures pricing argues for a strong relationship between futures prices and expected future spot prices. The presence of speculators in the futures market may seem to guarantee at least a general relationship between the two. For example, assume that 30-day corn futures are selling for $2.75 per bushel while the expected spot price of corn in 30 days is $2.60 per bushel. The speculator could go short in the futures contract, planning to buy corn in the spot market in 30 days at $2.60 and deliver the corn via the futures contract, collecting $2.75 per bushel. In the process, the trader would make $0.15 per bushel.

Should the futures price, with delivery at a specific point in time, merely equal the future spot price expected at the same future point in time? Even if the assets' characteristics in the spot market are identical to those specified in the futures contract, we see several good reasons why the futures price may only approximate the expected future spot price.

One reason is transaction costs. In the preceding example, say that transaction costs to go short in the futures contract amount to $0.25 per bushel. Now the speculative trade no longer appears profitable because the speculator can net only $2.50 per bushel while paying $2.60 per bushel.

Risk-Bearing Services of Speculators A more important reason why the futures price may only approximate the expected future spot price comes from the fact that both hedgers and speculators trade in the futures market. A hedger already holds a position in the asset's cash market and uses futures to reduce the

spread
Difference in prices of two futures contracts.

intracommodity spread
Difference in price between two futures contracts on the same asset but with different delivery dates.

intercommodity spread
Difference in price between two futures contracts on different but related assets.

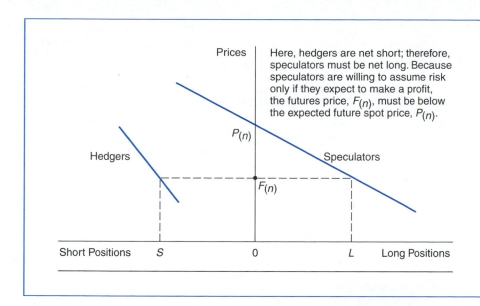

FIGURE 16.3

Futures Market with Both Hedgers and Speculators

Here, hedgers are net short; therefore, speculators must be net long. Because speculators are willing to assume risk only if they expect to make a profit, the futures price, $F_{(n)}$, must be below the expected future spot price, $P_{(n)}$.

risks associated with this cash position. A speculator holds no position in the cash market and seeks merely to profit from anticipated changes in prices. Therefore, hedgers are more risk-averse than speculators. In fact, speculators may be willing to assume some of the risk that hedgers are trying to avoid, if they can expect appropriate returns. This effect on the relationship between futures prices and expected future spot prices is best illustrated graphically.

Figure 16.3 illustrates a hypothetical futures market that includes both hedgers and speculators. The figure assumes that hedgers are net short. In other words, the sum of all the positions held by hedgers shows more short positions than long positions. For the market to function, therefore, speculators must be net long. As a futures contract's price declines, speculators should be willing to hold more long positions. At the same time, however, hedgers should be willing to hold fewer short positions.

Now, assume that P_n is the expected future spot, or cash, price of some asset n periods from today. If the futures price were to equal P_n, speculators would be willing to hold no position in the futures contract, because their goal is to make money by taking risk. To induce them to hold long positions in the futures, the futures price calling for delivery n periods from today, $F(n)$, must be below the expected spot price. The futures price has to clear the market, so the number of short positions desired by hedgers equals the number of long positions desired by speculators. The figure shows where $F(n)$ falls in the hypothetical market, relative to P_n. S is the number of short positions and L is the number of long positions; S must equal L for the market to clear.

What will happen over time as the delivery date approaches? If the expected future spot price remains unchanged, the futures price must rise, as shown in Figure 16.4. This rise in the futures price can be considered the expected return to speculators for assuming some of the risk that hedgers want to avoid. The tendency of futures prices to rise as the delivery date approaches was referred to by the legendary economist John Maynard Keynes as *normal backwardation*.[4]

---

[4]See John Maynard Keynes, *A Treatise on Money* (London: MacMillan, 1930).

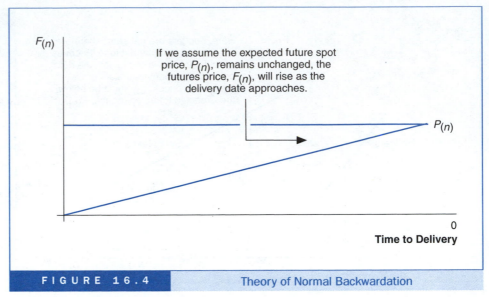

$F(n)$

If we assume the expected future spot
price, $P(n)$, remains unchanged, the
futures price, $F(n)$, will rise as the
delivery date approaches.

$P(n)$

0
Time to Delivery

FIGURE 16.4	Theory of Normal Backwardation

Notes: F_n is the futures price; P_n is the expected future spot price; 0 is the delivery date, at which time to delivery equals 0.

The reverse can also be true. If hedgers are net long, speculators must be net short. Therefore, for the market to clear, the futures price must be above the expected spot price, that is, $F(n) > P_n$. If expected spot prices do not change, the futures price should decline as the delivery date approaches. This process is sometimes referred to as *contango*.

Futures Prices and the Cost of Carry

cost of carry

Cost associated with storing an asset until the futures delivery date.

The other major theory of futures pricing argues that the price of a futures contract is merely the current spot price plus the **cost of carry**, the cost associated with storing the asset until the delivery date. In other words,

$$F_n = P(1 + c) \tag{16.1}$$

where F_n is the futures price, P is the spot price, and c is the net cost of carry (expressed as a percentage of the asset's value). The notion of cost of carry can also help to relate the price of a futures contract with a distant delivery date to the price of a contract on the same asset with a nearby delivery date. The price of the distant futures contract must equal the price of the nearby contract plus the cost of carrying the asset between the two delivery dates. At first glance, this formula appears to establish a relationship between the futures price, the spot price, and the cost of carry; otherwise, arbitrage opportunities would exist. For example, assume that the current spot price of gold is $320 per ounce and a three-month gold futures contract specifies a price of $346 per ounce. If the cost of carry for gold for three months is 5% (including storage, insurance, financing, etc.), an arbitrageur could profit from these prices, as shown:

Time	Transaction	Cash Flow
Today	1. Buy gold in the spot market for $320 per ounce.	−$320 per ounce
	2. Short 3-month gold futures for $346.	
Three months later	3. Pay storage cost (5% per ounce).	−$16 per ounce
	4. Deliver gold to satisfy futures contract; collect $346 per ounce	$346 per ounce

Net profits = $10 per ounce

This string of transactions would generate a risk-free profit of $10 per ounce. Of course, because other traders can do the same, these prices would not last long. Think about it this way: Who would be willing to sell gold today at $320 per ounce? Who would be willing to go long in a three-month futures contract at $346? Demand should push the spot price of gold upward or the three-month futures price downward, or both.

If futures prices are determined by the cost of carry, the basis may be either positive or negative, depending on whether the cost of carry is positive or negative. For most physical commodities—such as corn and crude oil—we would expect a positive cost of carry. In other words, it costs something to buy and store the commodities for a period of time. Therefore, if futures prices are related to the cost of carry, the basis for physical commodities should be negative.

What about the positive basis of T-bond futures, shown in Figure 16.2? The cost of carry for T-bonds is negative if short-term rates are lower than long-term rates. T-bonds pay coupon interest, even if they are held for only a short period of time, because interest accrues daily between coupon payment dates. If long-term rates exceed short-term rates, which they generally do, the amount of coupon income from T-bonds should exceed the cost of financing the bonds for a short period of time. Let's look at a simple example.

Assume that the price of a six-month T-bond futures contract and the spot price of an 8% T-bond are both 100 (or 100% of par). If the cost of financing T-bonds for six months equals 6% annually, one could profit by buying the bonds and shorting the six-month futures. In six months, the trader would deliver the bonds to satisfy the futures contract. The financing cost is 3% (6% of 100 divided by 2), so the effective cost is 103% (100 + 3). However, besides the 100% for the bonds at delivery, the trader also gets six months of coupon interest, 4% (8% divided by 2). This trade amounts to a riskless profit of 1% per bond (100 + 4 − 100 − 3). As in the prior gold example, this arbitrage situation would not last long in the real futures market.

In the real marketplace, several factors prevent the price of any futures contract from simply equaling the current spot price plus the cost of carry. For one, real-market trades impose transaction costs, which previous examples ignored. For another, characteristics of some assets may limit their storage (for example, orange juice may not last indefinitely in storage).

Restrictions on Short Sales Perhaps the most important complication to the cost of carry theory is that restrictions on short sales often limit spot market transactions. Think about the gold transaction discussed earlier. In that example, the following relationship created an arbitrage opportunity:

$$F_n > P(1 + c)$$

What would happen if the reverse were true: $F_n < P(1 + c)$. To profit, the arbitrageur would have to go short in the cash market, go long in the futures market, collect the storage cost, take delivery, and cover the short position in the cash market. Could someone really go short in the spot market for gold and collect the storage cost? It is hard to conceive of such a transaction for gold or any physical commodity.

Therefore, perhaps Equation 16.1 should be modified to state

$$F_n \le P(1 + c)$$

In other words, perhaps $P(1 + c)$ should be considered an upper boundary to the price of a futures contract.

Consider futures on other assets, however, such as T-bonds. Some traders can go short in T-bonds in the cash market; in fact, government bond dealers can go short almost as easily as they can go long. Even if it is possible to go short in the cash market, however, other restrictions limit short sales. The most common restriction is the need to keep some of the proceeds of a short position in a margin account. (This topic was discussed in Chapter 3.) Consequently, a trader cannot earn a market rate of return on the entire proceeds.

Which Theory of Futures Pricing Is Correct?

In our view, both theories are correct in the sense that both help us understand the relationship between current spot prices, expected future spot prices, and futures prices. Expected future spot prices clearly influence futures prices. At the same time, however, cost of carry relationships limit futures prices in relation to spot prices.

Which theory gives the most accurate price for a futures contract may depend on the asset. If trading in a contract faces few restrictions on short sales and hedgers are neither net short nor net long, futures prices are probably more closely related to costs of carry. Treasury note and bond futures probably fit in this group. However, if short sales face major restrictions and if hedgers are clearly net short or net long, futures prices are probably more closely related to expected future spot prices. Cost of carry, however, still restricts futures prices. Most physical assets probably fit more easily into this group.

USES OF FUTURES CONTRACTS

Having described the basic characteristics of futures contracts and their pricing, we now turn to a discussion of the general uses of futures contracts. We examine both speculative and hedging positions. Let's begin with several speculative positions.

Speculating with Futures

As discussed previously, speculators are traders who hold no cash position in the asset. They attempt to profit from expected price changes. The most basic speculative position is an outright position in a futures contract. The choice of the position, long or short, depends on the traders' expectations for future movements in the asset's price.

For example, suppose that a speculator decides that gold is currently overvalued because she sees no signs of inflation in most countries, the political situation is stable, the production of gold is well above consumption, and several countries appear to be selling some of their gold reserves. The speculator may decide to go short in June gold at $348 per ounce. The size of the contract is 100 ounces, so the initial value of one contract is $34,800. This position requires about a $3,000 margin deposit per contract.

Assume that the expectation is right. In two months, June gold is down to $320 per ounce. The speculator closes out the position by going long in June gold. In essence, she sold gold for $348 per ounce ($34,800 per contract) and bought it back at $320 per ounce ($32,000 per contract). This trade generated a profit of $28 per ounce ($2,800 per contract). On a $3,000 investment (assuming price changes while the position was open required no margin calls), the return is a rather healthy 93% ($2,800/$3,000).

What can go wrong? Lots, of course. Gold prices might defy reason and continue to rise. The trader may correctly perceive gold as overvalued but misjudge the timing of the price correction. If the market does not recognize that gold is overvalued until July, after she closes out the position, the move comes too late. Another potential risk is that gold might rise sharply after the trader goes short, causing a margin call. If she is unwilling or unable to deposit more cash, the position will be closed out. If gold then starts to fall, it is too late. All of this demonstrates that outright positions in futures are *highly* risky. Also, the potential loss is almost unlimited; one can easily lose much more than the initial margin deposit. Experienced futures traders understand that outright positions are risky, and as a result, most speculate using intracommodity and intercommodity spreads. Because spreads are unlikely to change dramatically, they are far less risky than outright positions. Let's look at some examples of both.

Intracommodity Spreads An intracommodity spread is a combination of a long position in one contract with a simultaneous short position in another contract on the same asset with a different delivery date. As an example, assume that today is January 6, 2003, and March 2003 crude oil is selling for $24.15 a barrel and June 2003 crude oil is selling for $22.74 a barrel—the spread is $1.41 a barrel. A speculator believes that oil prices are headed lower over the next month and this change in price will have a more substantial impact on the distant contract than the near-term contract. In other words, the spread between the March and June crude contracts should get wider. He would buy the March contract and sell the June contract. The details are shown in Table 16.5.

Notice that even though the trader lost money on the March contract, he made money on the trade because the spread did what was expected: It got larger. It increased from $1.41 per barrel to $2.01 per barrel.

Intercommodity Spread An intercommodity spread combines a purchase of one contract with a sale of another; the contracts have the same delivery date, but different, although related, assets underlie them. As in an intracommodity spread, the speculator hopes to profit from a change in the spread.

TABLE 16.5	Date	Transaction
Example of an Intracommodity Spread	January 30	1. Buy March crude oil at $24.15. 2. Sell June crude oil at $22.74.
	February 28	3. Sell March crude oil at $23.80. 4. Buy June crude oil at $21.79.
	Profit (loss)	5. March crude oil: Loss of $0.35 per barrel × 1,000 barrels = ($350) loss. 6. June crude oil: Profit of $0.95 per barrel × 1,000 barrels = $950 profit. Total profit = $600

TABLE 16.6	Date	Transaction
Example of an Intercommodity Spread	January 30	1. Buy March heating oil at 65.28 cents per gallon (42,000-gallon contract). 2. Sell March unleaded gas at 68.35 cents per gallon (42,000-gallon contract).
	February 28	3. Sell March heating oil at 75.28 cents per gallon. 4. Buy March unleaded gas at 73.35 cents per gallon.
	Profit (loss)	5. Profit on March heating oil = 10 cents per gallon × 42,000 gallons = $4,200 profits. 6. Loss on March unleaded gas = 5 cents per gallon × 42,000 gallons = ($2,100) loss. Overall profit = $2,100

Assume today is January 6, 2003. A trader observes that March heating oil is trading for 65.28 cents per gallon and March unleaded gasoline is trading for 68.35 cents per gallon. She believes that oil companies are about to reduce their production of heating oil while boosting their production of unleaded gasoline. At the same time, she believes that the demand for heating oil will remain high during February and early March. Consequently, the price of heating oil should rise relative to the price of unleaded gasoline. So, she would buy March heating oil and sell March unleaded gasoline. Details of this intercommodity spread are shown in Table 16.6.

Because heating oil became more expensive relative to gasoline, the trader ended up making money even though the prices of both commodities rose and she lost money on the unleaded gasoline contract.

Hedging with Futures

Futures, as you know, can help traders hedge cash positions. Ideally, the hedge should be constructed in such a way that

$$\Delta C + \Delta F = 0 \tag{16.2}$$

where ΔC is the change in the value of the cash position and ΔF is the change in the value of the futures position. No matter what happens to the price of the asset, the overall wealth remains unchanged. In reality, it is difficult to construct an ideal hedge, but a careful hedger may be able to come close.

TABLE 16.7

Example of a Short Hedge

Date	Transaction
May 1	Short 10 September corn contracts at $2.60 per bushel (5,000 bushels per contract).
September 15	1. Harvest 51,000 bushels of corn, sell in cash market for $2.40 per bushel.
	2. Buy 10 September corn contracts at $2.43 per bushel.
Profit (loss)	3. Cash market: Loss of 18 cents per bushel ($2.58 − $2.40) × 51,000 bushels = $9,180 loss.
	4. Future market: Profit of 17 cents per bushel × 10 contracts × 5,000 bushels = $8,500 profit.
	Overall loss = $680

Essentially, constructing a hedge requires a decision about what position to take in the futures market and in what contract (asset, delivery date, and number). The first decision is easy. The position in the futures market should be the *opposite* of the position in the cash market. In other words, if an increase in price in the cash market decreases the trader's wealth, it is a short position in the cash market. Consequently, the trader should go long in the futures market.

Deciding what contract to trade can be straightforward or something of a problem, depending on what asset the hedge must protect. Let's look at an example of both a short hedge and a long hedge.

Short Hedge A farmer may need a classic **short hedge**. Let's say it is springtime and an Iowa corn farmer just planted a crop for harvest in late September or early October. The farmer worries that the cash price of corn—currently $2.58 per bushel—will fall between planting and harvest time. Because the farmer is long in the cash market, the hedge requires a short position in the futures market. The farmer anticipates harvesting about 51,000 bushels of corn. Because each futures contract consists of 5,000 bushels, the farmer should short about 10 (51,000/5,000) September corn contracts.

The hedge turns out well, as shown in Table 16.7. The market justified the farmer's worries as corn fell in price between May and September. Because of the hedge, however, the losses in the cash market were almost totally offset by profits from the futures position.[5] Of course, few actual hedges turn out quite this well, but this example illustrates the logic behind the short hedge.[6]

Long Hedge Now, assume that today is March 1 and in two months a corporate treasurer must make a regular payment of DM100 million to a European supplier. Currently, the exchange rate between the dollar and the mark

short hedge

Short position in the futures market to offset a long position in the cash market.

----

[5]You may wonder why the farmer does not just go ahead and deliver corn to satisfy the futures contracts and collect $42.60 per bushel. The major reason is the cost of shipping the corn from the Iowa farm to the delivery location at a major export terminal (for example, New Orleans).
[6]Of course, had the price of corn risen between May and September the farmer would be better off by not hedging because that position ends up losing money in the futures market. However, the purpose of hedging, remember, is not to make money but to reduce risk.

TABLE 16.8	Date	Transaction
Example of a Long Hedge	March 1	Buy 800 June DM contracts at $0.5789 per DM (DM125,000 per contract).
	May 1	1. Buy DM100 million at a spot rate of $0.66 per DM, cost $66 million.
		2. Sell 800 June DM contracts at $0.6350 per DM.
	Profit (loss)	3. Loss in cash market: $0.06 per DM × DM100 million = $6 million loss.
		4. Profit in futures market: $0.0561 per DM × 800 × DM125,000 = $5.61 million profit.
		Total loss = ($390,000)

is DM0.60 per dollar; DM100 million is worth about $60 million. The treasurer worries that the value of the dollar will fall relative to the mark, meaning that the DM/dollar exchange rate will rise.

In essence, the firm is short in the cash market. The appropriate hedge, therefore, is a **long hedge**: Go long in DM in the foreign exchange futures market. Because each DM contract consists of DM125,000, the treasurer should buy 800 June DM contracts (DM100,000,000/DM125,000)—no May contract is available. The relevant information on the long hedge is shown in Table 16.8.

Had the treasurer not hedged, the the rise in the value of the DM relative to the dollar would have cost the company an additional $6 million to meet its May DM100 million obligation. The profits from the long hedge in DM futures reduced this loss to less than $400,000.

long hedge

Long position in the futures market to offset a short position in the cash market.

FINANCIAL FUTURES: A CLOSER LOOK

We already noted that trading in financial futures currently exceeds, by a wide margin, trading in futures on physical assets. Now, let's take a closer look at financial futures. First, we examine in more detail futures on money market instruments (T-bills and Eurodollars), coupon-bearing instruments (T-bonds and T-notes), and stock indexes. We also look at several ways to use financial futures both to speculate and to hedge.

Treasury Bill and Eurodollar Futures

T-bill and Eurodollar futures are traded on the IMM, which is part of the CME. Both contracts are similar in design, and futures on both T-bills and Eurodollars can be used to speculate on or hedge against short-term movements in interest rates. However, traders must recognize some important differences between the two contracts.

Treasury Bill Futures T-bill futures have delivery dates in March, June, September, and December. Any T-bill with a maturity of 90, 91, or 92 days at the time of delivery can satisfy the contract. All bills delivered, however, must have the same maturity. The face value of T-bills delivered, per contract, is $1 million. Price quotations are based on the IMM index:

$$IMM = 100\% - DY \qquad (16.3)$$

where DY is the discount yield on 90-day T-bills. (We discussed how to find the discount yield in Chapter 2.) The value of one T-bill contract is calculated as follows:

$$\text{Value of contract} = \$1,000,000\left[\frac{100 - (100 - IMM)(90/360)}{100}\right] \qquad (16.4)$$

where IMM is the IMM index value.

If the discount yield on T-bills were equal to 5%, the IMM index would equal 95. The value of one T-bill contract, with an IMM index of 95, would be

$$\$1,000,000\left[\frac{100 - (100 - 95)(90/360)}{100}\right] = \$987,500$$

The minimum price fluctuation in T-bill futures is one basis point (0.01%) in the discount yield, which translates to $25 per contract. If 91-day or 92-day bills are delivered, the price of the contract would be adjusted slightly by substituting the correct number of days into Equation 16.4.

Eurodollar Futures Eurodollar futures are based on Eurodollar bank deposits. As we described in Chapter 2, Eurodollar deposits are time deposits held in foreign banks or their U.S. branches. Even though federal law no longer limits the rates offered by U.S. banks, Eurodollar rates are still higher than comparable U.S. interest rates. This difference is caused, in part, by lack of deposit insurance on Eurodollar deposits.

The Eurodollar futures contract has a face value of $1 million, and its price is based on the three-month LIBOR (London interbank offered rate), the average interest rate offered by large London banks on Eurodollar deposits. We find the value of a Eurodollar futures contract in the same way as we find the value of a T-bill futures contract (Equations 16.3 and 16.4), with one major exception. Unlike T-bills, Eurodollars are not discount securities; rather, they are add-on instruments. Like most bank deposits, they pay interest on the amount deposited.

The add-on yield is calculated as follows:

(Interest/Purchase price)(360/Days to maturity)

The IMM index for Eurodollars is

100% − Add-on yield

The value of one Eurodollar contract is found using Equation 16.4. The other major difference between T-bill and Eurodollar futures is that Eurodollar futures are **cash settled**. Instead of allowing the short position to deliver an asset, all accounts that remain open on the last trading day are settled in cash at a LIBOR-based rate determined by the CME clearinghouse.

cash settled

No delivery of the asset actually occurs; all open accounts are settled in cash.

Treasury Bond and Note Futures

Futures contracts on T-bonds and T-notes (notes, five-year notes, and two-year notes), all of which are traded on the CBT, are virtually identical to each other, except for the deliverable instruments they specify. All T-bond and T-note contracts, with the exception of the two-year note contract, are based on securities with $100,000 in par value. (The two-year note's contract size is $200,000.) The prices of all bond and note contracts assume a coupon rate of 8%, and prices are stated in 32nds of a percent. If the price of June bond future is stated as 115-08, the decimal price is 115.25 (115 and 8/32), or $115,250 per contract.[7] The minimum price fluctuation is 1/32, or $31.25 per contract. Treasury note and bond futures have delivery dates in March, June, September, and December.

Conversion Factors and Invoice Amount As we just noted, all T-bond and T-note contracts are priced assuming an 8% coupon rate. Because the short position can deliver any Treasury security that meets the maturity requirements specified by the contract, regardless of the coupon rate, invoice amounts are adjusted by so-called conversion factors. The conversion factor is the price of the bond delivered, assuming a par value of $1 and a yield to maturity of 8%. Generally, bonds with coupon rates greater than 8% have conversion factors greater than 1, whereas bonds with coupon rates less than 8% have conversion factors less than 1.

If the short actually delivers securities to the long to fulfill the futures contract, the invoice amount equals

$$\begin{pmatrix} \text{Settlement price} \\ \text{as a percentage} \\ \text{of par} \end{pmatrix} \begin{pmatrix} \text{Number of} \\ \text{contracts} \end{pmatrix} (\$100,000) \begin{pmatrix} \text{Conversion} \\ \text{factor} \end{pmatrix} + \begin{matrix} \text{Accrued} \\ \text{interest} \end{matrix}$$

Assume that a short decides to deliver 10 T-bond contracts. The settlement price when the short established the position was 110-16 (110.5% of par). The short decides to deliver bonds with a coupon rate of 9% and a maturity of exactly 17 years three months. The conversion factor for these bonds is 1.0925, and accrued interest equals $22,500 (three months of interest, at 9% per year, on $1 million worth of bonds). The invoice is calculated as follows:

$$(1.105)(10)(\$100,000)(1.0925) + \$22,500 = \$1,229,712.50$$

Cheapest to Deliver One feature unique to T-bond and T-note futures is that some bonds and notes are cheaper to deliver than others because of the way in which conversion factors are computed. Essentially, the method of computing and using conversion factors assumes that all deliverable securities have the same yield to maturity. In reality, of course, they do not. Remember, the short initiates delivery and also chooses the instruments to deliver, assuming that they meet the

---

[7]Like price quotations in the cash market, T-bond and T-note futures prices are quoted in percentages of par value. A price of 11-08 translates into 11.25% of par value.

conditions of the contract. Logically, the short should choose the most advantageous instrument. The instrument that is cheapest to deliver is the one that costs the least compared with the futures price. Let's illustrate with an example. All the following bonds can be delivered against the March 2003 T-bond futures contract. (Prices and accrued interest as of January 6, 2003.)

	Bond A	Bond B	Bond C	Bond D
Price (per $100 par value)	89.3125	104.25	131.875	145.8125
Accrued interest (per $100 of par value)	2.75	1.5104	2.0573	5.1563
Cash price (per $100 par value)	92.0625	105.7604	133.9323	150.9688
Conversion factor	0.7761	0.9274	1.1795	1.3050
Adjusted cash price	118.6220	114.0397	113.5501	115.6849
Futures price	111.4375	111.4375	111.4375	111.4375
Ratio of adjusted cash price to futures price	1.0645	1.0234	1.0190	1.0381

Note: The adjusted cash price equals the cash price of the bond divided by its conversion factor.

The security that is cheapest to deliver has the lowest ratio of adjusted cash price to futures price. In our example, bond C is the cheapest to deliver. Determining which instrument is the cheapest to deliver is not difficult. As a result, a futures contract's price should closely match the price of the instrument that is cheapest to deliver as the first delivery date approaches.

Stock Index Futures

Stock index futures are contracts based on well-known indexes of common stocks. Today, the most actively traded stock index futures contract, based on the S&P 500, is traded on the CME. Delivery dates are December, March, June, and September. The futures price is quoted in the same manner as the index. The value of one futures contract is the index value multiplied by $500. (An index value of 780 would give one contract a value of $390,000.) Like Eurodollar futures, S&P 500 futures are cash settled.

One feature unique to stock index futures is the lack of any daily limits on price fluctuations, either upward or downward. In theory, a trader could lose an entire margin deposit during one trading day. However, in the wake of the 1987 market break, the futures markets instituted a set of procedures called *circuit breakers*. In periods of extreme stock market volatility, when the index rises or falls by a certain amount, the circuit breakers kick in and trading in stock index futures is suspended.

Program Trading Stock index futures faced criticism due to the controversial practice of program trading, computer-assisted trading of large blocks of stock simultaneously with stock index futures. Program trading attempts to take advantage of perceived pricing errors between the stock index (the cash market) and the stock index futures. Let's illustrate program trading with a hypothetical example.

The current index value is 765, and the index futures contract is trading for 795. Between now and the settlement date, in one year, the short-term rate of interest is 6% and the dividend yield is 2.5%. On the settlement date, the futures price and stock index will converge to the same value. Let's assume the index closes at 770 in one year.

Today, the trader borrows $382,500 (765 × $500) and buys the stocks in the index. Simultaneously, he goes short in the futures at 795. In one year, he sells the index stocks (collecting $385,000), repays the loan (paying $22,950 in interest), and collects the cash dividends ($9,562.50, or 2.5% of $382,500). He also closes out the futures position, buying the contract at 770. The profit from the futures trade is $12,500 [(795 − 770) $500]. Overall, he earns $887.50 ($12,500 + $9,562.50 − $22,950). The example assumes that the index is "cheap" relative to the futures. By buying the index and, at the same time, going short in futures, the trader locked in a profit. The position would make money regardless of whether the stock index were to rise or fall in value.

Note two points about the hypothetical example of program trading. First, transaction costs, which we ignored, would be considerable for all but large institutional investors. Second, the trader need not actually borrow the money today to purchase the index stocks. The short-term interest rate of 6% could also be considered the opportunity cost associated with tying up $382,500 in capital for a period of time.

As we noted, program trading is controversial. Some critics blame the technique for increasing volatility in the stock market. Some even lay much of the blame for the 1987 market break (Meltdown Monday) on program trading. The evidence that program trading contributes to stock market volatility or had a hand in the 1987 market break is, however, ambiguous at best.

Speculating and Hedging with Financial Futures

Financial futures futures create numerous opportunities to speculate on stock prices, interest rates, changes in the shape of the yield curve, and other market moves. As with all futures, most speculative trades in financial futures involve trading spreads. Financial futures can also be used to create both long and short hedges. A pension fund manager can use financial futures, for example, to hedge against declines in the portfolio's stock or bond prices.

In this section, we look at examples of a speculative trade in financial futures (an intracommodity spread using T-bond futures), a short hedge using T-bond futures, and a long hedge using S&P 500 futures. These examples are only three of dozens of speculative and hedging positions using financial futures.[8]

Intracommodity Spread Example Assume that today is February 1. Based on economic data, a trader believes that weak economic growth and modest inflation should force interest rates downward in the near future. As interest rates fall, of course, bond prices rise. Although a general decline in interest rates

[8]For more details, see *Treasury Futures for Institutional Investors* (Chicago: Chicago Board of Trade, 1990); and Donald Chance, *An Introduction to Options & Futures,* 3rd ed. (Fort Worth, TX: Harcourt, Inc., 1995).

Date	March Futures (prices in 32nds)	December Futures (prices in 32nds)	Spread (32nds)
February 1	Buy at 111-16.	Short at 110-00.	48
March 1	Sell to close at 114-00.	Buy to close at 112-00.	64
Profit (loss)	Profit of 2-16 per contract = $2,500 profit.	Loss of 2-00 per contract = ($2,000) loss.	16 per contract

TABLE 16.9

Intracommodity Spread Using T-Bond Futures

would affect all T-bond futures prices, the prices of futures for near-term delivery should rise more than the prices of futures for distant delivery.[9] The trader decides to buy five March T-bond futures contracts and, at the same time, sell five December T-bond futures. If interest rates were to decline as expected, with the position remaining open until March 1, the results would resemble those in Table 16.9.

The initial spread between the March and December bond contracts was 48/32 ($1,500 per contract). Even though the prices of both contracts rose as rates declined, the March contract rose more in price than the December contract. As a result, the spread between the two contracts widened to 64/32 ($2,000). The trader made 16/32 ($500) per contract, for a total profit of $2,500.

Example of a Short Hedge On February 1, a pension fund holds $10 million (measured by face value) of the 11% T-bond, currently priced at 145.8125 per $100 of par value—current value is $14,581,250. The fund manager is concerned about interest rates rising, and thus bond prices falling, over the next few weeks. To protect the portfolio, the manager constructs a short hedge using March T-bond futures. Because each T-bond futures contract has a face value of $100,000, the fund manager shorts 100 contracts at 111.4375. The market fulfills the fund manager's expectation, and interest rates rise over the next 30 days. By early March, the value of the fund's bonds declines by $90,625. The March futures, however, also fall; the short position produces a profit of $59,375, reducing the overall loss to $31,250. The details are shown in Table 16.10.

Although the the futures contracts reduced the fund's cash market loss by almost two-thirds, the fund manager did not construct an optimal hedge. A better tactic would consider that, as rates rise, the cash market instrument would show a greater dollar price change than the dollar change in price in the futures. Consequently, weighting the hedge by the conversion factor would have produced a better result. This scenario is also shown in Table 16.10. Had a weighted hedge been used, the loss would have been reduced to less than $13,000.[10]

---

[9]The reason relates to the relationship between bond futures prices and the cost of carry, which, remember, is negative, if short-term rates are less than long-term rates. See *Treasury Futures for Institutional Investors*, pp. 70–72.

[10]Weighting strategies can get quite sophisticated, depending on the instrument being hedged. See *Treasury Futures for Institutional Investors*, pp. 37–48.

TABLE 16.10
Short Hedge Example Using T-Bond Futures

A. Unweighted hedge

	Futures	Cash
February 1	Short 100 March T-bond contracts at 111.4375.	Hold $10 million (face value) of 11% bonds priced at 145.8125, or $14,581,250.
March 2	Buy 100 March T-bond contracts at 110.84375.	Hold $10 million of 11% bonds priced at 144.90625, or $14,490,625.
Profit (loss)	$59,375	($90,625)

B. Weighted hedge

(Face amount of bonds/Contract size)(Conversion factor) = Number of contracts
($10,000,000/$100,000)(1.3050) = 131 contracts
Profit on futures = 131($593.75) = $77,781.25
Loss in cash market = $90,625
Overall loss = $12,843.75

TABLE 16.11
Example of a Long Hedge Using S&P 500 Futures

	Futures	Cash
January 13	Go long in 24 March S&P 500 contracts at 780.	Will have $10 million for investment in March, current price = $50 per share.
March 15	Go short in 24 March S&P 500 contracts at 819.	Invest $10 million at $52.25 per share.
Profit (loss)	$468,000	($450,000)

Example of a Long Hedge On January 13, a corporate treasurer is reviewing investment plans for the pension fund contribution the company plans to make in March. The $10 million contribution will be invested in a pension fund at the fund's net asset value on the day of the contribution. Currently, the fund's net asset value is $50 per share, so the $10 million contribution would buy 200,000 shares. The treasurer is concerned about stock prices rising before March and decides to construct a long hedge using S&P 500 futures.

After deciding on a March delivery date, the treasurer must determine the number of contracts to buy. Assume that the current price of March S&P 500 futures is 780, for a current dollar value of $390,000 per contract (780 × 500). Dividing $390,000 into $10 million (the amount to be invested in March) gives 25.6. This answer is not the final one, however. Assume that the pension fund has a beta of 0.95, meaning that, historically at least, the pension fund is about 95% as volatile as the overall market. Weighting the hedge by the pension fund's beta gives 24.3 (0.95 × 25.6). Rounding off, the treasurer should buy 24 March S&P 500 futures at 780.

Details of this long hedge are shown in Table 16.11. The table shows the results if stock prices were to rise, as the treasurer feared, between January and March. This price move would boost March S&P 500 futures by 5%, to 819.

The price per share of the pension fund rose to $52.25. The loss in the cash market would amount to $450,000 ($2.25 × 200,000), and the profit in the futures market would amount to $468,000 (39 × $500 × 24). In this case, the treasurer ended up making a small profit, $18,000.

Of course, if stock prices were to fall rather than rise, the treasurer would lose money in the futures market and make money in the cash market. Remember, however, that the idea behind hedging is not to make money but rather to reduce the risk associated with a position in the cash market.

OPTIONS ON FUTURES

In 1982, the Commodity Futures Trading Commission allowed each futures market to begin trading options on one futures contract. The pilot program proved so successful that options on futures were permanently authorized in 1987. Today, options, both calls and puts, are available on most actively traded futures contracts.

Characteristics of Options on Futures

By now, you should be familiar with the characteristics of futures contracts. From Chapter 15, you should be familiar with the characteristics of call and put options. Putting them together, you will see how options on futures work. An option on a futures contract gives the holder the right, but not the obligation, to go long (with a call) or short (with a put) in a specific futures contract, at a specific price (the stated exercise price), until some point in the future (the option's expiration date). An option on a futures contract expires the month before the delivery month of the underlying futures contract, so a March 2000 T-bond call option expires in February.

As with all options, an option on a futures contract requires a seller (writer) for every buyer. The writer of a call option can be obligated to establish a short position in the futures, whereas the writer of a put option can be obligated to establish a long position in the futures. The most the buyer of an option on a futures contract can lose is the price he or she paid for the option. However, the option writer faces potentially unlimited losses.

Using Options on Futures

Almost all trading strategies that use stock options (whether for speculation or hedging) apply to options on futures as well. Much of the discussion in Chapter 15 transfers directly to options on futures. However, it would be useful to examine two basic strategies for options on futures: buying a call option instead of the futures contract, and using a call to protect a short position in the futures contract.

Buying a Call From Chapter 15 we know that the profit (or loss) from holding a call option on a futures contract until expiration is

$$\text{Profit (Loss)} = \text{Max}(0, F - E) - C$$

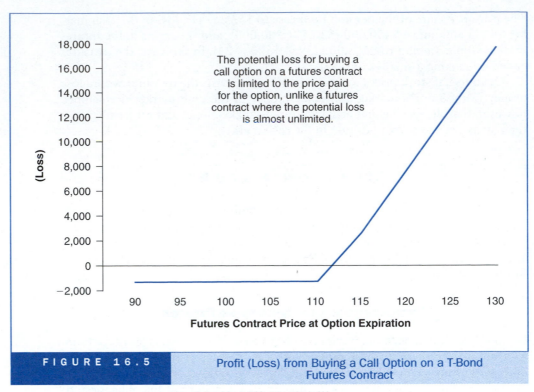

The potential loss for buying a call option on a futures contract is limited to the price paid for the option, unlike a futures contract where the potential loss is almost unlimited.

Futures Contract Price at Option Expiration

FIGURE 16.5   Profit (Loss) from Buying a Call Option on a T-Bond Futures Contract

Notes: Option price is 1-22, strike price is 111.

where F is the the price of the futures contract at expiration, E is the exercise price, and C is the price paid for the call option. Assume that someone buys a 111 March T-bond call at 1-22 (1 and 22/64, or $1,343.75). The profit or loss from buying one call, at various futures prices, is shown in Figure 16.5.

Buying the call can substitute for establishing a long position in the futures. Assume that a trader expects interest rates to decline before the end of February. She could go long in March futures at 111-14 or buy the call option on the March futures contract mentioned earlier ($E = 114$, $C = 1 - 22$). The profits and losses from both strategies, at various prices, are shown in Table 16.12.

If the price of March T-bonds were to fall from 111-14 to 100, the loss from holding the long position in the futures contract would be more than $11,400, compared with $1,343.75 from holding the option on the futures contract. The advantage of buying the call, as opposed to the futures contract, is the limit on the loss to the cost of the option ($1,343.75 in the example). The loss from a futures position is, at least technically, unlimited. Of course, the disadvantage of the call option is that it sacrifices some of the profit should T-bond prices rise as expected.

Using a Call Option to Protect a Short Futures Position Outright futures positions are risky. Consequently, most traders use spreads. An alternative to a spread is to combine an option on a futures contract with a futures position. For example, one could combine a call option with a short futures position. Let's look at an example.

TABLE 16.12

Buying a Call Option vs.
Buying a Futures Contract

Future Price (at option expiration)	Profit (Loss)	
	Futures	Call Option
$ 90	($21,437.50)	($1,343.75)
95	(16,437.50)	(1,343.75)
100	(11,437.50)	(1,343.75)
105	(6,437.50)	(1,343.75)
110	(1,437.50)	(1,343.75)
115	3,562.50	2,656.25
120	8,562.50	7,656.25
125	13,562.50	12,656.25
130	18,562.50	17,656.25

Note: The price of the futures contract, when the position was established is 111-14. The price of the call option is 1-22.

TABLE 16.13

Shorting a Futures Contract
and Buying a Call Option

Future Price (at option expiration)	Profit (Loss)		
	Futures	Call Option	Total
$ 90	$21,437.50	($1343.75)	$20,093.75
95	16,437.50	(1343.75)	15,093.75
100	11,437.50	(1343.75)	10,093.75
105	6,437.50	(1343.75)	5,093.75
110	1,437.50	(1343.75)	93.75
115	(3,562.50)	2,656.25	(906.25)
120	(8,562.50)	7,656.25	(906.25)
125	(13,562.50)	12,656.25	(906.25)
130	(18,562.50)	17,656.25	(906.25)

Note: The futures contract is shorted at 111-14. The call option is purchased for 1-64.

Assume that you short March T-bonds at 111-14 in expectation of falling bond prices. To protect the position, should prices rise, you also buy a 111 March call at 1-22. The profit and loss from the combination is shown in Table 16.13. Your loss is limited to slightly more than $900, regardless of how high T-bond prices go. However, the combination sacrifices profit should prices fall. The cost of the protection is $1,343.75, the price of the call option.

Now that you understand derivatives such as futures and options, read the Investment Insight on p. 458. It gives an account of a well-known investor, Warren Buffet's view on derivatives. He is skeptical about the use of derivatives and calls them "financial weapons of mass-destruction." His disdain of derivatives is accounted for through examples such as Long-Term Capital Management, a hedge firm that failed in 1998, requiring the Federal Reserve to provide an organized rescue. Enron is another of his examples that reinforce the dangers of derivatives.

INVESTMENT INSIGHT

Warren Buffet on Derivatives

Every year many investors eagerly await Warren Buffet's annual letter to shareholders of his firm Berkshire Hathaway. Buffet has been writing annual letters to Berkshire shareholders since 1965. Investors often pick apart the letter to provide insights into what the media-shy, Oracle of Omaha currently thinking about. In his 2003 letter to Berkshire shareholders, Buffet addresses two major issues. The first is corporate governance and CEO greed. Buffet has been a long-time critic of CEO compensation and loose corporate governance standards. In spite of new legislation and new regulations, Buffet still isn't convinced that any real, substantive reforms are likely in either area.

Buffet's other major topic in the 2003 letter concerned derivatives. In his letter, and a related article in *Fortune* magazine, Buffet characterized derivatives as financial weapons of mass-destruction. The explosion of derivative contracts, he believes, have created serious systemic risks to the United States and international financial system. Buffet admits that derivatives can serve a useful function by transferring risk from those who can't bear it to stronger hands. In doing so, derivatives can reduce, or even eliminate bumps from individual participants, stabilize the economy, and facilitate trade.

The problem, as Buffet sees it, is that "unless derivative contracts are collateralized or guaranteed, their ultimate value also depends on the creditworthiness of the counterparties to them." Herein lies the problem. According to Buffet large amounts of risk, particularly credit risk, have become concentrated in the hands of a few derivative dealers. These dealers, who are in turn owed huge amounts of money by non-dealer counterparties, are like a daisy change: The troubles of one could quickly bring down the others. Buffet uses the analogy of how, before federal deposit insurance, a run on one bank could lead to an overall bank panic.

As evidence he points to the case of Long-Term Capital Management (LTCM). This hedge firm, which failed in 1998, engaged in a series of highly levered, derivative transactions. At the beginning, LTCM engaged in fairly straight-forward, and limited risk, transactions. For example, in the early 1990s it bought Italian government bonds and simultaneously sold German bond futures to take advantage of what it believed was the undervaluation of the Italian lira. As time went on, however, LTCM entered into more and more complex derivative transactions. One, called a *total return swap,* creates 100% leverage in various markets, including stocks. A series of bad bets ultimately led to the failure of LTCM. Its failure caused such angst that the Federal Reserve organized a rescue effort. Investors, including banks, investment firms, and even corporations, lost hundreds of millions of dollars.

The failure of LTCM should have been a wakeup call concerning the dangers of derivatives—and the subsequent failure of energy trading firms such as Enron, should have reinforced the risks of derivatives. Buffet doesn't believe the market has learned its lesson and still sees danger ahead because of derivatives. Buffet ends his letter this way, "In our view, however, derivatives are financial weapons of mass destruction, carrying dangers that, while now latent, are potentially lethal."

Questions for Critical Thinking

1. How do derivatives, such as futures, provide legitimate risk-management functions?
2. Had the Fed not intervened, what impact could the failure of LTCM had on the financial system?

Source: Warren Buffet, "What Worries Warren," *Fortune,* accessed at the *Fortune* Web site, March 7, 2003.

SUMMARY

1. What are futures contracts?

Futures are real contracts that call for the sale of an underlying asset, at a point in the future, at a price agreed on today. Futures contracts have a short position (the party delivering the asset) and a long position (the person taking delivery of the asset). Both parties are required to post margin, which increases with gains and decreases with losses. Futures are available in agricultural commodities, precious metals, petroleum products, foreign currencies, interest-bearing instruments, and stock indexes.

2. How are futures contracts valued?

Futures traders pay attention not only to the price of the contract but also to the basis—the spread between the cash price and the futures price—and a variety of spreads, both intracommodity and intercommodity. Two general theories apply to futures pricing. The first says that the price of a futures contract relates to the expected future spot price of the asset. The second says that futures prices relate to the current spot price plus the cost of carry. Both theories aid in our understanding of futures pricing.

3. How do traders use futures?

Traders use futures either to speculate on the price of an asset or to hedge a cash position. Few successful futures traders trade outright positions, most trade spreads—buying one contract while selling another. Hedgers establish a position in the futures market that is the exact opposite of their position in the cash market. Thus losses in the cash market are offset by gains in the futures market and gains in the cash market are offset by losses in futures. Hedgers use futures not to make money but rather to reduce the risk of their cash positions.

4. What are financial futures?

Financial futures are currently the most popular type of futures. They are available on T-bills, Eurodollars, T-bonds, T-notes, and stock indexes, to name the most actively traded. Financial futures can be used to speculate on interest rates and stock prices. They can also be used to hedge cash positions in the stock and bond markets.

5. What are options on futures?

A call option gives the owner the right to establish a long position in the underlying futures at a specific price, and a put option gives the owner the right to establish a short position in the underlying futures at a specific price. Calls and puts can be used as substitutes for futures positions. They can also be used to reduce the risk of outright futures positions.

MINI CASE 1

This mini case constructs an intercommodity spread using futures on T-bonds and five-year T-notes. Assume that today is December 1. Between now and early next year, interest rates should fall. Further, the slope of the yield curve should remain essentially unchanged. Today, T-bonds are priced at 111 and five-year T-notes are priced at 107.

1. If interest rates do decline, what will happen to bond and note prices? What should happen to the spread between bonds and notes (both price and yield)?
2. What is the appropriate intercommodity spread if rates decline and the slope of the yield curve does not change?
3. Assume that rates fall as expected, and the position closes out with March notes selling for 113 and March bonds selling for 120-16. How much did the intercommodity spread make?

MINI CASE 2

This mini case sets up a hedge using a futures contract. Assume today is January 5. A company will receive payment from its Japanese customers on February 25. The payment will be denominated in Japanese yen and will be equal to ¥10 billion. The current yen-dollar exchange rate is (¥1 = $0.0092). The March yen futures contract (¥12.5 million per contract) is currently trading at $0.0094.

1. What change to the value of the dollar relative to the yen should the company be concerned about between now and late February? Explain.
2. What is the proper hedge using yen futures?

3. Assume that the spot exchange rate equals ¥1 = $0.0085 on February 25. On the same day, March yen futures are selling for 0.0083. How much did the company lose in the cash market and how much did it make in the futures market? How well did the hedge work out?

REVIEW EXERCISES

1. Describe the characteristics of a futures contract. How does a futures contract differ from a forward contract?
2. Why is futures trading considered a zero-sum game? Who makes money and who loses money if futures decline in price?
3. Who begins the delivery process? Does a long position have to take delivery of the asset?
4. What characteristics does an asset require to develop a viable futures market? Why has an active futures market developed in Treasury securities?
5. Describe the role of the clearinghouse. Why is the clearinghouse so important to the orderly functioning of a futures market?
6. What is *margin* in futures trading? What happens at the end of each trading day to a futures margin account?
7. Assume that a trader goes long in March T-bonds at 114-00 (114-0/32). The trader must post $4,000 in initial margin and maintain $3,000 in margin. What would happen to the account if March T-bonds were to settle the next day at 113-16? Would the trader face a margin call?
8. Describe open interest. Assume that A went short in 10 March T-bonds two weeks ago (B went long). Today, A went long in 5 March T-bonds (C went short). How much would open interest change?
9. What is basis? Why does basis have to equal zero on the delivery date?
10. Explain the differences between intracommodity and intercommodity spreads. Why are spreads important?
11. What is normal backwardation? What does normal backwardation assume about the net position of hedgers?
12. Explain cost of carry. Why is the cost of carry generally negative for T-bond futures? Illustrate with a numerical example.
13. Assume that the spot price of gold is $350 per ounce and the price of a three-month futures contract is $380. What do these prices imply about the cost of carry for gold? If the actual cost of carry were $5 per ounce per month, show how one could profit from these spot and futures prices.
14. What is an outright futures position? Assume you went short in March unleaded gasoline at 65 cents per gallon. How much would you make or lose if you close out your position at 62 cents per gallon?
15. If someone buys March corn and, at the same time, sells March wheat, what type of spread is traded? What does the trader expect to happen to the prices of corn and wheat between now and March?
16. What is the general idea behind hedging? What decisions about futures must the hedger make?
17. What are Eurodollars? Explain the differences between T-bill and Eurodollar futures.
18. What is the conversion factor in T-note and T-bond futures? Why does the conversion factor lead to the notion of the cheapest security to deliver?
19. Use the following information to find the invoice amount on a T-bond futures contract.

Settlement price	115-16
Conversion factor	1.1795
Size of contract	$100,000
Number of contracts	5
Accrued interest	−2.0573 per $100

20. What is program trading? If a trader believes that futures are overpriced, relative to the current index, how could he take advantage of this?
21. Assume that a trader is long in T-bonds in the cash market. What is she concerned about in the near term? What position should she establish in the futures market?
22. What are options on futures? Why would someone buy a put option as opposed to establishing a short position in the futures contract? Illustrate with a numerical example. (Assume that T-bonds futures are currently trading for 112 and a 112 put option is trading for 1-16.)

CRITICAL THINKING EXERCISES

The following exercise requires computer work. Open the Futures worksheet in the Data Workbook. It lists prices of T-bond and T-note futures, along with prices of call and put options on bond and note futures.

1. Assume you believe that interest rates will decline over the next few weeks. List some trades—using both futures and options—that you could make to take advantage of your expectation. Assume that you close out your positions after bond yields fall by 75 basis points and note yields fall by 50 basis points. Calculate the profit or loss from each trade you established.
2. Illustrate why an option is less risky than taking an outright position in a futures contract.
3. Construct a bull spread and a bear spread using options. What futures trade(s) would be similar to these option spreads? Illustrate your potential profit or loss from each trade.

THE INTERNET INVESTOR

1. Use a news Web site to find the seasonal supply and demand for a grain commodity. Determine whether it implies an expected rise or fall in the futures price for that commodity. Find the commodity in *The Wall Street Journal* and discuss whether your expectation was correct. Explain your answer.
2. Find any significant news items about a commodity or financial instrument (stock index or interest rate changes). Speculate what activity the news might stimulate and create a speculative position. Now create a scenario that requires a hedged position.
3. Ascertain today's general stock market performance by visiting a Web site with stock market information. Speculate on the impact to the stock index futures. How would you create a hedge using the spot price and the futures price?

PART 6

Modern Portfolio Theory

The next five chapters are devoted to a discussion of modern portfolio theory (MPT). We will discuss such topics as risk aversion, measuring risk and return (for both individual securities and portfolios), efficient frontiers, the capital asset pricing model, arbitrage pricing, and how to evaluate the performance of investment portfolios. The material in this section will probably seem more conceptual and theoretical than the material elsewhere in the text. However, we will show how modern portfolio theory can provide insight into many real-world investment situations. For example, the concept of diversification, the value of which is widely recognized by most investment professionals, really comes directly from MPT. Modern portfolio theory shows what diversification can do for investors (improve their risk/return trade-offs), and MPT helps us understand why diversification works (securities' returns are not perfectly correlated over time). Keep this in mind as you're reading the next five chapters.

17

Risk and Diversification

PREVIOUSLY . . .

We discussed derivative securities and how to evaluate risk and returns for options and futures. We learned to hedge by combining options with common stocks as well as combining various future contracts.

IN THIS CHAPTER . . .

Now that you have developed an understanding of bonds, common stocks, options, and futures, you may decide to invest in combinations of these various securities. Because it is not always possible to choose the stellar investments despite conducting every analysis possible, we recommend that you hedge your bets by not putting "all your eggs in one basket" or by diversifying. The chapter discusses risk and how investors are generally risk averse, as well as how to measure expected returns. Finally, we discuss how to measure portfolio risk and return.

TO COME . . .

If all risk-averse investors are likely to diversify and hold portfolios rather than just one or two stocks, then we can develop a model based on that idea. It is called the capital asset pricing model (CAPM).

CHAPTER OBJECTIVES

After reading Chapter 17, you should be able to answer the following questions:

1. What is risk aversion, and why are investors, as a group, risk averse?

2. What are the general investment implications of risk aversion?

3. Why is standard deviation a good measure of risk, and how does an investor compute standard deviations for both individual securities and portfolios?

4. What is the impact of security correlations on portfolio risk?

5. What are the benefits of diversification, and how can investors achieve them?

6. What is the meaning of efficient diversification and modern portfolio theory?

Two of the apparent truisms we discussed initially in Chapter 1, and touched on many times since, were (1) the positive relationship between historical returns and risk, and (2) the beneficial effects of investment diversification. Investment instruments that—at least over the past 65 years or so—exhibited higher rates of return also showed more variability around their average returns. You may recall from the historical data presented in Chapter 2 that common stocks, on average, returned more than Treasury bills (T-bills) since 1926 (13.1% versus 3.8% per year), but stock returns also showed far more volatility. Therefore, if an investor wants to increase expected returns, she or he must be willing to accept higher levels of risk. However, the historical evidence also suggests that owning a group of investment instruments can allow one to beat the risk/return trade-off, at least up to a point. In other words, owning five stocks will generally produce a better risk/return profile over time than owning one stock. Both of these truisms form the basis of modern portfolio and investment theory, as we discuss in more detail in this chapter. Many of the key ideas discussed here in Chapter 17 were touched on in previous chapters. In this chapter, we try to tie many of these ideas together and more formally develop the concepts of risk and diversification.

Chapter 17 begins with a discussion of risk aversion, why most investors are risk averse, and what risk aversion implies about the long-term relationship between risk and return. The discussion establishes the importance of risk. Next, we turn to a discussion of how to actually measure risk, a subject we mostly avoided up to this point. This discussion includes the problem of measuring historical versus expected risk, measuring risk for an individual security, and measuring risk for a group of securities (a portfolio). After a discussion of risk measurement, we turn to a detailed discussion of diversification and two types of risk, market risk and firm-specific risk. We examine diversification across securities and the fallacy of time diversification. Naive versus efficient diversification is scrutinized as well. A discussion of efficient diversification naturally leads to a discussion of modern portfolio theory, which concludes the chapter.

WHAT IS RISK AVERSION?

Suppose your state were to begin a new lottery today. For $5, you would have an equal chance of losing or winning $5. If you play the game, you have a 50/50 chance of coming out $5 richer or $5 poorer. The expected payoff is, of course, zero.[1] Would you play this new lottery game? You might answer yes as you are reading this page, but if you were playing with real money, you would probably answer no. If you play this lottery, you can actually expect to be worse off. The lottery involves obvious risk (the chance you may come away poorer), with no compensation for that risk. Now, suppose your state offered another new game. For $5, you would have an equal chance of winning nothing or winning $10. Now the expected payoff is $5; would you play the second game? Of course, not knowing you personally, we cannot answer the question definitively. We can say, however, that you are much more likely to play the second game than the first, because this second game offers some compensation for the risk involved with playing.

---

[1]Remember, the expected payoff is a weighted average of the possible outcomes. In this case, the expected payoff equals $0.50(-\$5) + 0.50(\$5)$.

As trivial as these lottery games sound, the two fundamental questions involved (would you play, and why?) are really the same questions all investors must answer when making investment decisions. For example, assume you could buy a T-bill for $1,000, hold it for a year and receive $1,060 (a 6% return). As we previously pointed out, T-bills are as close to a truly risk-free investment as you can get. Now, also assume that you could invest your $1,000 in shares of a high-risk junk bond fund. In a year, shares of the fund could be worth $1,500 (a 50% return), or only $500 (a minus 50% return); the expected return is 0%. Assuming each outcome provides about a 50/50 chance of occurring, which investment would you choose? Most investors would likely choose to invest in T-bills simply because the junk bond fund does not offer any compensation for its added risk. In fact, the expected payoff from the fund is less than the almost certain payoff from the T-bill investment ($1,000 versus $1,060). It is difficult to imagine any rational investor choosing the junk bond fund investment.

Make some changes to the example, however, and the decision becomes more interesting and ambiguous. Assume that the T-bill still offers an almost certain 6% return and the junk bond fund has the same two possible outcomes ($1,500 or $500), but change the probabilities of those outcomes occurring. Now, assume a 75% chance that the fund will be worth $1,500 in one year and only a 25% chance that it will be worth $500. The expected payoff becomes $1,250 (an expected return of 25%). Which would you choose in this situation? Some investors would choose to invest in the junk bond fund, and others would still choose to invest in T-bills.

Although this example is obviously simplified, it still serves to illustrate the important concept of **risk aversion** that was also discussed in Chapter 2. Most investors appear willing to pay to avoid risky situations. Paying to avoid risk is exactly what we do when we purchase insurance. We pay premiums to shift some, or even all, of the risk of owning a home, driving a car, and so forth, to the insurance company. To put the notion of risk aversion another way, most of us will voluntarily take risks only if we receive proper compensation for that risk. Risk aversion is, in turn, related to expected returns.

risk aversion

The notion that people need an incentive to voluntarily accept risk.

Risk Aversion and Expected Returns

Perhaps the most important implication of risk aversion is that an investment should show a positive relationship between expected returns and risk. Risk-averse investors will take risk only in exchange for sufficient compensation (i.e., returns). Therefore, higher-risk investments must offer risk-averse investors higher expected rates of return. If, at a certain price, a high-risk investment does not offer investors a sufficient expected rate of return, the price (or return) will have to fall (or rise). Now, assume that investors are, as a group, risk neutral. **Risk-neutral investors** would demand no relationship between risk and return. In fact, in a well-functioning market, all investments would be required to provide the same expected return, regardless of risk. Arbitrage would quickly eliminate any differences. As far-fetched as it sounds, consider the relationship between risk and return if investors are, as a group, risk takers. Because **risk takers** will pay to take risk, the relationship between expected returns and risk would be negative. In other words, high-risk investments would actually offer lower expected returns compared with safer investments!

risk-neutral investor

An investor whose utility function increases at a constant rate as wealth increases.

risk taker

An investor whose utility function increases at an increasing rate as wealth increases.

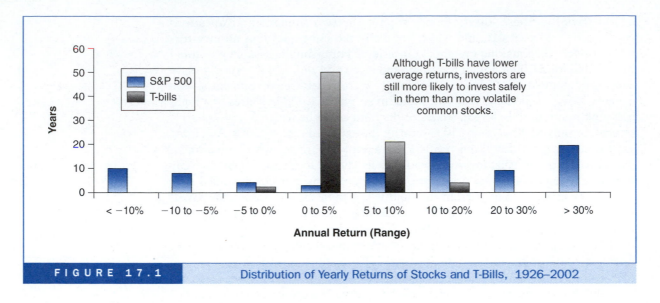

If our logical argument does not convince you that investors are risk averse, reviewing some of the historical evidence on risk and return might. Chapter 2 reviewed the long-term historical performance of the major investment instruments. We found that higher-risk investments historically returned more, on average, than lower-risk investments. For example, between 1926 and 2002, the return on common stocks in the United States—represented by the Standard & Poor's (S&P) 500—exceeded the return on U.S. T-bills by, on average, about 9.3% per year (13.1% versus 3.8%). By any conventional and reasonable measure, common stocks are more risky than T-bills. Figure 17.1 shows the distribution of yearly returns for both investments. Notice how the historical returns from T-bills are clustered together. For example, in 50 out of 77 years, T-bill returns ranged between 0% and 5%. By comparison, common stock returns exhibited far more variability. S&P 500 Index stocks earned more than 30% in 19 different years and lost more than 10% in 10 different years, between 1926 and 2002.

Relative Risk Aversion and Expected Returns

A little earlier we pointed out that some investors are probably more risk averse than others. In other words, investor A may be relatively more risk averse than investor B. What does this comparison imply about the relationship between risk and expected returns? The answer is quite straightforward: relatively more risk aversion increases the expected return investors demand for the same risk level. This notion is best illustrated with a simple example.

Let's say that investor A is relatively more risk averse than investor B. Figure 17.2 shows their hypothetical trade-offs between risk and expected return.[2] Level *f* represents the expected return from a risk-free asset (e.g., a T-bill). As the level of risk

---

[2]These trade-offs are referred to as indifference curves. An investor is indifferent between each point on the curve. In other words, each point (investment) offers an identical risk/return trade-off.

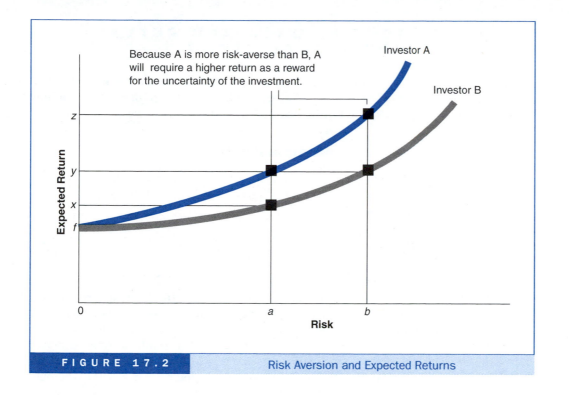

Because A is more risk-averse than B, A will require a higher return as a reward for the uncertainty of the investment.

FIGURE 17.2 Risk Aversion and Expected Returns

increases (say, to level *a*), the expected return for both investors increases, consistent with the notion of risk aversion. Notice, however, that the expected return for investor A (the more risk-averse investor) increases more (from level *f* to level *y*) than the expected return for investor B (from level *f* to level *x*). In fact, the risk level would have to increase all the way to level *b* before investor B's expected return would reach level *y*.

The notion of relative risk aversion helps to explain why certain investors hold only low-risk assets whereas others hold higher-risk assets. An investor who is relatively more risk averse may think that the compensation for holding, say, stocks, is not enough to justify their added risk. This investor would own mainly T-bills and certificates of deposit (CDs). However, another, relatively less risk-averse investor may think the compensation for owning stocks is enough to justify the added risk, and thus this person would own mainly stocks.

RECAPRECAP

We tried to show in this section that most investors are probably risk averse, although probably to varying degrees. Examples showed that investors would not take a gamble (risk) unless its expected payoff (or return) were to exceed that of a sure thing. Clearly, risk and expected return must be closely related. As a result, we can assume that investors prefer investments with higher expected returns and lower risk. Further, risk aversion is the basis on which we can make statements about investment choices, as you will see in Chapter 18. Given that risk and expected return are among the most striking features of the securities markets, and probably among the most important criteria in investment selection and analysis, the next question naturally becomes, how should (and can) risk and expected return be measured? We explore this issue in the next section.

| MEASURING RISK AND RETURN: |
| INDIVIDUAL SECURITIES |

In this section, we examine four topics: how to measure returns for individual securities, how to measure risk, how to calculate a standard deviation, and how investors can use risk and return measures to make security selections.

Measuring Returns

Back in Chapter 2, we discussed how to measure a one-year (or one-period) return for a security. Recall that the holding period return (HPR) for a stock i can be calculated as follows:

$$\text{HPR}_{i,t} = \frac{P_{i,t} - P_{i,t-1} + CF_{i,t}}{P_{i,t-1}} \quad \text{or} \quad \frac{P_{i,t} + CF_{i,t}}{P_{i,t-1}} - 1 \qquad (2.1)$$

where $P_{i,t}$ is the price in period t (e.g., year t), $P_{i,t-1}$ is the price in period $t - 1$, and $CF_{i,t}$ is the cash flow received in period t (dividends for common stock and interest for bonds). In this chapter let's use common stocks as examples with the understanding that the general concept can be applied to all securities. Suppose the closing stock price of stock i one year ago was $15, the owner received $1.00 in dividend income during the year, and today's closing price is $17.00. The one-year return is calculated as follows:

$$[(\$17.00 + \$1.00)/\$15.00] - 1 = 20\%$$

Also recall from Chapter 2 that we can measure ex-ante returns as in the following example. Someone is considering buying stock i today at its current price of $20.00 per share. In one year, the investor expects the stock to sell for $25.00 per share and pay a $1.00 dividend. In this case, the expected return (ER_i) would be measured by

$$ER_i = \frac{P_{i,t+1} - P_{i,t} + \text{DIV}_{i,t+1}}{P_{i,t}} \quad \text{or} \quad \frac{P_{i,t+1} + \text{DIV}_{i,t+1}}{P_{i,t}} - 1 \qquad (17.1)$$

where $P_{i,t}$ is today's price, $P_{i,t+1}$ is the expected price one period after t (usually one year), and $\text{DIV}_{i,t+1}$ is the expected dividend (which replaces the more generic cash flow or $CF_{i,t+1}$) in period $t + 1$.

Using Equation 17.1, we can compute the one-year return:

$$[(\$25.00 + \$1.00)/\$20.00] - 1 = 30\%$$

Now, even though Equations 2.1 and 17.1 are similar, a difference distinguishes them. The first computes an actual one-year return, whereas the second computes an expected one-year return. The expected return is based on a forecast (or guess) of future prices and dividends, and the holding period return is based on actual prices and dividends.

Now, let's consider the prior problem in a more sophisticated manner to account for several possible future prices. Assume that the investor is uncertain about the stock price one year from today; it may depend on the company's sales growth. (Assume that the dividend will pretty certainly be $1.00.) The following table represents the possibilities:

Sales Growth Rate	Price One Year from Today	Return
Above average	$30.00	55%
Average	25.00	30
Below average	20.00	5

(Note that the returns were computed using Equation 17.1.) Further assume a probability of each sales growth rate occurring next year, sometimes referred to as states of nature. The firm has a 30% chance of generating above-average growth, a 40% chance of average growth, and a 30% chance of below-average growth. We can now compute the expected return for stock i a little differently:

$$ER_i = \sum_{s=1}^{S} R_{i,s} \Pr(s) \qquad (17.2)$$

where R is the return for stock i in state s (above-average, average, or below-average sales growth) and $\Pr(s)$ is the probability of state s occurring. In our example,

$$ER_i = 0.55(30\%) + 0.30(40\%) + 0.05(30\%) = 30\%$$

Of course, it may be difficult, perhaps almost impossible, to forecast the future states of nature, the probability of each state occurring, and the rate of return from each state. Then why, you may ask, should anyone bother? The answer is that in making an investment decision, an analyst strives to obtain a future return for the stock and then to choose the stocks with the highest returns after adjusting for risk. Conceptually, it is important to recognize that investment decisions must be based on the return one expects to earn. It does little good to know what one could have earned (or the historical return); the critical value is the return from investing today, so investors strive to estimate future returns, or **ex-ante returns**.

In most cases, it is easier and more convenient to calculate actual, historical, or **ex-post returns**. The historical equivalent of the expected return, computed using Equation 17.2, is the average (or mean) return over a specified period of time. In Chapter 2, we discussed how to compute an average return from an actual return series. It is worth repeating here. The general formula for calculating an arithmetic mean return (AM_i) for stock i is

ex-ante returns
Forecasted or predicted returns.

ex-post returns
Historical returns.

$$AM_i = \frac{1}{T} \sum_{t=1}^{T} R_{i,t} \qquad (17.3)$$

where T is the number of time periods included in the sample and $R_{i,t}$ is the stock i return for period t (calculated using Equation 17.1).[3] A time period could be a

[3]When we use historical returns, we assume each return has a $1/n$ probability of occurring. This assumption is analogous to multiplying each return in Equation 17.2 by the probability $1/n$ of that return occurring.

day, a month, or a year. An example of how to calculate a mean return is presented later in the chapter in Table 17.2. The ending stock price for Lone Star Steakhouse (STAR) is given, along with the dividend (if any), on a monthly basis from November 2000 through November 2002. The monthly return is computed using Equation 17.1. Summing the monthly returns and dividing by T (number of months, or 24 in this example) completes the calculation. Thus, over the two-year period, STAR provided an average monthly return of 5.04%.[4]

Measuring Risk

Up to this point, we tried to discuss risk in a rather intuitive way. We relied on basic observations and conventional wisdom to distinguish between the riskiness of various securities. For example, in Chapter 2, we observed that the historical returns on common stocks exhibited far more variation over time than returns on long-term, high-quality corporate bonds. We argued that a stock, such as an electric utility stock, that pays a high dividend and grows at a slow predictable rate is probably a less risky investment over time than a cyclical stock (e.g., shares of an automobile manufacturer). In other words, the electric utility stock will show less variation in price and returns over most time periods. Although we have yet to precisely define investment risk and discuss how it can (and should) be measured, the term we keep coming back to is *variation,* or *dispersion,* around an average, or expected value. Now, we need to develop a risk measure that incorporates these intuitive observations into something more precise, allowing us to make risk comparisons between securities and portfolios.

Table 17.1 presents some data on returns for S&P 500 Index stock (including both dividends and capital gains) between 1980 and 2002. For each year, the table gives a yearly return, along with three common measures of variation (or dispersion) around that average value. The risk measures are based on monthly returns. Each could be thought of, and used, as a risk measure. Let's briefly examine each.

Range The range is simply the highest value minus the lowest value. In general, a larger range indicates greater risk. For example, during 1995, the monthly return for the S&P 500 index ranged between 4.105% and −0.500% (for a total of 4.60%). By contrast, during 1987, monthly returns ranged between 13.43% and −21.52% (for a total of 34.95%). Stock returns varied much more during 1987 than during 1995. In 2002, monthly returns ranged between 8.64% and −11.00% (for a total of 19.64%).

Number of Negative Outcomes In Table 17.1, this column gives the number of months during a year when the monthly return was less than zero.[5] For example, in eight months during 2000 the index generated negative monthly returns. By contrast, it had monthly returns less than zero in only two months during 1996.

---

[4]In Chapter 2, we saw how to annualize a monthly return. For STAR, if the average monthly return equals 5.04%, the annualized return equals

$$[(1 + \text{Monthly return})^{12} - 1] = (1.0504)^{12} - 1 = 80.41\%$$

It's a great return, given what the technology stocks returned. You have an opportunity to calculate Cisco's return later.

[5]Zero need not be the only benchmark. Another could be the number of periods the index earned less than the return, over the same time period, on a low-risk investment such as T-bills or bank CDs.

Year	Annual Return	Range	Number of Negative Returns	Standard Deviation
1980	32.42%	20.82%	2	18.31%
1981	−4.91	10.82	6	12.89
1982	21.41	17.79	6	19.14
1983	22.51	10.71	4	9.92
1984	6.27	16.59	5	10.01
1985	32.16	10.89	4	12.17
1986	18.47	15.70	4	17.94
1987	5.23	34.95	4	30.50
1988	16.81	8.01	4	10.07
1989	31.49	11.47	4	12.35
1990	−3.17	18.78	7	18.39
1991	30.55	20.49	3	16.00
1992	4.42	7.91	4	7.47
1993	7.06	6.69	4	5.93
1994	−1.54	8.34	5	10.61
1995	34.11	4.60	2	5.12
1996	20.26	11.91	2	10.83
1997	31.01	13.56	3	15.92
1998	26.67	22.61	3	21.48
1999	19.53	9.48	5	13.14
2000	−10.14	17.68	8	17.13
2001	−13.04	16.91	6	18.14
2002	−20.45	19.64	7	20.86

TABLE 17.1

Alternative Risk Measures Risk Measures Based on S&P 500 Index Monthly Returns

Notes: Standard deviation has been annualized; range is the highest monthly return that year minus the smallest monthly return; and number of negative returns is the number of months during the year with monthly returns less than zero.

Source: CRSP tapes (University of Chicago, 1998); and Yahoo Stock Index Quotes, 2000. Reproduced with permission of YAHOO! Inc. © 2003 by YAHOO! Inc. YAHOO! and the YAHOO! logo are trademarks of YAHOO! Inc.

Standard Deviation (or Variance) Standard deviation is a statistical measure of dispersion around the mean (average) of a distribution.[6] A higher standard deviation indicates a greater dispersion, or variation, around the mean. From Table 17.1, the year with the highest standard deviation of monthly returns was 1987 (30.50%); 1995 had the lowest standard deviation of monthly returns (5.12%). Investors believe that the market is more volatile today, and the standard deviation for 2002 confirms this belief, equalling 20.86%. However, it did not exceed the 1987 market volatility.

From the table, it would not be unreasonable to conclude that all risk measures are equally good. After all, it does seem to show a close relationship between all three measures. Years that show greater variation by one measure tend to show greater variation by the others, and the measures agree on less-variable years as

---

[6]The variance is the square of the standard deviation. Unlike standard deviation, however, variance does not have the same unit of measurement as the mean and thus is not as useful for comparisons.

well. Despite this apparent correlation, we argue that standard deviation is the superior measure of dispersion and thus security risk. Although range indicates the spread between the highest and lowest values, it says nothing about the distribution of returns in between. For example, how many values are closer to the high than the low? The number of negative returns indicates nothing about the range of the distribution, nor does it say anything about the returns that are greater than zero.

By contrast, the standard deviation provides rather full information about the distribution. For example, if we assume that the stock returns follow a normal distribution (a bell-shaped curve), one standard deviation from the mean accounts for about 67% of the possible returns, and two standard deviations from the mean account for 95% of the possible returns.

Calculating Standard Deviation

standard deviation

A statistic measuring the dispersion of a distribution around its mean; a measure of risk.

Standard deviation is a statistical measure of the dispersion, or variation, around the expected value, or mean, of a distribution. To illustrate further, let's go back to the earlier example in which the probability of a firm's sales growth being above average, average, or below average determined the expected return of 30%. Although the expected return is 30%, actual returns show dispersion around it. We can calculate the standard deviation (SD_i) of this expected future return (or ex-ante return):

$$SD_i = \left[\sum_{s=1}^{S} (R_{i,s} - ER_i)^2 Pr(s) \right]^{1/2} \tag{17.4}$$

where $R_{i,s}$ is stock i's return for state s, $Pr(s)$ is the probability of state s occurring, and ER_i is the expected return from the probability distribution.

The example data are provided here:

State of Sales Growth Rate	Probability of State	Return
Above average	30%	55%
Average	40	30
Below average	30	5

To use the formula, first subtract each return from the expected return, ER_i; next square the difference, then multiply by its probability; finally sum the products for each and take the square root:

$(R_{i,s} - ER_i)$	$(R_{i,s} - ER_i)^2$	$(R_{i,s} - ER_i)^2 Pr(s)$
(0.55 − 0.30)	(0.25)2 = 0.0625	0.0625(0.30) = 0.01875
(0.30 − 0.30)	(0.00)2 = 0.0000	0.0000(0.40) = 0.00000
(0.05 − 0.30)	(−0.25)2 = 0.0625	0.0625(0.30) = 0.01875
		0.0375
		$SD_i = \sqrt{0.0375} = 0.1936$

As for return measures, ex-ante standard deviations, not ex-post values, should guide investment decisions. The decision should depend on the risk expected from investing in the stock. A future, expected, or ex-ante risk is important to assess to decide how risky it will be to invest in this stock.

A historical standard deviation can also be calculated by using known ex-post returns. This approach may seem attractive, because historical returns can be measured more precisely and data on historical returns are more easily accessible. For historical returns, standard deviation is calculated as follows:

$$\text{SD}_i = \left[\frac{1}{(T-1)} \sum_{t=1}^{T} (R_{i,t} - \text{AM}_i)^2 \right]^{1/2} \qquad\qquad (17.5)$$

where T is the number of time periods (usually years or months) in a particular sample, $R_{i,t}$ is the return for period t, and AM_i is the mean return over the entire sample period.[7] An example of the mechanics of this calculation is presented in Table 17.2. The monthly returns we computed earlier for STAR are given in the first column. The second column gives the difference between each monthly return and the mean (5.04%). The third column squares the second column. Then, the third column is summed, divided by (24 − 1), or 23, and the square root taken. The result is a monthly standard deviation of 12.75%.[8]

Selecting Securities

Recall in Chapter 2 we discussed how investors can choose between securities by using the risk and return concepts developed in the preceding section. For a quick review, consider the following stocks:

Stock	Mean Return	Standard Deviation
A	12%	12%
B	12	10
C	14	12

Clearly, a risk-averse investor would find stock B a superior investment to stock A. B offers the same return (12%) but has less risk (a lower standard deviation) than A. Similarly, stock C is a superior investment to stock A. C has the same risk level (a standard deviation of 12%) but offers a higher return (14% versus 12%) than A. In general, we can say that if two securities have the same standard deviation but different expected returns, the security with the higher expected return is superior to the security with the lower expected return. A risk-averse investor will always choose the security with the higher expected return for securities with equal risk. Also, if two securities provide identical expected returns but different risk levels, the security with the lower standard deviation is superior to the security with the higher standard deviation. When one investment is clearly superior to another using mean return and standard deviation, it exhibits **mean-variance dominance** or is **mean-variance efficient**. In the example, B is mean-variance dominant over A.[9]

mean-variance dominance, or mean-variance efficient

Condition in which a stock or portfolio has the highest expected return for a given risk, or the lowest risk for a given expected return.

---

[7]Statistical theory suggests that one should divide by n for a population and divide by $(n-1)$ for a sample. Technically speaking, we should divide by $(n-1)$ because the return observation set is usually not the population but a sample of historical returns.

[8]Recall from Chapter 2 that the monthly standard deviation can be annualized as follows: multiply the monthly standard deviation, calculated using Equation 17.5, by the square root of 12. In the STAR example, the annualized standard deviation equals 44.17%.

[9]Variance equals the standard deviation squared [SD^2] and is also used as a risk measure. The relative level of risk between securities remains the same for the two measures, even if their scales differ.

TABLE 17.2					
Lone Star Steakhouse (STAR) Stock Risk Calculation					

Month t	End P_t	DIV$_t$	(1) HPR$_t$	(2) (HPR$_t$ − AM)	(3) $\sqrt{(\text{HPR}_t - \text{AM})^2}$
Nov-00	7.94		—	—	—
Dec-00	9.62		0.2116	0.1612	0.0260
Jan-01	8.38	0.13	−0.1154	−0.1658	0.0275
Feb-01	9.19		0.0967	0.0463	0.0021
Mar-01	9.28		0.0098	−0.0406	0.0016
Apr-01	12.05	0.13	0.3125	0.2621	0.0687
May-01	12.97		0.0763	0.0259	0.0007
Jun-01	12.99		0.0015	−0.0489	0.0024
Jul-01	10.9	0.13	−0.1509	−0.2013	0.0405
Aug-01	12.45		0.1422	0.0918	0.0084
Sep-01	10.8		−0.1325	−0.1829	0.0335
Oct-01	12.96	0.13	0.2120	0.1616	0.0261
Nov-01	13.83	0.01	0.0679	0.0175	0.0003
Dec-01	14.83		0.0723	0.0219	0.0005
Jan-02	19.5	0.15	0.3250	0.2746	0.0754
Feb-02	19.72		0.0113	−0.0391	0.0015
Mar-02	20.89		0.0593	0.0089	0.0001
Apr-02	19.5	0.15	−0.0594	−0.1098	0.0120
May-02	21.23		0.0887	0.0383	0.0015
Jun-02	23.59		0.1112	0.0608	0.0037
Jul-02	21.15	0.15	−0.0971	−0.1475	0.0217
Aug-02	19.98		−0.0553	−0.1057	0.0112
Sep-02	20.99		0.0506	0.0002	0.0000
Oct-02	20.84	0.15	0.0000	−0.0504	0.0025
Nov-02	20.26		−0.0278	−0.0782	0.0061

Sum = 1.2106   Sum = 0.3741
Mean = 0.0504   Sum/(T − 1) = 0.016267
St. Dev. = 0.127543

Note: HPR = $[(P_t - P_{t-1} + \text{DIV}_t)/P_{t-1}]$, and AM is the arithmetic mean of monthly returns.

The selection decision so far has been pretty straightforward. Let's make it more complicated. Which would you prefer, stock B or stock C? B has the smaller standard deviation but also the lower expected return. However, C has the higher expected return but also the higher standard deviation. Now, the selection decision is more ambiguous. You may prefer B to C (or C to B for that matter), but you really cannot say that one is superior to the other.

Another statistic, related to standard deviation, that may help to clarify some investment selection decisions is the **coefficient of variation (CV)**, which you also learned in Chapter 2. It can be used as a crude assessment of the risk/return trade-off of a security. Recall that CV equals the standard deviation divided by the mean (SD/AM). Statisticians use CV as a method of scaling standard deviations to account for differences in means. It measures the percentage of risk for every percentage return. Stock F in the following table has 0.67% of risk for every 1% of return. A lower CV indicates a better risk/return trade-off.

coefficient of variation (CV)

Standard deviation divided by the mean; a measure of an investment's risk per return trade-off.

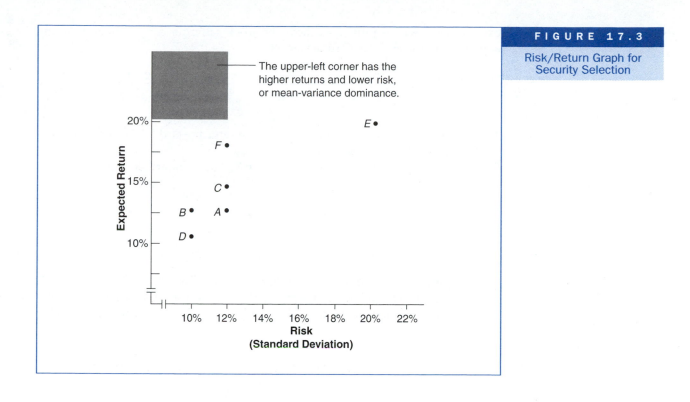

FIGURE 17.3

Risk/Return Graph for Security Selection

The upper-left corner has the higher returns and lower risk, or mean-variance dominance.

To see how the CV works, let's look at another hypothetical example:

Stock	Mean	Standard Deviation	CV
D	10%	10%	1.00
E	20	20	1.00
F	18	12	0.67

Again, the table gives little basis on which to choose between D and E. They have the same CV and, one could argue, offer the same risk/return trade-off. What about a choice between F and E or F and D? We really cannot say that F is superior to either E or D, but we can say that F offers a better risk/return trade-off (it has a lower CV). Why? Well, F has a lower mean than E (18% versus 20%), but it has substantially less risk as well (a standard deviation of 12% versus a standard deviation of 20%). Also, F does have a higher standard deviation than D (12% versus 10%) but offers a much higher mean return (18% versus 10%). We can display these results on a return/risk graph such as Figure 17.3. Generally, the stock that is farthest toward the upper-left corner usually offers the best risk/return trade-off. (See the shaded area in Figure 17.3.)

This section discussed the notion of risk and how to measure it, as well as the concept of ex-ante versus ex-post returns. Conceptually, we would like to measure risk and return ex-ante, but we usually calculate risk and return using

RECAPRECAP

ex-post data. We also discussed how the stock selection can be made by using expected returns and standard deviation risk.

Cisco (CSCO)	1998	1999	2000	2001	2002
HPR_t	142.88%	119.36	53.01	−45.73	−68.94

1. Calculate Cisco's ex-post (historical) mean return over the 1998–2002 period.
2. Calculate Cisco's standard deviation risk.
3. Consider the following stocks' returns, ER_i, and standard deviations, SD_i.

Stock	ER_i	SD_i
X	10%	15%
Y	10	12
Z	18	20

   Does any one stock dominate another? Explain why.
4. Using the data from Question 3, calculate the CV for stock Y and stock Z. Does one dominate the other? If not, what type of investor would choose Z over Y?

PORTFOLIO RISK AND RETURN

A portfolio is simply a group, or collection, of securities. When looking at a portfolio, the investor broadens the focus beyond the risk and return levels of the individual securities to evaluate the risk and return level of the group as a whole. How do we measure portfolio risk and return? Your initial answer might be that a simple combination of the risk and return levels of the individual securities would equal the portfolio risk and return. When it comes to calculating the mean, or expected, return from a portfolio, this answer is correct. The expected ex-ante return for a portfolio is defined as

$$ER_p = \sum_{i=1}^{N} X_i ER_i \qquad (17.6a)$$

The mean historical ex-post return from a portfolio is computed as

$$AM_p = \sum_{i=1}^{N} X_i AM_i \qquad (17.6b)$$

where ER_i and M_i are the expected and mean returns from security i, and X_i is the percentage of the portfolio invested in security i. An obvious condition of Equations 17.6a and 17.6b is that the sum of the Xs must equal 1.0.[10] Calculating the standard deviation for a portfolio of securities can also be relatively simple. In

---

[10]Normally, we would assume that all the Xs must be positive as well, and thus all would have values between zero and one. This assumption is not necessary if the possibility of short sales is allowed. In other words, it is possible that some Xs could be negative while others gave a partial sum greater than 1.0.

fact, the formulas presented in the prior section can be used in most cases. For example, the standard deviation of monthly returns shown in Figure 17.3 for the S&P 500 Index, which is, of course, a portfolio, was calculated using Equation 17.5. We simply calculated the portfolio return (i.e., the return for the S&P 500) for each time period and then found the standard deviation of those returns. Calculating portfolio standard deviations becomes more challenging when one must understand the impact of the interrelationships between the returns of the individual securities in the portfolio. We start with the simplest type of portfolio: one with two securities.

Standard Deviation of a Two-Security Portfolio

Let's begin by considering the following hypothetical example of the probability distributions for two individual stocks.

		Return	
State of the Economy	Probability	Stock A	Stock B
Good	0.30	+30%	+5%
Normal	0.40	+15	+10
Poor	0.30	+0	+15
Expected return		**+15%**	**+10%**
Standard deviation		11.7%	3.9%
Coefficient of variation		0.78	0.39

The expected return for each stock was calculated using Equation 17.2, and the standard deviations were calculated using Equation 17.4. For example, stock A's expected return is

$$0.30(30\%) + 0.40(15\%) + 0.30(0\%) = 15\%$$

as shown in bold type in the table.

Assume that company A builds and sells automobiles. The auto maker does better when the economy does better. Assume that company B makes antacids and aspirin, both of which may be in higher demand in a lousy economy. Further, suppose that the investor commits equal proportions of wealth to stocks A and B: 50% is invested in A and 50% in B. The return distribution for the portfolio of stocks A and B would be

State of the Economy	Probability	Portfolio Return
Good	0.30	17.5%
Normal	0.40	12.5
Poor	0.30	7.5
Portfolio expected return		12.5%
Portfolio standard deviation		3.9%
Portfolio CV		0.31

Notice that the expected return for the portfolio is simply a weighted average of the expected returns for the two stocks individually and is consistent with the result of Equation 17.6a. For example, the portfolio return under the good state of economy equals

$$0.50(30\%) + 0.50(5\%) = 17.5\%$$

The standard deviation, which was calculated using Equation 17.4, is not a simple weighted average as the expected return is. In fact, the standard deviation of this portfolio, 3.9%, is exactly the same as the standard deviation of stock B (the antacid and aspirin maker) and is considerably less than the standard deviation of stock A (the auto maker), even though half of the portfolio is made up of stock A.[11] Note that the portfolio CV is smaller than either stock A's or stock B's individual CV. How could this be?

The answer lies in the interrelationship between the return distributions for the two stocks. Notice that if the economy performs well, stock A has a higher return than expected and stock B has a lower return than expected. The situation is exactly reversed if the economy performs poorly. Statisticians refer to the interrelationship between probability distributions as **covariance (COV)**. The COV statistics for ex-ante returns are calculated as follows:

$$COV(A,B) = \sum_{s=1}^{S} (R_{A,s} - ER_A)(R_{B,s} - ER_B)Pr(s) \qquad (17.7)$$

where $R_{A,s}$ and $R_{B,s}$ are the returns for stocks A and B for the various states of the economy, s; ER_A and ER_B are the expected returns for A and B; $Pr(s)$ is the probability of occurrence of state s; and SD_A and SD_B are the standard deviations for stocks A and B.

In this example, the returns for the two stocks have negative covariance. In other words, as one stock's return gets larger, the other's return gets smaller, and vice versa. The actual covariance between the two stock returns is -0.0045.[12]

The preceding example was obviously concocted. Let's look at an example using some historical stock return data. If historical returns are used to calculate the covariance, the equation becomes

$$COV(A,B) = \frac{1}{(T-1)} \sum_{t=1}^{T} [(R_{A,t} - AM_A)(R_{B,t} - AM_B)] \qquad (17.8)$$

where T is the number of time periods (usually annual, quarterly, or monthly), $R_{A,t}$ and $R_{B,t}$ are returns over period t for stocks A and B, and AM_A and AM_B are mean returns for A and B.

Another statistical term that measures the interrelationship between two variables is called the **correlation coefficient**. It is interpreted just like the covariance;

covariance (COV)
Statistical measure of how two stock returns move together, or measure of comovement.

correlation coefficient
Statistical measure of comovement similar to the covariance; scaled to be between -1.0 and $+1.0$.

---

[11]The portfolio standard deviation is calculated as
$$SD_p = [(0.175 - 0.125)^2(0.30) + (0.125 - 0.125)^2(0.40) + (0.75 - 0.125)^2(0.30)]^{1/2}$$
$$= [0.0015]^{1/2} = 0.039 \text{ or } 3.9\%$$

[12]In our example, covariance is calculated as
$$[(0.30 - 0.15)(0.05 - 0.10)(0.30) + (0.15 - 0.15)(0.10 - 0.10)(0.40) +$$
$$(0.00 - 0.15)(0.15 - 0.10)(0.30)] = -0.045$$

however, the correlation is scaled so that its value can never be lower than -1.0 or higher than $+1.0$, or $-1.0 < \text{CORR}(A,B) < +1.0$. A positive sign implies that the two stocks generally move together, up or down, and the number between -1.0 to $+1.0$ conveniently provides the degree to which the two stocks covary together.

The equation for the correlation coefficient is

$$\text{CORR}(A,B) = \text{COV}(A,B)/\text{SD}_A\text{SD}_B \qquad (17.9)$$

For the preceding example, the correlation coefficient for stocks A and B is calculated as follows:

$$\text{CORR}(A,B) = (-0.0045)/(0.117)(0.039) = -1.0$$

A -1.0 means it is a perfect negative correlation and indicates that the two stocks, A and B, move in reverse direction (if one goes up, the other is expected to go down) and in a constant proportional amount. What would these statistics look like for real stocks using ex-post returns?

Table 17.3 presents monthly return data for Lone Star Steakhouse (STAR) and Krispy Kreme Doughnuts (KKD) from December 2000 to November 2002. At the bottom of each column, the table gives mean monthly returns, standard deviations of returns, and coefficients of variation for both stocks. (All means and standard deviations were calculated using Equations 17.3 and 17.5.) STAR had an average monthly return of 5.04%, with a standard deviation of 12.75% and a CV of 2.5298. KKD had an average monthly return of 4.50% with a standard deviation of 20.48% and a CV of 4.5511.

Column 4 gives the portfolio return, assuming half of the portfolio is invested in STAR and half in KKD, for each time period. At the bottom, the table lists the mean, standard deviation, and CV for the portfolio. Notice that the portfolio's average return, 4.77%, is exactly a weighted average of the mean returns for STAR and KKD, but the standard deviation, 13.63%, is not. It is less than KKD's standard deviation though it is slightly higher than STAR's. As in the prior example, the explanation for this lies in the interrelationship between STAR's and KKD's returns, which is measured by the covariance or correlation.

We next compute the covariance and correlation between the two sets of returns based on the historical ex-post return formulas for covariance and correlation (Equations 17.8 and 17.9). The calculation is detailed in Table 17.4. Columns 2 and 3 list the monthly returns for STAR and KKD. The fourth and fifth columns list the differences between each return and its respective mean. The sixth column is the product of columns 4 and 5, called the cross product. In this case the cross products seem both positive and negative, with 7 negatives out of 24 cross products. This result means that generally the two stock returns move in the same direction, when one goes up, the other goes up too. Column 6 is then summed and divided by $(24 - 1)$, or 23, giving the covariance (0.00807). Dividing the covariance by the product of the two standard deviations gives the correlation coefficient, $+0.309$. Thus, it appears that the two series of returns generally moved together during 2001 and 2002, although not always. This relationship is not surprising given that they are both in the food industry.

TABLE 17.3			
Portfolio Return Calculation			

(1) Month t	(2) STAR Return	(3) KKD Return	(4) Portfolio Return
Dec-00	0.2116	0.1857	0.1987
Jan-01	−0.1154	−0.2183	−0.1668
Feb-01	0.0967	0.1067	0.1017
Mar-01	0.0098	0.0028	0.0063
Apr-01	0.3125	0.1289	0.2207
May-01	0.0763	0.7992	0.4378
Jun-01	0.0015	0.0941	0.0478
Jul-01	−0.1509	−0.2950	−0.2229
Aug-01	0.1422	0.0940	0.1181
Sep-01	−0.1325	−0.0405	−0.0865
Oct-01	0.2120	0.1814	0.1967
Nov-01	0.0679	0.0652	0.0665
Dec-01	0.0723	0.1866	0.1294
Jan-02	0.3250	−0.0984	0.1133
Feb-02	0.0113	−0.0720	−0.0304
Mar-02	0.0593	0.1047	0.0820
Apr-02	−0.0594	−0.0654	−0.0624
May-02	0.0887	−0.0073	0.0407
Jun-02	0.1112	−0.1507	−0.0197
Jul-02	−0.0971	0.0982	0.0005
Aug-02	−0.0553	0.0042	−0.0255
Sep-02	0.0506	−0.1194	−0.0344
Oct-02	0.0000	0.0972	0.0486
Nov-02	−0.0278	−0.0012	−0.0145
Mean =	0.0504	0.0450	0.0477
St. Dev. =	0.1275	0.2048	0.1363
Coefficient of Variation			
CV =	2.5298	4.5511	2.8574

With these two examples serving as an introduction, let's look at the formula for finding the standard deviation of a two-security portfolio:

$$SD_p = [X_A^2 SD_A^2 + (1 - X_A)^2 SD_B^2 + 2X_A(1 - X_A)COV(A,B)]^{1/2} \qquad (17.10)$$

Remember from Equation 17.9 that

$$CORR(A,B) = COV(A,B)/SD_A SD_B$$

Rearranging terms gives

$$COV(A,B) = SD_A SD_B CORR(A,B)$$

This formula gives an alternative for the standard deviation of a two-security portfolio:

$$SD_p = [X_A^2 SD_A^2 + (1 - X_A^2)SD_B^2 + 2X_A(1 - X_A)(SD_A)(SD_B)(CORR(A,B))]^{1/2}$$
$$(17.11)$$

(1) Month t	(2) STAR Return	(3) KKD Return	(4) STAR (R − AM)	(5) KKD (R − AM)	(6) (4) × (5)
Dec-00	0.2116	0.1857	0.1612	0.1407	0.022681
Jan-01	−0.1154	−0.2183	−0.1658	−0.2633	0.043653
Feb-01	0.0967	0.1067	0.0463	0.0617	0.002852
Mar-01	0.0098	0.0028	−0.0406	−0.0422	0.001714
Apr-01	0.3125	0.1289	0.2621	0.0839	0.021987
May-01	0.0763	0.7992	0.0259	0.7542	0.019571
Jun-01	0.0015	0.0941	−0.0489	0.0491	−0.002399
Jul-01	−0.1509	−0.2950	−0.2013	−0.3400	0.068437
Aug-01	0.1422	0.0940	0.0918	0.0490	0.004496
Sep-01	−0.1325	−0.0405	−0.1829	−0.0855	0.015644
Oct-01	0.2120	0.1814	0.1616	0.1364	0.022050
Nov-01	0.0679	0.0652	0.0175	0.0202	0.000354
Dec-01	0.0723	0.1866	0.0219	0.1416	0.003101
Jan-01	0.3250	−0.0984	0.2746	−0.1434	−0.039385
Feb-02	0.0113	−0.0720	−0.0391	−0.1170	0.004578
Mar-02	0.0593	0.1047	0.0089	0.0597	0.000533
Apr-02	−0.0594	−0.0654	−0.1098	−0.1104	0.012113
May-02	0.0887	−0.0073	0.0383	−0.0523	−0.002005
Jun-02	0.1112	−0.1507	0.0608	−0.1957	−0.011889
Jul-02	−0.0971	0.0982	−0.1475	0.0532	−0.007841
Aug-02	−0.0553	0.0042	−0.1057	−0.0408	0.004309
Sep-02	0.0506	−0.1194	0.0002	−0.1644	−0.000025
Oct-02	0.0000	0.0972	−0.0504	0.0522	−0.002633
Nov-02	−0.0278	−0.0012	−0.0782	−0.0462	0.003612
Mean =	0.0504	0.0450		SUM =	0.185508
St. Dev. =	0.1275	0.2048		COV =	0.00806559
				CORR =	0.3088

TABLE 17.4

Covariance and Correlation Calculation

where X_A is the percentage of the portfolio invested in stock A, and $(1 − X_A)$ is the percentage of the portfolio invested in stock B. From Equation 17.10, you should see that the standard deviation of a two-security portfolio is really made up of three things: the standard deviation of stock A, the standard deviation of stock B, and the covariance between A and B.

Applying Equation 17.11 to the STAR-KKD example, the standard deviation of the portfolio (weighted one-half in STAR and one-half in KKD) is

$$SD_p = [(0.25)(0.1275)^2 + (0.25)(0.2048)^2 + 2(0.5)(0.5)(0.1275)(0.2048)(+0.309)]^{1/2} = 0.1363$$

This number is exactly the same as reported in Table 17.3 based on Equation 17.5! Because there are easier ways to compute the standard deviation of a two-security portfolio, how useful is Equation 17.11? As a simple calculation tool, perhaps not that useful. However, the most important feature of Equation 17.11 is that it explicitly shows that the standard deviation of a two-security portfolio is not simply the weighted average of the two individual standard deviations. The two securities' variations with each other must also be taken into account. You can see from Equation 17.11 that if the two securities move in opposite directions and thus have negative covariance and correlation, the standard deviation of the portfolio could be less than the standard deviation of either security individually. The portfolio could easily offer a better risk/return trade-off than the individual securities. It all depends on the correlation between the two sets of returns. We explore this issue in detail next.

Correlation and Portfolio Standard Deviation

The prior discussion showed, albeit indirectly, that the correlation between two sets of security returns can have a major impact on the risk of the resulting two-security portfolio. Let's look at the relationship in more depth. The relationship between correlation and portfolio standard deviation is best illustrated with an example.

Consider two securities, labeled A and B. Security A has an expected return of 12% and a standard deviation of 6%, whereas security B has an expected return of 20% and a standard deviation of 10%. Is one a better investment than the other? Not really. Both securities, for example, have the same CV (CV = 0.50). An individual may prefer one to the other, but no one can really say that one is better than the other.

Now, combine A and B into a portfolio. The expected portfolio return will be a simple weighted average of the two individual expected returns, or 16%, if one-half of the portfolio is invested in A and one-half is invested in B. We also know that the portfolio standard deviation will depend on the covariance, or correlation, between A and B. Let's look at three possible scenarios, summarized in Figure 17.4.

Figure 17.4 assumes that the returns for A and B move together perfectly and in the same direction [CORR(A,B) = +1.0]. In other words, the correlation coefficient between A and B equals +1.0. The **investment opportunity set** provides all the possible combinations of A and B and is graphed in Figure 17.4(a). Moving along the line from point A to point B, the percentage of the portfolio invested in A decreases whereas the percentage invested in B increases. Portfolio P_1 consists of one-half A and one-half B. Notice that portfolio P_1 has a standard deviation that is a weighted average of those of A and B, 8%. Because P_1 has an expected return of 16%, it has the same CV as A and B. Does P_1 offer a better risk/return trade-off than either A or B? No. In fact, none of the possible combinations of A and B, in this scenario, offer a better risk/return trade-off than the two individual stocks. If the correlation between any two stocks equals +1.0, then a better risk/return trade-off cannot be found; an investor can increase expected return only by increasing risk.

Now, pick a different stock, C, to pair with A, and assume for simplicity that C's return and risk are the same as B's, but its correlation with A equals zero. Suppose returns from A and C move completely independently of each other, or CORR(A,C) = 0.0. All the possible combinations of A and C are graphed in Figure 17.4(b). For example, portfolio P_2 consists of one-half A and one-half C. Portfolio P_2 also has an expected return of 16% but a standard deviation of only 5.8% and its CV equals 0.36. One could argue that P_2 offers a better risk/return trade-off because its CV is lower than those of A or C. P_2, for example, has only slightly less risk than A (5.8% compared with 6.0%) and a much higher expected return (16% versus 12%).

investment opportunity set

Possible combinations of stocks in a portfolio calculated by varying the percentage holdings in each stock.

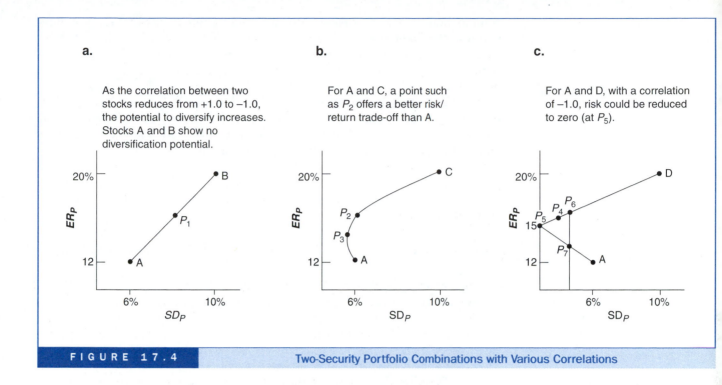

a.

As the correlation between two stocks reduces from +1.0 to −1.0, the potential to diversify increases. Stocks A and B show no diversification potential.

b.

For A and C, a point such as P_2 offers a better risk/return trade-off than A.

c.

For A and D, with a correlation of −1.0, risk could be reduced to zero (at P_5).

FIGURE 17.4	Two-Security Portfolio Combinations with Various Correlations

This potential to obtain a better risk/return trade-off by combining imperfectly correlated securities is called **diversification**. This case shows that any correlation between two stocks less than 1.0 indicates a potential to diversify. Graphically, the range of combinations between two stocks gives a nonlinear (bow-shaped) curve that allows diversification to occur. As Figure 17.4(b) shows, several possible combinations of A and C offer better risk/return trade-offs than either stock alone. A point such as P_3 has the minimum risk for a portfolio combination of A and C. Its expected return equals 14.1% (A's is 12.0%), and its risk equals 5.1% (A's is 6.0%). In fact, any combinations of A and C from P_3 to C offer better risk/return trade-offs than combinations between A and P3. Of course, the choice of the actual portfolio between P_3 and C depends on the amount of risk the investor is willing to take.

As a final scenario, let's assume that the two return series move together perfectly, although in opposite directions. Thus, A and D have perfect negative correlation [CORR(A,D) = −1.0]. Again, let us assume that D has the same return and risk as stock B.[13] The investment opportunity set for A and D is shown in Figure 17.4(c). Portfolio P_4 consists of one-half A and one-half D. Like P_1 and P_2, P_4 has an expected return of 16%, but its standard deviation is only 2.0%. Portfolio P_4 not only offers a better risk/return trade-off than A, but a risk-averse investor would actually prefer it—P_4 has a higher expected return and less risk than does stock A. In fact, a risk-averse investor would not choose any

diversification

Spreading your investment dollars among several different investments to reduce risk.

---

[13]In reality, perfect negative correlation is not possible, although negative correlation can be achieved using derivative securities in hedging (as described in Chapter 15). Generally, securities are positively correlated to each other; negative correlation is rare.

combination of A and D between point A and point P_5 because other combinations offer higher expected returns for the same level of risk, such as P_6 compared with P_7. Furthermore, portfolio P_5 is a combination of A and D (62.5% in A and 37.5% in D) that reduces the portfolio risk to zero with an expected return of 15.0%.

In summary, as the correlation coefficient decreases from 1.0 to -1.0, potential diversification benefits grow. Also, notice that diversification improves the risk/return trade-off only if the correlation is less than 1.0. Stated differently, as long as the correlation is less than 1.0, combinations of securities offer diversification potential.

Another way to see the effect of the correlation coefficient on the portfolio standard deviation (and diversification potential) is to examine Equation 17.11 again. Recall the formula,

$$SD_p = [X_A^2 SD_A^2 + (1 - X_A^2)SD_B^2 + 2X_A(1 - X_A)(SD_A)(SD_B)(CORR(A,B))]^{1/2}$$

Let's examine the three terms in the formula. The first term, $X_A^2 SD_A^2$, is always positive because both terms are squared, so it will only add to the portfolio risk. Similarly with the second term, $(1 - X_A)^2 SD_B^2$. The third term, $2X_A(1 - X_A)(SD_A)(SD_B)CORR(A,B)$, however, can be positive or negative because every term is positive except for the correlation coefficient, $CORR(A,B)$. The correlation coefficient can be negative, which would reduce portfolio risk. In fact, that is the result we found in the earlier examples; a low or negative correlation between pairs of stocks provides the greater diversification benefit or reduction in portfolio risk.

Investment Opportunity Set for a Two-Security Portfolio

An investment opportunity set that identifies the portfolio combinations is not difficult to define for a two-security portfolio. Apply Equation 17.6b to find AM_p and Equation 17.11 to find SD_p, varying the proportions invested in each security (X), as shown in the following example. Suppose that you already calculated the mean, AM_j, and standard deviation, SD_j, of each security, A and E, and their correlation coefficient, $CORR(A,E) = -0.20$.

Stock	AM_j	SD_j
A	12%	6%
E	20	10

Now, the investment combinations can be determined by varying the amount invested in A and E in Equations 17.6b and 17.11 (where X_A is the percentage invested in A and X_E is the percentage invested in E). Because the percentages invested must add up to 100%, X_E can be written as $(1 - X_A)$, and Equations 17.6b and 17.11 can be written as

$$AM_p = X_A(AM_A) + (1 - X_A)(AM_E)$$
$$SD_p = [X_A^2 SD_A^2 + (1 - X_A^2)SD_E^2 + 2X_A(1 - X_A)(SD_A)(SD_E)(CORR(A,E))]^{1/2}$$

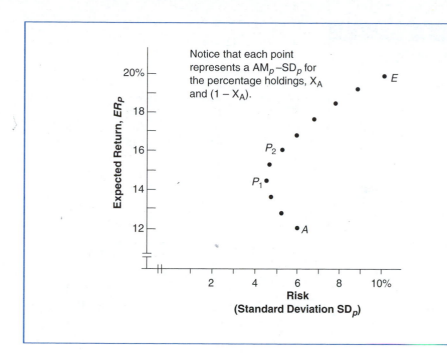

FIGURE 17.5

Two-Security Portfolio Combinations of Securities A and E

Note: P_1 is 70% in Security A and 30% in E. It is the minimum-variance portfolio. P_2 is 50% in Security A and 50% in E.

For example, if $X_A = 0.10$, then $(1 - X_A) = 0.90$. Plugging in these percentages,

$$AM_p = 0.10(12\%) + (0.90)(20\%) = 19.2\%$$

$$SD_p = [(0.10)^2(0.06)^2 + (0.90)^2(0.10)^2 + 2(0.10)(0.90)(0.06)(0.10)(-0.20)]^{1/2}$$
$$= 8.9\%$$

This calculation represents one point on the $AM_p - SD_p$ graph. To find several more combinations of securities A and E, just change the percentages X_A and $(1 - X_A)$. Figure 17.5 displays several combinations. Graphing the results in the table gives Figure 17.5, which resembles the curves in Figure 17.4.

One use of an investment opportunity set might be to find the **minimum variance portfolio**. Using calculus, solve for X_A and then for $(1 - X_A)$, the proportion invested in E. An investment of X_A in stock A and $(1 - X_A)$ in stock E provides the lowest portfolio risk:

minimum variance portfolio

Combination of stocks in a portfolio that gives the lowest portfolio standard deviation risk.

$$X_A = \frac{SD_E^2 - SD_A SD_E CORR(A,E)}{SD_A^2 + SD_E^2 - 2(SD_A)(SD_E)CORR(A,E)}$$

For our previous example, it is calculated as follows:

$$X_A = \frac{(0.10)^2 - (0.06)(0.10)(-20)}{(0.06)^2 + (0.10)^2 - 2(0.06)(0.10)(-0.20)} = 0.70$$

The proportion invested in E must equal $(1 - X_A)$ because the two securities must add to 100%:

$$X_E = (1 - X_A) = (1 - 0.70) = 30\%$$

TABLE 17.5	X_A	$(1 - X_A)$	AM_p	SD_p
Various Combinations of Securities A and E	0%	100%	20.0%	10.0%
	10	90	19.2	8.9
	20	80	18.4	7.8
	30	70	17.6	6.9
	40	60	16.8	6.0
	50	50	16.0	5.3
	60	40	15.2	4.8
	70	30	14.4	4.6
	80	20	13.6	4.8
	90	10	12.8	5.3
	100%	0	12.0	6.0

Note: AM_p is the portfolio's mean return and SD_p is the portfolio's standard deviation.

We can also find the portfolio expected return AM_p and risk SD_p for the percentage that provides the minimum risk portfolio. Again, using Equations 17.6b and 17.11,

$$AM_p = (0.70)(12\%) + (0.30)(20\%) = 14.4\%$$

$$SD_p = [(0.70)^2(0.06)^2 + (0.30)^2(0.10)^2 + 2(0.70)(0.30)(0.06)(0.10)(-0.20)]^{1/2}$$
$$= 4.6\%$$

Actually, the results in Table 17.5 already showed that the SD_p is lowest with 70% in security A and 30% in security E. Also, Figure 17.5 shows that these percentages are indeed the lowest-risk portfolio combination. By examining the SD_p in Equation 17.11 and Figure 17.5, it is clear that the risk can be reduced because SD_p is a nonlinear equation. It is also evident that correlation plays a major role in diversification. It is the only term in Equation 17.11 that contributes to reducing risk.

Standard Deviation of an *N*-Security Portfolio

Finding the standard deviation of a portfolio that contains more than two securities is a logical extension of what we discussed so far. Extending Equation 17.11 to N assets creates

$$SD_p = \left[\sum_{i=1}^{N} X_i^2 SD_i^2 + \sum_{i=1}^{N} \sum_{j=1}^{N} X_i X_j COV(i,j) \right]^{1/2} \tag{17.13}$$

where X_i is the percentage of the portfolio invested in security i (as before, the X values must sum to 1.0), SD_i is the standard deviation of security i, and $COV(i,j)$ is the covariance between security i and security j.

Now, Equation 17.13 may look horrible at first glance, but it is not as complicated as it seems. Like Equation 17.11, it states that the standard deviation of a portfolio is a function of two elements. The first element is the variances (the squares of the standard deviations) of the individual securities, and the second element is the covariances between each possible pair of securities. The double summation operator ($\Sigma\Sigma$) in the covariance element means that each covariance term appears twice. (Look at the covariance term.) The covariance appears once as $COV(i,j)$ and the second time as $COV(j,i)$. Because the order doesn't matter when we examine comovements, we know that $COV(i,j)$ equals $COV(j,i)$, which is why we multiply the covariance term by 2.

Let's use Equation 17.13 to calculate the standard deviation of a sample multi-stock portfolio. First, if the portfolio contains three securities (A, B, and C), Equation 17.13 becomes

$$SD_p = [X_A^2 SD_A^2 + X_B^2 SD_B^2 + X_C^2 SD_C^2 + 2X_A X_B COV(A,B) \\ + 2X_A X_C COV(A,C) + 2X_B X_C COV(B,C)]^{1/2} \qquad (17.14)$$

Notice that the equation contains three covariance terms because three pairs of securities (A and B, A and C, B and C) are possible.[14]

Suppose we add another stock, Yahoo! (YHOO), with a mean return of -0.93% and standard deviation of 25.05%, to STAR and Krispy Kreme (KKD). The portfolio consisting of one-third STAR, one-third KKD, and one-third YHOO and has a portfolio mean return that equals 2.87%. The portfolio's mean return, 2.87%, is simply a weighted average of the three stocks' mean returns. The portfolio's standard deviation, calculated using Equation 17.5, equals 12.99%. Notice that the portfolio standard deviation is much less than YHOO's and KKD's standard deviations, but similar to STAR's. It reduces the risk for YHOO and increases the return compared to YHOO's return. If the correlations are less than 1.0 (which it is for all three pairs of correlations), then the potential is present to reduce risk. This risk reduction is the benefit of diversification.

We can also find the portfolio's standard deviation using Equation 17.14. Recall that the correlation between STAR and YHOO equals $+0.3088$. (We went through the calculation in Table 17.4.) Using the same procedure, the correlation between STAR and YHOO equals 0.1405 and the correlation between KKD and YHOO equals 0.0572. The respective correlation coefficients show that the returns move together, generally but not perfectly. Each stock makes up one-third of the portfolio, and the respective standard deviations are 12.75% (STAR), 20.48% (KKD), and 25.05% (YHOO). Using Equation 17.14, the portfolio's standard deviation equals, not surprisingly, 12.99%. So if you own Internet stocks or glamour stocks like Krispy Kreme, it may be wise to diversify by combining with other stocks. It reduces Yahoo!'s and Krispy Kreme's risk while maintains risk that is close to STAR's.

Again, you may question the value of using Equation 17.13 to find the standard deviation of an N-asset portfolio. We agree that it is a computational device only, it is not that critical to memorize. However, as stated before, Equation 17.13 illustrates explicitly the impact of security correlation and covariance on portfolio risk. The standard deviation of a portfolio is not simply the weighted average of the standard deviations of the individual securities. The procedure for calculating the standard deviation of a portfolio also provides a good illustration of the concept of diversification.

---

[14]The number of possible pairs of securities equals: $N!/2!(N - 2)!$, where N is the number of securities. The ! sign means factorial, which mathematically is equal to $(1 \times 2 \times 3 \times 4 \times \ldots \times N)$. For example, $4! = (1 \times 2 \times 3 \times 4) = 24$. So, a 4-security portfolio would have $24/4 = 6$ covariance terms (each appearing twice), meaning six possible pairs of securities. A 10-security portfolio would have 45 covariance terms.

RECAPRECAP

This section discusses how to calculate portfolio return and risk. It also discusses the virtues of diversification and how the correlation coefficient between securities is the key factor to diversification. Diversification by investing in stocks with correlations less than 1.0 reduces the portfolio risk and possibly increases portfolio return.

5. Using the mean returns, standard deviation, and correlation displayed in Table 17.4 for STAR and KKD, calculate the portfolio return if you invest 40% in STAR and 60% in KKD.
6. Using the information from Table 17.4, calculate the portfolio standard deviation using Equation 17.11 if you invest 40% in STAR and 60% in KKD.

DIVERSIFICATION

When we discussed how to calculate the standard deviation of a portfolio in the prior section, we illustrated, albeit indirectly, two important points about diversification. They can be summarized as follows:

1. Diversification can improve the risk/return trade-off if the correlation between individual security returns in the portfolio is less than 1.0 (i.e., returns are not perfectly correlated).
2. The benefits of diversification increase as the correlation coefficient gets smaller (i.e., approaches −1.0).

The benefits of diversification appear to be obvious as shown in the prior examples. Further, the benefits of diversification may not be difficult to obtain. Let's now consider how to obtain the benefits of diversification in some realistic investment settings.

Diversification Across Securities

Perhaps the most straightforward way for investors to diversify is by spreading their investment funds across several different securities. We showed this approach already, both with manufactured and real return data. For example, we demonstrated that owning two stocks instead of just one can produce a risk/return trade-off that would be preferred by most risk-averse investors.

The benefits of diversification across securities are clearly shown in Figure 17.6. The data used to generate this graph were taken from the CRSP database. (We discuss the CRSP database in Appendix A.) From the CRSP database, one stock was randomly selected and then another stock was randomly selected, creating a portfolio of two stocks. Then another stock was randomly added to the portfolio, and so forth. (All portfolios are equally weighted combinations of the stocks.) Daily returns for each portfolio were then calculated. Notice how the portfolio standard deviation generally falls as the number of securities increases. The one-stock portfolio has an annualized standard deviation of 193.6%, the two-stock portfolio has an annualized standard deviation of 100.7%, and so forth.[15] By contrast, the 20-stock portfolio has a standard deviation of only 15.3%.

[15]For T trading days in a year, the annualized standard deviation equals the standard deviation of daily returns multiplied by the square root of T.

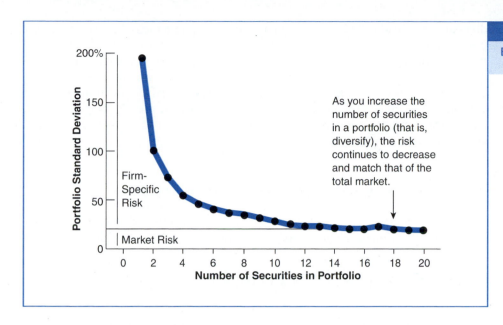

FIGURE 17.6

Example of Diversification
Across Securities

As you increase the number of securities in a portfolio (that is, diversify), the risk continues to decrease and match that of the total market.

This decreasing standard deviation occurs simply because returns between pairs of securities are not perfectly correlated. For example, the correlation coefficients between the first stock and the other 19 range from −0.10 to 0.09. Recall that some diversification potential exists as long as the correlation coefficient between two pairs of returns is less than 1.0.

Two Types of Portfolio Risk

The need to diversify leads to a distinction of two types of risk: market risk and firm-specific risk. Let's discuss the distinction between the two further.

Suppose you own just shares in Yahoo! stock in your investment portfolio. The return on the stock is affected by economic factors such as business cycles, the inflation rate, interest rates, and others (as discussed in Chapter 11), as well as factors that are firm-specific such as increased competition, managerial policies, and new innovations (as discussed in Chapters 12 and 13). Every stock return is affected by both kinds of factors in varying degrees.

Now, suppose you own two stocks, Yahoo! and Disney. Although these stocks are both affected by market-related factors (perhaps not to the same degree), their firm-specific factors may differ. For example, if the weather becomes extremely cold and rainy, sales receipts at Disney's theme parks may suffer, but you may spend more time surfing the net on Yahoo! The firm-specific factors can lead to offsetting returns between two stocks. Of course, this point is the crux of the power of diversification; as the number of stocks in a portfolio increases, the firm-specific risk becomes negligible. However, the market risk related to economic factors affects all stocks, so it cannot be eliminated through diversification, which can be seen in Figure 17.6. As diversification across securities increases, firm-specific risk decreases until the only risk left is the market risk.

The **market risk** that exists even with diversification is also called systematic risk or nondiversifiable risk. The **firm-specific risk** that can be eliminated by

market risk

Risk inherent in the market, such as business cycles, the inflation rate, interest rates, and other economic factors.

firm-specific risk

Risk specifically tied to the company such as labor contracts, new product development, and other company-related factors.

diversifying is also called diversifiable risk or nonsystematic risk. Two important points stem from this discussion: (1) a portfolio of stocks can virtually eliminate firm-specific risk; and (2) the only relevant risk is the market risk when portfolios are held because the firm-specific risk decreases to virtually zero.

A mathematical example can illustrate the power of diversification. The next section shows that as the number of securities increases, the effect of each company's standard deviation is virtually zero, and the portfolio risk is measured entirely by the covariance between the securities.

Mathematical Effects of Diversification

We can mathematically show that the standard deviations of securities have minuscule effects on portfolio standard deviation risk, SD_p, using Equation 17.13:

$$SD_p = \left[\sum_{i=1}^{N} X_i^2 SD_i^2 + \sum_{i=1}^{N} \sum_{j=1}^{N} X_i X_j COV(i,j) \right]^{1/2}$$

Suppose the standard deviation is squared to avoid the square root sign.

$$SD_p^2 = \sum_{i=1}^{N} X_i^2 SD_i^2 + \sum_{i=1}^{N} \sum_{j=1}^{N} X_i X_j SD_i SD_j COV(i,j)$$

Suppose we create a naive portfolio in which stocks are randomly chosen and invested in equal proportions. If the portfolio contains N stocks, each X equals $1/N$. The equation then becomes

$$SD_p^2 = \frac{1}{N} \sum_{i=1}^{N} \frac{1}{N} SD_i^2 + \sum_{i=1}^{N} \sum_{j=1}^{N} \frac{1}{N^2} COV(i,j)$$

It is difficult to figure out from the formula, but it contains N variances (SD_i^2) and $N(N-1)$ covariances. Now, just for simplicity (and also to make our point) suppose that each SD_i^2 is the same for each stock. It reduces the term to SD^2 (no subscript because they are all the same). Similarly, for the covariances, suppose they all equal COV, then SD_p^2 is calculated as follows:

$$SD_p^2 = \frac{1}{N} SD^2 + \frac{(N-1)}{N} COV$$

Now, we can really see the power of diversification. As the number of stocks, N, increases, $1/N$ decreases. When N becomes very large, $1/N$ becomes virtually equal to zero. It makes the standard deviation of each stock almost irrelevant. Similarly, the covariance term becomes more important as N increases because $(N-1)/N$ approaches 1.0 as N becomes large. Why? Because $(N-1)/N = 1 - (1/N) = 1$ as N becomes larger. This exercise shows that the standard deviation of stocks contributes almost no effect on the portfolio risk SD_p^2, and leaves the covariance between stocks as the only important term.

	Holding Period	Arithmetic Means (annualized)	Standard Deviation (annualized)	Coefficient of Variation	TABLE 17.6
S&P 500 Index	1 year	13.2%	20.1%	1.52	**Summary of Returns over Varying Holding Periods**
	2 years	12.2	14.5	1.19	
	5 years	11.0	8.4	0.77	
	10 years	11.1	5.5	0.50	
	25 years	11.1	2.4	0.21	
Treasury bonds	1 year	5.4	9.1	1.67	
	2 years	5.3	6.3	1.19	
	5 years	5.2	4.7	0.90	
	10 years	5.1	3.9	0.78	
	25 years	4.2	2.6	0.63	

Diversification Across Time

Table 17.6 presents mean annualized total returns from the S&P 500 Index and an index of long-term U.S. Treasury bonds (T-bonds) between the end of 1925 and the end of 2002, for different assumed holding periods. For 1-year holding periods, buying at the beginning of the year and selling at the end of the same year, the S&P 500 produced a mean annualized return of 13.2%. However, the data show considerable variation around this mean (SD = 20.1% and CV = 1.52). However, for 25-year holding periods (i.e., buying at the beginning of Year 1 and selling at the end of Year 25, reinvesting all dividends along the way), the mean annualized return from the S&P 500 was much less, 11.1%, but this return also showed far less variation about the mean (SD = 2.4% and CV + 0.21). In fact, the standard deviation and CV both fall consistently as the length of the holding period increases.

The same pattern is evident, although not as dramatic, for T-bond returns. For 1-year holding periods, long-term U.S. T-bonds produced a mean annual return of 5.4%, again with a fair amount of variation around the mean (SD = 9.1% and CV = 1.67). Increasing the holding period to 25 years, however, improves the risk/return profile. The mean annualized rate of return does fall to 4.2%, but the standard deviation, and thus the CV, fall even more (SD = 2.6% and CV = 0.63). As with stock returns, the standard deviation and CV fall consistently as the length of the holding period increases. This phenomenon, in which the annualized standard deviation declines as the time horizon increases, is called **time diversification**.

Many articles in the financial press attest to the benefits of time diversification. A *Wall Street Journal* article illustrates that longer holding periods have historically lowered the risks associated with stock investing, as Table 17.6 also illustrates.[16] The article shows that if the S&P 500 Index was held for only a 1-year period, the stock index return trailed a T-bill investment 40% of the time. If the stock

time diversification

Phenomenon in which the annualized standard deviation declines as the investment time horizon increases.

---

[16]Karen Slater, "Long Haul Investing: Riding Out the Risk in Stocks," *The Wall Street Journal*, December 16, 1991, p. C1.

index was held for a 5-year period, it trailed T-bills 31%; however, over a 20-year holding period, the stock index earns a higher return than T-bills 100% of the time.

If this benefit is real, an investor can reduce risk simply by increasing the investment period, a perfect tactic for retirement funds. Unfortunately, time diversification is a fallacy. It is true that the annualized standard deviation falls as the investment time horizon increases based on rates of return. It is also true, however, that the uncertainty compounds over a greater number of years, which implies that the total dollar return becomes more uncertain as the investment horizon becomes longer. Stated differently, the annualized standard deviation does not say anything about the total dollar return. As the holding period becomes longer, the risk of the total dollar return becomes greater. Most investors worry about the total dollar return on a retirement fund rather than the decreasing annualized standard deviation, so it is important to note that to feel safer with time diversification is illusory.

Ibbotson Associates provides evidence with real and simulated data that, although the confidence interval around the expected return narrows as investment period increases over time (i.e., the standard deviation around the mean decreases over longer investment periods), the confidence interval of the dollar return widens as investment periods increase (i.e., risk increases as the investment period lengthens).[17]

What is the point of this discussion? It is that investors must be careful when using these measures and not lose sight of the objective. To maximize long-term dollar return (perhaps for a retirement fund), one must be aware that risk increases for investments over longer periods, even if the standard deviation of the rate of return decreases. Perhaps a good example is Cisco Systems stock. Many investors considered Cisco stock to be a good investment because it is a market bellwether for technology stocks. Suppose you purchased 1,000 shares of Cisco in 1993 for about $0.90 (adjusted for stock splits). If you sold in 2000, its market price was about $82 per share, or your retirement fund would be worth about $82,000. If you waited until now, end of 2002, that same investment would be worth around $13,820. Holding the stock longer did not reduce your risk in dollar returns; instead it increased it and your ending wealth was much less. So the first lesson learned is to diversify and not invest in one stock. Remember all the other "dot-com" busts. The second lesson is to understand that longer investment horizon increases your uncertainty (risk) of its final dollar wealth.

Efficient Diversification

naive diversification

Technique in which an investor diversifies by randomly selecting securities for the portfolio investment.

efficient diversification

Technique in which an investor diversifies by finding the portfolio combinations that produce the highest return for a given risk or the lowest risk for a given return.

Most of the examples of diversification we discussed up to this point are examples of **naive diversification**. The stock selection technique we used to produce Figure 17.6 is a classic example of naive diversification: the stocks were added to the portfolio randomly. Although adding additional securities to a portfolio will generally improve its risk/return profile, it provides no guarantee that it will produce the best risk/return profile. In other words, naive diversification will not necessarily maximize return for a given level of risk, nor will it necessarily minimize risk for a given level of return.

By contrast, **efficient diversification** involves finding the portfolio combinations that produce the best risk/return profiles. It involves the use of mathematical techniques to search through all possible combinations of securities to determine which provide maximum expected returns for given risk levels or which subject the

[17]*SBBI 1998 Yearbook* (Chicago: Ibbotson Associates, 1998).

Harry Markowitz

In 1952, as an unknown 25-year-old graduate student at the University of Chicago, Harry Markowitz published an article entitled "Portfolio Selection" in the staid academic *Journal of Finance*. This article was considered to be so influential and innovative, both theoretically and practically, that Markowitz was awarded the Nobel Price in Economics in 1990. He is rightly regarded as one of the fathers of modern portfolio theory. Ironically, when he began his research, Markowitz had little interest in stocks or the stock market. A self-described nerd, Markowitz was more interested in applications of the relatively new field of linear programming. A chance meeting with a stock broker, who suggested Markowitz apply linear programming to the problems investors face, kindled his interest. A short time later, the dean of the University of Chicago Business School suggested that Markowitz read John Burr Williams's *The Theory of Investment Value,* then one of the most influential books on stocks. Intrigued with the notion that investors should be concerned with risk as well as return, Markowitz began work. The end result was a short, but brilliant article outlining the process by which investors can minimize risk for a given level of return, or maximize return for a given a level of risk, the cornerstone of modern portfolio theory. Markowitz also demonstrated how diversification can reduce portfolio risk, without significantly reducing a portfolio's expected return.

investor to the minimum amount of risk for given levels of return. In the process, all diversifiable risk is eliminated. These mathematical techniques are derived from a body of theory usually referred to as **modern portfolio theory (MPT)**.

The origins of MPT can be traced by an article published in 1952 by Harry Markowitz.[18] Markowitz argued that an investor could produce an optimal allocation of securities within a portfolio that would achieve the best possible risk/return trade-off. In other words, one can build a portfolio that minimizes risk for a given level of return or, alternatively, that maximizes expected return for a given level of risk. The basic technique used by Markowitz finds, for a given set of securities, what is called the *efficient frontier.* Portfolios that lie along the efficient frontier offer investors the optimal risk/return combinations; these portfolios are called **mean-variance efficient portfolios**.[19]

Let's illustrate an efficient frontier by considering a simple example with just three assets (A, B, and C), presented in Figure 17.7. Each asset is plotted based on its standard deviation and expected return. Notice that A and C have identical expected returns whereas B and C have identical standard deviations. Clearly, A is superior to C because it has less risk (i.e., a lower standard deviation) for the same expected return. By the same token, B clearly offers a superior risk/return trade-off compared with C because it has a higher expected return for the same level of risk. How can one choose between A and B? Although someone may prefer A to B, or vice versa, remember that no one can really say one is better than the other. In this simple example, A and B form endpoints along the efficient frontier.

modern portfolio theory (MPT)

A body of theory that includes the concept of diversification and measures security risk and return via the capital asset pricing model (CAPM).

mean-variance efficient portfolios

Portfolios that provide the highest return for a given risk or the lowest risk for a given return.

---

[18]See "Portfolio Selection," *The Journal of Finance,* March 1952, pp. 77–91. In 1990, Harry Markowiz, Merton Miller, and William Sharpe were awarded the Nobel Prize in Economics for their work developing MPT.

[19]In this text, we measure risk by portfolio standard deviation, SD_p, rather than variance, which equals SD_p^2. There is really no major difference between the two measures; the numerical value differs, but the relative risk level remains the same between securities or portfolios. To label a portfolio *mean-variance efficient* is the same as labeling it *mean-standard deviation efficient.* We will stick to the conventional phrase here and use *mean-variance efficient.*

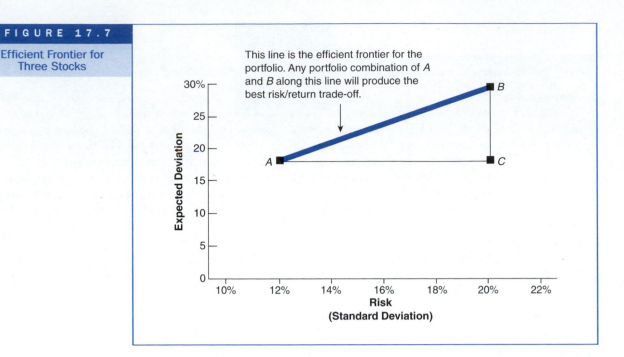

FIGURE 17.7

Efficient Frontier for Three Stocks

Assume that a straight line connects A and B. By definition, all the portfolios along that line would be combinations of A and B, and all, including A and B, would maximize expected return for a given risk level and minimize risk for a given expected return. All portfolios that lie along the efficient frontier produce the optimal risk/return trade-offs of all feasible combinations of the securities; at the same time, these efficient portfolios minimize nondiversifiable risk. Thus the Markowitz model allows an investor to reduce the number of feasible combinations under consideration to only those that lie along the efficient frontier, even though hundreds or even thousands of portfolios may remain.

How to Find an Efficient Frontier

The data necessary to find the efficient frontier for a set of securities, using the Markowitz model, consist of three items: the standard deviation of returns for each security, the mean (or expected) return for each security, and the correlation coefficient between returns for each possible pair. The Markowitz model can be used with either ex-ante (expected future) data or ex-post (historical) data.

The Markowitz model involves solving a set of mathematical equations to minimize portfolio standard deviation, subject to a minimum stated expected return. It does so by varying the percentages of the total portfolio invested in the individual securities. Computer software simplifies the work, which makes finding an efficient frontier relatively simple. Let's look at an example. Table 17.7 lists the data necessary to find an efficient frontier for five stocks: Wyeth, Boeing, Disney, Duke Power, and Texaco over five years. It gives the mean annualized monthly return and annualized standard deviation for each stock, along with the correlation coefficient for each pair of stocks.

Stock	Mean Return	Standard Deviation	Coefficient of Variance
Wyeth	17.46%	15.59%	0.89
Boeing	32.16	21.76	0.68
Disney	23.99	28.09	1.17
Duke Power	21.76	15.17	0.70
Texaco	22.53	14.59	0.65

	Correlation Matrix				
Stock	Wyeth	Boeing	Disney	Duke Power	Texaco
Wyeth	1.00				
Boeing	0.49	1.00			
Disney	0.52	0.69	1.00		
Duke Power	0.50	0.38	0.12	1.00	
Texaco	0.25	−0.04	−0.18	0.28	1.00

TABLE 17.7

Inputs Needed to Find an Efficient Frontier for Five Securities

Portfolio	Portfolio Mean Return	Portfolio Standard Deviation	Wyeth	Boeing	Disney	Duke Power	Texaco
1	23.13%	10.68%	7.29%	0.00%	14.05%	29.49%	48.27%
2	23.29	10.95	0.00	7.38	13.89	26.25	52.86
3	24.31	11.68	0.00	19.20	15.97	18.20	54.86
4	25.49	12.73	0.00	31.02	1.60	10.15	57.23
5	26.53	14.13	0.00	41.93	0.00	0.00	58.07
6	27.57	16.10	0.00	53.54	0.00	0.00	46.46
7	28.78	18.63	0.00	65.16	0.00	0.00	34.84
8	29.84	21.46	0.00	76.77	0.00	0.00	23.23
9	31.07	24.55	0.00	88.39	0.00	0.00	11.61
10	32.16	27.77	0.00	100.00	0.00	0.00	0.00
Equally weighted	23.43	14.03	20.00	20.00	20.00	20.00	20.00

Column group header: Percentage of the Portfolio Invested in (spanning Wyeth, Boeing, Disney, Duke Power, Texaco)

TABLE 17.8

Sample of Portfolio Combinations on the Efficient Frontier for the Five Securities

A spreadsheet application (e.g., Excel) can be used to identify the efficient frontier shown in Table 17.8. Ten portfolios create different combinations of the five stocks that lie along the efficient frontier; they are plotted along with an equally weighted portfolio of the five stocks. The relevant characteristics of the portfolios (mean returns, standard deviations, and percentages invested in each security) are also presented in Table 17.8. Notice that the equally weighted portfolio does not lie along the efficient frontier.

The 10 that do lie along the efficient frontier vary widely in their compositions. Portfolio 1 is the only one of the 10 that contains Wyeth (albeit only 7.29%). None of the 10 efficient portfolios contain all five stocks. In fact, portfolios 5 through 9 are made up of only two stocks (Boeing and Texaco). Portfolio 10 is even 100% Boeing! Of course, the Markowitz method does not guarantee that all

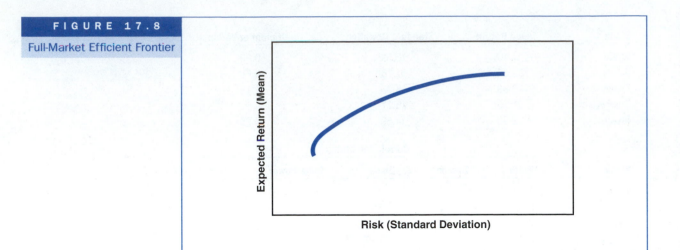

FIGURE 17.8

Full-Market Efficient Frontier

stocks will be included in all, or even any, efficient portfolios. The makeup of an efficient portfolio depends on the risk/return characteristics of the individual securities as well as the correlations between them.

By definition, remember, any portfolio that lies along the efficient frontier maximizes return for a given risk level and minimizes risk for a given return. To check trade-off relationship, let's compare the equally weighted portfolio to portfolios that lie along the efficient frontier. The equally weighted portfolio has about the same return as portfolio 2 (23.43% versus 23.29%) but a higher standard deviation (14.03% versus 10.95%). Similarly, the equally weighted portfolio has about the same standard deviation as portfolio 5 (14.03% versus 14.13%) but a lower mean return (23.43% versus 26.53%). Thus, most risk-averse investors would choose portfolio 2 or portfolio 5 over the equally weighted portfolio, because the efficient portfolios offer superior risk/return trade-offs. We cannot say, however, that risk-averse investors would choose portfolio 2 over portfolio 5, or vice versa.

This example considered only five stocks. Could an efficient frontier be computed for all publicly traded stocks? If so, what would its shape look like? The answer to the first question is yes; even though the amount of data required would be enormous, the mathematical process would be the same. As for the shape, most agree that the full-market efficient frontier would look something like Figure 17.8. It starts at the minimum risk portfolio and extends upward and to the right.

IMPLICATIONS FOR INVESTORS

Chapter 17 taught us that we must invest in several stocks to benefit from diversification. Also, we learned that a lower correlation (lower than 1.0) between securities gives us greater diversification benefits. However, we also found that by naively or randomly choosing 20 securities, we can achieve most of the benefits of diversification. Of course, many investors do not have the capital to invest in many stocks. Perhaps, this reason explains why mutual funds are so popular. They created a niche in the investment market by obtaining funds from several investors who may not have the ability to purchase several stocks. Mutual funds

INVESTMENT INSIGHT

Should Companies Diversify?

There are many stated reasons for why one company will acquire, or merge with, another company. In some acquisitions, companies acquire suppliers of key raw materials. In others, companies acquire competitors. In still others, companies will make acquisitions to fill in holes in their product lines. These are legitimate reasons for making an acquisition. However, sometimes, companies make acquisitions for no other reason than "diversification." In other words, the buyer purchases another company in an unrelated business. History is replete with examples of diversification-driven acquisitions. For example, during the 1980s, Philip Morris, now called Altria, spent billions of dollars acquiring two food companies, General Foods and Kraft, in an attempt to "diversify" away from tobacco.

What's the justification for a diversification-driven acquisition? The acquisition, presumably, will reduce the overall risk of the buying firm. Investors value diversification—we've discussed the benefits of diversification extensively—and will be willing to pay a premium for a diversified company. As a result, the buyer's stock price will rise. So, the acquisition creates value.

Well, that's the theory. The reality is often quite different. Although there are obvious benefits to diversification, it's important to remember that investors can easily diversify on their own. For an investor, much of the benefits of diversification can be achieved through something as simple as investing in shares of a mutual fund. So, why would an investor pay a premium for a diversified company? Good question. The answer is, investors probably wouldn't in most cases.

Not only can investors diversify more easily than companies, it is also much cheaper for an investor to diversify than it is for a company to diversify through acquisitions. The costs of investing in most mutual funds for an investor are relatively small. On the other hand, in order to acquire another company, the buyer has the offer shareholders of that company a price that is higher than the current market price (this is referred to as the merger premium). Altria paid shareholders of General Foods and Kraft billions of dollars in premiums.

The bottom line is that if the only motive for an acquisition is diversification, the acquisition is unlikely to add much value. In fact, these types of acquisitions more often than not reduce value. While Altria has stubbornly stuck to its "diversification" strategy, though it did spin off some of its stake in Kraft General Foods, there still are many analysts outside the company who believe that Altria is worth more broken up. In other words, the company would be worth more if its tobacco and food businesses were split up into two separate companies. Indeed, companies as diverse as AT&T, General Motors, and Kodak have recently sold businesses they acquired during attempts at "diversification."

Questions for Critical Thinking

1. Explain why a rational investor wouldn't normally pay a premium for shares of a diversified company.
2. Johnson & Johnson is a diversified health care company, something many analysts cite as a strength. Most believe the company's diversification efforts have created real value for shareholders. Why is a firm such as Johnson & Johnson an exception to notion that companies shouldn't diversify?

---

are ways in which resources (funds and talent) are pulled together so that all investors who purchase mutual funds are investing in several stocks via the funds.

The notion that risk-averse investors will invest in portfolios with optimal risk/return trade-offs is used in the next chapter to develop a risk/return relationship for securities. Chapter 18 provides a way to quantify security risk and develops a model called the capital asset pricing model (CAPM) to relate risk to return. You may ask, why is risk assessment important to security analysis? Only by quantifying a stock's risk can one determine a reasonable expected return (via CAPM) for the stock and then compare the predicted return with the CAPM required return to decide whether it is a good investment. Chapter 18 also covers security analysis and shows that it is similar to the fundamental analysis discussed in Chapter 14.

Now that you understand the concept of diversification, the Investment Insight on this page discusses whether companies should diversify. Particularly in the 1980s, firms acquired other companies in order to diversify. They reasoned that it reduced the overall risk of the acquiring firm and hence created value. It sounds reasonable; however, firm diversification by acquisition does not add value. Generally firms must pay more than the market price (premium) to gain control of another company, while investors can purchase shares in a company without paying a premium. Since investors can more easily and more cheaply diversify than companies, firm diversification generally will not add value to the acquiring firm.

SUMMARY

1. What is risk aversion and why are investors, as a group, risk averse?

Some simple lottery-type games suggest that most individuals are unlikely to play a risky game unless they receive some compensation for that risk. The reason is that most individuals probably have utility of wealth functions that increase at decreasing rates. Thus, a typical individual cares less about a $1 increase in wealth than a $1 decrease in wealth.

2. What are the general investment implications of risk aversion?

The most important implication of risk aversion is that risk becomes a dominant consideration in security selection. As a result, over time, a positive relationship should exist between risk and return. The historical record confirms that higher-risk investments, such as common stocks, returned more, on average, than lower-risk investments such as U.S. T-bills.

3. Why is standard deviation a good measure of risk, and how does an investor compute standard deviations for both individual securities and portfolios?

Among several alternative measures of risk, standard deviation is a good measure because it uses the entire return distribution and because it expresses, in a single statistic, the degree to which two securities have similar return distributions. We saw how to measure standard deviation for both individual securities and groups of securities (portfolios) using either historical return data (ex-post returns) or expected future returns (ex-ante returns). We looked at how to compare securities and portfolios based on their risk/return trade-offs.

4. What is the impact of security correlations on portfolio risk?

Several examples (with both real and concocted data) suggest that, although the expected (or mean) return for a portfolio is simply the weighted average of expected returns of the individual securities, the standard deviation of a portfolio is not a simple function of individual securities' standard deviations. The reason lies in the interrelationships (or correlations) between the return distributions of the securities.

5. What are the benefits of diversification, and how can investors achieve them?

Diversification can help investors achieve better risk/return trade-offs, reducing risk without significantly reducing expected returns. Diversification is possible as long as security returns are not perfectly correlated (their correlation coefficient is less than 1.0). Also, some actual historical data confirm that diversification is not a difficult goal for investors to achieve. Investors can easily diversify by spreading investment funds across several different investments. In doing so, they can eliminate firm-specific or diversifiable risk, leaving only market or systematic risk.

6. What is the meaning of efficient diversification and MPT?

We ended the chapter with a discussion of efficient diversification and the basics of MPT. MPT seeks the combinations of securities that offer optimal risk/return trade-offs, the so-called efficient frontier. An efficient frontier based on a set of five actual stocks verified that all portfolios that lie along the efficient frontier do indeed minimize risk for a given level of return and maximize return for a given level of risk.

MINI CASE 1

The purpose of this case is to provide practice calculating the mean, standard deviation, and CV, and to select stocks for a risk-averse investor. Open the Stock Returns worksheet in the Data Workbook. The file contains monthly returns for 50 stocks. To practice calculating the mean, standard deviation, and CV, and to select stocks for a risk-averse investor, use the data and a spreadsheet or calculator to answer the following questions:

1. What is the mean return for the first five stocks over the entire five-year period?
2. What is the standard deviation for each stock?
3. What is the CV for each stock? Which stock offers the best risk/return trade-off?
4. Graph the results of the five stocks on a risk/return graph (with ER-SD risk). Which one lies the farthest toward the northwest (upper-left) corner? What does its position imply?

MINI CASE 2

The purpose of this case is to create a two-security investment opportunity set. Open the Stock Returns worksheet in the Data Workbook. The file contains monthly returns for 50 stocks. Use the data on PepsiCo and Abbott Labs to answer the following questions.

1. What are the mean returns and standard deviations for both stocks?
2. What is the correlation coefficient for the pair?
3. Create a table like Table 17.5 and determine the portfolio return and standard deviation for various percentage holdings in PepsiCo and Abbott Labs. Start with 0% as X% for PepsiCo and change it by 10% increments.
4. Graph the results on an expected return/standard deviation graph.
5. Using the table and graph, find the proportional investment in PepsiCo and Abbott Labs with the minimum variance.
6. What are the exact proportions for the minimum variance portfolio?
7. What proportions would you invest in PepsiCo and Abbott Labs? Discuss.

REVIEW EXERCISES

1. How would you describe a risk-averse investor?
2. What does risk aversion imply about the long-term relationship between risk and return?
3. Suppose you have an option of investing $10,000 in T-bills to earn a guaranteed 4% annual return or investing in eBay, which recently went public. Suppose the stock has a 40% chance of earning 100% in a year and a 60% chance of going bankrupt within a year. Which investment would a risk-averse investor choose?
4. Suppose you invested in three stocks in 1999. Calculate the stocks' holding period returns:

Stock Name	Year-End 1998 Price	1998 Annual Dividends	Year-End 1999 Price
Toys "R" Us	$21.75	$0.00	$36.625
Tootsie Roll	39.625	0.29	36.25
Hewlett-Packard	83.75	0.48	96.00

5. Suppose you invested in the following three stocks during 1999. Calculate the stocks' holding period returns for

Stock Name	Year-End 1998 Price	1998 Annual Dividends	Year-End 1999 Price
Boeing	$78.375	$1.12	$ 92.875
Texaco	78.50	3.40	96.50
IBM	91.375	1.40	133.25

6. Suppose you invested in these three stocks during 1999. Calculate your holding period returns for the three stocks.

Stock Name	Year-End 1998 Price	1998 Annual Dividends	Year-End 1999 Price
STAR	$26.375	$0.89	$39.25
Duke Power	47.375	2.12	49.00
Disney	30.00	0.26	29.25

7. What is the difference between an actual holding period return and an expected return?
8. Suppose today is year t, last year was $t - 1$, and next year will be $t + 1$. The prices and disbursed cash dividends for a stock for these years are listed here:

Year	Price	Dividend
$t - 1$	$58	$1.00
t	65	1.50
$t + 1$	72	2.00

a. Calculate the actual holding period return.
b. Calculate the expected return.
9. Suppose today is year t, last year was $t - 1$, and next year will be $t + 1$. The prices and disbursed cash dividends for a stock for these years are listed here:

ear	Price	Dividend
$t - 1$	$42	$2.00
t	48	2.50
$t + 1$	53	3.00

a. Calculate the actual holding period return.
b. Calculate the expected return.
10. The following probabilities are given for each state of the economy and the respective stock returns:

		Returns	
State of Economy	Probability	Anheuser Busch	Toys "R" Us
Good	50%	+10%	+30%
Normal	30	+15	+20
Poor	20	+25	+ 5

a. What is the expected return for each state of the economy for each stock?
b. What is the standard deviation for each stock?

c. What is the portfolio expected return from investing 50% in each stock?
d. Calculate the correlation coefficient.
e. What is the portfolio standard deviation for an equally weighted portfolio of
    Anheuser Busch and Toys "R" Us?

11. The following probabilities are given for each state of the economy and the respective
    stock returns:

		Returns	
State of Economy	Probability	Johnson & Johnson	Disney
Good	70%	+ 5%	+40%
Normal	20	+12	+25
Poor	10	+20	+ 7

a. What is the expected return for each state of the economy for each stock?
b. What is the standard deviation for each stock?
c. What is the portfolio expected return from investing 50% in each stock?
d. Calculate the correlation coefficient.
e. What is the portfolio standard deviation for an equally weighted portfolio of
    Johnson & Johnson and Disney?

12. Five years of returns are given for PepsiCo and Hewlett-Packard:

Year	PepsiCo	Hewlett-Packard
1	32.22%	80.56%
2	27.24	65.41
3	20.88	11.10
4	29.47	28.14
5	56.70	69.39

a. Calculate the actual mean return for each stock.
b. Suppose someone invests 50% in each stock. Calculate the mean return for the
    portfolio using Equation 17.3 and again using Equation 17.6b.
c. Calculate the correlation coefficient between PepsiCo and Hewlett-Packard.
d. If someone invests 50% in each stock, calculate the portfolio standard deviation
    using Equation 17.5 and again using Equation 17.11.

13. Suppose you decided to invest 20% in PepsiCo and 70% in Hewlett-Packard. Using
    the data from Question 12, find the portfolio return and standard deviation.

14. Five years of returns are given for Toys "R" Us and Tootsie Roll:

Year	Toys "R" Us	Tootsie Roll
1	14.82%	21.45%
2	16.20	12.18
3	6.17	−6.24
4	−25.08	−10.18
5	−28.98	33.61

a. Calculate the actual mean return for each stock.
b. Suppose someone invests 20% in Toys "R" Us and 80% in Tootsie Roll.
    Calculate the mean return for the portfolio using Equation 17.3 and again using
    Equation 17.6b.

    c.   Calculate the correlation coefficient between Toys "R" Us and Tootsie Roll.

    d.   If someone invests 20% in Toys "R" Us and 80% in Tootsie Roll, calculate the portfolio standard using Equation 17.5 and again using Equation 17.11.

15. Suppose you decided to invest 10% in Toys "R" Us and 90% in Tootsie Roll. Using the data from Question 14, calculate the portfolio return and standard deviation.

16. Five years of return data are given for IBM and Texaco:

Year	IBM	Texaco
1	7.21%	9.83%
2	−10.97	10.81
3	13.07	12.72
4	32.17	−2.75
5	25.71	37.43

    a.   Calculate the actual mean return for each stock.

    b.   Suppose someone invests 50% in each stock. Calculate the mean return for the portfolio using Equation 17.3 and again using Equation 17.6b.

    c.   Calculate the correlation coefficient between IBM and Texaco.

    d.   If someone invests 50% in each stock, calculate the portfolio standard deviation using Equation 17.5 and again using Equation 17.11.

17. Suppose you decide to invest 30% in IBM and 70% in Texaco. Using the information from Question 16, calculate the portfolio return and standard deviation.

18. Two stocks, A and B, have expected returns of 10% and 25% with standard deviations of 15% and 20%, respectively. The correlation coefficient is +0.30. If one invests 40% in stock A and 60% in B, what are the portfolio expected return and standard deviation?

19. Determine the proportional investment in stocks A and B from Question 18 that provides the minimum variance portfolio.

    a.   What is the expected return of the minimum variance portfolio?

    b.   What is the standard deviation of the minimum variance portfolio?

20. Compare the two portfolios in Questions 18 and 19. Is one preferred over the other? Explain.

21. Two stocks, J and K, have expected returns of 20% and 30% with standard deviations of 25% and 35%, respectively. The correlation coefficient is −0.20. If one invests 30% in stock J and 70% in stock K, what are the portfolio expected return and standard deviation?

22. Determine the proportional investment in stocks J and K from Question 21 that provides the minimum variance portfolio.

    a.   What is the expected return of the minimum variance portfolio?

    b.   What is the standard deviation of the minimum variance portfolio?

23. Compare the two portfolios from Questions 21 and 22. Is one preferred over the other? Explain.

24. Suppose the two stocks, A and E, in Chapter 17 have a correlation coefficient equal to 0.0. Determine the proportional holdings in A and E that would give the minimum variance portfolio.

    a.   What is the portfolio's expected return?

    b.   What is the portfolio's standard deviation?

25. Suppose the two stocks, A and E, in Chapter 17 have a correlation coefficient equal to −1.0. Determine the proportional holdings in A and E that would give the minimum variance portfolio.

    a.   What is the portfolio's expected return?

    b.   What is the portfolio's standard deviation?

26. Suppose that two stocks, X and Y, have the following mean returns and standard deviations. The correlation between the two stocks is −0.50.

Stock	Mean Return	Standard Deviation
X	15%	8%
Y	25	14

Graph an investment opportunity set for these two stocks.
  a. Estimate the proportions of X and Y that make up the minimum variance portfolio from the graph.
  b. Calculate the proportions of X and Y that make up the minimum variance portfolio using Equation 17.12. How close was your estimate?

27. Suppose that two stocks, L and M, have the following mean returns and standard deviations. The correlation between the two stocks is 10.15.

Stock	Mean Return	Standard Deviation
L	13%	15%
M	21	25

Graph an investment opportunity set for these two stocks.
  a. Estimate the proportions of L and M that make up the minimum variance portfolio from the graph.
  b. Calculate the proportions of L and M that make up the minimum variance portfolio using Equation 17.12. How close was your estimate?

28. Explain why the correlation coefficients between securities are the key determinants of a portfolio's degree of diversification.

29. Suppose three stocks have the following risk and return characteristics:

Stock	Expected Return	Standard Deviation
X	0.05	0.08
Y	0.12	0.15
Z	0.12	0.15

The correlations between X and each of the other stocks are

$CORR(X,Y) = +0.35$
$CORR(X,Z) = -0.35$

  a. Based on portfolio theory, which combination, XY or XZ, is expected to have greater diversification benefits? Explain.
  b. Now, graph an investment opportunity set for X and Y versus X and Z.
  c. Do any combinations of XY dominate XZ? If so, show your answer on the investment opportunities on the risk/return graph.

30. Suppose four stocks have the following risk and return characteristics:

Stock	Expected Return	Standard Deviation
A	0.10	0.05
B	0.20	0.10
C	0.20	0.10
D	0.20	0.10

The correlations between A and each of the other stocks are

CORR(A,B) = +1.0
CORR(A,C) = +0.50
CORR(A,D) = −0.90

Graph an investment opportunity set for A and B, A and C, and A and D by the process described in Chapter 17. Which combination offers the greatest diversification benefits? Explain.

31. Suppose three stocks have the following risk and return characteristics:

Stock	Expected Return	Standard Deviation
J	0.15	0.15
K	0.35	0.30
L	0.25	0.30

The correlation coefficients between J and each of the other stocks are

CORR(J,K) = +0.05
CORR(J,L) = −0.15

Graph the investment opportunity sets for each portfolio, JK and JL. Over what proportional holdings does portfolio JK dominate JL? Do any combinations of proportional holdings show JL dominating JK? Show your answers on the graph and indicate the approximate proportional holdings for each portfolio.

32. What is the difference between market risk and firm-specific risk? Name two other terms for market risk. Name two other terms for firm-specific risk.

33. Suppose a manager of a fund must decide which of two stocks, B or C, to combine with stock A. The portfolio will hold 50% in A and 50% in B or C. The stocks' expected returns and risk characteristics are given here:

Stock	Expected Return	Standard Deviation	Coefficient of Variation
A	15%	15%	1.00
B	20	10	0.50
C	20	15	0.75

The correlation coefficient CORR(A,B) is +0.90 and CORR(A,C) equals −0.80. The manager concludes that B has a lower risk (and CV), so it is the obvious choice. Do you agree or disagree? Explain why.

34. Suppose a portfolio manager must decide which of two stocks, D or E, to combine with stock F. The portfolio will hold 40% in stock F and 60% in D or E. The stocks' expected returns and risk characteristics are given here:

Stock	Expected Return	Standard Deviation	Coefficient of Variation
F	12%	18%	1.50
D	24	30	1.25
E	24	28	1.17

The correlation coefficient CORR(D,F) is +0.50 and CORR(F,E) equals +0.00. The manager concludes that E has a lower risk and CV, so it is the obvious choice. Do you agree or disagree? Explain why. Show calculations to support your explanation.

CRITICAL THINKING EXERCISES

1. Open the Stock Price worksheet in the Data Workbook. The file contains month-end prices for STAR, KKD, and YHOO.
   a. Create a column to calculate the holding period return for each month for each stock.
   b. Calculate the mean return and standard deviation using the Excel spreadsheet common =AVERAGE(:) to calculate the mean and =STDEV(:) to calculate the standard deviation for the stock.
   c. Check to see that your results match the results presented in the file.
   d. Calculate a portfolio return with one-third proportional holdings in each stock, STAR, KKD, and YHOO. Create a column to calculate each monthly portfolio return, then calculate the portfolio mean and standard deviation. Now, calculate the portfolio mean and standard using Equations 17.3 and 17.14. Check your results with the results presented in the file.
2. Open the Stock Returns worksheet in the Data Workbook. The file contains monthly returns for many stocks. Use the data in the file choose five stocks (together in class) and answer the following questions.
   a. What are the mean returns, standard deviations, and pairwise correlation coefficients for the stocks?
   b. Display the five stocks' mean returns and standard deviation risk on a return-standard deviation risk graph.
   c. Choose two stocks and discuss your reasons for your choices.
   d. Create at least 10 portfolio combinations with your two stocks by varying the percentages invested in the two stocks. Remember, the percentages must sum to 100%.
   e. Which of your 10 portfolios appears to be the most "efficient" compared with the others? Justify your answer.

THE INTERNET INVESTOR

1. Find an Internet site that provides a chart of stock prices. Choose one Internet stock and one utility stock. Obtain daily stock price quotes for two months.
   a. Calculate daily holding period periods for each stock.
   b. Graph a distribution like Figure 17.1 where the x axis represents holding period returns in increments of 1% (that is, 0% to 1%, 1% to 2%, etc.) and the y axis represents the number of days the stock return fell in each percentage increment. Create one distribution for the Internet stock and another for the utility stock on the same graph.
   c. Which stock distributions appear riskier? Explain.
   d. Calculate range, number of days with negative returns, and standard deviation for each stock. Do these measures agree with your assessment in part (c)?
   e. Explain which measure provides more information.
2. Find an Internet site that provides historical monthly stock prices, starting from the most current month ended and going back 24 months. Possible sites are Yahoo (stock quotes), Microsoft Explorer, and AOL.
   a. Obtain closing stock prices (adjust for stock splits) and dividends for three stocks.
   b. Calculate monthly holding period returns, mean, and standard deviation for each stock.
   c. Graph the three stocks on a return-standard deviation risk graph.
   d. Use a spreadsheet to create an investment opportunity set with the three stocks.
   e. What combinations of these stocks would you invest in? Explain why.

18

Capital Asset Pricing Theory

PREVIOUSLY . . .

We developed portfolio theory and found that all rational risk-averse investors will diversify by holding several securities. Efficient diversification or attaining the highest return for the lowest risk can be created, and the choice of the risky portfolio is based on investor risk preference.

IN THIS CHAPTER . . .

We develop a method in which all rational risk-averse investors will choose portfolio *M*— labeled the market portfolio—as their choice of the risky portfolio. Given this premise, we are able to quantify security risk and develop the capital asset pricing model (CAPM). The CAPM can be used to value securities and conduct security analysis much like the fundamental analysis in Chapter 14.

TO COME . . .

Chapter 19 develops extensions of the CAPM as well as the arbitrage pricing theory (APT), which is another method to value securities. Chapter 19 can be omitted without loss of continuity. Chapter 20 applies the concepts developed in Chapter 18 to evaluate portfolios or mutual funds.

CHAPTER OBJECTIVES

After reading Chapter 18, you should be able to answer the following questions:

1. What is the capital market line (CML)?

2. How is the capital asset pricing model (CAPM) developed?

3. What is the difference between the standard deviation and beta risk measures?

4. How can an investor apply the CAPM to security analysis?

5. How do you estimate beta?

6. What are the good news and the bad news about beta?

In Chapter 17, we examined how a portfolio of securities can provide diversification, which offers the potential to reduce risk and increase return. In fact, we established that any rational investor would hold a diversified portfolio instead of one or two securities. This presumption raises the question: how can individual securities be priced when everyone holds combinations of securities? More specifically, you may be wondering how it will help with security selection, as discussed in Chapter 14.

Chapter 17 discussed securities only in the context of a portfolio. However, Chapter 17 developed two important ideas that link portfolio theory to a security risk/return relationship. It showed that risk-averse investors require higher returns to compensate them for risk. Further, investors who hold well-diversified portfolios eliminate firm-specific risk, so their only relevant risk is the market risk (also referred to as *systematic risk*).

This chapter develops techniques to measure market risk and security risk. By quantifying a security risk measure, we can determine a risk/return relationship for individual securities. The risk/return relationship is specified by the **capital asset pricing model (CAPM)**. It provides an objective way of determining the risk and return for each security in the context of portfolio diversification. The general notion presented in CAPM, that investors will accept higher risk only if compensated with higher returns, is also central to modern portfolio theory, as Chapter 17 showed.

> **capital asset pricing model (CAPM)**
>
> Equation that quantifies security risk and defines a risk/return relationship.

Before we embark on a development of the theory, let's discuss the assumptions. These assumptions are necessary to develop a model that provides a linear representation of the risk/return relationship; some assumptions are necessary to make decisions whereas others just simplify things. We admit that these assumptions may be unrealistic, but they help to simplify the model and to gain some insights on how security risk and return are related. Also, it is important to recognize that the value of the model resides in the insights it provides with respect to the real world and not in the realism of its assumptions. Later in Chapter 19, we discuss other developments of the model that relax some of the assumptions listed here; for now, however, we start by including all the assumptions to develop the original CAPM.

ASSUMPTIONS OF THE CAPITAL ASSET PRICING MODEL

Several assumptions are necessary in developing the capital asset pricing theory:

1. *Investors have homogeneous expectations.* This assumption says that everyone has equal information and the same perceptions about the securities and the market. It is necessary to ensure that everyone perceives the same efficient frontier. Otherwise, market equilibrium may not prevail.
2. *Capital markets are frictionless.* This assumption eliminates impediments that prevent investors from creating their optimal portfolios. It prevents additional costs or constraints (which may vary among investors) from affecting investment decisions to create frictionless markets. These listed restrictions include the following:
   a. No transaction costs, brokerage fees, or bid/ask spread fees exist.
   b. No taxes are payable.
   c. Securities can be divided in any proportions investors want to optimize their portfolios.
   d. One person's trading activity will not affect prices.

3. *Investors are rational and seek to maximize their expected utility functions.* This assumption allows us to determine investment choices for a standard group of risk-averse investors.
4. *Investment is for one period only.* This assumption is important to prevent future investment strategies from affecting today's prices. For example, if investment horizons vary from 2 years to 20 years, it may affect investment choices (and prices) today.
5. *All investors can borrow or lend at the risk-free rate.* This assumption simplifies the risk/return relationship. Without it, the risk/return relationship may be nonlinear.[1]

EFFICIENT FRONTIER AND THE OPTIMAL RISKY PORTFOLIO

In Chapter 17, we learned that the efficient frontier represents a series of portfolios that provide the highest return for a given risk or the lowest risk for a given expected return. See Figure 18.1.

As expected, a security's expected return (ER_s) and standard deviation (SD_s) will be inferior to those at any point on the efficient frontier, and hence any security will lie below the efficient frontier. Although an individual security may lie below the efficient frontier, it may be part of one (or several) of the portfolios on the efficient frontier. It may represent 5% of the value of a portfolio and 8% of another portfolio that lie on the efficient frontier.

A rational investor will always choose a portfolio that lies on the efficient frontier, but which one? Remember, a portfolio on the efficient frontier provides the maximum return for a given risk level, so the answer depends on an individual's preference for risk and return. Earlier in Chapter 17, we discussed the investor's utility function (or curve). Two investors with different utility functions will choose different risky portfolios. Figure 18.2 combines the efficient frontier with two investors' utility curves.[2]

Investor A, who is highly risk averse, chooses P_5, which exposes the portfolio to relatively low risk. Investor B, who is less risk averse, chooses P_{10}, which is riskier but also provides a higher return.[3] This illustration is helpful, but practically speaking, utility curves are difficult to assess. More important, they do not provide an objective portfolio choice. The portfolio chosen (and the percentage invested in each security) will differ depending on the individual's utility curve. For example, investor A's choice of P_5 may consist of 2% in STAR, whereas investor B's choice of P_{10} may have 35% invested in STAR. Besides, how often have you been asked by your stockbroker to describe your utility function?

---

[1]Economists and finance academics hold a biased expectation that the risk/return relationship should be a linear relationship. Also, only with a linear relationship can we separate personal (utility function) decisions from objective investment decisions. This point will be clearer after we discuss the portfolio separation theorem.

[2]Assumption 3, that investors are rational and maximize their utility functions, allows us to make portfolio choices for investors with different utility functions. Given this assumption, an investor will choose a risky portfolio that maximizes his or her utility function.

[3]Investor A may be a retired, middle-income individual, whereas investor B may be someone wealthy, such as Bill Gates.

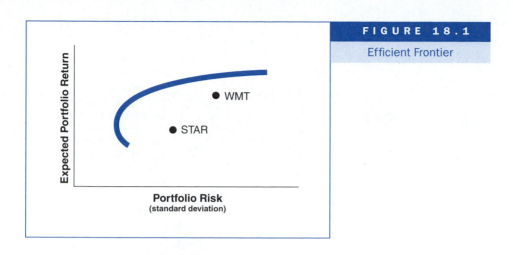

FIGURE 18.1

Efficient Frontier

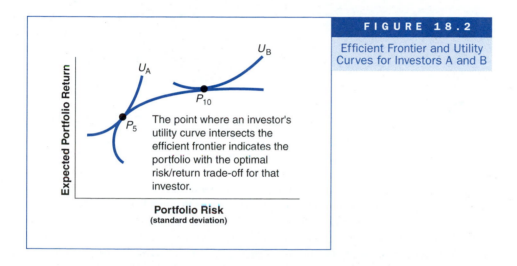

FIGURE 18.2

Efficient Frontier and Utility Curves for Investors A and B

Developing the Capital Market Line (CML)

To solve this problem, we introduce a risk-free asset, RF. The closest asset to a truly risk-free investment is a short-term U.S. Treasury bill. With a zero standard deviation, or risk, it lies on the y axis. Now, combine RF with a risky portfolio such as P_1. Figure 18.3 shows the combination between RF and P_1.

The combination of RF and P_1 is also a portfolio, and its expected return, ER_P, using Equation 17.6a, is calculated as follows:

$$ER_P = X(ER_{P_1}) + (1 - X)RF \tag{18.1}$$

where X is the proportion of wealth invested in the risky portfolio P_1 and $(1 - X)$ is the proportion invested in the risk-free asset RF. The standard deviation risk of the RF-P_1 combination can be calculated using Equation 17.11:

$$SD_P = [X^2 SD_{P_1}^2 + (1 - X)^2 SD_{RF}^2 + 2X(1 - X)SD_{P_1} SD_{RF} CORR(P_1, RF)]^{1/2}$$

FIGURE 18.3

Combination of the Risk-Free Asset RF and Risky Portfolios P_1 and P_2

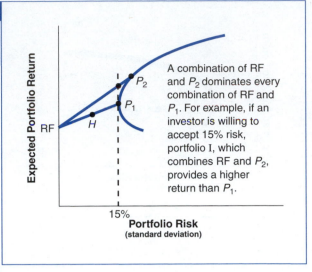

The last two terms equal zero because SD_{RF} equals zero by its definition, which leaves

$$SD_P = [X^2(SD_{P_1}^2)]^{1/2}$$
$$= X(SD_{P_1})$$

(18.2)

The standard deviation of the portfolio combination RF-P_1 is linear because the risk-free rate has a zero standard deviation.

The line between RF and P_1 can be interpreted in the same way as that between two-security combinations in Chapter 17. Point RF represents a 100% investment in the risk-free asset whereas point P_1 represents a 100% investment in the risky portfolio P_1. The halfway point, H, represents a 50% investment in each. Remember, investors want to maximize their expected returns for a given risk.

As shown in Figure 18.3, a combination of RF and P_2 dominates any point on the line created between RF and P_1. For example, suppose an investor is interested in maintaining a 15% risk level. He or she could invest 100% in P_1 or, better yet, invest 90% in P_2 and 10% in RF to reach point I. The P_2 and RF combination has the same 15% risk but a higher expected return, ER_P. Being rational, an investor would choose P_2 over P_1.

Of course, why stop there! Other combinations with RF, such as P_3, P_4, and so on, will dominate those before. As shown in Figure 18.4, portfolio M, where a tangent line from RF touches the efficient frontier, is the line that dominates any other line that can be drawn from RF to any point on the efficient frontier, even P_{10}. This line from RF to M is called the **capital market line (CML)**. The CML identifies all efficient portfolios and surpasses the old (curved) efficient frontier, except at point M. Recall that *efficient* means it has the highest expected return for a given risk, or the lowest risk for a given expected return. The CML is discussed in more detail later.

Like the earlier examples, the line represents percentage investment in RF and the risky portfolio M. For example, a point halfway between RF and M represents

capital market line (CML)

Line that describes the percentage holdings in the risk-free asset, RF, and the risky diversified market portfolio.

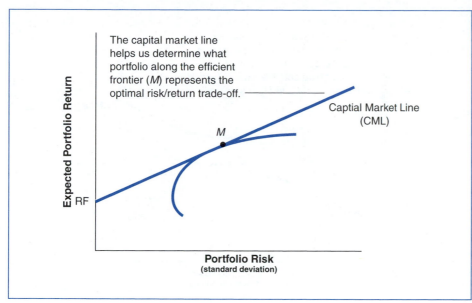

FIGURE 18.4

Combinations of the Risk-Free Asset RF and the Risky Portfolio *M*

The capital market line helps us determine what portfolio along the efficient frontier (*M*) represents the optimal risk/return trade-off.

Captial Market Line (CML)

M

RF

Expected Portfolio Return

Portfolio Risk
(standard deviation)

a 50% investment in RF and *M* each. Once an investor decides on a personally desirable combination of RF and *M*, he or she can calculate the expected portfolio return and its expected standard deviation risk by using Equations 18.1 and 18.2.[4] For 50% investments in each, the ER_P and SD_P are calculated as follows:

$$ER_P = (0.50)ER_M + (1 - 0.50)RF \tag{18.3}$$

$$SD_P = (0.50)SD_{P_1} \tag{18.4}$$

If RF equals 6% and ER_M equals 16% with an 8% SD_M, the portfolio expected return, ER_P, is 11% and SD_P is 4%.

$$ER_P = (0.50)(0.16) + (1 - 0.50)(0.06) = 0.11, \text{ or } 11\%$$
$$SD_P = (0.50)(0.08) = 0.04, \text{ or } 4\%$$

At point *M*, 100% is invested in the risky portfolio *M*. What about beyond point M? We defer this discussion until later to deal with the significance of the CML to investors who are choosing their optimal risky portfolios.

Remember the utility curves and how we determined which portfolio investors A and B would choose? A chose P_1 and B chose P_{10}. Now, recall from earlier discussions in Chapter 17 that investors gain utility as their utility curves move upward and to the left (toward the northwest). As shown in Figure 18.5, investor A's utility increases as the curve moves out from U_A to U'_A. U'_A is tangent to the CML and represents perhaps a 90% investment in *RF* and only 10% in the risky portfolio *M*. As we observed earlier, investor A is risk averse, choosing

---

[4]When using Equations 18.1 and 18.2, it is easiest to convert all percentages into decimals and later convert back to percentages if you prefer.

FIGURE 18.5

CML and Individual Utility
Curves

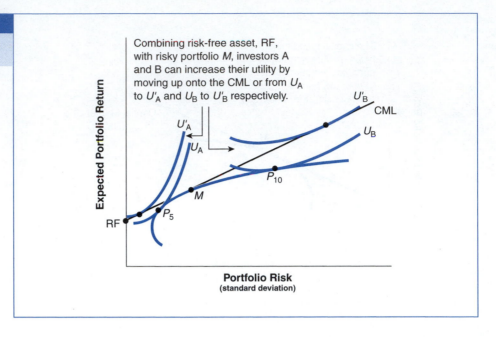

between RF and *M* consistently with his or her conservative utility function.
What about investor B?

B also increases his or her utility by moving from U_B to U'_B. B chooses to
invest −100% in RF and 200% in the risky portfolio *M*. What does it mean to
invest a negative percentage in RF? To be beyond *M*, it means that an investor
borrowed at the risk-free rate RF and invested more than 100% in portfolio *M*.
(A negative percentage allocation means borrowing.) In reality, it just means that
a person bought on margin or borrowed money to invest more wealth than he or
she has. Investor B is borrowing 100% at the risk-free rate and investing twice his
or her wealth (200%) in portfolio *M*. If $100 represents his or her invested
wealth, B borrows an additional $100 and invests $200 in *M*. This example
implies a 50% margin, borrowing half of what is invested. Investor B is definitely
not as risk averse as A and is willing to take more risk for a higher return.

Using the examples of investors A and B and their choices, we can segment
the CML between lenders and borrowers. For that reason, the CML is sometimes
called the **borrowing-lending line**.[5] The section between RF and *M* is called the
lending line, and beyond *M*, it is called the *borrowing line*. Why? Let's go back to
investor A—who invested 90% in RF and 10% in *M*. If A invests in RF, he or she
is basically lending money at the risk-free rate. Therefore, by investing 90% of his
or her wealth in RF, A is lending 90% of his or her wealth. Investor B, by investing −100% of his or her wealth in RF, is borrowing 100% of his or her wealth at
the risk-free rate. Figure 18.6 shows how the CML is segmented between lenders
and borrowers.

borrowing-lending line

Any point to the left of *M* on the
CML implies lending at RF, and
any point to the right of *M* on the
CML implies borrowing at RF.

---

[5]The CML relies on assumption 5, that everyone can borrow at the same rate as they lend, RF; otherwise, the borrowing-lending would be nonlinear.

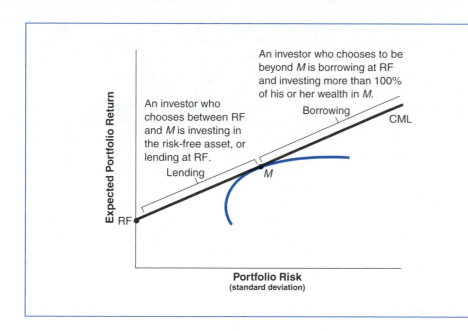

FIGURE 18.6

CML: The Borrowing-Lending Line

At this point, we make an important discovery. Both investors A and B will now choose to invest in the risky portfolio M along with the risk-free asset RF. Although they are diametrically different in their risk preferences, both investors will now choose M instead of P_1 or P_{10}. Notice that assumption 1 (homogeneous expectations) is critical here. If investors did not have homogeneous expectations, then even with the risk-free asset, investors A and B may perceive different efficient frontiers and choose different risky portfolios instead of M. Also, assumption 2 (frictionless markets) is necessary because impediments might lead investors to perceive different efficient frontiers based on their tax brackets or transaction fees.

Now, going back to the choice of portfolio M, we resolved the earlier problem of dealing with utility curves and different risk preferences. It now seems that all investors will choose the risky portfolio M; not P_1, P_2, P_5, or P_{10}, but M! This discovery is profound because we can now separate the risky portfolio choice from the subjective individual utility functions. This premise, called the **portfolio separation theorem**, states:

Individuals choose the risky portfolio independently of their utility functions. All risk-averse investors choose the same risky portfolio regardless of utility functions, then they decide on the combination of RF and the risky portfolio, based on their utility functions.

For example, investors A and B chose portfolio M as their risky portfolio despite their differences in risk aversion because M combined with RF is efficient. (It has the highest expected return for a given risk or the lowest risk for a given expected return.) Once M is chosen, the proportion (X) invested in RF and the balance invested in M depend on risk preference; how much risk is someone willing to take for a higher return? A invested only 10% in portfolio M, whereas B invested a whopping 200% in M. Note that their portfolio combinations of RF and M will have different ER_P and SD_P values, which can be calculated using Equations 18.1 and 18.2.

portfolio separation theorem

Allows investors to separate the decision of selecting the risky portfolio from the investor's risk preference (or utility curve).

The portfolio separation theorem emphasizes the importance of M as the only risky portfolio chosen by *all* investors. Because M is the only risky portfolio, it must include all traded assets from art, stamps, and coins to financial securities. If so, it is appropriate to call it the market portfolio. Also, if it contains all traded assets, it must be well diversified.

Furthermore, theoretically, the securities in the market portfolio are value weights of each security's proportion in the market portfolio. It is calculated as the security's total market value (price per share times the number of shares outstanding) divided by the total market value of all the securities in M. In practice, however, a proxy such as the Standard & Poor's (S&P) 500 Index, which is considered to be well diversified, substitutes for the market portfolio.

Finally, the CML that combines RF and M holds an important position, too. It defines all efficient portfolios, which are just combinations of RF and M. It can also be interpreted as a unique linear relationship between standard deviation risk, SD_P, and its expected return, ER_P, for all the RF-M choices for individuals. The equation of the CML is

$$ER_P = RF + \left[\frac{ER_M - RF}{SD_M} \right] SD_P \qquad (18.5)$$

where the y intercept (where the CML crosses the y axis) is RF and the slope equals $(ER_M - RF)/SD_M$. Keep this point in mind; it will be important in developing the CAPM.

Now, we have almost reached our goal, to find a model that shows how securities are priced. Recall that it is called the CAPM.

RECAPRECAP

The CML defines efficient combinations of RF and portfolio M. It defines only one optimal risky portfolio, M; all investors prefer to combine M with the risk-free asset RF. If M is preferred by all rational risk-averse investors, then it must be the market portfolio.

1. Suppose you prefer to invest 30% in portfolio M and 70% in the risk-free asset. If ER_M equals 16% and RF equals 6%, what is your portfolio's expected return, ER_P?
2. For the portfolio in Question 1, what is the portfolio risk, SD_P, if SD_M equals 8%?

So far, we developed only the portfolio M and justified why everyone will invest in M. If all rational risk-averse investors prefer only one risky portfolio, M (which is the market portfolio), then the risk that each security contributes to M is the only relevant risk for a security. The relevant risk of securities such as STAR, WMT, and DUKE is just what they contribute to M's risk. Figure 18.7 shows how all those securities are parts of the market portfolio M; and the next section discusses how to measure their risk, defined as each security's risk contribution to the market portfolio's risk.

CAPITAL ASSET PRICING MODEL

M must contain all tradable securities, as everyone invests only in M, and it must be well diversified. We also know from Chapter 17 that if everyone invests in a well-diversified portfolio, then only market risk is relevant. Any firm-specific risk is eliminated purely through portfolio diversification. Because everyone invests in

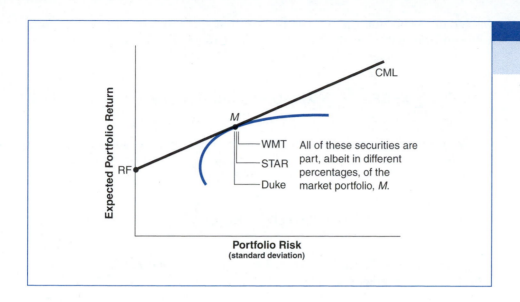

FIGURE 18.7

CML and Individual Securities

a well-diversified portfolio, M, by determining portfolio M's market risk, investors will know the risk level of their investment. Portfolio M's risk can be written as

Portfolio M's risk = Market risk

Further, because M is the only risky portfolio to consider, the relevant risk for each security is the amount of risk it contributes to M, or the security's market risk, ignoring firm-specific risk. If each security risk is stated as

Security risk = Total risk
= Market risk + Firm-specific risk

then we could restate portfolio M's market risk as

$$\text{Portfolio } M\text{'s risk} = \left(\begin{array}{c}\text{Security 1's} \\ \text{market risk}\end{array} + \begin{array}{c}\text{Security 2's} \\ \text{market risk}\end{array} + \cdots + \begin{array}{c}\text{Security } N\text{'s} \\ \text{market risk}\end{array}\right)$$

We are no longer interested in total risk (or standard deviation) of a security but in its risk contribution to the larger market portfolio.

Also, recall from Chapter 17 that, as the number of securities (N) increases, the security risk, SD, falls virtually to zero; the only relevant risk then is the security's covariance with the other securities in a well-diversified portfolio (in this case, the market portfolio M). We need to develop a measure of the security's risk contribution to the market portfolio, which we will call the security's relative risk measure.

Developing a Relative Risk Measure

Recall that Equation 17.13 defined the total risk of any portfolio p as

$$SD_P = \left[\sum_{i=1}^{N} X_i^2 SD_i^2 + \sum_{i=1}^{N}\sum_{j=1}^{N} X_i X_j COV(i,j)\right]^{1/2} \quad i \neq j$$

Instead of any portfolio, p, we will use Equation 17.13 to define the market portfolio and the risk contribution of security i to M. First, take the square of Equation 17.13 to ignore the square root sign. Rewrite it as

$$\text{SD}_P^2 = \sum_{i=1}^{N} X_i^2 \text{SD}_i^2 + \sum_{i=1}^{N} \sum_{j=1}^{N} X_i X_j \text{SD}_i \text{SD}_j \text{CORR}(i,j) \quad i \neq j \tag{18.6}$$

We will further rewrite Equation 18.6 by separating the summation over i from the summation over j, which adds up all the securities to make portfolio M. Now, we can identify security i's contribution to the market portfolio M as

$$\text{SD}_M^2 = \sum_{i=1}^{N} X_i \left[X_i \text{SD}_i^2 + \sum_{j=1}^{N} X_j \text{SD}_i \text{SD}_j \text{CORR}(i,j) \right] \tag{18.7}$$

Let's examine the term in brackets, which equals the total risk contribution of security i to the market portfolio M:

$$\begin{array}{c} \textbf{Total risk contribution} \\ \textbf{of security } i \end{array} = \left[X_i \text{SD}_i^2 + \sum_{j=1}^{N} X_j \text{SD}_i \text{SD}_j \text{CORR}(i,j) \right] \tag{18.8}$$

Equation 18.8 represents the total risk contribution of security i to the market portfolio M, in which the first term is $X_i \text{SD}_i^2$ and the second term, $X_j \text{SD}_i \text{SD}_j \text{CORR}(i, j)$, equals $X_j \text{COV}(i, j)$.[6] The first term measures the contribution of security i's total risk, multiplied by the proportion of security i in M; the second term measures the amount of risk security i contributes *to* security j and security j's proportion in portfolio M. By summing the $\text{COV}(i, j)$ over j

$$\left[\sum_{j=1}^{N} X_j \text{COV}(i,j) \right]$$

we are capturing how security i contributes to the risk of each of the other securities that make up the market portfolio M. The two terms together capture the total risk of security i in the market portfolio.

Now suppose that we want to measure the total risk of security i relative to the market portfolio risk, SD_M^2. Equation 18.8 can be rewritten as

$$\begin{array}{c} \textbf{Relative risk contribution} \\ \textbf{of security } i \end{array} = \dfrac{\textbf{Total risk contribution of security } i}{\textbf{Total risk of market portfolio } M}$$

$$= \frac{X_i \text{SD}_i^2}{\text{SD}_M^2} + \frac{\sum\limits_{j=1}^{N} X_j \text{SD}_i \text{SD}_j \text{CORR}(i,j)}{\text{SD}_M^2} \tag{18.9}$$

---

[6]Remember that $\text{CORR}(i,j)$ is defined as $\text{CORR}(i,j) = [\text{COV}(i,j)/(\text{SD}_i)(\text{SD}_j)]$, so we can rearrange terms and have $\text{COV}(i,j) = (\text{SD}_i)(\text{SD}_j)\text{CORR}(i,j)$.

Similar to the portfolio risk equation (Equation 17.13), this equation states that the relative security risk is composed of two types of risk: total risk of security i (SD_i^2) and its correlation (or covariance) with other securities. Because the market portfolio M consists of several thousand securities, each security's contribution, denoted by X_i, is very small, which makes $X_i SD_i^2 / SD_M^2$ virtually equal to zero. (Remember, this power of diversification was discussed in Chapter 17.)

The relative risk contribution of security i is then calculated as follows:

$$\text{Relative risk contribution of security } i = 0 + \frac{\sum_{j=1}^{N} X_j SD_i SD_j CORR(i,j)}{SD_M^2} \tag{18.10}$$

If the summation is taken over all securities j, it equals the risk of the market portfolio, and Equation 18.10 becomes

$$\text{Relative risk contribution of security } i = 0 + \frac{SD_i[SD_M CORR(i, M)]}{SD_M^2}$$
$$= \frac{SD_i}{SD_M} CORR(i, M) = \beta_i \tag{18.11}$$

Equation 18.11 says that the relative risk of security i equals security i's total risk relative to the market portfolio risk (SD_i/SD_M) multiplied by security i's risk contribution to the larger portfolio, M, measured by $CORR(i, M)$. This relative risk definition is better known as **beta**.

Because $CORR(i,M) = COV(i,M)/SD_i SD_M$, we can also rewrite Equation 18.11 as

beta

Measures the security risk or its volatility relative to the market portfolio. If beta is greater than 1.0, it is riskier than the market.

$$\text{Relative risk contribution of security } i = \frac{COV(i, M)}{SD_M^2} = \beta_i \tag{18.12}$$

Another definition of beta, β_i, is also used for security i. The relative risk contribution of security i equals β_i.

Now let's determine the beta for the market portfolio M. Using Equation 18.11,

$$\beta_M = \frac{SD_M}{SD_M} CORR(M,M)$$

Any variable must be perfectly correlated with itself, or $CORR(M,M) = +1.0$, so the market portfolio beta, β_M, equals 1.0. Because the market portfolio is a value-weighted average of all the traded securities, it says that an average security risk contribution is equal to 1.0. If security i's beta β_i is greater than 1.0, security i's risk contribution is higher than the average security or the market portfolio risk. If β_i is less than 1.0, then its risk contribution is less than the average security or the market portfolio risk. The market portfolio's beta can be used as a reference point for security risk. Let's continue our discussion on beta to obtain an intuitive feel about it and determine how to interpret it.

Understanding Beta

This section discusses the meaning and interpretation of beta. We start with a list of four ways to view beta and then discuss the difference between beta and the standard deviation risk (or total risk) of a stock.

1. All security betas are measured relative to the market portfolio beta, which equals 1.0. If a security beta is greater than 1.0, its risk is greater than the market portfolio's risk; if it is less than 1.0, its risk is less than the market portfolio's. The market beta of 1.0 serves as a reference point for security betas.
2. Alternatively, we can interpret a beta greater than 1.0 to mean that the security contributes more than average risk to the well-diversified market portfolio.
3. Also, the numerical value of beta, such as STAR's beta of 0.80, implies something about returns. If the return on the market portfolio changes by 1%, then STAR's return will move up or down by 0.80%. Therefore, high beta securities returns move more aggressively than the market portfolio whereas low beta securities are more conservative. Money managers create strategies to invest heavily in high beta stocks in bull markets. Using the same analogy, many will invest in money markets (risk-free assets) or low beta stocks when they expect bear markets or unpredictable conditions.
4. Finally because beta is a relative measure, the index used as a proxy for the market portfolio can make a big difference in the beta estimate. For example, if IBM were measured relative to the Dow Jones Industrial Average (DJIA), it would be closely correlated because the Dow is a price index made up of only 30 stocks. When the DJIA hit 6,319 on November 15, 1996, it was largely due to an eight point jump in IBM stock.[7] However, if IBM's beta is measured relative to the Wilshire 5000 index, IBM's beta may show less correlation, and so the beta estimate will be less than 1.0 measured relative to the Dow. This example just says that it is important to know what market index serves as a proxy for the market to measure each security beta.

Two Types of Risk Revisited Next, let's examine intuitively how to use the beta instead of standard deviation risk. In Chapter 17, we discussed two types of risk: market risk and firm-specific risk. Also, remember that a security's total risk is composed of market risk plus firm-specific risk. Now, we can define the relative market risk for a security as its beta, so the total risk of a security return can be divided into beta and firm-specific risk. Beta is also referred to as the systematic or nondiversifiable risk; it is the component of a security's risk that is associated with the market portfolio, M. Alternatively, it is the part of the security's risk that is inherent in the market, and the extent to which it moves with the system; hence, this systematic risk cannot be diversified away. By contrast, the firm-specific risk, or risk unique to the firm, can be eliminated simply by holding a well-diversified portfolio such as M; this risk is diversifiable risk. Often-cited sources of firm-specific risk are labor disputes or negotiations, product tampering (as in the Tylenol and Pepsi episodes), resignations of CEOs, and awards of government contracts.

Now, let's contrast investment decisions made by total risk versus beta. Suppose STAR's total risk, SD_{STAR}, is 10%, and Wal-Mart's, SD_{WMT}, equals 15%.

---

[7]*The Wall Street Journal,* November 19, 1999, pp. C1, C10.

Assume, for simplicity, that the expected return equals 20% for both securities. Based on what we said in Chapter 17, a risk-averse, rational single-security investor would prefer STAR with 10% total risk. However, now that the investor can hold a well-diversified portfolio such as M, the total risk is no longer relevant. Only the systematic risk (beta) or the risk that the security contributes to the large portfolio M is relevant.[8]

Suppose that total risk can be decomposed as follows for STAR and Wal-Mart:

$$\mathrm{SD_{STAR}} = 10\% \left\langle \begin{array}{l} \text{Systematic risk} = 8\% \\ \text{Diversifiable risk} = 2\% \end{array} \right.$$

$$\mathrm{SD_{WMT}} = 15\% \left\langle \begin{array}{l} \text{Systematic risk} = 4\% \\ \text{Diversifiable risk} = 11\% \end{array} \right.$$

Given that the two securities have the same expected return, an investor naively using the total risk measure would incorrectly choose STAR (which has a lower SD of 10%) when, in fact, Wal-Mart has a lower systematic risk of 4% as compared with STAR's 8%.

CAPM DERIVATION

A risk/return measure for securities can be developed now that we have an intuitive feel for the security's relative risk contribution. To take that final step to derive the CAPM, let's go back to the investment choice and reiterate some points. Remember, all risk-averse investors will invest in one risky portfolio, M. If so, portfolio M must be the market portfolio consisting of all traded securities. Recall that M is optimal because it lies on the CML and is preferred over all other risky portfolios. Now what does it take for M to be on the CML? To lie on the CML, it must have the same slope as the CML. From Equation 18.5,

$$\text{Slope of CML} = \frac{(ER_M - RF)}{SD_M}$$

This slope is interpreted as the market portfolio's ratio of reward $(ER_M - RF)$ to risk (SD_M).

What is the reward-to-risk ratio for a security? Let's first discuss how to measure reward for securities. Then we will cover risk.

Reward for Investing in a Security In Chapter 17, we found that risk-averse investors are enticed to invest in risky securities only if they are compensated for risk. Chapter 1 defined this risk/return relationship as

$$ER_i = RF + \text{Risk premium}$$

---

[8]We use systematic risk, defined as $\beta_i(SD_M)$, instead of beta because it provides a percentage risk measure comparable with total risk (which also is in percentage terms). Beta is a risk measured relative to the market portfolio, so it is an absolute number and cannot be compared with total risk given as a percentage.

The compensation for accepting risk is calculated as

$$ER_i - RF = \text{Risk premium}$$

The left side of the equation, $(ER_i - RF)$, is the reward for accepting risk. Now, how do we measure security risk?

Security Risk Recall that security i's risk is only relevant to the extent that it contributes to the market portfolio, M. That risk contribution is beta, β_i, also known as systematic risk, can also be defined as $\beta_i SD_M$. The term $\beta_i SD_M$ redefines security i's risk contribution to the market portfolio as a percentage rather than an absolute number, like beta. For example, if β_i equals 1.2 and SD_M equals 20%, security i's percentage risk contribution equals $\beta_i SD_M$ or $(1.2)(0.20) = 0.24$, or 24%. Now, we can define reward-to-risk ratios for a security.

Security's Reward-to-Risk Ratio Using this definition of the risk contribution of security i, its reward-to-risk ratio can be defined as

$$\text{Security } i\text{'s reward-to-risk ratio} = \frac{ER_i - RF}{\beta_i SD_M}$$

Because security i is part of the larger market portfolio, M, its reward-to-risk ratio must equal M's reward-to-risk ratio from the CML:

$$\frac{(ER_i - RF)}{\beta_i SD_M} = \frac{(ER_M - RF)}{SD_M} \tag{18.13}$$

Why? Remember that $\beta_i SD_M$ is security i's risk contribution to M. As this contribution increases, its reward must increase proportionately; otherwise M's reward-to-risk ratio would change and may no longer be optimal (that is, may no longer lie on the CML).[9] To be in market equilibrium and for M to maintain its optimal position, the reward-to-risk ratio for each security must maintain its proportion of the market portfolio's reward-to-risk ratio.

Risk/Return Relationship Now that we determined the relationship between reward-to-risk ratios necessary to maintain an optimal portfolio, M, we can use it to find a security's risk/return relationship. Solve Equation 18.13 for ER_i:

$$ER_i = RF + \beta_i(ER_M - RF) \tag{18.14}$$

Finally, we develop a risk/return measure for securities such as STAR. It is called the CAPM. The security risk premium, $\beta_i(ER_M - RF)$, equals the risk contribution to the market portfolio multiplied by the market portfolio's risk pre-

---

[9]We use calculus to prove this point. If you are interested in a mathematical proof, go to the following references. William Sharpe, "Capital Asset Prices: A Theory of Market Equilibrium," *Journal of Finance,* September 1964; John Lintner, "The Valuation of Risky Assets and the Selection of Risky Investments in Stock Portfolios and Capital Budgeting," *Review of Economics and Statistics,* February 1965; and Jan Mossin, "Equilibrium in a Capital Market," *Econometrica,* October 1966.

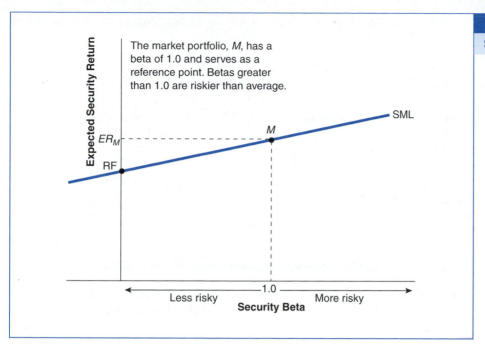

FIGURE 18.8

Security Market Line (SML)

The market portfolio, *M*, has a beta of 1.0 and serves as a reference point. Betas greater than 1.0 are riskier than average.

mium. This calculation makes sense because we presume that all risk-averse investors will purchase the market portfolio, so all security risk must be measured relative to the market portfolio risk. The CAPM is important because it allows us to quantify the *security's* risk premium and define a linear representation of the risk/return relationship for all securities and portfolios. This relationship comes from modern portfolio theory (MPT) because it relies on the idea that risk-averse investors will diversify away as much risk as they can; beyond that, expected return increases only with added risk. Because it is the minimum return compensation expected based on the beta risk, we will call it the "required return."

The CAPM (Equation 18.14) can also be displayed graphically; it provides the **security market line (SML)** displayed in Figure 18.8.

Notice that this graph uses beta, as opposed to standard deviation, as a measure of risk. The expected return equals the risk-free rate, RF, at zero beta; it increases as beta increases. The expected return when beta equals 1.0 is just the expected return on the market portfolio, ER_M. Because we have two points, RF at zero beta and ER_M at beta 1.0, we can draw a line to obtain the SML. Remember that Equation 18.14, the CAPM formula, creates the SML. To verify, let's find the equation of the line for the SML.

Recall that the equation of a line equals

$$Y = a + bX$$

security market line (SML)

Risk/return relationship for securities and a graphical representation of the CAPM.

where *a* is the *y*-intercept of the line, *b* is its slope, *X* is the independent variable, and *Y* is the dependent variable. For the SML, β_i, is the independent variable and ER_i is the dependent variable. What are the *y* intercept and the slope?

The y intercept is just the point at which the line crosses the y axis—RF in Figure 18.8. Recall that the slope is defined as

$$\frac{\text{Rise}}{\text{Run}} = \frac{\Delta Y}{\Delta X} = \frac{(ER_M - \text{RF})}{\beta_M}$$

For the SML, the slope equals $(ER_M - \text{RF})$, so the equation of the SML is

$$ER_i = \text{RF} + (ER_M - \text{RF})\beta_i$$

This equation for the SML equals Equation 18.14, the CAPM equation. The CML and SML sound similar at first, but in the next section we contrast the two lines to clear up any confusion.

Differences Between the CML and SML

Prior to this point, we introduced terms with two similar names, the capital market line (CML) and the security market line (SML). The latter graphs the CAPM equation. Now, let's contrast the two.

The lines differ in two ways. The most obvious is the risk measure; the CML measures risk by standard deviation, or total risk, whereas the SML measures risk by beta to find the security's risk contribution to portfolio M. The second difference is more subtle. The CML graph defines only efficient portfolios, whereas the SML graph defines both efficient and nonefficient portfolios and securities. Let's expand the discussion on these points.

Firm-specific risk or diversifiable risk for portfolios on the CML is theoretically zero because the CML contains only well-diversified, efficient portfolios. Even though it measures total risk (by standard deviation), it contains only market risk and no firm-specific risk. Also, remember that when the risk-free asset was introduced, all risk-averse investors preferred only one risky portfolio, the market portfolio M. All portfolios on the CML are just combinations of the risk-free asset and the market portfolio M.

The SML includes all portfolios and securities that lie on and below the CML. Because everyone invests in M, each security (or portfolio) risk is determined as its risk contribution to M. This risk contribution is defined as beta. Every security (or portfolio) on the SML exists only as part of M, and the relevant risk is the security's contribution to M's risk. Again, firm-specific risk is irrelevant to the SML, but for a reason different from the reason it is irrelevant to the CML.

RECAPRECAP

The CAPM (or its graph, the SML) provides a risk/return relationship for every security and portfolio. It measures risk as beta, a relative risk contribution to the market portfolio M, because all investors are assumed to hold only M as their risky portfolio choice. The total risk (or standard deviation) of a security is no longer relevant, because the firm-specific part of risk can be diversified away, leaving only beta. The CAPM quantifies the risk premium for securities as $\beta_i(ER_M - \text{RF})$ or the security risk contribution, β_i, multiplied by the market risk premium. The market beta equals 1.0 and serves as a reference point for other security betas. If a security's beta is greater than 1.0, then it is riskier than the average security, or the market portfolio; if its beta is less than 1.0, then it is less risky than the market.

3. Using Equation 18.11, calculate security i's beta if the correlation between the security and the market portfolio equals $+0.55$, $SD_i = 0.06$, and $SD_M = 0.35$.
4. Given the beta from Question 3, calculate security i's required return, ER_S, using the CAPM (or Equation 18.14) if $ER_M = 0.18$ and $RF = 0.03$.

Now that you have some insights on the development of the CAPM, let's apply this model to security analysis; this application will also promote a better understanding of the SML. The analysis essentially repeats the fundamental analysis conducted in Chapter 14. The only difference is that the CAPM replaces intrinsic values measured in dollars with expected returns measured in percentages. (We compare the two approaches later.) The next section illustrates how to conduct a security analysis using the CAPM.

CAPM AND SECURITY ANALYSIS

Suppose that a U.S. Treasury bond is currently yielding 3% and the current traded prices for STAR, Washington Water Power, Wal-Mart, and Echo Mining Co., as of 2002, are $21.00, $19.00, $54.00, and $22.00, respectively. Let's see how we can conduct security analysis using CAPM. This analysis is also an excellent alternative approach to value stocks that do not pay dividends.

Security Analysis

Value Line gives recent beta estimates for the four stocks of 0.80, 0.70, 1.10, and -0.20. Also, data from Ibbotson Associates give an average yield spread between the S&P 500 Index and the U.S. Treasury bill rate of 0.086. Given these data and Equation 18.14, we can estimate the required return for each of the four securities.

$$ER_i = RF + \beta_i(ER_M - RF) \tag{18.14}$$

For Lone Star Steakhouse (STAR):

$$ER_{STAR} = 0.03 + 0.80(0.086) = 0.10$$

For Washington Water Power (WWP):

$$ER_{WWP} = 0.03 + 0.70(0.086) = 0.09$$

For Wal-Mart (WMT):

$$ER_{WMT} = 0.03 + 1.10(0.086) = 0.125$$

For Echo Mining (MN):

$$ER_{MN} = 0.03 + -0.20(0.086) = 0.013$$

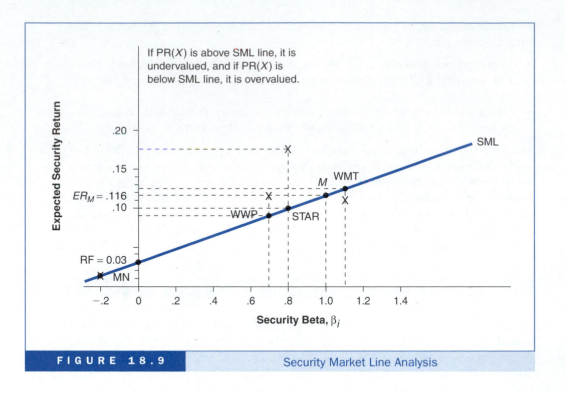

FIGURE 18.9   Security Market Line Analysis

Let's find these required returns on an SML graph, Figure 18.9. Because the SML is the graph for Equation 18.14 (the CAPM), they must all lie on the SML.[10]

The first three securities, those with positive betas, lie on the SML, and their corresponding required returns are greater than the risk-free rate, RF. What about Echo Mining Co., with its negative beta? What does it mean to have a negative beta and a corresponding ER_s less than RF? Although quite unusual, it is certainly possible. A negative beta means that the fund is negatively correlated with the market portfolio. This negative correlation can help to improve diversification benefits for the market portfolio. Remember the ultimate diversification benefit is derived from two assets that are perfectly negatively correlated (CORR = −1.0), which can reduce the combined portfolio risk to zero. To achieve this risk reduction, investors are willing to purchase the security even if it earns less than the risk-free rate RF.[11]

Next, we calculate the predicted return for each security based on today's price, $P_{i,t}$, a predicted price a year from today, $P_{i,t+1}$, and expected dividends during the coming year, $DIV_{i,t+1}$. Table 18.1 provides the data for the four securities.

---

[10]If a required return does not lie on the line, redo the calculations for Equation 18.14 or straighten your line. Remember, a required return must lie on the SML because the SML and Equation 18.14 (CAPM) are equal.

[11]Why might gold and other precious metals tend to be negatively correlated with the market portfolio? Typically, when a financial market is in a severe downturn (for example, a war or a depression), financial assets are riskier, sometimes even worthless, and a greater demand for tradable precious goods such as gold results. In Chapter 2, we reviewed evidenced that in the 1970s gold did well and stocks did poorly. During the 1980s and 1990s, stocks have on average outperformed gold. Gold made a comeback in 2000 and 2001.

Security Name	Today's Price, $P_{i,t}$	One-Year Predicted Price, $P_{i,t+1}$	Expected Dividends $DIV_{i,t+1}$	Beta β_i	Predicted Holding Period Return, PR_i	CAPM Required Return, ER_i
STAR	$21.00	$24.00	$0.65	0.80	0.174	0.10
WWP	19.00	20.04	1.24	0.70	0.12	0.09
WMT	54.00	60.00	0.21	1.10	0.115	0.125
MN	22.00	22.286	0.00	−0.20	0.013	0.013

TABLE 18.1	Prices, Dividends, and Predicted Holding Period Return

Predicted prices and dividends can be estimated by the procedure described in Chapter 11 on company analysis, which presented a procedure to estimate $P_{i,t+1}$ and $DIV_{i,t+1}$ to calculate PR_i. Of course, you may wonder whether every investor will make the same predictions. At this point, assumption 1—that all investors have homogeneous expectations—becomes important. It means that everyone has the same perceptions about securities and the market.

Now, this information will allow us to calculate an annual predicted holding period return, PR_i, for security i. A required return is calculated by Equation 11.19:

$$PR_i = (P_{i,t+1} - P_{i,t} + DIV_{i,t+1})/P_{i,t}$$

Predicted returns are calculated for each of the four securities.

$$PR_{STAR} = (\$24.00 - \$21.00 + \$0.65)/\$21.00 = 0.174$$
$$PR_{WWP} = (\$20.04 - \$19.00 + \$1.24)/\$19.00 = 0.120$$
$$PR_{WMT} = (\$60.00 - \$54.00 + \$0.21)/\$54.00 = 0.115$$
$$PR_{MN} = (\$22.286 - \$22.00 + \$0.00)/\$22.00 = 0.013$$

These predicted holding period returns are graphed onto Figure 18.9 with an X at the specified beta for each security. If X lies above the SML (or $PR_i > ER_i$), the security is undervalued; if X lies below the SML (or $PR_i < ER_i$), the security is overvalued. See Figure 18.9 again: STAR and WWP are undervalued, and WMT is overvalued. MN is priced as required by the CAPM.

Because the CAPM is an ex-ante (or expectation) model, it provides estimates of an appropriate future return, for a given risk, from investing today. Comparing this value to an expected return based on current and future market data, PR_i, suggests a decision rule. If a security seems likely to have a higher return than its risk level justifies ($PR_i > ER_i$), then it is undervalued and a good investment. However, a lower return than what its risk level justifies ($PR_i < ER_i$) suggests that a security is overvalued and not a good investment.

This analysis should sound familiar. It is like the intrinsic value method of fundamental analysis. Recall from Chapter 14 that we estimated an intrinsic value of a security and then compared it with the traded price. A traded price higher than the intrinsic value characterized an overvalued security; a price lower than the intrinsic value characterized an undervalued security. SML analysis is just another form of fundamental analysis, using percentage returns instead of

TABLE 18.2	**Fundamental Analysis**
Decision Rules for Fundamental Analysis and CAPM Security Analysis	V_{s0} is the intrinsic value of security s. P_{s0} is the current market price for security s. **CAPM Analysis** ER_s is the expected return according to the CAPM for security s. PR_s is the predicted return using the predicted market price, $P_{s,t+1}$, expected dividends, $DIV_{s,t+1}$, and the current price, $P_{s,t}$. **Decision Rules** $P_{s0} < V_{s0}$ implies $PR_s > ER_s$; security is undervalued. $P_{s0} > V_{s0}$ implies $PR_s < ER_s$; security is overvalued.

dollar values. However, because SML analysis measures predicted returns, it reverses the decision rule. Be careful not to confuse the two rules for SML and intrinsic value analyses! Because current price (on which intrinsic value is based) and expected return (on which SML analysis is based) are inversely related, the decision rules are reversed. The two analyses and their decision rules are summarized in Table 18.2.

Why do SML and intrinsic value analysis reverse their decision rules? The reason is that we assume that all investors predict the same price a year from now, $P_{i,t+1}$. Given this predicted price, SML analysis calculates a predicted holding period return, PR_i. If the return is higher than the required return according to the CAPM, it plots above the line, indicating that an investor can earn more than required. It also means that the investor paid less than required, making the security undervalued and a bargain.

If all investors agree that STAR is undervalued, demand for STAR will rise, driving the current price upward. The current price will go up just enough to allow investors to earn 10.0%, the required return justified by the stock's market risk as calculated via CAPM.

Let's address the question, how high will the price go? The analysis requires us to find the equilibrium price at which the investor would earn a justified return for the risk taken. Use the PR_i equation and solve for $P_{i,t}$:

$$\begin{aligned}PR_i &= (P_{i,t+1} - P_{i,t} + DIV_{i,t+1})/P_{i,t} \\ P_{i,t} &= (P_{i,t+1} + DIV_{i,t+1})/(1 + PR_i)\end{aligned} \qquad (18.15)$$

Now substitute the CAPM required return, ER_i for $PR_{i,t}$.

$$P_{i,t} = (P_{i,t+1} + DIV_{i,t+1})/(1 + ER_i) \qquad (18.16)$$

It does make sense that the current price should just equal the present value of future cash flows, $P_{i,t+1}$ and $DIV_{i,t+1}$. For STAR, the calculation is

$$P_{STAR} = (\$24.00 + \$0.65)/(1 + 0.10) = \$22.41$$

So STAR's current stock price will rise from $21.00 to about $22.41. At that price, STAR's stock price is at market equilibrium. Now it is neither undervalued nor overvalued but just equal to its intrinsic value. At $22.41 investors will earn the justified 10.0% required return based on CAPM.

All these calculations rely on an accurate beta value. In the next section, we discuss how to estimate beta and introduce two new terms, the *security characteristic line* and the *market model*.

In this section, we learned how to analyze securities using CAPM and predicted returns. This security analysis is analogous to the fundamental analysis discussed in Chapter 14. Using predicted returns, we found that if security i has a predicted return greater than the CAPM required return, then its expectation exceeds what is required, so it is a good investment. Also, we conclude that its predicted return is greater because you underpaid for the stock or it is undervalued. If security i has a predicted return less than the CAPM required return, then its expectation did not meet what is required, so it is not a good investment. Alternatively, if its predicted return is less, we can conclude that you overpaid for security i or it is overvalued. It is also effective for valuing stocks that do not pay dividends.

5. Suppose stock B has an estimated beta of $+1.30$. The market expected return equals 0.18 and the risk-free rate equals 0.05. What is stock B's required return via the CAPM?
6. Suppose you predict its price will increase to $90 in one year and dividends are expected to be $4.50 during that year. Stock B is currently trading for $80. What is its predicted return?
7. Is stock B a good investment? Discuss whether the stock is undervalued or overvalued.
8. Display stock B's required return and predicted return on a SML risk/return graph. Carefully label the risk-free rate, market portfolio, and stock B's returns.

ESTIMATING BETA

A beta estimate measures the changes of a security's return relative to the market return. A **security characteristic line** shows graphically this relationship between the return on the market portfolio, M, and a security return, $R_{i,t}$. The relationship can be estimated mathematically by a simple linear regression model called the **market model**:

$$R_{i,t} = \alpha_i + \beta_i R_{M,t} + e_{i,t} \tag{18.17}$$

security characteristic line

Defines the relationship between the security return and the market portfolio return.

market model

Simple regression equation used to estimate the relationship between the security return and the market portfolio return.

where α_i is the y-intercept estimate of the regression, β_i is the slope estimate for the regression line (also referred to as beta), $R_{M,t}$ is the return on the market portfolio in time t (usually measured in months or years), $R_{i,t}$ is the return on security i in time t, and $e_{i,t}$ is a random error term for the variation of security i's return around the regression line in time t.

Figure 18.10 graphs STAR's monthly returns for the 1998–2002 period. The parameter estimates, using ordinary least squares regression, give this market model equation:

$$R_{STAR,t} = 0.0285 + 0.76R_{M,t} + e_{STAR,t} \tag{18.18}$$

FIGURE 18.10

Regression Analysis to
Estimate Beta

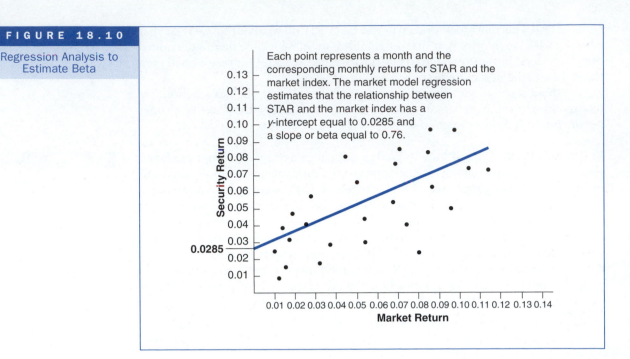

Each point represents a month and the corresponding monthly returns for STAR and the market index. The market model regression estimates that the relationship between STAR and the market index has a y-intercept equal to 0.0285 and a slope or beta equal to 0.76.

A statistical package estimates α_i and β_i as 0.0285 and 0.76. The slope coefficient, β_i is the estimate of systematic risk or beta. This confirms beta's role as the measure of volatility relative to the market return. If the market return changes by 1%, STAR's return will change by 0.76%, which is simply the definition of a slope. Alpha, α_i, also has a special interpretation; however, we reserve its detailed discussion until Chapter 21.

Information Service Beta Estimates

Many financial advisory firms such as Merrill Lynch, Value Line, and others provide estimates of beta. Table 18.3 displays a sample of securities and their betas, estimated by an ordinary least squares regression model. Notice that the utility stocks generally tend to have betas less than 1.0, the beta of the market portfolio. Because most consumption of gas and electricity is unrelated to market moves, these firms are typically not highly correlated to the market. Duke Power has a 0.11 beta whereas Washington Water Power has a 0.41 beta. Other betas are about 1.0, and some are much greater than 1.0; Charles Schwab's beta is more than twice the market level at 2.11. It makes sense for Schwab to be more volatile than the market because its business is pretty closely tied to trading volume, which tends to be high when the market is doing well. Betas tend to range from −0.9 to almost 4.0. Many high-technology firms have high betas, reflecting their participation in a risky, competitive industry. Advanced Micro Devices (2.04) and Hewlett-Packard (1.43) fall in this category. Securities with betas close to 1.0 are Lockheed (0.93), Philip Morris (0.89), Tootsie Roll (0.96), and Wal-Mart (1.07).

Security	Beta	R^2	SD_e^2
Abbott Labs	0.71	0.37	0.0520
Advanced Micro Devices	2.04	0.42	0.1346
Bank of America	1.18	0.29	0.1038
Barnett Banks	1.29	0.43	0.0848
Charles Schwab	2.11	0.44	0.1277
Duke Power	0.11	0.01	0.0496
Hewlett-Packard-Compaq	1.43	0.61	0.0652
Johnson & Johnson	0.86	0.52	0.0462
Kmart	1.41	0.69	0.0540
Lockheed	0.93	0.41	0.0637
Occidental Petroleum	0.82	0.42	0.0545
Orion Pictures	1.46	0.15	0.2000
Pennzoil	0.51	0.11	0.0831
Philip Morris	0.89	0.45	0.0561
Ralston Purina	0.58	0.31	0.0495
Tootsie Roll	0.96	0.39	0.0684
Toys "R" Us	1.19	0.54	0.0630
United Airlines	1.35	0.28	0.1238
Wal-Mart	1.07	0.61	0.0499
Washington Water Power	0.41	0.27	0.0380

TABLE 18.3

Beta Estimates
for Select Firms

Notes: $CORR(i,M)^2$ is the same as R^2 for a simple regression. SD_e^2 is the residual standard deviation or diversifiable risk.

Calculating Beta: Separating Systematic Risk from Diversifiable Risk

Using the market model, one can calculate systematic risk and diversifiable risk. Recall the market model:

$$R_{i,t} = \alpha_i + \beta_i R_{M,t} + e_{i,t}$$

The variance of this relationship, SD_i^2, would be calculated as follows:

$$SD_i^2 = \beta_i^2 SD_M^2 + SD_e^2$$

The previous equation has two terms. The first can be interpreted as a security's correlation with the market portfolio, or its systematic risk; the second term is interpreted as the portion of risk not explained by the independent variable, $R_{M,t}$. This term is the firm-specific or diversifiable risk. To simplify the equation, substitute in the definition for beta (Equation 18.11):

$$\beta_i^2 = (SD_i/SD_M)CORR(i,M)$$

It calculates β_i^2 as

$$\beta_i^2 = (SD_i^2/SD_M^2)(R^2)$$

where $\text{CORR}(i,M)^2$ is shortened to R^2. We can substitute the preceding definition of β_i^2 into the SD_i^2 equation and simplify as

$$\text{SD}_i^2 = (\text{SD}_i^2/\text{SD}_M^2)(R^2)(\text{SD}_M^2) + \text{SD}_e^2$$

The SD_M^2 cancels and the systematic risk equals $(\text{SD}_i^2)(R^2)$. It means that the diversifiable risk, SD_e^2, must be calculated as follows:

$$\text{SD}_e^2 = (1 - R^2)\text{SD}_i^2$$

It allows one to rewrite the total risk, SD_i^2, as

$$\text{SD}_i^2 = R^2(\text{SD}_i^2) + (1 - R^2)(\text{SD}_i^2)$$

R^2 is equal to $\text{CORR}(i,M)^2$ for a simple regression (one independent variable). It ranges from 0.0 to +1.0. As R^2 approaches 1.0, the explanatory power of the independent variable for the dependent variable increases. This relationship indicates how closely the security return correlates to the market return. A higher R^2 indicates a higher predictive power of the market return for the security return; it gauges the reliability of the beta estimate from the regression, helping the analyst to interpret Table 18.3.

Using the beta and R^2 data presented in Table 18.3 and given that SD_i^2 for Tootsie Roll (TOOT) is 0.1121, one can separate total risk into its systematic and diversifiable components for TOOT:

$$\text{SD}_{\text{TOOT}}^2 = 0.39(0.1121) + (1 - 0.39)(0.1121)$$

This equation can be interpreted to mean that 4.37% of TOOT's total risk (measured by $\text{SD}_{\text{TOOT}}^2$) is systematic risk and 6.84% of total risk is firm-specific or diversifiable risk. The formula gives a convenient way to find how much of total risk can be eliminated in a well-diversified portfolio. Furthermore, in regression analysis, R^2 measures the explanatory power of the independent variable ($R_{M,t}$) for the dependent variable ($R_{i,t}$); it indicates how much of the total variation of $R_{i,t}$ (denoted by $\text{SD}_{\text{TOOT}}^2$) is explained by variation in $R_{M,t}$.

Having described how to estimate beta, we can now show how to interpret its graphic representation, the security characteristic line. This explanation will reduce the confusion between the SML and the security characteristic line. They appear similar, but they perform different roles.

Differences Between the SML and the Security Characteristic Line

The most obvious difference is the variables graphed by the x axis and the y axis. The SML displays required return, ER_i, values for a cross section of securities on the vertical axis and betas on the horizontal axis. It shows the relationship of *two variables* for many securities. By contrast, the security characteristic line measures a security's returns on the vertical axis and the market portfolio's returns (usually S&P 500 returns) on the horizontal axis, using time series data, which show the relationship between the security's return and that of the market over time.

Given the difference in the variables, the slope and the y intercept are also different. The slope of the SML equals $(ER_M - RF)$ whereas the slope of the security characteristic line equals β_i. The y-intercept of the SML is the risk-free rate, RF, and the y intercept of the security characteristic line equals α_i. Because the relationships are different, the uses of the lines differ, too.

The security characteristic line is primarily used to determine how a security return correlates to a market index return. The R^2 that results from regressing the security return on the market index return indicates how well the market index return can explain the security return. A higher R^2 indicates greater explanatory power. Its other use is to estimate beta, which is the slope of the security characteristic line.

The SML, by contrast, is used for estimating the required return for a security relative to its risk measured by beta, β_i. The β_i value for the SML comes from the slope estimate of the security characteristic line. The security characteristic line estimates beta, and the SML graphs it. In Chapter 21, we explain how to interpret the slope of the SML as a reward-per-risk measure called the *Treynor measure*. That chapter shows that the y-intercept of the characteristic line, α_i, can be interpreted as a reward measure, too.

We conclude this chapter by reviewing some research studies and opinions about beta. What is the practical value of beta, and what are some of its problems?

GOOD NEWS AND BAD NEWS ABOUT BETA

Of course, researchers and practitioners have estimated beta since its discovery and found some good news and some bad news. They generally focus on two real issues. One is how well one can estimate beta, which is a purely statistical question. The other is how well one can predict future betas using past beta estimates. After all, the goal of security analysis is to measure its future systematic (beta) risk to determine what returns to expect.

Researchers and practitioners found that a single measure of the actual relationship between a security return and the market portfolio return is dubious at best. They found little correlation between security returns and market portfolio returns, which beta attempts to measure. Table 18.3 listed low R^2 values, which evaluated the explanatory power of the market portfolio's return for a security return. Duke Power, for example, has an R^2 of 0.01, and most are below 0.50. (The maximum is 1.0.) Studies found that portfolio betas have a much higher correlation with the market portfolio, so portfolio beta estimates may be more reliable than security beta estimates.[12]

The issue of measuring future betas can be addressed by summarizing Marshall Blume's study, "On the Assessment of Risk."[13] He shows that historical betas can be better predictors of future betas for large portfolios, even if they are unreliable for individual securities. His study correlated beta estimates for individual securities from July 1954 to June 1961 with estimates from July 1961 to

---

[12]For a more complete discussion, see Fischer Black, Michael C. Jensen, and Myron Scholes, "The Capital Asset Pricing Model: Some Empirical Tests," in Michael C. Jensen, ed., *Studies in the Theory of Capital Markets* (New York: Praeger Publishers, 1972).

[13]Marshall Blume, "On the Assessment of Risk," *Journal of Finance*, March 1971, pp. 1–10.

TABLE 18.4	Number of Securities in Portfolio	Correlation Coefficient[a]	R^{2b}
Correlation of Beta Estimates from One Time Period to a Subsequent Period	1	0.60	0.36
	2	0.73	0.53
	4	0.84	0.71
	7	0.88	0.77
	10	0.92	0.85
	20	0.97	0.95
	35	0.97	0.95
	50	0.98	0.96

[a]The correlation coefficient (CORR) ranges from -1.0 to $+1.0$ where $+1.0$ is a perfect correlation in which one variable (past beta) can perfectly predict the other (future beta).

[b]R^2 is the correlation coefficient squared. It has the same interpretation as the correlation but is limited to a range from 0.0 to $+1.0$.

Source: Marshall Blume, "On the Assessment of Risk" *Journal of Finance* (March 1971), pp. 1–10.

June 1968. His findings, reported in Table 18.4, show that correlations for single security beta estimates for the two periods of only 0.60 with an R^2 value of 0.36; if the number of securities in a portfolio increased from one to two, however, the correlation also increased to 0.73 with an R^2 of 0.53. When Blume included 50 securities in a portfolio and estimated its beta over the same two time periods, he found that the correlation increased to 0.98.

Table 18.4 suggests that as the number of securities in a portfolio increases, beta estimates become better predictors of subsequent-period beta estimates. Blume's study may suggest that historical betas are better predictors of future betas for mutual funds. However, other evidence suggests that mutual fund betas change because fund managers deliberately change the risk compositions of their funds. Remember, though, that the risk level must still comply with the portfolio objective, so it should change only within limits.

To summarize, the good news may be that portfolio (and mutual fund) betas are relatively stable. Analysts can use them with some degree of confidence. Be wary of security beta estimates, however.

Academics and practitioners alike seem doubtful as to the value of beta as a risk measure. In a shocking confession, an article by Eugene Fama and Kenneth French states that beta is nearly worthless as an explanation of a stock's relative performance over time. They suggest that strategies based on investing in stocks with low price-to-book ratios and small-capitalization firms produce better long-term performance than strategies based on beta.[14] The favored strategies basically look for firms selling cheaply compared with the book values of their assets, while avoiding those that sell way above their asset values. Also, firms with smaller market values appear to outperform firms with larger market values. These findings reduce the analytical value of beta to the point that some favor ignoring it, as discussed in the Investment Insight feature (page 536).

---

[14]Eugene Fama and Kenneth French, "The Cross-Section of Expected Stock Returns," *Journal of Finance,* June 1992, pp. 427–446.

Mark Hulbert, who follows investments newsletters, almost gleefully announces that "Beta Is Dead." He points out that beta is no longer regarded as sacred, allowing securities analysts to consider other strategies. Hulbert's work is to rank investment strategies; he believes that this task is more important with the loss of beta.

Although some merit can be found in ranking performance, Hulbert needs to be careful not to mislead investors. To say that beta is dead, making his task all the more important, may seem to be biased. In fact, we must be careful with analysts who dismiss betas too quickly. It still serves a purpose of quantifying risk. Moreover, it is important to remember that ranking past performance provides some information, but what worked during the 1980s and 1990s may not work in the decades to come. In Chapter 21, we discuss whether a money manager's past performance can predict future performance.

In response to Hulbert, another practitioner, Peter Bernstein, wrote an article, which appears in the Investment Insight box on page 537. Bernstein cautions readers against totally dismissing beta. He summarizes the implications of Fama and French's study and writes that even if beta may be pronounced dead, it does not invalidate the importance of the risk/return relationship. As we also emphasized, investors are smart enough to accept riskier investments only in exchange for compensation in the form of higher returns. (We called it a *risk premium*.) Based on this premise, Bernstein notes that small-capitalization stocks are riskier, so their stock returns must be higher. Also, stocks of firms with low price-to-book ratios would not sell cheaply if these companies were "prospering and growing"; this observation suggests that these firms, too, are unusually risky investments.[15] Because risk is an important factor in making investment decisions, even without a perfect measure of risk, one must incorporate some kind of risk measure to allow for these risk/return differences.

As Bernstein says, no one should despair just because beta was found to be less than perfect. It is still helpful in objectively quantifying risk and in recognizing a positive relationship between risk and return. Beta is still used by practitioners and academics alike. Recent developments point out weaknesses, but they do not invalidate the concept that higher risk implies a higher required return. Finally, understanding how risk measures are developed is helpful in discovering an underlying meaning of risk.

The next chapter expands on the CAPM and relaxes some of its assumptions to determine a more general risk/return relationship. Chapter 19 also examines some empirical studies of the CAPM and shortfalls of the studies, and it develops another measure of the risk/return relationship using arbitrage as its driving force.

IMPLICATIONS FOR INVESTORS

This chapter developed a risk/return relationship for stocks, the capital asset pricing model (CAPM), which enables investors to quantify risk for a stock and hence to evaluate the value of a stock relative to its risk level. We already know that a riskier stock should have a higher required return. Using the CAPM, we

---

[15]We discussed this point back in Chapter 14 when we explained the role of the price-to-book ratio in security analysis.

INVESTMENT INSIGHT

Beta Is Dead

Capital Ideas (Free Press, $24.95), by Peter Bernstein, the founder and first editor of the *Journal of Portfolio Management,* is a fine book and should be read by anyone wanting to understand modern Wall Street. Unfortunately for the book, almost as soon as it came out, the investment theory it highlights became discredited.

The book tells how the capital assets pricing model got its modest beginnings among a few upstart professors, took the rest of academia by storm, won Nobel Prizes for several economists, and in the process became standard operating procedure for institutional investors.

Bernstein's book was in bookstores only a few weeks when a revolutionary study was published by one of the heroes of Bernstein's story, University of Chicago Professor Eugene Fama. Fama and coauthor Kenneth French discovered that beta, a central analytical tool of the capital asset pricing model, is worthless as an explanation of stocks' relative performance over time.

Beta is a scoring system that rates individual stocks according to their volatility. The theory holds that the only way you can beat the market is by buying high-beta stocks—which also means you take a lot of risk. Despite several decades of confident academic assertions to the contrary, Professors Fama and French found that high-beta stocks don't do any better than low-beta stocks.

So far, other than an article by fellow columnist David Dreman (*Forbes,* Mar. 30, 1992), the reaction to Fama and French's study has been remarkably muted, but it means that the foundation of much of Wall Street's research has been yanked away. It leaves finance departments and business schools with the unsavory prospect of teaching theories to their students and then having to concede that those theories are wrong.

All this is reassuring for the individual investor, Despite the theoretical anarchy in academia and the cries of anguish from computer jocks whose programs are now pointless, beta's death gives the investor new hope. No longer can market-beating strategies be dismissed on the grounds that they must have incurred above-market risks. No longer can promising approaches be ignored because they don't conform to theoretical orthodoxy.

One of the best illustrations of this need for theoretical humility is the diversity of approaches pursued by the four investment letters that have beaten the market since 1980, when the *Hulbert Financial Digest* began tracking the industry's performance. Not only are their approaches theoretically distinct, some actually contradict each other. But in a world that recognizes more than one road to riches, this need not pose a problem.

For example, in first place since 1980 is Dan Sullivan's *The Chartist,* which utilizes only technical analysis. In second place is the *Value Line Investment Survey,* whose famed ranking system focuses on several different factors, such as price and earnings momentum. In third place is Martin Zweig's *The Zweig Forecast,* which uses a wide variety of technical, fundamental, and monetary indicators. And in fourth place is another Value Line service—*OTC Special Situations Survey,* which utilizes strictly fundamental valuation criteria.

That's pretty interesting, isn't it? Each of the four leading services uses an approach significantly different from the other three.

Or consider the outstanding performance of a newer letter. Editor Louis Navellier was trained in the intricacies of modern portfolio theory, and reportedly stopped short of completing his Ph.D. thesis only because he was impatient to begin applying his academic research to the investment world.

Navellier's success suggests that, even if beta is dead, the trip from gown to town is still worth making. Focusing on over-the-counter stocks, he has achieved a 37 percent compound annual return since the beginning of 1985 (when *HFD* began monitoring his performance), more than doubling the market's annualized total return over the same period. Navellier isn't surprised by Fama's findings. He tells me that his own research found no more than about a 30 percent correlation between a stock's performance and its beta.

How can we make sense of all this? One finance professor remarks that, in the wake of the Fama/French study, his profession today is where Newtonian physics was prior to Einstein: waiting and searching for a theory that makes sense of the markets, recognizing that previous explanations are woefully inadequate.

As a monitor of investment letter performance, perhaps I'm biased, but I believe advisory letters have a valuable role to play. Innovation comes more easily to letter editors than to institutions. And the lesson of Bernstein's book and Fama's research is the need for innovation and keeping an open mind.

Most of the myriad letters out there won't beat the market. That's why it is so crucial to monitor their performance rigorously and objectively, so that we can discover those methods that genuinely have promise. But we're all better off because so many of them are willing to try.

Source: Mark Hulbert, "Beta Is Dead," *Forbes,* June 22, 1992, p. 239. Reprinted by permission of Forbes Magazine © Forbes Inc., 1992.

INVESTMENT INSIGHT

If Beta Is Dead, Where Is the Corpse?

After Mark Hulbert's high compliment to my book, *Capital Ideas*, I hope I do not appear ungrateful if I take issue with his conclusions. He invokes the study by Professors Fama and French to assert that "beta's death gives the investor new hope. . . . No longer can market-beating strategies be dismissed on the grounds that they must have incurred above-market risks."

With all due respect, I think Mr. Hulbert may be reading more into the Fama-French study than is there.

The essential message of Fama-French is that long-term average returns are inversely correlated with price/book ratios and the size of a stock's market capitalization. In other words, small stocks do better than big ones, and stocks that sell cheaply relative to book value do better than those that sell at large premiums to book. As these two factors appear to dominate long-run performance, a stock's volatility relative to the market—its beta—loses its significance as a predictor of returns. As beta is often considered the most useful gauge of a stock's riskiness, the traditional linkage between risk and expected return appears to have crumbled. Hence, Mark Hulbert's good cheer.

Yet Fama-French cannot have sundered the relationship between risk and return unless we make the dangerous assumption that all investors are off their trolleys. Investors are not likely to take risks unless they expect returns above what they could expect on riskless investments. You do not drill for oil if all you can hope for is what a Treasury bill would provide. This requirement for higher returns from riskier investments pervades all investment decisions.

Consequently, investors tend to price riskier assets so that those assets will provide the higher returns demanded. In the long run and on the average, wildcat oil drillers earn more than investors in Treasury bills. When they do not, drilling dries up.

From this follows a second consequence. Predicting return is tough. But if return is related to risk, and if we can somehow measure risk, then risk will give us a guide to the probable rate of return! That upside-down use of the risk-return trade-off is what lent beta its attraction. Fama-French's demonstration that beta is a poor predictor of return is the source of Mr. Hulbert's cry of joy.

Yet beta has been moribund for some time as a predictor of returns, as many types of multifactor models have supplemented the single influence of the market on asset valuation. In addition, the current popularity of small-cap investing and of "value" strategies indicates that the professors were by no means the first to find an interesting road to the mother lode.

Thus, Mr. Hulbert neglects two elements of the Fama-French study. First, there is nothing in the Fama-French story to suggest that risk and return are unrelated. Fama and French focus on expected returns. The issue of whether small-cap and value stocks have outperformed because they are riskier than large companies and growth companies remains unresolved. This anomaly has haunted the Capital Asset Pricing Model, which is based on beta, for many years. But we do know that small companies are riskier than large companies. We also know that stocks do not sell at low prices relative to their assets if a company is prospering and growing. Although quantifying these risks is an elusive task, the Fama-French findings merely suggest that we do not yet have a good handle on calibrating risk.

Second, the implication that small-cap stocks and value stocks will *systematically* outperform after adjustment for risk flies in the face of common sense. The opposite conviction, that large-cap growth stocks would always outperform the market, led many prominent investment managers into Disasterville in the crash of 1974. These notions violate the one overriding lesson of investment theory. Do not put all your eggs in one basket. Tilting in one direction may be acceptable; abandoning diversification is perilous.

Investment is still a process of reading decisions under conditions of uncertainty. Risk is still the dominant consideration for investors. The stock market is still a volatile arena that does not feature free lunches. Make your choice, but never forget that you pay your money for doing so. There is nothing in Fama and French to contradict any of these truths or to overcome the nastiest truth of them all—that past performance, no matter how impressive, is no guarantee of future returns.

Source: Peter L. Bernstein, "If Beta Is Dead, Where Is The Corpse," *Forbes*, July 20, 1982, p. 343. Reprinted by permission of Forbes Magazine © Forbes Inc., 1992.

are able to conduct fundamental analysis using the required return versus the predicted return. Even though stock betas are relatively unstable, studies generally find portfolio betas to be relatively stable over time.

Even if beta measure of risk has its problems, investors recognize that risk must be accounted for when evaluating stocks, and although not perfect, beta is a start. The bottom line is to use beta wisely, knowing it has measurement problems.

SUMMARY

1. What is the capital market line (CML)?
By making a few assumptions about rational investors and capital markets and adding the risk-free asset, we can determine that all investors will choose M as their risky portfolio. The line that starts at the risk-free rate, RF, and extends to M is called the CML. It is also called the *lending-borrowing line* because it distinguishes between investors who lend and borrow at the risk-free rate, RF.

2. How is the capital asset pricing model (CAPM) developed?
Because all investors will invest in the same risky portfolio, M, we can show that each security risk should be measured by its contribution to the risk of the well-diversified portfolio M. The relative risk contribution of security i to portfolio M is defined by beta, β_i. It allows us to develop a model in which a security's required return, ER_i, equals $RF + \beta_i(ER_M - RF)$.

3. What are the differences between the standard deviation and beta risk measures?
We can now decompose the standard deviation, or total security risk, into two components: (1) systematic or beta risk, and (2) firm-specific or diversifiable risk. Because we assume that all investors hold well-diversified portfolios based on M, we can assume that they eliminate all diversifiable risk. Therefore, the only risk to consider for investment purposes should be the systematic risk.

4. How can an investor apply the CAPM to security analysis?
First, calculate a security's required return via the CAPM. It is the return that a security should earn, given its beta. Next, calculate the predicted holding period return, PR_i, and compare it with the required return estimated from the CAPM, ER_i. If $PR_i > ER_i$, then the security is undervalued; if $PR_i < ER_i$, then the security is overvalued.

5. How do you estimate beta?
Beta is estimated by a regression estimation process called the ordinary least squares method. The independent variable is the return on a proxy for the market portfolio (usually the S&P 500 Index); the dependent variable is the security's return. The slope of the resulting regression line equals beta.

6. What are the good news and the bad news about beta?
Research has found two items of bad news about beta. Security beta estimates demonstrate low explanatory power, and the predictability of a future beta is not especially good. In fact, some academics and practitioners believe that beta has all but lost its usefulness. The good news is that portfolio beta estimates are relatively reliable predictors of future portfolio betas; for a portfolio of approximately 20 stocks, beta's predictability is approximately 90% or better. These news flashes imply that, even if beta's power over the investment community has waned, some risk measure is still necessary to make good investment decisions.

MINI CASE 1

The objective of this mini case is to conduct a security analysis using SML. An assistant compiled the following data from various sources:

Security Name	Today's Price, $P_{i,t}$	Predicted Price After One Year $P_{i,t+1}$	Expected Dividends $DIV_{i,t+1}$	Risk Measure Beta, β_i
Bristol-Myers Squibb (BMY)	$22.78	$24	$1.14	1.25
IBM (IBM)	55.07	62	0.66	1.00
Cheesecake Factory (CAKE)	28.45	33	0.00	1.05

The market risk premium equals 0.086 and the risk-free rate (T-bill rate) is 0.02.

1. What required return does the CAPM give for each security?
2. Graph the SML and place each of the three securities along it.
3. Find the predicted return, PR_i, for each security.
4. Which stocks are overvalued or undervalued? Display the results on the graph in Question 2.
5. What is BMY's equilibrium price? What will happen to its price?
6. What is CAKE's equilibrium price? What will happen to its price?

MINI CASE 2

The objective of this mini case is to estimate betas and to interpret the market model regression. The 60 monthly returns for three stocks, BMY, IBM, and CAKE, are available on the data disk. Open Stock Returns file in the Data Workbook, and using software such as Excel, run a market model regression. Answer the following questions.

1. The market model is $R_{i,t} = \alpha_i + \beta_i R_{M,t} + e_{i,t}$. What are the beta estimates for BMY, IBM, and CAKE?
2. Interpret the R^2 values. How do they relate to the correlation coefficient, $CORR(i,M)$?
3. What is the total risk for each security?
4. What can we say about each security's systematic and diversifiable risks?

REVIEW EXERCISES

1. How do assumptions 1 through 5 help to develop the CAPM? Which ones are necessary and which just simplify the model?
2. You choose a risky portfolio, P_3, with an expected return of 0.12 and a standard deviation of 0.15. The risk-free rate, RF, equals 0.05. You want to invest 20% in RF and 80% in P_3.
   a. What is the RF-P_3 portfolio's expected return?
   b. What is the portfolio's standard deviation?
   c. Draw the CML for portfolio P_3.
3. What is the significance of introducing the risk-free asset to the investment opportunity set?
   a. What theorem results from introducing the risk-free asset and what is the significance of the theorem?
   b. What line results from the introduction of the risk-free asset?
   c. What is the significance of portfolio M in the line defined in Question (b)?

4. What two types of risk make up the standard deviation of a security return?
   a. Discuss the two types of risk.
   b. Why is only one relevant in the CAPM?
5. You expect United Airlines (UAL) to hit $11.54 per share with zero expected dividends this year. Its current price is $10.00, and your research sets UAL's beta at 1.25. The market risk premium is 0.086 with Treasury bills yielding 0.02. Is UAL a good investment? Conduct a security analysis using the CAPM and explain your answer.
6. American Airlines (AMR) is expected to hit $13.83 per share with zero expected dividends this year. Its current price is $12.88, and your research sets AMR's beta at 1.35. The market risk premium is 0.086 with Treasury bills yielding 0.02. Is AMR a good investment? Conduct a security analysis using the CAPM and explain your answer.
7. Display American Airlines' required and predicted returns on a SML graph. Include the risk-free asset and the market portfolio on the SML line.
8. Delta Airlines (DAL) is expected to hit $15.20 per share with $0.20 expected dividends this year. Its current price is $13.50, and your research sets DAL's beta at 1.45. The market risk premium is 0.086 with Treasury bills yielding 0.02. Is DAL a good investment? Conduct a security analysis using the CAPM and explain your answer.
9. Display Delta Airlines required and predicted returns on the SML graph. Include the risk-free asset and the market portfolio on the SML line.
10. The correlation coefficient of GM with the market portfolio is +0.80, SD_{GM} is 45%, and SD_M is 40%. The correlation between PepsiCo and the market portfolio is +0.50 and SD_{PEP} is 72%.
    a. Calculate separate betas for GM and PepsiCo.
    b. Compare the two and explain the results.
    c. What factors affect betas, and what can we conclude about how they affect GM and PepsiCo's betas?
11. The correlation coefficient of GE with the market portfolio is +0.65, SD_{GE} is 20%, and SD_M is 50%. The correlation between AT&T and the market is +0.45, and $SD_{AT\&T}$ is 0.60.
    a. Calculate separate betas for GE and AT&T.
    b. Suppose someone says, "Just looking at the correlation, you can tell that GE has a higher beta." Do you agree or disagree? Explain the differences.
12. You are given the following information about two stocks, A and B:

Stock	Current Price	Expected Price	Expected Dividends	Estimated Beta
A	$53.50	$60.00	$2.00	1.10
B	76.75	82.00	1.00	0.80

$(ER_M - RF) = 0.086$ and $RF = 0.02$

   a. Estimate the required returns using the CAPM.
   b. Estimate the predicted returns using the equation:

   $$PR_i = (P_{i,t+1} - P_{i,t} + DIV_{i,t+1})/P_{i,t}$$

   c. Which stock is overvalued or undervalued? Explain.
   d. Graph the two stocks' CAPM returns, the market portfolio, and the risk-free asset on the SML.
   e. Show the predicted returns for each stock on the graph.
   f. What is the equilibrium price for each stock?
13. You are given the following information about two stocks:

Stock	Current Price	Expected Price	Expected Dividends	Estimated Beta
X	$40.50	$53.00	$1.50	1.20
Y	62.75	78.00	0.80	2.20

$(ER_M - RF) = 0.07$ and $RF = 0.03$

   a.   Estimate the required returns using the CAPM.

   b.   Estimate the predicted returns using the equation:

$$PR_i = (P_{i,t+1} - P_{i,t} + DIV_{i,t+1})/P_{i,t}$$

   c.   Which stock is overvalued or undervalued? Explain.

   d.   Graph the two stocks' CAPM returns, the market portfolio, and the risk-free asset on the SML.

   e.   Show the predicted returns for each stock on the graph.

   f.   What is the equilibrium price for each stock?

14. You are given the following information about two stocks:

Stock	Current Price	Expected Price	Expected Dividends	Estimated Beta
W	$22.50	$26.00	$0.00	1.30
Z	35.00	46.00	0.00	1.50

$$(ER_M - RF) = 0.06 \text{ and } RF = 0.04$$

   a.   Estimate the required returns using the CAPM.

   b.   Estimate the predicted returns using the equation:

$$PR_i = (P_{i,t+1} - P_{i,t} + DIV_{i,t+1})/P_{i,t}$$

   c.   Which stock is overvalued or undervalued? Explain.

   d.   Graph the two stocks' CAPM returns, the market portfolio, and the risk-free asset on the SML.

   e.   Show the predicted returns for each stock on the graph.

   f.   What is the equilibrium price for each stock?

15. You expect stock of firm C to sell for $100 a year from now and to pay a $5.00 dividend during the year. If the stock's correlation coefficient with portfolio M is +0.40, $SD_C = 50\%$, $SD_M = 30\%$, $RF = 6\%$, and $ER_M = 15\%$, at what price should the stock sell today? Explain your results.

16. Firm G's stock is currently trading at $65, is expected to rise to $80 in a year and expects to pay dividends of $4.00 during the year. If the stock's correlation coefficient with the market portfolio equals −0.25, SD_G is 0.30, SD_M is 0.40, RF is 0.03, and ER_M equals 0.13, what is the predicted return and the CAPM required return for this stock? Should you invest in firm G's stock? Explain.

17. What is the intrinsic value for firm G, based on Question 16?

   a.   Conduct fundamental analysis and determine whether it is overvalued or undervalued.

   b.   Compare results with those found in Question 16.

   c.   How are the two methods analogous? Explain.

18. You are interested in estimating IBM's beta. IBM's correlation with the Dow Jones Industrial Average is +0.85, and SD_{IBM} equals 40% while SD_{DJIA} is 20%. You also decide to look into the Wilshire 5000 stock index as a proxy for the market portfolio. SD_W is 25%, and its correlation with IBM is +0.20.

   a.   Calculate IBM's beta with the Dow.

   b.   Calculate IBM's beta with the Wilshire 5000.

   c.   Why are the beta estimates for IBM so different?

19. The Dow's expected return is 30%, and Treasury bills are yielding 10%. Suppose the expected return of the Wilshire 5000 is 40%. Using the data given here and in Question 18, answer the following questions:

   a.   Calculate the CAPM return using the Dow as the market portfolio. Draw a SML with the Dow as the market portfolio.

   b.   Calculate the CAPM return using the Wilshire as the market portfolio. Draw a SML with the Wilshire 5000 as the market portfolio on the same graph as in part (a).

   c.   Suppose the predicted return for IBM, PR_i, equals 29%. Is IBM stock overvalued or undervalued using the respective required returns from part (a) and part (b)?

   d.   What is the drawback of using the wrong market index?

20. Microsoft's correlation with the Dow (DJIA) equals +0.55 whereas its correlation with the Wilshire 5000 Index is +0.65. Microsoft's SD equals 0.60, SD_{DJIA} is 0.20 and the Wilshire SD equals 0.30.

   a.   Calculate Microsoft's beta with DJIA.

   b.   Calculate Microsoft's beta with the Wilshire 5000 Index.

   c.   Under what condition would you use the beta calculated with the DJIA versus the Wilshire 5000 Index?

21. Suppose the DJIA's expected return equals 18%, the U.S. Treasury bill is expected to yield 3%, and the Wilshire 5000 Index's expected return is 20%.

   a.   Calculate Microsoft's required return using DJIA and information from Question 20.

   b.   Calculate Microsoft's required return using Wilshire 5000 Index and information from Question 20.

   c.   Suppose Microsoft trades at $54 today and it is expected to increase to $68 in one year. Microsoft pays no dividends. What is Microsoft's predicted return?

   d.   Conduct security analysis with each market index above.

   e.   Discuss possible problems when the wrong index is used.

22. Graph the two SMLs for Microsoft and the predicted return.

23. A security's standard deviation equals 20%, and its market model results are summarized as follows:

$$R_{i,t} = 0.03 + 1.32R_{M,t} + e_{i,t} \qquad R^2 = 0.35$$

   a.   What is the correlation coefficient between security i and the market portfolio?

   b.   What is the security's beta?

   c.   What are its systematic and diversifiable risks?

24. Suppose stock J has a total risk of 0.40 and a correlation with the market of +0.25. Stock K has a total risk of 0.50 and a correlation with the market of +0.85.

   a.   What are stock J's systematic and diversifiable risks?

   b.   What are stock K's systematic and diversifiable risks?

   c.   Your client thinks that stock J is less risky and wants to invest in J instead of K along with his or her diversified mutual fund. What would be your advice to him or her?

25. Firm XYZ, which invests in precious metals, has a beta of -0.54. What does it mean to have a negative beta? What are its benefits?

26. The following data for McDonald's (MAC), Waste Management (WM), and Abbott Labs (ABT) were compiled for your information:

Stock	Expected Return	Standard Deviation	Systematic Risk	Diversifiable Risk
MAC	0.10	0.122	0.068	0.054
WM	0.20	0.200	−0.005	0.205
ABT	0.05	0.080	0.075	0.005

Correlation coefficients: CORR(MAC, WM) = −0.60

CORR(MAC, ABT) = 0.25

CORR(WM, ABT) = 0.05

   a.   If a client wants to invest equal proportions in only two securities, which two would you recommend? Answer the question without performing any calculations, but based simply on your knowledge about portfolio theory. Explain in words.

b. Suppose your client already holds a well-diversified portfolio such as the S&P 500 Index. Which stock would you recommend? Why?

c. Your client says that WM is far too risky with a standard deviation of 0.20, especially compared with the other two firms' standard deviations of 0.12 and 0.08. How would you address his or her concern? Carefully explain, assuming that your client holds a well-diversified portfolio.

27. The following information has been compiled on United Airlines (UAL), Disney (DIS), and Johnson & Johnson (JNJ).

Stock	Expected Return	Standard Deviation	Systematic Risk	Diversifiable Risk
UAL	0.25	0.30	0.20	0.10
DIS	0.15	0.20	0.15	0.05
JNJ	0.30	0.26	−0.02	0.28

Correlation coefficients: CORR(UAL, DIS) = −0.60
CORR(UAL, JNJ) = 0.25
CORR(DIS, JNJ) = 0.05

a. Display the three securities on a total risk/return graph.

b. If a client wants to invest equal proportions in only two securities, which two would you recommend? Answer the question without performing any calculations, but based simply on your knowledge about portfolio theory. Explain in words.

c. Suppose your client already holds a well-diversified portfolio such as the S&P 500 Index. Which stock would you recommend? Why?

d. Your client says that JNJ is far too risky with a standard deviation of 0.26, especially compared with Disney's standard deviation of 0.15. How would you address his or her concern? Carefully explain, assuming that your client holds a well-diversified portfolio.

28. Show how the CAPM and the SML are identical.

29. What are the differences between the CML and the SML?

30. What are the differences between SML and the security characteristic line?

CRITICAL THINKING EXERCISES

1. Open the Stock Returns worksheet in the Data Workbook. The file contains 60 monthly returns for STAR and the S&P 500 Index. Use the LINEST command in Excel and run a regression equation (Equation 18.17) using STAR return as the dependent variable (Y) and the S&P 500 as the independent variable (X). Equation 18.17 is

$$R_{i,t} = \alpha_i + \beta_i R_{M,t} + e_{i,t} \qquad (18.17)$$

The Excel command is

=LINEST(y variable, x variable array, TRUE, TRUE).

Interpret the results for the y-intercept (α_i) and the slope (β_i)

2. Open the Stock Price worksheet in the Data Workbook. The file contains monthly returns for stocks along with a market index. It also contains Value Line estimates of the current prices, P_t, for the stock, expected earnings per share, EPS_{t11}, expected dividends per share, DIV_{t11}, and expected P/E ratios a year from today. Use the data and a spreadsheet program to answer the following questions:

a. Using the market model, estimate betas for the 10 stocks.

b. If Treasury bills are yielding 0.02 and the market risk premium equals 0.086, estimate the required return for each stock using the CAPM.

c. Each stock's predicted price, $P_{i,t+1}$, can be calculated by using $EPS_{i,t+1}(P/E_{i,t+1})$ from Equation 14.16 or using the EPS and P/E estimates provided in the far right column of Value Line. Calculate each stock's predicted return for the coming year.

d. Determine which stocks seem overvalued or undervalued. Explain.

e. Using the data provided and the required return calculated in part (b), estimate each stock's intrinsic value using one of Chapter 14's valuation models.

f. Determine which stocks are currently overvalued or undervalued. Explain.

g. Show that the results of part (d) and part (f) are consistent and really the same analysis.

http://ww   **THE INTERNET INVESTOR**

1. Go to an Internet site with stock prices and dividends and obtain daily and monthly prices and dividends paid for two stocks over a five-year period. Also obtain daily and monthly prices for the S&P 500 Index for the same time period.

    a. Calculate daily returns and monthly returns using the HPR equation for the two stocks and the S&P 500 Index.

    b. Using the LINEST function in Excel, run a market model regression for each stock using the daily returns.

    c. Repeat part (b) using monthly returns.

    d. Compare the beta estimates for each stock based on monthly and daily returns. What conclusions can you draw from the results?

2. Find an Internet site with net asset values (or prices) for mutual funds. Obtain monthly prices over a five-year period for a mutual fund and the S&P 500 Index.

    a. Calculate monthly returns using the HPR equation for the mutual fund and the S&P 500 Index.

    b. Using the LINEST function in Excel, run a market model regression for the mutual fund.

    c. Is the beta risk for the mutual fund close to 1.0? Explain theoretically whether it should be close to 1.0. If it isn't, provide a possible explanation as to why it may not be close to 1.0 (e.g., examine the composition of the mutual fund).

19

Extension of Capital Asset Pricing Theory[1]

PREVIOUSLY . . .	IN THIS CHAPTER . . .	TO COME . . .
We developed the capital asset pricing model (CAPM) and its application to security analysis. We presented several views regarding the status of the CAPM, many of which indicated that the CAPM and its beta risk measure was far from perfect.	We examine extensions of the CAPM and several empirical tests of the CAPM including Roll's critique of the CAPM empirical tests. Generally, we conclude that we must use the CAPM and its beta risk with care. This chapter also introduces the arbitrage pricing theory (APT), which is another way to view risk and return. Unfortunately, APT also has its drawbacks in application.	Next, we build on portfolio theory and the CAPM developed in Chapters 17 and 18 and develop ways to measure portfolio performance. These performance measures are applied to mutual funds and allow investors to choose the "best" performing mutual fund for their investment.

CHAPTER OBJECTIVES

After reading Chapter 19, you should be able to answer the following questions:

1. What is the zero-beta portfolio model?

2. What are some results of empirical tests of the capital asset pricing model?

3. What is roll's critique of the capital asset pricing model?

4. What is the arbitrage pricing theory?

---

[1]This chapter covers advanced material and can be omitted without loss of continuity.

We spent quite a bit of time and energy developing the capital asset pricing model (CAPM) in Chapter 18. The results can be summarized as follows:

1. Securities are priced in relation to their beta risk levels because all rational investors hold well-diversified portfolios equivalent to the market portfolio.
2. A security's total risk (standard deviation) is composed of two types of risk: beta risk and diversifiable risk.
3. Beta is estimated by a market regression model.
4. Beta estimates can accurately predict future portfolio betas but not individual securities' betas.

In this chapter, we turn to several other issues that can be viewed as extensions, or empirical tests, of the CAPM. Three issues are discussed, grouped under three topics: modifications of the CAPM, empirical tests and critiques of the CAPM, and arbitrage pricing theory (APT).

The first section deals with practical modifications to the CAPM. Recall that Chapter 18 required several restrictive assumptions to derive the CAPM. We discuss the Black's zero-beta model, which drops one particular assumption: that investors can borrow and lend at the risk-free rate.[2] This less restrictive model seems to produce results that conform more closely than those of the CAPM to empirical market performance.

This leads to a discussion of empirical tests of the CAPM and the more robust zero-beta model, followed by a critique of the CAPM. This section outlines the steps required to conduct the empirical tests to develop a clear idea of the procedures adopted by researchers and some appreciation of their tremendous efforts.

In Chapter 18 we discussed some problems with the CAPM; the second section continues that discussion with Roll's critique of the CAPM and its empirical tests.[3] Roll mathematically proves that the CAPM cannot be empirically tested (despite all the tests that researchers have conducted). His critique provides some insights on what researchers can test and what they have actually tested.

Finally, given the state of CAPM, the third section reviews Ross's alternative security pricing model called APT.[4] Ross uses the principle of arbitrage to develop a model with several factors and corresponding betas to price securities. The model's premise states that identical assets (assets of similar risk) must sell at identical prices. Stated differently, it says that each security return can give a price based on a linear combination of factors (or portfolios) that mimic that security's return. If the risk for the security and the linear combination of portfolios are equal, but the returns are not, the market will arbitrage the profits away to set identical prices for all identical assets. The last section of the chapter elaborates on the concept of APT.

Now, let's start with the zero-beta model, a modification of the CAPM.

---

[2]Fischer Black, "Capital Market Equilibrium with Restricted Borrowing," *Journal of Business,* July 1972, pp. 444–455.
[3]Richard Roll, "A Critique of the Asset Pricing Theory's Tests," *Journal of Financial Economics,* June 1977, pp. 129–176.
[4]Stephen Ross, "Return, Risk, and Arbitrage," in I. Friend and J. Bicksler, eds., *Risk and Return in Finance,* vol. 1 (New York: Ballinger, 1976).

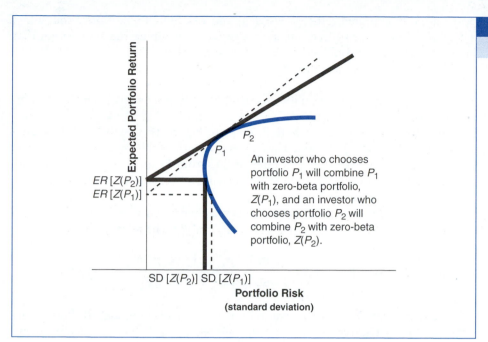

FIGURE 19.1

Zero-Beta Portfolio Model

An investor who chooses portfolio P_1 will combine P_1 with zero-beta portfolio, $Z(P_1)$, and an investor who chooses portfolio P_2 will combine P_2 with zero-beta portfolio, $Z(P_2)$.

MODIFICATIONS OF THE CAPM

As you perhaps noted, some of the assumptions required for the CAPM, as stated in Chapter 18, are quite restrictive. One particularly unlikely assumption states that all investors can borrow or lend at the risk-free rate, RF. If investors cannot all borrow at the same risk-free rate, some may choose risky portfolios based on their risk/return preferences (utility curves). This returns asset pricing theory to square one; recall that introducing the risk-free rate separated the objective choice of all investors to invest in portfolio M from the subjective choices of percentages to invest in the risk-free asset and portfolio M.[5] A common rate at which investors can borrow or lend allows them to adjust these percentages to achieve their own preferred combinations of risk and return. Without the common rate, they must choose different risky portfolios to meet their individual needs.

To address this problem, Black suggests that each investor create a personal combination of the chosen risky portfolio, P, and a portfolio of stocks that is uncorrelated to portfolio P, as shown in Figure 19.1. The portfolio that is uncorrelated to P is called the **zero-beta portfolio**. The zero-beta portfolio consists of a combination of securities with a beta equal to zero or with a zero correlation to the chosen risky portfolio P. The expected return of the zero-beta portfolio, $ER[Z(P)]$, is calculated as the weighted average return of all the securities in the portfolio. Notice that each risky portfolio has a different zero-beta portfolio associated with it. For example, consider P_1 and P_2 in Figure 19.1. An investor who chooses risky portfolio P_1 will choose $Z(P_1)$ as the uncorrelated zero-beta

zero-beta portfolio

Extension of the CAPM in which the risk-free asset is unnecessary and a more general risk/return relationship is developed with a portfolio uncorrelated to the market.

[5]Go back to reread portfolio separation theorem in Chapter 18 for a quick refresher if needed.

portfolio with expected return $ER[Z(P_1)]$ and risk $SD[Z(P_1)]$. Notice that $Z(P_1)$ may differ from the risk-free rate as is a result of dropping the assumption that investors can borrow and lend at the risk-free rate, RF.

Black's model has three major implications:

1. Any combination of portfolios on the efficient frontier will also be on the efficient frontier.
2. Any efficient portfolio, such as P_1 or P_2 in Figure 19.1, will have associated with it a zero-beta portfolio. The expected return of this zero-beta portfolio is found by the intersection of a tangent line from P_1 or P_2 with the y axis; its standard deviation (SD) is found by drawing a horizontal line from the intersection to the efficient frontier.
3. The expected return of any security i can be expressed as a linear relationship of any two efficient portfolios, such as P_2 and P_1. The relationship is

$$ER_i = ER_{P_1} + (ER_{P_2} - ER_{P_1})\left[\frac{COV(i,P_2) - COV(P_1,P_2)}{SD^2(P_2) - COV(P_1,P_2)}\right] \qquad (19.1)$$

These implications are sufficient to derive the zero-beta model. To find a market equilibrium risk/return relationship, aggregate the efficient risky portfolio choices of all investors, which becomes the market portfolio. Because any combination of efficient portfolios is itself efficient, the market portfolio identified in this way must be efficient. Into Equation 19.1, substitute the market portfolio M for the risky portfolio P_2 and the market portfolio's zero-beta portfolio $Z(M)$ for P_1. Note also that $COV[M,Z(M)]$ equals 0.0 by definition. By rearranging terms, Equation 19.1 simplifies to

$$ER_i = ER[Z(M)] + \{ER_M - ER[Z(M)]\}\left[\frac{COV(i,M)}{SD_M^2}\right] \qquad (19.2)$$

Recognize that $COV(i,M)/SD_M^2$ is beta, β_i. This substitution gives a revised expression of the risk/return relationship as

$$ER_i = ER[Z(M)] + \beta_i\{ER_M - ER[Z(M)]\} \qquad (19.3)$$

Figure 19.2 provides a graphic example of the zero-beta model described by Equation 19.3. Notice that the beta still equals 1.0 for the market portfolio; however, the y-intercept is equal to the expected return for the zero-beta portfolio, $ER[Z(M)]$, and the slope equals $ER_M - ER[Z(M)]$.

This equation is similar to the CAPM expressed in Equation 18.14. In fact, Equation 19.3 is simply a more general expression of the risk/return relationship.[6] If the CAPM truly defines the relationship between risk and return, empirically, the return on the zero-beta portfolio should equal RF. To determine

---

[6]This generalization is usually the case. Relaxing assumptions make a model more general, with the more restrictive model as a subset. Remember, this version of the asset pricing model no longer assumes that all investors can borrow or lend at the risk-free rate, RF.

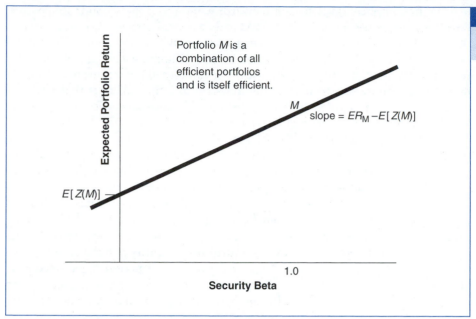

FIGURE 19.2

Risk/Return Relationship for
Zero-Beta Portfolio Model

whether $ER[Z(M)]$ equals RF, first define the market portfolio M, then mathematically solve for the associated zero-beta portfolio. For practitioners, this approach implies the possibility of a linear risk/return relationship, even if the y-intercept of the equation does not equal the risk-free rate. Simply identify a market index portfolio and mathematically solve for the return on the zero-beta portfolio, which need not equal RF.

In the next section, we outline the procedures by which researchers empirically tested the CAPM. In that process, they also tested the zero-beta model simply by determining whether $ER[Z(M)]$ equals RF. If not, a test would support the zero-beta model but not the CAPM.

EMPIRICAL TESTS AND CRITIQUE OF THE CAPM

Empirical Tests

Once a theory is developed, researchers test the model to determine how valid it is. To put it more scientifically, tests evaluate whether the hypothesis implied by the model can be refuted empirically. Before we discuss the procedure for testing the CAPM, let's talk about what is testable about the CAPM.

Unfortunately, along with its apparently unrealistic assumptions, any test of the CAPM must evaluate two implications jointly. If the data contradict the theory, the problem could arise from either of the following two implications, or both:

1. The risk/return relationship is consistent with the data.
2. The market is efficient.

The first implication is straightforward; what about the second? Remember, one of the major requirements of CAPM is that the efficient market prices securities based on all information and that market equilibrium prevails. The second implication of the CAPM is important because empirical testing assumes that securities are at equilibrium; an empirical test cannot tell failure due to a deficient model from failure due to market disequilibrium. Empirical tests that find evidence rejecting the CAPM lead to three possible consequences: (1) reject the CAPM, (2) label the market inefficient, or (3) both.

Given the evidence provided in Chapter 7 on market efficiency, it may be safe to assume that the market is relatively efficient and proceed with empirical testing. This jump past market efficiency is possible because the testing will consider several hundred *randomly* selected securities, which should eliminate any systematic inefficiencies such as small-firm effects or low price/earnings (P/E) ratio effects.[7] Several researchers conducted empirical tests of the CAPM.[8] The empirical studies followed a similar series of basic steps. First, a typical test uses the market model in a regression of excess returns for a security i on the excess return for the market portfolio, $(R_{M,t} - RF_t)$ over a 60-month period (**excess return** is defined as the difference between the risk-free rate and the return on security i or $(R_{i,t} - RF_t)$). This test is often called the **first-pass regression** because it is the first of two regressions in the CAPM empirical testing procedure. It estimates the beta for each security i. The test must run this regression individually for several hundred securities, with each **time series regression** calculated as follows:

$$(R_{i,t} - RF_t) = a_i + b_i(R_{M,t} - RF_t) + e_{i,t} \qquad (19.4)$$

Recall from the discussion of the market model that a time series regression compares time-based data (for example, returns over 60 months) for a single variable (for example, $R_{i,t}$). To distinguish between estimated betas and theoretical betas, we use b_i for an estimated beta and β_i for the theoretical beta.

In the second step of a test of the CAPM, the estimated beta values, b_j, serve as independent variables for **cross-sectional regressions**, which regress securities' mean excess returns $M(R_{i,t} - RF_t)$ on their b_j values. This test is called the **second-pass regression** because it is the second set of regressions run to test the CAPM.

The cross-sectional regression is calculated as

$$M(R_{i,t} - RF_t) = \gamma_0 + \gamma_1 b_i \quad i = 1, 2, 3, \ldots, N \qquad (19.5)$$

where N equals the number of securities in the sample, $M(R_{i,t} - RF_t)$ is the mean of the security return minus the risk-free rate (Treasury bill rate) over the entire testing period; b_i is the estimated beta from the first pass regression; γ_0 is the y-intercept of the second-pass regression; and γ_1 is the slope of b_i. This regression

---

excess return

Return over and above the required return estimated by the CAPM; actual return minus the CAPM return.

first-pass regression

Time series regression used to estimate beta for a security and used for empirically testing the CAPM.

time series regression

Regression analysis using data for variables (stock return versus market index return) over time.

cross-sectional regression

Regression analysis using data at a given time for many stocks.

second-pass regression

Method used to empirically test the CAPM, in which the beta estimate from a time series regression is imposed as an independent variable for a second cross-sectional regression.

---

[7]Remember that small-firm or low P/E ratio effects can skew results only if securities are sorted by size or P/E.

[8]Two of the first empirical studies were J. Lintner, "Security Prices, Risk, and Maximal Gains from Diversification," *Journal of Finance,* December 1965, pp. 587–615; and M. H. Miller and M. Scholes, "Rate of Return in Relation to Risk: A Reexamination of Some Recent Findings," in M. C. Jensen, ed., *Studies in the Theory of Capital Markets,* (New York: Praeger, 1972).

is cross-sectional because the regression data consist of several hundred securities' returns regressed on their corresponding beta values, b_i.

We add a second independent variable, SD_e^2, which represents diversifiable or firm-specific risk, to determine whether this factor affects security returns. This variable gives the following regression:

$$M(R_{i,t} - RF_i) = \gamma_0 + \gamma_1 b_i + \gamma_2 SD_e^2 \qquad (19.6)$$

The theoretical CAPM model in Chapter 18 is stated as

$$ER_i = RF + \beta_i(ER_M - RF) \qquad (18.4)$$

It can be rewritten as

$$ER_i - RF = \beta_i(ER_M - RF)$$

If the mean excess return for the security estimates the ex-ante expected excess return for the security, Equation 19.6 equals Equation 18.14. Therefore, if the CAPM correctly describes the risk/return relationship for securities,

$$\gamma_0 = 0 \quad \gamma_1 = (ER_M - RF) \quad \gamma_2 = 0$$

Unfortunately, the empirical results are far from satisfying. Lintner and Miller and Scholes all found that

1. γ_0 was statistically significantly different from zero.
2. γ_1 was statistically significantly less than the mean market portfolio excess return, or $M(R_{M,t} - RF)$.
3. γ_2 was statistically significantly different from zero.

These findings should not provoke despair, however. Black, Jensen, and Scholes suggested that the poor results could stem from measurement errors for b_i values, which serve as independent variables in the second-pass regressions.[9] These authors reasoned that measurement errors in the b_i estimates caused biases in the second-pass regression and hence reduced the power of the tests. They improved the empirical technique by evaluating security portfolios instead of individual securities in the second-pass regressions. The researchers created a three-step procedure to reduce estimation errors and applied the new technique to data from 1931 to 1965.

Step 1. Based on 60 months of return data (for example, from 1931 to 1935) for each security, estimate a security beta. If the sample includes 600 securities, rank the estimated 600 security betas in descending order. Divide these betas into 10 portfolios and identify the firms that belong in each portfolio.

Step 2. Estimate betas for the 10 portfolios created in step 1. Conduct the regression on results for a different time period (for example, 1936 to 1940) so that

---

[9]F. Black, M. C. Jensen, and M. Scholes, "The Capital Asset Pricing Model: Some Empirical Tests," in M. C. Jensen, ed., *Studies in the Theory of Capital Markets* (New York: Praeger, 1972).

FIGURE 19.3

Empirical Findings for the CAPM

Source: F. Black, M. C. Jensen, and M. Scholes, "The Capital Asset Pricing Model: Some Empirical Tests," in M. C. Jensen, ed., *Studies in the Theory of Capital Markets* (New York: Praeger, 1972).

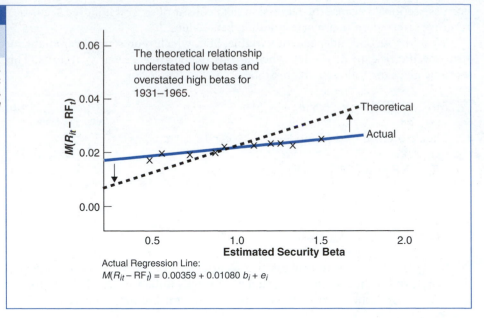

The theoretical relationship understated low betas and overstated high betas for 1931–1965.

Actual Regression Line:
$$M(R_{it} - RF_t) = 0.00359 + 0.01080\ b_i + e_i$$

the measurement errors for security betas are independent of any measurement errors in portfolio betas. This step is the first-pass regression described earlier. Estimating betas for portfolios reduces the variance of the error term or SD_e^2. Stated differently, portfolios are more highly correlated with the market portfolio than with individual securities.

Step 3. Run the second-pass regression on the 10 portfolios' excess returns, averaged over another time period (for example, 1941).

Figure 19.3 summarizes the results. Black, Jensen, and Scholes found that the theoretical CAPM relationship understated low betas and overstated high betas over the period from 1931 to 1965. The zero-beta model seemed to fit the data better than the CAPM did, although it failed to give consistent results. The researchers also found that the average zero-beta portfolio return is much greater than the risk-free rate. Undaunted by the poor findings, these authors continue to pursue the modified version of the CAPM, or the zero-beta model.

The major difficulty with this test of the CAPM is the use of ex-post data to evaluate ex-ante returns. Even if the test results are less than perfect, therefore, one could attribute the difference to the fact that historical data do not determine ex-ante results. For example, Black, Jensen, and Scholes split their second-pass regression over several subperiods. They found that from April 1957 to December 1965, ex-post data gave a regression line with a slightly negative slope, as displayed in Figure 19.4. In reality, of course, a negative risk/return relationship is impossible. Would you invest in a security for which you expected a lower return for greater risk? In an efficient market, investors would sell those securities, forcing their prices to decline until the securities earned returns commensurate with their risk levels. This result emphasizes the fact that expectations (like the weather forecasts) may not match actual results.

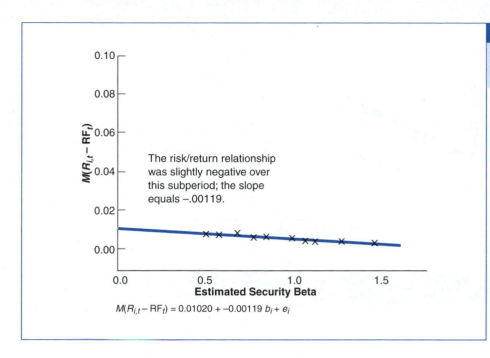

FIGURE 19.4

Empirical Findings for the CAPM: April 1957 to December 1965

Source: F. Black, M. C. Jensen, and M. Scholes, "The Capital Asset Pricing Model: Some Empirical Tests," in M. C. Jensen, ed., *Studies in the Theory of Capital Markets* (New York: Praeger, 1972). Copyright © 1972 Praeger Publishers. Reproduced with permission of Greenwood Publishing Group, Inc., Westport, CT.

We reviewed some obvious problems revealed by empirical tests of the CAPM. The next section outlines even more damaging evidence from these kinds of empirical tests.

Critique of the CAPM

To add to the chorus of detractors, Richard Roll provides a critique of the CAPM and creates doubt about the value of empirical testing and results of CAPM.[10] His critique can be summarized in six premises.

1. *Limits on tests.* The only testable implication from the CAPM is whether the market portfolio is mean-variance efficient (that is, whether it lies on the efficient frontier).

2. *Linear risk/return relationship.* If the market portfolio is mean-variance efficient, mathematical relationships require that the beta risk/return relationship (graphed by the security market line, SML) is exactly linear. Once the market portfolio is established as efficient, the second-pass regression adds nothing; the relationship must be linear. However, it creates further problems, outlined in the next three premises.

3. *Market portfolio composition.* The true composition of the market portfolio is unobservable, so it is impossible to test the first two premises accurately. Conceptually, the true market portfolio should consist of all traded assets, which includes common stocks, bonds, preferred stocks, real estate, art, and

---

[10]Richard Roll, "A Critique of the Asset Pricing Theory's Tests," *Journal of Financial Economics,* June 1977, pp. 129–176.

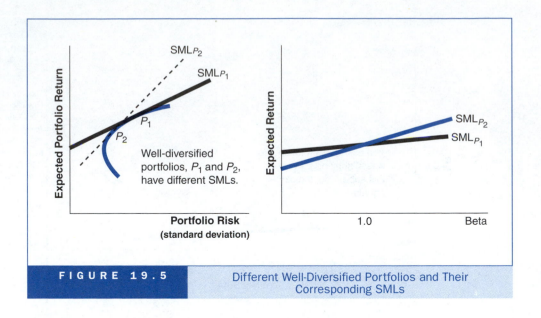

FIGURE 19.5   Different Well-Diversified Portfolios and Their Corresponding SMLs

any other traded assets. Could professional baseball, basketball, and football players fall under the category of traded assets?

4. *Range of SMLs.* The vast market proxies offer an infinite number of ex-post mean-variance efficient portfolios, each with an SML that tracks an exact linear beta risk/return relationship. Essentially, every efficient portfolio has a different SML. Therefore, each security *i* has a different beta estimate, based on the efficient portfolio with which it is correlated. Using different sample portfolios as market proxies, even if they are mean-variance efficient, will produce different beta estimates for each security; these differences can be significant. Figure 19.5 displays individual SMLs for two different efficient portfolios, P_1 and P_2 (SML_{P_1} and SML_{P_2}).

5. *Market efficiency effects.* In a nutshell, Roll states that using a substitute, such as the Standard & Poor's (S&P) 500 Index, for the market portfolio creates two problems:
   a. Even if the proxy is mean-variance efficient, it does not accurately represent the true market portfolio.
   b. Even if the proxy is not efficient, the true market portfolio may still be efficient.

6. *Conflicts between proxies.* Finally, more confusion may arise when different substitutes for the true market portfolio may be closely correlated, even though some may be efficient and others not. This difference leads to varying conclusions with regard to the beta risk/return relationship. Remember, efficient portfolios give perfectly linear beta risk/return relationships, whereas inefficient portfolios give linear estimates that fail to line up perfectly.

What can we conclude about the empirical test results presented earlier? The empirical tests confirmed only that their substitutes for the market portfolio were not mean-variance efficient. The researchers certainly did a lot of work, but they did not test the CAPM!

Roll convincingly showed that the CAPM is untestable, but this argument does not make it valueless. The general agreement is that the CAPM has its merits and should be used carefully. Although some controversy remains about its merits, many still regard it as a useful tool. It does provide a theoretical justification for the risk/return relationship, and it does describe a quantifiable measure of risk. Although the CAPM's beta requires cautious use, some will argue that having an inexact quantifiable risk measure is better than having none at all. Peter Bernstein's comments in the Chapter 18 Investment Insight box summarize the consensus; the CAPM is a useful framework in which to see how riskier investments provide higher returns.[11]

While Roll was adding to the demise of the CAPM, Stephen Ross was developing an alternative way to look at asset pricing. His work culminated in the APT, discussed in the following section.

ARBITRAGE PRICING THEORY

Given the theoretical and empirical problems with the CAPM, some researchers turned to alternative theories to explain asset pricing. Stephen Ross used the old idea of arbitrage to develop another view of asset returns. The resulting *arbitrage pricing theory (APT)* is a way to price securities. Although its final equation seems an extension of the CAPM, its logical development is different. The CAPM stems from utility theory concepts of investor preference for risk and return, whereas APT is built on the principle of arbitrage.

Concept of Arbitrage

The general arbitrage principle states that two identical securities (or goods) should be bought and sold at identical prices. You might also say that if one invests nothing, one should get nothing in return.[12]

Although it sounds pretty straightforward, an example can help illustrate its application to securities. Remember the concept of selling short? Suppose one could borrow a stock with no margin requirements or transaction costs and sell it for $69. The proceeds of the sale could finance a purchase of the stock for $69, which would constitute a zero investment, and it would generate zero profits. For every dollar gained (or lost) in the long position, the investor would lose (or gain) the same amount in the short position. For instance, if the example stock were to rise to $70, the long position would make $1, but the short position would lose $1. This situation eliminates any possibility of profits from arbitrage. Investing nothing gains nothing.

Now, look at an example that offers arbitrage opportunities but still requires no investment. The theory holds that this situation will disappear quickly as arbitrageurs' trades drive prices toward equilibrium. Suppose that two stocks, A and B, have identical risk levels. If stock A is expected to earn 12% and stock B 10%,

arbitrage principle

Process in which an investor buys the lower-priced asset and sells the higher-priced asset, both similar in risk, and captures the difference as arbitrage profits.

---

[11]The Investment Insight box in Chapter 18 reprints Peter Bernstein's article, "If Beta Is Dead, Where Is the Corpse?"

[12]It sounds similar to the old adage "nothing ventured, nothing gained," or the slogan from aerobics classes, "no pain, no gain."

careful trading can create arbitrage profits. Because all investors perceive stocks A and B to have identical risk, an arbitrageur can sell short $100 of B and invest long $100 in A and receive a $2 in arbitrage profits:

	Today	One Year Later
Short position in B	$100	$100(1 + 0.10) = ($110)
Long position in A	($100)	$100(1 + 0.12) = $112
Investment	$ 0	Net profits = $2

Of course, if this result is a sure thing, why stop with $100? Arbitrageurs will sell B and buy A to make unlimited profits while investing no money until the prices of stocks A and B reach equality.[13] This simple example of arbitrage leads us into a discussion of how the principle can suggest a model for security prices in the context of developing a single-factor APT.

Single-Factor APT

single-factor APT model

Risk/return relationship in which one variable (or factor) is related to the stock return and is used to measure stock risk.

Let's formulate a **single-factor APT model** to describe how arbitrage operates. Suppose that ex-post returns, $R_{i,t}$, are generated according to some stochastic relationship described as

$$\tilde{R}_{i,t} = E_{0,t} + \beta_{i,t}\tilde{F}_{1,t} + \tilde{e}_{i,t} \quad \text{for } i = 1, 2, \ldots, N \tag{19.7}$$

where $E_{0,t}$ is the security's expected return if $\beta_{i,t}F_{1,t}$ equals zero; $\tilde{F}_{1,t}$ is a factor (which we will call F1) that affects stock i's ex-post return for year t; $\beta_{i,t}$ is the sensitivity (systematic risk or beta) of stock i to factor F1; $\tilde{e}_{i,t}$ is the firm's stock price movement that is uncorrelated to F1. (It is essentially the firm-specific risk for year t.) $E(\tilde{e}_{i,t})$ is assumed to equal zero.

The F1 factor can be decomposed into two types of factors: (1) a factor expected by investors ($EF_{i,t}$) and (2) an unexpected factor ($\tilde{f}_{1,t}$). Rewrite Equation 19.7 more explicitly:

$$\tilde{R}_{i,t} = E_{0,t} + \beta_{i,t}(EF_{1,t} + \tilde{f}_{1,t}) + \tilde{e}_{i,t} \tag{19.8}$$

where $EF_{1,t}$ is F1's expected effect on stock i's ex-post return for year t and $\tilde{f}_{1,t}$ is the effect of the unanticipated change in stock i's ex-post return, which is also uncorrelated to $e_{i,t}$.

Finally, rewrite Equation 19.8 as

$$\tilde{R}_{i,t} = ER_{i,t} + \beta_{i,t}\tilde{f}_{1,t} + \tilde{e}_{i,t} \tag{19.9}$$

where $ER_{i,t}$ equals stock i's expected return, or $(E_{0,t} + \beta_{i,1}EF_{1,t})$.

An example may help to clarify this relationship between $EF_{1,t}$ and $\tilde{f}_{1,t}$. Suppose that stock i is Johnson and Johnson (JNJ) and factor F1 represents the change in the rate of inflation. If the change in inflation rate is zero, JNJ's return is 10% ($E_{0,t}$ = percent).

---

[13]Other investors quickly catch on to this type of scheme, and their demand for the stock with the lower price drives prices toward equality. (Academics refer to this process as *market equilibrium*.)

Suppose, however, that everyone believes that inflation will increase by 3% ($EF_{1,t}$ is 3%). Because stocks tend to suffer during periods of high inflation, JNJ should decline. If JNJ's beta relative to the F1 factor equals -1.5, its return is expected to fall by 4.5% ($-1.5 \times 3\%$) and its expected return, ER_{JNJ}, equals 5.5%:

$$ER_{JNJ} = 10\% + [-1.5(3\%)] = 5.5\%$$

Remember, however, that 3% is only a predicted change in F1. If the actual change in the rate of inflation is equal to $+4\%$, so that $\tilde{f}_{1,t}$ is $+1\%$, the effect on JNJ's actual, realized return is

$$ER_{JNJ} = ER_{JNJ} + [-1.5(1\%)] = 5.5\% - 1.5\% = 4.0\%$$

The difference between actual and expected inflation causes the actual, realized return (R_{JNJ}) to be 1.5% lower than the expected return, ER_{JNJ}; the stockholder expects 5.5% but realizes only 4.0%.

Now, what is $\tilde{e}_{i,t}$, the firm-specific effect on the stock's actual return? The variable $\tilde{e}_{i,t}$ might measure the effects of the hackers shutting down Yahoo!'s Web site for several hours (the incident occurred in February 2000 and affected Yahoo!, eBay, and E*TRADE) or for JNJ litigation on a product that causes side effects. This effect would cause the actual return to differ from ER_{JNJ}. Notice the difference between $\tilde{e}_{i,t}$ and $\tilde{f}_{1,t}$: The latter captures the effect of F1 that is not predicted correctly (unexpected inflation), whereas $\tilde{e}_{i,t}$ captures the firm-specific effect, which is not captured by $\tilde{f}_{1,t}$ and is uncorrelated to $\tilde{f}_{1,t}$.

Single-Factor APT for a Well-Diversified Portfolio

Next, let's discuss the risk/return relationship for a well-diversified portfolio. Start with the same ex-post relationship (Equation 19.9), but modify it for a portfolio:

$$\tilde{R}_{p,t} = ER_{p,t} + \beta_{p1}\tilde{f}_{1,t} + \tilde{e}_{p,t} \qquad (19.10)$$

One benefit of diversification is elimination of virtually all firm-specific risk, as described in Chapter 17. Recall from that chapter that the effect of a security's standard deviation, SD_i, on a well-diversified portfolio's standard deviation, SD_P is virtually zero; the only relevant risk is the covariance of each security with the portfolio. Another way of saying it is that the standard deviation of unexpected, ($\tilde{e}_{p,t}$), or firm-specific risk equals zero. Because the expected value of firm-specific risk, $E(\tilde{e}_{p,t})$, equals zero and its standard deviation, $SD(\tilde{e}_{p,t})$, is zero, the actual effect on the portfolio return of $\tilde{e}_{p,t}$ must equal zero for a well-diversified portfolio. The ex-post return relationship for a well-diversified portfolio becomes[14]

$$\tilde{R}_{p,t} = ER_{p,t} + \beta_p\tilde{f}_{1,t} \qquad (19.11)$$

---

[14]It involves constructing portfolios so that $E(\tilde{e}_{p,t})$ equals zero. Also, remember from statistics that if an expected value is zero and actual values show no deviation from its (standard deviation is zero), then all the values that make up $e_{p,t}$ must be zero.

Well-diversified portfolio risk equals[15]

$$SD_P^2 = \beta_P^2 SD_{f,1}^2 \quad \text{or} \quad SD_P = \beta_P SD_{f,1}$$

The APT imposes three conditions:

1. No wealth is invested.
2. A portfolio can eliminate firm-specific risk, $\tilde{e}_{p,t}$. (Of course, it is possible by holding a well-diversified portfolio.)
3. If arbitrage opportunities exist, the market can without risk or cost arbitrage the profits to eliminate any discrepancies between any combinations of portfolios or securities at the same risk level.

If these conditions hold, it follows mathematically that portfolio expected return, $ER_{p,t}$, has a linear relationship with beta, β_p

$$ER_{p,t} = E_{0,t} + \beta_p EF_{1,t} \tag{19.12}$$

An example may be helpful here. The following example shows both the rationale for security return and how the arbitrage process is truly risk-free; the dollar payoff is the same, regardless of any unanticipated changes in the portfolio return. Based on that premise, the example shows that Equation 19.12 follows from the assumptions of the single-factor APT.

Suppose that a single-factor model defines expected and realized returns as

Realized return: $\tilde{R}_{p,t} = ER_{p,t} + \beta_p \tilde{f}_{1,t}$
Expected return: $ER_{p,t} = E_{0,t} + \beta_p EF_{1,t}$

Suppose, also, that three portfolios C, D, and K have expected returns of 14%, 16%, and 17% with $\beta_{p,1}$ (systematic risk) measures of 0.7, 1.7, and 1.2, respectively. So, portfolio K has a systematic risk of 1.2 and an expected return of 17%. Investing 50% of your wealth in C and 50% in D gives a systematic risk of combined portfolio CD as

$$\beta_{CD} = X_c\beta_{C,1} + (1 - X_C)\beta_{D,1} \tag{19.13}$$

where X_C is the proportion invested in portfolio C. For the example,

$$\beta_{CD} = 0.50(0.7) + (1 - 0.50)(1.7) = 1.2$$

---

[15]Portfolio risk can be shown mathematically as
$$SD_P = \beta_P SD_{f,1}$$
Recall that
$$SD_P^2 = \beta_P^2 SD_{f,1}^2 + SD_e^2$$
Having established that SD_e^2 is virtually zero for a well-diversified portfolio, then
$$SD_P^2 = \beta_P^2 SD_{f,1}^2$$
Taking the square root gives
$$SD_P = \beta_P SD_{f,1}$$

TABLE 19.1
Arbitraging Portfolio K with Portfolio CD

A. Investment Today

	Dollar Investment	Systematic Risk
Sell Portfolio CD short:		
Short Portfolio C	$ +50	−0.35
Short Portfolio D	+50	−0.85
Buy Portfolio K	−100	+1.20
Net investment	$ 0	Net risk 0.00

B. One Year Later
Unanticipated Changes

Realized Dollar Payoffs

$\tilde{f}_{1,t}$ $= INV + INV(ER_{p,t} + \beta_{p,1}\tilde{f}_{1,t})$

Low $\tilde{f}_{1,t}$
C: Dollar payoff = −{$50 + $50[0.14 + 0.7(−0.03)]}	$−55.95
D: Dollar payoff = −{$50 + $50[0.16 + 1.7(−0.03)]}	−55.45
K: Dollar payoff = $100 + $100[0.17 + 1.2(−0.03)]	113.40
Net profits	$ + 2.00

Expected $\tilde{f}_{1,t}$
C: Dollar payoff = −{$50 + $50[0.14 + 0.7(0)]}	$−57.00
D: Dollar payoff = −{$50 + $50[0.16 + 1.7(0)]}	−58.00
K: Dollar payoff = $100 + $100[0.17 + 1.2(0)]	117.00
Net profits	$ + 2.00

High $\tilde{f}_{1,t}$
C: Dollar payoff = −{$50 + $50[0.14 + 0.7(10.05)]}	$−58.75
D: Dollar payoff = −{$50 + $50[0.16 + 1.7(10.05)]}	−62.25
K: Dollar payoff = $100 + $100[0.17 + 1.2(10.05)]	123.00
Net profits	$ + 2.00

Portfolio CD has the same systematic risk as portfolio K; however, its expected return equals 15%. Using Equation 17.6a, the portfolio expected return is

$$ER_{CD} = X_C(ER_C) + (1 − X_C)(ER_D)$$
$$= 0.50(0.14) + (1 − 0.50)(0.16) = 0.15, \text{ or } 15\%$$

This example presents an arbitrage opportunity because portfolios K and CD have the same systematic risk ($\beta = 1.2$), but K's expected return is 17%, whereas CD's is 15%. Arbitrage with no risk and no investment can be constructed by selling short $100 of portfolio CD and using the proceeds to buy $100 of portfolio K. This trade results in zero investment and zero risk, as displayed in the first part of Table 19.1.

Now, let's see what happens a year from today if the unanticipated change ($\tilde{f}_{1,t}$) equals −3%, 0%, or 5%. Table 19.1 displays the results of the realized dollar payoffs, calculated as

$$\text{Dollar payoff} = INV + INV(ER_{p,t} + \beta_{p,1}\tilde{f}_{1,t}) \tag{19.14}$$

where INV is the dollar amount invested (\$100 in the example) and $(ER_{p,t} + \beta_{p,1}\tilde{f}_{1,t})$ is the actual realized return, from Equation 19.11. These results show that the dollar payoffs are exactly the same regardless of the unanticipated changes; whether the model's single factor changes by -3%, 0%, or 5%, the net profits equal \$2. This example shows the meaning of risk-free arbitrage; the technique guarantees a known dollar payoff a year from today, regardless of the unanticipated changes. This situation allows arbitrageurs to exploit mispricing between portfolios of equal systematic risk until the profits become zero (that is, the portfolios' returns become equal).

The risk caused by the unanticipated changes, $\tilde{f}_{1,t}$, can be eliminated by constructing two portfolios (CD and K) that have offsetting effects; therefore, $\tilde{f}_{1,t}$ is not relevant in pricing a security if it can be eliminated with off-setting arbitrage portfolios. It suggests removing $\tilde{f}_{1,t}$ from Equation 19.11:

$$\tilde{R}_{p,t} = ER_{p,t} + \beta_{p,1}\tilde{f}_{1,t}$$

If so, the realized return, $\tilde{R}_{p,t}$ can be best described by the expected return, $ER_{p,t}$. Recall, however, that $ER_{p,t}$ is defined by Equation 19.12 as

$$ER_{p,t} = E_{0,t} + \beta_{p,1}EF_{1,t}$$

Intuitively, if one portfolio (K) can be replicated by combinations of other portfolios, its expected return can be described by Equation 19.12.

Let's rework the example of portfolios C, D, and K to develop another intuitive technique to evaluate returns describing the arbitrage process. Suppose the realized returns for portfolio K and portfolio CD are defined by Equation 19.11 as

$$\tilde{R}_{K,t} = ER_{K,t} + \beta_{K,1}\tilde{f}_{1,t} \quad \text{and} \quad \tilde{R}_{CD,t} = ER_{CD,t} + \beta_{CD,t}\tilde{f}_{1,t}$$

Because ER_K equals 0.17 and $\beta_{K,1}$ equals 1.2, rewrite portfolio K's realized return as

$$\tilde{R}_{K,t} = 0.17 + 1.2\tilde{f}_{1,t}$$

Portfolio CD's $ER_{CD,t}$ equals 0.15 and its $\beta_{CD,1}$ equals 1.2, and its realized return is calculated as

$$\tilde{R}_{CD,t} = 0.15 + 1.2\tilde{f}_{1,t}$$

Because the portfolio combination in CD has the same systematic risk of 1.2 but earns only 15%, an arbitrageur will sell CD short and buy portfolio K with the proceeds of the short sale giving a net investment of zero. The results is as follows:

Buy portfolio K	$\tilde{R}_{K,t} = (0.17 + 1.2\tilde{f}_{1,t})$
Sell short portfolio CD	$-\tilde{R}_{CD,t} = -(0.15 + 1.2\tilde{f}_{1,t})$
Arbitrage profits	$(\tilde{R}_{K,t} - \tilde{R}_{CD,t}) = +0.2$

The arbitrage generates a 2% profit. Notice, also, that the effects of any unanticipated changes, $\tilde{f}_{1,t}$, are offset no matter what that number is: -3%, 0%,

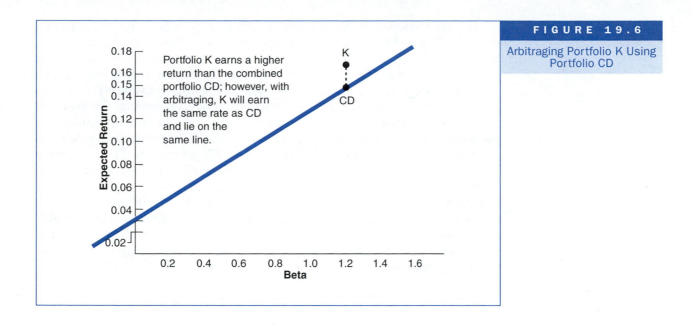

FIGURE 19.6

Arbitraging Portfolio K Using Portfolio CD

or 5%. It means that the arbitrage investment risk is zero. Because all arbitrageurs are guaranteed to realize this profit, they will continue to make these trades until portfolio K's price rises enough to reduce its return to 15%.

Generally, if a portfolio (for example, K) with a higher return can be replicated as a combination of other portfolios (for example, C and D), arbitrage profits exist. However, arbitrageurs quickly eliminate this mispricing between portfolios. For that reason, all portfolios with the same systematic risk must lie on the same line, defined by Equation 19.12. Stated differently, portfolios with the same systematic risk must have the same expected return.

The linear relationship for portfolios CD and K may be

$$ER_{p,t} = 0.03 + 1.2(0.10) = 0.15, \text{ or } 15\%$$

This relationship is displayed in Figure 19.6.

The risk/return relationship defined by Equation 19.12 needs one last modification. The systematic risk factor in Equation 19.12 can be normalized so that the average $\beta_{p,1}$ equals 1.0. The general normalized risk/return relationship becomes

$$ER_{p,t} = E_{0,t} + \beta_{p,1}(ER_{1,t} - E_{0,t}) \tag{19.15}$$

where $E_{0,t}$ is the expected return for the portfolio if the systematic risk for the portfolio is zero; $\beta_{p,1}$ is the systematic risk for a portfolio (equal to 1.0 for the average systematic risk for F1); and $(ER_{1,t} - E_{0,t})$ is F1's risk premium.

This normalization allows us to interpret APT's measure of systematic risk like the CAPM's beta. If systematic risk is greater than 1.0, the portfolio's systematic risk is higher than the average of all portfolios; if it is less than 1.0, the portfolio is less risky than average. Again, it provides a reference point for factor F1's systematic risk.

Having developed an intuitive feel for arbitrage, we make a leap by induction to apply the principle to valuation of securities. If a well-diversified portfolio can be valued by Equation 19.12, what about individual securities? Each security must also follow Equation 19.12 as long as arbitrageurs can create well-diversified portfolios to mimic a security's extraordinary return. Put differently, if JNJ were compensating investors for firm-specific risk such as product tampering [for example, if $SD(e_i) \neq 0$], shrewd investors could create combinations of other stocks in a portfolio that would have the same systematic risk level as JNJ. They would sell the portfolio short and buy more JNJ, driving JNJ's price upward until its return came to equal the portfolio's, or until JNJ's $SD(e_i)$ would no longer affect its security return.

Therefore, if a security return could be recreated by a combination of other securities' returns (in a portfolio), no arbitrage profits would remain and all securities would be priced to reflect only the systematic risk associated with the factor. Then Equation 19.15, which we have applied only to well-diversified portfolios, can be extended to security i's return:

$$ER_{i,t} = E_{0,t} + \beta_{i,1}(ER_{1,t} - E_{0,t}) \quad \text{for } i = 1, 2, \ldots, N \tag{19.16}$$

This equation should look vaguely familiar. It resembles the CAPM formula, if some assumptions are made. We see in the next section that the single-factor APT model and the CAPM take on exactly the same form, but we also examine differences between the two processes.

Single-Factor APT and the CAPM

Because $\beta_{i,1}$ is defined as a security's sensitivity to factor F1, this APT variable has the same definition as beta in the CAPM. Given a single-factor APT model and defining F1 as the market portfolio M, the term $ER_{1,t} - E_{0,t}$ in Equation 19.16 becomes $ER_{M,t} - RF_t$. Also, if $E_{0,t}$ equals RF, it makes Equation 19.16 equal to

$$ER_i = RF + \beta_{i,M}(ER_M - RF)$$

The term $(ER_M - RF)$ is the market risk premium, and $\beta_{i,M}$ is security i's systematic risk relative to the market portfolio M.

The result is the same formula as the CAPM. However, the process of arriving at the final formula is quite different; the APT model uses the arbitrage principle, whereas the CAPM uses utility theory. Let's discuss how the APT develops the single-factor model.

Development of the Single-Factor APT

In Chapter 17, we found that risk-averse investors are enticed to invest in risky securities only if they are compensated for risk. Even in Chapter 1, we defined a risk/return relationship as

$$ER_i = RF + \text{Risk premium}$$

The compensation for accepting risk equals

$ER_i - RF$ = Risk premium

The left side of the equation, $ER_i - RF$, is the reward for accepting risk. How can one measure security risk?

Recall from the previous section that systematic risk is the only relevant risk for a well-diversified portfolio because a portfolio diversifies away any firm-specific risk. Therefore, a reward-to-risk ratio for a well-diversified portfolio can be defined as

$$\text{Reward-to-risk ratio} = \frac{(ER_p - RF)}{\beta_p}$$

In market equilibrium, the reward-to-risk ratios for all well-diversified portfolios must be equal, otherwise market forces would arbitrage any profits until they reached equality. In essence, the reward-to-risk ratio must increase proportionately or else arbitrage opportunities, as described earlier, are possible. If so, arbitrageurs will eliminate any discrepancies in portfolios with arbitrage profits. For two well-diversified portfolios, G and Q,

$$\frac{(ER_G - RF)}{\beta_G} = \frac{(ER_Q - RF)}{\beta_Q}$$

Now, what about securities? If securities' returns can be duplicated by combinations of other portfolios, in market equilibrium, they too must have reward-to-risk ratios that equal those of the portfolios. For example, suppose a well-diversified portfolio, M, can combine other securities so that its systematic risk is the same as security i. Their reward-to-risk ratios must be equal.

$$\frac{(ER_i - RF)}{\beta_i} = \frac{(ER_M - RF)}{\beta_M}$$

If not, arbitrage would drive them into equality. Suppose that security i's reward-to-risk ratio equals 0.8, whereas the ratio of the combination portfolio M equals 0.6.

$$\frac{(ER_M - RF)}{\beta_M} = \frac{(0.12 - 0.06)}{1.0} = 0.6$$

$$\frac{(ER_i - RF)}{\beta_i} = \frac{(0.30 - 0.06)}{0.30} = 0.8$$

Investors who notice that security i has a greater reward-to-risk ratio than portfolio M will purchase security i and sell portfolio M short until the two reward-to-risk ratios become equal. This relationship says simply that as risk increases, reward must increase in the same proportion for every security in the market; otherwise mispricing occurs. However, arbitrage quickly corrects any mispricing to prevent a security from earning a reward out of proportion to its risk.

If securities can be combined into a portfolio that duplicates the return of security i, but with a different reward-to-risk ratio, arbitrage will occur. In the end, most securities and portfolios have a single reward-to-risk ratio:

$$\frac{(ER_j - RF)}{\beta_j} = \frac{(ER_i - RF)}{\beta_i} = \frac{(ER_M - RF)}{\beta_M}$$

In equilibrium, all securities, including portfolios, must have the same reward-to-risk ratio or

$$\frac{(ER_i - RF)}{\beta_i} = \frac{(ER_M - RF)}{\beta_M}$$

Remember that if beta is normalized, the average beta equals 1.0, where the average portfolio is represented by a well-diversified portfolio M. Therefore, the reward-to-risk ratio is

$$\frac{(ER_i - RF)}{\beta_i} = \frac{(ER_M - RF)}{1.0}$$

Solve for ER_i to determine the risk/return relationship for security i:

$$ER_i = RF + \beta_i(ER_M - RF)$$

If portfolio M is defined as the market portfolio, beta, β_i is security i's risk contribution to the market portfolio and $(ER_M - RF)$ is the market risk premium.

You probably recognize Equation 19.17 as the CAPM from Chapter 18; however, the process of developing the formula using APT is different from that in Chapter 18, which used utility theory and the capital market line (CML). The next section outlines the differences between the single-factor APT and the CAPM.

Differences Between the Single-Factor APT and the CAPM

Four major differences separate the single-factor APT and the CAPM:

1. The APT is appealing because it relies only on the premise that arbitrage will preclude any mispricing in a rational capital market, maintaining market equilibrium. The CAPM relies on utility theory and risk aversion to develop the risk/return relationship, giving CAPM a less intuitive basis than the APT.
2. The development of the single-factor APT assumes a well-diversified portfolio that affects returns on individual securities. The APT does not rely on any unobservable market portfolio, as the CAPM does.
3. However, the CAPM does have its strengths. Its development shows that all traded securities will lie on its risk/return line; the APT guarantees that diversified portfolios must lie on the line, but individual securities may diverge somewhat. It recognizes the possibility of small mispricing errors, although it is virtually impossible for most securities to systematically deviate from the APT's risk/return line.
4. Both models have drawbacks that become apparent when conducting empirical tests. The CAPM is not testable because no one can observe the true market portfolio, whereas the APT does not define its factors, nor does it rely on a set number of factors.

Both models have weaknesses and strengths, so it is impossible to say that one model is clearly better. However, both models help the analyst to quantify a risk premium and both define risk/return relationships useful in evaluating securities for investment decisions.

The final step we take is to develop a multifactor APT, which assumes that many factors are significant in explaining security returns. We start with a two-factor APT and generalize to the N-factor APT. In either case, the underlying principle is the same; the only difference is the initial premise that more than one factor can affect an ex-post security return.

APT with Multiple Factors

The concept of security pricing based on arbitrage can extend to more than one factor. In fact, introduction of several factors says only that security j's return depends on more than one force, so it can be recreated by holding a linear combination of different factors. Using the same arbitrage principle, we show that if a security's return can be mimicked by combining several stocks in a portfolio, no arbitrage profits remain. We begin by extending the single-factor relationship to a two-factor relationship.

Two-Factor APT A two-factor APT extends the single-factor APT by defining a security's realized returns and expected returns as

Realized return: $\quad \tilde{R}_{i,t} = ER_{i,t} + \beta_{i,1}\tilde{f}_{1,t} + \beta_{i,2}\tilde{f}_{2,t} + \tilde{e}_{i,t}$ $\qquad$ (19.18)

Expected return: $\quad ER_{i,t} = E_{0,t} + \beta_{i,1}EF_{1,t} + \beta_{i,2}EF_{2,t}$ $\qquad$ (19.19)

where $E_{0,t}$ is security i's expected return if it is uncorrelated to F1 and F2; EF_1 and EF_2 are the factors' expected effects, based on F1 and F2, respectively; $\tilde{f}_{1,t}$ and $\tilde{f}_{2,t}$ are the effects of unanticipated changes in stock i's ex-post return, which are uncorrelated to $e_{i,t}$ ($\tilde{f}_{1,t}$ and $\tilde{f}_{2,t}$ are also uncorrelated); $\beta_{i,1}$ and $\beta_{i,2}$ are the systematic risk effects of F1 and F2, respectively; finally, $\tilde{e}_{i,t}$ is the firm-specific risk, which is uncorrelated to F1 and F2.

Well-diversified portfolios can eliminate firm-specific risk through diversification, so their realized returns are calculated as follows:

Realized return $\quad \tilde{R}_{p,t} = ER_{p,t} + \beta_{p,1}\tilde{f}_{1,t} + \beta_{p,2}\tilde{f}_{2,t}$ $\qquad$ (19.20)

Again, an example can illustrate that the effects of unanticipated changes $\tilde{f}_{1,t}$ and $\tilde{f}_{2,t}$ are offset in arbitrage, leaving the expected return, $ER_{p,t}$, in a linear relationship with systematic risk, or beta, as defined in Equation 19.19.

Suppose that two portfolios, P and Q, have the following systematic risks to F1 and F2 and expected returns, ER_P and ER_Q:

Portfolio	$\beta_{p,1}$	$\beta_{p,2}$	$ER_{p,t}$
P	0.1	0.2	0.05
Q	0.3	0.6	0.18

Investing 300% in portfolio P would give the following risk levels and expect return:

$$\beta_{p,1} = 3(0.1) = 0.3$$
$$\beta_{p,2} = 3(0.2) = 0.6$$
$$ER_{p,t} = 3(0.05) = 0.15$$

Notice that portfolio P's risk levels are now equal to those of portfolio Q, but its return is lower (15% versus 18%). This situation suggests a strategy of selling short a dollar of portfolio P for every dollar invested in portfolio Q, resulting in the following realized returns for portfolios P and Q:

Realized return for investment in portfolio Q	$\tilde{R}_{Q,t}$	$= (0.18 + 0.3\tilde{f}_{1,t} + 0.6\tilde{f}_{2,t})$
Realized return for short sale of portfolio P	$-\tilde{R}_{P,t}$	$= -(0.15 + 0.3\tilde{f}_{1,t} + 0.6\tilde{f}_{2,t})$
	$(\tilde{R}_{Q,t} - \tilde{R}_{P,t})$	$= +0.03$

Again, the unanticipated effects, $\tilde{f}_{1,t}$ and $\tilde{f}_{2,t}$, offset each other for well-diversified portfolios, generating a 3% arbitrage profit. The arbitrage will continue until the expected returns from the portfolios are equal, so the two-factor APT for a well-diversified portfolio can be described by

$$ER_{p,t} = E_{0,t} + \beta_{p,1}EF_{1,t} + \beta_{p,2}EF_{2,t}$$

This equation assumes that most securities' returns can be replicated as combinations of other securities or portfolios, so arbitrage profits will be virtually zero for securities, too. If so, security i's expected return can also be written as a linear relationship of the beta risks of the two factors:

$$ER_{i,t} = E_{0,t} + \beta_{i,1}EF_{1,t} + \beta_{i,2}EF_{2,t}$$

As in the single-factor APT, standardizing each beta can set the average beta equal to 1.0 for each factor's beta. The standardized two-factor APT is calculated as follows:

$$ER_{p,t} = E_{0,t} + \beta_{p,1}(EF_{1,t} - E_{0,t}) + \beta_{p,2}(EF_{2,t} - E_{0,t}) \tag{19.21}$$

where $E_{0,t}$ is the expected return value when all factors equal zero; $(EF_{1,t} - E_{0,t})$ and $(EF_{2,t} - E_{0,t})$ are risk premiums for factors F1 and F2, respectively; $\beta_{i,1}$ and $\beta_{i,2}$ are systematic risks for factors F1 and F2, respectively.

The two-factor APT is derived much like the single-factor APT. The only difference is that it includes more than one factor to describe the realized return.

N-Factor APT Now, suppose that N factors describe the realized return for a security. Security j's realized return equals

$$\tilde{R}_{j,t} = E_{0,t} + \beta_{j,1}(EF_{1,t} + \tilde{f}_{1,t}) + \beta_{j,1}(EF_{2,t} + \tilde{f}_{2,t}) + \cdots$$
$$+ \beta_{j,N}(EF_{N,t} + \tilde{f}_{N,t}) + \tilde{e}_{j,t}$$

where $k = 1, 2, \ldots, N$ representing the k factors; where the $EF_{k,t}$ terms are the expected values of the k factors in period t. The $\tilde{f}_{k,t}$ terms are the unexpected values of the k factors in period t, $\tilde{e}_{j,t}$ is the firm-specific risk that is uncorrelated to any of the unexpected $f_{j,t}$ values; $\beta_{j,k}$, are the sensitivities or systematic risks associated with each of the k factors; $E_{0,t}$ is the expected return value when each of the N factors equals zero.

First, separate and collect the expected values of all the k factors as one term and the unexpected values as the second term:

$$\tilde{R}_{j,t} = (E_{0,t} + \beta_{j,1}EF_{1,t} + \beta_{j,2}EF_{2,t} + \ldots + \beta_{j,N}EF_{N,t}) \\ + (\beta_{j,1}\tilde{f}_{1,t} + \beta_{j,2}\tilde{f}_{2,t} + \ldots + \beta_{j,N}\tilde{f}_{N,t}) + \tilde{e}_{j,t}$$

(19.22)

Because the first term in parentheses can be defined as the expected return for all the factors that are correlated with security j, make the following substitution:

$$ER_{j,t} = (E_{0,t} + \beta_{j,1}EF_{1,t} + \beta_{j,2}EF_{2,t} + \ldots + \beta_{j,N}EF_{N,t})$$

Inserting this term into Equation 19.22 gives

$$\tilde{R}_{j,t} = ER_{j,t} + (\beta_{j,1}\tilde{f}_{1,t} + \beta_{j,2}\tilde{f}_{2,t} + \ldots + \beta_{j,N}\tilde{f}_{N,t}) + \tilde{e}_{j,t}$$

(19.23)

This formula says that if an expected return on a security can be recreated by factors and their systematic risks, arbitrageurs will price the two the same, assuming they pay no transaction costs. The security's realized return must then equal its expected return, which is explained by many factors, plus the unanticipated changes of those factors. Therefore, each $\beta_{j,k}$ is composed of two components: the part of security return that is sensitive to and explained by factor $F_{k,t}$ and the part that is sensitive, but not explained by $F_{k,t}$; the second part is captured by a random term, $\tilde{f}_{k,t}$. The unpredictable component can be unexpected factor outcomes $(\tilde{f}_{k,t})$ or unexpected firm-specific events $(\tilde{e}_{j,t})$. If a factor to explain a security return were an industry index, an unanticipated outcome might be a new drug breakthrough; a firm-specific outcome could be a product-tampering episode. Again, if the three conditions outlined for the single-factor APT model hold, virtually no arbitrage opportunities exist, implying the relationship

$$ER_{j,t} = E_{0,t} + \beta_{j,1}(EF_{1,t} - E_{0,t}) + \beta_{j,2}(EF_{2,t} - E_{0,t}) + \ldots \\ + \beta_{j,N}(EF_{N,t} - E_{0,t})$$

(19.24)

where $EF_{k,t} - E_{0,t}$ is the risk premium for the kth factor; $E_{0,t}$ is the expected return value when all N factors equal zero (this value is uncorrelated to all the factors); $\beta_{j,k}$ equals the systematic risk or beta of security j with the kth factor. Also, each factor must be uncorrelated with the other factors (that is, $CORR(F1,F2) = 0.0$). The same relationship must hold for other pairs of factors.

This formula says that each factor, F_k, captures an independently different effect and its sensitivity is measured by its corresponding beta, $\beta_{j,k}$. The only requirement is that the number of factors must be less than the number of securities being evaluated. Researchers found that three to six factors can eliminate virtually all arbitrage opportunities.[16]

Final Synopsis of APT

multifactor APT model

Risk/return relationship in which many variables (or factors) are related to the stock returns and are used to measure the stock risk.

The **multifactor APT model** is more robust than the CAPM because it allows for several factors that may affect security returns and it avoids the need to identify a true market portfolio. However, it has some empirical problems of its own. The factors are not well defined, so the analyst must empirically attempt to identify the factors significant in describing security returns. This need creates two types of problems: (1) the factors may change, depending on the sample of securities used to ascertain them; and (2) factors may change over time.

Researchers found that increasing the sample size also increases the number of factors that significantly affect security returns. The question of what the factors are is difficult to resolve. Furthermore, the number of factors appears to vary, not only with the sample but with time periods as well.

An alternative strategy is to define factors that appear to be plausible descriptions of security returns. For example, Chen, Roll, and Ross tested specified factors and found that a large part of a security's return can be explained by four factors: (1) differences between yields to maturity on long-term and short-term Treasury securities, (2) inflation rates, (3) differences between yields to maturity on BB-rated corporate bonds and Treasury bills, and (4) growth of industrial production (or gross national product).[17]

In conclusion, extensive research continues toward determining the appropriate risk measures, but both academics and practitioners agree that risk level is an important component in making good investment decisions.

IMPLICATIONS FOR INVESTORS

Generally, these extensions of CAPM define risk slightly differently. However, the extensions of CAPM and the APT all tell us that risk is an important component of evaluating investments and that we should account for it by using models or theory helpful in quantifying it. Most investors resort to the CAPM despite its shortcomings to measure risk and allow for other qualitative factors in order to determine the risk level of each investment.

SUMMARY

1.   What is the zero-beta portfolio model?
The zero-beta portfolio model relaxes the CAPM's assumption that all investors can borrow and lend at the risk-free rate, RF. It results in a similar linear, beta risk/return relationship; however, it replaces the risk-free asset with a zero-beta portfolio, or a stock portfolio that is uncorrelated to the market portfolio.

---

[16]Richard Roll and Stephen Ross, "An Empirical Investigation of the Arbitrage Pricing Theory," *Journal of Finance*, December 1980, pp. 1073–1103.
[17]Nai-Fu Chen, Richard Roll, and Stephen Ross, "Economic Forces and the Stock Market," *Journal of Business*, September 1986, pp. 383–404.

2. What are some results of empirical tests of the CAPM?

Empirical findings for the CAPM are less than satisfactory. Major findings indicate that (1) actual beta risk/return relationships are flatter than theory suggests, (2) the y-intercept does not equal the risk-free rate, RF, and (3) the slope for the SML was slightly negative during some periods in 1957 to 1965.

3. What is Roll's critique of the CAPM?

Roll mathematically proves that the CAPM cannot be empirically tested because any efficient portfolio will have an exactly linear beta risk/return relationship, as described by the CAPM. Unless the analyst can identify an ex-ante market portfolio (which is impossible), no one can test the CAPM. One can test only whether the proxy for the market portfolio is mean-variance efficient.

4. What is the APT?

The APT is based on the theory that identical assets must be priced exactly the same, otherwise, investors will arbitrage the profits to zero. Ross developed an alternative way of viewing asset pricing based on this principle. His model is more robust than the CAPM and incorporates a formula exactly like the CAPM. However, the process of arriving at the final formula is quite different. (CAPM uses utility theory, and APT uses arbitrage theory.) Also, the APT can include multiple factors.

REVIEW EXERCISES

1. What assumption of the CAPM is relaxed to develop the zero-beta portfolio model?
2. What are the general results of the empirical tests for the CAPM and zero-beta portfolio model?
3. How would you explain the negative risk/return relationship that is documented for the April 1957 to December 1965 period?
4. What are the premises of Roll's critique of the CAPM?
5. According to Roll, what are the implications of the empirical results provided by Black, Jensen, and Scholes?
6. The chapter example on portfolios CD and K shows the dollar payoffs if $\tilde{f}_{1,t}$ equals $-3\%, 0\%,$ and 5%. What are the dollar payoffs if $\tilde{f}_{1,t}$ equals -5% and 2%?
7. The chapter example on portfolios CD and K shows the dollar payoffs if $\tilde{f}_{1,t}$ equals $-3\%, 0\%,$ and 5%. What are the dollar payoffs if $\tilde{f}_{1,t}$ equals -10% and $+10\%$?
8. What are the conceptual differences between the single-factor APT and the CAPM?
9. Suppose that one factor affects ex-post realized returns and expected returns. The systematic risk, $\beta_{p,1}$, and expected returns for three well-diversified portfolios, A, B, and X, are given in the following table.

Portfolio	$\beta_{p,1}$	$ER_{p,t}$
A	1.2	0.15
B	0.3	0.06
X	0.9	0.11

If you invest in portfolio B and in portfolio X, what arbitrage profits can you gain when you hedge the BX portfolio with portfolio A? Create a table similar to Table 19.1. Show the realized dollar payoffs at unanticipated changes of -8% and $+12\%$.

10. Suppose that two factors affect ex-post realized returns and expected returns. The systematic risks, $\beta_{p,1}$ and $\beta_{p,2}$ and expected returns for two well-diversified portfolios, R and S, are given in the following table.

Portfolio	$\beta_{p,1}$	$\beta_{p,2}$	$ER_{p,t}$
R	0.5	0.3	0.07
S	1.0	0.6	0.09

a. Write the expected return and systematic risk relationship for portfolios R and S.
b. Write the realized return and systematic risk relationship for portfolios R and S.
c. Do these portfolios offer any arbitrage opportunities? If so, how would you construct the arbitrage?

11. Suppose that two factors affect ex-post realized returns and expected returns. The systematic risks, $\beta_{p,1}$ and $\beta_{p,2}$ and expected returns for two well-diversified portfolios, X and Y, are given in the following table.

Portfolio	$\beta_{p,1}$	$\beta_{p,2}$	$ER_{p,t}$
X	0.2	0.4	0.16
Y	0.1	0.2	0.09

a. Write the expected return and systematic risk relationship for portfolios X and Y.
b. Write the realized return and systematic risk relationship for portfolios X and Y.
c. Do these portfolios offer any arbitrage opportunities? If so, how would you construct the arbitrage?

CRITICAL THINKING EXERCISES

This exercise requires computer work. Open the CAPM worksheet in the Data Workbook. The betas are estimated using the S&P 500 index as the market proxy. Suppose these mutual funds represent portfolios identified in the first-pass regression. Run the second-pass regression described by Equation 19.5 and answer the following questions. Recall Equation 19.5 is

$$M(R_{i,t} - RF_t) = \gamma_0 + \gamma_1\beta_i \quad \text{for } i = 1, 2, \ldots, N$$

a. What should γ_0 and γ_1 equal if the mutual fund returns follow the CAPM relationship?
b. What are the estimates for γ_0 and γ_1? Do they support the CAPM relationship? Explain.
c. Graph the actual regression line and the theoretical relationship. What conclusions can you draw from the difference?
d. According to Roll's critique of the CAPM, what do the results imply about the market proxy, the S&P 500?

THE INTERNET INVESTOR

Go to an Internet site with stock quotes for five years. Obtain monthly stock price quotes and dividends paid for a stock and for index quotes for the Dow Jones Industrial Average (DJIA) and the S&P 500 Index. Calculate returns using the formula: $R_{I,t} = \ln(P_{I,t} + DIV_{i,t}) - \ln(P_{i,t-1})$ for the five-year period.

1. Run a market model regression for the stock return using the DJIA as the market portfolio.
2. Run the market model regression for the stock return using the S&P 500 index as the market portfolio.
3. Compare the beta estimates and determine the SD of the regression residual.
4. What can you conclude given the critique of the CAPM?

PART 7

Investment Management

Part 7 discusses how investment portfolios should be managed and serves as a logical capstone for the book. Chapter 20 sets out a systematic procedure by which investment portfolios are built and managed. Chapter 21 describes in detail how portfolio performance can be evaluated.

20

Building and Managing an Investment Portfolio

PREVIOUSLY . . .

Together the prior three chapters developed something we call modern portfolio theory (MPT). We discussed concepts such as diversification, efficient frontiers, beta, and arbitrage pricing.

IN THIS CHAPTER . . .

We describe how investment portfolios should be constructed and managed, whether the investor is an individual or an institution, and whether the investor takes an active approach to investing or more of a passive approach. This chapter, along with the next chapter, attempts to tie together the many themes and issues we covered up to this point.

TO COME . . .

We conclude our journey through the world of investments with a discussion of how to evaluate the performance of investment portfolios.

CHAPTER OBJECTIVES
After reading Chapter 20, you should be able to answer the following questions:

1. What is the process of building and managing an investment portfolio?

2. How is an investment policy developed?

3. How do capital market assumptions affect the investment process?

4. What is asset allocation?

5. What does monitoring a portfolio involve?

In a sense, everything in the prior 19 chapters sets the stage for these final two chapters. We described risk and return, the wide array of investment alternatives, how securities are bought and sold, how to analyze bonds and common stocks, the purpose of derivative securities, and modern portfolio theory. All of these topics are combined when building and managing an investment portfolio.

Building and managing an investment portfolio requires that every investor make a series of decisions and complete a set of tasks. The investor must establish investment objectives in light of constraints, preferences, and circumstances. Expectations concerning the future performance of various investment instruments must be formed. Investment funds must be allocated and performance evaluated. The overall goal of this process is the creation of an investment portfolio that comes as close as possible to meeting the investor's objectives. Ultimately, the success of any investment program should be judged by the performance of the portfolio, not the performance of the individual investments that make up the portfolio.

In this chapter, we outline the step-by-step process of building and managing an investment portfolio. Even though the specifics obviously will vary widely from investor to investor, the basic process is always the same, regardless of whether the investor is an individual or an institution; whether the investor wants to take an active approach or a passive approach; whether the investment horizon is 5 years or 50 years; and whether an investor has $10,000 to invest or $10 million to invest.

CONSTRUCTING AND MANAGING A PORTFOLIO

An outline of the steps in the process of building and managing a portfolio is shown in Figure 20.1. The outline is fairly general because specifics will vary from investor to investor. Yet all investors follow the same steps, and follow them in the order shown. The first step is the development of an investment policy. An investment policy blends three elements: (1) the investor's objectives, (2) the constraints faced by the investor, and (3) any investor preferences.

Investment objectives are defined in terms of the investor's required return and risk tolerance. Both are heavily influenced by the investor's characteristics. For example, is the investor an individual or an institution? If the investor is an institution, what kind of institution (profit or not-for-profit)? If the investor is an individual, what are his or her personal characteristics (such things as age and income)? What kind of time horizon does the investor have (short term or long term)? Constraints include the degree of risk aversion, legal or regulatory constraints, the investor's tax situation, and so forth. Preferences include any unique needs or circumstances.

Because investing is never done in a vacuum, the investor must also formulate some expectations concerning the financial markets. For example, how will stocks perform over the investment horizon, relative to bonds and money market instruments? Often investors base their expectations on historical performance data—data we reviewed frequently throughout the book—because, of course, ex-post returns are the only actual returns we ever have. Remember, however, the past is never a guarantee of the future, and the use of historical return data can be problematic. It must be used carefully and appropriately.

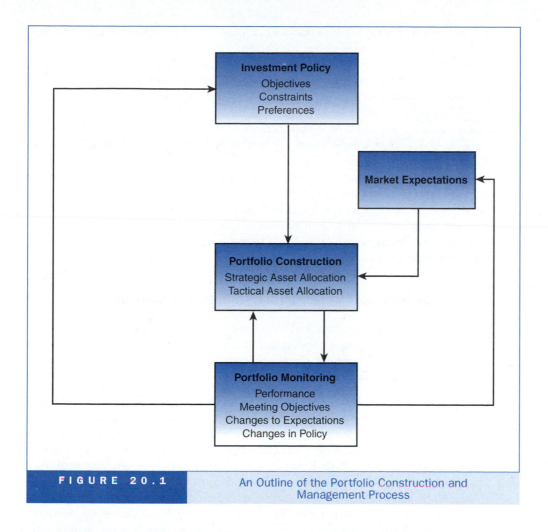

FIGURE 20.1
An Outline of the Portfolio Construction and Management Process

Portfolio construction is the next step in the process. By combining investment policy, along with market expectations, strategic and tactical asset allocations decisions can be made. The investor determines the general mix of investments (strategic asset allocation) along with specific investments within each general category (tactical asset allocation). Issues such as diversification and risk/return optimization are also factors in asset allocation decisions.

The final step in the process is portfolio monitoring. Whether the investor takes an active approach or more of a passive one, the performance of the portfolio should be measured and evaluated. Part of this step includes a determination of whether the investment objectives are being met. If investment objectives are not being attained in a satisfactory manner, then changes to the portfolio need to be made. The investor should return to the portfolio construction step.

The process shown in Figure 20.1 is not a one-way street—it is more of a circle. For one thing, investor characteristics often change over time. For example, individual investors get older. As they get older, their needs and objectives will also change. The investment objectives of a 30-year-old, investing for retirement, are markedly different from the investment objectives of a 65-year-old who is about to retire. Changes in investor characteristics lead to changes in investment policy which, in turn, affect asset allocation.

Financial market expectations can also change. A sharp rise in interest rates, for example, will likely affect asset allocation, even if investment policy remains essentially unchanged.

DEVELOPING AN INVESTMENT POLICY

investment policy

A set of guidelines that specifies actions to be taken to achieve the investor's objectives, within the constraints imposed by or on the investor.

The first step in the process of building a portfolio is to develop an investment policy. An **investment policy** is a set of guidelines that specifies actions to be taken to achieve the investor's objectives, within the constraints imposed by or on the investor. Both individual and institutional investors should develop investment policies. Some important differences distinguish individual investors from institutional investors. Let's review some of these differences.

Differences Between Individuals and Institutions

Investment professionals often deal with both individual investors as well as institutional investors (such as a pension fund or a not-for-profit organization). Even though the overall investment process is essentially the same for both types of investors, important differences include the following:

- *Time horizon.* Individuals obviously don't live forever, so an individual investor's time horizon is a function of where that person is in his or her life cycle (e.g., just beginning a career or just about to retire). Individuals can be short-term investors or long-term investors depending on where they are in the life cycle. On the other hand, most institutions are long-term investors. An institution may have some short-term needs yet still have a long-term horizon.
- *Changes in investor characteristics.* As individuals process through the life cycle, the investor characteristics change dramatically, investors age, incomes rise, and so on. Institutions, by their very nature, rarely have a life cycle. Consequently, their characteristics change little, if at all, over time.
- *Risk and behavior.* As a *general* rule, individual investors are more risk averse than institutional investors. Many individuals view risk as only the possibility that they may lose money. Institutions often take a broader view of risk and deal with risk in a more rational manner than do individual investors; individual investors tend to be more emotional. Conventional wisdom seems to suggest that individual investors, often less experienced than institutional investors, are more prone to falling into the bubble trap and to panicking when prices plunge. However, experience seems to suggest otherwise— institutional investors are just as likely as individual investors to fall into the bubble trap.
- *Reasons for investing.* Individuals often have specific reasons for investing. Such things as buying a home, sending a child to college, or retiring early. The reasons institutions are investing, on the other hand, may be much more general. As a result when developing a profile for an institutional investor, you need to consider not just the characteristics of the institution, but also the characteristics of those who may benefit from the institution's investments.

- *Regulatory and legal constraints.* Institutions are subject to numerous legal and regulatory constraints when making investment decisions. Individuals, on the other hand, have much more freedom when it comes to investing. Common sense, rather than laws or regulations, is the guiding force for individuals.
- *Taxes.* Taxes are an important consideration for individuals, because virtually all personal investing has tax implications. Taxes are often much less important for institutional investors. Many, in fact, are tax exempt.

Formulating Investment Objectives

In general, the three investment objectives are growth in capital, preservation of capital, and current income. As we noted previously, inflation erodes investment returns. Consequently, all three objectives should be thought of in real, not nominal terms. If growth in capital is an objective, capital should grow at a rate exceeding the rate of inflation; if capital is to be preserved, it should be preserved in real terms; and if current income is an objective, it should keep pace with the rate of inflation over time.

All investors must prioritize these three objectives. No single investment instrument is perfect. Money market instruments, for example, preserve capital and produce modest amounts of current income, but they provide no opportunity for capital growth. Common stocks have the potential for substantial capital growth, but many provide little if any current income. And, of course, stock prices don't always go up.

How the investor prioritizes capital growth, capital preservation, and current income depends on the characteristics of the investor and the reason(s) for investing. For individual investors, some important characteristics include age, income, martial status, number of dependents, existing assets and liabilities, insurance protection, and current pension benefits. Some of the reasons individuals give for investing include buying a home, sending children to college, or a financial secure retirement.

Prioritizing investment objectives involves a trade-off between risk and return. Obviously all investors want high returns, with low risk, but it doesn't work that way in the real world. A recurring themes throughout this book is that risk and return are positively related. Higher returns come at a price, higher risk. Blending individual characteristics with the reasons for investing suggests the proper trade-off between risk and return. Several hypothetical examples will help to illustrate this point.

Mark's Retirement Mark is 25 and just starting his career. Like most employers today, Mark's employer offers a so-called benefit contribution retirement plan. In a defined contribution plan, both Mark and his employer make contributions to Mark's retirement account. Mark has a fair degree of control over where the retirement assets are invested. Contributions are tax deductible and investment profits are tax deferred. Mark would like to retire at age 60 and figures he needs to accumulate at least $1.5 million in his retirement account by then.[1]

---

[1]Think Mark's goal is ambitious? It's not. If you started working today, the experts will tell you that you need save a minimum of $1 million (in constant dollars) by the time you retire. Company pensions and Social Security will meet only a fraction of your retirement needs.

Prioritizing Mark's investment objectives is straightforward. Mark is clearly a long-term investor (his time horizon is 35 years). Current income is not an issue at this point, nor is preservation of capital. His clear objective is growth in capital. If Mark and his employer are contributing $6,000 a year to his retirement account, Mark needs to earn a minimum of about 9.6% per year in order to meet his goal. Because Mark is a long-term investor he can afford to take risks. He is in a position of being able to mostly ignore the day-to-day, even the year-to-year volatility in the financial markets.

Kim's Daughter's College Education Here's another simple example. Kim is in her early 40s and wants to have enough money saved in five years to send her daughter to college. Kim believes that she needs about $35,000 in cash at that time and is saving $6,100 per year. What are her investment priorities? Like Mark, current income is not an issue for Kim. On the other hand, unlike Mark, Kim has a much shorter term investment horizon. Even though she needs some growth in capital, she needs to earn about 6.5% per year—preservation of capital is also important. Compared to Mark, Kim can't take as much risk and needs to be more conservative with her investments.

Constraints

constraints

Limitations imposed on the portfolio construction process.

Constraints are limitations imposed on the portfolio construction process. Constraints can be self-imposed (imposed by the investor) or can be imposed by others. Investors must operate within constraints and preferences when developing an appropriate investment policy. As we noted earlier, constraints can vary widely from investor to investor, and the constraints faced by individual investors are different from those faced by institutional investors. Some of the major constraints facing both types of investors are discussed next.

Time Horizon When developing an investment policy, all investors need to consider the investment time horizon. For an individual investor, age and the reasons for investing often determine the time horizon. Consider the examples in the prior section. Mark's time horizon is fairly long (30 to 35 years) while Kim's time horizon is fairly short (5 years). As a *general* rule, the longer the time horizon, the more risk the investor can afford to take.

Liquidity Needs The liquidity needs of investors vary widely. Depending upon individual circumstances liquidity needs can be quite high or quite low. An older investor's liquidity needs, for example, might be higher than average. He or she might need liquid assets to meet unexpected medical or long-term care expenses.

Liquidity, as you probably remember from earlier chapters, is defined the ability to turn an asset into cash at a price close to the asset's "true" value. Virtually all financial assets are liquid. However, the price at which shares of common stock can be turned into cash may be unacceptable to the investor. Consequently, investors with greater liquidity needs should keep a greater portion of their portfolios in money market instruments or other near cash assets.

Taxes As we noted earlier in the chapter, virtually all investment decisions made by individual investors have tax implications. As a *general* rule, the higher the investor's marginal tax bracket, the larger the role played by taxes in investment decisions. Some of the pertinent tax issues include the following:

- Long-term capital gains are taxed at a lower rate than ordinary investment income (dividends and interest).
- Only realized capital gains are subject to taxes; unrealized gains are not taxed until the asset is sold.
- Most retirement programs offer substantial tax benefits. Contributions may be tax deductible, and investment returns are usually tax deferred.
- The market value of any investments are part of a person's estate. Federal estate tax rates are much higher than income tax rates.

Although taxes are an important consideration in individual investment decisions, you have to be careful not to allow the tax tail to wag the investment dog. Focusing solely on taxes, at the expense of all other factors, can lead to poor investment decisions.

Regulatory and Legal Constraints Other than those relating to taxes, few legal or regulatory requirements restrict on individual investment decisions. Institutional investors, on the other hand, are subject to extensive regulatory and legal constraints, at both the federal and state levels. Most institutions invest money for the benefits of others—a pension fund, for example, invests money on behalf of current and future beneficiaries. Those who invest money for the benefit of others are subject to something known as the **prudent person rule**. This rule states that the institution should act as a prudent person would when making investment decisions. Unfortunately, legal interpretations of the prudent person rule tend to vary widely from state to state.

An important piece of legislation governing institutional investors in the Employment Retirement Income Security Act (ERISA). Among other things, ERISA set up rules and standards governing employer-sponsored retirement plans, whether these plans are traditional pension plans (so-called defined benefit plans) or retirement savings plans such as 401(k) plans (so-called defined contribution plans).

prudent person rule
A principle that guides institutions to act as a prudent person would when making investment decisions.

Special Needs, Circumstances, and Goals It is not uncommon for investors to have special needs, circumstances, or goals that affect investment decisions. For example, an older investor might want to leave a substantial estate to children or grandchildren. His or her investment choices will obviously be constrained by this goal.

In summary then, formulating an investment policy is a process by which an investor's circumstances and investment objectives are blended with a set of constraints. The resulting investment policy will go a long way in determining the appropriate asset allocation. The investment policy isn't the only input into the asset allocation decision, however. We also need to form some expectations concerning the financial markets.

FINANCIAL MARKET EXPECTATIONS

In the process of forming expectations concerning the financial markets, we can form both *macro-expectations* and *micro-expectations*. **Macro-expectations** involve forming expectations of the future performance for the broad financial

macro-expectations
Expectations of the future performance for broad categories of financial assets.

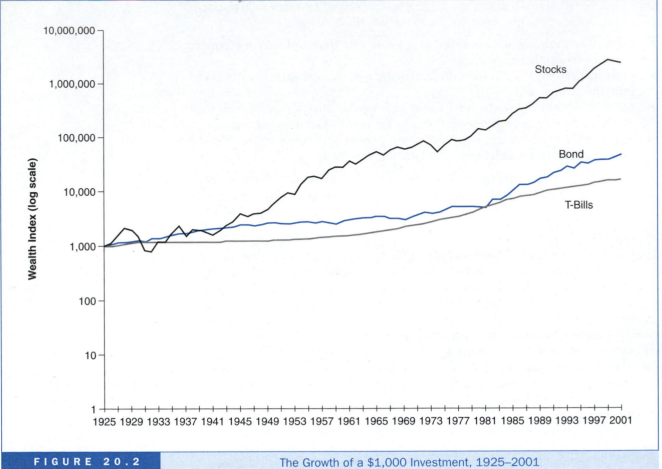

FIGURE 20.2   The Growth of a $1,000 Investment, 1925–2001

micro-expectations

Expectations of the future performance of groups or individual
securities within the broad
categories.

asset categories (stocks, bonds, and money market instruments). **Micro-expectations**
involve the formation of expectations of the future performance of groups and
individual securities within the broad asset categories (for example, the future
performance of small company stocks relative to large company stocks).

Macro-Expectations

A starting point for macro-expectations is the historical record on financial market returns. We summarized much of the historical record throughout the book,
but it is still worth reiterating the two key results.

1. Stocks outperformed bonds and Treasury bills by substantial margins (see
   Figure 20.2). A $1,000 investment in large-company stocks made at the end
   of 1925 was worth in excess of $2.1 million by the end of 2001. By con-
   trast, a $1,000 investment in bonds made at the end of 1925 was worth less
   than $47,000 by the end of 2001. Treasury bills did even worse. In fact,

	Large Stocks	Small Stocks	Bonds	T-bills
Mean return	12.6%	17.3%	5.5%	3.8%
Standard deviation	20.2	33.1	9.0	3.2
Highest return	54.0	142.2	40.4	14.7
Lowest return	−43.3	−58.0	−9.2	0.1
Number of positive periods	54 out of 76	53 out of 76	55 out of 76	76 out of 76

TABLE 20.1

Historical Returns from Stocks, Bonds, and Money Market Instruments, 1926–2001 (annual returns)

	Holding Period			
	1 Year	5 Years	10 Years	20 Years
Mean	12.6%	11.0%	11.2%	11.3%
Standard deviation	20.2	8.4	5.5	3.6
High	54.0	27.5	20.1	17.6
Low	−43.3	−12.5	−0.9%	3.1
Number of positive periods	54 out of 76	65 out of 72	65 out of 67	57 out of 57

TABLE 20.2

The Impact of Holding Period Length on Risk and Return from Large Stocks

Note: All returns are annualized.

Treasury bill returns, on average, barely kept pace with the rate of inflation since the mid 1920s.

2. Stock returns show much more year-to-year variability than either bond or Treasury bill returns (see Table 20.1). This variability is reflected in higher standard deviations and greater ranges between the highest and lowest annual returns. The standard deviation of stock returns is more than twice the standard deviation of bond returns.

However, the historical record also clearly shows that much of the year-to-year variability in stock returns disappears over longer holding periods. We can clearly see the relationship between volatility and holding period by looking at the data shown in Table 20.2. Notice how both the standard deviation and range drop dramatically as the length of the holding period increases. For example, between 1926 and 2001, negative stock returns occurred in 22 years out of a total of 76 years. On the other hand, in no rolling 20-year period out of a total of 57 periods were stock returns negative. Further, the spread of annual returns between the best 20-year period and the worst 20-year period is only about 14.5%. By contrast, the spread in returns between the best year and the worst year for large stocks is almost 100%.

If we go back even further in time we notice that stock returns over long periods of time show remarkable consistency. Take a look at Table 20.3. It shows the nominal and real compound average annual returns from common stocks over varying periods between 1802 and 2000. Notice that the real compound average annual return from common stocks hovered around 7%.

Another way of analyzing historical returns is to calculate the probabilities associated with actually earning various rates of returns. If we make the assumption that historical returns are normally distributed, then we can calculate probabilities

TABLE 20.3		Compound Average Annual Return	
A Summary of Stock Returns Since 1802	Period	Nominal	Real
	1802–1870	7.1%	7.0%
	1871–1925	7.2	6.6
	1926–2001	10.2	6.9
	1802–2001	8.3	6.9

TABLE 20.4		Holding Period			
Probabilities of Earning Minimum Rates of Return	Average Annual Return of at Least	1 Year	5 Years	10 Years	20 Years
	0%	73.3%	90.6%	98.0%	99.9%
	5	64.6	76.4	87.2	96.1
	10	55.1	54.9	58.8	64.3
	15	45.2	31.8	24.5	15.2

based on the mean and standard deviation of each return series.[2] The probabilities for large stock investments, for varying holding periods, are shown in Table 20.4. Notice the impact of the length of the holding period on the probabilities of earning specific rates of return. If you hold stocks for only one year the odds of earning 5%, or more, are about 65%. On the other hand, if you hold stocks for 20 years, the odds of earning at least 5% per year are greater than 97%. Historical data would give virtually no chance of earning negative returns if you invest your money for 20 years. Investing your money in stocks for only year means a 25% chance you will lose money.

So, will these patterns hold over the next year, the next 5 years, the next 30 years, or the next 100 years? If you are a short-term investor, should you avoid stocks. On the other hand, if you have a long-term time horizon, should you invest most of your money in stocks? Obviously no one knows with any certainty what the future will hold, which is part of the risk associated with all investment decisions.

Although our crystal ball isn't any clearer than anyone else's, we do have some observations and caveats that should help investors form macro-expectations concerning the future returns from financial assets.

• We believe that one clear lesson from the historical record is that stocks are better long-term investments than other financial assets. We don't believe that observation will change anytime in the foreseeable future. Real stock returns will continue to average between 6% and 8% per year. Real bond returns will likely average between 3% and 5% per year. Of course, we are not suggesting that stocks will outperform other financial assets next year, or over the next

---

[2]Statistical analysis of historical security returns indicates that the series are fairly close to being normally distributed.

five years. But over longer periods of time—10 to 30 years—we believe stocks will earn substantially higher returns than either bonds or money market instruments.

- Long-term returns are far more predictable or, if you will, less uncertain than short-term returns. Be careful not to place too much emphasis on short-term trends or patterns. For example, just because stocks fared poorly since the end of 1999, doesn't mean that they will continue to do poorly over the next few years. At the same time, don't assume that a period of above-average returns will be followed by a period of below-average returns, or vice versa.
- The historical record is just that—it's a record of what happened, not what will happen. Because the financial markets are forward-looking by nature, the past is never a guarantee of the future. If you believe, as we do, that stock prices follow earnings in the long run, future stock returns will be driven by future corporate profits. Interestingly, over long periods of time increases in corporate profits, like stock returns, have been fairly consistent.

Micro-Expectations

If macro-expectations deal with expected returns from general categories of financial assets, micro-expectations deal with expected returns from groups within the general categories. For stocks, for example, examples of micro-expectations include the expected return from large-company stocks relative to small-company stocks, the expected return from domestic stocks relative to international stocks, or the expected return from growth stocks relative to value stocks. An example of micro-expectations for bonds include the expected return on junk bonds relative to investment grade bonds. Micro-expectations can also be used to select individual securities and to time markets.

As we discussed in the prior section, most investors base their macro-expectations on the historical record. We could base micro-expectations on the historical record as well, but the historical record is far more muddled at the micro-level than it is at the macro level. Take, for example, the performance of large-company stocks versus the performance of small-company stocks. On average, between 1926 and 2001, small stocks have returned about 4% a year more than large stocks (16.9% versus 12.7%). Further, small stocks outperformed large stocks in 42 out of the 76 years. Over longer holding periods, small stocks still beat large stocks. For rolling 20 year holding periods, small stock returns averaged almost 15% per year. By contrast, large stock returns averaged about 11% per year. Out of the 57 rolling 20-year periods between 1926 and 2001, small stocks beat large stocks in all but five of the periods.

Over the last couple of decades, however, the pattern reversed and large stocks often outperformed small stocks. Take a look at the chart shown in Figure 20.3. It shows the compound average annual returns from large and small stocks over varying periods ending on December 31, 2001. Over the 20 years ending on December 31, 2001, large stocks averaged a return of 15% per year. By contrast, returns from small stocks averaged only 12.2% per year. On the other hand, during the years 1999–2001, small stocks regained their dominant position over large stocks.

So what does the future hold? Will small stocks continue their comeback and return to a dominant position relative to large stocks, or will large stocks

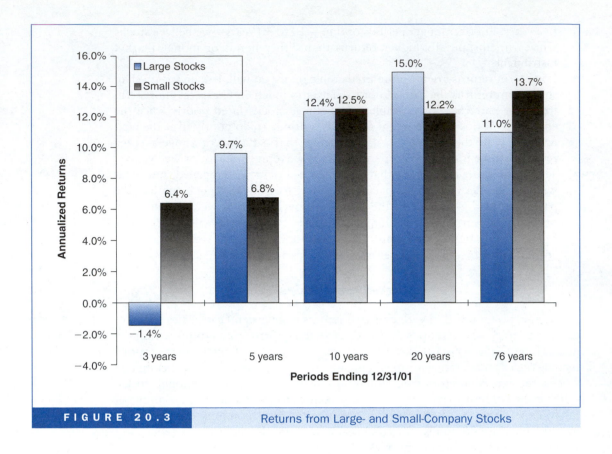

outperform small stocks, as they did during most of the 1990s? Frankly, your guess is as good as anyone else's. We tend to think that small stocks are poised for a comeback, but our conviction isn't terribly strong. We place a lot more confidence in our macro-expectation that stocks will continue to outperform bonds than our micro-expectation that small stocks will begin again to outperform large stocks. Micro-expectations, in addition to being more problematic, simply require much more careful analysis and research.

One way to avoid problems associated with forming micro-expectations is by simply investing in index funds. A 30-year-old investor saving for retirement might invest 80% of her money in a stock index fund and the other 20% in a bond index fund. Index funds, as we know, mimic the broad market and have become extremely popular with investors. The Investment History box on page 585 describes the origins of index funds.

ASSET ALLOCATION

asset allocation

Decisions regarding the percentage of funds to be invested in various financial assets.

Asset allocation involves decisions regarding the percentage of funds to be invested in various financial assets (stocks, bonds, and money market instruments). Asset allocation is the most important part of the portfolio construction

INVESTMENT HISTORY

A Brief History of Index Funds

Index funds—mutual funds designed merely to track a specified index—are extremely popular investment choices today. The largest and oldest index mutual fund, the Vanguard 500 Index fund, has more than $100 billion in assets, ranking it among the five largest stock mutual funds. Investors are attracted to index funds due to their low fees, high tax efficiency, and their ability to routinely outperform most managed mutual funds.

What to many people is one of the greatest inventions of all time, does not have a long history. In the early 1970s, several banks and investment firms began experimenting with indexing. One of the first was a $6 million index account constructed for Samsonite Corporation's pension fund by Wells Fargo Bank. Most investment professionals, however, initially dismissed the idea of indexing as silly. The magazine *Pensions & Investments* awarded its "Dubious Achievement Award" in 1972 to Batterymarch Financial Management of Boston for its index-based investing program. It took until 1975 before Batterymarch attracted its first index client.

By the mid-1970s, however, things began to change. Index fund pioneer and mutual fund maverick John Bogel, argued that three seminal articles, published in the early to mid-1970s by distinguished authors, helped to legitimize the idea of index investing. All three articles pointed out that active investment managers—those managing pension funds and mutual funds—failed to outperform the overall market on a consistent basis. One of authors, the highly respected Charles Ellis, managing partner of Greenwich Associates, wrote, "The investment management business is built upon a simple and basic belief: professionals can beat the market. That premise appears to be false." In fact, Ellis argued, once you subtract the fees col-

lected by professional money managers, most will consistently underperform the market.

These articles, along with his familiarity of the research on the consistency of mutual fund performance, led John Bogel to create the first index mutual fund, what is now the Vanguard 500 Stock Index fund. In 1974, Bogel formed his own mutual fund company, the Vanguard Group. His philosophy was to offer investors low-cost funds. Bogel believed then, and still believes today, that in the long run, low-cost funds outperform high-cost funds. In his mind, an index fund was the closest one could get in a real-world framework to zero-cost investing.

It took a while for Bogel's new invention to catch on. Of course, the 1970s weren't the best of decades for stock investors. Even during the 1980s, however, index funds grew slowly. It really wasn't until the mid-1990s, that the average investor "discovered" index funds, helped along by the popular press. A headline in an issue of *Money* magazine in 1995 read, "Bogel wins: Index funds should be the core of most portfolios today." Today, index funds account for more than 7% of all mutual fund assets (up from less than 3% in 1995).

Questions for Critical Thinking

1. Some argue that index funds are essentially a phenomenon of bull markets and that investors will return to actively managed funds during bear markets. Given the recent market decline, do you agree or disagree with that statement?

2. What are the major advantages and disadvantages of index funds? How would you explain them to a novice investor?

---

process because the way in which funds are allocated among various financial assets determines the investor's return and risk exposure.

As we noted in Chapter 1, asset allocation decision come in two forms: strategic asset allocation and tactical asset allocation. In strategic asset allocation decisions are made regarding the general mix of investments that will make up the investor's portfolio. For example, the result of strategic asset allocation could be a portfolio consisting of 70% stocks, 20% bonds, and 10% money market instruments. Tactical asset allocation involves selecting specific investments within each of the general categories of stocks, bonds, and money market instruments. For instance, within the 70% of the portfolio invested in stocks, a tactical asset allocation decision might result in half of the funds being invested in large stocks and half in small stocks.

Strategic asset allocation is based on the investor's objectives, return requirements, time horizon, and risk preferences. In general, investors whose main objective is growth in capital will allocate a large share of their investment funds to common stocks. Investors whose main objective is capital preservation, will allocate less of their funds to common stocks, and more to bonds and money market instruments.

Macro-expectations also play a role in strategic asset allocation decisions. An investor who believes, for example, that bonds are attractive at the present time might choose to allocate a larger share of his portfolio to bonds, and a smaller share to stocks, than he would normally.

When it comes to tactical asset allocation decisions, micro-expectations play a prominent role. If, for example, an investor believes that small stocks will begin again to outperform large stocks, the investor might allocate a larger share of the portfolio to small stocks, and a smaller share to large stocks. Tactical asset allocation also deals with individual security selection and market timing.

Which is more important, strategic or tactical asset allocation? According to several studies, strategic asset allocation dominates tactical asset allocation. One study found that virtually all of variation in pension plan returns could be explained by strategic asset allocation decisions.[3]

The Life Cycle Approach to Asset Allocation

According to many investment professionals and financial planners, asset allocation on the part of individuals should be heavily influenced by the person's age, or stage of the life cycle. The life cycle approach to asset allocation is appealing because the financial position, investment objectives, and constraints of a 60-year-old investor are likely to be different from those of a 25-year-old investor.

Jack Bogel, founder and senior chairman of the Vanguard Group (the nation's second-largest mutual fund company), advocates a simple asset allocation model based on two factors. They are the age of the investor, and the whether the investor is in an "accumulation" stage or a "distribution" stage. Investors who are in the accumulation stage have as their main objective, growth in capital. Investors who are in the distribution stage have preservation of capital and current income as their primary investment objectives.

Bogel's model is illustrated in Figure 20.4. Younger investors who are in the capital accumulation stage have long-term investment horizons. They have no immediate need for their money and, therefore, can afford to take greater risks in exchange for higher returns. Consequently these investors should allocate a large portion of their portfolios to common stocks—perhaps as high as 80% or 90%. The balance of their funds should be invested in bonds or money market instruments. Age plays a role for investors in the accumulation stage. The older the investor, the lower the percentage that should be invested in common stocks. However, even older investors who are in the capital accumulation stage should still invest a majority of their funds in common stocks.

Investors who are in more of a distribution stage have more immediate needs for their money. Short-term volatility and losses are far more significant for an

---

[3]These studies are cited and discussed in John Bogel, *Common Sense on Mutual Funds* (New York: John Wiley & Sons, 1999), pp. 67–69.

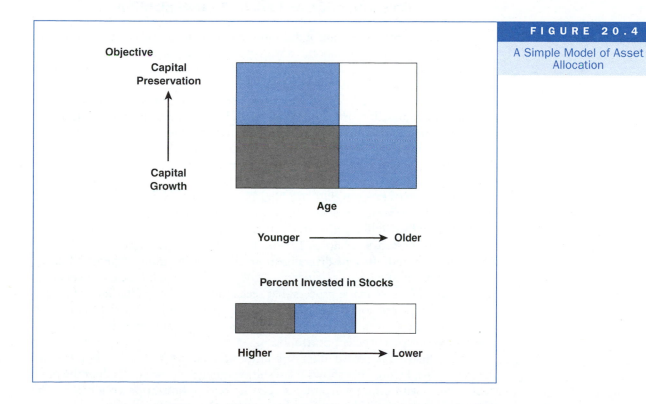

FIGURE 20.4

A Simple Model of Asset Allocation

investor in the distribution stage than for one in the accumulation stage. A retired person, for example, may depend on a relatively fixed amount of capital to generate sufficient income to meet his or her daily needs. As a result investors in the distribution stage should allocate less to stocks, and more to bonds and money market instruments. The appropriate mix might be something like 50% stocks, 30% bonds, and 20% money market instruments. Again, the older the investor, the lower the percentage that should be invested in common stocks.

Older investors must be careful not to become too conservative and allocate all of their funds to money market instruments or bonds. Capital growth is still important even for a 65-year-old, recently retired investor. Here's why. First, although bonds historically produced the highest current income of any financial asset, the interest income paid by a bond doesn't increase over. Considering inflation, real interest income actually declines. The income paid by stocks, on the other hand, historically tends to rise at about the rate of inflation. Consequently, over about a 10-year period, the dividend income from stocks will generally exceed the interest income from bonds. Second, a 65-year-old still has a fairly long investment horizon. According to actuarial statistics a 65-year-old in good health has a life expediency of almost 20 years. Financial planners will tell you that you should plan on living into your 90s. Even the 65-year-old, according to the experts, should still allocate 40% to 50% of his or her portfolio to common stocks. The Investment Insight box on page 589 lists some suggested portfolios for investors at varying stages of their life cycles.

Diversification and Portfolio Optimization

As you no doubt remember, one of the important investment truisms is that diversification is beneficial. Diversification is a way of reducing a portfolio's risk without significantly reducing its expected return. All portfolios should, therefore, be diversified. When making asset allocation decisions, the investor needs to ensure an adequate level of diversification. Investing 80% of your retirement money in your company's common stock, and 20% in Treasury bills, is probably not adequate diversification.

Fortunately, it is not difficult to achieve a reasonable level of diversification. As we showed, even a portfolio of five or six stocks will be fairly well diversified. One of the main advantages of investing in mutual funds is diversification. The typical mutual fund holds several hundred different securities. Index funds, another popular choice today, are also by their very nature well diversified. Investing 80% of your retirement funds in a stock index fund and the other 20% in Treasury bills will likely give you a pretty high level of diversification.

As we discussed is Chapter 17, the two types of diversification are naive diversification and efficient diversification. Any combination of financial assets will likely result in naive diversification. On the other hand, efficient diversification is more of a systematic process that seeks to find the combinations of investments inefficient portfolios that minimize risk for a given level of return or maximize return for a given level of risk. Investors can allocate their funds in such a way as to construct efficient portfolios.

Using historical return data for large stocks, small stocks, bonds, and Treasury bills, Figure 20.5 shows the resulting efficient frontier.[4] Each of the portfolios along with efficient frontier meets the two optimization conditions. The portfolio labeled A on the efficient frontier has the same mean return as a portfolio consisting of 100% large stocks (12.6%), but has a lower standard deviation (17.2% versus 20.2%). Portfolio A consists of approximately 56% large stocks, 27% small stocks, and 17% bonds.

---

[4]The efficient frontier was constructed using the Optimal Portfolio worksheet in the Wizard Workbook.

INVESTMENT INSIGHT

Some Suggested Retirement Portfolios

One of the major goals people have for investing is a financially secure retirement. Achieving that requires  careful planning and proper asset allocation. The following are some suggested retirement portfolios.

Katie, age 25

Growth and income stock funds 15%

International stock funds 15%

Bonds 10%

Growth stock funds 60%

Michele, age 50

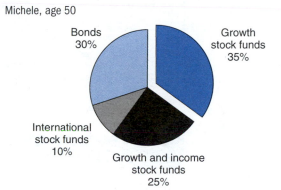

Bonds 30%

Growth stock funds 35%

International stock funds 10%

Growth and income stock funds 25%

Steven, age 38

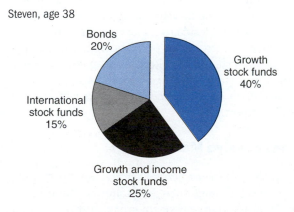

Bonds 20%

Growth stock funds 40%

International stock funds 15%

Growth and income stock funds 25%

Walter, age 62

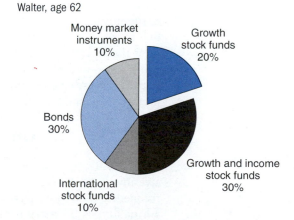

Money market instruments 10%

Growth stock funds 20%

Bonds 30%

International stock funds 10%

Growth and income stock funds 30%

Questions for Critical Thinking

1. What is the relationship between holding period and the percentage of the portfolio invested in stocks?

2. For long-term investors, why should any of the portfolio be invested in bonds?

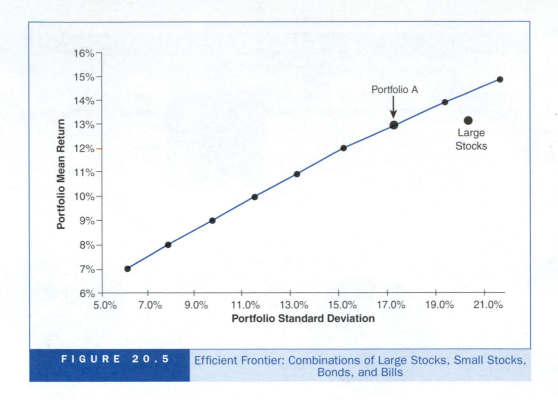

FIGURE 20.5 Efficient Frontier: Combinations of Large Stocks, Small Stocks, Bonds, and Bills

MONITORING PORTFOLIOS

The last step in the portfolio construction and management process consists of monitoring the investment portfolio. Monitoring a portfolio involves measuring its performance and assessing how well it is meeting investment objectives. In the process of monitoring a portfolio, the investor may decide to make changes to the portfolio due to poor performance or a conclusion that the portfolio failed to adequately meet the investor's objectives. Investors should also keep tabs on changing market conditions—and resulting changes to macro- or micro-expectations—and investor circumstances. Changes in an investor's circumstances or market conditions may necessitate changes to the investment portfolio.

Active vs. Passive Management

Back in Chapter 1 we discussed the difference between active investors and passive investors. Investors who actively manage their portfolios buy and sell more frequently than more passive investors. Active investors may shift funds between various types of instruments due to shifts in macro- or micro-expectations. To plan these moves, they tend to monitor the performance of their investments more closely, and they may be more concerned about short-term performance than passive investors.

A passive investor, however, tends to buy a portfolio of securities and keep it mostly intact for a long period of time. This investor may be less inclined to make changes to the portfolio in response to changes in macro- or micro-expectations.

Only a significant change to the investor's circumstances will lead to a significant adjustment to the investor's portfolio.

Because active investors make more changes to their investments than passive investors, active investors incur higher transactions costs and may pay more in taxes. Consequently, active investors should earn higher returns than passive investors. Does it pay to be an active investor? We pondered this question frequently throughout this book, and our feet are planted firmed in the middle. Some evidence supports arguments in favor of active investing, but equally compelling evidence favors passive investing. Index funds, perhaps the pinnacle of passive investing, often outperform the average actively managed mutual fund.

Changes in Investor Circumstances

One thing that both active and passive investors agree upon is that changes in an investor's circumstances may alter an investor's objectives or constraints, and lead to changes in asset allocation. Some of the more obvious circumstances that can change for individuals include the following:

- *Getting older.* As investors age, their time horizons get shorter. A shorter time horizon means the investor needs to be somewhat more conservative. As a general rule, accumulation of capital becomes less important relative to preservation of capital as investors age.
- *Increases in wealth.* The wealth of an investor can change dramatically over time. Changes in wealth can lead to changes in investment objectives and constraints. For example, an increase in wealth may make an investor less risk averse. Increases in wealth usually push investors into higher tax brackets, and tax issues become a more important consideration in the investment process.
- *Changes in family status.* The investment objectives of someone who is single are necessarily different from the investment objectives of someone who supports a family.

Rebalancing

Whether someone is a passive or an active investor, it may be necessary to rebalance the investor's portfolio at times. Rebalancing means adjusting your investments to return to your target asset allocation. Although it sounds complicated, rebalancing is actually a fairly simple process. Let's look at an example.

rebalancing
Adjusting the contents of a portfolio to return to the investor's target asset allocation.

Maria's target asset allocation is 75% stocks and 25% bonds. Two years ago, she invested $75,000 in a stock index fund and invested 25% in a bond index fund. Over the next two years, the stock index fund had a total return of 45% while the bond index fund had a total return of 4.5%. Now, Maria has more than 75% of her money invested in stocks and less than 25% invested in bonds. Here's the math:

Stock index fund	Beginning value = $75,000	Ending value = $75,000 × 1.45 = $108,750
Bond index fund	Beginning value = $25,000	Ending value = $25,000 × 1.045 = $26,125
Total portfolio	Beginning value = $100,000	Ending value = $134,875
	(75% stocks, 25% bonds)	(81% stocks, 19% bonds)

To return to her target asset allocation (75% stocks, 25% bonds), Maria needs to rebalance her portfolio. She could either sell some shares of her stock fund, and buy bond fund shares, or allocate slightly more of any new investment dollars to bond funds until she reaches her target allocation.

Performance Measure and Evaluation

Measuring and evaluating the performance of an investment portfolio is a critical part of the investment process. Periodically *all* investors must sit down and carefully measure and evaluate the performance of their investments. As we noted, passive investors may do this kind of evaluation less frequently than active ones, but it is a task that even the most passive investor cannot avoid. When it comes to measuring and evaluating performance, concerns focus around such issues as overall performance, relative performance, cost, and risk. You need to ask yourself whether your investment plan is working and whether it is adequately meeting your investment objectives. If you conclude that your portfolio isn't meeting your objectives, or isn't performing well, it may be time to consider some changes.

Measuring and evaluating performance is a logical conclusion to the study of investments. In the following, and concluding chapter, we consider how to go about measuring and evaluating the performance of investment portfolios.

SUMMARY

1. What is the process of building and managing an investment portfolio?
The process of building and managing an investment portfolio consists of a series of steps, the details of which can vary from investor to investor. The first step is the development of an investment policy, which blends the investor's objectives, the constraints faced by the investor, and any preferences the investor has. The investment policy, along with expectations concerning the future performance of the financial markets, are considered when making strategic and tactical asset allocation decisions. The final step of the process is portfolio monitoring. Such things as poor performance, changes in the investor's circumstances, and changing market expectations can lead to changes in the investor's asset allocation.

2. How is an investment policy developed?
An investment policy blends the investor's objectives with the investors constraints and preferences. Both individual and institutional investors should develop investment policies, but many important differences also distinguish institutional from individual investors. In general, the three investment objectives are growth in capital, preservation of capital, and current income. How an investor prioritizes these three objectives depends on the reasons for investing and the characteristics of the investor. Prioritizing investment objectives involves a trade-off between risk and return. Constraints are limitations imposed on the portfolio construction process. Examples of constraints include the time horizon, liquidity needs, taxes, regulatory constraints, and unique needs or preferences.

3. How do capital market assumptions affect the investment process?
You cannot make investment decisions without forming some expectations concerning the future performance of the financial markets. Investors can form both macro- and micro-expectations. Macro-expectations involve forming expectations of the future performance for broad financial asset categories (stocks, bonds, and money market instruments). Micro-expectations involve the formation of expectations of the future performance of groups and individuals within the broad asset categories. Investors tend to form expectations based on the historical performance record. Even though aspects of the record have been relatively consistent over time, the past is never a guarantee of the future.

4. What is asset allocation?

Asset allocation involves decisions regarding the percentage of an investor's funds to be invested in various financial assets. The two types of asset allocation are strategic and tactical asset allocation. Strategic asset allocation concerns decisions regarding the general mix of investments that will make up the portfolio. Tactical asset allocation involves selecting specific investments within each of the general categories. Asset allocation decisions are heavily influenced by the investment policy and financial market expectations. One popular approach to asset allocation for individual investors is the so-called life cycle approach. Younger investors, whose primary objective is capital accumulation, should invest a high proportion of their funds in common stocks. Older investors, whose primary objective is capital distribution and preservation, should invest a smaller proportion of their funds in common stocks. Another factor guiding asset allocation decisions is diversification; all investor's should strive to hold diversified portfolios.

5. What does monitoring a portfolio involve?

Monitoring a portfolio involves measuring its performance and assessing how well it is meeting investment objectives. In the process of monitoring a portfolio, an investor may decide to make changes due to poor performance or a conclusion that the portfolio is not adequately meeting investment objectives. Changes in the investor's circumstances and market expectations may also lead to portfolio changes. Investors use one of two general approaches to portfolio management. Active investors are more apt to make more frequent changes to their portfolios than passive investors who buy and hold. All investors need to periodically rebalance their portfolios if the actual asset allocation differs significantly from the target asset allocation.

REVIEW EXERCISES

1. Explain the steps involved in the construction and monitoring of an investment portfolio. Is the process a one-way street?

2. Define an *investment policy*. List some of the differences between individual investors and institutional investors.

3. What are the three main investment objectives? Which objective is most important for a young person investing for retirement?

4. Jill is 25 and wants to begin a retirement investment program (she plans to retire in 40 years at age 65). If Jill believes she needs at least $2.5 million to retire, how much does she need to invest each year between now and then if she can earn 10% annually? Convince Jill that she should invest most of her retirement savings at least initially in common stocks.

5. John is 65 and plans to retire within the next six months. Currently, John has $2.2 million in his 401(k). What is John's primary investment objective? Would investing 100% of his money in bonds or money market instruments be a mistake? Why or why not?

6. List some of the constraints faced by individual and institutional investors. Which type of investor is subject to more regulation?

7. Explain the difference between macro-expectations and micro-expectations. How do most investors form their expectations?

8. What is the difference between strategic asset allocation and tactical asset allocation? Give an example of each. Explain how asset allocation is affected by an investor's life cycle.

9. What steps are involved in portfolio monitoring? Give some reasons why even a passive investor might make some changes to his or her portfolio.

10. Define *rebalancing*. John wants to maintain an asset allocation of 70% stocks and 30% bonds. Five year ago, he invested $70,000 in a stock index fund and $30,000 in a bond index fund. Over the past five years stocks returned a compounded annual average of 11.1% while bonds' compound average annual return was 5.1%. What is John's current asset allocation? What changes should he make?

CRITICAL THINKING EXERCISE

This exercise requires computer work. In the Data Workbook, available on the text Web site (http://hearth.swlearning.com), is a worksheet entitled Security Returns. The worksheet provides annual returns from large stocks, small stocks, Treasury bonds, and Treasury bills between 1950 and 2001. Use these returns to answer the questions associated with the following case study.

Scott and Shelly are both 45. Their combined annual income is $110,000. Currently the combined balance in their retirement accounts is $500,000. They are each saving about $7,500 a year (including employer contributions). Bonds make up 60% of their investments, stocks 30%, and money market instruments 10%. Scott and Shelly describe themselves as "conservative" investors. They would like to retire in about 20 years. A financially secure retirement is their main investment goal (they have sufficient resources to meet other major financial goals).

1. Based on the information provided, how much do you believe Scott and Shelly will need in their retirement accounts by the time they retire? (Most financial planners argue that people need an annual retirement income that is close to their pre-retirement income. Financial planners also suggest developing retirement plans based on the assumption that people will live to be age 90.)
2. Based on the case information along with the historical data on stock and bond returns, do you believe Scott and Shelly are saving enough each year?
3. What is your recommended asset allocation? What kind of risk/return characteristics will it have? What kinds of changes to the portfolio should be made as Scott and Shelly age?

THE INTERNET INVESTOR

1. A number of "retirement planners" are available today. Some are software programs you install on your PC while others are Internet-based. Visit the one of the major personal finance-oriented Web sites (such as MSN Money Central at http://moneycentral. msn.com) and, using your expected situation or that of a friend, go through the retirement planner. Write a brief report on your experience.
2. When developing an investment policy, and allocating assets, investors need to consider their tolerance for risk, along with other individual characteristics. Visit the Web site www.schwab.com and click on "Investor Profile Questionnaire." How much would this exercise, in your opinion, help an investor with asset allocation decisions?
3. Asset allocation can be confusing for many investors, especially novices. A variety of Web sites provide interactive guides to help investors with asset allocation decisions. Go to www.fidelity.com/planning and complete the asset allocation planner. Write a brief report discussing your reaction to the exercise.

21

Evaluating Investment Performance

PREVIOUSLY . . .	IN THIS CHAPTER . . .	TO COME . . .
We described how investment portfolios should be constructed and managed, beginning with the formation of an investment policy, which, along with market expectations, determines asset allocation decisions. Portfolio monitoring is the final step in the process.	We discuss how the performance of investment portfolios should be measured and evaluated. We apply the concepts and measures of risk and return developed in prior chapters to measure risk-adjusted portfolio performance. By applying these measures, we can determine, historically, which portfolios outperformed the market.	With this last chapter, we hope you enjoyed your journey through the world of investments.

CHAPTER OBJECTIVES

After reading Chapter 21, you should be able to answer the following questions:

1. What issues are important when evaluating investment performance?

2. How are risk and return measured?

3. What are three measures of risk-adjusted performance?

4. How good is past performance as a predictor of future performance?

Warren Buffet is arguably the world's most famous investor. He is also one of the wealthiest. His company, Berkshire Hathaway, is essentially an investment holding company. It owns 100% of several companies and large minority positions in several others. Buffet's investment philosophy has always been to concentrate his investments in a handful of companies whose businesses, in his view, are fairly easy to understand and predict. He likes stocks of companies with recognizable brand names and always buys stocks with the intention of holding them for long periods of time. Berkshire's largest stock holdings included American Express, Coca-Cola, Gillette, and Wells Fargo. Berkshire is Coke's largest single shareholder. Berkshire also owns controlling interests in two large insurance companies: GEICO and General Re. By his own admission, Buffet doesn't understand technology very well. He claims that he can't forecast what the technology business will look like in 10 years, nor which companies will still be around, which is the reason he tends to avoid technology stocks.

During the late 1990s, some began to wonder whether the "Sage of Omaha" was losing his magic touch. Over a three-year period, from the end of 1996 to the end of 1999, the performance of Berkshire Hathaway shares lagged that of the S&P 500. During 1999, the value of Berkshire shares actually fell by more than 20%, while the S&P 500 rose by almost 19%. Critics contended that Buffet's approach to stock picking and his avoidance of technology stocks were out of date.

Even though some suggested that Buffet's time had passed, many others believed Buffet's approach to investing was as sound as ever. Some mutual fund managers, in fact, used the dip in Berkshire's stock as an opportunity to buy additional shares. According to Buffet's defenders, what happened during the late 1990s, 1999 in particular, was merely an aberration not the beginning of a long-term trend.

In retrospect, Buffet looks pretty smart. The bubble in technology stocks broke in early 2000. As the overall market dropped during the rest of the year, the value of Berkshire shares rose and finished 2000 up 38%. While the S&P 500 dropped by more than 25% during the next two years, the value of Berkshire shares remained relatively constant. Over the past decade, the average annual return from Berkshire is almost twice the average annual return from the S&P 500.

The debate over whether Buffet had lost his golden touch illustrates many of the issues confronting investors when evaluating the performance of investment portfolios. Being able to properly evaluate the performance of investment portfolios is critical if investors are to make intelligent choices. How to properly evaluate investment performance is the subject of this final chapter. Although we will focus on evaluating the performance of mutual funds in this chapter, the material applies to any investment portfolio.

PERFORMANCE EVALUATION ISSUES

At the outset, you should be aware that no universally agreed-upon set of standards exists for the evaluation of investment portfolios. Government regulators and industry organizations recently adopted policies designed to make it easier for investors to evaluate and compare performance. For example, the Association for Investment Management and Research (AIMR) adopted a minimum set of

INVESTMENT INSIGHT

Standards for Reporting Portfolio Performance

The Association for Investment Management and Research (AIMR) prepared a list of standards in 1993 regarding how portfolio performance should be reported. These standards, which apply to any investment portfolio, include the following:

- Returns reported are total returns (holding period returns).
- Ten years of annual returns should be reported.
- All fees and expenses should be subtracted from gross portfolio returns.
- Cash and cash equivalents are to be included when calculating returns.
- Time-weighted returns are to be included, at least quarterly, and linked geometrically.

The Securities and Exchange Commission has a set of requirements on how mutual fund returns are reported in the fund's prospectus. Among these requirements are the following:

- Total returns over varying periods of time (one year, three years, five years, etc.) are provided.
- All fees and expenses are subtracted from gross returns.
- For comparison purposes, returns from a benchmark (such as the appropriate market index) are to be included.
- A graph comparing the quarter-to-quarter volatility in the fund's returns relative to the market benchmark is required.

Questions for Critical Thinking

1. What is the overall purpose of AIMR performance reporting suggestions and recent SEC regulations? Do you think these suggestions and recommendations help ordinary investors?
2. What additional reporting requirements would you recommend?

Sources: Association for Investment Management & Research, U.S. Securities and Exchange Commission.

---

portfolio presentation performance standards in 1993.[1] The AIMR standards, as well as standards described by the Securities and Exchange Commission, are listed in the Investment Insight box on this page.

With this lack of firm standards in mind, you need to consider a number of factors when evaluating the performance of mutual funds or any other investment portfolio. To illustrate these factors, let's consider the following example. Over the past three years, the Yacktman fund averaged an annual return of 15.9%.[2] During the same period the MFS International New Discovery fund averaged an annual return of about −2.3%. If you are considering investing some of your IRA money in the one of these two stock funds, what should you think about?

Time Periods

Whenever you evaluate performance, and especially when you compare the performance of one mutual fund to another, the time periods must be consistent. You may see two different mutual funds both advertising in the same publication that they were the top-performing fund. How can they both make that claim? Simply because each fund used a different time period when promoting its performance.

---

[1]AIMR controls and operates the Certified Financial Analyst (CFA) program. All CFAs are members of AIMR and are, therefore, subject to its standards. Many security analysts, mutual fund managers, and other investment professionals are CFAs. We briefly describe the CFA program in Appendix B.
[2]The three years ending September 30, 2002.

TABLE 21.1 Proper Performance Benchmarks for Mutual Funds	

Type of Fund	Market Benchmark
Large stock fund	S&P 500 index
Midcap stock fund	S&P Midcap 400 index
Small stock fund	Russell 2000 index
International stock fund	Morgan Stanley EAFE index
Taxable bond fund	Lehman Brothers aggregate bond index
Tax-exempt bond fund	Lehman Brothers municipal bond index

Examining different time periods can lead to different performance results and rankings. Consider the two funds we just mentioned. Based on three-year returns, the Yacktman fund is clearly superior; after all, the MFS International New Discovery fund's average annual return was negative. However, if we examine five-year returns, the results look quite different. Over the past five years ending on September 30, 2002, the average annual return from the Yacktman fund is only 5.4% compared to 12.3% for the MFS International New Discovery fund.

One other point to remember about time periods: we argue that performance over longer time periods—5 years, 10 years, or even longer—is usually more meaningful than performance over short periods, say, 1 or 2 years. A common investment mistake is to chase returns based on short-term historical performance.

Appropriate Benchmark

In and of themselves, returns tell you little unless you compare them to appropriate benchmarks. For mutual funds the obvious benchmarks are group average and the appropriate market index. Going back to our two funds, compared with their group averages, the MFS International New Discovery fund actually did slightly better than the Yacktman fund (based on three-year returns). Even though the MFS fund's average annual return was negative, it was still about 12.3% per year higher than its group average. The Yacktman fund's average annual return beat its group average by about 12% per year.

The appropriate market index is also another performance benchmark to which you can compare the performance of an investment portfolio. For stock funds, the most commonly used market benchmark is the Standard & Poor's 500 index. Yet the S&P 500 is not the appropriate benchmark for *some* types of stock funds. For instance, the MFS International New Discovery fund is classified as a foreign stock fund, meaning it invests in stocks of companies located outside the United States. Consequently, its appropriate market benchmark is one of the international stock indexes, such as the Morgan Stanley EAFE index. Over the five years ending on September 30, 2002, the MFS fund beat the index by about 14.4% per year. Table 21.1 lists the appropriate market index for a variety of mutual funds.

Risk

A theme we stressed throughout this book is that investors cannot ignore risk when making investment choices. Investors need to realize that risk and return are positively related. Investors need to compensated, in the form of higher returns, for higher risk. Perhaps the Yacktman fund's superior three-year performance resulted simply because it was riskier than the average fund. Consequently, careful review of the risk of each fund is necessary, as is evaluation of whether the fund's *risk-adjusted returns* are adequate.

We describe methods for evaluating risk-adjusted returns a little later in the chapter. As for one measure of risk, the Yacktman fund's beta is less than 1.0, indicating that it has less systematic, or market risk than average.

Objectives and Constraints

In the prior chapter we discussed how investment objectives and constraints are blended to form an investment policy, which in turn significantly affects asset allocation decisions. Investment performance should always be evaluated within the context of the portfolios objectives and any constraints faced by the portfolio manager. For example, many international stock funds are prohibited from investing in U.S. stocks, even if the U.S. market looks more attractive than international markets.

Here's another example. For the three years ending in 1993, Fidelity Asset Manager, an asset allocation fund, beat the S&P 500 by about 4% per year, even though the fund had less than half of its portfolio invested in stocks.[3] Investors responded by pouring billions of dollars into the fund. Things turned sour for Asset Manager, however. In both 1994 and 1995, the fund averaged an annual return of less than 5%, compared to 18% for the S&P 500. Those who were disappointed with the performance of Asset Manager, and redeemed hundreds of thousands of shares, failed to understand the fund's primary objective. Asset Manager, like all asset allocation funds, attempts to produce consistent returns over long periods of time, not beat the stock market.

Those who stayed the course with Asset Manager were rewarded. Since 1995, the fund showed a fairly steady performance from year to year. It also held up well in the face of the bear market in stocks than began in 2000. Over the past three years, 2000–2002, Fidelity Asset Manager beat the S&P 500 by an average of almost 10% per year.

MEASURING RISK AND RETURN

We need to review again how to properly measure risk and return when evaluating the performance of investment portfolios. If you need to further refresh your memory, reread Chapters 2, 17, and 18.

Return

The best measure of the return from an investment is its total, or holding period, return. In Chapter 2, we defined the holding period return, or HPR_t, as follows:

$$HPR_t = \frac{P_t - P_{t-1} + CF_t}{P_{t-1}}$$

---

[3]Asset allocation funds hold a combination of stocks, bonds, and money market instruments. The percentage invested in each asset category is adjusted to reflect the manager's assessment of changing market conditions.

where P_t is the price at the end of the period (month, quarter, year, etc.), P_{t-1} is the price at the beginning of the period, and CF_t is the amount of cash received from the investment during the period.[4]

From the holding period return we can construct a total return index that measures the change in an investors wealth over a period of time. The total return index is calculated as follows:

$$I_t = I_{t-1}(1 + \text{HPR}_t)$$

where I_{t-1} is the index value at the end of the prior period. The initial index value is set at some arbitrary number (1, 10, 100, 1,000, etc.).

Because returns vary over several periods of time, we also may want to calculate average returns. As we noted in Chapter 2, the two measures of "average" returns are the arithmetic mean (AM) and the geometric mean (GM). The arithmetic mean is calculated as follows:

$$\text{AM} = \frac{1}{T}\sum_{t=1}^{T}\text{HPR}_t$$

where T is the number of observations.[5] The geometric mean is calculated as:

$$\text{GM} = \left[\prod_{t=1}^{T}(1 + \text{HPR}_t)\right] - 1$$

Both averages are useful. The arithmetic mean is the "typical" return during a period of time. The geometric mean, on the other hand, is the average compound return and measures the actual change in wealth.

Risk

We defined *risk* as some uncertainty that exists as to what an investment's actual return will be over some period in the future. The greater the uncertainty, the greater is the risk. In general, risk is associated with the variability of returns. The more variable the returns are, the more risky the investment.

One way of measuring the risk of an investment is to calculate the standard deviation of returns. Standard deviation measures the dispersion of a distribution around its mean. Higher standard deviations, indicate more variability in the returns, and thus a more risky investment. Standard deviation is found as follows:[6]

$$\text{SD} = \left[\frac{1}{T-1}\sum_{t=1}^{T}(\text{HPR}_t - \text{AM})^2\right]^{1/2}$$

[4]In Chapter 2 we described how to adjust a holding period return for inflation.
[5]We described in Chapter 2 how to annualize the arithmetic mean if it was calculated using something other than annual return data—monthly or quarterly returns, for example.
[6]In Chapter 2 we showed how to annualize the standard deviation if it was calculated using something other than annual return data.

One of the cornerstones of modern portfolio theory (MPT), which we discussed starting in Chapter 2, and continued in detail in Chapter 17, is that the total risk of an investment can be broken into two parts. The first part, called *unsystematic risk*, can be eliminated through diversification that comes about when a security is added to a portfolio. The second part, called *systematic risk*, cannot be eliminated through diversification. Standard deviation measures total risk. A measure of systematic, or market risk is what we call beta. Beta is calculated as follows:

$$\beta_j = \text{CORR}(M,j)\frac{\text{SD}_j}{\text{SD}_M}$$

where $\text{CORR}(M, j)$ is the correlation between returns for investment j and the appropriate market portfolio, SD_j is the standard deviation of returns for investment j, and SD_M is the standard deviation of returns for the market. By definition the market has a definition of 1.0. An investment with a beta less than 1.0 has less systematic risk than the market while an investment with a beta greater than 1.0 has more systematic risk than the market.

With respect to portfolios, you can measure the degree to which the portfolio is diversified, meaning the degree to which unsystematic risk has been eliminated. You compute the correlation between returns for the portfolio and returns for the market portfolio, $\text{CORR}(M, p)$. The square of the correlation coefficient, known as R^2, tells you the percentage of the portfolio's total risk that is systematic risk. The closer R^2 is to 1.0, the more diversified the portfolio.

Risk and Return Measures for the Legg-Mason Value Trust

As an illustration, let's calculate some risk and return measures for the Legg-Mason Value Trust, a large-stock mutual fund. Figure 21.1 shows cumulative wealth indexes, based on quarterly returns, for the Legg-Mason Value Trust and the S&P 500 beginning at the end of 1994 and continuing through the end of the third quarter of 2002.

First, we calculate the arithmetic mean and the standard deviation for both return series. The results are shown in the following table.

	Legg-Mason Value Trust	S&P 500
Arithmetic mean (annualized)	16.3%	10.1%
Standard deviation (annualized)	22.8%	17.8%
Cumulative return (change in wealth)	+206%	+103%

The Legg-Mason Value Trust had a higher average annual return than did the S&P 500 during this period. Each dollar invested in the Legg-Mason Value Trust at the end of 1994 was worth slightly more than $3 by the end of the third quarter of 2002. By contrast, each dollar invested in the S&P 500 grew to slightly more than $2 during the same period. At the same time, however, the Legg-Mason fund's quarterly returns were more variable. This variability is reflected in the higher standard deviation—22.8% versus 17.8%—and suggests that the Legg-Mason fund has more risk than does the S&P 500. Whether the

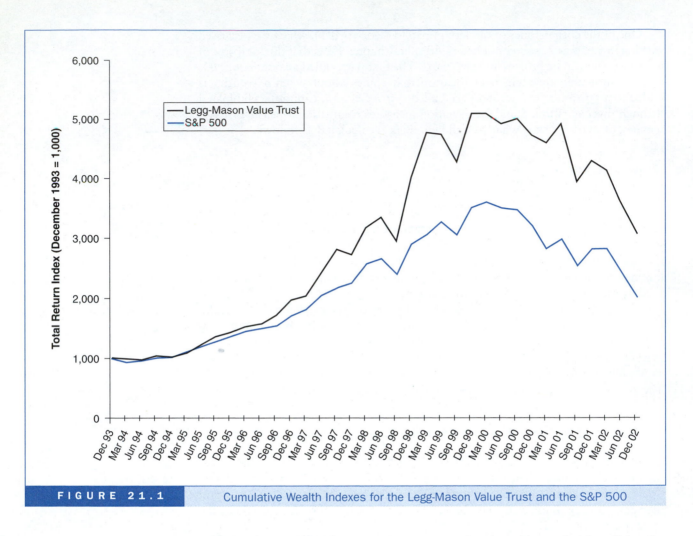

FIGURE 21.1 Cumulative Wealth Indexes for the Legg-Mason Value Trust and the S&P 500

additional return is adequate compensation for the additional risk will be discussed in the next section.[7]

The correlation of returns between the Legg-Mason fund and the S&P 500 is .901. Thus, the Legg-Mason fund has a beta of

$$\beta_{\text{Legg-Mason}} = .901(.228/.178) = 1.15$$

The fund's R^2 is $(.901)^2 = .81$. So the Legg-Mason fund has more systematic risk than the overall market (its beta is greater than 1.0). Coupled with its higher standard deviation, it does appear as though the Legg-Mason fund is riskier than the overall market. Moreover, about 81% of the fund's total risk is systematic; the rest, about 19%, is unsystematic. Whether the Legg-Mason fund is adequately diversified is something we examine in the next section.

---

[7]We should also note that Bill Miller, manager of the Legg-Mason Value Trust, has the distinction of having the longest winning streak on Wall Street. He is the only mutual fund manager who outperformed the S&P 500 in each of the past 12 calendar years.

ASSESSING RISK-ADJUSTED PERFORMANCE

Modern portfolio theory provides three ways of assessing risk-adjusted performance. All are named after their respective author. They are the Treynor measure, the Sharpe measure, and Jensen's alpha. Even though all three measures have their basis in modern portfolio theory, they are each a little different. Let's examine each performance measure individually.

Treynor Performance Measure

The **Treynor measure** is essentially a reward-to-risk ratio.[8] It is calculated as follows:

$$T_p = \frac{AM_p - RF}{\beta_p} \qquad\qquad (21.1)$$

Treynor performance measure

A reward-to-risk ratio in which the average risk-adjusted return from a portfolio is divided by the portfolio's beta.

where AM_p is the mean return from a portfolio over a period of time, RF is the risk-free rate, and β_p is the portfolio's beta.

The Treynor measure is based on the capital asset pricing model (CAPM) and security market line (SML) discussed in Chapter 18. Recall that the SML for a portfolio is defined by

$$ER_p = RF + \beta_p(ER_M - RF)$$

where ER_p is the expected (or required) return from the portfolio and ER_M is the expected return from the market. We can rewrite the security market line as

$$(ER_p - RF) = \beta_p(ER_M - RF) \qquad\qquad (21.2)$$

Essentially Equation 21.2 states that a portfolio's risk premium equals the portfolio's beta multiplied by the market risk premium. Dividing both sides of Equation 21.2 by beta gives us

$$(ER_p - RF)/\beta_p = (ER_M - RF) \qquad\qquad (21.3)$$

The left side of Equation 21.3 is the Treynor measure for portfolio p (ER_p replaces AM_p). The right side of Equation 21.3, as you probably remember from Chapter 18, is the slope of the security market line. It's also the Treynor measure for the market since, by definition, the market has a beta of 1.0.

When calculating the Treynor measure, we use the actual, or ex-ante mean return from a portfolio. In a sense we're comparing actual performance to expected performance. Therefore, if a portfolio's Treynor measure equals that of the market, then the portfolio lies along the SML. We would conclude that the portfolio's risk-adjusted performance was equal to what it should be, given its beta risk. Therefore, the portfolio neither outperformed, nor underperformed the market on a risk-adjusted basis, which is shown graphically in Figure 21.2.

---

[8]Jack Treynor, "How to Rate Management of Investment Funds," *Harvard Business Review,* January/February 1965, pp. 119–138.

FIGURE 21.2

Interpreting the Treynor Measure

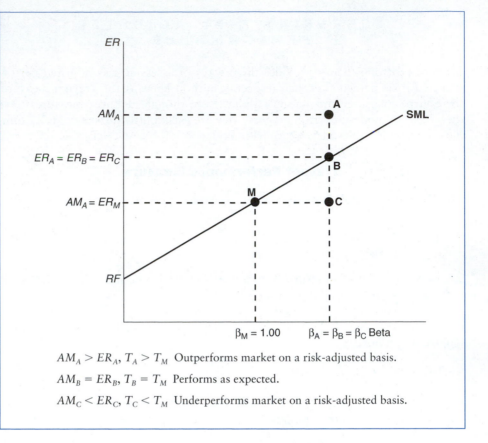

$AM_A > ER_A$, $T_A > T_M$ Outperforms market on a risk-adjusted basis.

$AM_B = ER_B$, $T_B = T_M$ Performs as expected.

$AM_C < ER_C$, $T_C < T_M$ Underperforms market on a risk-adjusted basis.

On the other hand, if the portfolio's Treynor measure is higher than the market's, the portfolio lies above the SML. In that case, we would conclude that the portfolio's risk-adjusted performance was higher than expected, given its beta risk, and the portfolio outperformed the market on a risk-adjusted basis (see Figure 12.2). Finally, if the portfolio's Treynor measure is less than the market's, the portfolio lies below the SML. The portfolio underperformed the market on a risk-adjusted basis, meaning that its actual return was less than expected given its beta risk. This relationship is also shown graphically in Figure 21.2.

Okay, lets see how the Legg-Mason fund performed on a risk-adjusted basis. We need to calculate its Treynor measure and the Treynor measure for the S&P 500. We use the return on short-term T-bills as the proxy for the risk-free rate. Between 1994 and 2002, T-bill returns averaged about 5% per year. The Treynor calculations are shown as follows:

Legg-Mason fund: $T_{\text{Legg-Mason}} = (16.3\% - 5\%)/1.15 = .983$

S&P 500: $T_{\text{S\&P 500}} = (10.1\% - 5\%)/1.00 = .501$

The Legg-Mason fund lies above the SML and outperformed the market on a risk-adjusted basis. By how much did it outperform the market on a risk-adjusted basis? To lie along the SML, the Legg-Mason's Treynor measure must equal the market's, at .501. A little bit of arithmetic tells us that, given a beta of 1.15, the Legg-Mason fund's average return would need to be approximately 10.8% per year in order for its Treynor measure to equal that of the market. Subtracting the fund's actual average annual return, 16.3%, from its expected annual return, 10.8%, tells us that the Legg-Mason fund outperformed the market on a risk-adjusted basis by about 5.5% per year.

Sharpe Performance Measure

The **Sharpe measure** is similar to the Treynor in that it is a reward-to-risk ratio.[9] Instead of using beta as the risk measure, Sharpe substituted total risk, standard deviation. The Sharpe measure is calculated as follows:

Sharpe performance measure

A reward-to-risk ratio in which the average risk-adjusted return from a portfolio is divided by the portfolio's standard deviation.

$$S_p = (AM_p - RF)/SD_p \qquad (21.4)$$

where SD_p is the portfolio's standard deviation.

Sharpe's logic for using total risk instead of just systematic risk lies with the assumption behind beta risk. Beta risk assumes that a portfolio is totally diversified, with no remaining unsystematic risk. Sharpe argues that a portfolio manager who doesn't hold a well-diversified portfolio shouldn't be rewarded for exposing investors to unsystematic risk. In other words, a portfolio could have a relatively low beta, but a high standard deviation simply because the portfolio isn't well diversified.

Unlike the Treynor measure, which is based on the security market line, the Sharpe measure is based on the capital market line (CML). In Chapter 18 we defined the capital market line as

$$ER_p = RF + [(ER_M - RF)/SD_M]SD_p$$

where SD_M is the market standard deviation. We can rewrite the CML as

$$(ER_p - RF) = [(ER_M - RF)/SD_M]SD_p \qquad (21.5)$$

Dividing both sides of Equation 21.5 by the portfolio standard deviation give us

$$(ER_p - RF)/SD_p = (ER_M - RF)/SD_M \qquad (21.6)$$

The left-hand side of Equation 21.6 is the Sharpe measure for the portfolio (with ER_p replacing AM_p). The right-hand side of the equation is the Sharpe measure for the market (again with ER_M replacing AM_M).

As with the Treynor measure, actual returns are used to calculate the Sharpe measure. Again we are in essence using the Sharpe measure to compare actual returns to expected returns. If a portfolio's Sharpe measure equals that of market's, then the portfolio lies along the capital market line (see Figure 21.3). It means that the portfolio's return equals what would be expected, given the portfolio's standard deviation (total risk).

---

[9]William Sharpe, "Mutual Fund Performance," *Journal of Business,* January 1966, pp. 119–138.

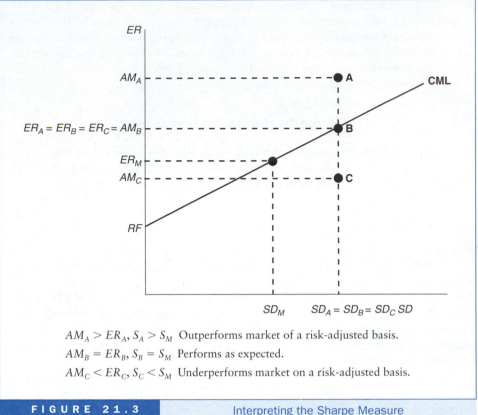

$AM_A > ER_A, S_A > S_M$ Outperforms market of a risk-adjusted basis.

$AM_B = ER_B, S_B = S_M$ Performs as expected.

$AM_C < ER_C, S_C < S_M$ Underperforms market on a risk-adjusted basis.

FIGURE 21.3   Interpreting the Sharpe Measure

If the portfolio has a higher Sharpe measure than the market's, then the portfolio lies above the CML. The portfolio's actual return exceeds its expected return, given the total risk of the portfolio. On the other hand, if the portfolio's Sharpe measure is less than the market's, then the portfolio lies below the CML. The portfolio's actual return is less than the expected return, given the total risk of the portfolio. Both cases are illustrated in Figure 21.3.

Let's compute the Sharpe measure for the Legg-Mason fund and the Sharpe measure for the S&P 500. We again use the return from T-bills as the proxy for the risk-free rate. The mean annual return from T-bills during this period was about 5%. The Sharpe measure calculations are as follows:

Legg-Mason: $S_{\text{Legg-Mason}} = (16.3\% - 5\%)/22.8\% = .50$

S&P 500: $S_{\text{S\&P 500}} = (10.1\% - 5\%)/17.8\% = .29$

Because the Sharpe measure for the Legg-Mason fund exceeded the Sharpe measure for the S&P 500, the Legg-Mason fund's actual return will be higher than expected, given its level of total risk, and falls above the capital market line. For the Legg-Mason to have a Sharpe measure equal to that of the market's, its annual return would average only about 11.6%. Given its actual average annual return of 16.3%, the Legg-Mason Fund beat the market on a risk-adjusted basis by about 4.7% per year.

You may recall that according to the Treynor measure, the Legg-Mason fund outperformed the market by an average of about 5.5% per year on a risk-adjusted basis. However, according to the Sharpe measure, the Legg-Mason beat the market by approximately 4.7% per year. Why the difference? The answer goes back to the risk measure used and the issue of diversification. The Treynor measure uses beta risk while the Sharpe measure uses total risk. According to the R^2 statistic, which measures diversification, the Legg-Mason fund is not totally diversified, if it were the R^2 would be close to 1.0. The fund has a R^2 of .81 meaning almost 20% of its total risk is unsystematic.

Jensen's Alpha

The third measure of risk-adjusted performance is called **Jensen's alpha**.[10] As with the Treynor measure, Jensen's alpha is derived from the capital asset pricing model (CAPM) and the security market line. We start again with CAPM:

$$ER_p = RF + \beta_p(ER_M - RF)$$

Then subtract RF from both sides of the equation:

$$ER_p - RF = \beta_p(ER_M - RF)$$

which leads us back to Equation 21.2 again. Now let's add another variable, called alpha, to Equation 21.2.

$$ER_p - RF = \alpha_p + \beta_p(ER_M - RF) \tag{21.7}$$

Jensen's Alpha

A reward-to-risk measure; a positive alpha indicates superior risk-adjusted performance.

In order for Equations 21.2 and 21.7 to equal one another, alpha must equal zero. When the y-axis is defined as the portfolio risk premium ($ER_p - RF$), rather than the portfolio's expected return, the SML's intercept is equal to zero (see Figure 21.4). What happens if alpha isn't equal to zero? If alpha is positive, then the portfolio is returning more than it should, given its level of beta risk. In that case, the portfolio lies above the security market line. On the other hand, if alpha is negative then the portfolio's return is less than it should be, given its level of beta risk, and the portfolio lies below the SML. So how is alpha estimated?

In Chapter 18 we described something we called the *characteristic line*. The characteristic line is a regression equation in which the return from a security, or portfolio, is the dependent, or Y variable, while the return from the market is the independent, or X variable. We used the characteristic line as another way of estimating beta, because beta is the slope of the characteristic line.

By making one small modification we can use the characteristic line to estimate alpha. The modified characteristic line is

$$HPR_p - RF_t = \alpha + \beta(HPR_M - RF_t) \tag{21.8}$$

where α and β are estimated using least squares regression, HPR_p is the holding period return from the portfolio, HPR_M is the holding period return from the market, and t refers to time periods (months, quarters, or years).

---

[10]Michael Jensen, "The Performance of Mutual Funds in the Period 1945–1964," *Journal of Finance,* May 1968, pp. 389–415.

FIGURE 21.4

Interpreting Jensen's Alpha

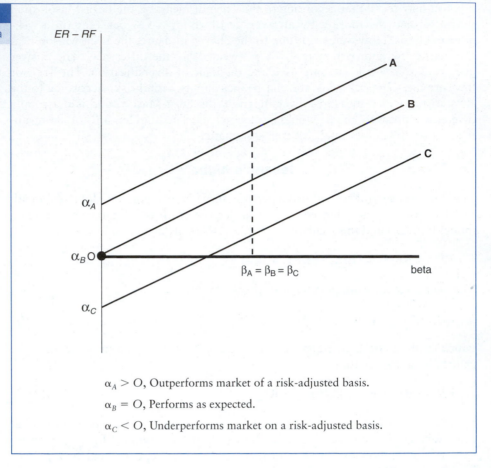

$\alpha_A > O$, Outperforms market of a risk-adjusted basis.

$\alpha_B = O$, Performs as expected.

$\alpha_C < O$, Underperforms market on a risk-adjusted basis.

Let's come up with an estimate of alpha for the Legg-Mason fund using the same set of quarterly returns. The resulting alpha is .012, indicating that the actual quarterly returns from the Legg-Mason fund were higher than the quarterly returns expected given the fund's level of beta risk. In other words, the positive alpha suggests that the Legg-Mason fund outperformed the market on a risk-adjusted basis.

Comparing Treynor, Sharpe, and Jensen

To assist in our comparison of the three portfolio performance measures, Table 21.2 lists the performance of 10 stock mutual funds, along with the performance of the S&P 500 and T-bills. (We used returns from what was a happier period for most investors the 1990s!) The three performance measures are calculated for each mutual fund and the measures are ranked from 1 (best) to 10 (worse).

The first thing you should recognize is that the Treynor measure and Jensen's alpha are closely related to one another, due to the simple fact that both are directly derived from the capital asset pricing model and the security market line. In fact, you perhaps already noticed that Jensen's alpha is equal to the "excess" return earned by a portfolio (the actual return minus the expected return, given

Fund	Mean Return	Standard Deviation	Beta	r-square	Performance Measures			Ranks		
					Treynor	Sharpe	Jensen	Treynor	Sharpe	Jensen
AIM Value	28.8%	23.4%	1.03	0.89	0.23	1.02	0.04	6	5	6
Berger 100	26.2	30.7	1.22	0.71	0.17	0.69	−0.02	8	8	8
Dreyfus Appreciation	22.5	20.1	0.99	0.93	0.18	0.87	−0.02	7	6	7
Fidelity Fund	29.1	21.9	0.99	0.93	0.24	1.10	0.05	4	2	4
PBHG Select Equity	50.0	72.1	1.54	0.33	0.29	0.62	0.15	1	9	1
Safeco Equity	19.3	18.4	0.88	0.89	0.16	0.78	−0.03	9	7	9
Scudder Large Company Growth	33.7	26.6	1.12	0.88	0.26	1.08	0.07	3	3	3
Strong Growth & Income	31.9	22.7	1.01	0.93	0.27	1.19	0.07	2	1	2
T. Rowe Price Dividend Growth	13.5	14.0	0.66	0.77	0.13	0.61	−0.04	10	10	10
Vanguard US Growth	29.2	22.9	1.03	0.92	0.23	1.06	0.04	5	4	5
S&P 500	24.3	20.6	1.00	1.00	0.19	0.94	0.00			
Treasury bills	5.0									

TABLE 21.2 Performance Measures for 10 Stock Mutual Funds

the portfolio's beta risk). We can see this point by simply rearranging Equation 21.7, and substituting actual returns for expected returns.

$$\alpha_p = AM_p - RF - \beta_p(AM_M - RF) \tag{21.8}$$

where AM_M is the arithmetic mean return from the market proxy (e.g., the S&P 500).

Because the Treynor measure and Jensen's alpha are so closely related to one another, they will always give you the same ranking when you are comparing the performance of several portfolios. As an example, take a look at Table 21.2. Notice that the top-ranked fund based on the Treynor measure (PBHG Select Equity) also has the highest Jensen's alpha. The fund with the lowest Treynor measure (T. Rowe Price Dividend Growth) also has the lowest Jensen's alpha.

Where differences in rankings can occur is between Treynor/Jensen and the Sharpe measure. The Sharpe measure, remember, is based on the notion that all portfolios *should* be diversified and, consequently, standard deviation rather than beta is the appropriate risk measure. Let's go back to the funds shown in Table 21.2. By and large, the rankings based on Treynor/Jensen and Sharpe are fairly consistent, with one notable exception. The PBHG Select Equity fund is the highest-ranked fund based on the Treynor/Jensen measures; it is one of the lowest ranked funds based on the Sharpe measure. According to the Treynor/Jensen measures, the PBHG Select Equity fund outperformed the market on a risk-adjusted basis. However, the Sharpe measure says the fund underperformed the market on a risk-adjusted basis. Why? The answer lies in the fact that the fund is not well diversified—its R^2 is only .33—and it contains a great deal of unsystematic risk.

The PBHG Select Equity fund has, by far, the highest mean return and the highest standard deviation of any of the 10 funds listed in Table 21.2. With a standard deviation of about 72%, the PBHG Select Equity fund carries more than twice as much total risk as any of the other nine mutual funds. Next on the list is the Berger 100 fund with a standard deviation of about 31% and more than three times as much total risk as the S&P 500. Although the PBHG Select Equity fund has the highest beta of the 10 mutual funds, its beta indicates that it has about 1.5 as much systematic risk as the overall market.

So if you use the SML to determine the PBHG Select Equity fund's required return, you would come up with $5.0\% + 1.54(24.3\% - 5.0\%) = 34.7\%$, which is much less than the fund's actual return, 50.0%. On the other hand, if you use the capital market line the fund's required return is $5.0\% + [(24.3\% - 5\%)/20.6\%]72.1\% = 72.6\%$. Based on the capital market line, the PBHG Select Equity fund's actual return was more than 22% less than its required return, given its level of total risk.

Before you conclude that the PBHG Select Equity manager hasn't managed the fund properly, you should take into account the fact that the fund isn't designed to be diversified. As is made quite clear in the prospectus, the fund places large bets on a handful of stocks. Investors are warned that the fund's strategy will likely result in a nondiversified portfolio, one that is riskier than the "average" mutual fund.

The choice of whether to rely on the Treynor/Jensen measures or the Sharpe measure may depend on portfolio objectives. If the portfolio is designed to be diversified, then the Sharpe measure is probably the better performance measure. On the other hand, if the portfolio isn't designed to be diversified, then the Treynor measure (or Jensen's alpha) should be used.

PAST AND FUTURE PERFORMANCE

All of the performance measures just discussed use historical returns, so they evaluate *historical* performance. Of course, history may not repeat itself, at least during a particular investment horizon. Thus, the results from using ex-post data even in a theoretically sound technique are dubious at best if the past is not a guarantee of the future. Does the past predict the future? As we have seen before, and will seen again, the answer is, alas, both yes and no.

Here's some anecdotal evidence on the consistency of mutual fund returns. Table 21.3 lists the top 10 performing stock mutual funds based on the three years ending December 31, 1998. We then report the subsequent performance of 1998's stars over the next three-year period (1999–2001). As you can see, the results are mixed. Only two of 1998's stars outperformed the average stock fund over the subsequent three-year period (1999–2001).

After an extensive examination of mutual fund returns, John Bogel argues that the performance of individual mutual funds tends to revert toward the mean. In his words, "There is a profound tendency for the returns of high-performing funds to come down to earth, and, almost as inevitably, for the returns of low-performing funds to come up to earth."[11] Here's some of his evidence. Bogel ranked equity mutual funds by performance during the 1970s and divided the rankings into quartiles. The top quartile beat the S&P 500 by an average of 5% per year. The bottom quartile, by contrast, underperformed the S&P 500 by about 4% per year. Bogel then calculated the performance of these funds during the 1980s. Funds in the top quartile, based on

[11]John Bogel, *Common Sense on Mutual Funds* (New York: John Wiley, 1999), p. 226.

Fund	Average Annual Return	
	1996–1998	1999–2001
Rydex OTC	48.5%	−2.1%
MFS Strategic Growth	45.3	1.2
Janus Twenty	42.8	−3.5
Legg-Mason Value Prime	41.1	6.2
Reynolds Blue Chip Growth	37.7	−10.8
Delaware Investments Aggressive Growth	36.9	1.5
Transamerica Premier Equity	36.7	1.5
MFS Massachusetts Investors Growth	36.4	1.4
Weitz Hickory	35.3	2.8
Van Kampen Growth	34.6	12.0
Average Stock Fund	18.5	4.2

TABLE 21.3

Subsequent Three-Year Performance of 1998's Top-Performing Funds

1970s' performance, slightly underperformed the S&P 500 during the 1980s. On the other hand, funds in the bottom quartile, based on 1970's performance, actually did better in 1980s, relative to the S&P 500, than they did in the 1970s.

However, evidence also suggests that investors should not ignore past performance. (We looked at some of it in Chapter 7.) A study of pension fund managers concluded that money managers with outstanding records are better bets for future gains than those with dismal past performance records.[12] The study measured the results of investing with managers whose performance records over the previous three years placed them in the top 25% of all pension funds. This strategy produced a 2.1% greater annual return than investing with managers whose performance records for the previous three years placed them in the bottom 25%.

We emphasized throughout this chapter that investors, when analyzing investment performance, should consider *both* return and risk. Several scientific studies of mutual funds returns used measures of risk-adjusted performance when assessing how well past performance predicted future returns. One extensive study of stock mutual fund returns found strong evidence of persistence in risk-adjusted performance over time.[13] Using the Sharpe measure performance, the study found that the best predictor of future risk-adjusted performance turned out to be past risk-adjusted performance. However, another scientific study found evidence to the contrary—that past risk-adjusted performance wasn't an especially good predictor of future risk-adjusted performance.[14]

So what can you conclude from all of this conflicting evidence? We believe the primary lesson is that even though past performance isn't a perfect predictor of future performance, it must not be ignored. Consistently good risk-adjusted performance over a long period of time at least tilts the odds of success in the investor's favor.

---

[12]Josef Lakonishok et al., "The Structure and Performance of the Money Management Industry," *Brookings Papers on Economic Activity*, 1992, pp. 339–391.

[13]James Philpot, *Performance-Related Characteristics of Mutual Funds*, Ph.D. dissertation, University of Arkansas, Fayetteville, AR, 1994.

[14]Mark Carhart, "On the Persistence in Mutual Fund Performance," *Journal of Finance*, March 1997, pp. 57–82.

1. What issues are important when evaluating investment performance?

Whenever performance is evaluated, the time periods must be consistent with one another. In addition, performance over longer periods of time often provides more useful information than short-term performance. Performance needs to be compared to the appropriate market benchmark and should be adjusted for risk. Finally, investment objectives and any constraints imposed on the portfolio need to be taken into consideration.

2. How are risk and return measured?

Historical performance is evaluated so the appropriate measure of investment return is the holding period return. A total return index, along with the arithmetic and geometric means, also provides useful information. The standard deviation of returns should be calculated along with the portfolio's beta and R^2 measure. Beta measures systematic risk and R^2 measures the degree to which the portfolio is diversified.

3. What are three measures of risk-adjusted performance?

All three measures of risk-adjusted performance are derived from modern portfolio theory. The Treynor measure is a reward-to-risk ratio. If the portfolio's Treynor measure is greater than that of the market benchmark, then the portfolio's return exceeded its expected return, given the portfolio's beta risk. The Sharpe measure is another reward-to-risk ratio. Instead of using beta, the Sharpe measure uses standard deviation. If a portfolio's Sharpe measure exceeds that of the market, then the portfolio's actual return exceeded its expected return, given the portfolio's total risk. Jensen's alpha is based on the capital market asset pricing model. The expected value of alpha is zero. A positive alpha indicates that portfolio's actual return exceeded its expected return, given the portfolio's beta risk.

4. How good a predictor is past performance of future performance?

All measures of portfolio performance are based on historical returns. Are historical returns good predictors of future returns? The answer is perhaps both yes and no since existing evidence supports both positions. A portfolio manager who exhibits good, consistent performance over a long period of time at least improves the odds of success for the investor.

1. List the issues you need to consider when evaluating the performance of a portfolio. How could two different mutual funds both claim to be the "top-performing fund?"
2. What is a market benchmark? What is the appropriate benchmark for a small stock fund? For a large stock fund?
3. Explain how returns should be measured. What does standard deviation measure? What does beta measure?
4. Assume that a portfolio has a standard deviation of 15%. The market portfolio has a standard deviation of 15%. If the portfolio has a beta of .80, what is the portfolio's R^2? How well diversified is the portfolio?
5. Compare and contrast the Treynor, Sharpe, and Jensen performance measures? What is Sharpe's rationale for using standard deviation instead of beta?
6. Assume a portfolio has a beta of .80 and a mean return of 20%. The market has a mean return of 20%. If the risk free rate is 5%, what is the portfolio's Treynor measure? Where does the portfolio lie relative to the security market line?
7. Using the information provided in the prior problem, find Jensen's alpha. Interpret Jensen's alpha.
8. A portfolio has a mean return of 25% and a standard deviation of 25%. The market portfolio has a mean return of 20% and a standard deviation of 18%. The risk-free

rate is 5%. Find the portfolio's Sharpe measure. Did the portfolio outperform or underperform the market on a risk-adjusted basis?

9. Assume a portfolio has a Treynor measure of .35 and a Sharpe measure of .25. The market has a Treynor measure of .20 and a Sharpe measure of .30. Explain why the portfolio out performed the market based on one measure, but under performed the market based on the other. Is the portfolio's R^2 close to 1.0? Why or why not?

10. Is past performance a good guide to future performance? Why is the long-term track record more important than the short-term track record?

CRITICAL THINKING EXERCISES

1. This exercise requires library/Internet research. Using a well-known source of mutual fund information, such as Morningstar or the February issue of *Money* magazine, review data for the five-year period (1998–2002). Measured in terms of total return, find the five best-performing stock mutual funds each year (ignore international and sector funds). Record each fund's name and its total one-year return. Also, record the average total return for each fund's group (e.g., large growth funds or small value funds), as well as the total return for the appropriate market benchmark.
    a. How did each fund on your list do the following year? For example, how did the top-performing fund in 1998 do in 1999?
    b. Do these one-year returns show any consistent patterns? In other words, do one year's top-performing funds perform well the next year. Discuss your findings.
    c. Assume you buy the best-performing fund from the prior year on January 1 and hold it for the next 12 months—so you would own 1998's top-performing fund during 1999, for example. How well do you think this strategy would work?
2. This exercise requires computer work. Open the Stock Returns worksheet in the Data Workbook (available on the text Web site, http://hearth.swlearning.com). The worksheet contains 10 years of monthly returns for 50 stocks, the S&P 500, and T-bills. Use the data to form five portfolios each consisting of five stocks. You can use whatever criteria you wish when forming the portfolios. Evaluate the performance of each portfolio.

THE INTERNET INVESTOR

1. Visit one of the main investment-oriented Web sites—such as MSN Investor (http://investor.msn.com). Search for recent performance data for the three mutual funds discussed in the chapter (Legg-Mason Value Trust, MFS International New Discovery, and Yacktman). How has each fund performed in recent months?
2. The Morningstar Web site (www.morningstar.com) provides an extensive database of mutual fund performance. Choose 10 different stock mutual funds. Visit the Morningstar site and collect the following information: mean return, standard deviation, beta, and R^2. Collect the same information for the S&P 500. (You can use an index fund as a proxy for the S&P 500.) Also, find the average return on T-bills. Use these data to calculate the Treynor, Sharpe, and Jensen performance measures for each fund.
3. By now, your Web surfing skills should be pretty good. Search the Web, especially the investment-oriented Web sites and try to answer this following question: Has the Sage of Omaha (Warren Buffet) continued to regain his investment touch? (*Hint:* The best gauge of Buffet's investment performance is the performance of his company Berkshire Hathaway.)

Appendix A: Sources of Investment Information

The purpose of this appendix is to help you sort through the massive amount of information available to investors today, from economic data to financial news to information on specific companies. We describe both objective sources of investment information and subjective sources of information. We define an objective source as one that provides information and data but no opinions or analyses. A subjective source generally provides both data and opinions.

Before starting, note that this appendix is not meant to be comprehensive. Also understand that the information needs of investors vary substantially. Sources that are important to certain professional or institutional investors may offer little or no value for small individual investors. Many small investors can satisfy all their information needs with general interest periodicals, newspapers, and popular Web sites.

SOURCES OF STATISTICAL DATA

A variety of government and private organizations compiles and publishes all kinds of economic and industry data. The amount of these data is staggering. You can find the number of housing starts in the United States between 1947 and today, the profits of electric and gas utilities over the past 20 years, or the current yield on Canadian government bonds. Most sources of such information provide objective data (e.g., historical economic statistics) rather than subjective opinions and analyses. We start by examining government sources of statistical data about economy-wide and industry-specific conditions and trends.

Government Publications

Several U.S. federal agencies, international organizations, and foreign governments compile and publish statistical data. Some series are reported monthly, some quarterly, and some annually. For some series, historical data going back many years may be available. Several examples follow.

Survey of Current Business The U.S. Department of Commerce publishes the *Survey of Current Business* each month to review recent developments in the U.S. economy (and to a lesser extent, the world economy) and to present data on such things as gross domestic product (GDP), industrial production, employment, wages, and interest rates. The *Survey* also contains detailed data on conditions in specific industries. The *Survey* reports current data and limited historical data, typically going back a couple of years.

Besides the *Survey*, every two years the U.S. Commerce Department *publishes Business Statistics*, which provides longer-term historical economic data. You could find data, for example, on steel production or the unemployment rate from about 1947 to the present.

Federal Reserve Bulletin The *Federal Reserve Bulletin* is published monthly by the Board of Governors of the U.S. Federal Reserve System. It is the investor's primary source for current monetary and banking data. The *Bulletin* also presents several other financial data series, both domestic and international.

In addition to banking and financial data, the *Bulletin* also contains articles, written by the staff of the Board of Governors, on contemporary monetary and banking issues. Announcements, congressional testimony by board members, and so forth are also printed in the *Bulletin*.

International Publications Several international organizations can provide detailed data on world economies, including the International Monetary Fund (IMF), United Nations, and World Bank. In addition, the governments of most developed countries, such as Canada, publish statistical data regularly. An example of this type of publication is *International Financial Statistics*, published by the IMF. It provides data, on a country-by-country basis, on such things as inflation, industrial production, unemployment, and main components of the country's GDP.

The average investor may have little interest in these types of international data, but some professionals might be interested. For example, say an analyst for a big Wall Street investment firm follows a company that generates a high percentage of its sales in Europe. Obviously, the prospects for that company, and therefore the investment potential of its stock, will be closely tied to the economic outlook in Europe.

Nongovernmental Sources

Economic data are also available from nongovernmental sources such as financial institutions, investment firms, securities exchanges, and trade associations. In fact, many of these private organizations provide some of the data that appear in government publications such as the *Survey of Current Business*. Furthermore, many investment advisory services, such as Standard & Poor's and brokerage firms, publish extensive economic data. Unlike government sources of economic data, however, these sources often provide subjective commentary along with statistical information. For example, they may provide data that suggest that European economic growth is accelerating and then answer the question of what it means for European stocks.

NEWSPAPERS AND PERIODICALS

Most investors probably get the bulk of their information from newspapers and periodicals. You are probably already familiar with *Barron's, The Wall Street Journal, Business Week*, and such, but hundreds of more-specialized publications are published that interest certain investors.

Newspapers

Most daily newspapers report some business and economic news, although the quality and quantity of coverage can vary widely. Many daily papers, even in larger cities, tend to concentrate on local business news, with some exceptions. The *New York Times,* for example, provides extensive, well-respected coverage of national business and economic news. Many investors prefer daily business newspapers for more in-depth financial information.

The Wall Street Journal is arguably the best-known, most widely quoted business publication in the world. It is also one of the oldest. Founded in 1885, the *Journal* provides detailed coverage of business and economic news, both nationally and globally. The *Journal* publishes Asian and European editions as well. The paper carries extensive price quotations for stocks, bonds, options, futures, and mutual funds. It also reports earnings announcements, dividend declarations, new product information, management changes, and other current business news.

Barron's, like *The Wall Street Journal,* is published by Dow Jones & Company. *Barron's* is a weekly newspaper that covers a wide range of investment topics. A typical issue contains a review of the week's major business and economic developments, interviews with professional investors, recent analyst opinions on stocks, and columns on commodities, mutual funds, options, and so forth. *Barron's* also publishes thorough price quotations on all major types of investments, as well as detailed technical information.

Periodicals

Dozens of periodicals seek to serve the information needs of investors. They include general interest periodicals such as *Newsweek* and *Time;* business periodicals such as *Business Week, Forbes,* and *Fortune;* and international periodicals such as *The Economist.* All contain news and analysis of contemporary business and economic issues. The business periodicals tend to focus more narrowly on investing, providing articles on specific companies, consumer trends, economic forecasts, and so forth.

Trade periodicals may also interest certain investors. These publications of various trade associations provide in-depth coverage of specific industries and segments of the economy. Two examples of trade periodicals are *Air Transport World* and *Public Utilities Fortnightly.*

In addition to the general business press, some well-known periodicals deal more heavily with personal investing and others aspects of personal finance. These publications include *Money* magazine, *Smart Money,* and *Worth.*

INVESTMENT ADVISORY SERVICES

To supplement published information, investors can consult private companies that specialize in providing investment information and advice. These include the large, well-known financial information services such as Standard & Poor's, brokerage firms such as Merrill Lynch, and investment newsletters with names such as the *Professional Tapereader.* The cost of these services varies. Many large public and college libraries offer at least some of these publications to patrons.

Clients of brokerage firms may have access to some of this information free of charge. Purchasing many of these services as an individual can be quite expensive. A yearly subscription to a typical newsletter costs between $200 and $300. An annual subscription to *The Outlook,* a publication of Standard & Poor's, costs almost $300. Any investor should carefully evaluate the cost and benefit of buying any of these publications.

Moody's and Standard & Poor's

Moody's Investors Service and Standard & Poor's (S&P) provide similar publications and information services covering a wide range of investment topics. Moody's and S&P provide both objective information and subjective analysis. For example, Moody's and S&P both publish basic reference volumes covering most public corporations. Moody's *Manuals* group company information by industry for banking, industrial, international, transportation, and public utility firms. These publications and S&P's *Corporation Reports* provide detailed historical and current information on revenue, earnings, capitalization, major news developments, and so forth. Moody's and S&P update these reference volumes continuously throughout the year. Both also publish regular reports on the economy and specific industries. S&P's two-volume *Industry Surveys,* for example, provide valuable industry information.

Moody's *Bond Survey* is another example of the many reports and publications of these advisory services. This weekly publication provides extensive information on and analysis of the bond market. A typical issue of the *Bond Survey* includes a list of new bond issues, data on interest rates, and bond ratings under review. In addition to its *Corporation Reports,* S&P publishes *Stock Reports,* two-page summary reports on most public companies. Updated quarterly, these reports provide basic financial information (e.g., revenue, assets, dividends), as well as brief assessments of companies' future prospects.

Two other S&P publications are *The Outlook* and *Investor's Monthly.* Unlike *Stock Reports,* these publications tend to offer more subjective analysis of the financial markets and specific stocks and contain less statistical data. A typical issue might analyze conditions in the overall market, make changes in stock recommendations, and highlight special situations

Value Line

One of best-known and most widely followed investment advisory services, Value Line, follows more than 1,700 individual stocks in 98 industries. Each weekly report spotlights one or two industries and the companies in those industries. A new report is prepared on each company and industry approximately once every three months. Although Value Line reports a great deal of objective information, most investors view it primarily as a source of subjective analysis.

Many users of Value Line rely on several summary measures. Two especially important numbers appear in the upper left-hand corners of its company reports: timeliness (probable price performance in the next 12 months) and safety (probable safety in the future). To develop its timeliness ranking, Value Line uses a computer model to rank each of the 1,700 or so stocks it follows, with higher ranks indicating better investment potential. The service assigns ranks of 1 and 5 to the top 100 and bottom 100 stocks, respectively. Ranks of 2 and 4 identify the next 300 stocks from the top and bottom, respectively. The remaining, middle group of about 900 stocks get timeliness ranks of 3. A similar procedure is used to assign safety rankings. We discussed the performance of investment strategies based on the Value Line rankings in Chapter 7.

Brokerage Firms

In Chapter 6, we discussed the difference between full-service brokerage firms, such as Merrill Lynch, and discount firms, such as Charles Schwab. Other than their commission rates, the major difference between the two is the full-service firm's offer of investment advice and information. All full-service firms, for example, maintain lists of stocks that they recommend. Brokers at full-service firms often use some of the sources already discussed (e.g., S&P and Value Line). Often, however, they rely more on reports prepared by their firm's analysts.

Every major full-service brokerage firm employs a group of security analysts, each of whom concentrates on specific industries or stocks. Each major firm, for example, has at least one analyst who follows Chrysler and the auto industry. Brokerage firms also employ economists, market strategists, technical analysts, bond market analysts, and even weather forecasters to fully serve their clients.

One issue we discussed in Chapter 6 deals with the objectivity of brokerage firm research. Research, in and of itself, doesn't generate revenue; brokerage commissions and investment banking fees do. Critics contend that brokerage firm research is not objective. Evidence of this criticism recently emerged. For instance, several firms admitted tailoring investment recommendations to assist investment banking deals. Regulations now in place help to better ensure the independence and objectivity of brokerage firm research analysts. Nevertheless, a good rule of thumb is "buyer beware."

Mutual Fund Rating Services

Several investment advisory services follow mutual funds almost exclusively. Three of the most firmly established mutual fund rating services are CDA/Wisenberger, Lipper Analytical Services, and Morningstar. In 1993, Value Line began offering a mutual fund rating service similar to the company's well-respected stock rating service. Mutual fund rating services all present objective information and historical results for mutual funds; some also make subjective recommendations.

Newsletters

Investors can subscribe to dozens of investment newsletters. Some of the better-known newsletters include *The Zweig Forecast, The Prudent Speculator, The Chartist,* and *Elliott Wave Theorist.* Newsletters provide subjective analysis and opinion rather than objective information. Newsletters tell investors, for example, what they should buy, what they should avoid (or sell), and whether to hold stocks or cash. Many, although not all, newsletters rely on technical analysis to make their investment recommendations. Subscriptions to investment newsletters are generally fairly expensive and many newsletters have less-than-stellar track records when it comes to the quality of their advice.

COMPUTER-BASED INFORMATION SOURCES

One of the most significant developments in recent years is the growth of computer-based sources of investment information. These services allow computer users to access large information databases without having to go to the library or turn a page. Computer-based sources can be divided into two groups: historical databases and online services, including the Internet. Historical databases provide users with financial information on disks or computer tapes, updated periodically.

Traditional Computer Databases

Several computer databases have been around for a number of years. Many universities and large institutions subscribe to these databases, which require mainframe computers. COMPUSTAT, a service of Standard & Poor's, maintains a body of historical financial information on thousands of companies, as well as industry and economic data. It can provide either annual data going back as many as 20 years, or quarterly data going back as many as 20 quarters.

Another established computer database is CRSP, developed by the Center for Research in Security Prices at the University of Chicago. CRSP produces computer tapes, updated annually, that report monthly and daily historical security price returns on approximately 5,000 NYSE, AMEX, and over-the-counter stocks. Dividends and closing prices are also included. Some of the series go back as far as 1926.

PC Products

Today, the personal computer is an excellent alternative. PC services include both online services and databases. For example, in the early 1990s, Standard & Poor's created a compact disk version of Compustat for use on a personal computer. Called Research Insight, it contains most of the information found on the mainframe version of Compustat. Research Insight offers several report and chart builders that can be used in conjunction with Microsoft Excel.

The Internet

For investors, the Internet is one of the greatest information sources currently available. What is more, much of the information obtainable from the Internet is free to users. All you need is Internet access and one of the popular Web browsers. Your college or university probably has both. Most colleges and universities provide high-speed Internet access to students.

The amount of information available on the Internet is staggering, and it is growing daily. Getting started is often the hardest part. A good place to begin is one of the major search engines, such as Google (www.google.com) or one of the major investment-oriented Web sites, such as MSN Investors (http://money central.msn.com).

An excellent source of company information is the SEC's Edgar database (www.sec.gov/edgar). Attached to the SEC's homepage, Edgar is an electronic library of SEC filings. If you want to study the most recent annual report for a company, you can find it on Edgar. Another source of information are company homepages. You can read about new products or study the annual report. Microsoft's Web site (www.microsoft.com), for example, lets you download its latest annual report as an Excel file.

Critical Thinking Exercise

This exercise requires library and/or Internet research. For the following list of 12 data items, identify an information source from the multiple sources available, collect the most recent data you can find, and answer any questions asked.

1. Breakdown of Canadian GDP into the four major components (private consumption, net exports, government spending, and private investment).
2. Japanese and U.S. savings rates. Collect the most recent year's data and data for 1985. Be sure to define *savings rate*.
3. Distribution of U.S. population by age group and projected change in each age group to the year 2005.
4. Performance of the Weitz Value mutual fund from 1990 through the most recent year you can find.
5. U.S. retail sales (seasonally adjusted and not seasonally adjusted). Obtain overall data and sales for specific types of retailers (e.g., discount stores).
6. Revenue, operating expenses, and net income of U.S. electric and gas utilities (overall industry data). Collect the most recent year's data and data for 1990.
7. Stock price index for the computer industry from 1990 through the most recent year. Be sure to specify how the computer industry is defined.
8. Exchange rates between the U.S. dollar and the Japanese yen and between the U.S. dollar and the German mark from 1990 through the most recent year.
9. Earnings and dividends for The Gap from 1990 through the most recent year. Could you construct a total return index using these data?
10. Projection of earnings for The Gap for next year. Why are The Gap's earnings expected to rise or fall?
11. Most recent balance sheet and income statement for Wal-Mart Stores.
12. Industry ratios and averages for the airline industry.

Appendix B: Careers in Investments

Many readers may be interested in working in the investments field; it can be a rewarding career. Although it is difficult to estimate the number of full-time investment professionals, a good guess would be several hundred thousand, at least. For example, Merrill Lynch, the nation's largest brokerage and investment company, employs about 40,000. As another example, Fidelity Investments, the world's largest mutual fund company, which also operates a large discount brokerage firm, employs nearly 10,000 people. Of course, not all of these workers are engaged in investment management, but a majority probably are.

In this appendix, we look briefly at some of the career opportunities in the investments field. Before we begin, however, consider the following points. First, competition for most jobs in the investments field is intense. Institutions have many high-quality applicants from whom to choose. Second, the number of investment professionals is not growing especially rapidly; in some job categories, the number of workers may actually be declining. Several well-known investment firms cut staff in recent years. As a result, you must be flexible in your job search. You must be willing to relocate, be willing to start at the bottom, and be prepared to work hard. Finally, you should be aware that many positions in the investments field require federal or state licenses.

WHO EMPLOYS INVESTMENT PROFESSIONALS?

The obvious employers of investment professionals are brokerage firms, investment banking firms, life insurance companies, pension funds, and mutual funds. Ask your librarian for sources that list the addresses and phone numbers of these organizations. Also, don't forget about banks. Many investment professionals begin work in bank trust departments. Also, many large banks have active bond-trading operations, especially for municipal bonds. Even large, nonfinancial corporations employ investment professionals to manage such areas as investor relations and pension plans.

BROKERAGE AND SALES POSITIONS

The first job that probably comes to mind in the investment field is that of a stockbroker (now called an *account executive* in most brokerage firms). Account executives work mainly with individual investors, though some may handle accounts for small institutional investors as well. Account executives provide advice, execute orders, and help maintain records. Account executives who work for full-service firms such as Merrill Lynch earn most of their compensation through commissions on trades. Successful account executives can do quite well financially, earning six-figure annual incomes. Brokers at discount brokerage firms, on the other hand, are salaried employees. They are responsible for maintaining records, providing price quotations, and executing orders; these services are, of course, important. The distinction between full-service and discount brokerage firms was described in Chapter 3.

Large investment firms also employ salespeople who deal mainly with institutional investors and other workers who execute orders (traders). In any case, a successful account executive or investment salesperson possesses effective selling skills, along with some interest in finance. New account executives often have prior sales or business experience.

A growth area today is the sale of 401(k) and other similar defined contribution retirement plans to employers. Most employers replaced traditional pension plans with defined contribution plans. Large investment firms and mutual fund companies actively market these plans.

ANALYSTS AND PORTFOLIO MANAGERS

Security analysts work for a variety of organizations studying stocks, bonds, options, futures, and so forth. Analysts write research reports for distribution to their organizations' clients. Most analysts specialize in particular securities. Stock analysts, for example, specialize in specific industries and companies, following the pattern described in Chapters 11–14. Analysts work for large banks, brokerage firms, life insurance companies, mutual funds, and pension funds. The analyst whose name appears on a research report usually has a staff to assist him or her. Many analysts begin their careers by doing tedious grunt work for the senior analyst. Top analysts can easily command six- or seven-figure salaries.

Portfolio, or money managers, in the view of many, represent the pinnacle of the investments field. Portfolio managers are responsible for managing large pools of funds and work for mutual funds and other large, institutional investors. Most managers have staffs of assistant managers and analysts. The compensation of a top portfolio manager can easily exceed $1 million annually.

INVESTMENT BANKERS

As we discussed in Chapter 3, investment bankers act as intermediaries between issuers of securities and investors. They also advise corporate and government clients on financial strategies. Investment bankers often lead large staffs and are well compensated.

FINANCIAL PLANNERS

In order to help them deal with personal finance issues, including estate planning, taxes, insurance, and investments, many individuals turn to financial planners. Financial planners come from a variety of backgrounds, including accounting and insurance sales. Some work for insurance companies, investment firms, banks, and even public accounting firms. Other financial planners work independently. The demand for financial planners increased dramatically in recent years, which coincided with the growth in defined contribution retirement plans. Earnings of top financial planners easily reach into six figures.

Financial planner is still a loosely defined term, however. Almost anyone, regardless of qualifications, can call himself or herself a financial planner. Recently, efforts led to the development of a professional designation for financial planners. The Certified Financial Planner designation means that an individual meets education and experience requirements, and demonstrates a minimum level of knowledge and competence about subjects such as taxes, life insurance, and estate planning. More than 25,000 individuals today hold CFP certificates, and we suggest that anyone with an interest in becoming a financial planner obtain a CFP certificate. For more information, contact the CFP Board, 1700 Broadway, Suite 2100, Denver, CO, 80290-2101; (303) 830-7500; www.cfp-board.org.

CHARTERED FINANCIAL ANALYSTS

Approximately 20,000 chartered financial analysts (CFAs) are licensed in the United States. Obtaining a CFA designation enhances the prestige of an investment professional such as a security analyst or portfolio manager, much as a CPA designation enhances the prestige of an accounting professional. To obtain a CFA designation, you must pass a series of three comprehensive examinations (Levels I, II, and III) over a three-year period. You must also meet certain educational and experience requirements to reach each level.

Although a CFA designation is not necessarily a requirement to get into the investments field, there is little question that the designation is valued by most investment organizations. It is rare today to find a top analyst or portfolio manager who isn't a CFA. For more information, contact the Association for Investment Management and Research, PO Box 3668, Charlottesville, VA 22903-0668; (804) 980-3668; www.aimr.com.

We wish you the best of luck on whatever career path you decide to take.

CHAPTER 2

1. 33%
2. Historical returns are ex-post returns.
3. Inflation adjusted real return is 29.1%.
4. Measured in yen, 16.7%; measured in dollars, 12.2%.
5. $10,000 invested at the beginning of the period would have been worth in excess of $21,300 by the end of year 5. Total return during the five year period equals approximately 113.5%.
6. Arithmetic mean equals 17.5%; geometric mean equals 16.4%.
7. The annualized three-year return equals 13.4%.
8. Credit risk is the risk that the financial health of the issuer will change causing the value of the security to rise or fall; interest rate risk is the risk interest rates will change causing the value of the security to change; market risk is the risk reflected in the daily fluctuations in security prices.
9. 15.9%.
10. 15.8% and 16.9%.
11. Stock A: mean is 18.6%, standard deviation is 23.0%, and coefficient of variation is 1.23.
    Stock B: mean is 18.8%, standard deviation is 28.1%, and coefficient of variation is 1.50.
12. The portfolio return each year is a weighted average of the annual returns for the two individual stocks.
13. The portfolio mean return is 18.7%, its standard deviation is 14.2%, and its coefficient of variation is 0.76. The portfolio is diversified and represents a better risk-return tradeoff than either individual stock (lower standard deviation and coefficient of variation.)

CHAPTER 9

1. $854
2. $851.55
3. $872.55

4. 12.17%
5. 4.387 years; 4.1 years
6. $20.50 increase for $1,000 face value bond

CHAPTER 10

1. The forward rate on a one-year bond, one year from today is 6.64%; the forward rate on a two-year bond, one year from today is 6.50%.
2. The investor would sell one two-year bond (receiving $89.05) and buy 1.063 three-year bonds (paying $89.05). In two years, the investor would owe $100; in three years he or she would receive $106.30. The one-year return is 6.3%.

CHAPTER 13

1. The compound average annual growth rate is 15.8%; the forecast of 2003 earnings is $2.55.
2. The estimated earnings regressions equals: $-203.224 + .1025(\text{year})$; the forecast of 2003 earnings equals $1.71.
3. Of the two, the forecast derived from the compound average annual growth rate is probably more accurate. The forecast derived from the regression is actually lower than the firm's 2002 earnings.
4. The impact of both changes (faster same store sales growth and a lower gross profit margin) reduces Kohl's estimated earnings to $1.65 per share (compared to the original forecast of $1.90. As noted in the chapter, the earnings forecast appears more sensitive to changes in the firm's gross margin than to changes in same store sales growth.

CHAPTER 14

1. $Vso = (\$.80)/(.09 - .075) = \$53.33$
   $Vso = (\$1.84/.09)\{1 + [(.075 - (.09)(.4348)]/(.09 - .075)\} = \$69.33$
2. Since the market price ($48.49) < IV ($53.33), KO is undervalued and a good investment.
3. KO is a growth company if ROE > ERs. Since ROE = 13% and ERs = 9%, it is a growth company.
4. Yes, KO is a growth stock because it is undervalued.
5. $\$.64(1 + g)^4 = \$1.10$ $g = (1.71875)^{1/4} - 1 = 14.5\%$
6. $\$1.13(1 + g)^4 = \$1.93$ $g = (1.70796)^{1/4} - 1 = 14.3\%$
7. $g = .116 \times [1 - (1.20/2.10)] = .0497$
8. $ERs = .02 + 0.70(.086) = .0802$
9. $Vso = \$1.20/(.08 - .05) = \$40$
10. Since the market price ($35) < Vso ($40), the stock is undervalued and a good investment.
11. DIV1 = $0.84; DIV2 = $1.01; DIV3 = $1.21; DIV4 = $1.45; DIV5 = $1.74; Vs5 = $95.80
    $Vso = \$0.75 + \$0.804 + \$0.861 + \$0.923 + \$0.988 + \$54.357 = \$58.683$

12. P/E = \$35/\$2.10 = 16.67x
13. MV/BV = \$35/\$11 = 3.18x
14. $Vso = (26 \times \$2.35)/(1 + .11)^3 = \$61.10(.7312) = \$44.67$
    At a market price of \$32.71, CAKE is undervalued.
15. $\$32.71 = (26 \times EPS3)(.7312)$ Solve for EPS3 = \$0.92
    $\$0.60(1 + g)^3 = \$0.92$ $g = (1.533)^{1/3} - 1 = 15.3\%$

CHAPTER 17

1. $M_s = 40.12\%$
2. $SD_s = 95.22\%$
3. Y dominates X because it has a lower risk for the same return.
4. $CV_Y = 1.2$ $CV_Z = 1.11$ No, one does not dominate. A more risk averse investor would choose Z over Y.
5. $ER_p = 4.716\%$
6. $SD_p = 14.687\%$

CHAPTER 18

1. $ER_p = .30(16\%) + .70(6\%) = 9.0\%$
2. $SD_p = .30(8\%) = 2.4\%$
3. SD_i should be 0.60 not 0.06; $\beta_i = (+.55)(.60/.35) = 0.94$
4. $ER_s = .03 + 0.94(.18 - .03) = 17.1\%$
5. $ER_s = .05 + 1.30(.18 - .05) = 21.9\%$
6. $PR = (\$90 - \$80 + \$4.50)/\$80 = 18.125\%$
7. Since PR (18.125\%) $< ER_s$ (21.9\%), we should not invest.
8. Graph 2 points: RF = .05 with beta = 0 and ERM = .18 and beta = 1.0.
   Also the stock should *lie exactly on* the SML with $ER_s = .219$ and beta = 1.30.

Name and Organization Index

Note: **Boldface** text and page numbers refer to key terms. *Italic* page numbers refer to exhibits (tables, figures, and feature boxes).

Subject Index

Note: **Boldface** text and page numbers refer to key terms. *Italic* page numbers refer to exhibits (tables, figures, and feature boxes).